"The great merit of Köstenberger's and Patterson's volume is its three-dimension account of biblical interpretation. The authors rightly focus on the history, literature, and theology of the Bible—what they call the hermeneutical triad. Call it hermeneutics in real 3-D. A three-stranded hermeneutical cord may not be easily broken, but it's easy to grasp by following this introductory textbook. Another merit is the authors' reminder that biblical interpretation is not only about method but about virtue: a heart-felt humility before the divine text is as important as any heady procedure."

—Kevin J. Vanhoozer,
Blanchard Professor of Theology, Wheaton College Graduate School

"I am filled with admiration. I learned much from this vigorous book. It is a work of great clarity that summarizes the best principles of general hermeneutics with the best principles of biblical interpretation. Professor Köstenberger's and Patterson's students are lucky to have such a trenchant and learned guide—and so are the readers of this fine book."

—E. D. Hirsch, Jr.,
Professor Emeritus of Education & Humanities,
University of Virginia and Founder, Core Knowledge Foundation

"There are certain topics of must-reading for serious Bible students—hermeneutics is at the top. There are certain books of must-reading for a topic—Andreas Köstenberger's work on hermeneutics is one of them. It is clear, concise, and yet deep, and manages to cover most of the needed areas. Thus it becomes an invaluable guide for the student working through the labyrinth of issues that make up the task of biblical interpretation. It will enable the reader to bridge the gap from understanding biblical portions in their original cultural context and from showing their relevance to a modern audience. I recommend it very highly."

—Grant Osborne,
Professor of New Testament, Trinity Evangelical Divinity School

"*Invitation to Biblical Interpretation* is destined to become the standard textbook for colleges and seminaries for the foreseeable future. It is simply the best work available in the field of biblical hermeneutics. It is comprehensive in its breadth and in depth at all the right places. And it is well written! I will be certain to make it my anchor text as I teach biblical hermeneutics."

—Daniel L. Akin, President,
Professor of Preaching and Theology,
Southeastern Baptist Theological Seminary

"Andreas Köstenberger and Richard Patterson, two brilliant and experienced interpreters of Holy Scripture, have produced a first-rate volume on biblical hermeneutics. Distinctive in its approach, with a focus on the "hermeneutical triad," this monumental publication is encyclopedic in its thoroughness, masterful in its organizational design, and skillful in its pedagogical emphasis. The clear discussions in each chapter, followed by helpful and informative bibliographies, will make this book a rich resource for students, scholars, and pastors for years to come. I am truly excited about the publication of *Invitation to Biblical Interpretation*."

—David S. Dockery,
President, Professor of Christian Thought & Tradition, Union University

"I am truly impressed. This introduction to hermeneutics covers all the bases, and I mean all of them. Read this book and you will be well prepared for the task of serious interpretation."

—Tremper Longman,
Robert H. Gundry Professor of Biblical Studies, Westmont College

"This introduction to hermeneutics is outstanding in several ways: It takes full account of the unique divine authorship of the Bible; it is clear, readable, and doctrinally sound; it attends to the spiritual state of the interpreter; it provides detailed guidance for understanding the historical background, literary and linguistic features, and theological significance of each text; it is coauthored by an Old Testament and a New Testament professor; and it insists that right interpretation must end in application to life. It is an excellent book that will be widely used as a standard textbook for years to come."

—Wayne Grudem,
Research Professor of Theology and Biblical Studies, Phoenix Seminary

"This book on biblical interpretation combines training in exegesis with a basic knowledge of hermeneutics. It urges careful consideration of historical, literary, and theological issues. Thus, historically, it includes helpful chronological charts, and much on cultural history. Its literary focus includes canon, genre, and language. Its theological dimension includes application. Genre is crucial: thus narrative, poetry and wisdom are distinguished in the Old Testament; and parable, epistles, and apocalyptic, in the New. Why responsible interpretation requires toil and labor receives careful explanation. This book contains plenty of common sense, sanity, and love of Scripture. I commend it especially to students, teachers, and even pastors, as helping all of us to use the Bible responsibly and fruitfully."

—Anthony C. Thiselton,
Professor of Christian Theology, University of Nottingham

"A major task—perhaps *the* major task—of hermeneutics is to clarify the meaning of texts. This work by Köstenberger and Patterson not only succeeds brilliantly in elucidating the fundamental principles and processes of biblical hermeneutics but itself is a model of how a book ought to be written. Its conception, organization, systematic development, and applications—all work together to make this the finest contribution of its kind to biblical scholarship. There is no stodginess or impenetrable "academese" here. Layman and scholar alike will find it to be a virtual treasure house of sane and sensible hermeneutical practice."

—Eugene H. Merrill,
Distinguished Professor of Old Testament Studies, Dallas Theological Seminary

"Don't be misled by the title; this is no typical hermeneutics primer. Here, in considerable detail, covering both introductory and more advanced topics, and interacting with the most current and classic scholarship, is a one-stop shopping resource for the entire exegetical process for the most capable seminary students, pastors, and teachers. Particularly distinctive and/or helpful are the discussions of Old Testament chronology, interpreting Revelation, discourse analysis, grammatical fallacies, biblical theology, and homiletical method. Warmly recommended."

—Craig L. Blomberg,
Distinguished Professor of New Testament, Denver Seminary

"This is a well-written, clear, and thorough book on the principles of biblical interpretation for the whole Bible. It would be an excellent book for an upper-level hermeneutics course at the college level or an introductory hermeneutics course at the seminary level. Pastors will also find this a useful book to get an overview of the interpretative principles for different parts of the Bible from which they are preparing to preach. Seminary students and pastors will also benefit from the concluding chapter that applies the interpretative approach of the book to the task of preaching. The authors rightly contend that hermeneutics is to be viewed through the triadic lens of history, literature, and theology. This is not so much a theoretical approach to hermeneutics but a competent hands-on guide for interpreting the different kinds of literature that one encounters in the Bible. In this respect, each chapter helpfully concludes with a sample passage in which the principles discussed in the chapter are applied and illustrated, followed by study questions for the student and important bibliographical resources pertaining to the chapter. This is one of the best general and most thorough introductions to interpreting the English Bible that I have read. While paying attention to the details of interpretative method, it reflects a robust view of the absolute truth of Scripture."

—Gregory K. Beale,
Professor of New Testament and Biblical Theology,
Westminster Theological Seminary

"Köstenberger's *Invitation to Biblical Interpretation* is just that, a rich invitation to engage Scripture as God's Word, making appropriate use of all available tools. His triadic approach is fresh and helpfully non-reductive. This work is wide-ranging and in touch with contemporary scholarly trends while written and produced in a thoroughly accessible way for student, pastor, and professor. Highly recommended."

—Craig Bartholomew,
Professor of Religion and Theology, Redeemer University College

"In this triad dance of history, literature, and theology, as they move across the floor of biblical interpretation, Köstenberger and Patterson excel at sorting through and clearly presenting massive amounts of material across a wide spectrum of cognate disciplines. Written in a down-to-earth style, the book is as accessible as it is broad, as practical as it is informed on contemporary discussions of these difficult matters. From the particulars of Greek grammar and discourse analysis to helpful introductions on canon, biblical theology, and appropriate application, here one again and again finds a welcome orientation to the bread-and-butter concepts, sound practices, and tools needed for handling the biblical text responsibly and the spiritual posture for approaching it reverently. I am impressed and looking forward to putting this book in the hands of my students, who will find here a rich, expansive resource from which to draw guidance for years to come."

—George H. Guthrie,
Benjamin W. Perry Professor of Bible, Union University

"*Invitation to Biblical Interpretation* offers a thorough, scholarly, Scripture-honoring approach to biblical hermeneutics that lays the foundations for genuine expository preaching. Under its "hermeneutical triad" of the preaching text's historical setting, literary dimensions, and theological message, the book provides a balanced approach even as it explores most of the topics discussed in contemporary biblical hermeneutics. It is well researched and documented and clearly written and illustrated. This student-friendly book is not only an excellent text for a seminary course in biblical hermeneutics but is equally useful for independent study. I highly recommend this book for all who desire to preach and teach the Word faithfully and accurately."

—Sidney Greidanus,
Professor of Preaching Emeritus, Calvin Theological Seminary

"This is indeed a warm invitation to interpret the Bible responsibly, passionately, and practically. Showing readers how to explore the context, literature, and theology of the biblical books, the authors provide a guide to all phases of interpretation. The work climaxes in particularly helpful instructions on how to move from study of the text to crafting of the sermon. Novices should not be put off by the size of the volume. Although comprehensive in scope and breadth, the style of writing and the practical helps at the end of each chapter ensure that the concepts conveyed will be readily grasped even by non-professionals. If students of Scripture are seeking a single volume to which they can turn for practical assistance in interpretation, this is the book to get. Thank you, Kregel Publishers, for making their work available to us."

—Daniel I. Block,
Gunther H. Knoedler Professor of Old Testament, Wheaton College

"This book distills a wealth of wisdom from two seasoned scholars whose expertise spans both Testaments. Chapters are up to date without succumbing to the trendy. There is attention to both the theory and practice of interpreting Scripture, obligatory given the title. But the novel element of this volume is at least twofold. (1) It unabashedly privileges Scripture as recording a *history* that produced *literature* which conveys *theology* of eternal redemptive importance. (2) It strikes a balance between these three elements in a readable and engrossing style. No book on this subject can do everything. But this one is without peer as a classroom resource supporting the triadic reading it calls for at a level that is neither brutally rudimentary nor unrealistically advanced. It will enhance the teaching of this subject and draw students into the excitement of navigating hermeneutical frontiers."

— Robert W. Yarbrough,
Professor of New Testament, Covenant Theological Seminary

"The field of biblical interpretation and hermeneutics is vast and complicated, and those outside of the field might be forgiven for thinking that it renders any aspiration to reading, understanding, and preaching the Bible to be little more than a fool's errand. That is why it is great, as one such amateur, to be able to recommend this new book by Andreas Köstenberger and Richard Patterson. In clear, thoughtful chapters, the authors guide the reader through the dense thickets of theory, and yet never stray from the principal task of imparting the knowledge and techniques which will make the Bible more understandable and, above all, more preachable. Everyone—from the humblest Bible reader to the most accomplished preacher—will find something here to benefit them and to unlock yet more of the riches of God's Word for their lives and ministries. A book for both teachers and students."

—Carl Trueman,
Dean, Westminster Theological Seminary

"Laid out as a seminary class book, this is a thoroughly researched, up-to-the-minute didactic treatise on the method and disciplines—historical and canonical, literary and linguistic, theological and applicatory—of biblically valid biblical interpretation. It is a superb resource that deserves a place on every preacher's shelf."

—J. I. Packer,
Lord of Governors Professor of Theology, Regent College

"Here is the answer for the student who wants the results of sound scholarship in the field of hermeneutics without having to negotiate all the philosophical debates that have so come to dominate the subject. For the theological student (and the serious Bible reader) Köstenberger and Patterson have assembled a logically organized, comprehensive yet uncomplicated, guide to interpreting the Bible. This book not only provides an excellent basic course in hermeneutics, but it will serve students and those who preach and teach the Bible as an invaluable and practical reference handbook."

—Graeme Goldsworthy,
Visiting Lecturer in Hermeneutics, Moore College

"Andreas Köstenberger and Richard Patterson have produced a comprehensive yet accessible introduction to biblical hermeneutics, chock full of helpful examples of the exegetical process. Approaching the Bible through the hermeneutical "triad" of history, literature, and theology, the authors take into account the nature of Scripture as divine discourse delivered through human authors in diverse genres and historically-embedded cultures, contexts, and languages. The volume is well researched, well organized, and clearly written, an excellent text for seminary or college level courses on biblical interpretation."

—Mark L. Strauss,
Professor of New Testament, Bethel Seminary San Diego

"Since the Scriptures are the Word of God, it is imperative that we interpret them accurately. Köstenberger and Patterson have provided a comprehensive work, full of wisdom and good sense, which will enable readers to be skilled interpreters of Scripture. The authors do not merely explain the rules of hermeneutics, but they also provide many helpful examples, so that the reader also learns a significant amount of biblical theology in this invaluable textbook."

— Thomas R. Schreiner,
James Buchanan Harrison Professor of New Testament Interpretation,
The Southern Baptist Theological Seminary

"It is important to understand what this book is not. Despite its size, it is not a comprehensive guide to advanced hermeneutics. Rather, its size stems from the fact that it is a thorough introduction to (mostly) common sense elements that go into faithful biblical interpretation, diligently worked out with many examples. The step-by-step approach will be too mechanical if anyone thinks that in real life such sequences guarantee an accurate and mature grasp of what the Bible says, but it will be an enormous help to those who are taking their first steps toward recognizing the many elements that go into sound interpretive judgment."

—D. A. Carson,
Research Professor of New Testament, Trinity Evangelical Divinity School

"Biblical interpretation is a delicately balanced and widely expansive field of study. This volume, replete with explanations, charts, diagrams, study questions, assignments, and sample texts, reflects this reality. Köstenberger and Patterson structure their approach on the belief that Scripture is meant for our instruction, and their hermeneutical triad of history, literature, and theology provides the functional structure for achieving this goal. Obviously designed out of the authors' many years of classroom teaching, teachers and preachers and serious students of Scripture will find this volume to be indeed an *Invitation* to a lavish feast of biblical understanding."

—C. Hassell Bullock,
Franklin S. Dyrness Professor of Biblical Studies *Emeritus*, Wheaton College

"Köstenberger and Patterson have put together a significant volume on biblical interpretation. It covers three important areas of interpretation: the historical context of God's revelation, the literary dimensions of the text, and the theological nature of God's communication to us. Attention to these three dimensions opens up the world of Scripture. The authors provide ample examples and encouragements to enter the world of the text. This is a book all students of the Bible will want to read in order to meet God afresh through his written Word."

—Willem A. VanGemeren,
Professor of Old Testament, Trinity Evangelical Divinity School

"This book is yet another gift from one of my favorite biblical scholars. Can there be anything more important than learning how to correctly interpret and apply the Bible?"

—Pastor Mark Driscoll,
Mars Hill Church, The Resurgence, The Acts 29 Church Planting Network

"The task of interpreting the word of the Lord is fraught with peril, and it has been since our primeval ancestors took hermeneutical direction from a demon. This book, written by two of the most significant biblical scholars in Christianity today, is a sure and steady pathfinder through the most difficult aspects of reading, interpreting, and communicating the Bible. Read this book and prepare yourself to hear afresh the Spirit speaking in the Scriptures."

—Russell D. Moore,
Dean, The Southern Baptist Theological Seminary

"Here is a hermeneutics textbook aimed squarely at instructing students in the essentials of how to interpret the Bible. It avoids jargon laden, philosophical discussion on the relationship between the reader and the text, but instead gives the student an objective method for finding what a text means. Yet it is not simply a "how-to" book; it demonstrates that each biblical text must be read as a representative of the biblical world and not just as words and sentences to be analyzed. A text should be interpreted by a kind of triangulation, seeing it from its historical, literary, and theological *context*. This in turn allows the student to grasp that text's historical, literary, and theological *meaning*. Along the way, Köstenberger and Patterson give students a complete but concise introduction to the concepts that make up the world of biblical hermeneutics."

— Duane Garrett,
John R. Sampey Professor of Old Testament Interpretation,
The Southern Baptist Theological Seminary

"*Invitation to Biblical Interpretation* may easily become the new standard hermeneutics textbook for seminaries and evangelical universities. Köstenberger and Patterson faithfully guide readers across the vast and diverse terrain of the biblical canon. They expertly provide readers with all the necessary historical, literary, and theological tools for the task of exegesis as part of the interpretive journey. Along the way, they point out relevant signposts and occasionally stop to dig deeply into the text with probing insights. They begin with the broad scope of the canon and brilliantly interweave matters of general and special hermeneutics while managing to present a robust hermeneutical theory. This comprehensive hermeneutics textbook rivals, and may even surpass, the well-respected works by Fee and Stuart or Duvall and Hays."

"The authors have provided a treasure trove of information, methods, procedures, and insights that will benefit anyone who wants to read the Bible seriously and delve deeply into its riches. Fully equipped with examples and cautions, the book will guide readers judiciously under the careful tutelage that Köstenberger and Patterson bring to the task of interpretation informed by their long years of experience."

"Hermeneutics is without a doubt a difficult course to teach. Köstenberger and Patterson have made that task a little easier now with their impressive textbook on the subject. Their clear, objective method for interpreting the Bible is built around the "hermeneutical triad," studying Scripture in terms of its historical setting, literary and linguistic features, and theological message. User friendly and example rich, *Invitation to Biblical Interpretation* will help theological students to become better interpreters of the Bible. A fine work!"

"This volume is well conceived and well written. It presents introductory and advanced concepts in a systematic way that makes it suitable for college or seminary use. Its authors are trustworthy veteran scholars and master teachers. I recommend it highly to teachers, students, pastors, and lay teachers."

"*Invitation to Biblical Interpretation* is a welcome addition for those who seek to move beyond the hermeneutical "basics" to even more serious consideration of the biblical text. Its emphasis on the "hermeneutical triad" of history, literature, and theology results in a comprehensive approach to biblical interpretation that leaves few, if any, stones unturned. It provides ample bibliography and guides students in developing their own personal biblical and theological libraries. Finally, Köstenberger and Patterson insist the exegete move beyond interpretation to application and proclamation—a good reminder that hermeneutics should never become an end in itself, but a tool to life change."

—Bryan Beyer,
Professor of Old Testament, Columbia International University

"In *Invitation to Biblical Interpretation*, Andreas Köstenberger and Richard Patterson condense their many years of teaching hermeneutics into an engaging and faithful interpretive guide. Much thought has gone into designing a textbook with maximum utility for the classroom. I highly commend this fine new book."

—Robert L. Plummer,
Associate Professor of New Testament Interpretation,
The Southern Baptist Theological Seminary

"Hermeneutics textbooks can sometimes occlude rather than reveal the meaning of the Bible. *Invitation to Biblical Interpretation* brilliantly illumines the Scriptures by rightly paying attention to their historical, literary and theological horizons. It is insightful, lucidly written, and thorough. I am certain this resource will become a standard text for many universities, seminaries, and theological colleges."

—Heath Thomas,
Assistant Professor of Old Testament & Hebrew,
Southeastern Baptist Theological Seminary
Fellow in Old Testament Studies, The Paideia Centre for Public Theology

"Greek and Hebrew are invaluable tools for exegesis. However, without a consistent, informed, balanced approach to interpreting Scripture, their use can become a pretext for eisegesis instead of exegesis. The text then becomes whatever the reader wants it to mean and the biblical languages can be sorely abused. Köstenberger and Patterson have crafted an extraordinary volume that takes scholarly concepts from advanced hermeneutics books and simplifies them for the striving seminary student (and even the undergraduate student) to understand. They delineate difficult concepts in tangible ways for sound and effective exegesis. This book should get widespread use in classes among seminary and undergraduate biblical interpretation courses. I highly recommend it."

— David A. Croteau,
Associate Professor of Biblical Studies, Liberty University

"Köstenberger and Patterson have provided us a well-rounded and sound hermeneutical method, clearly explaining the historical, literary, and theological dimensions. It is evident that this volume is the result of years of in-depth and careful study. Students and pastors alike will gain a wealth of knowledge and insight from this book. Köstenberger and Patterson have given us an invitation to study the Bible and we would do well to accept their offer."

—Benjamin L. Merkle,
Associate Professor of New Testament and Greek,
Southeastern Baptist Theological Seminary

"Wedding clarity with grace, precision with pastoral sensitivity, Köstenberger and Patterson have provided us with an introduction to biblical interpretation that is firm in conviction without being strident in tone. The hermeneutical triad of history, text, and theology, presented in a way that moves from the big picture (canon) to the specifics (words) and thus assumes from the start a coherent, unified, and divinely governed narrative, will achieve its goal—producing workers who need not be ashamed but rightly handle the word of truth."

—Dane Ortlund,
Senior Editor, Crossway Books

"Between the covers of this book you'll find impressive coverage of primary and secondary sources related to the interpretation of the Bible, competent engagement with topics relevant to the hermeneutical task, and a student-friendly package made easy for teachers to deploy. This faithful exploration of the hermeneutical triad of history, literature, and theology deserves wide reading and heavy use."

—Jim Hamilton,
Associate Professor of New Testament,
The Southern Baptist Theological Seminary

"Part biblical history, part OT and NT introduction, part genre, form, and literary analysis, part linguistic method, part biblical theology, and part contemporary application—Köstenberger and Patterson provide for the beginning evangelical student a one-stop textbook that is competent, conservative, and contextually oriented at every turn. Showing the crucial interrelationship of history, text, and theology, their work provides a solid place for the new student to stand in order to reach for the Scriptures for the first time!"

—Scott Hafemann,
Mary F. Rockefeller Distinguished Professor of NT,
Gordon-Conwell Theological Seminary

INVITATION TO
BIBLICAL
INTERPRETATION

Exploring the Hermeneutical Triad of
History, Literature, and Theology

ANDREAS J. KÖSTENBERGER
RICHARD D. PATTERSON

There are added resources available for this book on the Kregel website: www.kregeldigitaleditions.com, including an overview chart, a syllabus shell, chapter quizzes, and presentation slides in PowerPoint format. Some of these aids are also accessible from www.biblicalfoundations.org.

Invitation to Biblical Interpretation: Exploring the Hermeneutical Triad of History, Literature, and Theology

© 2011 by Andreas J. Köstenberger and Richard D. Patterson

Published by Kregel Publications, a division of Kregel, Inc., P.O. Box 2607, Grand Rapids, MI 49501.

Library of Congress Cataloging-in-Publication Data
Köstenberger, Andreas J., 1957-
    Invitation to biblical interpretation : exploring the hermeneutical triad of history, literature, and theology / by Andreas J. Köstenberger and Richard D. Patterson.
    p. cm.
    1. Bib—Textbooks. I. Patterson, Richard Duane. II. Title.
    BS476.K67 2011
    220.601—dc23
                                                                    2011039897
ISBN 978-0-8254-3047-3

Printed in the United States of America
12 13 14 15 / 5 4 3 2

To all faithful interpreters of God's Word,
Augustine, Luther, Calvin, Schlatter,
and to our colleagues and students
who strive to do their best to study
to show themselves approved by God,
correctly handling the word of truth
(2 Tim. 2:15)

CONTENTS

PREFACE

WRITING A HERMENEUTICS TEXT is not an easy task. Having taught courses on biblical interpretation on the college, graduate, and doctoral levels for many years, we can attest to the fact that hermeneutics is one of the hardest subjects to teach—but also one of the most important. The present volume is dedicated to all serious students of Scripture who are willing to do whatever it takes—even master the biblical languages, if God provides the opportunity—to understand God's Word and to teach it faithfully to others.

We gratefully acknowledge the loving support of our wives, Margaret and Ann, during the process of writing this volume. They have faithfully stood by our side for many years. Thank you so much! Thanks are also due the students who patiently endured various stages of drafts and penultimate versions of this manuscript. Your feedback has made this a better book that is hopefully more helpful to new generations of students. We are also grateful to Jim Weaver of Kregel Publications for commissioning the volume.

I (Andreas Köstenberger) would also like to express my gratitude to my esteemed colleague and friend, Dick Patterson, for embarking with me on the adventure of writing this text. I could not have asked for a better collaborator, equally conversant with and committed to exploring the historical, literary, and theological dimensions of Scripture. It has been a great privilege to work with you, Dick, and your seasoned scholarship sets a wonderful example for others to emulate.

I would also like to acknowledge the debt of gratitude I owe to those who, by instruction and example, taught me how to interpret the Bible: my first hermeneutics teacher, Robertson McQuilkin; my Greek exegesis instructor, William Larkin; my advanced hermeneutics teacher, Grant

Osborne; and my doctoral mentor, D. A. Carson. While I have charted my own course, standing on the shoulders of these spiritual giants has enabled me to see farther than I would otherwise have been able to see. Especially Grant Osborne's *Hermeneutical Spiral* and D. A. Carson's *Exegetical Fallacies* have made a lasting impact on me, and in many ways this volume represents a tribute to the formative influence of these men.

I (Dick Patterson) would like to express my gratitude to my distinguished and well-respected colleague and friend, Andreas Köstenberger, for his vision, direction, and dedication to the completion of this text. I have profited from my interaction with the fruits of his dedicated scholarship and have enjoyed collaborating with him in our mutual concern for the "hermeneutical triad." It has been my privilege to be asked to serve with you, Andreas. Your wide-ranging expertise and commitment to Christ have set a high standard for all of us to follow.

I would also acknowledge the contributions to my training by the excellent graduate faculty at UCLA in my early days, such as Giorgio Buccellati, and my dear mentor and professor of Greek and theology, Marchant King, all of whom not only provided vital information, but also shared both their love of the subject matter and their lives with me. I also acknowledge the contributions of so many colleagues in the Evangelical Theological Society, whose commitment to Christ and his Word have served as motivating examples to me to make God's Word my guidebook for life (Ps. 119:111).

Finally, both of us would like to express our gratitude to Liz Mburu, Corin Mihaila, and Alan Bandy for writing serious first drafts of the chapters on the Gospels and parables, the Epistles, and the apocalyptic material. Michael Travers penned a serious first draft of the chapter on figurative language, and Scott Kellum did the same with the final chapter on application (special thanks are due Scott, who did so on very short notice and with distinction). Chip McDaniel contributed some material on Hebrew word study, and Mark Catlin did the same for the chapter on historical background. Mark also went the extra mile and competently prepared the indexes. John Burkett, the director of our writing center, kindly read the entire manuscript and made several helpful suggestions for improvement.

Soli Deo gloria.

A PERSONAL NOTE

TO TEACHERS, STUDENTS, AND

READERS

THIS BOOK IS TRYING to teach a simple method for interpreting the Bible. It involves preparation, interpretation, and application. The method for interpretation is built around the hermeneutical triad, which consists of history, literature, and theology. In essence, our core proposal is this: for any passage of Scripture, you will want to study the historical setting, the literary context, and the theological message. Before saying a bit more about the hermeneutical triad and how it works in practice, it may be helpful to say a word about how this text relates to previous hermeneutics texts.

This is now at least the third geometric figure used in a hermeneutical context. First came the hermeneutical circle (the notion that one's understanding of a text in its entirety provides the proper framework for understanding the individual parts and vice versa). Then came the hermeneutical spiral (the notion that "biblical interpretation entails a spiral from text to context, from its original meaning to its contextualization or significance in the church today").[1] Now, at long last, comes the hermeneutical triad: the proposal that history, literature, and theology form the proper grid for biblical interpretation.

---

1. Grant Osborne's definition on p. 22 of his book *The Hermeneutical Spiral: A Comprehensive Introduction to Biblical Interpretation.* 2d ed. (Downers Grove: InterVarsity, 2006).

While the terminology is new—to my knowledge, I am the first to use the term "hermeneutical triad"—the actual practice of studying Scripture in terms of history, literature, and theology is certainly not. To the contrary, there is a growing number of scholars who discuss the study of Scripture from this vantage point. Tremper Longman and Raymond Dillard, for example, in their *Introduction to the Old Testament*, routinely discuss a given Old Testament book under the rubrics of "Historical Background," "Literary Analysis," and "Theological Message." Perhaps most notably, N. T. Wright, in several of his writings such as in *The New Testament and the People of God*, uses this classification.

In fact, Wright is a master in this. In both his work on Jesus and Paul, he grounds his study in extensive historical research of Second Temple and first-century Judaism. He also continually speaks of the "story of Israel" and the "Christian story," incorporating a plethora of insights from recent literary study; but most of all Wright prioritizes theology, seeking to discern the divine message in his study of the historical and literary dimensions of the biblical text. In this way of conceiving the hermeneutical task, we stand completely united with Wright (though we differ with him on a few interpretive details!). We also concur with Wright that critical realism (the notion that texts can and do accurately represent external objects, properties, and events) is the best way to capture the essence of the approach to be taken in biblical study.

Kevin Vanhoozer, in his influential work, *The Drama of Doctrine*, writes, "First, in order to do justice to these texts, we must approach them on several levels: historical, literary, and theological." In many ways, the present volume represents a biblical-theological realization of Vanhoozer's proposal of a "canonical-linguistic approach." Thus, by speaking of a hermeneutical triad, we are tapping into well-established interpretive theory and practice.

These three proposals—the hermeneutical circle, the hermeneutical spiral, and the hermeneutical triad—are not mutually exclusive, nor is one necessarily superior to the other. In fact, each geometric figure conveys a valid insight. The hermeneutical circle establishes the exceedingly important interpretive principle of understanding each part of Scripture in light of the whole biblical message. The hermeneutical spiral underscores the importance of moving from the ancient text to the contemporary context. Without application, interpretation is not complete. The hermeneutical triad, for its part, points to the triadic structure of the interpretive task, noting that the biblical interpreter is faced with three inescapable realities: history, the text (i.e. literature), and theology (divine revelation). God has revealed himself in history, and the biblical texts require skilled interpretation, with careful attention being given to the text's canonical location, genre characteristics, and linguistic features (including word meanings and grammatical relationships).

By starting with the big picture or broadest category, canon, and moving from there to genre (still a very broad category) and finally to the study of a concrete literary unit in its discourse context (with careful attention being given to the specific words used), our method embodies the principle of interpreting the parts (words) in light of the whole (canon and genre). By moving all the way from history (the historical-cultural grounding of a given biblical passage) to contemporary application (the final chapter of our book), we heed the key concern of the proponents of the hermeneutical spiral—that interpretation is not complete until we apply our interpretive insights to our own lives and those of our congregations.

Having said this, there is a pronounced difference between the flow adopted in our book and the conventional course of action. Many books, *The Hermeneutical Spiral* being a typical example, move from general to special hermeneutics, based on the premise that as a piece of human communication, the Bible should be interpreted like any other piece of writing: study the words, break down the syntax, look at the historical setting, and so forth (general hermeneutics). After this, they move into special hermeneutics: studying the various biblical genres both literarily and theologically. In this book, we turn the conventional wisdom on its head: rather than moving from general to special hermeneutics, we move from special to general. In doing so, we are building on the enormous amount of recent scholarship on the importance of the canon, theology, metanarrative, and Scripture as "theodrama." (We also follow the elementary hermeneutical principle, mentioned above, of interpreting the parts in light of the whole.)

As a result, we don't start with words; we start with the canon. For example, this is also how we would interpret, say, a play by Shakespeare. We don't just analyze the words in a given sentence; we first try to learn more about Shakespeare, his background, the time in which he wrote, surveying his major works, and so on, before finally settling on a particular play. Even then we might read a good summary before eventually delving in and starting to read the play. When we encounter a given word with which we are unfamiliar, we would not stop reading, because we are more concerned about following the general flow than identifying individual word meanings. Thus we don't start with analyzing the details of the biblical text (word study); we start with the whole (canon).

What is more, we also don't start out pretending the Bible is just like any other book, because we don't believe it is. Rather, our purpose here is not to study just any form of human communication; our purpose is to study the Bible—the inerrant, inspired Word of God. This conviction governs our presentation from the very outset and is maintained throughout the entire volume. Ultimately, this is *God's* canon, conveyed in the genres intended by *God*, and communication of *God's* discourses using *God's* words (without, of course, denying human instrumentality, style, and authorship). Thus, we don't introduce the notion of the Bible being "special" at some point later in the interpretive process (as if it were immaterial to the early stages of general hermeneutics) but put it front and center in the organization of the book.

By comparison, other books such as the classic *How to Study the Bible for All Its Worth* by Gordon Fee and Douglas Stuart, essentially jump right into interpreting the different genres of Scripture, which rightly occupies a central part in any hermeneutical method for interpreting Scripture and also forms a sustained and central part of the present volume. *Grasping God's Word*, another popular textbook, coauthored by J. Scott Duvall and J. Daniel Hays, utilizes the metaphor of the interpretive journey and adopts a more pragmatic, didactic approach, starting with identifying sentences, paragraphs, and discourses before addressing historical and literary context as well as word studies, and moving to application. Only then, specific New and then Old Testament genres are discussed (a rather idiosyncratic order).

In our book, we, too, use the metaphor of an interpretive journey through the canonical landscape. We do make a concerted effort, however, to ground our proposed interpretive method more rigorously in hermeneutical theory, specifically the importance of canon and genre, and the primacy of special over general considerations in the interpretation of Scripture. It is not that words and grammar are not important—they are. It is more a matter of determining what is the proper framework for interpretation—the canon and genre or individual words and grammar— and how to best translate our choice into a given interpretive method. In this regard, unlike *The Hermeneutical Spiral*, which moves from word study to syntax, we chose to move from the study of biblical discourse (chapter 12) to the study of individual words, semantic field study (chapter 13), based on the common linguistic premise that the discourse context is primary for determining word meaning. With this comparison of other methods and an all-too-brief rationale for our own method, we now describe the hermeneutical triad in more detail.

The first element of the hermeneutical triad is history. Studying the historical setting provides a proper grounding, since all Scripture is rooted in real-life history. God revealed himself in history, and the genres and language in which God chose to reveal himself reflect the historical context.

Second comes literature. Studying the literary context is the focus of Bible study, since Scripture is a piece of writing, a text that has three major components: (1) canon; (2) genre; and (3) language. In studying the literary dimension of Scripture, we locate a passage's place in the canon, determine its genre, and interpret it in keeping with its genre characteristics, doing justice to the language used (which normally will involve outlining the passage to determine its flow of thought and performing relevant word studies).

Third is the climax of biblical interpretation: theology. While the biblical message is grounded in history and conveyed through literature, exploring the theology of a given passage of Scripture is the ultimate goal in interpretation, since, as mentioned, Scripture is first and foremost God's revelation or self-disclosure to us.

The sevenfold method we are proposing looks therefore like this:

Step 1: Preparation
Step 2: History
Step 3: Literature: Canon
Step 4: Literature: Genre
Step 5: Literature: Language
Step 6: Theology
Step 7: Application and Proclamation

By way of brief explanation, interpretation starts with the interpreter. This requires heart preparation. To be successful, the interpretive task also requires the use of a proper method. Depending on the task at hand, the method we are proposing is as simple as possible and as complex as necessary. Just as interpretation begins with the interpreter, it ends with the interpreter. While not technically part of interpretation, application is therefore absolutely vital. What is more, once the interpreter has properly understood and applied God's Word, he doesn't stop there, but teaches or preaches it to others (2 Tim. 2:2).

We have tried and tested the materials in this book for years in various settings. We want to be helpful to teachers in the classroom, so at the beginning of every chapter, we include a simple chart of the hermeneutical triad that tells readers exactly where they are in the seven-step process mentioned above.

A teacher working with a 14-week semester may want to combine chapters 3 and 4 (on the Old and New Testament canon) and/or chapters 12 and 13 (on discourse context and word meanings), though this is probably not ideal, since these chapters are loaded with important content and also require students to practice what they've learned. Alternatively, an instructor may want to assign students to read chapter 14 on figurative language concurrently with chapter 6 on poetry or chapter 11 on apocalyptic literature.

In essence, professors will use the first class period to introduce students to the method used in the book (built around the hermeneutical triad). The second class period will be devoted to historical-cultural background (chapter 2), followed by two lessons on the Old and New Testament canon (chapters 3 and 4). That way, students will first develop a grasp of the overall biblical storyline and its historical development before getting bogged down in the details of exegesis. This will also ensure that, as mentioned, they will interpret the parts (their specific passage) in light of the whole (the drama of Scripture and its salvation-historical, redemptive framework).

The bulk of the semester will be taken up with a study of the various genres of Scripture, in canonical order: Old Testament historical narrative, poetry and wisdom, prophecy, New Testament historical narrative (Gospels and Acts), parables, epistles, and apocalyptic literature (Revelation) (chapters 5–11). We believe this nicely follows the canon survey in chapters 3 and 4.

After this, students will learn more specifically to read a passage in its larger discourse context (chapter 12), to conduct a word, or better still, semantic field study, to avoid the most common exegetical fallacies (chapter 13), and to interpret figurative language (chapter 14). The book culminates in a chapter on biblical theology (chapter 15) and a chapter on personal application (chapter 16), which includes practical sections on how to use Bible study tools and on moving from text to sermon genre by genre.

One more comment: Some teachers will be used to introducing word study and sentence diagramming early on in the process. If so, no problem. They can simply start with chapters 12 and 13—or start with chapters 1 and 2 and then follow up immediately with chapters 12 and 13. The chapters in this book are largely self-contained, though we did put them in what to us seemed to be the most intuitive and methodologically preferable order. Teachers and students may rearrange the chapters any way they like. The important thing is not so much the exact order of the seven steps but whether in the end justice has been done to the study and application of a given passage.

Beyond this, we welcome questions, comments, or suggestions for improvement; we would love to hear from those who use this book. Who knows, if the book meets a need and is well received, there may even be a second (and third, and fourth) edition, and we will be glad to incorporate any helpful suggestions to make this an even better book and one that is even more helpful to teachers and students alike. Contact us at akostenberger@sebts.edu or profpatterson@frontier.com. We would also like to encourage the use of the resources available on the Kregel website: www.kregeldigitaleditions.com, including a syllabus shell, chapter quizzes, and presentation slides in PowerPoint format (also posted at www.biblicalfoundations.org).

Throughout the book, we use the metaphor of our method—the hermeneutical triad—serving as a compass on our interpretive journey through the canonical landscape. Thanks for joining us on this exciting journey of life-giving discovery and adventure. May God richly bless all who serve him and study his Word.

Your fellow servants,
Andreas Köstenberger and Dick Patterson

COMPLETE OUTLINE

Preface
A Personal Note to Teachers, Students, and Readers
Complete Outline
Abbreviations

PREPARATION: THE WHO, WHY, AND HOW OF INTERPRETATION

Chapter 1: Welcome to the Hermeneutical Triad: History, Literature, and Theology
  A. Chapter 1 Objectives
  B. Chapter 1 Outline
  C. Introduction
  D. The Need for Skilled Biblical Interpretation
  E. The Cost of Failed Biblical Interpretation
  F. The Characteristics of the Biblical Interpreter
  G. The Purpose and Plan of This Book
  H. The History of Biblical Interpretation and the Hermeneutical Triad
    1. The Old Testament, Jesus, and the Early Church
    2. The Apostolic Fathers and the Apologists
    3. The Schools of Alexandria and Antioch
    4. Jerome and Augustine
    5. The Medieval Period
    6. The Reformation and the Enlightenment
    7. The Modern Period
  I. The Hermeneutical Triad

J. Guidelines for Biblical Interpretation: Overall Method
K. Key Words
L. Study Questions
M. Assignments
N. Chapter Bibliography

INTERPRETATION: THE HERMENEUTICAL TRIAD

PART 1—The Context of Scripture: History

Chapter 2: Setting the Stage: Historical-Cultural Background
A. Chapter 2 Objectives
B. Chapter 2 Outline
C. Introduction: History and Hermeneutics
D. Chronology
   1. Old Testament Period
      a. Primeval Period
      b. Patriarchal Period
      c. From the Exodus to the United Monarchy
      d. Divided Monarchy
      e. Exile and Return
   2. The Second Temple Period
      a. Babylonian and Persian Periods
      b. Hellenistic Period
      c. Maccabean Period
      d. Roman Period
   3. The New Testament Period
      a. Jesus
      b. Early Church and Paul
      c. Rest of the New Testament
E. Archaeology
   1. Old Testament
   2. New Testament
F. Historical-Cultural Background
   1. Primary Sources
      a. Ancient Near Eastern Literature
      b. Old and New Testament Apocrypha

PART 2—The Focus of Scripture: Literature

UNIT 1: CANON

Chapter 3: The Old Testament Canon: The Law, the Prophets, and the Writings

G. Covenant
   1. Covenant Types
   2. Key Chain of Covenants Culminating in the New Covenant
   3. Applicability of the Covenants
   4. Guidelines for Understanding the Old Testament Covenants
H. Coordinating Old Testament Themes
   1. Rule of God and the Concept of Messiah
   2. Relation of God and of the Messiah to the Law, the Exodus, and the Covenants
   3. Role of Messiah in the New Covenant
   4. Relation of Old Testament Messianism to the New Testament
   5. Righteousness and Faith
I. Guidelines for Understanding the Nature and Relevance of Messianism
J. Key Words
K. Study Questions
L. Assignments
G. Chapter Bibliography

Chapter 4: The New Testament Canon: The Gospels, Acts, Epistles, and Apocalypse
A. Chapter 4 Objectives
B. Chapter 4 Outline
C. Introduction
D. New Testament Canon
E. Gospels and the Gospel
F. Book of Acts and the Early Church
G. Epistles, Christ, and the Churches
H. Apocalypse and the Revelation of the Word
I. Conclusion
J. Guidelines for Interpreting the New Testament Canon
K. Key Words
L. Study Questions
M. Assignments
N. Chapter Bibliography

UNIT 2: GENRE

Chapter 5: Enjoying a Good Story: Old Testament Historical Narrative
    A. Chapter 5 Objectives
    B. Chapter 5 Outline
    C. Nature of Biblical Narrative
    D. Modes of Old Testament Historical Narrative
       1. Stories
       2. Accounts
       3. Reports
    E. Elements of Old Testament Historical Narrative
       1. External Elements
       2. Internal Elements
          a. Setting
          b. Plot
          c. Characterization
    F. Narrative Style
       1. Dialogue
       2. Repetition
       3. Highlighting
       4. Irony
       5. Satire
    G. Sample Exegesis: 1 Kings 19
    H. Guidelines for Interpreting Old Testament Narrative
    I. Key Words
    J. Study Questions
    K. Assignments
    L. Chapter Bibliography

Chapter 6: Words of Wisdom: Poetry and Wisdom
    A. Chapter 6 Objectives
    B. Chapter 6 Outline
    C. Nature and Characteristics of Biblical Poetry
       1. Parallelism
          a. Similar Parallelism
          b. Antithetic Parallelism
          c. Progressive Parallelism

ABBREVIATIONS

Bible Versions
MT   Masoretic Text
LXX   Septuagint

Bible Translations
ESV   English Standard Version
HCSB   Holman Christian Standard Bible
NIV   New International Version

Patristic and Medieval Works
Eusebius, *Hist. Eccl.*   Eusebius, *Historia Ecclesiastica* (*Ecclesiastical History*)
Nicholas of Lyra, *In Gal.* Nicolas of Lyra, (*On Galatians*)

Periodicals
AASOR   *Annual of the American Schools of Oriental Research*
AUSS   *Andrews University Seminary Studies*
BA   *Biblical Archaeologist*
BAR   *Biblical Archaeology Review*
BASOR   *Bulletin of the American Schools of Oriental Research*
Bib Sac   *Bibliotheca Sacra*
BBR   *Bulletin for Biblical Research*
CJ   *Classical Journal*
CTR   *Criswell Theological Review*
EvQ   *Evangelical Quarterly*
HTR   *Harvard Theological Review*

Int	*Interpretation*
IBS	*Irish Biblical Studies*
JAOS	*Journal of the American Oriental Society*
JBL	*Journal of Biblical Literature*
JETS	*Journal of the Evangelical Theological Society*
JNES	*Journal of Near Eastern Studies*
JSNT	*Journal for the Study of the New Testament*
JSOT	*Journal for the Study of the Old Testament*
LW	*Living Word*
NovT	*Novum Testamentum*
NTS	*New Testament Studies*
ST	*Studia theologica*
TJ	*Trinity Journal*
TynBul	*Tyndale Bulletin*
VT	*Vetus Testamentum*
WTJ	*Westminster Theological Journal*
WW	*Word and World*
ZAG	*Zeitschrift für Alte Geschichte*

Series and Reference Works

AB	Assyriologische Bibliothek
AGJU	Arbeiten zur Geschichte des antiken Judentums und des Urchristentums
BDAG	*Greek-English Lexicon of the New Testament and Other Early Christian Literature*
BDB	*A Hebrew and English Lexicon of the Old Testament*
BDF	*A Greek Grammar of the New Testament and Other Early Christian Literature*
BECNT	Baker Exegetical Commentary on the New Testament
BTNT	Biblical Theology of the New Testament
BZAW	Beihefte zur Zeitschrift für die alttestamentliche Wissenschaft
CBET	Contributions to Biblical Exegesis and Theology
CRINT	Compendia rerum iudaicarum ad Novum Testamentum
DJG	*Dictionary of Jesus and the Gospels*
FRLANT	Forschungen zur Religion und Literatur des Alten und Neuen

HALOT	*The Hebrew and Aramaic Lexicon of the Old Testament*
ICC	International Critical Commentary
JSNTSupp	Journal for the Study of the New Testament Supplement Series
JSOTSupp	Journal for the Study of the Old Testament Supplement Series
LEC	Library of Early Christianity
LNT	Library of New Testament Studies
MNTC	Moffatt New Testament Commentary
NAC	New American Commentary
NIBC	New International Biblical Commentary
NICNT	New International Commentary on the New Testament
NICOT	New International Commentary on the Old Testament
NIDNTT	*New International Dictionary of New Testament Theology*
NIGTC	New International Greek Testament Commentary
NIVAC	NIV Application Commentary
NSBT	New Studies in Biblical Theology
NTOA	Novum Testamentum et Orbis Antiquus
OBO	Orbis biblicus et orientalis
OTL	Old Testament Library
PNTC	Pillar New Testament Commentary
SAHS	Scripture and Hermeneutics Series
SacPag	Sacra Pagina
SBLDS	Society of Biblical Literature Dissertation Series
SBLSS	Society of Biblical Literature Supplement Series
SNTSMS	Society for New Testament Studies Monograph Series
SBT	Studies in Biblical Theology
STL	Studies in Theological Interpretation
TB	Theologische Bücherei: Neudrucke und Berichte aus dem 20. Jahrhundert
TDNT	*Theological Dictionary of the New Testament*
TDOT	*Theological Dictionary of the Old Testament*
TNTC	Tyndale New Testament Commentaries
WBC	Word Biblical Commentary
WUNT	Wissenschaftliche Untersuchungen zum Neuen Testament

PREPARATION:
The Who, Why, and How of
Interpretation

CHAPTER 1 OBJECTIVES

1. To convince the reader of the need for, and the rewards of, skilled interpretation.

2. To persuade the reader of the cost of failed biblical interpretation.

3. To set forth the essential characteristics of the biblical interpreter.

4. To preview the purpose and plan of this book.

5. To review briefly the history of biblical interpretation.

6. To introduce the student to the hermeneutical triad of interpreting Scripture.

CHAPTER 1 OUTLINE

A. Chapter 1 Objectives

B. Chapter 1 Outline

C. Introduction

D. Need for Skilled Biblical Interpretation

E. Cost of Failed Biblical Interpretation

F. Characteristics of the Biblical Interpreter

G. Purpose and Plan of This Book

H. History of Biblical Interpretation and the Hermeneutical Triad

I. The Hermeneutical Triad

J. Guidelines for Biblical Interpretation: Overall Method

K. Key Words

L. Study Questions

M. Assignments

N. Chapter Bibliography

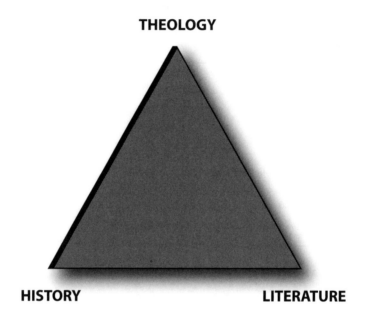

Chapter 1

WELCOME TO THE HERMENEUTICAL TRIAD: HISTORY, LITERATURE, AND THEOLOGY

INTRODUCTION

COME ON IN, AND STAY for a while! Make yourself at home, and acquire vital skills in understanding the most important book ever written—the Holy Scriptures. The volume you are holding in your hands invites you to embark on the quest of sound biblical interpretation or as it is also called, "hermeneutics."[1] As in Jesus' parable of the wedding feast, the invitation goes out to all who care to listen. And as in Jesus' parable, the terms are not set by those invited but by the one who issues the invitation and by the book to be interpreted.

In our quest to understand the Bible, *author*, *text*, and *reader* each have an important part to play.[2] Every document has an author, and the resulting

---

1. "Hermeneutics" refers to the study of the methodological principles of interpretation, in particular, in the Bible. The term originates from the Greek god Hermes, who served as herald and messenger of the other gods and whose portfolio included commerce, travel, invention, and eloquence. The term "hermeneutics" was used by the important Greek philosopher Aristotle in his work *Peri Hermeneias*, one of the earliest surviving philosophical works in the Western tradition to deal with the relationship between language and logic.
2. See esp. Grant R. Osborne, *The Hermeneutical Spiral: A Comprehensive Introduction to Biblical Interpretation*, 2d ed. (Downers Grove: InterVarsity, 2006), Appendices 1 and 2.

text is shaped by his or her intention. It is this authorial intention the interpreter must aim to recover. The text is not "just there," left to be interpreted any way a given reader chooses. When my wife talks to me, I dare not give her words my own preferred meaning. The rules of proper communication demand that I seek to understand the meaning *she* intended to convey.

It follows that the text of Scripture, likewise, is not neutral, that is, malleable to a great variety of interpretations that lay equal claim to represent valid readings of a given passage (as is common in various postmodern, reader-response approaches to biblical interpretation).[3] Nor is the text autonomous, that is, a law unto itself, as if it existed apart from the author who willed and wrote it into being (as is held by various narrative or literary approaches).[4] It is an authorially shaped and designed product that requires careful and respectful interpretation.

There is therefore an important ethical dimension in interpretation. We should engage in interpretation responsibly, displaying respect for the text and its author.[5] There is no excuse for interpretive arrogance that elevates the reader above text and author. The "golden rule" of interpretation requires that we extend the same courtesy to any text or author that we would want others to extend to our statements and writings. This calls for respect not only for the intentions of the human authors of Scripture but ultimately for God who chose to reveal himself through the Bible by his Holy Spirit.[6]

This volume is based on such respect both for the ultimate author of Scripture and for its human authors. We are committed to taking the text of Scripture seriously and to practicing a hermeneutic of listening and perception.[7] We aim to take into account the relevant historical setting of a given passage and to pay close attention to the words, sentences, and discourses of a particular book. We purpose to give careful consideration

---

3. The classic treatment of validity in interpretation in the context of affirming the primacy of authorial intention is E. D. Hirsch, *Validity in Interpretation* (New Haven: Yale University, 1973).

4. See Kevin J. Vanhoozer, "A Lamp in the Labyrinth: The Hermeneutics of 'Aesthetic Theology,'" *TJ* 8 (1987): 25–56.

5. See esp. Kevin J. Vanhoozer, *Is There a Meaning in This Text? The Bible, the Reader, and the Morality of Literary Knowledge* (Grand Rapids: Zondervan, 1998).

6. For an introductory treatment, see "The Nature and Scope of Scripture," Chap. 1 in Andreas J. Köstenberger, L. Scott Kellum, and Charles L. Quarles, *The Cradle, the Cross, and the Crown: An Introduction to the New Testament* (Nashville: B&H, 2009).

7. A dictum posited by the theologian Adolf Schlatter (see further below).

to the theology of the Bible itself and to interpret the parts in light of the canonical whole.[8] Last but not least, we seek to operate within the proper framework of the respective genres of Scripture.

Why would we want to take the time and exert the effort to learn to interpret Scripture correctly? First of all, we will want to do so because we are seekers of *truth* and because we realize that truth sets free while error enslaves.[9] Many cults have arisen because of their flawed interpretation of Scripture.[10] There is an even more powerful motivation, however: embarking on the quest for accurate biblical interpretation out of our *love* for God, his Word, and his people.[11] If you and I truly love God, we will want to get him know him better, and this involves serious study of his Word.

As seekers of truth and as lovers of God and others, then, we set out to discover revealed truth and to acquire biblical wisdom as one sets out to mine gold and precious stones.[12] Our conviction that God's Word is the most precious commodity there is fuels a desire to extract even the last ounce of meaning from the biblical text no matter how much effort or learning it takes to recover it. In our quest for revealed divine truth, we will be prepared to pay whatever price it takes to hear God speak to us in and through his Word and to proclaim his life-giving message authentically and accurately to others.

---

8. These component parts of proper biblical interpretation form the backbone of the present volume.

9. As Jesus told his would-be followers, "If you hold to my teaching, you are really my disciples. Then you will know the truth, *and the truth will set you free*" (John 8:31–32).

10. A great recent tool in this regard is *The Apologetics Study Bible*, ed. Ted Cabal (Nashville: B&H, 2007). See also Gleason L. Archer, *New International Encyclopedia of Bible Difficulties* (Grand Rapids: Zondervan, 1982); Walter C. Kaiser Jr., Peter H. Davids, F. F. Bruce, and Manfred T. Brauch, *Hard Sayings of the Bible* (Downers Grove: InterVarsity, 1996); and the forthcoming *Holman Apologetics Bible Commentary* (Nashville: B&H).

11. See in this context N. T. Wright's advocacy of a "hermeneutic of love" (*The New Testament and the People of God* [Minneapolis: Fortress, 1992]). Just as love "affirms the reality and otherness of the beloved" rather than attempt to "collapse the beloved into terms of itself," a hermeneutic of love "means that the text can be listened to on its own terms, without being reduced to the scale of what the reader can or cannot understand at the moment" (p. 64).

12. See Jesus' parables of the hidden treasure and the pearl (Matt. 13:44–46) and his statement, "Therefore every teacher of the law who has been instructed about the kingdom of heaven is like the owner of a house who brings out of his storeroom new treasures as well as old" (Matt. 13:52). See also Psalms 9 and 119 and the depiction of wisdom in Proverbs 1–9.

NEED FOR SKILLED BIBLICAL INTERPRETATION

"Do your best," Paul wrote in his final missive to his foremost disciple, "to present yourself to God as one approved, a workman who does not need to be ashamed and who correctly handles the word of truth" (2 Tim. 2:15). In a day when people are confronted with a flood of information and are struggling to keep up and set priorities, Paul's words bring into sharp focus what ought to be our primary object of study: Scripture, "the word of truth." Like Peter, we ought to say, "Lord, to whom shall we go? You have the words of eternal life" (John 6:68). We ought to be driven by a hunger and thirst for righteousness (Matt. 5:6); we ought to be longing for the life-transforming, "living and active" word of God (Heb. 4:12).

To unpack Paul's above-cited words yet further, we need to work hard at interpreting Scripture. We must "do our best" as "a worker." Biblical interpretation is even *hard* work. The one who wants to master the handling of God's Word must be like the apprentice of a master crafts person. Over time, and through practice, that apprentice will learn to skillfully use many tools. Likewise, the biblical interpreter must know what interpretive tools to use and how to use them. This is what it means to "correctly handle" the word of truth.

While the analogy holds well between the realm of craftsmanship and biblical interpretation, the argument nonetheless is clearly from the lesser to the greater. If it is important for crafts people to wield their tools skillfully, how much more important it is for those who are called to handle God's "word of truth" with utmost care and expertise. No sloppy or shoddy work will do. Everything must be done in proper sequence, appropriate proportion, and with the purpose of producing an end product that pleases the one who commissioned the work. Background information, word meanings, the context of a given passage, and many other factors must be judiciously assessed if a valid interpretation is to be attained.

Also, no worker labors without regard for the approval of the one who assigned a particular task. Once again, the argument is from the lesser to the greater: for in the case of biblical interpretation, the one to whom we have to give an account is none other than God himself. It is *his* approval we are seeking, for if God approves, no one else's approval, or disapproval, ultimately matters. Our love for God and our conviction that God's Word is so precious that we ought to spare no effort to comprehend it as precisely as possible will be powerful motivators as we embark on our interpretive journey. In so doing, we will long to hear God's words of approval, "Well done, good and faithful servant. Enter the joy of your master."

COST OF FAILED BIBLICAL INTERPRETATION

Not only are there great rewards for faithful biblical interpretation, there is also a considerable cost if we fail in this effort. This cost, too, is mentioned in 2 Timothy 2:15. It is shrinking back in shame at God's judgment by the one who is unwilling to acquire the skills needed to interpret Scripture accurately. The equivalent of improper biblical interpretation is shoddy workmanship, due either to the lack of skill or carelessness. In the area of hermeneutics, this translates into fallacies arising from neglect of the context, prooftexting, *eisegesis* (reading one's preferred meaning *into* the text rather than deriving it by careful study *from* the text), improper use of background information, and other similar shortcomings.[13]

Scripture is replete with examples of those who failed in the task of biblical interpretation and were severely chastised, because their failure did not merely bring ruin on these individuals themselves but also on those they taught and influenced. In the verses immediately following 2 Timothy 2:15, the apostle makes reference to two such individuals by the name of Hymenaeus and Philetus. According to Paul, these men "have wandered away from the truth,"[14] "say[ing] that the resurrection has already taken place" (2 Tim. 2:17–18). As Paul pointed out, these false teachers were "destroy[ing] the faith of some" (2 Tim. 2:18). Interestingly, Hymenaeus is already mentioned in Paul's first letter to Timothy, where the apostle wrote that he had handed this man over to Satan so that he might learn not to blaspheme (1 Tim. 1:20). Yet, sadly, Hymenaeus persisted in twisting and distorting the word of truth.

From this we learn, among other things, that biblical interpretation is not an individualistic enterprise. Rather, it takes place in the community of believers, and the failure or success of the interpretative task affects not merely the interpreter but other believers as well. Note also that, as is often the case with cults—ultimately inspired by Satan, the master distorter and

---

13. See the discussion of exegetical fallacies in chapter 13 below.
14. Compare the reference to "the word of truth" in 2 Timothy 2:15.

twister of Scripture (see Gen. 3:1–5)—there is a kernel of truth in the assertion that "the resurrection has already taken place." Christ did in fact rise from the dead as "the firstfruits of those who have fallen asleep" (1 Cor. 15:20), and all believers can expect to be raised in the future (1 Cor. 15:51–53; 1 Thess. 4:14–18).

But Scripture makes clear that this resurrection is still future, and to say that "the resurrection has already taken place" suggests that rising from the dead is spiritualized and transferred completely into the present. Yet this resembles more closely the Greek notion of the immortality of the soul than the biblical teaching of the resurrection of the body. The problem of Hymenaeus and Philetus, therefore, seems to have been that they improperly imposed their Hellenistic philosophical and cultural conceptions onto Scripture, resulting in an "over-realized eschatology" that failed to acknowledge the future reality of believers' bodily resurrection according to the pattern of Christ.[15]

This brief example shows that biblical interpreters are charged with a sacred task: handling Scripture with accuracy. They are entrusted with a sacred object, God's Word of truth, and their faithfulness or lack thereof will result in God's approval or in personal shame. God's Word commands our very best because, in the ultimate analysis, it is not a human word, but the Word of God. This means that our interpretive enterprise must rest on a robust doctrine of biblical revelation and a high view of Scripture—as Jesus taught, Scripture is "the word of God" and thus "cannot be broken" (John 10:35). Though conveyed through human means, using human language and thought forms, Scripture is ultimately the product of divine inspiration and therefore completely trustworthy.

CHARACTERISTICS REQUIRED
OF THE BIBLICAL INTERPRETER

Rather than adopting a critical stance toward Scripture, we should

---

15. The presentation above is admittedly rather basic. For detailed discussions of the rather complex issues involved in the interpretation of 2 Timothy 2:17–18 and the heresy in view, see especially George W. Knight, *Commentary on the Pastoral Epistles*, NIGTC (Grand Rapids: Eerdmans, 1992), 413–14; William D. Mounce, *Pastoral Epistles*, WBC 46 (Nashville: Thomas Nelson, 2000), 527–28; and I. Howard Marshall, *The Pastoral Epistles*, ICC (Edinburgh: T&T Clark, 1999), 750–54 (with further bibliographic references).

rather submit to it as our final authority in all areas of life. An essential quality required of the biblical interpreter is therefore *humility*. As Adolf Schlatter pointed out decades ago, we must stand "below" Scripture rather than arrogantly asserting our right to critique Scripture in light of our modern or postmodern presuppositions and preferences.[16] Instead of accepting only the teachings we find acceptable in keeping with contemporary sensibilities, we should be prepared to conform our presuppositions and preferences to the teachings of Scripture and to act accordingly. We must come to Scripture willing to obey what it says.

Part of this humility is acknowledging our finiteness and need for instruction and correction. As Paul wrote in his final letter to Timothy, "All Scripture is God-breathed and is useful for teaching, rebuking, correcting and training in righteousness, so that the man of God may be thoroughly equipped for every good work" (2 Tim. 3:16–17). Proper instruction and, if necessary, correction are therefore a function of Scripture itself, though God may choose to administer these through those who rightly interpret the Bible and teach it to others (cf. 2 Tim. 2:2).

Note also that biblical interpretation is not an end in itself but interpretive competence equips the interpreter for "every good work" (2 Tim. 3:17; cf. Eph. 2:10). Rather than being exclusively, or even primarily, a scholarly pursuit, interpretation is required of every believer. While it is true that God has given to the church certain individuals who are to serve as teachers and pastors (Eph. 4:11), he expects *every* believer to progress toward spiritual maturity (Col. 1:28–29). For this reason, we all should assume responsibility for our spiritual growth and make every effort to grow in our ability to handle God's Word accurately and with increasing skill (2 Pet. 3:17–18).

Another quality that is essential for the biblical interpreter is to *listen carefully* to the Word and to study it *perceptively*. This is what Adolf Schlatter called a "hermeneutic of perception." In a time when listening is largely a lost art and many are approaching Scripture primarily for the purpose of validating their own predetermined conclusions, this is a much-needed reminder. Schlatter observed that "it is not the interpreter's

---

16. See the anecdote recounted in Köstenberger, Kellum, and Quarles, *Cradle, the Cross, and the Crown*, 52.

own theology or that of his church and times that is examined but rather the theology expressed by the New Testament itself."[17] He continued:

> It is the historical objective that should govern our conceptual work exclusively and completely, stretching our perceptive faculties to the limit. We turn away decisively from ourselves and our time to what was found in the men through whom the church came into being. Our main interest should be the thought as it was conceived *by them* and the truth that was valid *for them*. We want to see and obtain a thorough grasp of what happened historically and existed in another time. This is the internal disposition upon which the success of the work depends, the commitment which must consistently be renewed as the work proceeds.[18]

In James' words, and in keeping with Old Testament wisdom, interpreters should be "quick to listen" and "slow to speak" (Jas. 1:19). As the ancient preacher pointed out, "Guard your steps when you go to the house of God. Go near to listen rather than to offer the sacrifice of fools . . . Do not be quick with your mouth, do not be hasty in your heart to utter anything before God. God is in heaven and you are on earth, so let your words be few" (Eccl. 5:1–2). Deplorably, the opposite is far more common: people are often quick to air their opinions but slow to hear the actual Word of God. Listening to Scripture requires discipline, self-restraint, wisdom, and love for God.

One final set of desirable (in fact, essential) attributes for biblical interpreters: they should be *regenerate* (that is, have experienced spiritual rebirth) and be *Spirit-filled and led*.[19] The role of the Spirit in biblical interpretation warrants extended treatment,[20] but for a start read Paul's concise treatment in 1 Corinthians 2:10b–16:

---

17. Adolf Schlatter, *The History of the Christ*, trans. Andreas J. Köstenberger (Grand Rapids: Baker, 1997), 18 (emphasis original).
18. Ibid.
19. On the role of faith in interpretation, see Gerhard Maier, *Biblical Hermeneutics* (trans. Robert W. Yarbrough; Wheaton: Crossway, 1995), chap. 11.
20. For a representative treatment, see Daniel P. Fuller, "The Holy Spirit's Role in Biblical Interpretation," in *Scripture, Tradition, and Interpretation* (ed. W. Ward Gasque and William LaSor; Grand Rapids: Eerdmans, 1978), 189–98. See also Roy B. Zuck, *Basic Bible Interpretation: A Practical Guide to Discovering Biblical Truth* (Colorado Springs: David C. Cook, 1991), 22–26.

The Spirit searches all things, even the deep things of God. For who among men knows the thoughts of a man except the man's spirit within him? In the same way no one knows the thoughts of God except the Spirit of God. . . . The man without the Spirit does not accept the things that come from the Spirit of God, for they are foolishness to him, and he cannot understand them, because they are spiritually discerned. The spiritual man makes judgments about all things, but he himself is not subject to any man's judgment . . .

While Paul wrote these words in order to address a specific issue in the Corinthian church that we cannot fully address here,[21] his remarks are also highly relevant for all of us who embark on our interpretive journey. If we do not have the Spirit—or if we have the Spirit but do not listen to him and depend on him for spiritual insight from God's Word—our interpretations will invariably fall short. Only the interpreter who depends on the Holy Spirit in his interpretive quest will likely be successful in discerning God's special, Spirit-appraised revelation.

While a given interpreter may indeed be devoid of faith and the Holy Spirit and still understand some of the words in Scripture, he will lack the spiritual framework, motivation, and understanding to grasp a given passage in its whole-Bible context. What is more, he will not be able to carry out what Scripture asks of him, because it is only regeneration and the Holy Spirit that enable him to do so. For this reason, anyone who has a sincere desire to understand the Bible will want to make sure that he or she is the kind of person who can receive God's words of truth.[22]

PURPOSE AND PLAN OF THIS BOOK

Foundational to the plan of this book is the conviction that those who want to succeed in the task of biblical interpretation need to proceed within a proper interpretive framework, that is, the hermeneutical triad, which consists of the three elements interpreters must address in studying any given biblical passage regardless of its genre: a book's *historical setting*

---

21. For competent, representative treatments see David E. Garland, *1 Corinthians*, BECNT (Grand Rapids: Baker, 2003), 90–103; and Gordon D. Fee, *The First Epistle to the Corinthians*, NICNT (Grand Rapids: Eerdmans, 1987), 97–120.
22. To prepare your heart for the sacred task of interpreting Scripture, you may want to meditate on passages such as Psalms 1, 8, 9, 19, 139, or Isaiah 57:15; 66:1–2.

(chapter 2), its *literary dimension* (chapters 3–14), and its *theological message* (chapter 15).[23] Since Christianity is a historical religion, and all texts are historically and culturally embedded, it is important that we ground our interpretation of Scripture in a careful study of the relevant historical setting. Since Scripture is a text of literature, the bulk of interpretive work entails coming to grips with the various literary and linguistic aspects of the biblical material. Finally, since Scripture is not merely a work of literature but inspired and authoritative revelation from God, the goal and end of interpretation is theology. Using the hermeneutical triad as a compass will ensure that Bible students stay on track in their interpretive journey.

As an interpreter sets out to explore a particular biblical text, he will first research its historical setting (studying what is often called "introductory matters"). After grounding his study in the real-life historical and cultural context of the biblical world, he will orient himself to the canonical landscape. This will place a given passage in its proper salvation-historical context. Next, he will consider the literary genre of a passage. He should imagine the different genres found in Scripture as topographical features such as valleys, mountain ranges, or plains, each of which exhibit characteristic features and call for appropriate navigational strategies. Finally, he will take a close look at the specific linguistic features of a text—larger discourse context, important word meanings, and figurative language where appropriate.

It will be useful to have several road maps on the interpretive journey, depending on the type of terrain encountered: Old Testament historical narrative (chapter 5), poetry and wisdom (chapter 6), prophecy (chapter 7), New Testament narrative (the Gospels and Acts; chapter 8), parables (chapter 9), Epistles (chapter 10), and apocalyptic literature (chapter 11). Using the hermeneutical triad, then, will serve as an overall method for studying any passage of Scripture. As a result, the interpretive apprentice will be well on the way to becoming a skilled worker who does not need to be ashamed, having developed the necessary skills for handling God's Word. Before we proceed, therefore, we will introduce you to the hermeneutical triad of history, literature, and theology, which will serve as our compass on our interpretive journey throughout this book, and briefly review the history of biblical interpretation.

---

23. A "triad" may be defined as a union or group of three, such as a three-tone chord. In our case, the "hermeneutical triad" draws attention to the triadic structure of biblical interpretation consisting of the study of history, language, and theology.

HISTORY OF BIBLICAL INTERPRETATION
AND THE HERMENEUTICAL TRIAD

Interpreters of Scripture are faced with three inescapable realities in their interpretive practice: (1) the reality of history, or more specifically, salvation history, that is, the fact that God's revelation to humans, which is conveyed by the biblical texts, took place in a real-life time and space continuum; the writings of Scripture did not come into being in a vacuum; they were written by people with specific beliefs, convictions, and experiences; (2) the existence of texts containing that revelation that require interpretation (literature); and, last but not least, (3) the reality of God and his revelation in Scripture (theology). Each of these realities, in turn, comprises one aspect of the hermeneutical triad.

THEOLOGY

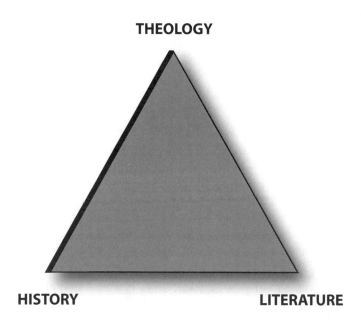

HISTORY   **LITERATURE**

1.1. The Hermeneutical Triad²⁴

---

24. Note that the first letters of "Theology," "History," and "Literature"—that is, T, H, and L—form the mnemonic "THeoLogy." If genre, canon, and language are included as well (see below), the word is "THeoLoGiCaL"—we must give attention to Theology, History, and Literature, which consists of Genre, Canon, and Language.

In essence, therefore, the interpretive task consists of considering each of the three major dimensions of the hermeneutical triad—history, literature, and theology—in proper balance, with the first two elements—history and literature—being foundational and with theology at the apex. While discerning the spiritual message of Scripture—theology—is the ultimate goal of biblical interpretation, an appreciation of the historical-cultural background of a particular text and a proper understanding of its literary features are essential. As the following thumbnail sketch will show, however, the history of interpretation demonstrates that interpreters have not always been successful in giving proper attention to each of the three elements in the hermeneutical triad.[25]

Old Testament, Jesus, and the Early Church

The earliest instances of biblical hermeneutics are found in Scripture itself. In some cases, later Old Testament authors referred back to and further developed earlier Old Testament themes.[26] There are also abundant examples of Jewish interpretation, including those found in the sectarian literature at Qumran (the Dead Sea Scrolls).[27] The New Testament contains abundant references to Old Testament passages, both in form of explicit quotations and by way of allusions and echoes.[28] While there is some variety in the ways in which later biblical authors appropriated earlier texts, ranging from promise-fulfillment to typology, analogy, and, in rare instances, allegory,[29] what all these instances have in common is es-

---

25. I also urge you to read chap. 1 in Köstenberger, Kellum, and Quarles, *Cradle, the Cross, and the Crown,* which will provide you with an excellent framework for studying Scripture with regard to the vital matters of canon, textual transmission, translation, and inspiration.
26. See esp. D. A. Carson and H. G. M. Williamson, *It Is Written: Scripture Citing Scripture* (Cambridge: Cambridge University Press, 1988). See also Michael Fishbane, *Biblical Interpretation in Ancient Israel* (Oxford: Clarendon, 1984).
27. This is a vast field of study. For a survey and bibliographic references, see Köstenberger, Kellum, and Quarles, *Cradle, the Cross, and the Crown,* chap. 2. See also Richard N. Longenecker, *Biblical Exegesis in the Apostolic Period,* 2d ed. (Grand Rapids: Eerdmans, 1999), chap. 1.
28. See esp. G. K. Beale and D. A. Carson, eds., *Commentary on the New Testament Use of the Old Testament* (Grand Rapids: Baker, 2008); and Longenecker, *Biblical Exegesis in the Apostolic Period.* See also R. T. France, *Jesus and the Old Testament* (London: Tyndale, 1971); and Richard B. Hays, *Echoes of Scripture in the Letters of Paul* (New Haven: Yale University Press, 1989).
29. See David L. Baker, *Two Testaments, One Bible* (3d ed.; Downers Grove: InterVarsity, 2010).

sentially two elements: (1) the recognition of dual authorship, that is, the fact that behind any human author of Scripture stands the divine author, God himself; and (2) a respect for the original intention of these authors, both divine and human, in the process of interpretation and application.

The first of these aspects is bound up with important biblical doctrines such as revelation, inspiration, and inerrancy, which flow plainly from Scripture's own self-attestation and underlie the use of Scripture by Jesus, Paul, and the early church.[30] The second aspect involves intricate issues related to discerning the New Testament use of the Old Testament which will occupy us in greater detail in a later chapter.[31]

To this, we may add a third, all-important element: the promised coming of the Messiah in the Old Testament and the hermeneutical axiom undergirding the entire New Testament: that Jesus of Nazareth was that Messiah—Jesus, who was born of a virgin, lived a sinless life, and had gathered the Twelve as his new messianic community; Jesus, who died, was buried, and rose from the dead on the third day; Jesus, who was exalted and ascended to the Father, now through his Spirit directs the church's mission, and will one day return to gather his people and judge the unbelieving world, ushering in the eternal state.[32]

Apostolic Fathers and the Apologists

The Apostolic Fathers—including Clement of Rome (died A.D. 101), Ignatius (A.D. 35–110), and Polycarp (A.D. 69–155), as well as writings such as the *Diduche* and the *Shepherd of Hermas*—built on these scriptural precedents and affirmed that the Messiah predicted in the Old Testament had now come in the person of Jesus of Nazareth.[33] The Apologists—Justin Martyr (A.D. 100–165), Irenaeus (c. 130–c. 200), and Tertullian (c. 160–c.

---

30. See Norman L. Geisler, ed., *Inerrancy* (Grand Rapids: Zondervan, 1980), esp. the essay by Paul Feinberg; D. A. Carson and John D. Woodbridge, eds., *Scripture and Truth* (Grand Rapids: Zondervan, 1983), esp. the essay by Wayne Grudem; and D. A. Carson, *Collected Writings on Scripture* (Wheaton: Crossway, 2010), with reference to a forthcoming 2-volume edited work, tentatively titled *The Scripture Project*, to be published by Eerdmans.
31. Chapter 15: Making the Connection: Getting Our Theology from the Bible.
32. See esp. the canonical survey in Chapters 3 and 4 below.
33. On patristic exegesis, see esp. Charles Kannengiesser, *Handbook of Patristic Exegesis*, 2 vols. (Leiden/Boston: Brill, 2004). See also the relevant essays in Alan J. Hauser and Duane F. Watson, eds., *A History of Biblical Interpretation*, Volume 1: *The Ancient Period* (Grand Rapids: Eerdmans, 2003).

225)—defended Christianity against pagan Romans, non-messianic Jews, and Christian sects or heretics such as Marcion who sought to pit the God of the Old Testament against that of the New Testament. In essence, these early defenders of the Christian faith maintained that both Testaments were unified around Christ as their center and that all of Scripture must be interpreted within an overarching christological framework. Biblical interpretation in this period exhibited a wide range of approaches from literal to typological (historical correspondence between a type and an anti-type), midrashic (commentary), and allegorical.

Schools of Alexandria and Antioch

The most noted proponent of the school of Alexandria—a major ancient center of learning located in Egypt—was the church father Origen (A.D. 185–253). As the head of the Catechetical School in Alexandria, Origen presided over the flourishing of the allegorical method of biblical interpretation. Origen addressed himself primarily to Gentiles with an interest in philosophy. In an effort to demonstrate the supremacy of Christianity, he attempted to show that Christ was the supreme human and religious source of knowledge. According to Origen, Christ himself had spoken in the Old Testament, and the Old Testament message anticipated the best in Greek philosophy. Another Alexandrian writer, Clement (c. 150–c. 215), distinguished between historical and theological (spiritual) elements (*Stromateis* Book I, chap. 28). While appreciating the historical nature of the Mosaic narratives, he also featured instances of "spiritualizing" interpretations (e.g. *Stromateis* Book I, chap. 21).[34]

The exegetical school of Antioch, represented by Theophilus, who became bishop of Antioch in about A.D. 169, and later John Chrysostom (A.D. 354–407), differed markedly from the Alexandrian approach. In fact, the contrast between the two schools explains some of the most foundational issues in biblical interpretation. At the core, the difference between these two schools hinged on their approach to the biblical writings as *history*. While the Alexandrian school resorted to allegorical readings in which history took second place to an interpreter's perceived spiritual

---

34. See Klein, Blomberg, and Hubbard, 38–39, who point out that, like Philo, Clement believed that Scripture had a twofold meaning: "like a human being, it has a body (literal) meaning as well as a soul (spiritual) meaning hidden behind the literal sense" (p. 38).

significance of a given Old Testament character or event, the Antiochenes proceeded in the conviction that the primary level of exegesis was the historical one.

Consequently, while the Alexandrian school set aside the literal historical meaning where it was thought to conflict with an interpreter's moral or intellectual sensibilities, the Antiochene school was committed to interpreting the biblical texts literally wherever possible. At the same time, the Antiochenes did allow for a fuller sense alongside the historical one in the case of messianic psalms and prophecy. In their interpretive restraint and their awarding of primacy to the historical, grammatical level of biblical interpretation, the School of Antioch constitutes an important precursor for the historical-grammatical interpretation propagated during the time of the Reformation.

Jerome and Augustine

The great scholar Jerome (A.D. 347–420) translated the Bible into Latin, a version commonly called the Vulgate, which reigned supreme as the church's Scripture for the next 1,000 years. Having lived intermittently in Antioch, Jerome spent the last 35 years of his life in Bethlehem (A.D. 386–420). In a sense, Jerome combined the best of both the Alexandrian and the Antiochene schools. On the one hand, "He made it clear to his successors that the Old Testament was an oriental book written in an oriental language and set in the oriental past. At the same time he fervently expressed the belief that the coming of Jesus showed that the Old Testament was a book of illumination and hope for all mankind."[35]

The church father Augustine (A.D. 354–430) is notable especially for his theological masterpiece *The City of God*. In this landmark work, written soon after the sacking of Rome by the Goths in the year 410, Augustine replied to the pagan criticism in his day that the fall of Rome was a result of the city's embrace of Christianity and the abandonment of its pagan set of deities. In his discussion of the earthly and the heavenly city, Augustine maintains utmost respect for the historicity of the events recorded in the Old Testament. As the city of God on the earth, the church

---

35. John Rogerson, "The Old Testament," in *The History of Christian Theology*, Volume 2: *The Study and Use of the Bible*, by John Rogerson, Christopher Rowland, and Barnabas Lindars (Grand Rapids: Eerdmans, 1988), 46.

still contains both good and bad, a state of affairs only remedied at the second coming of Christ. While there are instances of spiritualizing interpretation in Augustine, "the impressive thing about *The City of God* is that it is an attempt to take the Old Testament seriously as history and to consider how secular and sacred history are to be regarded in relation to each other."[36] Jerome and Augustine stand as towering figures in biblical interpretation and remain unsurpassed for at least the next 600 years.

Medieval Period

In the following centuries, which witnessed the contributions of Cyril of Alexandria (archbishop of Alexandria, A.D. 412–444), Gregory the Great (pope, A.D. 590–604), and the Venerable Bene (c. 672–735), among others, the allegorical and mystical interpretations of the Old Testament reached a climax. The remainder of the Middle Ages, however, saw a renewed interest in the historical interpretation of Scripture. This is evident particularly in the school of the Abbey of St. Victor in Paris. Proponents of this school include Hugh, who taught at St. Victor from 1125 until his death in 1142, and his student Andrew who taught there until 1147 and again from 1155 until 1163, both of whom pursued primarily the historical, literal sense.

While the method goes back at least as far as John Cassian (A.D. 360–435),[37] medieval exegesis is known primarily for its pursuit of the fourfold sense of Scripture: (1) literal (or historical), (2) allegorical (or spiritual), (3) tropological (or moral), and (4) anagogical (or future; from the Greek *anagogē*, "leading up to"). Nicolas of Lyra (1270–1340) memorably cites the following distich (a unit of verse consisting of two lines) in around 1330:

> The letter teaches events; allegory, what you should believe; the moral sense, what you should do, anagogy, what to hope for.[38]

---

36. Ibid., 52.
37. "The one Jerusalem can be understood in four different ways, in the historical sense as the city of the Jews, in allegory as the church of Christ, in *anagogē* as the heavenly city of God 'which is the mother of us all' (Gal 4:26), in the tropological sense as the human soul." John Cassian, *Conferences*, trans. Colm Luibheid (New York: Paulist, 1985), 160. See also, similarly, Augustine, *De Genesi ad litteram* 1.1.
38. In the original Latin, *Littera gesta docet, quid credas allegoria, Moralis quid agas, quo tendas anagogia.*Nicholas of Lyra, *In Gal.* 4, 3 (Bible de Douai, 6, Anvers [1634], 506),

The literal sense is the historical-grammatical sense. The allegorical sense (including typology) is the spiritual sense thought to lie beneath the surface of the text. The tropological sense pertains to the moral lessons that can be drawn from Scripture. The anagogical sense is concerned with the end-time implications of a given passage.

Some among medieval interpreters, such as the aforementioned Hugh of St. Victor, stressed the literal sense, while others, such as Bernard of Clairvaux (1090–1153), favored a more spiritual interpretation. Yet others, such as Thomas Aquinas (1225–1274), sought to hold these aspects in tension.[39] But in many cases, all four senses were affirmed alongside each other and were seen as viable, albeit diverse, ways of grasping the meaning of Scripture. To the extent that authorial intent receded into the background and the interpreter's own way of thinking took over the interpretive enterprise, however, textual meaning was obscured and a proper contextual reading of Scripture gave way to a type of mysticism that used Scripture merely as a springboard for the pursuit of higher, "loftier" goals of progressing in the interpreter's spirituality.

Reformation and the Enlightenment

Biblical interpretation at the beginning of the sixteenth century, the eve of the Reformation, was still largely controlled by the notion of a fourfold sense of Scripture. The literal sense was the historical sense that recounted God's dealings with Israel and the church. The spiritual sense involved relating the message of Scripture to Christ, with interpreters seeking to make moral application to people's everyday lives. The great Reformers, Martin Luther and John Calvin, operated in the wake of the revival of classical learning, epitomized by the scholarship of Erasmus of Rotterdam (1466/69–1536).[40]

Luther (1483–1546) is well known for insisting on the principle of *sola Scriptura* (Latin for "Scripture alone") over against the Roman Catholic practice of awarding church tradition a role equal to (if not greater than)

---

cited in Henri de Lubac, *Medieval Exegesis*, Volume 1: *The Four Senses of Scripture* (trans. Mark Sebanc (Grand Rapids: Eerdmans, 1998), 1. The saying is thought to originate with Augustine of Dacia (Denmark) in his *Rotulus pugillaris* (1206).

39. Rogerson, "Old Testament," 70–73.
40. Klein, Blomberg, and Hubbard, *Introduction to Biblical Interpretation*, 47, cite the popular sixteenth-century saying, "Erasmus laid the egg and Luther hatched it."

Scripture. He also held that Scripture is its own best interpreter (*Scriptura sui interpres*), which meant that the study of Scripture took precedence over patristic commentary or ecclesiastical authority. Luther also rejected medieval allegorical interpretation and affirmed, with Aquinas, that Scripture had one essential meaning, the historical sense.[41]

Thus, in Luther's distinctive approach, the fourfold sense collapsed: "If there was a literal sense that referred to Christ, there was no need for spiritual senses in order to find him in the text."[42] In the Old Testament, Luther discovered a rich history of faith that was able to instruct believers on how to conduct their Christian lives. At the same time, Luther distinguished between law and gospel and held that the Old Testament law, as law, is not normative for Christians today. When interpreting the prophets, Luther affirmed the literal sense in which a given text referred to Christ. Luther also noted that because the Holy Spirit guides the interpreter, the resulting interpretation is a properly "spiritual" interpretation.

Calvin (1509–1564), for his part, was more systematically oriented than Luther. He also showed greater concern to establish the meaning of the text by the aid of secular knowledge. At the same time, as in the case of Luther, Calvin's primary concern lay with the literal, historical sense of the text. Calvin also affirmed a subjective element in interpretation, "the internal witness of the Holy Spirit."[43] Within this framework, his interpretation was christological. The difference between the Testaments Calvin saw primarily as one of administration, in which the Old Testament remained incomplete and contingent on New Testament revelation. The law, especially the Ten Commandments, retained relevance because they were in accordance with natural law.

During the period of the Enlightenment, interpreters became increasingly skeptical toward the supernatural element of Scripture, such as the miracles performed by Moses and Jesus.[44] Increasingly, human reason questioned the very possibility of miracles, and anti-supernaturalism largely prevailed. A new view of science led to an interpretation of the biblical cre-

---

41. At the same time, Luther took up the typological interpretation found in the New Testament. See Klein, Blomberg, and Hubbard, *Introduction to Biblical Interpretation*, 47.
42. Rogerson, "Old Testament," 78.
43. For background sources, see Klein, Blomberg, and Hubbard, *Introduction to Biblical Interpretation*, 48, n. 106.
44. For an excellent account of this development, see William Baird, *History of New Testament Research*, Vol. One: *From Deism to Tübingen* (Minneapolis: Fortress, 1992).

ation and miracle stories as "myths." This included Jesus' resurrection, even though Paul and other New Testament writers made clear that the resurrection is essential to the Christian faith. This rationalistic mind-set gave rise to a pronounced skepticism toward the scriptural data and led to the development of the historical-critical method with its various criteria for assessing the historicity of biblical texts.[45]

Modern Period

A more detailed treatment would rehearse the rise of historical criticism from Richard Simon (1638–1712), a Roman Catholic priest considered by many the "father of biblical criticism," to F. C. Baur (1792–1860), the leader of the Tübingen School, to Julius Wellhausen (1844–1918), the chief advocate of the documentary hypothesis of the composition of the Pentateuch (positing sources he designated "J" [Jahwist], "E" [Elohist], "D" [Deuteronomist], and "P" [Priestly redactor]), the history-of-religions school, and the various quests for the historical Jesus.[46]

Perhaps the most important figure in the modern period is the German theologian and philosopher Friedrich Schleiermacher (1768–1834), whom many consider to be the father of modern hermeneutics.[47] Grounded in his conviction that religious faith was rooted in a person's feeling of dependence on God, Schleiermacher contended that interpretation consisted of both an objective and a subjective element, grammatical as well as psychological. The former involved studying the text's overt message as conveyed by its words, sentence structure, and so forth; the latter entailed an attempt to reconstruct the author's psyche as he wrote. Schleiermacher's notion of authorial intention is universally discredited today because the only access to a given author's state of mind is the text itself. That said, there is much value in seeking to ascertain an author's intended meaning by careful study

---

45. See Edgar Krentz, *The Historical-Critical Method*, Guides to Biblical Scholarship (Philadelphia: Fortress, 1975); and Roy Harrisville and Walter Sundberg, *The Bible in Modern Culture: Theology and Historical-Critical Method from Spinoza to Käsemann* (Grand Rapids: Eerdmans, 1995). For a critique, see Gerhard Maier, *The End of the Historical-Critical Method*, trans. Edwin W. Leverenz and Rudolph F. Norden (St. Louis: Concordia, 1977).

46. For the latter, see the concise summary in Köstenberger, Kellum, and Quarles, *Cradle, the Cross, and the Crown*, 111–16.

47. See, e.g., Osborne, *Hermeneutical Spiral*, 468.

of the text. In fact, apart from authorial intent, validity in interpretation is a virtual impossibility.[48]

Following Schleiermacher, modern biblical interpretation of the historical-critical variety has been increasingly characterized by an anti-supernatural bias and historical skepticism on the part of most of its proponents.[49] Deplorably, this negative, critical stance toward Scripture had the effect of undermining the credibility of the biblical record as it tended to blunt the notions of biblical revelation, inspiration, and authority.[50] In most proponents of the historical-critical method, the question of history became detached from the biblical text, and the question of whether or not a given event actually took place became the singular preoccupation of biblical scholars.[51] Thus assessing the historicity of events recorded in Scripture replaced the task of studying the actual text of the Bible, a development trenchantly chronicled in Hans Frei's *Eclipse of Biblical Narrative*.[52] In this the "historical-critical method" became unduly preoccupied with the question of history at the expense of an engagement with the Bible's literary and theological aspects.

In the wake of Frei's work, however, the pendulum swung to the other extreme. Increasingly, historical skepticism regarding the

---

48. For helpful discussions, see Robert H. Stein, "The Benefits of an Author-Oriented Approach to Hermeneutics," *JETS* 44 (2001): 451–66; and Jerry Vines and David Allen, "Hermeneutics, Exegesis, and Proclamation," *CTR* 1 (1987): 309–34 (both articles are also available online).

49. For surveys of the history of hermeneutics see Anthony C. Thiselton, *The Two Horizons* (Grand Rapids: Eerdmans, 1979); idem, *Hermeneutics: An Introduction* (Grand Rapids: Eerdmans, 2009); Klein, Blomberg, and Hubbard, *Introduction to Biblical Interpretation*, chap. 2; and Osborne, *Hermeneutical Spiral*, App. 1 and 2 (only the modern period starting with Schleiermacher).

50. But see the able critiques of these trends by North American scholars B. B. Warfield, W. H. Green, W. J. Beecher, and others. See Klein, Blomberg, and Hubbard, *Introduction to Biblical Interpretation*, 54.

51. In historical Jesus studies, scholars frequently drove a wedge between the "Jesus of history" (i.e. Jesus during his earthly ministry) and the "Christ of faith" (the Jesus in whom the first Christians believed), as if these were of necessity different and in conflict with one another. In this context, scholars often spoke about the "Easter faith" of Jesus' followers and claimed that their faith led them to attribute features to Jesus that he never claimed to possess during his earthly ministry. See, e.g., Martin Kähler, *The so-called historical Jesus and the historic, biblical Christ*, trans. Carl E. Braaten (Philadelphia: Fortress, 1964 [1896]).

52. Hans W. Frei, *The Eclipse of Biblical Narrative* (New Haven/London: Yale University Press, 1974).

historicity of the events depicted in the Bible led to a mere literary study of Scripture as any other book.[53] In this approach, aptly labeled "aesthetic theology" by Kevin Vanhoozer, students of Scripture focused unilaterally on the various literary features of the biblical text while excluding historical questions from the scope of their research.[54] Biblical scholarship was reduced to narrative criticism or various other forms of literary criticism, and while interesting literary insights were gained, Scripture's historical dimension was unduly neglected, resulting in an imbalanced interpretation once again. Postmodernism has further built on this "aesthetic turn" in biblical studies and questioned the very notion of objective history, viewing the question of truth merely in terms of human convention rather than as correspondence to facts and reality.[55] Reader-response approaches and deconstructionism, likewise, set aside authorial intention and held that textual meaning was determined subjectively by the reader or denied the possibility of a stable notion of meaning altogether, resulting in a plurality of theologies and readings with no objective standard to adjudicate between more or less valid interpretations.[56]

Other approaches set aside the question of historicity while continuing to be concerned with theology, whether in existentialist or other terms.[57] Adherents to this school of thought maintained that theological truth was not contingent on the truthfulness of Scripture in depicting various phenomena and events. The resurrection was redefined as a person's existential

---

53. Again, see Baird, *History of Research*, Vol. 1, for a thorough account of the historical roots of this phenomenon.
54. Vanhoozer, "Lamp in the Labyrinth." See also Andreas J. Köstenberger, "Aesthetic Theology—Blessing or Curse? An Assessment of Narrative Hermeneutics," *Faith & Mission* 15/2 (1998): 27–44.
55. See on this question Andreas J. Köstenberger, ed., *Whatever Happened to Truth?* (Wheaton: Crossway, 2005), in particular the trenchant critique of postmodernism by J. P. Moreland. See also D. A. Carson, *The Gagging of God: Christianity Confronts Pluralism* (Grand Rapids: Zondervan, 1996).
56. See esp. Osborne, *Hermeneutical Spiral*, App. 1 and 2; Hirsch, *Validity in Interpretation*.
57. See, e.g., the effort by the German theologian Rudolf Bultmann (1884–1976) to "demythologize Scripture" in order to salvage an existentialist core of the Christian message that appealed to modern people. See Rudolf Bultmann, *New Testament Mythology and Other Basic Writings*, ed. Schubert M. Ogden (Philadelphia: Fortress, 1984); Karl Jaspers and Rudolf Bultmann, *Myth & Christianity: An Inquiry into the Possibility of Religion without Myth* (Amherst, NY: Prometheus, 2005).

experience of new life through faith apart from the historical resurrection of Jesus. Regeneration following faith in Christ was recast as the result of an existential encounter with God occasioned by the reading of Scripture, and so on. These are examples of a pursuit of theology that is inadequately built on the foundation of the historical dimension of Scripture. While theology, as mentioned, is rightly viewed as the pinnacle of biblical interpretation, it must be built on a proper understanding of the historical, linguistic, and literary aspects of Scripture if a valid, balanced interpretation is to be achieved.[58] This, in turn, brings us back to the hermeneutical triad.

HERMENEUTICAL TRIAD

Only an approach to the study of Scripture that properly balances history, literature, and theology will be adequate to the task. As Charles Scobie aptly noted, "In much contemporary literary criticism, historical study of the original author of a text has been set aside as irrelevant." He went on to say that in biblical studies, any total abandonment of historical study "would be a major disaster that would cast the interpreter adrift on a sea of subjectivity."[59]

For this reason the hermeneutical triad, which includes historical study, will prove to be a useful guide for mastering the general skills required for biblical interpretation and for following the special rules applied to the various genres of Scripture. Rather than being pitted against one another, history, literature, and theology each have a vital place in the study of the sacred Word.

Regardless of the passage of Scripture, the interpreter needs to study (1) the historical setting; (2) the literary context (including matters of canon, genre, and language); and (3) the theological message, that is, what

---

58. A more promising (though not entirely unproblematic) recent development is the movement advocating a return to the theological interpretation of Scripture. See esp. Daniel J. Treier, *Introducing Theological Interpretation of Scripture: Recovering a Christian Practice* (Grand Rapids: Baker, 2008); and Kevin J. Vanhoozer, ed., *Dictionary for Theological Interpretation of the Bible* (Grand Rapids: Baker, 2005). See also the brief initial assessment in the opening section of Andreas J. Köstenberger, "Of Professors and Madmen: Currents in Contemporary New Testament Scholarship," *Faith & Mission* 23/2 (2006): 3–18.

59 Charles H. H. Scobie, *The Ways of Our God: An Approach to Biblical Theology* (Grand Rapids: Eerdmans, 2003), 33.

the passage teaches regarding God, Christ, salvation, and the need to respond in faith to the Bible's teaching.

The interpretation of Scripture, in turn, is not the end in itself but only a means to an end: the application of biblical truth to life. Using proper interpretive tools and resources and finding a path from text to sermon for each biblical genre are important. Thus sound interpretation becomes the solid foundation for the application and proclamation of biblical truth to life.

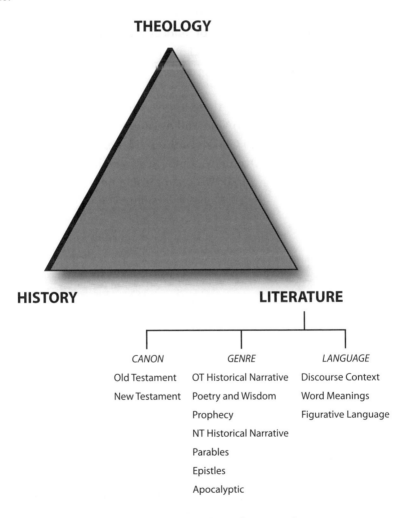

1.2. The Hermeneutical Triad in Detail

From the above observations, then, flows naturally a method for interpreting and applying any passage of Scripture. Those who hone their understanding of this method will develop several vital skills, including the following set of interpretive and communicative competencies:

1. historical-cultural awareness;
2. canonical consciousness;
3. sensitivity to genre;
4. literary and linguistic competence;
5. a firm and growing grasp of biblical theology; and
6. an ability to apply and proclaim passages from every biblical genre to life.

Acquiring and polishing these skills will be well worth the effort. Doing so will bring glory to God and great blessing to the Bible student and through him or her to God's people. To this end, the "Guidelines for Biblical Interpretation: Overall Method," depicted below in both a chart and step-by-step listing, will be followed throughout this volume.[60]

---

60. For an excellent work that grounds biblical preaching in the three component parts of the hermeneutical triad (history, literature, and theology), see Sidney Greidanus, *The Modern Preacher and the Ancient Text: Interpreting and Preaching Biblical Literature* (Grand Rapids: Eerdmans, 1988).

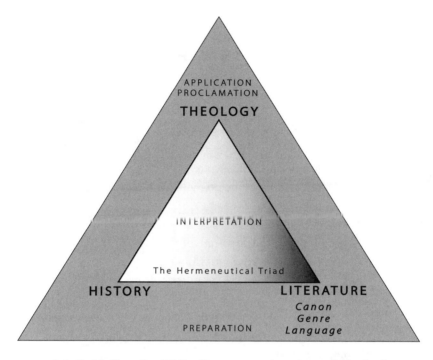

1.3. Guidelines for Biblical Interpretation: Overall Method

GUIDELINES FOR BIBLICAL INTERPRETATION: OVERALL METHOD

I. PREPARATION:
Prepare yourself for the interpretive task by recognizing your own presuppositions. Pray for God to open your mind to understand the Scriptures. Approach your task with a proper method for biblical interpretation—the hermeneutical triad.

II. INTERPRETATION:
1. Determine the historical setting of the passage and identify relevant cultural background issues (history).
2. Locate your passage in the larger canonical context of Scripture (literature/canon).
3. Determine your passage's literary genre and use appropriate interpretive principles for interpreting each given genre (literature/genre).
4. Read carefully and seek to understand an entire passage in its larger discourse context, conducting a full-fledged discourse analysis if possible (literature/language/discourse context).
5. Conduct a semantic field study of any significant terms in a passage (literature/language/word meanings).
6. Identify any figurative language in a passage and interpret figures of speech in keeping with proper principles of interpretation (literature/figurative language).
7. Identify the major theological theme(s) in a passage and determine the passage's contribution to the understanding of the character and plan of God in dealing with his people (theology).

III. APPLICATION & PROCLAMATION:
Assess the contemporary relevance of a passage and make proper application to your life and to the life of the church today.

KEY WORDS

Aesthetic theology: mere literary study of Scripture

Alexandrian School: interpretive approach that preferred allegorical to historical interpretation

Antiochene School: interpretive approach that preferred historical to allegorical interpretation

Dual authorship: human and divine authorship of Scripture

Eisegesis: reading one's preferred meaning into the text

Exegesis: deriving one's interpretation from the text

Fourfold sense of Scripture: method of medieval exegesis that pursued the literal, allegorical, tropological, and anagogical sense of Scripture

Hermeneutics: discipline concerned with the proper theory and practice of textual interpretation

Hermeneutic of perception: interpretive approach that prizes careful listening to the text

Historical-critical method: interpretive approach whose primary concern is the assessment of the historicity of events recorded in Scripture, often with negative results

Scriptura sui interpres: Reformation dictum that Scripture is its own best interpreter

STUDY QUESTIONS

1. Why is it so important to interpret Scripture accurately? Cite Scripture to support your answer.

2. What are some of the results if people fail to interpret Scripture responsibly? Again, support your answer with scriptural references.

3. Name at least three characteristics required of the interpreter of Scripture and support your answer with Scripture.

4. What are the three realities with which the interpreter finds himself confronted, and how do these realities form the "hermeneutical triad"?

5. What happens when interpreters neglect any one or two of the three elements of the "hermeneutical triad"? Illustrate your answer by giving examples from the history of biblical interpretation.

ASSIGNMENTS

1. Give examples from Scripture and from your own personal experience that illustrate the benefits of proper biblical interpretation and/or the cost of failed biblical interpretation.

2. Make up a chart tracing the history of biblical interpretation, including major interpretive schools or individual interpreters, dates, and pertinent characteristics. If possible, supplement the information provided in this chapter with additional research into the history of biblical interpretation.

3. Discuss the importance of each of the three major aspects of the hermeneutical triad—history, literature, and theology—as well as the importance of canon, genre, and language. Show how neglect of one or two of these aspects results in imbalanced interpretation and point out how this can be harmful in distorting the proper understanding of the biblical text.

4. Reflect upon and provide a detailed commentary on each of the following interpretive competencies: historical-cultural awareness, canonical consciousness, sensitivity to genre, literary and linguistic competence, a grasp of biblical theology, and the ability to apply and communicate biblical truth.

CHAPTER BIBLIOGRAPHY

Carson, D. A. *Exegetical Fallacies*. 2d ed. Grand Rapids: Baker, 1996.

Grudem, Wayne A., gen. ed. *The ESV Study Bible*. Wheaton: Crossway, 2008.

Klein, William W. *Handbook for Personal Bible Study: Enriching Your Experience with God's Word*. The Navigators Reference Library. Colorado Springs: NavPress, 2008.

Klein, William W., Craig L. Blomberg, and Robert L. Hubbard, Jr *Introduction to Biblical Interpretation*. Rev. ed. Nashville: Thomas Nelson, 2004.

Osborne, Grant R. *The Hermeneutical Spiral: A Comprehensive Introduction to Biblical Interpretation*. 2d ed. Downers Grove: InterVarsity, 2006.

Plummer, Robert L. 40 *Questions about Understanding the Bible*. Grand Rapids: Kregel, 2009.

Schlatter, Adolf. *The History of the Christ: The Foundation of New Testament Theology*. Translated by Andreas J. Köstenberger. Grand Rapids: Baker, 1997.

Tenney, Merrill C., gen. ed.; Moisés Silva, rev. ed. *The Zondervan Encyclopedia of the Bible*. 5 vols. Grand Rapids: Zondervan, 2009.

Vanhoozer, Kevin J. Is *There a Meaning in This Text? The Bible, the Reader, and the Morality of Literary Knowledge*. Grand Rapids: Zondervan, 1998.

_____. *The Drama of Doctrine: A Canonical-Linguistic Approach to Christian Theology*. Louisville: Westminster John Knox, 2005.

Wright, N. T. *The New Testament and the People of God*. Christian Origins and the Question of God 1. Philadelphia: Fortress, 1996.

INTERPRETATION:
The Hermeneutical Triad

PART 1

THE CONTEXT OF SCRIPTURE:
HISTORY

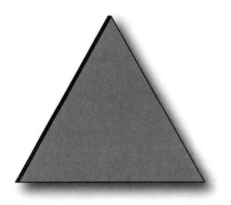

CHAPTER 2 OBJECTIVES

1. To impress upon the student the crucial importance of under-
    standing the historical-cultural background of a given biblical
    passage.

2. To assure the student of the trustworthiness of the biblical record.

3. To direct the student's attention to the need for determining the
    author's purpose regarding the specific details he has chosen to
    record.

4. To provide a set of interpretive guidelines for applying the prin-
    ciples embedded in the historical-cultural data of the Bible to con-
    temporary social and political problems.

CHAPTER 2 OUTLINE

A. Chapter 2 Objectives
B. Chapter 2 Outline
C. Introduction: History and Hermeneutics
D. Chronology
    1. Old Testament Period
        a. Primeval Period
        b. Patriarchal Period
        c. From the Exodus to the United Monarchy
        d. Divided Monarchy
        e. Exile and Return
    2. Second Temple Period
        a. Babylonian and Persian Periods
        b. Hellenistic Period
        c. Maccabean Period
        d. Roman Period
    3. New Testament Period
        a. Jesus
        b. Early Church and Paul
        c. Rest of the New Testament
E. Archaeology
    1. Old Testament
    2. New Testament
F. Historical-Cultural Background
    1. Primary Sources
        a. Ancient Near Eastern Literature
        b. Old and New Testament Apocrypha
        c. Old Testament Pseudepigrapha
        d. Dead Sea Scrolls
        e. Other Relevant Primary Sources
    2. Secondary Sources
G. Conclusion
H. Sample Exegesis (Old Testament): 1 Kings 17–18
I. Sample Exegesis (New Testament): Luke 2:1–20
J. Guidelines for Interpreting Biblical Historical-Cultural Backgrounds
K. Key Words
L. Study Questions
M. Assignments
N. Chapter Bibliography

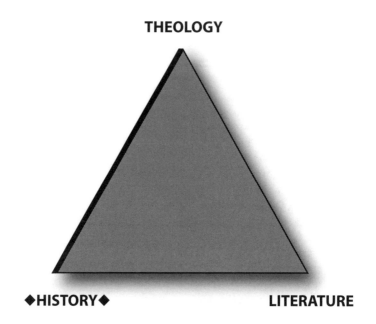

Chapter 2

SETTING THE STAGE:
HISTORICAL CULTURAL
BACKGROUND

INTRODUCTION: HISTORY AND HERMENEUTICS

IN ORDER FOR THE INTERPRETATION of Scripture to be properly grounded, it is vital to explore the historical setting of a scriptural passage, including any cultural background features. An informed knowledge of the historical and cultural background is imperative also for applying the message of Scripture. J. Scott Duvall and J. Daniel Hays put the issue well:

> Since we live in a very different context, we must recapture God's original intended meaning as reflected in the text and framed by the ancient historical-cultural context. Once we understand the meaning of the text in its original context, we can apply it to our lives in ways that will be just as relevant.[1]

---

1. J. Scott Duvall and J. Daniel Hays, *Grasping God's Word*, 2d ed. (Grand Rapids: Zondervan, 2005), 100.

Emphasizing the importance of historical information, of course, does not mean that every available piece of background data will necessarily be germane for the interpretation of a given biblical passage. The relevance of a particular piece of background information must to be carefully weighed and assessed. Certainly, background information should never override what is stated explicitly in the text. In fact, lack of judiciousness in selecting background information has led some to disparage the use of historical-cultural data in scriptural interpretation altogether (surely an overreaction).

For our present purposes, the most important hermeneutical question relates to the relationship between history and literature, the first and second element in the hermeneutical triad. Literature, in the ancient Greek and Hebrew languages, immediately reinforces the notion of texts, different from our own, with unique historical and cultural development. These texts not only require translation into a understandable language (English) but also the study of historical-cultural aspects embedded within them since both the biblical languages and other parts of biblical culture and history are inextricably intertwined.

Indeed, it is commonly acknowledged that it is vital to study Scripture in its proper context, and that context, in turn, properly conceived, consists of both historical and literary facets; so there is no need to justify the necessity of responsible historical research as part of the interpretive process. Suffice it to say that the necessity of historical research underlies major reference works such as study Bibles, Old and New Testament introductions, commentaries, and other standard reference works.

However, historical research has been given a bad name by the practitioners of the historical-critical method, which has been largely undergirded by an anti-supernatural bias that has consistently cast aspersions on the historicity of much of the biblical material.[2] In reaction to the excesses of the historical-critical method, some have advocated a strict literary reading of Scripture while leaving aside the question of historical referentiality.[3] While surmounting the difficulty of alleged historical

---

2. See William Baird, *The History of New Testament Research*, 2 vols. (Minneapolis: Fortress, 1992, 2002). See also Eta Linnemann, *Historical Criticism of the Bible: Methodology or Ideology?*, trans. Robert W. Yarbrough (Grand Rapids: Baker, 1990).
3. Hans W. Frei, *The Eclipse of Biblical Narrative: A Study in Eighteenth and Nineteenth Century Hermeneutics* (New Haven: Yale University Press, 1980).

discrepancies, this proposed method, too, is not without its problems, because it unduly severs the vital (in fact, inevitable) connection between the biblical texts and their historical-cultural embeddedness.[4]

What is more, postmoderns believe that impartial, objective history-writing is impossible. The view of history as events "as they actually happened" has given way to the realization that all historiography is of necessity subjective. In addition, postmodern critiques frequently lodge the charge that much of history is written by those who prevailed in the struggle for power and authority. Thus history-writing is often viewed as a tool of oppression wielded by the powerful against the disenfranchised. In this context, all historiography, including the biblical records, are viewed with suspicion, and widespread skepticism rules the day.[5]

Despite the views of postmoderns, history is here to stay. After all, Christianity is a historical religion, at whose heart is a historical event, the resurrection of Jesus Christ (see esp. Paul's comments in 1 Corinthians 15). Unless Jesus rose from the dead *historically*, we are not saved but remain in our sin (1 Cor. 15:16–19). In a memorable interchange in the pages of the *Trinity Journal*, Carl F. H. Henry and Hans Frei debated this very question, and Frei, who espoused a focus on the text to the detriment of history in interpretation, found it difficult to affirm unequivocally that Jesus rose from the dead not merely *textually*, but *historically*.[6]

---

4. For an exceedingly helpful chronicling of the relevant issues and of the movement from author to text to reader in the field of hermeneutics, see Grant R. Osborne, "Appendix 1: The Problem of Meaning: The Issues" and "Appendix 2: The Problem of Meaning: Toward a Solution," in *The Hermeneutical Spiral: A Comprehensive Introduction to Biblical Interpretation*, 2d ed. (Downers Grove, IL: InterVarsity, 2006), 465–521.
5. Helpful treatments of postmodernism include D. A. Carson, *The Gagging of God: Christianity Confronts Pluralism* (Grand Rapids: Zondervan, 1996); J. P. Moreland, "Truth, Contemporary Philosophy, and the Postmodern Turn," in Andreas J. Köstenberger, ed., *Whatever Happened to Truth?* (Wheaton, IL: Crossway, 2005), 75–92; and Millard J. Erickson, *Truth or Consequences: The Promise and Perils of Postmodernism* (Downers Grove, IL: InterVarsity, 2001).
6. Carl F. H. Henry, "Narrative Theology: An Evangelical Appraisal," *TJ* 8/1 (1987): 3–19; Hans Frei, "Response To 'Narrative Theology: An Evangelical Appraisal,'" *TJ* 8/1 (1987): 21–24. See also Kevin J. Vanhoozer, "A Lamp In The Labyrinth: The Hermeneutics Of 'Aesthetic' Theology," *TJ* 8.1 (1987): 25–56; Andreas J. Köstenberger, "Aesthetic Theology—Blessing or Curse? An Assessment of Narrative Hermeneutics," *Faith & Mission* 15/2 (1998): 27–44.

This shows how important it is not to unduly divide the historical and literary dimensions of Scripture but to keep them in proper balance, as is integral to the hermeneutical triad used in the present volume. The very fact that the triad consists of history, literature, *and* theology shows the need for historical research to be balanced by a proper focus on the text (literature) and sufficient attention being given to theology (that is, God's self-revelation in the sacred, historically embedded text). Conversely, Bible students should avoid both the excesses of the historical-critical method and the reductionism of unmitigated literary approaches that set themselves over against historical research.

CHRONOLOGY

Reading the Bible reveals the great distance in time between the events recorded in Scripture and today; in its pages are not only events of long ago but also customs that are quite foreign. In order to grasp their significance an understanding of the people, events, and customs of the Bible in their proper historical milieu is necessary.[7] The remainder of the chapter provides surveys of biblical chronology, archeology, and historical-cultural background research, beginning with a general historical framework for biblical interpretation using biblical chronology.[8]

OLD TESTAMENT PERIOD

From the internal biblical data, we can establish dates for Old Testament chronology. A key passage is 1 Kings 6:1, which mentions the fourth year of Solomon's reign as the 480th year after the exodus.[9] Correlation

---

7. Among the best resources are John Walton, ed., *Zondervan Illustrated Bible Backgrounds Commentary: Old Testament*, 5 vols. (Grand Rapids: Zondervan, 2009); and Clinton Arnold, ed., *Zondervan Illustrated Bible Backgrounds Commentary: New Testament*, 4 vols. (Grand Rapids: Zondervan, 2001). See also excellent study Bibles such as the NIV Study Bible, the ESV Study Bible, and the HCSB Study Bible.

8. For a helpful, more detailed survey of biblical history, see P. E. Satterthwaite, "Biblical History," in T. Desmond Alexander and Brian S. Rosner, eds., *New Dictionary of Biblical Theology: Exploring the Unity & Diversity of Scripture* (Leicester, UK: InterVarsity, 2000), 43–51.

9. The following survey will focus on the internal data for establishing a framework for biblical chronology. Externally, the chronological framework for the ancient Near

of data from external sources with the biblical record places this date at 967 B.C. Utilizing other biblical information, we can determine a rather well-established general chronology for the Old Testament, stretching from the birth of Abram in 2166 B.c. to the end of the Old Testament era in the closing decade of the fifth century B.C.[10] An accurate chronology thus provides the interpreter with the necessary framework for interpreting a given Old Testament passage in its historical context.[11]

Primeval Period

Primeval history covers the period between Genesis 1–11, encompassing the time span between Creation to the birth of Abram. Despite the fact that we cannot determine with any degree of finality dates for primeval history, Genesis 1–11 is a crucial part of biblical history, reflecting not mere textual realities but historical realities that have served to shape the present world. The world in which we live is the one that God created as good, the one corrupted by the Fall, the one in which God established his covenant with Noah, and the one in which God made his promise to Abraham. If these are not historical realities, then the Christian faith is merely one among many mythological understandings of the world. True faith is rooted in a text that reveals not merely literary but also *historical* reality.

East has been rather well ascertained by means of data from two sources: (1) the Greek geographer Ptolemy's Canon, which lists the names of the rulers of Babylon from 747 B.C. to the second century A.D.; and (2) a record of the names of those who occupied the office of *limmu* (or *eponym*) in ancient Assyria.

10. J. Barton Payne, "Chronology of the Old Testament," in *The Zondervan Pictorial Encyclopedia of the Bible*, ed. Merrill C. Tenney and Moisés Silva, 5 vols., rev. ed. (Grand Rapids: Zondervan, 2009), 1.846–65; Richard D. Patterson, "The Divided Monarchy: Sources, Approaches, and Historicity," in *Giving the Sense: Understanding and Using Old Testament Historical Texts* (ed. David M. Howard,, Jr. and Michael A. Grisanti; Grand Rapids: Kregel, 2003), 182–83.

11. Further information comes from Mesopotamian and Egyptian sources such as royal annals, king lists, and histories that detail particular events between political powers, which can be found in James H. Breasted, ed., *Ancient Records of Egypt*, 5 vols. (London: Histories & Mysteries of Man, 1988); William W. Hallo and K. Lawson Younger Jr., *The Context of Scripture*, 3 vols. (Leiden: Brill, 1997, 2000, 2002); David D. Luckenbill, *Ancient Records of Assyria and Babylonia*, 2 vols. (Chicago: University of Chicago Press, 1926); James B. Pritchard, ed., *Ancient Near Eastern Texts*, 3d ed. (Princeton: Princeton University Press, 1969); Kenton L. Sparks, *Ancient Texts for the Study of the Hebrew Bible: A Guide to the Background Literature.* (Peabody, MA: Hendrickson, 2005).

Historical realities are communicated through a text, and by its very nature, a text is selective in what it records. For this reason, no full history of every incident exists. Rather, the biblical authors recorded the most significant historical events for understanding who God is, what he is doing in the world, and what he calls humanity to do in response. Thus, the biblical text provides the interpretive framework for understanding human history. What is more, the biblical story line focuses particularly on salvation history, that is, the record of God's mission in carrying out his plan of redemption for sinful humanity in and through the Messiah. This section on chronology seeks to understand that history as given by the biblical text.

Though Genesis 1–2 as a narration of how God, as the Creator, fashioned the universe is doubtless a central part of the author's purpose, the creation narrative is within the larger context of the purpose of the five books of Moses (the Pentateuch) as a whole. This purpose is to demonstrate to Israel that their covenant God, Yahweh, is also the Creator of the entire universe. In this context, locating the creation of the world at an exact point of time in the past is secondary to understanding the creation narrative in the context in which it was originally written, namely, the early stages of Israel being constituted as a nation as part of its relationship with Yahweh, the Creator and God who had established his covenant with, first Noah, then Abraham, and now Moses.

Subsequent to this creation is the fall of humanity into sin. Though God created all things as "good," Adam's sin brings death to all creation; yet God at once begins to make provision for overcoming death and restoring all things by speaking of the promised seed, a child from Eve who will end sin's rule (Gen. 3:15). Despite God's promise to end sin's reign by crushing the head of the serpent, the primeval period demonstrates that humanity spiraled downward until "[t]he LORD saw how great man's wickedness on the earth had become, and that every inclination of the thoughts of his heart was only evil all the time" (Gen. 6:5).

In the midst of this world of sin, God keeps a remnant of people who are faithful to him. In the flood narrative, all flesh is destroyed, except for Noah's family (Genesis 6–9); thus, the promise of the seed endures. Following the flood, the Noahic covenant confirms that God will sustain the natural cycle in order to set a firm stage for the redemption of all things by the promised seed (Genesis 9). The story of the tower of Babel serves to show the need for the redemption of all nations (Genesis 10–11). The answer for creation's plight and the nations' deliverance will come through God's covenant with Abraham.

Patriarchal Period

Most of the patriarchal period is set in the archaeological era known as the Middle Bronze Period (c. 2000–1600 B.C.).[12] In the biblical literature, the patriarchal period begins in Genesis 12 with God's calling of and covenant with Abram and carries through the lives of Abraham, Isaac, Jacob, and Joseph until the end of Genesis (2092–1877/6 B.C.). Much of the biblical literature, including the material covering the patriarchal period, is written to demonstrate God's faithfulness to the promises he made to Abra(ha)m in Genesis 12, 15, and 17.

The Hebrew people, and therefore God's covenant promises and the deliverance of all that God had created, face a great challenge through the people's bondage in Egypt (1876–1447 B.C.). The book of Exodus opens up with the Hebrews growing so numerous that the Egyptian pharaoh decrees the slaughter of all the newborn male children, and thus the promise of the seed is threatened. Yet "God heard their groaning, and God remembered his covenant with Abraham, with Isaac, and with Jacob" (Exod. 2:24).

From the Exodus to the United Monarchy

God remembers the covenant through the exodus of the Hebrew people from Egypt, arguably the most important event for the constitution of the nation of Israel (1447/6 B.C.).[13] Through the exodus and the Mosaic cov-

---

12. There is substantial evidence that the names of the patriarchs are not mythical, legendary, or invented names. Instead, they are well attested in the extrabiblical literature of the period, such as the texts from Tell Ebla and the tablets from Tell Mar. See Kenneth A. Kitchen, *The Bible in Its World* (Downers Grove: InterVarsity, 1978), 68.

13. For the debate concerning the date of the biblical exodus, see John J. Bimson, *Redating the Exodus and Conquest* (Sheffield: University of Sheffield, 1981); Ralph K. Hawkins, "Propositions for Evangelical Acceptance of a Late Date Exodus Conquest: Biblical Data and the Royal Scarabs from Mt. Ebal," *JETS* 50 (2007): 31–46; James K. Hoffmeier, *Israel in Egypt* (New York: Oxford University Press, 1996), 164–98; idem, "What is the Biblical Date for the Exodus? A Response to Bryant Wood," *JETS* 50 (2007): 225–47; Kenneth A. Kitchen, *On the Reliability of the Old Testament* (Grand Rapids: Eerdmans, 2003), 65–79; Carl G. Rasmussen, "Conquest, Infiltration, Revolt,

enant established at Sinai, God calls Israel into being as a nation set apart for him. God then continues to be faithful to his covenant promises by taking the people across the Jordan to settle the land that he promised Israel's forefathers (1407/6 B.C.).[14] The period of the judges ensues as God continually raises up leaders to bring Israel back to faithfulness to the covenant (1367–1064 B.C.).[15] The united monarchy then begins with the anointing of Saul as king (1044 B.C.) and consists of the reigns of Saul, David, and Solomon. With regard to biblical literature, this time period proved to be significant because the Psalms and wisdom literature flourished during this time period as David and Solomon became the archetypal psalmist and embodiment of wisdom, respectively.

The period of the united monarchy also proved to be significant with respect to the covenant promises of God. God made a covenant with David, saying,

> When your days are over and you rest with your fathers, I will raise up your offspring to succeed you, who will come from your own body, and I will establish his kingdom. He is the one who will build a house for my Name, and I will establish the throne of his kingdom forever (2 Sam. 7:12–13).

This covenant with David continued God's faithfulness to his prior covenants, specifying that the promised seed, God's Messiah, would come in and through the line of David (see Matt. 1:1–17). Later, Solomon builds the temple as the place where God has chosen to make his name dwell (957 B.C.). After Solomon's death, the nation is divided into the northern and the southern kingdoms, called Israel and Judah.

---

or Resettlement," in *Giving the Sense*, 143–59; William H. Shea, "The Date of the Exodus," in *Giving the Sense*, 236–55; Bryant G. Wood, "The Rise and Fall of the 13th-century-Conquest Theory," *JETS* 48 (2005): 475–88; idem, "The Biblical Date for the Exodus is 1446 BC: A Response to James Hoffmeier," *JETS* 50 (2006): 164–98

14. Bryant G. Wood, "The Rise and Fall of the 13th-Century Exodus-Conquest Theory," *JETS* 48/3 (2005): 488.

15. For details, see John J. Bimson, *Redating the Exodus and Conquest* (Sheffield: University of Sheffield, 1981), 223; Eugene H. Merrill, *Kingdom of Priests* (Grand Rapids: Baker, 1987), 141–88; Andrew E. Steinmann, "The Mysterious Numbers of the Book of Judges," *JETS* 48/3 (2005): 491–500.

Divided Monarchy

The era of the divided monarchy encompasses the period from the death of Solomon until the collapse of the northern and southern kingdoms in 722 B.C. and 586 B.C, respectively. This is a lively time in the history of the ancient Near East, which sees the ascendancy of the Neo-Assyrian Empire (745–612 B.C.), the rise of the Neo-Babylonian (or Chaldean) Empire (626–539 B.C.), and a brief resurgence of Egypt (664–525 B.C.). Israel's location in the midst of these competing powers provides frequent pressure upon the twin kingdoms. That pressure will lead to Israel and Judah's breaking of the covenant and her spiritual apostasy and worship of other gods. Breaking the covenant, in turn, means that Israel and Judah incur the curse of the Mosaic covenant exile from the promised land (586–516 B.C.).

Exile and Return

As mentioned, the northern kingdom (Israel) is exiled by the Assyrians in 722 B.C., and the southern kingdom (Judah) follows suit when it falls into Babylonian captivity. If the exodus serves as the paradigmatic event of redemption, the exile represents the paradigmatic event of judgment. Though it is Israel's—not God's—unfaithfulness that issues in divine judgment, now that the Jews have gone into exile they question God's faithfulness to his covenant. God promised that Israel would be in the land permanently, that his name would dwell in the temple indefinitely, that David would have a son on the throne forever, and that all nations would be blessed through Israel. Yet, other nations took Israel captive in judgment and destroyed the temple. Nevertheless, in spite of Israel's failure to fulfill her side of the covenant arrangement, God would prove faithful.

In due course, God calls the Persian ruler, Cyrus, to defeat the Babylonians who captured Israel (Isaiah 44:24–45:7), and he issues a decree to bring God's people back to the Promised Land (538 B.C.). Subsequently, the people begin to rebuild the temple in 536 B.C. Under the ministries of Ezra and Nehemiah, the temple is completed in 516 B.C. God proves faithful, and the people are restored from exile. Though the temple is rebuilt, however, it is not as glorious as Solomon's temple, nor does the glory of God descend to take up his presence there again. God's fulfillment of his promises awaits a future time.

2.1. BIBLE CHRONOLOGY: 2167–430 B.C.		
DATE	EVENT/PERSON	SCRIPTURE
2167–1992	Abraham	Genesis 11:26–25:11
2092–1877/76	Patriarchal Age	Genesis 12–50
1876–1447	Bondage in Egypt	Exodus 1–12:30
1447/6	The Exodus	Exodus 12:31–15:21
1407/6	Entrance into Canaan under Joshua	Joshua
1367–1064	Period of the Judges	Judges
1064–1044	Samuel	1 Samuel 7:2
1044–1004	Saul	1 Samuel 10; cf. Acts 13:21
1011–971	David	2 Samuel 5:5
971–931	Solomon	1 Kings 11:42
931	Division of the Kingdom	1 Kings 12:19
722	Assyrian Exile	2 Kings 17:6
605	First deportation to Babylon	Daniel 1
598	Second Deportation to Babylon	2 Kings 24: 2 Chronicles 36
586	Third deportation to Babylon	Jeremiah 38–45
538	Decree of Cyrus allowing return	Ezra 1–4
520	Work on temple renewed under Darius	Haggai; Ezra 5–6
483–74	Xerxes and Esther; Purim	Esther
458	Return of Ezra to Jerusalem	Ezra 7–10
444	Artaxerxes allows Nehemiah to return	Nehemiah
430	End of Old Testament prophetic period	Malachi

SECOND TEMPLE PERIOD

Students of Scripture should not ignore the intertestamental period, or as it is more commonly called today, the Second Temple period (named after the time between the rebuilding of the temple after the return from exile in 516 B.C. and its destruction by the Romans in A.D. 70).[16] The world of the Gospels is very different from the one at the close of the Old Testament. Much has happened, and this interim period is attested to, not by biblical material but by extrabiblical literature (i.e., a variety of apocryphal and pseudepigraphical material, such as 1 and 2 Maccabees). Thus we encounter in the Gospels various Jewish sects—the Pharisees, the Sadducees, the Herodians, and the Zealots— whose roots lie in events that transpired in the centuries preceding the Incarnation, for the most part during the Maccabean revolt and its aftermath.

Babylonian and Persian Periods

The cataclysmic event transpiring toward the end of Old Testament history is the Babylonian captivity of God's people Israel. Despite the return of a small Jewish remnant to Jerusalem, this deportation resulted in Israel losing its independent nation status and in its being subject to rule by a successive string of empires. The Babylonians (Nebuchadnezzar) had wrested control from Egypt at the famous battle of Carchemish at the Euphrates in 605 B.C. (Jer. 46:2). In the year 539, Darius the Mede seized power (Dan. 5:30), soon replaced by the Persian Cyrus, who in 538 issued a decree allowing the Jews to return. Subsequent years saw the rebuilding of the temple and the returns of Ezra and Nehemiah to Jerusalem and their religious reforms.

Hellenistic Period

In 333, the Greeks (Alexander the Great) took over world domination at the battle of Issus. Alexander's acquisition of Palestine in the following year (332) had far-reaching impact on the Jews owing to his policy of Hellenization,

---

16. Only the briefest survey of the origins and basic beliefs of these groups and the history of the Second Temple period can be given below. For a fuller treatment of the history, literature, and theology of the Second Temple period, see Andreas J. Köstenberger, L. Scott Kellum, and Charles L. Quarles, *The Cradle, the Cross, and the Crown: An Introduction to the New Testament* (Nashville: B&H, 2009), Chapter 2. See also Michael E. Stone, ed., *Jewish Writings of the Second Temple Period*, CRINT (Minneapolis: Augsburg, 1984); Larry R. Helyer, *Exploring Jewish Literature of the Second Temple Period* (Downers Grove: InterVarsity, 2002); and James C. VanderKam, *An Introduction to Early Judaism* (Grand Rapids: Eerdmans, 2001).

that is, the spread of Greek language and culture. Long after the Greeks had been defeated by the Romans, the reach of Hellenistic culture continued. The Romans essentially adopted the Greek pantheon (spectrum of gods). The Greek translation of the Old Testament, the Septuagint (LXX), prepared in the third century B.C., became the version used by the early Christians and most frequently cited by the New Testament writers (cf. *The Letter of Aristeas*). The New Testament would be written, not in Hebrew or Aramaic, but in Greek. Several of Jesus' disciples, such as Philip or Andrew, though from Galilee, had Greek names. Even the name of the Jewish ruling council, "Sanhedrin," is a transliteration of the Greek word for "gathering."

After Alexander's death in 323 B.C., his empire was divided, issuing in two major dynasties: the Ptolemies in Egypt and the Seleucids in Mesopotamia and Syria. After a century-long struggle for control of Palestine between these two empires, the Seleucids (Antiochus) seized control in 198. Things came to a head during the reign of Antiochus Epiphanes IV (175–164 B.C.), whose radical Hellenization program culminated in the erection of a statue of Zeus and the sacrifice of a pig in the Jerusalem sanctuary, an act that stirred Jewish outrage and galvanized national resistance led by Mattathias and his five sons Judas (Maccabeus; 166–60 B.C.), Jonathan (160–143 B.C.), Simon, John, and Eleazar, known as the Maccabees or the Hasmoneans.

Maccabean Period

The Maccabean revolt succeeded in reversing Antiochus' policy. The temple was rededicated in 164 B.C. (the Feast of Dedication; see John 10:22), and in 142 B.C. Judah became independent until the Romans conquered Palestine under Pompey in 63 B.C. The second century B.C. was a period of considerable ferment in Jewish life. Nationalism was rife, and several movements emerged that continued to exist until the time of Jesus, such as the Sadducees (aristocracy) and the Pharisees (religious reformists, persecuted by Alexander Jannaeus who ruled 103–76 B.C.). The Dead Sea community likewise arose during the mid-second century B.C., rejecting what it considered to be the corrupt Jerusalem priesthood (led by the "Wicked Priest"; e.g., 1QpHab 11.2–8) and rallying around the enigmatic "Teacher of Righteousness" (e.g., 1QS 1.5–11).[17]

---

17.   For a helpful overview see James C. VanderKam, *The Dead Sea Scrolls Today* (Grand Rapids: Eerdmans, 1994), 100–104.

2.2. BIBLE CHRONOLOGY: 333 B.C.–A.D. 37		
DATE	**PERSON/EVENT**	**SIGNIFICANCE**
333 B.C.	Alexander the Great seizes world domination	Hellenization
198 B.C.	Seleucids seize control of Palestine	Hellenization (continued)
175 61 D.C.	Antiochus Epiphanes IV rules Palestine, radical program of Hellenization	"Abomination causing desolation"
164 B.C.	Maccabean revolt, rededication of Temple	Feast of Dedication
142 B.C.	Judah becomes independent	Rise of Sadducees, Pharisees, Dead Sea community
63 B.C.	Roman general Pompey conquers Palestine	Roman vassal rulers in charge of Palestine at time of Christ
31 B.C.–A.D. 14	Emperor Augustus presides over "Golden Age" of Rome	Roman peace (*Pax Romana*; compared with Christ; Luke 2:1)
5 B.C.	Birth of Christ	Virgin birth
4 B.C.	Death of Herod the Great	Slaughter of infants, head of Herodian dynasty
A.D. 14–37	Emperor Tiberius	Ruled when Jesus began ministry and when he was crucified

Roman Period

After Pompey's conquest of Palestine in 63 B.C., a series of local rulers were put in charge of the provinces of Palestine. At the time of Jesus' birth in 5 B.C., Herod the Great ruled the region, though he died soon afterwards (4 B.C.) and was succeeded by Archelaus. In Jesus' day, Herod Antipas was in charge of Galilee (Mark 6:14; Luke 13:32). The great Emperor Augustus (31 B.C.–A.D. 14) presided over a golden period of peace (the *Pax Romana*) and prosperity (as well as rising corruption and decadence), which provided a poignant counterpoint to the humble birth of Christ (Luke 2:1). When John the Baptist and Jesus commenced their ministries, the rule had passed to Emperor Tiberius (14–37; cf. Luke 3:1) who was still in charge at the time of Jesus' crucifixion in the spring of 33, with Pontius Pilate serving as the procurator or prefect of Judea.[18]

NEW TESTAMENT PERIOD

Jesus

For the purpose of interpreting the New Testament, a brief discussion and survey of its underlying chronology is helpful. Especially important is the dating of the life of Jesus, in particular the crucifixion, and the life of Paul and related events. The two major questions with regard to the chronology of Jesus' life pertain to the dating of his birth and death.[19]

Regarding his birth, the most likely date is December of 5 B.C.[20] Herod's death in 4 B.C. provides the *terminus ad quem* (latest possible date) in this regard. An error in the computation of the modern reckoning of time in the Middle Ages is responsible for the fact that Jesus' birth does not fall in the year 1, as might be expected, but is dated 5 B.C.

---

18. As attested by the famous "Pilate inscription" (see below). For a helpful discussion of the date of Jesus' crucifixion, see *The ESV Study Bible* (Wheaton: Crossway, 2008), 1809–10. See also the discussion below.
19. For a fuller discussion, see Chapter 3 in Köstenberger, Kellum, and Quarles, *Cradle, the Cross, and the Crown*.
20. Cf. Paul L. Maier, "The Date of the Nativity and the Chronology of Jesus' Life," in *Chronos, Kairos, Christos: Nativity and Chronological Studies Presented to Jack Finegan*, ed. J. Vardaman and E. M. Yamauchi (Winona Lake, IN: Eisenbrauns, 1989), 113–30.

2.3. CHRONOLOGY OF JESUS' LIFE		
EVENT	APPROXIMATE DATE	SCRIPTURE REFERENCE
Jesus' Birth	5 B.C.	Matt. 1:18–25; Luke 2:1–20
Death of Herod the Great	April/March 4 B.C.	Josephus, *Ant.* 17.6.4 §167
Beginning of John the Baptist's Ministry	A.D. 29	Luke 3.1–3 pars.
Beginning of Jesus' Ministry	Fall 29	John 1:19–51
Jesus' First Passover	Spring 30	John 2:13–22
Jesus' Second Passover	Spring 31	Matt. 12:1 pars.
Jesus at Feast of Tabernacles	Fall 31	John 5
Jesus' Third Passover	Spring 32	John 6
Jesus at Feast of Tabernacles	Fall 32	John 7–8
Jesus at Feast of Dedication	Winter 32	John 10:22–39
Final Passover, Crucifixion, Resurrection, Ascension, Pentecost	Spring 33	Gospels passion narratives; Acts 1–2

Luke (3:1) writes that John the Baptist began his ministry in the fifteenth year of Tiberius Caesar's reign (A.D. 14–37), which places the beginning of the Baptist's, and of Jesus', ministry at A.D. 29.[21] If Jesus was born in 5 B.C., he would have been 33 years old, which comports well with the statement in Luke 3:23 that Jesus was "about thirty years old" when he started his ministry.

A date of 29 for the start of Jesus' ministry, in turn, requires a date of 33 for the crucifixion, since the Gospels record Jesus attending as many as four Passovers (three of which are mentioned in John; see chart above). Thus, of the two major possibilities suggested for the dating of Jesus' ministry, 26–30 or 29–33, the latter is preferred.[22]

Early Church and Paul

The book of Acts, on a canonical as well as a historical level, provides a wonderful transition between the life of Jesus (the Gospels) and the New Testament epistles, most notably the 13 letters of Paul. The following chart represents an effort to construct a Pauline chronology on the basis of the book of Acts, Paul's epistles, and extrabiblical data,[23] a helpful tool in interpreting Paul's letters within their proper historical framework.

Rest of the New Testament

The above two charts cover Jesus and the Gospels, the book of Acts, and Paul's Epistles (it should be added that the Synoptic Gospels were most likely written prior to the destruction of the temple in the year A.D. 70, while John dates in all probability to the 80s or early 90s). A framework for the rest of the New Testament writings is also needed.[24]

---

21. Cf. Harold Hoehner, *Chronological Aspects of the Life of Christ* (Grand Rapids: Zondervan, 1977), 31–37, and B. Messner, "'In the Fifteenth Year' Reconsidered: A Study of Luke 3:1," *Stone-Campbell Journal* 1 (1998): 201–11, with reference to the Roman historians Tacitus (*Ann.* 4.4) and Suetonius (*Tiberius* 73), both of whom date the beginning of Tiberius' reign to A.D. 14 (the precise date is August 19, the day of Emperor Augustus' death).

22. See esp. Hoehner, *Chronological Aspects;* idem, "Chronology," *DJG* 118–22; and C. J. Humphreys and W. G. Waddington, "The Jewish Calendar, a Lunar Eclipse, and the Date of Christ's Crucifixion," *TynBul* 43 (1992): 331–51, esp. 335.

23. For a fuller discussion, see Chapter 9 in Köstenberger, Kellum, and Quarles, *Cradle, the Cross, and the Crown.*

24. For treatments of introductory matters for all New Testament books see D. A. Carson and Douglas J. Moo, *An Introduction to the New Testament,* rev. ed. (Grand Rapids: Zondervan, 2005); and Köstenberger, Kellum, and Quarles, *Cradle, the Cross, and the Crown.*

2.4. CHRONOLOGY OF PAUL'S LIFE AND LETTERS		
EVENT	APPROXIMATE DATE	SCRIPTURE REFERENCE
Paul's Birth		
Jesus' Crucifixion, Resurrection, Ascension, and Pentecost	Spring 33	Gospels passion narratives; Acts 1–2
Paul's Conversion	34	Acts 9:1–19
First Missionary Journey	47–48	Acts 13–14
Authorship of **Galatians**	48	
Jerusalem Council	49	Acts 15
Second Missionary Journey Antioch to Corinth **Thessalonian Letters** from Corinth Appearance before Gallio	49–51	Acts 16–18 Acts 18:11 Acts 18:12
Third Missionary Journey 3-Year Stay in Ephesus "Severe letter" **1 Corinthians** "Sorrowful letter" **2 Corinthians** (from Macedonia) Stay in Corinth Romans (from Corinth)	51–54 53/54 54/55 55	Acts 19–21 Acts 20:31 1 Cor. 5:9, 11 Acts 19:10 2 Cor. 2:4; 7:8 Acts 20:1–2 2 Cor. 13:1–2 Rom. 16:1–2, 23
Jerusalem Arrest	55	Acts 21–23 Acts 21:27–40
Imprisonment in Caesarea Defense before Felix, Festus, Agrippa	55–57	Acts 24–27
Journey to Rome Voyage and Shipwreck Winter in Malta	57–58	Acts 27 Acts 28:1–10

2.4. CHRONOLOGY OF PAUL'S LIFE AND LETTERS (CONTINUED)		
EVENT	**APPROXIMATE DATE**	**SCRIPTURE REFERENCE**
First Roman Imprisonment Prison Epistles: **Colossians, Philemon, Ephesians, Philippians**	58–60	Acts 28:11–30
Paul's Release	60	
Further Travels **1 Timothy** **Titus**	60–66	
Great Fire of Rome, Persecution of Christians under Emperor Nero	64	
Paul's Arrest and ***Second Roman Imprisonment*** **2 Timothy**	66	
Paul's and Peter's Martyrdoms	66/67	
Outbreak of Jewish War	66	
Destruction of Jerusalem	70	

James, a Jewish-Christian work written by one of Jesus' half-brothers, the head of the Jerusalem church, was likely written around the time of the Jerusalem Council in the early 50s. The epistle of Jude, authored by James' brother and half-brother of Jesus, may also be dated to the 50s. Jude, in turn, was possibly used by Peter in 2 Peter 2, which suggests dates in the 60s for Peter's two epistles.

The book of Hebrews was almost certainly composed prior to the destruction of the Jerusalem temple in the year 70. It is hard to imagine why the author would not have mentioned the temple's destruction if it had already taken place by the time of writing, since this would have provided strong support for his contention that old-style Judaism had now been superseded—and fulfilled—in Jesus and the Christian faith.

The Johannine corpus, finally, consisting of the Gospel, John's three epistles, and the book of Revelation, most likely in this order clusters around the 80s and 90s, with Revelation closing the entire canon of Scripture. Thus the canonical framework for New Testament interpretation spans from the Gospels to the historical narrative of Acts to the Epistles and to the concluding Apocalypse.[25]

ARCHAEOLOGY

Old Testament

Archaeology has steadily increased the understanding of ancient Near Eastern history and culture beginning with the decipherment of the Rosetta Stone in the nineteenth century. This amazing discovery provided the key to the ancient Egyptian language and gave the impetus for further unraveling the tangled strands of the history of the ancient Near East. Space does not permit a cataloging of all the pioneering efforts in Near Eastern archaeology, but special mention should be made of Sir Flinders Petrie whose excavations at Tell el Hesi (some 15 plus miles northeast of Gaza) laid the foundation for all subsequent archaeological excavations. Building on several significant discoveries in the early twentieth century, the quest for knowledge of the ancient Near East blossomed between the first two world wars. Steady progress continues up to our own time with scholars of many nations contributing to the discipline.[26]

Although a vast number of tells or mounds of debris remain totally or partially unexcavated, archaeology has contributed significantly to the understanding of the biblical record. In some cases, the Old Testament Scriptures are confirmed by archaeology. In others, our lack of information with regard to difficulties becomes illumined, while in still other cases the biblical data are supplemented by ongoing discoveries. Some of these have been mentioned above in the discussions of the patriarchal period, the era of the exodus, and the time of the Judges.[27]

---

25. See Chapter 11.
26. Contemporary findings are regularly available in such leading periodicals as the *AASOR, BA, BAR, BASOR*, the *Near East Archaeological Society Bulletin*, and *Artifax*.
27. See further the several excellent articles on these periods by Richard Averbeck, Carl Rasmussen, Mark Rooker, William Shea, and Bryant Wood in *Giving the Sense*, 115–59, 217–99.

With regard to the time of the united monarchy, the biblical description of Solomon's Temple finds confirmation in the excavation of similarly laid-out temples of ancient Syro-Palestine. Further information concerning Solomon's building activities comes from the excavations at Hazor, Megiddo, and Gezer. There Solomon's fortifications and building activities involved the use of casemate walls and ashlar masonry, and gates having six chambers, three on each side. This type of construction, typical of the Solomonic era, illustrates the accuracy of the biblical record in 1 Kings 9:15 that it was Solomon who built the walls around these cities.[28]

With regard to the time of the divided monarchy, numerous discoveries aid in the fuller understanding of the biblical record in this period (931–841 B.C.). In the first part of this era, Pharaoh Sheshonq I of Egypt's twenty-second dynasty (biblical Shishak) invaded Israel (1 Kgs. 14:25–26). Sheshonq's own account has been found in the great temple at Karnak. In it he lists more than 150 Palestinian cities that he attacked and despoiled.[29]

In the middle period of Old Testament history (841–640 B.C.), the Assyrian King Shalmaneser III (859–825 B.C.) records the capitulation of King Jehu of Israel on his well-known Black Obelisk: "The tribute of Jehu, son of Omri." This information supplements that which the biblical record provides concerning Jehu's reign (2 Kgs. 9:1–10:36). The familiar account of King Sennacherib of Assyria's siege of Jerusalem in which he lost 185,000 men due to the Lord's intervention (2 Kgs. 19:35–36) also falls into this period. Sennacherib's version of this event during his third campaign attempts to paint a more positive picture by claiming that Hezekiah paid him a heavy tribute in order to get him to leave Jerusalem.[30] Concerning Hezekiah, Sennacherib declares, "As for Hezekiah, the Jew . . . Him, like a caged bird, in Jerusalem, his royal city, I shut up."[31]

One of the more intriguing problems with regard to the fall of the northern kingdom concerns the identity of "So King of Egypt" (2 Kgs. 17:4). Because no pharaoh is listed bearing this name, some have suggested

---

28. 1 Kings 9:15: "Here is the account of the forced labor King Solomon conscripted to build the LORD's temple, his own palace, the supporting terraces, the wall of Jerusalem, and Hazor, Megiddo and Gezer." See further Hoerth, *Archaeology*, 281–88.
29. See Breasted, *Ancient Records of Egypt, 4*, 348–55. See also William Petrie, *Egypt and Israel* (London: Society for Promoting Christian Knowledge, 1911) and especially, Hoerth, *Archaeology*, 300–302.
30. See Luckenbill, *Ancient Records of Assyria and Babylonia*, 2:120–21.
31. Ibid, 2:143.

that the biblical record is inaccurate or in error.[32] Several suggestions for harmonizing the biblical record with Egyptian data have been put forward.[33] For example, A. R. Green has equated biblical "So" with a certain Pharaoh Piankhy of Egypt's twenty-fifth dynasty whose growing power may have appealed to King Hoshea of Israel who therefore sent "envoys" to him as possible help against the Assyrians.[34] Green's proposal, like that of some others, does demonstrate the value of archaeological and historical research and show that scholars should not discount the biblical record so hastily.

One further example of this is Daniel's mention of King Belshazzar of Babylon (Daniel 5). This was considered by previous generations to be one of the most obvious errors in the Bible, for ancient historians mentioned Nabonidus as Babylon's last ruler. Yet subsequent information discovered in the Babylonian clay tablets proved not only the existence of Belshazzar, but also indicated that because Nabonidus, his father, was absent for long periods from Babylon, he left the affairs of state to Belshazzar. Critical denial of the existence of Belshazzar has now largely disappeared.

Confirmation of the biblical record for the third period (640–586 B.C.) concerning the scriptural record of Daniel's captivity at the hands of King Nebuchadnezzar II of Babylon in 605 B.C. comes from the Babylonian chronicles. In that year after his victory over the Assyrians and Egyptians at Carchemish, Nebuchadnezzar swept westward, but due to the death of his father Nabopolasser he returned to Babylon to secure the throne. Having done so, he rejoined his troops and marched "unopposed through Hatti Land."[35] Such data harmonized well with the biblical accounts in Daniel 1:1–2 and 2 Chronicles 36:6–7.[36]

---

32. See G. H. Jones, *1 and 2 Kings,* New Century Biblical Commentary (Grand Rapids: Eerdmans, 1984), 2:546–47; D. B. Redford, "Studies in Relations Between Palestine and Egypt During the First Millennium B.C.," *JAOS* 93 (1973): 3–17.

33. See, for example, Kenneth A. Kitchen, *The Third Intermediate Period in Egypt* (Warminster, England: Aris & Phillips, 1973), 371–76; H. Goedicke, "The End of So, King of Egypt," *BASOR* 17 (1963): 64–66; J. Day, "The Problem of 'So, King of Egypt' in 2 Kings xvii.4," *Vetus Testamentum* 42 (1992): 289–301.

34. A. R. Green, "The Identity of King So of Egypt: An Alternate Interpretation," *JNES* 52 (1993): 99–108.

35. See Donald J. Wiseman, ed. *Chronicles of the Chaldaean Kings* (London: Trustees of the British Museum, 1956), 69.

36. Illumination concerning the Babylonian advance against Judah in 598–597 B.C. is also available from the Lachish Ostraca, which detail the advance of the Babylonians southward into Judah and from the Babylonian chronicles that record events

The above examples are but a brief sample of the many instances in which the biblical record has been verified, illumined, or supplemented by the archaeologist's spade. For this reason the interpreter does well in taking archaeological data into account in his or her use of the historical-cultural leg of the hermeneutical triad.

New Testament

In recent years archaeology has made a significant contribution to a better understanding of various geographical and topographical features of the New Testament, and detailed archaeological information is available regarding many sites mentioned in the New Testament.[37] This section briefly addresses relevant historical, cultural, and archaeological issues for New Testament interpretation pertaining to the life of Jesus, Paul, and the New Testament writings.[38]

Charlesworth lists what he considers to be the seven most important contributions made by archaeology to Jesus research:

1. Archaeological evidence that Jesus was crucified on the rock now seen inside the Church of the Holy Sepulchre

2. The remains of a crucified man named Jehohanan[39]

---

relative to Judah's progressive demise at the end of the seventh century and Jerusalem's (second) deportation in 597 B.C.

37. See esp. "Archeology and Geography," *DJG* 33–46; E. Stern, ed., *The New Encyclopedia of Archaeological Excavations in the Holy Land*, 4 vols. (New York/London: Simon & Schuster, 1993); E. M. Meyers, ed., *The Oxford Encyclopedia of Archaeology in the Near East*, 5 vols. (New York/Oxford: Oxford University Press, 1997); and A. Negev and S. Gibson, eds., *Archaeological Encyclopedia of the Holy Land*, rev. ed. (New York/London: Continuum, 2001). See also "Archaeology and the Bible," in *ESV Study Bible*, 2591–94.

38. The existence of Jesus itself is established beyond reasonable doubt by witnesses otherwise hostile to the Christian faith. The Roman historian Suetonius refers to Claudius' expulsion of the Jews on account of disturbances related to "Chrestus" (i.e. Jesus; Claudius 25.4; cf. Acts 18:2). Another Roman historian, Tacitus, writes that "Christus, from whom the name ['Christians'] had its origin, suffered the extreme penalty during the reign of Tiberius at the hands of one of our procurators, Pontius Pilatus" (*Annals* 15.44). Josephus, a Jewish historian, makes reference to the trial of "James, the brother of Jesus who was called the Christ" (*Ant.* 20.9.1 §§200–203). The Babylonian Talmud asserts that, "On the eve of the Passover Yeshu [Jesus] was hanged" (*b. Sanh.* 43a).

39. The man is estimated to have been 24 to 28 years old, and his remains date roughly to Jesus' day and were found in Jerusalem in 1968. Cf. James H. Charlesworth, "Jesus

3. The Praetorium, the official residence of the Roman governor: Pilate's dwelling was probably in the Upper City and not in the Fortress of Antonia

4. The Pool of Bethesda described in John 5:2–9[40]

5. The Temple Mount: monumental pre-70 structures located south of the southern retaining wall of the Temple

6. The walls and gates of Jerusalem

7. Pre-70 synagogues at Gamla, Masada, and the Herodium, and possibly at Jericho.[41]

To these, we may add the Pilate inscription ("Pontius Pilate, prefect of Judea") discovered in 1961 in Caesarea Maritima;[42] the tombs of Annas and Caiaphas and the Caiaphas ossuary (bearing the name of Joseph Caiaphas);[43] the James ossuary (bearing the inscription "James, the son of Joseph, the brother of Jesus");[44] and the Alexamenos graffiti ("Alexamenos worships his god").[45] Though archaeologists do not always agree on the way in which they interpret archaeological findings and their relevance

---

and Jehohanan: An Archaeological Note on Crucifixion," *Expository Times* 84 (1972–73): 147–50.

40. Cf. esp. Urban C. von Wahlde, "Archaeology and John's Gospel," in *Jesus and Archaeology*, ed. James H. Charlesworth (Grand Rapids: Eerdmans, 2006), 560–66.

41. Cf. James H. Charlesworth, "Jesus Research and Archaeology: A New Perspective," in *Jesus and Archaeology*, 27–37, with reference to idem, *Jesus within Judaism: New Light from Exciting Archaeological Discoveries*, ABRL 1 (Garden City, NY: Doubleday, 1988), who lists additional discoveries in Nazareth, Cana, Bethsaida, the Galilean Boat, Caesarea Maritima, Jerusalem, Peter's house in Capernaum (?), and Sepphoris. See also many of the other essays in *Jesus and Archaeology*.

42. Cf. Andreas J. Köstenberger, *John*, ZIBBC 2.165.

43. Cf. Zvi Greenhut, "Burial Cave of the Caiaphas Family" and Ronny Reich, "Caiaphas Name Inscribed on Bone Boxes," *Biblical Archaeology Review* 18 (1992): 28–36, 38–44, 76.

44. Though the authenticity of the inscription is debated. Positive are Hershel Shanks and Ben Witherington, *The Brother of Jesus* (San Francisco: HarperSanFrancisco, 2003); more cautious is Craig A. Evans, *Jesus and the Ossuaries* (Waco: Baylor University Press, 2003); skeptical is Charlesworth, *Jesus and Archaeology*, 48.

45. Cf. Everett Ferguson, *Backgrounds of Early Christianity*, 2d ed. (Grand Rapids: Eerdmans, 1993), 560–61.

to Jesus, no archaeological discovery has disproved any information regarding Jesus given in the canonical Gospels.

With regard to Paul and the New Testament writings, major excavations have been conducted in many of the cities where Paul ministered and where the early Christian mission unfolded. This includes important sites such as Ephesus and Corinth.[46] Particularly important is the Gallio Inscription, which allows us to date Gallio's governorship in the province of Achaia to between the summer of the year 51 and the summer of 52. Most likely, therefore, the Jews brought charges against Paul in the summer or fall of the year 51 per Acts 18:12. With Paul's ministry in Corinth spanning 18 months (Acts 18:11) and his departure from Corinth taking place sometime after the Gallio incident, Paul's arrival in Corinth can be dated to early 50. Thus the Gallio inscription, as one of the few reasonably fixed dates in New Testament history, provides an anchor for an absolute chronology of Paul's life, letters, and ministry.[47]

HISTORICAL-CULTURAL BACKGROUND

Doing justice to the historical dimension of Scripture entails not only a careful consideration of chronology and archeology but involves also sensitivity to various aspects in the biblical text related to historical-cultural background.

---

46. On Ephesus, see Helmut Koester, ed., *Ephesos: Metropolis of Asia* (Valley Forge, PA: Trinity, 1995); and Peter Scherrer et al., eds., *Ephesus: The New Guide*, rev. ed., trans. Lionel Bier and George M. Luxon (Selçuk: Österreichisches Archäologisches Institut, 2000); on Corinth, see David E. Garland, *1 Corinthians*, BECNT (Grand Rapids: Baker, 2003), 1–13.

47. See the chronology of Paul above. See also Ferguson, *Backgrounds*, 549–50. Another important artifact corroborating New Testament information is the Erastus inscription, which reads, "Erastus in return for his aedileship laid [the pavement] at his own expense," and which most identify as referring to the person mentioned by Paul in Romans 16:23 as the city's *oikonomos* (aedile?; see also 2 Timothy 4:20; and Acts 19:22; for a helpful discussion see Garland, *1 Corinthians, 11–12*). Many other pieces of information pertaining to Roman government officials mentioned in the Book of Acts and to a variety of other historical and cultural data referred to in the New Testament letters are illumined by extrabiblical data as well (see esp. the *Zondervan Illustrated Bible Backgrounds Commentary*) and the relevant commentary literature as well as various reference works mentioned in the Bibliography at the end of this chapter). Another fascinating area of study is that of ancient coins illustrating the background of early Christianity. See Jon Yonge Akerman, *Numismatic Illustrations of the New Testament* (Chicago: Argonaut, 1966); R. S. Yeoman, *Moneys of the Bible* (Racine, WI: Whitman, 1961).

For example, Paul's discussion of divisions in the Corinthian church in 1 Corinthians 1–4 is significantly predicated upon first-century Greco-Roman rhetorical schools and conceptions of leadership. Understanding of Paul's references to wealth and prosperity as well as sexual immorality in the same epistle is significantly aided by understanding that Corinth was a wealthy seaport with a vast amount of immorality associated with it.

Or take John's Gospel, for example. Among many other historical-cultural background features, John's account includes both a wedding (John 2:1–12) and a funeral (John 11:1–44).[48] Jewish weddings were important social occasions, usually lasting seven days, and the family of the groom was responsible to accommodate the guests during the festivities. Cana was less than ten miles from Nazareth where Jesus grew up, which may explain why Jesus' mother Mary as well as Jesus himself were invited to the wedding. If Mary was a family friend of the groom's family, this may also explain why she intervened when the wine had run out; she tried to save her friends the social embarrassment that came from failing to provide for the wedding guests. Thus the heart of the dilemma with which Jesus is presented is better understood by knowing Jewish wedding customs. The same can be said for the funeral for Lazarus, where we see Mary "seated" in the house (11:20), in keeping with the customary mourning for a loved one.

Grant Osborne helpfully surveys the areas for research involved in historical-cultural background study. These include geography, politics, economics, military and war, and various cultural practices and religious customs.[49] Without the historical-cultural background lying behind a given book of Scripture, its study will often be insufficient and superficial. For this reason it is important that students are familiar with the vast array of primary and secondary sources that are available for the exploration of the historical-cultural background of the Old and New Testaments.

Primary Sources

Pride of place with regard to the primary sources for biblical study belongs to the scriptural documents themselves. The Old and the New Testaments often include references to the historical setting of a given passage. The

---

48. For more detailed discussions of the historical-cultural background to John 2:1–12 and 11:1–44, see Andreas J. Köstenberger, "John," in *Zondervan Illustrate Bible Backgrounds Commentary*, 2.23–27 and 106–13.
49. Osborne, *Hermeneutical Spiral*, 161–67.

book of Esther, for instance, opens with the following introduction: "This is what happened during the time of Xerxes, the Xerxes who ruled over 127 provinces stretching from India to Cush. At that time King Xerxes reigned from his royal throne in the citadel of Susa, and in the third year of his reign he gave a banquet for all his nobles and officials. The military leaders of Persia and Media, the princes, and the nobles of the provinces were present" (Esth. 1:1–3). By providing this historical setting for the story of Esther, the biblical author shows great care to locate this story in the period following the Assyrian and Babylonian exiles.

There are also some very interesting extrabiblical sources that confirm and supplement the information provided in the biblical book of Esther. One such source is the Greek historian Herodotus (490–425 BC), who portrayed Xerxes "as an ill-tempered, impatient monarch with a wandering eye for women."[50] This illustrates that while the biblical documents must remain primary, extrabiblical information can be used in tandem and can helpfully illuminate aspects of the biblical story that may lie in the background and be assumed by the biblical writer.

There are many relevant primary sources for the study of the historical-cultural background of Scripture,[51] and a Bible student does not have to enroll in a Ugaritics course or become a specialist in ancient Near Eastern languages, because most good study Bibles, commentaries, and reference tools already provide the salient historical-cultural background information from the primary sources. Nevertheless, a survey of the primary sources increases appreciation for the types of sources available for illuminating the historical-cultural background of the Old and New Testament writings.

Ancient Near Eastern Literature
If authorial intention is the locus of meaning, then understanding the context within which the author wrote his text is of utmost importance. Because literature arises within and also forms and shapes culture, an attempt to understand the ancient culture through its literature, and in turn literature through its culture, is vital. Ancient Near Eastern literature provides

---

50. Tremper Longman and Raymond B. Dillard, *An Introduction to the Old Testament*, 2d ed. (Grand Rapids: Zondervan, 2007), 216, with reference to Edwin Yamauchi, "The Archaeological Background of Esther," *BibSac* 137 (1980): 104.

51. Part of the following survey is adapted from Köstenberger, Kellum, and Quarles, *Cradle, the Cross, and the Crown*, 81–84.

access to the cultural context within which the biblical authors wrote the Old Testament. Certainly, this access is limited and imperfect, but the wealth of ancient Near Eastern literature available provides access nonetheless.[52] Faithful interpreters of Scripture must exhaust any means possible to understand what God communicates in Scripture through the human author to his original audience. To be sure, abuses have occurred, especially in the area of Old Testament background studies. These abuses, however, do not represent faithful and diligent interpretations and ought not to scare us away from seeking to understand the ancient world of Scripture.

From law to prophecy and from proverbs to historical narrative, texts from the ancient Near East contain nearly every genre of literature in the Old Testament, as the abbreviated list below demonstrates. These texts, covering over two millennia, come from all over the ancient Near East including Egypt, Mesopotamia, Anatolia, and Persia in languages including Ugaritic, Akkadian, Sumerian, Hittite, and Egyptian. Assyriologists, Egyptologists, and many other scholars have done considerable work to make many of these texts accessible to the layman and scholar alike. Though an exhaustive list of ancient Near Eastern texts is not possible here, what follows is a few key texts for understanding the Old Testament and a list of resources for further study of the ancient texts and, therefore, the context of Scripture.[53]

The Pentateuch

Creation
- Enuma Elish
- Atrahasis

---

52. The two standard texs for reading ancient Near Eastern primary sources are Hallo and Younger, *Context of Scripture; and* Pritchard, *Ancient Near Eastern Texts.* For sources that include texts and discussion concerning those texts, see Bill T. Arnold and Bryan E. Beyer, eds., *Readings from the Ancient Near East: Primary Sources for Old Testament Study* (Grand Rapids: Baker Academic, 2002); Jeffrey J. Niehaus, *Ancient Near Eastern Themes in Biblcal Theology* (Grand Rapids: Kregel, 2008); Sparks, *Ancient Texts for the Study of the Hebrew Bible;* and John H. Walton, *Ancient Near Eastern Thought and the Old Testament: Introducing the Conceptual World of the Hebrew Bible* (Grand Rapids: Baker Academic, 2006).

53. This list follows the structure provided by Arnold and Beyer, *Readings from the Ancient Near East*, which helpfully categorizes the ancient Near Eastern texts in relation to the biblical parallels. Other categorizations are certainly possible. For a categorization of the texts according to their ancient Near Eastern genres, see the sources listed above.

Flood
- Gilgamesh

Law Codes
- Laws of Hammurapi
- Hittite Laws

Covenants/Treaties
- Mari Covenant Ritual
- Treaty between Mursilis and Dupp-Teshub

Cultic Texts
- Ritual of the Substitute King
- Instructions for Cultic Officials and Temple Personnel
- New Year Festival at Babylon

Historical Books

Royal Records from Mesopotamia
- Tiglath-pileser III
- Senacharib
- Cyrus Cylinder
- Chronicles and Other Historiographic Lists
- Sumerian King List
- Babylonian Chronicles

Other Hebrew Incriptions
- Siloam Tunnel Inscription

Poetic Books

Wisdom Literature
- Babylonian Theodicy
- Instruction of Merikare
- Instruction of Amenemope
- Hymns and Prayers
- Hymn to Enlil
- Prayer to Ishtar
- Psalm to Marduk

Prophetic Books

Prophecies
- Mari Prophecy

- Marduk Prophecy

Lamentations

- Lamentation over the Destruction of Ur
- The Old Testament and New Testament Apocrypha

Old and New Testament Apocrypha

The Greek word "apocrypha" originally meant "things that are hidden."[54] The designation "apocrypha" may also refer to the mysterious or esoteric nature of some of the contents of these books or to their spurious or heretical nature (or both). The writings comprising the Old Testament Apocrypha included in this category represent several different genres:

1. historical writings (1 Esdras, 1–2 Maccabees);
2. moralistic novels (Tobit, Judith, Susanna, Bel and the Dragon);
3. wisdom or devotional literature (Wisdom of Solomon; Sirach, also called Ecclesiasticus; Prayer of Manasseh; Prayer of Azariah; Song of the Three Young Men);
4. pseudonymous letter (Letter of Jeremiah); and
5. apocalyptic literature (2 Esdras).

Except for 2 Esdras, these writings are found in the Septuagint. The Apocrypha are also included in the Vulgate (the Latin translation of the Bible prepared in the fourth century by Jerome) either as part of the Old Testament or as an appendix but that are not part of the canonical Scriptures.[55] Because of their inclusion in the Vulgate, the books of the Apocrypha were considered part of Scripture by the medieval church. In 1546, the Council of Trent declared them canonical except for 1–2 Esdras and the Prayer of Manasseh.[56]

---

54. David A. deSilva, "Apocrypha and Pseudepigrapha," in Craig A. Evans and Stanley E. Porter, eds., *Dictionary of New Testament Background: A Compendium of Contemporary Biblical Scholarship* (Downers Grove, IL: InterVarsity, 2000), 58; see the entire entry on pp. 58–64, including additional bibliographic references.
55. The following survey is indebted to Bruce M. Metzger, "Introduction to the Apocrypha," in *The Oxford Annotated Apocrypha*, exp. and rev. ed., ed. Bruce M. Metzger (New York: Oxford University Press, 1977), xi–xxii. See also Craig A. Evans, *Ancient Texts for New Testament Studies: A Guide to the Background Literature* (Peabody, MA: Hendrickson, 2005), 1–8.
56. On issues related to the canonicity of the Old Testament Apocrypha and Pseudepigrapha, see Norman L. Geisler and William E. Nix, *A General Introduction to the Bible*, rev. and exp. ed. (Chicago: Moody, 1986), chap. 15.

Apart from the Old Testament Apocrypha of the Second Temple period, there are also New Testament Apocrypha that emerged in the second and subsequent centuries of the Christian era, consisting of spurious Gospels, Acts, and Apocalypses.[57] Many of these writings have in common the underlying motivation to fill in perceived gaps in Scripture, frequently resulting in heterodox (false) teaching. This is the case both with the writings commonly grouped together as Apocrypha and with other Jewish Second Temple literature assembled under the amorphous rubric of Pseudepigrapha.[58]

Old Testament Pseudepigrapha

The Pseudepigrapha (from *pseudos*, "false," and *graphein*, "write") encompass the following types of literature:

1. apocalyptic and related literature (1–2 Enoch; 2–3 Baruch, 4 Ezra, Sibylline Oracles);

2. testaments (Testaments of the Twelve Patriarchs);

3. pseudonymous epistle (Letter of Aristeas);

---

57. See especially J. K. Elliott, *The Apocryphal New Testament* (New York: Oxford Univ. Press, 2005); and William Schneemelcher, ed., *New Testament Apocrypha*, 2 vols., trans. R. McL. Wilson (Louisville/London: Westminster John Knox, 2003). Contrary to Bart D. Ehrman (*Lost Scriptures* [New York: Oxford University Press, 2005] and *Lost Christianities* [New York: Oxford Univ. Press, 2005]) who followed Walter Bauer (*Rechtgläubigkeit und Ketzerei im ältesten Christentum* [Tübingen: Mohr, 1934]; *ET Orthodoxy and Heresy in Earliest Christianity*, eds. Robert A. Kraft and Gerhard Krodel [Philadelphia: Fortress, 1971]), the New Testament Apocrypha were not for a time put side by side with the canonical New Testament writings and only later disqualified by the early Catholic church. See especially Darrell L. Bock, *The Missing Gospels: Unearthing the Truth behind Alternative Christianities* (Nashville: Nelson, 2006); Craig A. Blaising, "Faithfulness: A Prescription for Theology," *JETS* 49 (2006): 6–9; Paul Trebilco, "Christian Communities in Western Asia Minor into the Early Second Century: Ignatius and Others as Witnesses against Bauer," *JETS* 49 (2006): 17–44; and Andreas J. Köstenberger and Michael J. Kruger, *The Heresy of Orthodoxy: How Contemporary Culture's Fascination with Diversity Has Reshaped Our Understanding of Early Christianity* (Wheaton: Crossway, 2010).

58. See James H. Charlesworth, ed., *The Old Testament Pseudepigrapha*, 2 vols. (Garden City, NY: Doubleday, 1983, 1985); Bruce N. Fisk, "Rewritten Bible in Pseudepigrapha and Qumran," in *Dictionary of New Testament Background*, 947–53.

4. wisdom or devotional literature (Psalms of Solomon; Odes of Solomon; Psalm 151);

5. expansions of Old Testament material (Jubilees; Joseph and Aseneth; Jannes and Jambres; Assumption of Moses, Martyrdom and Ascension of Isaiah); and

6. religious novels and philosophical treatises (3–4 Maccabees).[59]

The evaluation of Second Temple literature has been variously positive and negative. On the positive side, the historical information provided by books such as 1 Maccabees provides an indispensable source for this particular period in Jewish history. Also, while not inspired or authoritative, many of these writings reflect the various religious beliefs of the Jewish people in the intertestamental period and thus provide helpful background information for the study of the New Testament.

On the negative side, scholars have stressed that some of the teaching in these writings are heterodox, that is, not in conformity with the doctrines affirmed in the canonical books. For example, 2 Maccabees teaches one to pray for the dead, and Tobit contains elements of magic and syncretism. This calls for discernment and a clear demarcation between the Old Testament and the apocryphal and pseudepigraphical writings.[60] In this regard, it is interesting to note that the New Testament Letter of Jude

---

59. Helpful resources on the contents of the apocryphal and pseudepigraphical literature include the following works. On the Apocrypha, see the introductions in Metzger, *Annotated Apocrypha*; cf. Evans, *Ancient Texts for New Testament Studies*, chap. 1; David A. deSilva, *Introducing the Apocrypha: Message, Context, and Significance* (Grand Rapids: Baker, 2002). On the Pseudepigrapha, see the introductions in Charlesworth, *Old Testament Pseudepigrapha*; and Evans, *Ancient Texts for New Testament Studies*, chap. 2. On both, see Michael E. Stone, ed., *Jewish Writings of the Second Temple Period*, CRINT 2 (Assen: Van Gorcum/Philadelphia: Fortress, 1984); George W. E. Nickelsburg, *Jewish Literature Between the Bible and the Mishnah* (Philadelphia: Fortress, 1981); Emil Schürer, *The History of the Jewish People in the Age of Jesus Christ (175 BC–A.D. 135)*, rev. and ed. Geza Vermes, Fergus Millar, and Matthew Black, 3 vols. in 4 (Edinburgh: T&T Clark, 1973, 1979, 1986, 1987), 3.1; deSilva, "Apocrypha and Pseudepigrapha"; and the relevant sections in Larry R. Helyer, *Exploring Jewish Literature of the Second Temple Period: A Guide for New Testament Students* (Downers Grove, IL: InterVarsity, 2002).

60. See Köstenberger, Kellum, and Quarles, *Cradle, the Cross, and the Crown,* chap. 1.

makes reference to several pseudepigraphical writings, most notably 1 Enoch.

Dead Sea Scrolls

The discovery of the Dead Sea Scrolls constituted the major archeological find related to biblical studies in the twentieth century.[61] The Qumran writings include both biblical manuscripts, which predate the previously earliest extant Old Testament manuscripts by as many as a thousand years, and sectarian writings. The former includes all Old Testament books except for Esther, and the latter consists of writings such as the Damascus Document (CD); the Community Rule or Manual of Discipline (1QS); Thanksgiving Hymns (1QH); the War Scroll (1QM); the Habakkuk Pesher (1QpHab), and the Temple Scroll (11QTemple).[62] The biblical documents discovered at Qumran, including the famous Isaiah Scroll, have provided scholars with early readings of the Hebrew Scriptures, which has enabled them to make progress in ascertaining the original reading of specific Old Testament passages.

In addition, the Dead Sea Scrolls provide a fascinating glimpse into the life of a Jewish sect that most likely arose in the Maccabean era around the middle of the second century B.C. and continued through the first Jewish revolt in A.D. 66–73.[63] The precise identity of the group responsible for the Qumran literature remains uncertain. Most likely, the original im-

---

61. See especially John C. Trever, *The Dead Sea Scrolls: A Personal Account* (Grand Rapids: Eerdmans, 1977). Other helpful works include Geza Vermes, *The Dead Sea Scrolls: Qumran in Perspective*, rev. ed. (Philadelphia: Fortress, 1977); James C. VanderKam, *The Dead Sea Scrolls Today* (Grand Rapids: Eerdmans, 1994); and Florentino García Martínez and Julio Trebolle Barrera, *The People of the Dead Sea Scrolls: Their Writings, Beliefs and Practices,* trans. Wilfred G. E. Watson (Leiden: Brill, 1995); the selected excerpts in Barrett, *New Testament Background,* chap. 9; and Michael O. Wise, "Dead Sea Scrolls: General Introduction," in *Dictionary of New Testament Background,* 252–66.

62. See Florentino García Martínez, *The Dead Sea Scrolls Study Edition,* 2 vols. (Grand Rapids: Eerdmans, 2000); James C. VanderKam, *An Introduction to Early Judaism* (Grand Rapids: Eerdmans, 2000); Lawrence H. Schiffman and James C. VanderKam, eds., *Encyclopedia of the Dead Sea Scrolls,* 2 vols. (Oxford: University Press, 2000); James H. Charlesworth, ed., *The Bible and the Dead Sea Scrolls,* 3 vols. (Waco: Baylor Univ. Press, 2006); Robert A. Kugler and Eileen M. Schuller, *The Dead Sea Scrolls at Fifty* (Atlanta: Scholars Press, 1999); Schürer, *History of the Jewish People,* 380–469; Evans, *Ancient Texts for New Testament Studies,* chap. 3; and relevant entries in *Dictionary of New Testament Background.*

63. See Köstenberger, Kellum, and Quarles, *Cradle, the Cross, and the Crown,* 70–73.

petus for the group's departure from Jerusalem and its withdrawal to the Dead Sea region was the corruption of the Jerusalem priesthood during the Maccabean period. It is likely that the Jewish high priest at the time of the community's formation is referred to in the Qumran literature as the "Wicked Priest" in contrast to the "Teacher of Righteousness" (see 1QpHab 1:13; 2:2; 8:7; 11:4–5), who presumably was the founder of the community.[64]

It is important to note that the Dead Sea Scrolls do not portray mainstream Judaism or Jewish attitudes during this era. This isolated community was a sect that defined itself over against the Jerusalem establishment and engaged in its own distinctive religious and communal practices. These included a particular method of interpreting Scripture, the *pesher* method, which appropriated biblical material with reference to the community's contemporary situation (e.g., the *"Habakkuk pesher"*).[65] Also, there is no reference to the New Testament or to Jesus in the Dead Sea Scrolls. Thus these documents should be regarded as Jewish rather than Christian writings.[66]

The community's critical stance toward the corrupt Jerusalem priesthood thus provides an antecedent for Jesus' challenge of the corruption of the Jerusalem temple ritual during his ministry (Matt. 21:12–17; John 2:13–22). The community's use of Scripture also provides a fascinating precedent for John the Baptist's self-identification as "a voice crying in the wilderness" (cf. Isa. 40:3). The Dead Sea community appropriated the same passage of Scripture with reference to itself.[67] The Qumran community and documents provide a helpful backdrop for understanding aspects of the Old and the New Testament.[68]

---

64. As mentioned above, Schürer (*Jewish History in the Age of Jesus Christ*, 2:587), for example, suggests that the Jewish high priest Jonathan was the person called the "Wicked Priest" in the Dead Sea Scrolls.

65. See Richard N. Longenecker, *Biblical Exegesis in the Apostolic Period*, 2d ed. (Grand Rapids: Eerdmans, 1999), 24–30.

66. Against erroneous claims in the tabloids and in popular literature such as Dan Brown (*The Da Vinci Code* [New York: Doubleday, 2003], 245), who claimed that the Dead Sea Scrolls are among "the earliest Christian records."

67. See Andreas J. Köstenberger, "John," in *Commentary on the New Testament Use of the Old Testament*, eds. G. K. Beale and D. A. Carson (Grand Rapids: Baker, 2007), 421, 425–28.

68. See James H. Charlesworth, ed., *John and the Dead Sea Scrolls* (New York: Crossroad, 1990); Kugler and Schuller, *Dead Sea Scrolls at Fifty*; Charlesworth, *Bible and*

Other Relevant Primary Sources

In addition to the above-mentioned primary sources, there are several other important background resources that are relevant for Old and New Testament studies. These include rabbinic literature (including the Mishnah, the Talmuds, and the Tosefta), the Hellenistic philosopher Philo, the Jewish historian Josephus, the Targums (Aramaic paraphrases of the Old Testament), the New Testament Apocrypha, and Greco-Roman sources. There are several helpful bibliographies and primary source collections available that make these resources more accessible to the diligent student of Scripture.[69]

Secondary Sources

The inquisitive interpreter of the Bible has a plethora of secondary resources at his or her disposal today. The best study Bibles on the market, such as the *ESV Study Bible*, the *NIV Study Bible*, or the *HCSB Study Bible*, to name but a few, are often a great place to start. There are also several specialized background commentaries available that provide specific background information in easily accessible fashion, such as the *Zondervan Illustrated Bible Backgrounds Commentary*, which covers both the Old and the New Testaments.

An excellent secondary source is often a good Old or New Testament introduction such as Longman and Dillard or Hill and Walton for the Old Testament and Köstenberger, Kellum, and Quarles, or Carson and Moo for the New Testament. In addition, students will do well to consult first-rate commentaries which, in addition to exegetical discussions, will also cover the relevant historical-cultural background material.

With regard to the New Testament use of the Old, the *Commentary on the New Testament Use of the Old Testament* edited by G. K. Beale and D. A. Carson deserves pride of place. Other helpful types of secondary sources include Bible atlases, Bible dictionaries and encyclopedias, Old and New Testament histories, and special studies in ancient life and culture.

---

the Dead Sea Scrolls; and the helpful discussion in Evans, *Ancient Texts for New Testament Studies*, 3–6.

69. See esp. David W. Chapman and Andreas J. Köstenberger, "Jewish Intertestamental and Early Rabbinic Literature: An Annotated Bibliographic Resource," *JETS* 43 (2000): 577–618 (also available online at www.biblicalfoundations.org); see also Barrett, *New Testament Background*; Sparks, *Ancient Texts for the Study of the Hebrew Bible*; and Evans, *Ancient Texts for New Testament Studies*.

Increasingly, there is also much useful information conveniently available on the internet. See the appendix in this volume and other similar compilations of helpful background sources.[70]

CONCLUSION

Christianity is a historical religion, and Scripture presupposes that God revealed himself in human history. This requires that Bible students have a sensitivity to historical factors, both chronological timelines and historical-cultural customs that have a bearing on biblical interpretation. Many helpful tools can assist in this endeavor, from technical commentaries to Bible handbooks to the more recent genre of Bible background commentaries.[71]

While studying historical-cultural customs is of great value, often the Bible student is faced with the important question of cultural relativity vs. normativity. How is the modern interpreter to understand and apply biblical injunctions that are given in the context of social norms that may no longer be in effect? Grant Osborne registers the following helpful comment in describing the interpreter's task in assessing the ancient historical-cultural background:

> Therefore, the task of the receptor in the modern cultural framework is to recapture the total framework within which the sacred writer communicated and to transfer that message to our own day. The cultural aspects presupposed in the passage help interpreters get behind the words to the underlying message, understood by the original readers but hidden to the modern reader.[72]

---

70. See, e.g., Duvall and Hays, *Grasping God's Word*, 107–16.; Köstenberger, Kellum, and Quarles, *Cradle, the Cross, and the Crown*, 97–99; and Osborne, *Hermeneutical Spiral*, 167–73. See also Arnold and Beyer, *Readings from the Ancient Near East*; Walter A. Elwell and Robert W. Yarbrough, eds., *Readings from the First-Century World* (Grand Rapids: Baker, 1998); and Ferguson, *Backgrounds*.

71. As a starting point, see the Chapter Bibliography at the end of this chapter. See also the lists of recommended resources posted at www.biblicalfoundations.org. An area of biblical background that is not to be missed is the study of ancient coins. See esp. David Hendin, *Guide to Biblical Coins*, 5th ed. (New York: Amphora, 2001); Ya'akov Meshorer, *A Treasury of Jewish Coins* (New York: Amphora, 2001); and Kenneth Bressett, *Money of the Bible* (Atlanta: Whitman, 2007).

72. Osborne, *Hermeneutical Spiral*, 166.

The student may well ask, "Were these customs meant to be permanently binding or not?"[73] The answer is not always readily apparent, and often there is a certain amount of diversity of opinion among biblical interpreters. We suggest the following three general guidelines.

1. Some cultural matters mentioned in the Old Testament clearly are limited in application and are not repeated in the New Testament. For example, per the book of Hebrews, this includes the entire Old Testament sacrificial system and the Levitical priesthood, both of which found their fulfillment in Christ.

2. Some Old Testament cultural standards are repeated later on in the Bible and thus continue to be valid. The Ten Commandments, for example, are repeated in the New Testament (except for the Sabbath commandment) and for this reason continue to apply, though they are deepened by the New Testament. Or take the repeated Old Testament commands to show concern for the poor. At harvest time, people were to leave some of the grain for the poor (Lev. 23:22). Similarly, the New Testament calls on believers to provide for those in need (e.g., 1 Cor. 16:1; 1 Tim. 5:3).

3. In many cases, biblical customs contain an underlying principle that remains applicable today. The biblical custom of employing a kiss as a conventional greeting, for example (see, e.g., Gen. 33:4; 2 Sam. 19:39; Luke 7:35; Rom. 16:16), may find application in today's handshake or hug. In these cases, we seek to discern and apply the underlying principle involved in the cultural expression.

SAMPLE EXEGESIS (OLD TESTAMENT): 1 KINGS 17–18

First Kings 17–18 provides one of the most popular and riveting tales in all of Scripture. Yahweh and his prophet Elijah confront Baal and his prophets. Prior to chapter 17, Ahab becomes king of Israel following the death of Omri and does "more evil in the eyes of the Lord than any of

---

73. In addition to these comments, see also the more detailed discussion of matters pertaining to application in Chapter 16 below.

those [kings] before him" (1 Kgs. 16:30). Ahab marries Jezebel, daughter of the king of the Sidonians, and so began "to serve Baal and worship him. He sets up an altar for Baal in the temple that he built in Samaria" (1 Kgs. 16:31–32). Within the context of Ahab bringing widespread Baal worship to Israel after marrying Jezebel the Sidonian woman, Yahweh's great confrontation with Baal takes place. Our understanding of the conflict between Yahweh and Baal is significantly deepened when we understand Baal in his ancient Near Eastern context.

First Kings 17:1 sets the stage for the rest of pericope:

> Now Elijah the Tishbite, from Tishbe in Gilead, said to Ahab, "As the Lord, the God of Israel, lives, whom I serve, there will be neither dew nor rain in the next few years except at my word."

The basic thrust of Elijah's words seems evident: God is alive, and he will keep his word. Yet understanding the historical-cultural context enriches the meaning of the passage. Elijah's statement pertains not merely to the identity of Yahweh but addresses very poignantly the nature of Baal.

Baal was a prominent storm god in the ancient Near East, and in Phoenicia in particular.[74] Thus, the promise that there would be no rain except by the power of Yahweh was not an arbitrary promise to show Yahweh's power in general, but a more direct statement concerning Yahweh's power *over* Baal. As the storm god, Baal ought to be able to make it rain, and thus bring life, in spite of this promise from Elijah. Ugaritic texts support the fact that a correlation exists between Baal as storm god and Elijah's promise that there will be neither dew nor rain. In an ancient depiction of the Baal Cycle, the language of dew and rain is linked explicitly with the storm god Baal:

> Seven years Baal is absent,
> Eight, the Rider of the Clouds
> No dew, no rain,
> No swirling of the deeps,
> No welcome voice of Baal.[75]

---

74. Paul R. House, *1, 2 Kings*, NAC (Nashville: Broadman & Holman, 1995), 215.
75. Leah Bronner, *The Stories of Elijah and Elisha: As Polemics Against Baal Worship*, Pretoria Oriental Series, ed. A. Van Selms, vol. VI (Leiden: Brill, 1968), 68.

In this text, Baal's absence causes "no dew" and "no rain." Baal's absence is due to his death. The god Mot, which means "death," consumes Baal, killing him. While Baal is dead, there is no rain, and therefore no life. The return of rain would signify that Baal is alive again. So, after Mot kills Baal, El longs for Baal to return in order that the land may bring life yet again:

> Let the heavens rain oil,
> The wadis run with honey,
> Then I will know that Mightiest B[aal] lives,
> The Prince, Lord of the Earth is alive.[76]

Drought signifies Baal's death. The return of rain signifies that Baal is alive again.

In light of these texts, 1 Kings 17:1 takes on new import. Elijah's statement is not simply a statement of Yahweh's power, but also a direct challenge to the power of Baal. In the midst of the drought that will come, Yahweh still lives though Baal is dead. As the story will go on to demonstrate, Baal does not provide rain and life; Yahweh does. Only Yahweh, as Creator and Sustainer, properly provides for his creatures.

Yahweh's provision for Elijah in the midst of the drought (1 Kgs. 17:2–24), therefore, takes on new significance. Yahweh commands Elijah to go to the Kerith Ravine where Elijah will drink from the brook and ravens will feed him. Yahweh controls nature. After the brook dries up, Yahweh commands Elijah to go to Zarephath of Sidon. It ought not be lost on us that Yahweh commands Elijah to go to Zarephath of *Sidon*. Jezebel, through whom Baal worship entered into Israel with her marriage to Ahab, is the daughter of Ethbaal king of the Sidonians. Elijah enters into Zarephath, the very heart of Baalism. Yahweh will confront Baal on Baal's home turf. The story continues to demonstrate that Yahweh is the God of life and rules over all creation, while Baal is indeed dead with no hope of returning.

Zarephath is a place riddled by death. Drought has overtaken the land. Elijah encounters a widow, whose life is defined by death. When Elijah meets her, she has no food and is preparing her last meal before she dies. While Elijah is with the widow, her son dies. In the land of Baal, death

---

76. Simon B. Parker, ed., *Ugaritic Narrative Poetry*, SBL *Writings from the Ancient World* 9 (Atlanta: Scholars Press, 1997), 157.

reigns. Yet Yahweh, who lives, brings life, providing life for Elijah through the widow. Yahweh miraculously continues to provide food for Elijah, the widow, and her son from a small amount of flour and oil. Yahweh revives the boy through Elijah. In the midst of Baal's death, Yahweh brings life. Yahweh's life brackets Baal's death through the widow's statement in verse 12, "As surely as the Lord your God lives," and Elijah's declaration in verse 23, "Look, your son is alive!" Set against the backdrop of Canaanite belief that Baal's death caused the current drought, the story is not merely about Yahweh's ability to sustain in hard times. This story makes a much stronger statement: Baal is dead; Yahweh lives.

Understanding the story in this way does take the suspense out of the showdown between Yahweh and Baal on Mount Carmel. The confrontation began in 1 Kings 17:1, and the verdict has already been delivered. Anxious suspense is replaced by confidence and faith in God. As the account moves toward the public display of Yahweh's superiority, the reader should not be surprised at Elijah's confidence and faith in God. Yahweh has already proved faithful to his word and superior to Baal. A full understanding of the confrontation beginning in 17:1, however, is possible only through a grasp of the historical-cultural context. Even so, the historical context affords even more for understanding the present passage.

Greater clarity and understanding concerning the events on Mount Carmel ensue when the account is understood in its historical-cultural context. The challenge that Elijah proposes would have struck those who worship Baal as eminently suitable because it fits in well with Baal's powers. As the storm god, Baal could send fire from heaven (lightning) to set fire to the altar erected by his prophets. As Baal's prophets cry out to Baal, calling him to arouse and bring fire to the altar they have set up, Elijah seemingly mocks their attempts by ridiculing their "god." Elijah's words may be pouring ridicule at their god, but the biblical text does not indicate that Baal's prophets took exception to this ridicule. George Saint-Laurent suggests that though Baal's prophets are made to look ridiculous; "Elijah has good reason to refer to Baal being 'pre-occupied' in terms of the Baal-cycle, which speaks of a very busy god indeed, concerned about a wide variety of matters."[77] Saint-

---

77. George E. Saint-Laurent, "Light From Ras Shamra on Elijah's Ordeal Upon Mount Carmel," in *Scripture in Context: Essays on the Comparative Method*, ed. Carl D. Evans, William W. Hallo, and John B. White (Pittsburgh: Pickwick, 1980), 132–33.

Laurent shows that within the Baal cycle, Anat cannot find Baal at his house when he is off hunting on a journey, and that Canaanite gods do indeed sleep and need to be awakened.[78] Once again, Elijah's words are not arbitrary mocking, but designed to pointedly reveal who Yahweh is *over* Baal.

What is more, Baal's prophets cutting themselves is also a practice attested in the Baal cycle. When the gods El and Anat find that Baal is dead, they likewise cut themselves:

> Then Beneficent El the Benign
> Descends from his seat, sits on the footstool,
> [And] from the footstool, sits on the earth.
> He pours dirt on his head for mourning,
> Dust on his crown for lamenting;
> For clothing he puts on sackcloth
>
> With a stone he scrapes his skin,
> Double-slits with a blade.
> He cuts cheeks and chin,
> Furrows the length of his arm.
>
> He plows his chest like a garden,
> Like a valley he furrows the back.
>
> He raises his voice and cries:
> "Baal is dead! What of the peoples?
> The Son of Dagan! What of the multitudes?
> After Baal I will descend to Hell."
>
> Then Anat goes about hunting,
> In every mountain in the heart of the earth,
> In every hill [in the he]art of the fields.
>
> She comes to the pleas[ant land of] the outback,
> To the beautiful field of [the Realm] of Death;
> She com[es] upon Baal fall[en to ear]th.

---

78. Ibid., 133.

[For clothing] she puts on sack[cloth,]
With a stone she scrapes her skin,
Double-[sl]its [with a blade.]

She cuts cheeks and chin,
[Furrows] the length of her arm.

She plows her chest like a garden,
Like a valley she furrows her back:

"Baal is dead! What of the peoples?
The Son of Dagan! What of the multitudes!
After Baal we will descend to Hell."[79]

Baal's death breeds more death, which is one of the themes in 1 Kings 17–18. Of course, in stark contrast to the prophets of Baal's feeble attempts to arouse their dead god, Elijah calls upon the one who lives. Yahweh immediately responds in order to show that he is the one true God. Once Yahweh publicly displays his superiority, he brings rain to show that he is not only superior to Baal but that Baal is no god at all. Yahweh, not Baal, is the Lord of all creation and the God of life. Yahweh rules in life, while death rules over Baal.

SAMPLE EXEGESIS (NEW TESTAMENT): LUKE 2:1–20

The well-known account of Jesus' birth in Luke's Gospel provides an excellent example of the importance of studying the historical and cultural setting of Scripture. The passage begins with reference to a decree issued by Caesar Augustus. Luke deliberately places the birth of Christ during the reign of the Roman Emperor.[80] *Historical research* reveals that Augustus (31 B.C.–A.D. 14) was the first and (many believe) the greatest Roman emperor. He presided over what is commonly called the "Golden Age" of Rome and prided himself on having inaugurated an era of peace,

---

79. Parker, *Ugaritic Narrative Poetry*, 149–51.
80. See also Luke 3:1–3 where the beginning of John the Baptist's and Jesus' public ministries are placed in "the fifteenth year of the reign of Tiberius Caesar" (v. 1), the Emperor who succeeded Augustus and who reigned from A.D. 14–37.

the so-called *Pax Romana* ("Roman peace"). Augustus was deified subsequent to his death, and coins refer to him as *Divi filius* ("Son of divinity" or "divine Son").[81]

This historical evidence is highly relevant for a discerning reading of Luke's birth narrative in keeping with his authorial intention. By placing Jesus' birth under the aegis of Augustus's reign, Luke almost certainly sought to establish a comparison and contrast between Augustus, the Roman Emperor, on the one hand, and Christ, the Jewish Messiah, on the other. Jesus, too, came to bring "on earth peace to men" as the angels proclaimed (Luke 2:14). While Augustus ruled over "the entire . . . world" (v. 1), the angel's good news would be "for all the people" (v. 10). Jesus, unlike Augustus, truly was the "Son of God." Even the term "Savior" may invoke Roman imperial language, according to which the Emperor was considered to be a "savior" of his people.

Another interesting historical datum provided by Luke is that the census undertaken here was "the first census that took place when Quirinius was governor of Syria" (v. 2). According to ancient historians, Quirinius was legate over Syria in A.D. 6–9 after Archelaus, the son of Herod the Great, had been removed from office (Josephus, *Ant.* 18.1.1–2 §§1–11; cf. Tacitus, *Annals* 2.30; 3.22–23, 48; Strabo, *Geography* 12.6.5). Since Jesus was born during the reign of Herod the Great (who, according to reliable records, died in 4 B.C.), some say that Luke must be in error. However, it is much more likely that the available evidence is too limited to draw firm conclusions. In light of Luke's remarkable accuracy where his data can be confirmed from other sources, it is probable that the census was either taken before Quirinius became governor (a possible reading of the adverb translated "first" in the NIV) or that Quirinius was already in some sort of governing post prior to assuming this role officially in A.D. 6.[82]

---

81. For additional information, see Ferguson, *Backgrounds*, 25–30. On p. 198, Ferguson notes that "from the time of Tiberius temples were dedicated to the divinized Augustus." See also Werner Eck, *The Age of Augustus*, trans. Deborah Lucas Schneider (Oxford: Blackwell, 2003).

82. See "Sidebar 3.1: Luke and Quirinius" in Andreas J. Köstenberger, L. Scott Kellum, and Charles L. Quarles, *The Cradle, the Cross, and the Crown: An Introduction to the New Testament* (Nashville: B&H, 2009); "Excursus 2: The Census of Quirinius (2:1–2)," in Darrell L. Bock, *Luke 1:1–9:50*, BECNT (Grand Rapids: Baker, 1994), 903–9..

In some of the complexities of historical reconstruction, the most crucial point made by Luke in Jesus' birth narrative should not be missed: God sovereignly and providentially used the decree of the Roman Emperor to move the parents of Jesus the Messiah from Nazareth in Galilee to Bethlehem in Judea, the place where, according to Old Testament prophecy, the Messiah was to be born (Mic. 5:2; cf. Matt. 2:6). This may well be one of the most profound ironies of all of human history: the Roman Emperor's decree brought about the will of God in having Jesus the Messiah born in Bethlehem, "the town of David" (vv. 4, 11)![83] The central storyline in the grand meta-narrative of Scripture—the coming of God's promised Messiah to provide salvation from sin and death—thus finds its culmination in the emperor's decree and Jesus' subsequent birth in the city of David.[84]

Even this brief thumbnail sketch of the historical background of Luke's account of Jesus' birth shows the considerable reward that accrues for those who diligently research the historical setting of a given story found in Scripture. In addition, Luke's narrative surrounding the birth of Jesus is also rich in *cultural details* that need to be studied carefully. To begin with, Jesus' parents, Joseph and Mary, went from Nazareth to Bethlehem. As any good map of the Holy Land will indicate, the distance between these two cities, as the crow flies, is about 60 miles. If, as was customary, Joseph and Mary did not travel the most direct route through Samaria but journeyed east of the Jordan River, the distance would have been closer to 90 or 100 miles. Traveling such a considerable distance would have constituted a severe hardship for a woman such as Mary late in her pregnancy.

The reference to Jesus as Mary's "firstborn" in verse 7 also invokes Jewish cultural custom. Darrell Bock gives as many as five possible interpretations, noting that "a reference to the general rights of Jesus as a firstborn is likely" (see esp. vv. 23–24).[85] Of course, the biblical record also indicates that Jesus was *literally* the first born, in the sense that Mary, subsequent to Jesus' birth, also had other children besides Jesus (cf. Matt. 12:46–47; Luke 8:19–20). Verse 7 also contains three other important words that are significantly illumined by cultural background research: (1) Mary's wrapping of

---

83. See also the reference to salvation coming from "the house of his servant David" in Zechariah's Song in 1:69.
84. David, for his part, was the original recipient of God's promise that he would establish his kingdom forever (2 Sam. 7:12–13).
85. Bock, *Luke 1:1–9:50*, 207.

Jesus "in cloths"; (2) her placing of Jesus "in a manger" (see also v. 16, where
this becomes an important piece of identification for the shepherds); and
(3) the statement that "there was no room for them in the inn."

The swaddling cloths reflect the Jewish custom "to take strips of
clothes and bind them around the child to keep the limbs straight."[86] The
manger was probably a feeding trough for animals, which suggests that
Jesus was born in some kind of animal room. This may have been either
a stable or possibly a cave.[87] But how should we understand Luke's reference to the inn? Luke 22:11 uses the same expression to refer to a guest
room in a house, while a related term is found in the "Parable of the Good
Samaritan" in 10:34 where it denotes a formal inn. Since, unlike in 10:34,
no inn-keeper is mentioned by Luke in the birth narrative, perhaps the
reference in verse 7 is to "some type of reception room in a private home
or some type of public shelter."[88] Since there was no room there, Jesus'
parents sought refuge elsewhere. What all these background details have
in common is that they jointly point to the humble circumstances of Jesus'
birth. In keeping with Luke's consistent emphasis on the poor and lowly,
the evangelist shows how Jesus humbled himself to provide salvation for
sinners (see esp. 19:7; cf. Phil. 2:5–8).[89]

Careful historical research and an awareness of ancient cultural customs are indispensable aids in interpreting a given passage of Scripture in
keeping with its original context and authorially intended message. While
Luke's first readers may have been more aware of some of these pieces of
information than readers are today, all who want to understand Scripture must strive, to the best of their ability, to present themselves to God
as those approved, skilled in research and the correct handling of God's
word (2 Tim. 2:15). The specific details, of course, will vary according to
a specific passage, but more often than not, historical research is essential
for understanding the full authorial meaning of Scripture. Fortunately,
there are many helpful resources, whether study Bibles, good commentaries, or other reference works, to aid us in this task.[90]

86. Bock (ibid.), with reference to other sources.
87. See the discussion in ibid., 208.
88. Ibid.
89. See "Table 6.3: Jesus and the Lowly in Luke's Gospel" in Köstenberger, Kellum, and
    Quarles, Cradle, the Cross, and the Crown, 286.
90. See the chapter bibliography and the appendix at the end of this volume.

GUIDELINES FOR INTERPRETING
HISTORICAL-CULTURAL BACKGROUND

1. Determine the scope of the historical account. Look for links with other scriptural passages, especially those relating to the same event(s).

2. Compare the biblical record with external data for additional information and illumination.

3. Consider the author's purpose(s) in recording the event(s) he has selected.

4. Remember that historical events are descriptive of morality and conduct but not always prescriptive.

5. Make appropriate application(s) of the underlying lesson or principle involved in the event or custom recorded in the text.

6. Recognize that the biblical historical and cultural accounts are sacred and trustworthy records of what actually occurred.

KEY WORDS

Divi filius: "divine Son," title for Roman emperors such as Augustus

Gallio inscription: ancient artifact mentioning the name of the governor of Achaia by that name

Graffiti: informal sketch or scribbling

Maximalist-minimalist debate: controversy as to whether the Bible is an accurate source of historical-cultural background information

Ossuary: ancient bone box containing the remains of a deceased

Second Temple period: period between the rebuilding of the temple subsequent to the return from the exile and the destruction of the temple in A.D. 70

Terminus ad quem: latest possible date

STUDY QUESTIONS

1. What is the value of studying the historical-cultural background of a particular portion of Scripture, and how does the study of the historical-cultural background fit within the overall approach taken in the book?

2. Does everyone agree that the truthfulness of Scripture is borne out by historical-cultural background data, and how do you assess the trustworthiness of the biblical record?

3. Why is it important to identify the chronology of major Old Testament events?

4. What are some important Old Testament dates that provide a general framework for the study of the Old Testament? Read through the presentation of Old Testament chronology and take note of major dates, such as the date of the exodus, the time of the judges, the beginnings of the Israelite monarchy, and the exiles.

5. How is it possible to determine the dates of the beginning of Jesus' ministry and of the crucifixion? What are the options and what are the most likely dates?

6. What are the major dates pertaining to the book of Acts and the ministry of Paul, including his letters? Why is it helpful to be aware of this general chronology in interpreting these portions of Scripture?

7. What are some of the most significant finds that are corroborating the truthfulness of the Old and New Testament records, and how does that increase our confidence in the reliability of Scripture?

8. What are the relevant guidelines for applying principles embedded in the historical-cultural data to political and social problems?

ASSIGNMENTS

1. Discuss 2 Kings 17:1–6 on the basis of the data of Israelite and ancient Near Eastern history. Assuming the maximalist position, write a summary of the value and limitations of such information to the immediate and following context of the passage.

2. Utilizing the data from both biblical and ancient Near Eastern history as well as the archaeological findings of the period, discuss 1 Kings 9:15–19. How does such evidence confirm, illumine, or supplement the biblical record?

3. Historical/cultural information is also of great value to Old Testament books other than those traditionally recognized as "historical books." In that regard, discuss the value of data from biblical and ancient Near Eastern historical and archaeological evidence as to the date and accuracy of the information in the book of Jonah.

4. Engage in a study of the relevant historical-cultural background for interpreting John 2:13–3:21 (the unit comprising Jesus' first visit to Jerusalem in John's Gospel). Take inventory of any items of a historical-cultural nature that require further study. Then, use resources such as the *ESV Study Bible* or the *Zondervan Illustrated Bible Backgrounds Commentary* to illumine the historical-cultural background of this passage of Scripture.

5. Produce a chart relating Paul's letters to his ministry as narrated in the book of Acts. Where possible, estimate dates and write down any other relevant information. To complete this assignment, you may use resources such as a good New Testament introduction or a study Bible. Make sure not just to copy down the information you find but engage in first-hand study of the New Testament data and be able to support your conclusions with biblical and (where available) extrabiblical evidence.

CHAPTER BIBLIOGRAPHY

Arnold, Bill T. and Bryan E. Beyer, eds. *Readings from the Ancient Near East: Primary Sources for Old Testament Study*. Grand Rapids: Baker Academic, 2002.

Arnold, Clinton E., ed. *Zondervan Illustrated Bible Backgrounds Commentary: New Testament*. 4 vols. Grand Rapids: Zondervan, 2002.

Bauckham, Richard. *The Jewish World around the New Testament*. Grand Rapids: Baker, 2008.

Beyerlin, Walter, ed. *Near Eastern Religious Texts Relating to the Old Testament*. Philadelphia: Westminster, 1978.

Breasted, James H., ed. *Ancient Records of Egypt*. 5 vols. London: Histories & Mysteries of Man, 1988.

Burge, Gary M., Lynn H. Cohick, and Gene L. Green. *The New Testament in Antiquity: A Survey of the New Testament within Its Cultural Contexts*. Grand Rapids: Zondervan, 2009.

Chapman, David W. and Andreas J. Köstenberger. "Jewish Intertestamental and Early Rabbinic Literature: An Annotated Bibliographic Resource." *Journal of the Evangelical Theological Society* 43 (2000): 577–618.

Charlesworth, James H., ed. *The Old Testament Pseudepigrapha*. 2 vols. Garden City: Doubleday, 1983.

_____, ed. *Jesus and Archaeology*. Grand Rapids: Eerdmans, 2006.

Evans, Craig A. *Ancient Texts for New Testament Studies*: A Guide to the Background Literature. Peabody, MA: Hendrickson, 2005.

Ferguson, Everett. *Backgrounds of Early Christianity*. 2d ed. Grand Rapids: Eerdmans, 1993.

Hallo, William W. and K. Lawson Younger Jr. *The Context of Scripture*. 3 vols. Leiden: Brill, 1997, 2000, 2002.

Helyer, Larry R. *Exploring Jewish Literature of the Second Temple Period: A Guide for New Testament Students*. Downers Grove, IL: InterVarsity, 2002.

Hoerth, Alfred J. *Archaeology and the Old Testament*. Grand Rapids: Baker, 1998.

Hoffmeier, James K. *Israel in Egypt*. New York: Oxford, 1996.

Howard, David M. Jr. and Michael A. Grisanti, eds. *Giving the Sense: Understanding and Using Old Testament Historical Texts*. Grand Rapids: Kregel, 2003.

Kaiser, Walter C. Jr. *A History of Israel*. Nashville: B&H, 1998.

Keener, Craig S. *The IVP Bible Background Commentary: New Testament*. Downers Grove: InterVarsity, 1993.

Kitchen, Kenneth A. *The Bible in Its World*. Downers Grove: InterVarsity, 1978.

Luckenbill, David D. *Ancient Records of Assyria and Babylonia*. 2 vols. Chicago: University of Chicago Press, 1926.

Martínez, Florentino Garcia. *The Dead Sea Scrolls Study Edition*. 2 vols. Grand Rapids: Eerdmans, 2000.

_____. *The Dead Sea Scrolls Translated*. Translated by Wilfred G. E. Watson. Leiden: Brill, 1994.

Matthews, Victor H. and Don C. Benjamin. *Old Testament Parallels*. New York: Paulist, 1991.

Merrill, Eugene H. *Kingdom of Priests: A History of Old Testament Israel*. 2d ed. Grand Rapids: Baker, 19872008.

Meyers, E. M., ed. *The Oxford Encyclopedia of Archaeology in the Near East*. 5 vols. New York/Oxford: Oxford University Press, 1997.

Millard, Alan. *Discoveries from Bible Times*. Oxford: Lion, 1997.

Negev, A. and S. Gibson, eds. *Archaeological Encyclopedia of the Holy Land*. Rev. ed. New York/London: Continuum, 2001.

Nickelsburg, George W. E. *Jewish Literature Between the Bible and the Mishnah*. Philadelphia: Fortress, 1981.

Pritchard, James B., ed. *Ancient Near Eastern Texts*. 3d ed. Princeton: Princeton University Press, 1969.

Schürer, Emil. *The History of the Jewish People in the Age of Jesus Christ: 175 B.C.–A.D. 135*. Rev. and ed. Geza Vermes, Fergus Milar, and Matthew Black. 3 vols. in 4. Edinburgh: T&T Clark, 1973, 1979, 1986, 1987.

Sparks, H. F. D., ed. *The Apocryphal Old Testament*. Oxford: Clarendon, 1985.

Sparks, Kenton L. *Ancient Texts for the Study of the Hebrew Bible: A Guide to the Background Literature*. Peabody, MA: Hendrickson, 2005.

Stern, E., ed. *The New Encyclopedia of Archaeological Excavations in the Holy Land*. 4 vols. New York/London: Simon & Schuster, 1993.

Stone, Michael E., ed. *Jewish Writings of the Second Temple Period*. CRINT 2. Assen: Van Gorcum/Philadelphia: Fortress, 1984.

VanderKam, James C. *The Dead Sea Scrolls Today*. Grand Rapids: Eerdmans, 1994.

Vermes, Geza. *The Dead Sea Scrolls in English*. 4th ed. London: Penguin, 1991.

Walton, John H., Victor H. Matthews, and Mark W. Chavalas. *The IVP Bible Background Commentary: Old Testament*. Downers Grove: InterVarsity, 2000.

Walton, John H., ed. *Zondervan Illustrated Bible Backgrounds Commentary: Old Testament*. 5 vols. Grand Rapids: Zondervan, 2009.

Wiseman, Donald J., ed. *Chronicles of Chaldaean Kings*. London: Trustees of the British Museum, 1956.

PART II

THE FOCUS OF SCRIPTURE:
LITERATURE

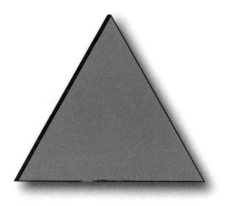

UNIT 1: CANON

CHAPTER 3 OBJECTIVES

1. To acquaint the student with three key themes, which provide a proper orientation to the Law, Prophets, and Writings of the Old Testament.

2. To acquaint the student with the nature and culmination of the Law in the new covenant.

3. To acquaint the student with concept of redemption in the exodus event and their contribution to the new covenant.

4. To acquaint the student with the God-man relationship in the Old Testament covenants and the culmination of the covenants in the new covenant.

5. To enable the student to appreciate the sovereign rule of God in relation to the people of Old Testament times and the importance of the promise of a coming Messiah and his relation to the new covenant.

6. To give the student a perspective on the Old Testament that prepares him for understanding the New Testament revelation.

CHAPTER 3 OUTLINE

A. Introduction
B. Canon and Canonical Interpretation
   1. Canon
   2. Canonical Interpretation
C. Law
   3. Types of Law
   4. Terms for the Law
   5. Transmission of the Law
   6. Applicability of the Law
   7. Guidelines for Applying the Old Testament Law
D. The Exodus
   1. Setting of the Exodus
   2. Transmission of Exodus Account
   3. Culmination of the Exodus in the New Covenant
   4. Applicability of the Exodus
   5. Guidelines for Understanding the Exodus
E. Covenant
   1. Covenant Types
   2. Key Chain of Covenants Culminating in the New Covenant
   3. Applicability of the Covenants
   4. Guidelines for Understanding the Old Testament Covenants
F. Coordinating Old Testament Themes
   1. Rule of God and the Concept of Messiah
   2. Relation of God and of the Messiah to the Law, the Exodus, and the Covenants
   3. Role of Messiah in the New Covenant
   4. Relation of Old Testament Messianism to the New Testament
   5. Righteousness and Faith
   6. Guidelines for Understanding the Nature and Relevance of Messianism
G. Key Words
H. Study Questions
I. Assignments
J. Chapter Bibliography

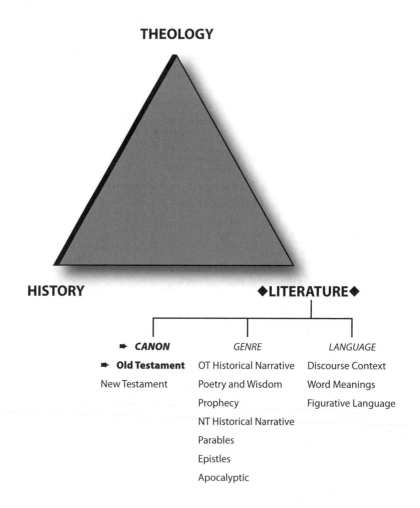

THEOLOGY

HISTORY   ◆LITERATURE◆

➡ *CANON*   *GENRE*   *LANGUAGE*

➡ **Old Testament**   OT Historical Narrative   Discourse Context

New Testament   Poetry and Wisdom   Word Meanings

                       Prophecy   Figurative Language

                       NT Historical Narrative

                       Parables

                       Epistles

                       Apocalyptic

Chapter 3

THE OLD TESTAMENT CANON: THE LAW, THE PROPHETS, AND THE WRITINGS

INTRODUCTION

NOW THAT WE HAVE PROPERLY grounded our study of Scripture by investigating its historical setting, we are ready to turn to an exploration of the second element of the hermeneutical triad: literature, the major focus of our interpretative journey. In keeping with the bedrock hermeneutical principle of interpreting the parts in light of the whole, we will proceed from the larger *canonical framework* to the *literary genre* and from there to specific *linguistic features* of various passages of Scripture. As Kevin Vanhoozer has reminded us, the biblical canon is a coherent whole, a "theo-drama."[1] N. T. Wright, likewise, has drawn attention to the important function of the overarching storyline of Scripture on the interpretation of individual passages.[2] Outside of the Christian camp, postmodernists have emphasized the importance of meta-narratives and

---

1. Kevin J. Vanhoozer, *The Drama of Doctrine: A Canonical-Linguistic Approach to Christian Theology* (Louisville: Westminster John Knox, 2005).
2. N. T. Wright, *The New Testament and the People of God* (Minneapolis: Fortress, 1992).

151

worldview.[3] For this reason we will do well to develop a good grasp of the biblical story line as a whole before looking at specific genre characteristics and linguistic features of a particular text of Scripture.

This chapter will consider the three major parts of the Old Testament revelation: the Law, the Prophets, and the Writings. The next chapter will survey the canonical landscape of the New Testament. The collected writings in the Law, the Prophets, and the Writings form the Old Testament canon. The word "canon" is ultimately derived from a Hebrew root qāneh meaning "reed." Because some reeds could be used to measure things, this nuance became eventually part of the meaning of the Greek kanōn, denoting a *standard*. In time, the word was used for a *group of books* that were measured by certain standards and deemed authoritative.

Although the Old Testament canon grew gradually over more than a millennium, when the individual writings were completed, they were often immediately recognized and accepted as divinely authoritative (e.g., Exod. 24:3–4, 7; Deut. 4:1–2; 31:9–11, 24–26; Josh. 1:7–9; 8:35). Time and again, the prophets claimed that they had received a divine revelation and declared that they spoke for the Lord (e.g., 1 Kings 17:13–14; Isa. 1:1; 6:1–13; Jer. 1:4–19; Ezek. 2:1–3:4; Jonah 1:1; 3:1; Hab. 1:1; Zech. 1:1; Mal. 1:1; etc.). Many recognized the Old Testament writings as authoritative (1 Kings 16:34; 2 Kings 14:6, 25; 23:1–3; Ezra 5:1–2; Neh. 9:30; Isa. 34:16; Dan. 9:2), including Jesus (Matt. 5:17–20; 23:34–35), the apostles (e.g., Acts 2:17–21, 25–26, 34–35; Rom. 1:2–3; 11:2; 2 Pet. 1:19–21), and others in the New Testament (e.g., Luke 1:1–4; 24:27, 32, 45; Heb. 2:6–9; 5:5–6; 8:8–12; etc.).

Moreover, careful historical inquiry and research have demonstrated that at each step of its formation the Old Testament accurately represents the area and era with which it is concerned. Its truthfulness in the case of data that can be verified further suggests that where it claims to be the word of the Lord, the Old Testament can be trusted. It is also of interest to note that phrases such as "thus says the Lord" and "God/the Lord said" occur thousands of times. When one adds to this the fact that individuals responding positively to the Bible's teachings and standards experience a

---

3. See the excellent treatment of D. A. Carson, *The Gagging of God: Christianity Confronts Pluralism* (Grand Rapids: Zondervan, 1996).

life-changing spiritual condition, this indicates that the Old Testament canonical books transcend mere human invention.

In what follows, we shall therefore proceed on the firm foundation that the Old Testament canonical writings are what they claim to be— God's authoritative revelation to humankind as revealed through chosen human instruments. Indeed, God himself is the basic unifying factor of the Old Testament. From its first verse (Gen. 1:1) until the closing verse of the Jewish Scriptures (2 Chron. 36:23), the Old Testament speaks of God as the Creator and sovereign Ruler of all things. The early narrative in Genesis tells of humanity's fall and God's provision for our redemption based on the principle of substitutionary sacrifice (Gen. 3:21; 22:8–14). The book of Genesis also contains the promise of the consummation of earth's history in a coming victorious Redeemer (Gen. 3:15; 49:10). These truths of humanity's fall and God's redemption will guide our interpretive journey through the Old Testament revelation, but an understanding of the canon and canonical interpretation set the proper interpretive framework for our thematic discussion.

CANON AND CANONICAL INTERPRETATION

Canon

In interpreting the Old Testament, it is beneficial to develop a grasp of the Old Testament canon and canonical interpretation. There are at least two reasons for this. In the first place, the complexities of the term "canon" need to be rightly understood when interpreting the Old Testament. In the second place, the idea of "canonical" interpretation has gained a good degree of currency in scholarship and should be properly understood for its prospects for biblical interpretation.

As mentioned before, "canon" is that term that is used to describe the body of authoritative Old Testament books from Genesis to Malachi. "Canon" is often described as simply a list of authoritative books. This idea, however, may imply that the "canon," then, is an arbitrary list of books that at some point in the second century B.C. was simply agreed upon and compiled together. In fact, however, the canon of the Old Testament is much more than a mere list of books. The canon represents a body of texts that has influenced each other in the formation and development of the full body. Put another way, some books have been received in a particular way by others and in turn ought to shape the way in which we read these other books.

A couple of examples explain what is meant by *canon*. One is found in the book of Deuteronomy. The leadership laws of Deuteronomy 16:18–20 and 17:1–18:22 set the stage for how readers ought to evaluate the leaders of Israel in Joshua–Kings. This is because the writer of Joshua to Kings seems to be aware of Deuteronomy and is further guided and theologically constrained by the theology of Deuteronomy. Thus the book of Deuteronomy sets a norm that shapes both the composition and evaluation of the remainder of Joshua to Kings. Another example of this is the relationship between 1–2 Kings and 1–2 Chronicles. These two histories of Israel are similar at places, indicating that the writer of Chronicles knows of, and is guided by, the book of Kings. And yet, Chronicles goes its own way at points as well, building upon the theological message of Kings and constructing its own.

What this shows is that the canon of the Old Testament is not an arbitrary list of books thrown together or decided upon in a haphazard manner. Rather, biblical writers were constantly informed and constrained by God's Word during the process of constructing the full body of the Old Testament. The idea that the canon is simply a list of books actually underplays the way that books influenced others; rather, the canon is an entity that indicates this inner-textual interdependence and logic.

Interpretatively, this means that the reader must learn to read the Old Testament in light of the Old Testament. A very useful way to begin this reading process is to habituate oneself into the foundational first five books of the Old Testament (the Pentateuch) and to look for the terminology, idioms, and imagery of this language as it is picked up in the other portions of the Old Testament. Then you will be able to work outward to the rest of the Old Testament and explore other ways the Old Testament depends upon, and is shaped by, the Old Testament (like Kings' influence upon Chronicles).

Along with the complexity of the term *canon*, the interpreter must be aware of the range and arrangement of books in the Christian canon of the Old Testament. Interpreters of the Old Testament ought to be aware of the two primary versions: the ancient Hebrew witness, which is represented by a tripartite division of Law (*Torah*), Prophets (*Neviim*), and

Writings (*Kethuvim*), and then the Greek translation of Hebrew originals. The Hebrew version is represented in its most complete form in what is commonly called the MT (Masoretic Text), while the latter version is found in what is commonly called the LXX (Septuagint), although these terms can be misleading and the readers should consult some of the specialist sources cited below. Important to consider is the fact that, strictly speaking, the term "Septuagint" applies only to the original Greek translation of the Pentateuch.[4] Other books need to be identified as "Old Greek" translations. The nature of the translation technique (whether more literal or periphrastic) varies from book to book and needs to be assessed as such. Both textual witnesses are challenging, and for further research on the subject one should consult the available scholarly resources.[5]

For our purposes, it will suffice to note differences between two major versions. In the Hebrew version, the *Torah* contains the first five books of the Old Testament including Genesis, Exodus, Leviticus, Numbers, and Deuteronomy. The *Neviim* includes Joshua, Judges, 1–2 Samuel, 1–2 Kings, Isaiah, Jeremiah, Ezekiel, and the Minor Prophets (also called the Book of the Twelve: Hosea, Joel, Amos, Obadiah, Jonah, Micah, Nahum, Habakkuk, Zephaniah, Haggai, Zechariah, and Malachi). The *Kethuvim* includes Psalms, Proverbs, Job, the Song of Songs, Ruth, Lamentations, Ecclesiastes, Esther, Daniel, Ezra, Nehemiah, and 1–2 Chronicles.

Extant Greek manuscripts, however, are arranged in different ways and converge with and diverge from the Hebrew, depending upon which major manuscript one reads. Three important major extant Greek versions of the Old Testament are Codex Vaticanus (B), Codex Siniaticus (א), and Codex Alexandrianus (A).[6] In all these Greek manuscripts, the opening order coheres with the Hebrew (Genesis–Deuteronomy). Also, in A, B, and א, what follows should be construed as a span of historical books (Joshua–Chronicles, with some other books interspersed in B and א). Following upon these historical books are poetical books (Psalms–Job) in B,

---

4. For a discussion, see Karen Jobes and Moisés Silva, *Invitation to the Septuagint* (Grand Rapids: Baker, 2000).

5. Ernst Würthwein, *The Text of the Old Testament: An Introduction to the Biblia Hebraica*, 2d ed. (Grand Rapids: Eerdmans, 1994); Emmanuel Tov, *Textual Criticism of the Hebrew Bible*, 2d rev. ed. (Minneapolis: Augsburg Fortress, 2001); Jobes and Silva, *Invitation to the Septuagint*; N. F. Marcos, *The Septuagint in Context: Introduction to the Greek Version of the Bible* (Atlanta: Society of Biblical Literature, 2009).

6. For other important versions, see Jobes and Silva, *Invitation to the Septuagint*.

but A and ℵ follow with prophetic books (Book of the Twelve–Ezekiel). Finally, B concludes with prophetic books, while A and ℵ conclude with poetical books (like the Hebrew order).[7]

Differences and similarities between the Hebrew and Greek orders should be considered, but not overplayed. One must remember that the New Testament authors seemed to be aware of both Greek and Hebrew versions of the Old Testament, and so it would be a good idea to be at least aware of both. Despite the differences in versions, the order of Law, Prophets, and Writings appears to be quite old and likely is the arrangement known by Jesus and the apostles (cf. Luke 24:44). Incidentally, this arrangement seems to be preferred by A and ℵ, but this point should not be pressed too far.

Canonical Interpretation

Having addressed idea of canon, it is now possible to discuss briefly the matter of canonical interpretation. Since the work of Brevard Childs, *canonical interpretation* means an approach that explores and evaluates the very nature of the Old Testament as the sacred Scripture of the church and a living and active text that addresses each new generation.[8] For Childs, this means exploring the larger shape of biblical texts:

1. By restoring the best text of particular books (through textual criticism).

2. By assessing the development of the text towards the "final form" of the book or larger blocks of material (assessing the gradual development of, say, the Psalms or the Book of the Twelve).

3. By assessing the nature of the "final form" of the book or block of material—why it is shaped the way it is (for instance, why Psalms 1–2 were placed at the beginning of the Psalter) and

---

7. For a useful discussion of the orders, see Greg Goswell, "The Order of the Books of the Hebrew Bible," *JETS* 51 (2008): 673–88; idem, "The Order of the Books in the Greek Old Testament," *JETS* 52 (2009): 449–68.
8. See esp. Brevard S. Childs, "An Interview with Brevard S. Childs," www.philosophy-religion.org/bible/childs-interview.htm.

what this shaping means theologically. That is to say, Childs is not interested solely in the "bits and pieces" of material (i.e., Psalms 1–2 alone), but rather in how each of the bits works corporately to produce the theological texture and message of the whole work (the book of Psalms).

4. By assessing the way in which the canon of the Old Testament constrains and opens theological horizons for interpretation in both the Greek and Hebrew text traditions (as briefly discussed above).

5. By relating the Old Testament and New Testament as discreet but unified witnesses to God in Christ Jesus.[9]

Practically, Childs has been the most significant proponent of this approach, and Christopher Seitz, amongst others, has carried his work forward.[10] Childs's approach, in particular, should not be confused with a "critical method" such as redaction criticism or form criticism. Canonical interpretation is a faithful effort to hear the way in which God addresses his people in and through the text of Scripture as it testifies to God in Christ. This is not a method (even though it builds perhaps upon the work of historical criticism) but a practice of theological reading.

Childs's and Seitz's understanding of canonical interpretation differs from others. For instance, Sanders's approach to canonical interpretation observes the way in which canon creates and authorizes communities of faith, to which Childs responds that this way of looking at the Old Testament is entirely too anthropocentric when the Scriptures necessitate a theocentric reading practice, recognizing the Old Testament as the

---

9. Brevard Childs, "The Canon in Recent Biblical Studies: Reflections on an Era," *Pro Ecclesia* 14/1 (2005): 26–45. See also the helpful analyses of Anthony Thiselton ("Introduction: Canon, Community, and Theological Construction") and Christopher Seitz ("The Canonical Approach and Theological Interpretation") in *Canon and Biblical Interpretation*, ed. Craig Bartholomew, Scott Hahn, et al., SAHS 7 (Grand Rapids: Zondervan, 2006), 1–32, 58–110.

10. Christopher R. Seitz, *Prophecy and Hermeneutics: Toward a New Introduction to the Prophets*, STL (Grand Rapids: Baker, 2007); idem, *The Goodly Fellowship of the Prophets: The Achievement of Association in Canon Formation* (Grand Rapids: Baker, 2009).

revelation of God.[11] Yet Childs confirms the importance of communities that receive this revelation.

What is more, the approach of John Sailhamer builds upon Childs's canonical approach, but should be identified as "compositional" rather than canonical in the fashion of Childs. Sailhamer observes the final shape of the text—that is, the way in which large blocks of text (such as the Pentateuch) have been put together or composed—with little concern for the history of the construction of the text or the reading communities who would have actually received it.[12] Sailhamer's approach has not been as influential as has Childs, in part perhaps because it verges on a version of New Criticism that disassociates the historicity of the text from its originating author and readers. This lack of historical rigor distances his approach from Childs's rendering of canonical interpretation, which is more robust because it rightly considers both the historical background and the larger theological fabric of the Old Testament as Scripture.[13]

Both the history of construction as well as reading communities remain vitally important for Seitz and Childs in their understanding of canonical interpretation, as one may see in Childs's Exodus and Isaiah commentaries and in Seitz's commentaries on Isaiah.[14] So while Sanders's and Sailhamer's works are related to Childs's version of canonical interpretation, they remain distinctive and exhibit tendencies from which Childs's work diverges.

Why is canonical interpretation important for reading and understanding the Bible? First of all, it recognizes that the Old Testament, in particular, is a body of text that spans approximately 700–1,000 years of

---

11. See James A. Sanders, *Canon and Community: A Guide to Canonical Criticism* (Philadelphia: Fortress, 1984); Childs, "Canon," 31–34.

12. John H. Sailhamer, *The Meaning of the Pentateuch* (Downers Grove: InterVarsity, 2009); idem, *Introduction to Old Testament Theology: A Canonical Approach* (Grand Rapids: Zondervan, 1995); idem, *The Pentateuch as Narrative* (Grand Rapids: Zondervan, 1992). However, it is unduly restrictive to minimize the value of historical background information in interpreting Scripture. See further the comments below.

13. Brevard S. Childs, *Introduction to the Old Testament as Scripture* (Philadelphia: Fortress, 1979), 75–83; idem, *Introduction to Old Testament Theology in a Canonical Context* (Philadelphia: Fortress, 1985), 1–19.

14. Brevard S. Childs, *Exodus*, OTL (Louisville: Westminster John Knox, 2004 [1974]); idem, *Isaiah*, OTL (Louisville, Westminster John Knox, 2001); Christopher R. Seitz, *Isaiah 1–39*, Interpretation (Louisville: John Knox, 1989); idem, "Isaiah 40–66," in *New Interpreter's Bible*, ed. Leander Keck (Nashville: Abingdon, 2001).

history in terms of textual formation. From the times of Moses to Ezra, the Old Testament has been constructed in particular ways and cannot be said to have been put together all at once in the post-exilic period (e.g., after 539 B.C.). Canonical interpretation takes account of this history of textual formation, but it does not stop there. The history of textual formation is understood to testify to God himself and to his self-disclosure in and through the Scripture. One cannot stop interpreting at, say, Psalm 1 or 2, because these Psalms have been incorporated into the larger sweep of the book of the Psalter for a distinctive theological purpose. Canonical interpretation enables the interpreter to ask questions about the text in relation of the part to the whole in a sophisticated way. It moves the interpreter away from naive reading practices and enables one to read with the contours of the text itself to hear God's address more clearly.

As an example of the canonical interpretation approach, Christopher Seitz, in his research into the Book of the Twelve, sees that each individual prophetic book from Hosea to Malachi remains important in its own right and needs to be interpreted as such. This means that the interpreter pays attention to the history of the text, its theological purpose, its distinctive theological themes, and so on; but in so doing, the interpreter notes that a number of features tend to bind these books together.

Seitz here draws upon previous research that has found these binding elements are thematic ties, catchwords, and intertextual allusions. While others have been suggested,[15] the most prominent thematic tie evidenced throughout the Book of the Twelve is the "Day of the LORD." This language can be seen prominently in Hosea 9:5; Joel 3:4; Amos 5:18–20; Obadiah 15; Micah 2:4; Habakkuk 3:16; Zephaniah 1:7–16; Haggai 2:23; Zechariah 14:1; and Malachi 4:1.[16] Another possible thematic tie is that of "return" (šûb). This language occurs prominently across several books: Hosea 3:5;

---

15. Note the following: (a) sin-punishment-restoration theme (Paul House, *The Unity of the Twelve*, JSOTSup 77 [Sheffield: Sheffield Academic Press, 1990]); (b) A multivocal set of themes: covenant-election, fidelity-infidelity, fertility-infertility, turning-returning, justice and mercy of God, kingship of God, Temple/Zion, nations as enemies/allies (Terence Collins, "The Scroll of the Twelve," in *The Mantle of Elijah*, BS 20 [Sheffield: Sheffield Academic Press, 1993], 65). Collins's identified "themes," however, tend toward the literary category of *motif* rather than *theme*.

16. David L. Petersen, "A Book of the Twelve?" in *Reading and Hearing the Book of the Twelve*, ed. James D. Nogalski and Marvin A. Sweeney, SBLSS 15 (Atlanta: SBL, 2000), 8–10.

5:4; 6:1, 2, 11; 7:10; 8:13; 9:3; 11:5; 12:6; 14:1-2; Joel 2:12–13; 3:1, 4, 7; Amos 4:6, 8–11; 9:11; Obadiah 15; Micah 2:8; 4:8; 5:3; Nahum 2:2; Zephaniah 2:7, 10; 3:20; Zechariah 1:3, 16; 4:1; 8:3; 9:12; 10:6, 9; and Malachi 3.7. In each of these instances cited above, those in bold indicate the semantics of šûb as "restore" while the others indicate the semantics of šûb as "return/turn."

What is more, there are a number of ways that the Twelve can be seen to cohere *structurally* as well as thematically. In the first instance, as has long been recognized, there is a deliberate repetition of "catchword chains" that bind books together: Hosea 14:2//Joel 2:12; Joel 4:16//Amos 1:2; Amos 9:12//Obadiah 19; Obadiah 1//Jonah (messenger to nations); Jonah 4:2//Micah 7:18–19//Nahum 1:2–3; Nahum 1:1//Habakkuk 1:1; Habakkuk 2:20//Zephaniah 1:7; [17] as well as Zephaniah 3:20//Haggai 1:2, 4 (through the repetition of the word "time").[18] These catchword chains may indicate that the Book of the Twelve is designed so that each part is to be read with a conscious understanding of the whole.

Another way that the Twelve reads together is through the repetition of Exodus 34:6–7:

> The LORD, the LORD, the compassionate and gracious God, slow to anger, abounding in love and faithfulness, maintaining love to thousands, and forgiving wickedness, rebellion and sin. Yet he does not leave the guilty unpunished; he punishes the children and their children for the sin of the fathers to the third and fourth generation.

This text, as van Leeuwen notes, contains "an elaboration of the name YHWH expressing the bipolar attributes of mercy and retributive justice."[19] The repetition of this text through the corpus of the Twelve is evidenced in either citation or wordplay, drawing upon it: Hosea 1:6 (mercy of God no longer operative through wordplay); Joel 2:13 (recalls the verses

---

17. See Aaron Schart, "Reconstructing the Redaction History of the Twelve Prophets," in *Reading and Hearing the Twelve*, 34–48, esp. 35–36.

18. James Nogalski, *Literary Precursors to the Book of the Twelve*, BZAW 217 (Berlin: de Gruyter, 1993), 215; *Redactional Processes in the Book of the Twelve*, BZAW 218 (Berlin: de Gruyter, 1993).

19. Raymond C. van Leeuwen, "Scribal Wisdom and Theodicy in the Book of the Twelve," in *In Search of Wisdom: Essays in Memory of John G. Gammie*, ed. Leo Perdue, B. B. Scott, and W. J. Wiseman (Louisville: Westminster John Knox, 1993), 32.

as a call to repentance due to God's compassion); Jonah 3:9; 4:2 (cites the verse as a kind of lament over the compassion of God); Micah 7:18–20 (cites the verses to display the compassion of God); Nahum 1:2–3a. In light of these binding features, Seitz avers that the Book of the Twelve—in terms of individual books as well as a whole—must be taken seriously. The individual books need to be taken seriously and interpreted as such. And yet, as a whole, the Book of the Twelve remains coherent and teaches several valuable theological lessons:

1. God's history is a providentially ordered whole in that different books from different time periods work together to reveal God working sovereignly to bring about his purposes in history.

2. The nations have a different, but parallel and by no means neglected, place in God's economy.

3. There are a number of models of obedience (Joel, Habakkuk, and Jonah) that teach about faith in God in times of trouble and the virtue of faithful prayer.

4. Theological themes such as "Day of the Lord" are related in terms of tradition history, but they exceed these historical confines when related to one another in the Minor Prophets, which act as a lens by which to perceive the theological focus of these themes.

5. God is shown to be just and patient in history, but God's call for repentance and faith in him is vital for understanding his divine character. This is shown in the embedded allusions to Exodus 34 throughout the Book of the Twelve.[20]

Thus, in canonical perspective, the Twelve offers a micro- and macro-theological message. Both levels need to be addressed and embraced for a full-orbed understanding of God's Word. The question is

---

20. Seitz, *Prophecy and Hermeneutics*, 189–219, esp. 214–16.

that of balance—proper interpretation will attend to both levels in a way that addresses and incorporates the full testimony of the canonical Old Testament.

There are a variety of ways of doing this. Attending to theological themes is one way, and space will be given to this in this chapter, particularly to the vital themes of law, exodus, covenant, and other coordinating themes. Another way of dealing with both levels is to attend to the distinctive language that appears in and across bodies of text. We have already given examples of this in our discussion on Deuteronomy and Joshua–Kings on the one hand and in the rich interaction of language in the Book of the Twelve on the other. The point is that coherent canonical interpretation will attend to the particularities of the text at smaller and larger levels itself and allow the text to shape interpretation, rather than the other way around.

LAW

As the interpreter comes to the books of Exodus through Deuteronomy, he or she must remember that the word translated "law" (Hebrew tôrâ) means basically "instruction." The Hebrew Torah includes Genesis through Deuteronomy and is also known as the five books of Moses. Genesis thus provides a narrative background not only for the four books that follow but its message is foundational for the whole Old Testament.

There are three primary themes that form the focal points of the Old Testament: God's *law*, the *exodus*, and *covenant*. These three major concepts embody the principles of righteousness (law), redemption (exodus), and the believer's relationship to God (covenant). Indeed, it is these three themes that God brings together at Mount Sinai (Exod. 19:3–6) and that Moses later charges the Israelites to remember and pass on to subsequent generations (Deut. 6:4–12). Moses sums them up as follows:

> In the future, when your son asks you, "What is the meaning of the stipulations, decrees and laws the LORD our God has commanded you?" tell him: "We were slaves of Pharaoh in Egypt, but the LORD brought us out of Egypt with a mighty hand. Before our eyes the LORD sent miraculous signs and wonders—great and terrible—upon Egypt and Pharaoh and his whole household. But he brought us out from there to bring us

in and give us the land that he promised on oath to our forefather. The LORD commanded us to obey all these decrees and to fear the LORD our God, so that we might always prosper and be kept alive, as is the case today. And if we are careful to obey all this law before the LORD our God as he has commanded us, that will be our righteousness." (Deut. 6:20–25)

In obeying these commands, Israel will enjoy "a true and personal relationship with the covenant God . . . which not only would be a spiritual reality, but would be seen in the lives of the people of God."[21]

The applicability of Old Testament law to New Testament believers is one of the most controversial issues in biblical theology. Questions such as "Is the Old Testament law still in effect?" and "How much of it, if any, is still binding on Christians?" continue to trouble believers today. We shall begin to address these issues by examining the law's Old Testament setting.

Types of Law

The Old Testament laws covered virtually every aspect of human conduct. For example, the various laws concerned matters such as the needs of special classes in society (e.g., Exod. 22:22–24; Lev. 19:9–10, 33–34; Deut. 23:15–16), business dealings (e.g., Deut. 23:19–21), agriculture (e.g., Exod. 23:9–10; Lev. 25:1–24), and land and property rights (e.g., Deut. 19:14; 25:5–10). Laws of a religious or ceremonial nature were also included, such as regulations concerning the Sabbath (e.g., Exod. 31:12–17), sacrificial offerings (Leviticus 1–7), stated feasts (Num. 28:11–15; Deut. 16:1–15), and places of worship (Deut. 12:1–14). In addition, there were laws governing the personal lives of the people (e.g., Lev. 12–15; Deut. 12:15; 14:3–21). All these laws were designed to remind the Hebrews that they were a people specially chosen by God and that they were called to be a holy, just, and morally responsible people of God (Deut. 14:1–2).

Traditionally, some have classified these laws as to whether they are moral, civil, or ceremonial in nature. Others have classified them as to whether they are laws based upon legal precedents (casuistic laws) or laws

---

21. Peter C. Craigie, *The Book of Deuteronomy*, NICOT (Grand Rapids: Eerdmans, 1976), 175.

prescribing absolute religious and moral standards for the smooth running of society (apodictic laws). The difficulty of assigning individual laws to specific categories has made scholars consider an alternative approach. Increasingly, they are beginning to view Old Testament laws in relation to the narrative context in which they are found. Thus Watts points out, "The narrative context of Pentateuchal law confirms that the Torah is intended to be read as a whole and in order. Unlike law, narrative invites, almost enforces, a strategy of sequential reading, of starting at the beginning and reading the text in order to the end."[22]

Therefore, rather than reading Old Testament laws in order to decide to which category they belong or which of these laws are absolute and universally binding standards or which are ethically and historically limited to Israel, the careful interpreter should see them as part of the broad narrative in which they are found (Exod. 12:1; Deut. 34:12). Moreover, as Duvall and Hays point out, "The law is not presented by itself as some sort of timeless universal code. Rather, it is presented as part of the theological narrative that describes how God delivered Israel from Egypt and established them in the Promised Land as his people."[23] Therefore, all the laws are to be treated as the expression of the will and high moral standards of a sovereign and holy God. They are designed for a redeemed people specially chosen to represent him and reflect his character in their lives (Lev. 19:1). In addition, their narrative setting places them in juxtaposition with our other two focal themes, the exodus event and covenant stipulations (cf. Exod. 19:1–6).

Terms for the Law

The law of Israel was known by several different terms, such as: "Law of the Lord" (Exod. 13:9); "Book of the law of God" (Josh. 24:26); "Law of Moses" (2 Kings 23:25); "Book of the law of Moses" (2 Kings 14:6); "the law which Moses set" (Deut. 4:44); "Book of the law" (Josh. 1:8); and "the law" (Deut. 1:5) or "this law" (Deut. 31:9). Whatever the precise term, the teachings of the law were to be passed on and read regularly and obeyed (Deut. 31:10–13; Josh. 1:6–9).

---

22. James W. Watts, *Reading Law: The Rhetorical Shaping of the Pentateuch* (Sheffield: Sheffield Academic Press, 1999), 29.
23. J. Scott Duvall and J. Daniel Hays, *Grasping God's Word*, 2d ed. (Grand Rapids: Zondervan, 2005), 320.

Transmission of the Law

The Old Testament Scriptures point out that the law was read and transmitted to those who remained faithful to the Lord and to the spirit of the law (e.g., Josh. 8:31–35; 2 Kings 23:1–3, 24–25; Ezra 8:1–3; Neh. 9:6–15). Accordingly, the importance of the law (as well as of the exodus and covenant) is stressed in the poetic writings (e.g., Psalms 78; 119). Note, for example, the following texts:

> The law of the LORD is perfect,
> > reviving the soul.
> The statues of the LORD are trustworthy,
> > making wise the simple. (Ps. 19.7)
> Where there is no revelation,
> > the people cast off restraint;
> but blessed is he who keeps the law. (Prov. 29:18)

The prophets also stressed the importance of remembering and keeping the law, as well as the danger of transgressing it (e.g.,Isa. 42:20–25; Jer. 7:21–24; Hos. 8:12; Amos 2:4). But it is Jeremiah who encapsulates both the importance of the law and its relation to the other two basic Old Testament themes:

> "This is the covenant I will make with the house of Israel
> > after that time," declares the LORD.
> "I will put my law in their minds
> > and write it on their hearts.
> I will be their God,
> > and they will be my people.
> No longer will a man teach his neighbor,
> > or a man his brother, saying, 'Know the LORD,'
> because they will all know me,
> > from the least of them to the greatest," declares the Lord.
> > (Jer. 31:31–34)

In this text, Jeremiah prophesies that although the Torah will find continuity in the future, its provisions will be written on the heart rather than serve as an external law code. Moreover, Jeremiah hints that what was unique to Israel will be universally available at that point; there will be an intimacy of fellowship unmatched in previous times.[24] Since this is an internal rather than external reality, Jeremiah makes clear that it is the theological principles inherent in the specific laws that are in view.

Applicability of the Law

To be sure, the law was originally designed for Israel. Yet the realization that its theological and moral principles are embedded in the new covenant puts the applicability of the law into proper perspective. For Christ, the mediator of the new covenant, later stressed the importance of the principles of the law for the believer's life. Also, it is he who supplies the ability to keep and apply the Law to believers under the terms of the New Testament revelation. Nevertheless, although the old Mosaic Law has been superseded by a new covenant (cf. Jer. 31:31–34; Ezek. 37:24–28; with Gal. 2:15–16), the underlying theological and moral principles are timeless and continue to be in effect (cf. Matt. 5:17). As Klein, Blomberg, and Hubbard observe:

> First, we believe that God intends it [the Law] to serve as a paradigm
> of timeless ethical, moral, and theological principles. . . . Second, to
> properly interpret Law properly the student must discover the timeless
> truth it conveys.[25]

Thus the applicability of the law for Christians is channeled through the light of the new covenant established by Christ.

It is important for us to note that where the New Testament deals with specific Old Testament laws, they are to be given special regard. A case in point is the Ten Commandments. Although written specifically for Israel, the theological principles in them are implicit in texts that antedate the revelation at Mount Sinai and are found in various places in the New Testament. Note the following selective chart of relevant texts:

---

24. See further Walter C. Kaiser Jr., *Toward an Old Testament Theology* (Grand Rapids: Zondervan, 1978), 231–35.
25. William W. Klein, Craig L. Blomberg, Robert L. Hubbard Jr., *Introduction to Biblical Interpretation*, rev. ed. (Nashville: Thomas Nelson, 2004), 345–46.

3.1. THE TEN COMMANDMENTS AND UNDERLYING PRINCIPLES			
COMMANDMENTS			PRINCIPLES
Exodus	Deuteronomy	Pre-Sinai	New Testament
Exod. 20:2–6	Deut. 5:7	Gen. 17:1; Exod. 3:14	Acts 14:10–15; 1 Cor. 8:4
Exod. 20:4–6	Deut. 8–10	Gen. 35:3–4	2 Cor. 6:16; 1 John 5:20–21
Exod. 20:7	Deut. 5:11	Gen. 24:3	Matt 6:5–13
Exod. 20:8–11	Deut. 5:12–13	Gen. 2:2–3	1 Cor. 16:2
Exod. 20:12	Deut. 5:16	Gen. 46:29; 50:1–5	Matt. 19:18; Eph 6:1–3
Exod. 20:13	Deut. 5:17	Gen. 4:6–12, 15; 9:5–6	Matt. 19:19; Rom. 13:9
Exod. 20:14	Deut. 5:18	Gen. 39:9	Matt. 19:18; Rom. 13:9
Exod. 20:15	Deut. 5:19	Gen. 27:36; 31:5	Matt. 19:18; Rom. 13:9; Eph. 4:28
Exod. 20:16	Deut. 5:20	Gen. 39:16 18	Matt. 19:18; Rom. 13:9; James 4:11–12
Exod. 20:17	Deut. 5:21	Gen. 26:10	Rom. 7:7; 13:9–10

Even here, as elsewhere, however, the teachings inherent in the Old Testament law must be viewed through the lens of the New Testament revelation. It is important for the student of Scripture to realize that the whole Bible, including the Old Testament law, has much to teach us concerning Christian living. Indeed, "The Old Testament legal material contains rich *principles* and *lessons* for living that are still relevant when interpreted through New Testament teaching."[26]

---

26. Duvall and Hays, *Grasping God's Word*, 324.

GUIDELINES FOR APPLYING THE OLD TESTAMENT LAW

1. As with any biblical text or passage, determine what the law meant to its original hearers or readers.

2. Determine the theological and moral principles inherent in the particular law.

3. Determine whether the law has been commented on by Jesus or the New Testament writers. If so, how has the law been modified (e.g., the Sabbath vs. Sunday worship)?

4. Granted the underlying theological or moral intention of the law and its New Testament application (if any), determine how this law applies to contemporary culture (e.g., the issues of slavery, business practices, women's dress, etc.).

5. Make proper personal application relying on the Holy Spirit's guidance.[27]

THE EXODUS

By referring to the exodus as part of an event, we are emphasizing that Israel's deliverance out of Egypt was but the first part of a whole movement that took God's people from Egypt to the Promised Land (Exod. 3:16–17). We will trace not only this event but also the transmission of the story of the exodus in the Old Testament books, noting in particular its inclusion in the details of the new covenant.

Setting of the Exodus

Israel's exodus from Egypt forms the climax of the contest between Moses and the Egyptian pharaoh (Exod. 3:1–12:36). The account of Israel's

---

27. See the helpful discussion in Roy B. Zuck, *Basic Bible Interpretation* (Wheaton: Victor, 1991), 279–92.

deliverance from Egypt is told in a well-structured narrative that portrays the various stages of Israel's journey: from Egypt to Succoth (Exod. 12:37–13:19); from there through the Re(e)d Sea (Exod. 13:20–15:21); and on in succession to the oasis at Elim (Exod. 15:22–27); to the Desert of Sin (Exod. 16:1–36); to Rephidim (Exod. 17:1–18:27); and on to Mount Sinai (Exod. 19:1–2).

The account of the events during the encampment before Mount Sinai (Exod. 19:3–Num. 10:10) forms a pivotal episode in the narrative of the exodus. For as we have seen, it was there that the stipulations of the law were delivered to Israel (cf. Exod. 20:1–17). As noted, however, the exodus would not be complete until God brought his people through the wilderness and into the Promised Land (Num. 10:11–Josh. 21:43). The full narrative thus ends only when Israel has entered and taken possession of the land of Canaan.

It is important to note that both Israel's actual deliverance out of Egypt and the details regarding its settling in the Promised Land are part of one grand narrative telling of God's gracious acts on behalf of his people. Note the following key texts:

> I have come down to rescue them from the hand of the Egyptians and to bring them up out of that land into a good and spacious land, a land flowing with milk and honey . . . (Exod. 3:8)

> After the LORD brings you into the land of the Canaanites and gives it to you, as he promised on oath to you and your forefathers . . . (Exod. 13:11)

> Not one of all the LORD'S good promises to the house of Israel failed; every one was fulfilled. (Josh. 21:45)

Rather than viewing the Law or the exodus as isolated accounts that have been pieced together at some late date, understanding both as part of one complete narrative allows the interpreter to see the importance of each as well as to realize that the value of the whole narrative is greater than the sum of its individual parts. Perceptive students have doubtless noted that details regarding God's covenant act are also pertinent to the story of the giving of the Law, which in turn forms part of the exodus account (cf. Exod. 19:1–6). We will consider this aspect of the narrative later in the chapter.

Transmission of the Exodus Account

Various aspects of the exodus narrative have come down to us in individual remembrances recorded in the Old Testament as part of the completed canon. Thus details may be gleaned from passages such as Exodus 15:1–18, 21; Deuteronomy 33:2; Judges 5:4-5; Psalms 18:7–15 (cf. 2 Sam. 22:8–16); 68:5–7; 77:16–20; 144:5–6; and Habakkuk 3:3–15. The antiquity of these texts is attested in that all of them are told in early Hebrew poetry. In these texts special attention is called to God's provision of victory for Israel over the Egyptians at the Re(e)d Sea and the successful crossing of the Jordan River (e.g., Exod. 15:1–18, 21; Ps. 77:16–20; Hab. 3:3–15).

God instructed the people that specific details of the story of the exodus out of Egypt were to be remembered and passed on to subsequent generations (cf. Exod. 13:1–13). Note the place of the Passover as part of the exodus story:

> In days to come, when your son asks you, "What does this mean?" say
> to him, "With a mighty hand the LORD brought us out of Egypt, out
> of the land of slavery. When Pharaoh stubbornly refused to let us go,
> the LORD killed every firstborn in Egypt both man and animal. This
> is why I sacrifice to the LORD the first male offspring of every womb
> and redeem each of my firstborn sons. And it will be like a sign on
> your hand a symbol on your forehead that the LORD brought us out of
> Egypt with his mighty hand." (Exod. 3:14–16)

Later writers also often commented on God's deliverance of his people in the exodus, sometimes as mere historical fact (e.g., Num. 1:1; Josh. 24:5–13) and at other times as a witness of the people's ingratitude and infidelity (e.g., Num. 21:5; Hos. 11:2–3; Mic. 6:1–5), for which God's judgment must surely come (e.g., Amos 2:6–16). On some occasions, the Lord called attention to the exodus while delivering specific stipulations of the Law to his people (e.g., Lev. 23:43; 25:54–55). The remembrance of the exodus also served as a source for spiritual instruction in various matters (e.g., Deut. 6:20–25) as well as in challenges to live righteously before the Lord (e.g., Deut. 6:2–12; 1 Sam. 12:6–8).

God's faithful believers often remembered the Lord's provision in the exodus in their praises (e.g., Pss. 66:3–6; 114; 135:8–9) and prayers to God (2 Sam. 7:23; Isa. 63:7–15). Note, for example, Habakkuk's words of praise in introducing his poems concerning the exodus:

LORD, I have heard of your fame;
  I stand in awe of your deeds, O LORD.
Renew them in our day,
  in our time make them known;
  in wrath remember mercy. (Hab. 3:2)

Unfortunately, the exodus was also transmitted in warnings to the people of impending judgment for their failure to remember God's past deliverances and goodness to them (e.g., Jer. 2:5–9; 7:21–29; 11:14–17). Nevertheless, God assured his people that after the threatened judgment that would come in the form of expulsion from the Promised Land by way of captivity, with humble repentance and surrender to God there would come restoration to God's favor and a return to the land (e.g., Isa. 61:1–4; Jer. 16:14–15; Ezek. 20:32–38). Thus the exodus motif becomes a message of comfort to God's people and hope (e.g., Isa. 40:1).

One of the most interesting passages in which the exodus is mentioned is Jeremiah 32. Although it was the eve of Jerusalem's fall to the Neo-Babylonian king Nebuchadnezzar, God instructed Jeremiah to buy the field belonging to his cousin Hanamel (Jer. 32:8). Having done so (vv. 8–15, 25), Jeremiah prayed to the Lord (vv. 16–19), especially recalling God's mighty work in the exodus event (vv. 20–22) and the people's subsequent infidelity that was about to cause their captivity (vv. 23–24). God confirmed to Jeremiah his intention to bring judgment to the people (vv. 26 35) but also pointed to a better hope—the restoration of a repentant, God-fearing people to the Promised Land (vv. 36–39). In connection with this hope God assured Jeremiah that in the future he would make a new covenant with his people.

I will make an everlasting covenant with them: I will never stop doing good to them, and I will inspire them to fear me, so that they will never turn away from me. I will rejoice in doing them good and will assuredly plant them in this land with all my heart and soul. (Jer. 32:40–41)

Culmination of the Exodus in the New Covenant

As we have just seen, like the Law, the exodus finds it climax in the new covenant (cf. Jer. 31:31–37). Although there were exoduses in historic Old Testament times (Ezra 1:1–2:70; 8:31–36), the thrust of the exodus as wedded to the new covenant involves a greater future exodus of God's people from the entire world. The temporal setting is eschatological. It will indeed be an even greater exodus than that original one.

> So then, the days are coming, declares the LORD, "When people will no longer say, 'As surely as the LORD lives, who brought the Israelites up out of Egypt,' but they will say, 'As surely as the LORD lives, who brought the descendants of Israel out of the land of the north and out of all the countries where he had banished them. Then they will live in their own land.'" (Jer. 23:7–8)

This will involve the release of God's people from all lands.

> Do not be afraid, for I am with you;
> I will bring your children from the east
> and gather you from the west.
> I will say to the north, 'Give them up!'
> and to the south, 'Do not hold them back.'
> Bring my sons from afar
> and my daughters from the ends of the earth—
> everyone who is called by my name,
> whom I created for my glory,
> whom I formed and made. (Isa. 43:5–7)

God himself will go before them and provide for them (Isa. 43:16–21; 52:12). His ransomed people will return with singing (Isa. 35:10) to enjoy everlasting gladness in full fellowship with the Lord in the ancient land of promise (Isa. 65:17–25). As a restored, faithful, and blessed people they will be an avenue of salvation for all people:

> I will make you a light for the Gentiles,
> that you may bring my salvation to the ends of the earth. (Isa. 49:6)

Thus the exodus motif finds it full significance in being wedded to the new covenant.

Applicability of the Exodus
The initial exodus event bore witness to God's redemptive power.

During the exodus, God, Israel's Redeemer, brought his people to himself. What was experienced nationally was also true of a great many of God's faithful believers such as Moses, Aaron, Joshua, and Caleb. Indeed, the exodus bore testimony to both God's sovereignty and his redemption. Theologically, the exodus symbolized the truth of God's redeeming grace.[28] This truth has theological implications not only for the exodus motif but for our perspective on the law. For, as we noted previously, the law was designed specifically for God's redeemed people. Moreover, because the exodus finds its culmination in the new covenant, the availability of God's redemption now takes on universal proportions. As wedded to the new covenant, it prepares the readers of Scripture for the New Testament message of redemption by which all people may experience an exodus from the realm of sin and darkness in order to enter the realm of light and God saving grace.

> . . . giving grace to the Father, who has qualified you to share in the inheritance of the saints in the kingdom of light. For he has rescued us from the dominion of darkness and brought us into the kingdom of the Son he loves, in whom we have redemption, the forgiveness of sins. (Col. 1:12–14)

As F. F. Bruce points out, "the Exodus provides for the rest of the biblical record a form of language and imagery for communicating the message of salvation."[29]

The exodus message of hope thus finds its ultimate reality in the inauguration of the new covenant mediated by Jesus Christ (Matt. 26:27–29; 2 Cor. 3:6; Hebrews 8). As we will see in the following chapter, the motif of the exodus will be reflected in many of the messages of the New Testament. It will only reach its final goal in the eschatological era as reflected in the imagery and symbolism of the Apocalypse (e.g., Rev. 14:1–5).

---

28. See the informative and helpful discussion by Geerhardus Vos, *Biblical Theology* (Grand Rapids: Eerdmans, 1954), 127–29.
29. F. F. Bruce, *This Is That: The New Testament Development of Some Old Testament Themes* (Exeter: Paternoster, 1968), 32.

GUIDELINES FOR UNDERSTANDING THE EXODUS

1. Examine the story of Israel's deliverance from Egypt in the light of the full narrative of the exodus event.

2. Note the transmission of the exodus and its culmination in the new covenant.

3. Note the importance of the exodus in the teachings inherent in the Law and the covenant structure of the Old Testament.

4. Take notice of the underlying theological principle of redemption in the exodus and its importance to the new covenant.

5. Note the importance of the exodus event as wedded to the new covenant as a preparation for the New Testament revelation.

6. Apply the principles inherent in the exodus to the Christian message and the missionary responsibility for all believers.

COVENANT

The concept of "covenant" is an old one in the ancient Near East stretching back nearly five millennia.[30] It is inextricably bound to the needs of treaty-making and law. From Sumer in Mesopotamia to Ebla in the western Fertile Crescent and from the third to the first millennium B.C., literally scores of such documents have been found in various formats.[31] From this data, we are able to see the variety of details incorpo-

---

30. The classic treatment of covenant in Old Testament theology is in Walter Eichrodt, *Theology of the Old Testament*, trans. J. A. Baker (Philadelphia: Westminster, 1961).

31. For excellent discussions concerning treaty and covenant-making, see Kenneth A. Kitchen, *Ancient Orient and the Old Testament* (Chicago: InterVarsity, 1966), 90–102; *The Bible in Its World* (Downers Grove: InterVarsity, 1977), 79–85; "The

rated in such works in the individual cultures and across the spectrum of a substantially long time period. Careful research reveals that the biblical covenants may now be safely placed in relation to their closest cultural setting and specific era. As a result, it may be concluded that "the treaty forms fit the times when the Bible places the narratives. In short, this typology of treaties provides *factual* material that broadly substantiates the Biblical chronology."[32]

Covenant Types

The information gained from historical inquiry enables us to isolate two basic types of treaties that have important ramifications for their interpretation in the covenantal conventions of the Old Testament.[33] Before turning to a consideration of these two types, we will do well to remember that the covenant concept is already present (but not fully developed as such) in people's early relationship with God. Having placed the first man in the Garden of Eden, the sovereign God informed Adam of the stipulations attendant to life in the garden and the curse/penalty for breaking the terms of covenant life.

> And the LORD God commanded the man, "You are free to eat from any tree in the garden, but you must not eat from the tree of the knowledge of good and evil, for when you eat of it you will surely die." (Gen. 2:16–17)

Although God is a beneficent sovereign in his relationship to Adam, it is clear that the man was to learn matters of faith, faithfulness, and obedience through a simple test of his character and will. With the failure of the first human pair to keep the agreement, specific curses attended to the prescribed penalty were imposed (Gen. 3:14–19).

Patriarchal Age: Myth or Mystery?" *BAR* 21/2 (1995): 52–56; *On the Reliability of the Old Testament* (Grand Rapids: Eerdmans, 2003), 283–307; Meredith Kline, *Treaty of the Great King* (Grand Rapids: Eerdmans, 1963); idem, *The Structure of Biblical Authority* (Grand Rapids: Eerdmans, 1972).

32. Kitchen, "Patriarchal Age," 56.
33. It should also be noted that although no fully developed parity treaty/covenant (in which equal participants agree to certain conditions) is attested in the Old Testament, the concept can be seen in several of the covenant agreements recorded in biblical texts (e.g., Gen. 21:27; 31:43–54; 1 Sam. 20:3–17).

The first of the two prevalent types of covenants is known as the *Suzerain Treaty*. In it, the enacting party imposes covenant stipulations upon the vassal state. Several elements are standard in this form:

1. a title/preamble naming the parties involved;

2. a historical prologue tracing past relations between the covenanting parties;

3. the basic stipulations to be kept by the vassal;

4. a statement concerning the deposition of the covenant in an appropriate place as well as the periodic reading of the covenant;

5. a list of the witnesses who attend the making of the treaty/covenant; and

6. the sanctions to be imposed by the superior party, including revocation of the covenant, should the vassal fail to keep its terms.

This type of treaty/covenant also contained a list of blessings and curses attendant to its ratification and maintenance by the vassal.

The suzerainty-type treaty is found in the Old Testament in connection with the Sinaitic (or Mosaic) covenant and its renewal in Deuteronomy and in Joshua 24. Exodus 20 begins with a clear preamble and historical prologue:

> I am the LORD your God, who brought you out of Egypt, out of the land of slavery. (Exod. 20:2)

The basic stipulations follow in the Ten Commandments (Exod. 20:3–17). Other specific stipulations may be seen in the various laws mentioned earlier in the chapter. Provision for periodic reading may be seen in Moses' reading of the Book of the Covenant to the people (Exod. 24:7). Likewise, the blessings and curses attached to the covenant are found in Leviticus 26:3–43.

Many scholars have pointed out that the most fully developed example of a suzerainty-type treaty may be seen in the book of Deuteronomy. Here most of the covenant elements are clearly present:

1. preamble (1:1–5);

2. historical prologue (1:6–3:29);

3. basic (4:1–11:32) and specific stipulations (12:1–26:19);

4. covenant sanctions in the forms of blessings and curses (chap. 28);

5. instructions concerning the reading and deposition of the covenant (31:9–13, 24–26; cf. 32:44–47); and

6. statements as to the witnesses to the covenant (31:19–22; 32:1–43).

The Sinai treaty was apparently renewed in later times such as at Mount Ebal, where once again the covenant words were read aloud (Josh. 8:30–35) and at Shechem (Josh. 24:1–27). In the latter instance, most of the covenant elements are present: (1) preamble vv. 1–2a); (2) historical prologue (vv. 2b–13); (3) stipulations (vv. 14–15); covenant enactment and deposition (vv. 21, 25–26); (4) blessings and curses (vv. 19–20); and (5) witnesses (vv. 22, 27). The passage also contains an example of covenant oath (vv. 14–18). Still later, Josiah led the people in a time of covenant renewal where public reading of the covenant was followed by covenant enactment and oaths (2 Kgs. 23:1–3).

It is crucial for the interpreter of suzerainty-type covenants to understand that all such covenants depict God as the sovereign regulator of the covenant. The covenant was also conditional, its continuity as well as the blessings and curses embedded in it being contingent upon the people's response and obedience to the terms of the covenant. It is important, too, to see that the sovereign God who affixed the covenant was not an overbearing despot but a gracious Lord who was providing a means for blessing his people. Their keeping of the terms of the covenant was not only for God's glory and as a testimony to his redemptive grace, but was intended for their good (Exod. 19:4–6; cf. Deut. 5:23–33).

A full understanding of the nature and provisions of the suzerainty treaty/covenant will enable you to grasp the difference between this type of covenant and the other major type that God made with his people: the *royal grant* type. Recent research concerning covenant and treaty forms in the ancient Near East has discerned two types of royal grants.[34] In the first type, a beneficent king would often freely bestow certain privileges or benefits to a vassal or servant for faithful and loyal service. In the second, which could be termed a reconfirmation grant/treaty/covenant made by the king or his successor(s), continued compliance with the terms of the original grant was obligatory for the grant to remain in effect in order to be beneficial for the grantee and/or his heirs. As we will see, some effect of the difference between these two types of royal grants may be seen in the Old Testament covenants. A royal grant covenant traditionally contained the following elements: (1)

1. a preamble noting the parties involved;

2. a statement of the covenant's provisions or promises;

3. certain stipulations for the full enjoyment of the benefits of the covenant; and

4. a record of covenant enactment and/or oaths taken while putting the covenant into force. A covenant sign could also accompany the making of the covenant.

Several royal grant types are found within the pages of the Old Testament. The first occurs in God's dealing with Noah (Gen. 9:1–17). In the Noahic covenant, we note the following typical elements:

---

34. Notable examples may be found in the excellent studies by Gordon Johnston: "The 'Unconditional' & 'Conditional' Passages in the Abrahamic Covenant in the Light of Ancient Near Eastern Royal Land Grants & Grant Treaties" (paper presented to the Pentateuch Study Group Section, National Meeting of the Society of Biblical Literature, Boston, 2008); and idem, "'Unconditional' and 'Conditional' Features of the Davidic Covenant in the Light of Ancient Near Eastern Grants and Grant Treaties" (paper presented to the Historical Literature Study Group, Annual Meeting of the Evangelical Theological Society, Providence, RI, 2008).

1. a preamble telling of God's grant to Noah and his sons (Gen. 9:1a);

2. God's provisions for/promises to them (vv. 1b–3, 7);

3. prescribed stipulations (vv. 4–6);

4. covenant enactment (vv. 8–11a) together with a divine oath (v. 11b); and

5. the accompanying sign of the rainbow (vv. 12–17).

Although the grant was made to Noah and his sons, the wide-ranging and perpetual provisions in the covenant indicate that Noah and his sons were the mere representatives of a mankind that was to recognize, appreciate, and enjoy the blessings of a gracious God (v. 17b). The stipulations made it clear that although those who were benefited could fail to appropriate or enjoy God's goodness, the Lord would not revoke the terms of the covenant (cf. vv. 11–17).

It is crucial for the interpreter to grasp the basic distinction between the suzerainty (conditional) and royal grant (unconditional) types of covenants. For only then will he or she come to realize the exceedingly great provisions and promises God has granted to his own. One other formal distinction between these two types of covenants is found in the formulae used in relation to them. Thus in the suzerainty type, the customary formula is "cut a covenant" (e.g., Deut. 5:3), while in the royal grant type verbs such as "set/establish/confirm/make" a covenant are typically found (e.g., Gen. 9:12, 17; 17:2).

Although some have suggested that the Abrahamic covenant was conditional in nature, the evidence strongly suggests that it was unconditional, a royal grant type. God's gracious promises to Abraham were felt even before any formal covenant arrangement (Gen. 12:2–3). What is more, the formal covenant was anticipated in God's promise to Abram to give the land of Canaan to him and his descendants as an everlasting possession (Gen. 12:6–7; 13:14–17), a pledge that was later confirmed in a covenantal sign (Gen. 15:17–19).

It is in Genesis 17, however, that we find the full formal covenant privileges that the Lord bestowed upon Abraham. Here we can see typical elements of the royal grant treaty type: (1) covenant parties (v. 1a); (2) covenant enactment (vv. 2, 7); (3) covenantal provisions/promises (vv. 5–8); (4) stipulations (vv. 1b, 9a); and (5) a threefold covenant sign involving the change of the names of Abram and Sarai to Abraham and Sarah, the rite of circumcision (vv. 9b–14), and the promise of a son for them in their old age. God also bound himself to Abraham through two unchangeable acts: a theophany (Gen. 15:17) and his solemn word—the "I will" of chapter 17. The promises to Abraham were reiterated to him later because of his obedience to God's command (Gen. 22:15–18).

Another royal grant type may be found in 2 Samuel 7:8–16 (cf. 1 Chron. 17:7–14). Here again we find clear evidence of the elements of royal grant type covenant-making: (1) covenant parties (vv. 8, 11); (2) preamble (vv. 8–9); (3) provisions/promises (vv. 8–10, 12–14a, 15–16); (4) covenant enactment (v. 11); and (5) stipulations (v. 14b). Again, the provisions are guaranteed in the unchangeable promise of God himself. As we will note below, the promises to David are reiterated and enlarged upon by several of God's prophets.

Doubtless the grandest of all of the royal grant types is the new covenant (Jer. 31:31–37). Here we also see the typical elements inherent in such covenants: (1) the parties involved (v. 31); (2) covenant provisions (vv. 32–34); (3) covenant enactment (v. 33); and (4) a sign of the covenant (vv. 35–37). The terms or provisions of the new covenant are repeated in Jeremiah 32:36–44, where Jeremiah earlier was instructed to enact a sign of the validity of God's good intensions toward his people by purchasing his cousin's field on the eve of Jerusalem's captivity (Jer. 32:6–15).

As we have seen previously, the culmination of the law and exodus also take place in the new covenant, an agreement that brings together both suzerainty and royal grant covenant types.

Key Chain of Covenants Culminating in the New Covenant

Although both suzerainty and royal grant covenants held distinctive purposes for Israel, it is the latter that particularly directs our attention to the central emphasis of the completed Old Testament canon; for the royal grant covenants contain the Lord's unconditional, gracious promises for believers of all ages. God's promised never again to send a universal flood upon the earth as given in the covenant with Noah. Significant as that covenant and its provisions are, a royal grant-type covenant is a golden thread stitching together the whole scriptural fabric. This is found in the unfolding revelations in the Abrahamic, Davidic, and new covenants. For by these God graciously revealed successively greater promises.

When God instructed Abram to come out of his own country and go to the land he would show him, he promised him great blessings by which all people could eventually be blessed (Gen. 12:1–3). In later encounters, the Lord granted to Abram and his descendants the land of Canaan as their possession in perpetuity (Gen. 12:6–7; 13:14–17). Abram consistently showed his faith and faithfulness to God through a consistent pattern of spiritual growth in his worship practices at each stage of his growing relationship with the Lord (Gen. 12:8–9; 13:18; 22:13–14). When the Lord promised aged Abram a son and heir who would grow into a great number of descendants (Gen. 15:1–5), therefore, it is characteristic of the man to read: "Abram believed the LORD, and he credited it to him as righteousness" (Gen. 15:6). As Ross correctly observes, "Abram accepted the Word of the Lord as reliable and true and acted in accordance with it; consequently the Lord declared Abram righteous and therefore acceptable."[35] This promise to Abraham was subsequently reinforced by a theophany, which served as a sign guaranteeing the fulfillment of God's Word (Gen. 15:17–21).

In the details of the covenant in Genesis 17, however, elements of conditionality may be seen, for it is stipulated that Abraham must continue in faithfulness to Yahweh and his heirs must do so also (vv. 2, 9). Moreover, the rite of circumcision was obligatory for all male members (vv. 10–11). Hence, some have suggested that Genesis 17 is an example of the second type of royal grant arrangement. It must not be forgotten, however, that the promises in the original details of the Abrahamic covenant were not made by an earthly ruler, but by God whose word and faithfulness are certain (Ps. 100:5; 119:89–90).[36] Indeed, the Lord assures Abraham that

---

35. Allen P. Ross, *Creation and Blessing* (Grand Rapids: Baker, 1988), 310. Abram's example of living out his active fellowship with the living God lies behind the prophetic dictum in Habakkuk 2:4, which is taken up and commented upon by Paul (Rom. 1:17; Gal. 3:11) and the writer to the Hebrews (Heb. 10:35–39). The force of the Greek text in Paul's writings underscores the fact that those who are justified by faith are those who find and experience true life. See further Richard D. Patterson, *Nahum, Habakkuk, Zephaniah* (Chicago: Moody, 1991), 219–23; reprint edition, Biblical Studies Press, 2003, 200–3.

36. See the full discussions in David Noel Freedman, "Divine Commitment and Human Obligation," *Int* 18 (1964), 419–31; and Bruce K. Waltke," The Phenomenon of

the covenant he is making with him is an "everlasting covenant between me and your descendants after you for the generations to come, to be your God and your descendants after you" (Gen. 17:7). Not only was the land of Canaan to belong to the family of Abraham, but God's blessings upon Abraham would be beneficial to many people (cf. Gen. 12:2; 22:17–18). As Kaiser correctly observes, "The . . . climactic element in the promise was that Abraham and each successive son of promise were to be the source of blessing: indeed, they were to be the touchstone of blessing to all other peoples."[37] Although some descendants might alienate themselves from the blessings of the covenant (Gen. 17:14), the covenant would remain inviolable.[38]

That the Abrahamic covenant did continue through Abraham's heirs is immediately apparent. For God promised that the covenant would pass on directly to Isaac (Gen. 17:19). This, in turn, becomes part of a key theme found in many places in the Old Testament. Indeed, the God of Abraham became the God of Isaac (Gen. 26:1–6) and the God of Abraham and Isaac became the God of Jacob (Gen. 28:10–15; 31:42; 32:9). Thereafter, the promises inherent in the Abrahamic covenant could be symbolized by the phrase, "The God of Abraham and Isaac and Jacob" (Gen. 50:24; Exod. 3:6, 15, 18; 4:5; 6:8; 32:15; Lev. 26:42; Deut. 6:10; 9:5; 30:20; 34:4; 1 Kings 18:36; 2 Kings 13:23; Ps. 105:8–11; Jer. 33:26).

It is imperative, therefore, for the interpreter to see both the perpetuity and inviolability of the Abrahamic covenant. For its remembrance continued down into New Testament times, where applications of its further benefits were made by Jesus (Matt. 22:32); the virgin Mary (Luke 1:55); John the Baptist's father Zechariah (Luke 1:72–75); Stephen (Acts 7:30–32); and Paul (Gal. 3:29).

Although the Abrahamic covenant was to remain in effect in perpetuity, it was channeled through a specific heir—King David (2 Sam. 7:11–16; 1 Chron. 17:10–14). Through the prophet Nathan God gave words of assurance reminiscent of the Abrahamic covenant that he would establish David's line and kingdom as an everlasting reality (2 Sam. 7:16). In so

---

Conditionality within Unconditional Covenants, " in *Israel's Apostasy and Restoration*, ed. Avraham Gileadi (Grand Rapids: Baker, 1988), 123–39.

37. Walter C. Kaiser Jr., *Toward an Old Testament Theology* (Grand Rapids: Zondervan, 1978), 91.

38. As we shall note below, the same condition is found in the Davidic covenant.

doing, the Lord declared that David's heir would enjoy a filial relationship with God.

That David understood that his covenant with God would extend into the future is certain in his reaction to God's promise: "You have spoken concerning the future of the house of your servant" (2 Sam. 7:19; cf. vv. 27–29). David goes on to remark, "And this is a revelation [or instruction/ law] for mankind, LORD God" (v. 19b; HCSB). To that effect, Kaiser notes eight instances of wordings that are common to the Abrahamic and Davidic covenants and then suggests that this was a "Charter for Humanity."[39] David appears to agree with such an idea, for at a later time he would declare his understanding of the covenant to be an everlasting one:

> Is not my house right with God?
> Has he not made with me an everlasting covenant,
> arranged and secured in every part? (2 Sam. 23:5)

The psalmist also recognizes the continuance of the Davidic covenant by citing God as saying:

> I will maintain my love to him forever,
> and my covenant with him will never fail.
> I will establish his line forever,
> his throne as long as the heavens endure. . . .
>
> Once for all, I have sworn by my holiness—
> and I will not lie to David—
> that his line will continue forever
> and his throne endure before me like the sun;
> it will be established forever like the moon,
> the faithful witness in the sky. (Ps. 89:28–29, 35–37)

Like the Abrahamic covenant, benefits of the Davidic covenant could be forfeited, yet the covenant itself would remain in force (Ps. 89:30–34). Many of David's royal heirs would fail as would the nation they ruled, but ultimately the divine promise would prevail. It would appear, then,

---

39. Kaiser, *Old Testament Theology*, 152–55.

that in accordance with an ancient promise God would provide a royal heir through the line of Judah (Gen. 49:10), Jacob's son and a descendant in the line of Abraham. The promises and provisions in the Abrahamic covenant thus find a distinct relationship to the Davidic covenant. As we have noted, the Abrahamic covenant remained in effect, but this added provision to it provided a distinct linkage with the Davidic covenant. As Kaiser observes, "Thus the ancient plan of God would continue, only now it would involve a king and a kingdom. Such a blessing would also involve the future of all mankind."[40]

The ancient Abrahamic covenant, now channeled through the line of David, Judah's heir, was yet to be wedded to another all-embracing covenant. We have noted previously that the themes of the Law and the exodus event find their culmination in the new covenant (Jer. 31:31–37). The perceptive interpreter has probably noticed that these themes were also linked to the theme of covenant earlier (e.g., Exod. 19:3–6; Deut. 6:1–22). It is significant to note that Israel's deliverance out of Egypt and the subsequent giving of the Mosaic covenant/Law are implicitly linked with the Abrahamic covenant in the term "house of Jacob" (Exod. 19:3). Therefore, it comes as no surprise to see that all of the above themes that we have studied come together under one grand new covenant.

The new covenant, however, is not limited to Jeremiah 31:31–37. Besides the applicability of Jeremiah 32 to the provisions in the new covenant, there are other passages that provide further information.[41] In Jeremiah 33:14–26, the Lord's promises in the new covenant to include the terms and provisions of the Davidic covenant. In words reminiscent of the fixed perpetuity found in Jeremiah 31:35–37,

> This is what the LORD says: "If I have not established my covenant with day and night and the fixed laws of heaven and earth, then I will reject the descendants of Jacob and David my servant and will not choose one of his sons to rule over the descendants of Abraham, Isaac, and Jacob." (Jer. 33:25–26)

---

40. Ibid, 155.
41. Aaron Kligerman, *Old Testament Messianic Prophecy* (Grand Rapids: Zondervan, 1957), 83, observes that "[t]he New Covenant is referred to no less than seven times in Isaiah."

Here we see the amplification of the prophecies in Jeremiah 32 that mentioned the return of the people in a new exodus as part of the guarantees in the new covenant (cf. Jer. 32:36–41; 33:6–9). We also note the combining of the promises in the new covenant with the covenants made with Abraham and David.

Ezekiel likewise prophesies regarding a new exodus for God's people (Ezek. 34:11–14) and regarding the role of David's heir (vv. 22–24), as well as the establishing of a new covenant with Israel (vv. 25–30). God promises that in connection with the new covenant he will give Israel "a new heart and put a new spirit in you" (Ezek. 36:26) in order that they will be able to keep his laws (vv. 27–29; cf. Jer. 31:33–34). All of this comes together most clearly in Ezekiel 37. In this passage, Ezekiel prophesies that in the days of the new covenant there will be a new exodus (v. 21) and return to the land (vv. 22–23) in fulfillment of the promises in the Abrahamic covenant (v. 25). Moreover, as in the Davidic covenant David's heir will rule over God's people (vv. 24–25) and "they will follow my laws and be careful to keep my decrees" (v. 24). Then they will enjoy everlasting gladness of life and worship in God's presence forever (vv. 26–27).

Just as the law and the exodus event find their culmination in the new covenant, so also does the covenant concept. Not only does the Abrahamic covenant remain in effect with its provisions for blessings for all of God's people, but the principles of the Sinai covenant will be lived out from the heart of redeemed new covenant believers (Ezek. 37:21 23). In accordance with the provisions of the Davidic covenant, God's people will once again live in the land, as was promised in the Abrahamic covenant, where the king who is David's heir now rules (v. 25). The new covenant is also called a "covenant of peace" (Isa. 54:10; Ezek. 34:25). In accordance with its name it will be a time of great universal peace (cf. Isa. 2:2–4; Ezek. 37:26) and security (Ezek. 34:27), and God's people will live in fellowship with God (Jer. 31:34; Ezek. 37:23) and enjoy his blessings (Isa. 61:8–9) forever (Ezek. 27:26). Here we see the outworking of God's plan for humanity as expressed in the Abrahamic covenant (Gen. 12:3).

Truly, then, the new covenant is the capstone of all the previous covenants, as well as the culmination of the provisions in the Law and the principle of redemption resident in the exodus event. Yet even here, as we will see below, there are further features to examine, which will make the new covenant the stepping stone to the New Testament revelation.

3.2. MAJOR BIBLICAL COVENANTS			
COVENANT	**FUNCTION**	**TYPE**	**CONTENT**
Noahic	Universal	Royal grant	No more universal flood
Abrahamic	Foundational	Royal grant	Land, seed, blessing
Mosaic	Conditional	Suzerain treaty	Blessings and curses
Davidic	Royal, messianic	Royal grant	Built on Abrahamic covenant
New	Culmination	Royal grant	Predicted by Prophets

Applicability of the Covenants

Just what significance do covenants have for today's believers? The theological principles that undergird the law as found in the conditional Mosaic (or Sinai) covenant still have validity today. This is because they have been transmitted by way of the new covenant into the teachings of the New Testament. Moreover, Jesus declared that he came to fulfill the law (Matt. 5:17). By this he meant that in himself the law and Mosaic covenant find their full meaning. Its principles therefore become realized because today's believers have been taken into union with Christ, enabling them by the power of the indwelling Christ to live in accordance with God's timeless standards (cf. John 17:22–23; Gal. 2:20; Col. 1:27).

As for the royal grant type of unconditional covenants, all people enjoy the provisions of the Noahic covenant in that they may be assured that God will not allow a worldwide flood to again cover the earth. The Abrahamic covenant remains in effect and has been incorporated into the new covenant; the same is true for the Davidic covenant. Thus both the Abrahamic and Davidic covenants find their development and culmination in the new covenant due to God's plan, which was progressively revealed across the centuries.

It is the new covenant, therefore, that brings together the essential provisions of the earlier covenants by incorporating their major planks into its finished construction. The new covenant is already in effect because of the finished work of Jesus Christ (Matt. 26:27–29; 2 Cor. 3:6; Hebrews 8). This does not mean, however, that all of the terms of the new covenant are completely fulfilled. Rather, some of its provisions, such as the rule of David's heir over a restored Israel, remain unfulfilled. Therefore, we may think of the new covenant as fulfilled in the New Testament revelation in the sense of being made fuller even though all of its provisions have not been totally met or brought to completion. Building on the suggestion of George Ladd, R. T. France caught the significance of this by calling a prediction in the new covenant termed "fulfilled" in the New Testament a "fulfillment without consummation."[42] The point, then, is that Christ understood that the terms of the New Testament were being fulfilled through his ministry, which in turn inaugurated the last days (cf. 1 Tim. 4:1–2; Heb. 1:1–2; 1 Pet. 1:18–20; 1 John 2:18).

In every way, therefore, the message of the covenants is applicable to Christian living. For it reminds us of the need for faithful and obedient service (cf. Gen. 22:15–18) and the necessity of living holy and righteous lives (Gen. 17:1; Lev. 19:1; Deut. 5:6–21; 6:1–3) before the Lord with all our heart (1 Kings 2:1–4). As embedded in the new covenant, the promises, provisions, and theological truths inherent in the covenants find their richest relevance in Christ's provisions for the believer (Gal. 2:20). The blessings that the believer now enjoys as well as those to which he looks forward in the culmination of the eschatological era should also serve as a missionary imperative for sharing the gospel with a needy and lost world (2 Cor. 5:16–20).

---

42. See R. T. France, *Jesus and the Old Testament* (London: Tyndale, 1971), 162.

GUIDELINES FOR UNDERSTANDING
THE OLD TESTAMENT COVENANTS

1. Determine whether the covenant under consideration is conditional or unconditional.

2. Note the primary provisions within the covenant.

3. Take particular notice of the progressive revelation attached to the unconditional covenants, especially those with Abraham and David as incorporated in the new covenant.

4. Consider the role of the new covenant as preparation for the New Testament.

5. Make proper application of the theological principles in the covenants to today's Christian living.

COORDINATING OLD TESTAMENT THEMES

Rule of God and the Concept of Messiah

Although we have featured three primary themes that serve as important focal points for understanding the Old Testament revelation, it must not be forgotten that the most important figure and force in the Old Testament is God. As the Creator and Ruler of nature, as Job recognized long ago (Job 38–41; cf. Ps. 104:1–30), he is also the Ruler of mankind's history and the one who brings it to its final consummation (Isa. 46:10).

A corollary to this truth is the theme of God's plan through his Anointed, the coming Messiah. Although the presence of messianic themes has been the subject of great debate, we conclude with Jewish tradition that there was an expanding message concerning a Messiah during

Old Testament times.[43] Certainly Daniel's reference to the Messiah the Ruler (Dan. 9:25) establishes the reality of the messianic concept toward the end of the Old Testament canon. Indeed, the hope of a coming king who would deliver Israel from its enemies and establish a kingdom over which he would rule in righteousness runs through the Old Testament and was an increasingly vivid hope in Israel. To be sure, kings (2 Sam. 5:6), priests (Exod. 29:7; Lev. 7:36), and prophets (1 Kgs. 19:16) were anointed in ancient Israel, but "the chief element in the conception of the Messiah in the OT is that of the king."[44]

Although many have attempted to show that the idea of an anointed king in Israel was derived from the surrounding nations (cf. Deut. 17:14), the existence of the concept of a royal kingship from the early period of Israel's history (Gen. 49:10) and its persistence and growth throughout Israel's history are capable of a better understanding. Thus Van Groningen remarks, "Messianic revelation is, to sum up, at the very heart of God's covenantal self-revelation. It is the central strand of the written record of that revelation of covenantal relationship between the sovereign God and his created, redeemed, and restored viceregents."[45]

If, then, the messianic ideal is part of God's plan for the outworking of earth's history, one would expect a gradual unfolding of that plan to be revealed. Although the term "Messiah" may not always be present, such a concept may be found in the early days of man's history. Thus Genesis 3:15 has long been understood as a proto-messianic prophecy:

> And I will put enmity
> between you and the woman,
> and between your offspring and hers;
> he will crush your head,
> and you will strike his heel.

---

43. E.g., S. H. Levey, *The Messiah: An Aramaic Interpretation, The Messianic Exegesis of the Targum*, Monographs of the Hebrew Union College 2 (Cincinnati: Hebrew Union College Press, 1974); Herbert W. Bateman IV, Gordon H. Johnston, and Darrell L. Bock, *Jesus the Messiah* (Grand Rapids: Kregel, 2011).

44. James Crichton, "Messiah," in *The International Standard Bible Encyclopedia*, ed. James Orr (Grand Rapids: Eerdmans, 1952), 2040.

45. Gerard Van Groningen, *Messianic Revelation in the Old Testament* (Grand Rapids: Baker, 1990), 72.

Kenneth Mathews observes, "Our passage provides for the mature reflection that points to Christ as the vindicator of the woman (cf. Rom 16:20). There may be an allusion to our passage in Gal 4:4, which speaks of God's Son as 'born of a woman.' Specifically, Paul identified Christ as the 'seed' ultimately intended in the promissory blessing to Abraham (Gal 3:16), and Abraham's believing offspring include the church (Rom. 4:13, 16–18; Gal 3:8)."[46] The early concept of a coming king/ruler is also found in Numbers 24:22:

> I see him, but not now;
> I behold him, but not near.
> A star will come out of Jacob;
> a scepter will rise out of Israel.

In another early passage, the king was to be the one whom God would choose (Deut. 17:15).

The role of a coming king/Messiah became a prominent theme in the first millennium B.C. It is found in many of the Psalms (e.g., Pss. 2:2, 4–7; 89:20–37; 110:1–2)[47] and especially in the prophets (e.g., Isa. 7:13–17; 9:6–7; 11:1–9; 41:8–20; 42:1–7; 52:13–53:12; 61:1–3; Jer. 23:5–7; 33:15–18; Ezek. 34:20–31; 37:20–28; Dan. 7:13–14; 9:25–26; Zech. 12:10–14). Giving God his rightful place in the Scriptures is basic to proper interpretation. Seeing his plan to sum up all things in his sent one, the Messiah, is not only vital to understanding the Old Testament but also for viewing the Old Testament as preparation for the New Testament revelation.

Relation of God and of the Messiah to the Law, the Exodus, and the Covenants

The presence of the Lord permeates the Old Testament. It is he who is also the sovereign Ruler and providential Overseer of the themes of law, exodus, and covenant in the Old Testament. Thus the Lord is the author of the Law, which he designed not only for the orderly regulating of society

---

46. Kenneth A. Mathews, *Genesis 1–11:26*, NAC (Nashville: B & H, 1996), 247–48.
47. See Gerald H. Wilson, "Psalms and Psalter: Paradigm for Biblical Theology," in *Biblical Theology: Retrospect and Prospect*, ed. Scott J. Hafemann (Downers Grove: InterVarsity, 2002), 100–10.

but for mankind's individual good (Exod. 19:5; 20:22–23:19; Num. 27:1–30:16; Deut. 5:32–6:2; 6:3–30:10).

He is the author of man's redemption as well, having not only provided the initial means for fallen humanity's deliverance from sin and restoration to the Lord's favor (Gen. 3:21; cf. 4:2–4; 8:20–22) but the maintenance of fellowship with himself through the sacrificial system, as detailed particularly in the Levitical legislation. As Israel's Redeemer, God delivered his people out of Egypt (e.g., Exod. 19:4; 20:2); led them on their journey from Egypt to Canaan (Exod. 40:36–38; Num. 10:11; 33:50; Josh. 1:1–3:17); and settled them in the Promised Land (Josh. 21:43–45). Not only was God Israel's national liberator but the Redeemer of each believing Israelite (cf. Job 19:23–27, Jer. 31.31–34).

It was God who authored and entered into covenants with his people, whether in terms of a conditional covenant (Exod. 19:3; Deut. 6:13–25) or as a freely given unconditional grant in perpetuity (e.g., Gen. 9:12–17; 17:1–8; 2 Sam. 7:11–16; Ps. 89:27–19:23–27; Jeremiah 29, 35–37; Isa. 54:10; Jer. 31:31–37; 33:13–22; Ezek. 34:23–31; 37:20–27).

An important feature of God's covenantal relationship with Israel is the person of the Messiah. The fulfillment of the promises inherent in the Abrahamic covenant as expanded in the prophecy concerning the line of Judah (Gen. 49:10) became more clearly identified in terms of the Davidic covenant. It would be David's heir *par excellence* who as the Servant of the Lord would assume the throne of the promised kingdom (Jer. 23:5–7). As the prophesied coming king (cf. Gen. 49:10 with Ezek. 21:27), he will also constitute the central figure of the new covenant through which God's plan of the ages to bring in everlasting peace and righteousness will be realized (Isa. 11:1–9; Jer. 33:15–16; Ezek. 34:25–31; 37:22–28; Mic. 4:1–5).

Roll of the Messiah in the New Covenant

The plan of God to rule through the Messiah is a significant feature of the new covenant. As we have seen, the themes of law, exodus, and covenant all come to their climax in the new covenant. We have also noted that the promised Messiah plays the key role in the realization of the new covenant. Therefore, it may be expected that he may bear some relation to those themes that find their culmination in it.

The law prescribed how a person should live before a holy God. In the coming Messiah, people would find their supreme example of godly living (Isa. 42:1–7). The means for coming into a right relationship with God symbolized in the sacrificial system receive their effective power in the Messiah, the mediator of the new covenant. Vern Poythress suggests that the sacrificial system was but a shadow of the reality of the coming Messiah, Jesus Christ:

The shadow was not itself the reality, but a pointer to Christ who was the reality. Yet the shadow was also like the reality. And the shadow even brought the reality to bear on people in the Old Testament. As they looked ahead through the shadows, longing for something better, they took hold of the promises of God that he would send the Messiah. The promises were given not only verbally but symbolically, through the very organization of the tabernacle and its sacrifices.[48]

An example is the symbolism of the Day of Atonement, by which Israel's sins could be confessed and forgiven (Lev. 16:1). The ritual connected with the Day of Atonement involved two goats. One was slain "for the sin offering of the people" (Lev. 16:15). Then Aaron was to "lay both hands on the head of the live goat and confess over it the wickedness and rebellion of the Israelites—all their sins—and put them on the goat's head" (v. 21). The goat was released into the wilderness, symbolizing the removal of people's sin: "As the sacrifice of the first goat signified the means of reconciliation with God, namely, by the death and the sprinkled blood of a vicarious offering, so the dismissal of the second goat typified the effect of the expiation in the removal of the sin from the presence of the holy God. Together these two features of the sin offering indicate the full meaning of atonement."[49] That which was symbolized in the worship practice of the Day of Atonement would become realized in the Messiah, the mediator of the new covenant; for he would suffer death for the people's sin (Isa. 52:13–53:12) yet be victorious over it (Ps. 16:8–11; cf. Acts 2:25–35; Hos. 13:14).

Israel's exodus from Egypt demonstrated that God himself could only accomplish its deliverance. A helpless Israel needed a redeemer. Its deliverance on the night of Passover was therefore evidence of the power and sovereign grace of God. As we have seen, the theological principle underlying the exodus event was that of redemption. When Israel lived in

---

48. Vern S. Poythress, *The Shadow of Christ in the Law of Moses* (Phillipsburg, NJ: Presbyterian & Reformed, 1991), 11.
49. Charles R. Erdman, *The Book of Leviticus* (New York: Revell, 1951), 75.

slavery in Egypt, it was God who redeemed his people and brought them for himself. This reality was memorialized in the observance of the Passover. Here, too, the theme of Messiah would find its ultimate fulfillment. "The Old Testament observance of the Passover not only looked back to a previous redemption from bondage but also looked forward to the coming of the Lamb of God who would deliver Israel from bondage to sin. . . . As the Passover brought an enslaved people into a new life of liberty and rest, so Christ anticipated that through His death believers would be brought into a new life of peace and rest."[50]

We have stressed repeatedly the central significance of the new covenant as the culmination of the Law and exodus event. The same is true of God's covenants with Israel. Here again the importance of God's redeeming work is felt, for under the terms of the new covenant the Lord will again redeem his people from slavery in foreign lands (cf. Isa. 61:3, 11-12). The role of the Messiah is particularly significant here. He who was destined to be Israel's restorer (Isa. 49:5) would become its Redeemer. Of him it is prophesied:

> The Spirit of the Sovereign LORD is on me,
> because the LORD has anointed me
> to preach good news to the poor.
> He has sent me to bind up the brokenhearted,
> to proclaim freedom for the captives
> and release from darkness for the prisoners,
> to proclaim the year of the LORD'S favor
> and the day of vengeance of our God
> to comfort all who mourn,
> and provide for those who grieve in Zion. (Isa. 61:1–3)[51]

In accordance with the terms of the new covenant, therefore, the Messiah would be a royal Redeemer. He will restore and comfort his people, defeat all his foes (Zech. 14:1–5) and establish his universal kingdom (Dan. 7:13–14; cf. Ps. 2:7–9; 110:1–2).

---

50. J. Dwight Pentecost, *The Words and Works of Jesus Christ* (Grand Rapids: Zondervan, 1981), 425. It is doubtless no coincidence that Jesus' atoning sacrifice came at the height of the Passover season (Luke 22:7–8; 1 Cor. 5:7).
51. Note Christ's application of Isaiah 61:1–2a to his earthly ministry (Luke 4:18–19).

It is important, then, for the biblical interpreter to note that his or her starting point is crucial for the understanding of the Scriptures. When we approach the Bible as God's authoritative revelation and make God's disclosure of his person and works the central feature of our research, we are in a position to grasp his overall design of the ages.[52] It is by giving God his rightful place of sovereignty that many otherwise difficult texts take on proper perspective. Rather than traveling the dark path of doubt, as critics so often have done, we can appreciate a given text in the light of God's plans.

Relation of Old Testament Messianism to the New Testament

The climax of God's plan for the consummation of earth's history as contained in the new covenant, whose central figure is the Messiah, provides the grand perspective for viewing the New Testament revelation. It is the person and work of Messiah in terms of the new covenant which serves to prepare New Testament readers for the person and work of Jesus Christ.

In the New Testament, Jesus Christ is declared to be the long-expected Messiah. This is seen from the very onset. Thus the angel announced to the virgin Mary that Jesus "will reign over the house of Jacob forever; his kingdom will never end" (Luke 1:33). John the Baptist's father Zechariah declared that God "has raised up a horn of salvation for us in the house of his servant David . . . to show mercy to our fathers and to remember his holy covenant, the oath he swore to our father Abraham" (Luke 1:69–73). The subsequent New Testament revelation reinforces that understanding repeatedly (e.g., John 1:41; Rev. 11:15). Christ is indeed the central figure of the New Testament revelation in fulfillment of God's plan for the redemption and eternal welfare of humankind, as well as the consummation of all things (Col. 1:15–20). As the writer of Hebrew declares,

> In the past God spoke to our forefathers through the prophets at many times and in various ways, but in these last days he has spoken to us by his Son, whom he appointed heir of all things and through whom he made the universe. The Son is the radiance of God's glory and the exact

---

52. Vern S. Poythress, *God-Centered Biblical Interpretation* (Phillipsburg, NJ: Presbyterian & Reformed, 1999), 10, remarks, "People can do all kinds of crazy things with the Bible. But if we would profit spiritually, we must reckon with what God himself requires."

representation of his being, sustaining all things by his powerful word. After he had provided purification for sins, he sat down at the right hand of the Majesty in heaven. (Heb. 1:1–3)

In accordance with the prophesied promise of the new covenant of an inward reality that guarantees the knowledge of God and proper conduct before him, New Testament believers have been taken into living union with the risen Christ (Gal. 2:20; Ezek. 2:19–22): "A believer is 'in Christ' by virtue of being united to Him by faith; and through such union with Him he shares in His saving power and comes under His sovereign authority. . . . Thus it may be said both that Christ is in believers and that they are in Him."[53]

As those who have entered into a new relation under terms of the new covenant, today's believers have the double assurance that because the principles of God's law are written within them (Jer. 31:33–34), and because Christ in whom the Law finds its fulfillment has taken them into union with himself, they have the ability to live in accordance with the principles of God's high moral standards. What is more, as those united to Christ they have the privilege of being his ambassadors to those who are yet in bondage to sin (2 Cor. 5:17–21). Like Jesus' disciples whom he commissioned and sent out to carry on the message of redemption (John 20:21–22), we are to "go and make disciples of all nations" (Matt. 28:19). Also like Jesus' original followers, we are to go in the power of the Holy Spirit (1 Cor. 2:1–5, 12–13; 2 Cor. 3:1–6; cf. Ezek. 36:26).

Righteousness and Faith

One important guiding principle for the way in which we today ought to read the Old Testament is the study of how the New Testament writers themselves read the Hebrew Scriptures. If we want to be biblical in our hermeneutical practice, there is no better place to look than the hermeneutical approach of the biblical writers themselves. As we do so, we discover, as mentioned, the significance of the Old Testament concepts of law, exodus, and covenant, and the relation these concepts sustain with

---

53. I. Howard Marshall, *The Work of Christ* (Grand Rapids: Zondervan, 1969), 85–86. For helpful treatments of the doctrine of union with Christ, see A. H. Strong, *Systematic Theology* (Philadelphia: Judson, 1954), 793–809; Wayne Grudem, *Systematic Theology* (Grand Rapids: Zondervan, 1994), 840–50.

the expectation of a Messiah fulfilled in the person and work of the Lord Jesus Christ.

In particular, it appears that the New Testament writers centered their discussion on the gospel defining the proper attainment of righteousness through faith. This is nowhere clearer than in Paul's preface to his letter to the Romans, where the apostle refers at the very outset to "the gospel of God—the gospel he promised beforehand through his prophets in the Holy Scriptures regarding his Son . . . Jesus Christ our Lord" (Rom. 1:1–4). What is more, at the end of this preface Paul specifically cites the prophet Habakkuk: "For in this gospel a righteousness from God is revealed, a righteousness that is from faith[fulness] to faith, just as it is written: 'The righteous will live by faith'" (Rom. 1:17; cf. Hab. 2:4).

Thus Paul found the essence of his gospel—which in fact was *God's* gospel—already revealed and proclaimed in the Old Testament prophetic Scriptures. Righteousness—a right standing before God—came through faith "apart from law," a reality "to which the Law and the Prophets testify" (Rom. 3:21). Reaching back even farther than the prophet Habakkuk, Paul found the gospel of righteousness through faith already in the Law—in the first book of the Pentateuch, the book of Genesis. "What does the Scripture say? 'Abraham believed God, and it was credited to him as righteousness'" (Rom. 4:3; see also Gal. 3:6; cf. Gen. 15:6). Thus Paul emphatically stated that the Law and the Prophets agreed: a right standing before God could only be attained by faith, not by human works.

This faith, importantly, is to be directed to God's Messiah, Jesus Christ. Truly understood, the Law pointed to him. Rather than being a mere collection of legal requirements, the Law's ultimate orientation was prophetic. Thus not only the Prophets, but also the Law anticipated the coming of the Messiah and the redemption provided by his substitutionary atoning sacrifice. As Paul writes,

> This righteousness from God comes through faith in Jesus Christ to all who believe. There is no difference, for all have sinned and fall short of the glory of God, and are justified freely by his grace through the redemption that came by Christ Jesus. God presented him as a sacrifice of atonement, through faith in his blood (Rom. 3:23–25).

This provision of salvation for humanity in and through the atoning sacrifice of his Son, in turn, allowed God to be both righteous and justify those who had no righteousness in themselves: "he did it to demonstrate his justice at the present time, so as to be just and the one who justifies those who have faith in Jesus" (Rom. 3:26). This need for salvation through faith in Christ apart from human works also unites God's chosen people, Israel, and non-Jews (Gentiles)—"for all have sinned and fall short of the glory of God." Thus the stage is set for the creation, in Christ, of a new body of believers, the church, made up of believing Jews and Gentiles, an entity Paul elsewhere calls the "body of Christ" (see, e.g., Eph. 3:6; 5:23, 29–30).

GUIDELINES FOR UNDERSTANDING THE RELEVANCE OF MESSIANISM

1. Determine which passages contain a messianic relevance. Look for relevant terminology or the presence of thematic connections with biblical references to the Messiah.

2. Evaluate the passage's contribution to God's plan in accordance with the coming of Messiah under the terms of the new covenant.

3. Note the distinctive forms of the Messiah's ministry and compare them to the earthly ministry of Jesus.

4. Avoid the temptation to be overzealous with finding the pre-incarnate presence of Christ in the Old Testament, such as in every place the term "the angel of the Lord" occurs.

KEY WORDS

Covenant: an agreement between two parties presented either as the will or intentions of a superior to an inferior or an agreement between equals.

Exodus event: historical details concerning God's deliverance of the Hebrews out of Egypt, his guidance of them through the wilderness, and eventual bringing them into the Promised Land.

Law: in the Bible an expression of God's will and moral standards for human conduct delivered as instructional material.

Messiah: God's promised anointed divine representative who would deliver his people and rule as king in earth's final state.

New covenant: in Old Testament prophesies, God's future bestowal of blessings upon his redeemed people in the Promised Land.

Old Testament canon: that body of writings accepted as reflecting divine inspiration and authority.

Royal grant treaty: privileges or benefits granted by a king to a vassal or servant for faithful and loyal service.

Suzerainty treaty: an agreement whereby the enacting party imposes covenant stipulations upon a vassal.

STUDY QUESTIONS

1. What are the three parts of Old Testament revelation?
2. Genesis contains the major story of the Scripture as a whole. What is this story that needs to be kept in mind in the interpretation of the whole Old Testament revelation?
3. What are the three primary themes that form the basic focal point of the Old Testament? What principles do they embody?
4. What are the traditional ways to classify the laws? What better way might there be to view the law which draws it together with the two other focal themes of the Old Testament?
5. How does Jeremiah 31:31–34 help us understand that the law, though containing external commands to be obeyed, embodies deeper theological principles?
6. What is the principle underlying a given commandment listed as one of the Ten Commandments?
7. What are the guidelines for applying the Old Testament law?
8. How is the exodus motif included in the new covenant?
9. What are the guidelines for understanding the exodus?
10. How can the relationship between the various covenants be diagrammed?
11. What are the guidelines for understanding Old Testament covenants?
12. What are the coordinating themes of Old Testament revelation? Explain their relevance, giving particular attention to the role of the Messiah to the interpretation of the Bible as a whole.

ASSIGNMENTS

1. As noted, the Old Testament law code was designed to remind God's chosen and redeemed people that they were to be a holy, just, and morally responsible people before God. Moreover, these laws were to be treated as expressions of the high moral standards of Israel's sovereign and holy God. Based upon these principles, write a short exposition of Deuteronomy 6:1–9, a passage which contains the well-known *Shema* of Israel.

2. Discuss the relevance of the first two commandments in Exodus 20:2–6 to Christian living. What other biblical theme is also of crucial importance as seen in the setting and context of the original commandments?

3. As demonstrated, the exodus motif is of crucial significance to the development and understanding of the biblical revelation. Explain the relevance of this theme to the Christian's standing and experience before God. What prominent attribute of God is central in the narrative of the original exodus event and its subsequent expressions?

4. Distinguish the basic differences between suzerainty and royal grant treaty types. How is such information important to the understanding of the biblical presentation of the covenants?

5. Based upon the information in this chapter, discuss the importance of the new covenant to the basic Old Testament themes of law, exodus, and covenant. How is this applicable to normal Christian living?

6. Identify key verses and/or passages in each of the three sections of the Old Testament—Torah, Prophets, and Writings—concerning the coming of the Messiah.

7. Write a short summary of the role of the Messiah to each of the basic themes of the Old Testament: law, exodus, and covenant. How does all of this relate to the New Testament revelation concerning Jesus Christ and to vital Christian living?

8. Explain the ramifications of Paul's teachings regarding the gospel and the doctrines of righteousness and faith.

CHAPTER BIBLIOGRAPHY

Beckwith, Roger T. "The Canon of the Old Testament." In *The Origin of the Bible*. Edited by Philip Wesley Comfort. Wheaton: Tyndale, 2003.

_____. "Formation of the Hebrew Bible." Pp. 39–86 in *Mikra*. Edited by Martin Jan Mulder. Philadelphia: Fortress, 1988. Repr. Peabody, MA: 2004.

Blenkinsopp, Joseph. *Wisdom and Law in the Old Testament*. Rev. ed. Oxford: Oxford University Press, 1995.

Clements, Ronald E. "Law and Promise." In *The Flowering of Old Testament Theology*. Edited by Ben C. Ollenburger, Elmer A. Martens and Gerhard F. Hasel. Winona Lake, IN: Eisenbrauns, 1992.

Eichrodt, Walther. *Old Testament Theology*. Translated by J. A. Baker. Philadelphia: Fortress, 1961.

Fairbairn, Patrick. *The Revelation of Law in Scripture*. Winona Lake, IN: Alpha, 1979.

Freedman, David N. "The Song of the Sea." Pp. 179–86 in *Pottery, Poetry, and Prophecy*. Winona Lake, IN: Eisenbrauns, 1980.

Goswell, Greg. "The Order of the Books in the Hebrew Bible." *JETS* 52 (2009): 449–66.

_____. "The Order of the Books in the Greek Old Testament." *JETS* 51 (2008): 673–88

Kaiser, Walter C. Jr. *Toward an Old Testament Theology*. Grand Rapids: Zondervan, 1978.

Kitchen, Kenneth A. *On the Reliability of the Old Testament*. Grand Rapids: Eerdmans, 2003.

Kligerman, Aaron. *Old Testament Messianic Prophecy*. Grand Rapids: Zondervan, 1957.

Pao, David W. *Acts and the Isaianic New Exodus*. Grand Rapids: Baker, 2000.

Patterson, Richard D. "The Song of Redemption." *WTJ* 57 (1995): 453–61.

_____. "Victory at Sea: Prose and Poetry in Exodus 14–15." *BibSac* 161 (2004): 42–54.

Patterson, Richard D. and Michael E. Travers. "Contours of the Exodus Motif in Jesus' Earthly Ministry." *WTJ* 66 (2004): 25–47.

Poythress, Vern S. *The Shadow of Christ in the Law of Moses.* Phillipsburg, NJ: Presbyterian & Reformed, 1991.

Robertson, O. Palmer. *The Christ of the Prophets.* Phillipsburg, NJ: Presbyterian & Reformed, 2004.

Schreiner, Thomas R. *The Law & Its Fulfillment.* Grand Rapids: Baker, 1993.

Van Groningen, Gerard. *Messianic Revelation in the Old Testament.* Grand Rapids: Baker, 1990.

Von Rad, Gerhard. *Old Testament Theology.* Translated by D. M. G. Stalker. New York: Harper & Row, 1962.

Watts, James W. *Reading Law: The Rhetorical Shaping of the Pentateuch.* Sheffield: Sheffield Academic Press, 1999.

Wegner, Paul D. Pp. 101–18 in *The Journey from Texts to Translations.* Grand Rapids: Baker, 1999.

CHAPTER 4 OBJECTIVES

1. To acquaint the student with various theories concerning the New Testament canon.

2. To help the student assess the relative places of the Gospels, the Acts, the Epistles, and the Apocalypse in the New Testament canon.

3. To provide a synthesis of the theology of the New Testament, focusing on the fulfillment of biblical prophecy in Christ and discussing other major New Testament themes.

4. To provide a framework for the interpretation of individual New Testament passages by giving the student a sense of whole in which light to interpret any of the parts.

5. To demonstrate the harmonious relationship between the three elements in the hermeneutical triad—history, literature, and theology—in biblical interpretation.

6. To give the student confidence that there is underlying theological unity amidst the diversity of the biblical writers' witness.

CHAPTER 4 OUTLINE

A. Introduction

B. New Testament Canon

C. Gospels and the Gospel

D. Book of Acts and the Early Church

E. Epistles, Christ, and the Churches

F. Apocalypse and the Revelation of the Word

G. Conclusion

H. Guidelines for Interpreting the New Testament Canon

I. Key Words

J. Study Questions

K. Assignments

L. Chapter Bibliography

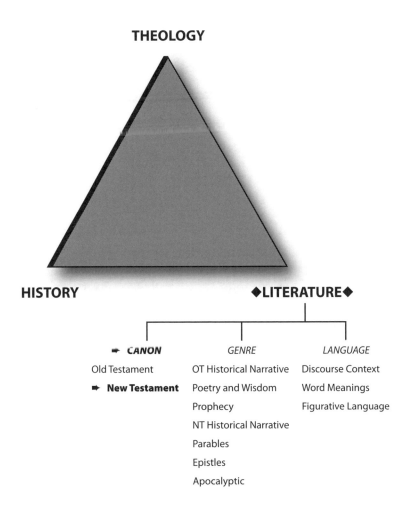

THEOLOGY

HISTORY

◆LITERATURE◆

➡ *CANON*   *GENRE*   *LANGUAGE*

Old Testament   OT Historical Narrative   Discourse Context

➡ **New Testament**   Poetry and Wisdom   Word Meanings

     Prophecy   Figurative Language

     NT Historical Narrative

     Parables

     Epistles

     Apocalyptic

Chapter 4

THE NEW TESTAMENT CANON: THE GOSPELS, ACTS, EPISTLES, AND APOCALYPSE

INTRODUCTION

HE SAID TO THEM, 'How foolish you are, and how slow to believe all that the prophets have spoken! Did not the Messiah have to suffer these things and then enter his glory?' And beginning with Moses and all the Prophets, he explained to them what was said in all the Scriptures concerning himself. . . They asked each other, 'Were not our hearts burning within us while he talked with us on the road and opened the Scriptures to us'?" Soon thereafter, "He said to them, 'This is what I told you while I was still with you. Everything must be fulfilled that is written about me in the Law of Moses, the Prophets and the Psalms.' Then he opened their minds so they could understand the Scriptures. He told them:

> This is what is written: The Messiah will suffer and rise from the dead on the third day, and repentance for the forgiveness of sins will be preached in his name to all nations, beginning at Jerusalem. You are witnesses of these things. I am going to send you what my Father has promised; but stay in the city until you have been clothed with power from on high (Luke 24:25–27, 32, 44–49; cf. Acts 1:4–8).

The above-cited Scripture passages from Luke, the salvation-historical theologian of the New Testament *par excellence*, provide us with the theology of the Bible in a nutshell: Christ, the Messiah, spoken of in "all" the Scriptures, that is, in all the major canonical divisions of the Old Testament, as one who would suffer and rise on the third day, prophecies that were fulfilled in the person of the Lord Jesus Christ, who in turn sent the Holy Spirit from the Father so that his followers could serve as witnesses from Jewish to Gentile territories, to the ends of the earth. Here is the heart of the theology of the Old Testament—the message about the Christ—and here is the heart of New Testament theology: the fulfillment of the Old Testament message about the Christ in Jesus of Nazareth, the Son of God.[1]

The various parts of the Christian canon all cohere and contribute to this overall purpose of showing the fulfillment of the Old Testament hope and message in Christ: the Gospels narrate the life of Jesus of Nazareth, focused on his death and resurrection; the Book of Acts continues this narration by showing what Jesus continued to do in and through the mission of the early church (the implication of Acts 1:1); the Epistles are documents fleshing out the fulfillment of Christ's vision, "On this rock I will build my church" (or, perhaps more accurately, "my messianic community," Matt. 16:18); and the Apocalypse brings the canon to a glorious exclamation point by focusing all eyes on the triumphant return of the Lamb of God—turned Lion of Judah—who judges the world and gathers the elect to be with him in heaven forever.

Now the fact that, properly conceived, Christ is the center of all Scripture does not mean that every chapter and every verse in Scripture are narrowly focused on Christ as if every verse of the Bible needed to be read messianically in a strict sense.[2] We must beware of an overly simplistic theology that finds Christ, somewhat anachronistically, in places in the Old Testament where finding him there would involve some major hermeneutical twisting and maneuvering. Nor does Christ as the unifying center of Scripture mean that the biblical writers are

---

1. For a helpful treatment along these lines see Kevin J. Vanhoozer, *The Drama of Doctrine: A Canonical-Linguistic Approach to Christian Theology* (Louisville: Westminster John Knox, 2005).
2. See on this the treatment of the Messiah in the previous chapter.

completely uniform in their presentation of the coming of Christ (the Gospels) or of the implications of his coming (the Epistles). Within this unity, we clearly encounter a refreshing and stimulating diversity reflecting the various personalities, vantage points, and theological perspectives of the respective New Testament writers.[3] Nor does it mean that we should pit Jesus against the Bible and claim that the former, rather than the latter, is central. After all, it is only through Scripture that we know Jesus in the first place, and Jesus himself cited the Scriptures as testifying to himself and averred that Scripture cannot be broken (John 10:35).[4]

In the present chapter, we will not be able to—or need to—probe every nook and cranny of the New Testament in detail. This would be to attempt to write a full-fledged New Testament theology, which is clearly beyond the scope of this volume.[5] The purpose of the following treatment is rather to provide a general framework that can serve as a point of reference for the interpretation of specific biblical passages. In the previous chapter, we have laid the foundation for the present chapter by surveying the landscape of Old Testament theology. The present chapter picks up where the previous one left off and endeavors to scout out the canonical landscape of the theology of the New Testament. After a few preliminary comments on the New Testament canon itself, we will treat, in turn, the Gospels and the gospel; the Book of Acts and the early church; the Epistles, Christ, and the churches; and the Apocalypse and the revelation of the Word.

---

3. On unity and diversity in the New Testament, see esp. Andreas J. Köstenberger, "Diversity and Unity in the New Testament," in *Biblical Theology: Retrospect & Prospect*, ed. Scott J. Hafemann (Downers Grove: InterVarsity, 2002), 144–58; and David Wenham, "Appendix: Unity and Diversity in the New Testament," in George E. Ladd, *A Theology of the New Testament*, rev. ed. (Grand Rapids: Eerdmans, 1993), 684–719.

4. See the blog "Jesus and the Bible," posted at www.biblicalfoundations.org in response to Daniel B. Wallace.

5. For recent attempts see Frank Thielman, *Theology of the New Testament* (Grand Rapids: Zondervan, 2005); I. Howard Marshall, *New Testament Theology* (Downers Grove: InterVarsity, 2004); and Thomas R. Schreiner, *New Testament Theology: Magnifying God in Christ* (Grand Rapids: Baker, 2008). Still helpful are George E. Ladd, *A Theology of the New Testament* and Adolf Schlatter's two-volume New Testament theology, *The History of the Christ* (Grand Rapids: Baker, 1997) and *The Theology of the Apostles* (Grand Rapids: Baker, 1999).

NEW TESTAMENT CANON

At the very outset of our brief discussion, a look at the present shape of the New Testament canon will prove instructive.[6] The New Testament canon first features the Gospels or, more precisely still, four documents presenting the one gospel according to four witnesses, Matthew, Mark, Luke, and John.[7] The order should not necessarily be taken as an indication of the chronological order of writing, however.[8] More likely, Matthew's Gospel was chosen to be first because it starts out with the genealogy of Jesus Christ and thus provides a fitting transition from the end point of the Old Testament and a proper entry point into the story of the New Testament, which is essentially the story of the Lord Jesus Christ.[9]

John may have been placed last among the four Gospels in light of the fact that his Gospel was almost certainly the last Gospel to be written. As such, it is interposed between the two writings by Luke included in the New Testament, the Gospel of Luke and the Book of Acts. Cumulatively,

---

6. For detailed discussions, see Andreas J. Köstenberger, L. Scott Kellum, and Charles L. Quarles, *The Cradle, the Cross, and the Crown: An Introduction to the New Testament* (Nashville: B&H, 2009), Chap. 1, esp. pp. 2–31; F. F. Bruce, *The Canon of Scripture* (Downers Grove: InterVarsity, 1988); Bruce M. Metzger, *The Canon of the New Testament: Its Origin, Development, and Significance* (Oxford/New York: Oxford University Press, 1987); Lee M. McDonald, *The Formation of Christian Biblical Canon*, rev. and exp. ed. (Peabody, MA: Hendrickson, 1996); Paul D. Wegner, *The Journey from Texts to Translations* (Grand Rapids: Baker, 1999); and Greg Goswell, "The Order of the Books of the New Testament," *JETS* 53 (2010): 225–241, with further bibliographic references.

7. Recent efforts to expand the New Testament to include other Gospels such as the Gospel of Thomas (viz. the Jesus Seminar's *The Five Gospels*; cf. the popular novel *The Da Vinci Code*) are misguided. See Michael Green, *The Books the Church Suppressed* (Grand Rapids: Kregel, 2006); J. Ed Komoszewski et al., *Reinventing Jesus* (Grand Rapids: Kregel, 2006); Darrell L. Bock, *The Missing Gospels* (Nashville: Thomas Nelson, 2006); and Andreas J. Köstenberger, *The Da Vinci Code: Is Christianity True?* (Wake Forest, NC: SEBTS, 2006).

8. Note also the so-called "Western" order (found in codices Bezae and Washington, the Chester Beatty codex known as $\mathfrak{P}^{45}$), grouping the Gospels as follows: Matthew, John, Luke, and Mark, perhaps in an effort to give pride of place to the Gospels attributed to apostles. See Goswell, "Order of the Books of the New Testament," 229, n. 23.

9. Note that Luke's Gospel, too, includes a genealogy of Jesus Christ, but not at the beginning of the book (cf. Luke 3:23–38). Goswell, "Order of the Books of the New Testament," 228, n. 21) with reference to Trobisch, makes the interesting suggestion that, canonically speaking, Luke's reference to previous attempts at writing an account of what Jesus said and did can be understood as referring to the Gospels of Matthew and Mark.

the four Gospels—or the gospel according to these four witnesses—contribute to the New Testament canon its very foundation, the narrative of the birth, life, ministry, death, and resurrection of Jesus Christ. As Adolf Schlatter understood, the story (or history; the German word *Geschichte* can mean either) of Jesus Christ is properly conceived as "The Foundation of New Testament Theology."[10]

Some, such as Rudolf Bultmann, have in fact argued that Jesus Christ should be considered a mere presupposition rather than properly a part of New Testament theology on the basis of their belief that the "Jesus of history" (Jesus as he actually walked the earth) and the "Christ of faith" (the Jesus the early church believed in and wrote about) are different figures entirely. Much more likely, however, the early church's teaching—indeed, the teaching of the apostles—is inextricably rooted in the teaching and life of the so-called "historical Jesus" himself. In fact, it is Jesus' teaching and his resurrection that generated what has been called "Easter faith," that is, the Spirit-aided recognition that Jesus in his own person is the Messiah predicted in the Old Testament.

This realization, in turn, accounts well for the presence of the book of Acts in the New Testament canon subsequent to the four Gospels. For it is the book of Acts that presents the continuing mission of Jesus in and through the church in the power of the Holy Spirit (Acts 1:1; cf. John 14–16). According to Luke–Acts, there is therefore no Bultmannian dichotomy between the historical Jesus and the Christ of faith. Rather, Luke–Acts upholds the essential salvation-historical unity between Jesus' completed mission and the church's mission as it began at Pentecost and continues through the book and until this very day.[11] The book of Acts thus shows how there was continuity between Jesus and the early church and how what started out in the life of a Galilean itinerant preacher who was crucified outside of the city of Jerusalem became a world religion that reached the ends of the then-known earth represented by the capital of the world empire, Rome.

The narration of the spread of Christianity in the book of Acts, in turn, encapsulates and provides the framework for the Epistles that follow

---

10. See the subtitle of his work *The History of the Christ*.
11. For a thorough treatment of the biblical theology of mission see Andreas J. Köstenberger and Peter T. O'Brien, *Salvation to the Ends of the Earth*, NSBT 11 (Downers Grove: InterVarsity, 2002).

in the New Testament canon. Peter, Paul, John, and James, all authors of New Testament epistles, are all featured in the book of Acts, which thus provides the life-setting (or perhaps better, ministry-setting) of the latter New Testament writings. Paul's ministry dominates the latter half of the book of Acts, which records the establishment of several strategic local congregations by Paul's missionary activity, and it is letters to these very congregations that form the backbone of the Pauline corpus in the New Testament. Specifically this includes Paul's letters to the Galatians, the Thessalonians, the Corinthians, and the Ephesians (though not Romans or Colossians, churches Paul did not plant), as well as his letters to Timothy (though not Titus or Philemon, individuals not mentioned in Acts). It also includes James' one, Peter's two, and John's three epistles (though not Hebrews, whose author is unknown, and Jude, James' less well-known brother).[12]

It is this focus on the apostles as Jesus' appointed representatives that proved decisive in the church's recognition of the New Testament canon. Matthew and John were accepted on account of their apostolic authorship, Mark and Luke (as well as Acts) on account of the authors' connection to leading apostles (Peter and Paul, respectively). Paul's letters were accepted on the basis of his apostolic office (as well as Hebrews, possibly on the basis of its putative, commonly accepted Pauline authorship). Others were the Petrine and Johannine epistles, plus the letters of James and Jude owing to their connection to Jesus as his half-brothers and, in James' case, his leading role in the Jerusalem church and at the Jerusalem council (Acts 15; Galatians 2). Apostolicity, and, by extension, the "rule of faith" (the *regula fidei*, that is, the apostles' teaching), was the overriding criterion as the church recognized the divine inspiration and supernatural authority of the various books that came to make up the New Testament canon.

This is true also for the last book of the New Testament, the Apocalypse, which purports to be from John "the seer," whom the early church took to be none other than John the apostle (the Gospel) and John "the elder" (the Epistles). Just as the Gospels in general, and the Gospel of

---

12. For thorough treatments of the historical setting, literary features, and major theological themes in each of these writings, see Köstenberger, Kellum, and Quarles, *Cradle, the Cross, and the Crown.*

Matthew in particular, provide a fitting entry point into the story of Jesus, so the book of Revelation constitutes a fitting conclusion, depicting, as it does, Jesus' glorious return (his "Second Coming," variously called *parousia* ["coming"] or *epiphaneia* ["revelation"] in the New Testament). Jesus' return and his subsequent judgment of the world and gathering of his elect (his covenant community) to be with him forever in heaven provide proper closure to the biblical story line which began with Creation and the Fall and concludes with the new creation and the restoration of all things in Christ.[13]

The above summary of the coherent nature of the New Testament canon and the interrelationship of its various constituent parts obtains regardless of the specific ways in which the New Testament canon commonly affirmed today came to be officially and widely recognized. Traditionally, the canonical process has been conceived as a gradual process culminating in the fourth century. There is also evidence for an earlier compilation of the New Testament canonical books.[14] In its current, final form, the canon of the New Testament with its 27 books constitutes a coherent and unified whole that serves as the proper overall frame of reference for the interpretation of individual New Testament passages.[15]

---

13. On the "new creation" motif in the New Testament see esp. Gregory Beale, "The New Testament and New Creation," in Hafemann, *Biblical Theology*, 159–73; see also the same author's "The Eschatological Conception of New Testament Theology," in *Eschatology in Bible & Theology*, ed. Kent E. Brower and Mark W. Elliott (Downers Grove: InterVarsity, 1999), 11–52; and *The Temple and the Church's Mission*, NSBT 17 (Downers Grove: InterVarsity, 2004; though we cannot endorse all of his interpretations).

14. David Trobisch, *The First Edition of the New Testament* (Oxford/New York: Oxford University Press, 2000), proposes that a second-century editorial circle was responsible for issuing a "canonical edition" of the 27 books commonly affirmed to be part of the New Testament. As evidence Trobisch cites the pervasive presence of so-called *nomina sacra*, that is, contracted words for deity, and the near-universal use of the codex rather than the scroll. He also notes the uniform order of the early scriptural codices—Gospels, Acts, General Epistles, Pauline Epistles (including Hebrews), and Revelation—and the uniformity of titles of individual books. Note, however, the critique of aspects of Trobisch's view by Andreas J. Köstenberger, "'I Suppose' (*oimai*): The Conclusion of John's Gospel in Its Literary and Historical Context," in *The New Testament in Its First Century Setting*, ed. P. J. Williams et al. (Grand Rapids: Eerdmans, 2004), 80–81, n. 31.

15. For a thorough treatment of the New Testament canon, see Köstenberger, Kellum, and Quarles, *Cradle, the Cross, and the Crown*, Chap. 1.

GOSPELS AND THE GOSPEL

As mentioned, the four biblical Gospels all present the one gospel of salvation in Jesus Christ according to four major witnesses, Matthew, Mark, Luke, and John.[16] Goldsworthy helpfully notes that all four Gospels root Jesus' mission at the very outset in the Hebrew Scriptures (i.e. the Old Testament).[17] This has important canonical implications. Consider the way in which the four Gospels open:

Matthew 1:1: A record of the genealogy of Jesus Christ the son of David, the son of Abraham . . .

Mark 1:1–2: The beginning of the gospel about Jesus Christ, the Son of God. It is written in Isaiah the prophet . . .

Luke 1:1–4 refers to previous accounts of the life of Jesus and relates Jesus' coming to David and Abraham (Luke 1:27, 54–55)

John 1:1–3: In the beginning was the Word, and the Word was with God, and the Word was God. . . . Through him all things were made . . .

Thus Matthew begins with Jesus' family tree, with Abraham, David, and the exile as major junctures, whereby Abraham and David are the major recipients of God's promises and the exile marks Israel's failure to receive the blessings associated with these promises. Mark roots the coming of John the Baptist, Jesus' forerunner, in the prophetic message of Isaiah and Malachi. John is the God-appointed, Scripture-fulfilling messenger who will prepare the way for Jesus the Messiah. Similar to Matthew, Luke, likewise, anchors Jesus' coming in the Old Testament promises made to Abraham and David; the Baptist is linked to Elijah (Luke 1:17). John, finally, reaches back all the way to creation through the pre-incarnate Word, Jesus Christ.

The same is true for the first epistle and first letter by Paul in the New Testament canon, the book of Romans. There Paul speaks of "the gospel he [God] promised beforehand through his prophets in the Holy Scriptures regarding his Son, who as to his human nature was a descendant of

---

16. Cf. Martin Hengel, *The Four Gospels and the One Gospel of Jesus Christ* (Valley Forge, PA: Trinity Press International, 2000). On the gospel, see also Andreas J. Köstenberger, "The Gospel for All Nations," in *Faith Comes by Hearing: A Response to Inclusivism*, ed. Christopher W. Morgan and Robert A. Peterson (Downers Grove: InterVarsity, 2009), 201–19. See also the discussion of the "fourfold Gospel" in Goswell, "Order of the Books of the New Testament."

17. Cf. Graeme Goldsworthy, *According to Plan: The unfolding revelation of God in the Bible* (Leicester, UK: Inter-Varsity, 1991), 107–9.

David, and who through the Spirit of holiness was declared with power to be the Son of God by his resurrection from the dead: Jesus Christ our Lord" (Rom. 1:2–4). The important point made by Paul is that the gospel, rather than being a recent innovation, was promised beforehand through the prophets in the Old Testament Scriptures.

The Apocalypse, too, presents Christ in keeping with Old Testament characters and imagery (e.g., Rev. 1:17–3:22).

When we read the Gospels, we are struck by the centrality of Jesus, and here particularly his crucifixion and resurrection.[18] All four Gospels culminate in the Passion narrative, and all cohere and concur in presenting Jesus' sacrifice as substitutionary and atoning. Thus the Gospels form the perfect backdrop for Paul's statement in 1 Corinthians:

> For what I received I passed on to you as of first importance: that Christ died for our sins according to the Scriptures, that he was buried, that he was raised on the third day according to the Scriptures" (1 Cor. 15:3–4).

Not what the church believed about Jesus, but the person of Jesus himself is the towering presence in all four Gospels.[19] Not only is Jesus called God (John 1:1, 18; 20:28; Phil. 2:6; Titus 3:4–5), both Paul and Peter apply Old Testament references to Yahweh unhesitatingly to Jesus. The author of Hebrew claims Jesus is not only the final revelation of God but also the exact representation of his being (Heb. 1:1–3).

With regard to Jesus' message, at least in the synoptic Gospels the theme that dominates is that of the kingdom of God (Mark 1:15; cf. the kingdom parables chapters in Matthew and Luke). God's kingdom, in keeping with his promises to David (e.g., 2 Sam. 7:14), represents a fulfillment of Old Testament promises to Israel. "Kingdom" also conveys the notion of God's reign or rule over his people, and in Jesus, God's kingdom is already present (Luke 17:21).[20]

The Gospels provide both the *complement to the Old Testament* and constitute the *foundation of the New Testament canon*. All four Gospels

---

18. Cf. D. A. Carson, *The Gagging of God: Christianity Confronts Pluralism* (Grand Rapids: Zondervan, 1996), 257–64.
19. Ibid., 257.
20. Ibid., 260–63.

take their conscious point of departure from the Hebrew Scriptures and from God's acts in history and his promises to his chosen servants.[21] The Gospels, in turn, constitute the quarry from which the early church, Paul, and the other New Testament authors draw their formulation of the Christian gospel (esp. Rom. 1:2–4; 1 Cor. 15:3–4).[22] The book of Revelation, finally, shows that the kingdom of the world has now become the kingdom of God's Christ (Rev. 11:15).

BOOK OF ACTS AND THE EARLY CHURCH

The book of Acts not only sustains important links with the Gospel of Luke (cf. Acts 1:1), it also is significantly founded on and continues the narration of Jesus' mission in the four Gospels (cf. John 21:25 and Acts 1:1). Thus in its canonical embeddedness and strategic placement, the book of Acts registers the important claim that the life and mission of the early church is grounded in the life and mission of Jesus Christ himself. In this way, the various commissions of Jesus to his disciples recorded in the Gospels (Matt. 28:18–20; Luke 24: 46–49; John 20:21–22) issue organically in the early church's pursuit of its mission (cf. esp. Luke 24:46–53 and Acts 1:1–11). This point is also integral to the structure of John's Gospel where Jesus is shown to anticipate his exalted status with God subsequent to the crucifixion and resurrection (his "glorification") and hence speaks to his followers about their future mission (the Farewell Discourse [John 13–17]).[23]

---

21. Beyond this, it is possible that the New Testament canon exhibits a parallel structure to the Old Testament canon, "so that the Gospels correspond to the Pentateuch, Acts to the Historical Books, the letters to the Poetic Books, and Revelation to the Prophetic Books" (Goswell, "Order of the Books of the New Testament," 225–26). Thus the Pentateuch comprises a biography of Moses while the Gospels (plus the "fifth" book, Acts) contain a biography of Jesus. See also Christopher R. Seitz, who suggested that the three-part structure of the Hebrew Bible has influenced the shape of the New Testament canon (*The Goodly Fellowship of the Prophets: The Achievement of Association in Canon Formation* [Grand Rapids: Baker, 2009], 103).
22. As Robert W. Wall put it, the Gospels are "the subtext for all the writings that follow in the New Testament" ("The Significance of a Canonical Perspective of the Church's Scripture," in *The Canon Debate*, ed. L. M. McDonald and J. A. Sanders [Peabody, MA: Hendrickson, 2002], 536). See also Eugene E. Lemcio, "The Gospels within the New Testament Canon," in *Canon and Biblical Interpretation*, Scripture and Hermeneutics 7, ed. Craig Bartholomew *et al.* (Grand Rapids: Zondervan, 2006), 123–45.
23. See Andreas J. Köstenberger, *John*, BECNT (Grand Rapids: Baker, 2004), 395–98, 419.

The most important ingredients of New Testament theology contributed on a canonical level by the book of Acts are the following. First, the mission of the church is conducted in the power of the Holy Spirit subsequent to his coming at Pentecost (Acts 2). While the Holy Spirit is mentioned repeatedly in the Gospels, especially in the Gospel of Luke, these references are either focused exclusively on Jesus as the Spirit-anointed Messiah (e.g., Luke 4:18–19, citing Isa. 60:1–2) or anticipatory with regard to his future ministry in and through Jesus' followers (e.g., John 7:37–39; 14:16–18, 26; 15:26–27; 16:7–15; 20:22). The book of the Acts of the Apostles is in reality the book of the Acts of the Holy Spirit (cf. Acts 1:2, 5, 8, etc.).

The book of Acts, second, also marks a new kind of relationship sustained between believers and Jesus. Rather than fearing God (the Father) as Old Testament believers did, and rather than physically leaving their familiar surroundings and following Jesus during his earthly ministry as his first followers did, believers in the church age sustain a vital, organic relationship with God the Father and Jesus in and through the Holy Spirit (note the trinitarian dimension, on which see John 14 and 15).

This scenario, in turn, involves *prayer* to the exalted Jesus in the church's pursuit of her mission (which is still Jesus' mission; cf., e.g., John 14:12–13; Acts 4:24–31). The fact that Jesus has not relinquished his mission but entrusted it to his followers under the direction of the "other helping presence," the Holy Spirit, means that they are to serve as his authorized and duly commissioned representatives—as his *witnesses* (Luke 24:48; Acts 1:8; John 15:26–27)—rather than exalt themselves as originators of the gospel message or set themselves off against Jesus in any way.[24]

Third, the book of Acts is first and foremost about *mission*, about God's irresistible, inexorable pursuit of lost sinners with the gospel of forgiveness and salvation in the Lord Jesus Christ. Thus the book of Acts marks the beginning of the fulfillment of Jesus' words that before the end would come the gospel must first be preached to all nations (Mark

---

24. This insight marks the burden and finding of the monograph on mission by Andreas J. Köstenberger, *The Missions of Jesus and the Disciples according to the Fourth Gospel* (Grand Rapids: Eerdmans, 1998).

13:13 and parallels). In keeping with and in initial fulfillment of Jesus'
words, the book of Acts narrates the spread of the gospel from Jerusalem to Judea, Samaria, and the ends of the earth (Acts 1:8), culminating in Paul's preaching of the gospel in Rome, the empire's capital
(Acts 28:30–31).

This, in turn, took place in fulfillment of the Old Testament prophetic
vision (Acts 28:26–27, citing Isa. 6:9–10), according to which the gospel
would spread beyond Israel to the nations (cf. Rom. 1:16). This movement
is already evident in the Gospels in several ways:

1. within the Gospel of Matthew, there is a movement from Jew to
   Gentile (cf. Matt. 10:6, 15:24; 28:16–20);[25]

2. from Matthew as focused on the fulfillment of Old Testament
   messianic predictions to Israel to the Gospels of Mark and
   Luke, both of which address a primarily Gentile audience (be
   it Roman as in the case of Mark or a more universally Gentile audience as in the case of Luke; note that the Book of
   Acts itself narrates the spread of the gospel to the non-Jewish
   world);

3. the Gospel of John features Jesus' mission to the Jews, the Samaritans, and Gentiles *in nuce* (in a nutshell) in chapters 2, 3,
   and 4;

4. of all the Gospels, John is perhaps most keenly focused on
   the universal nature of the gospel and on the sole requirement of faith in Jesus as Messiah for salvation (see, e.g., John
   3:16);

5. while the mission of Jesus in all four Gospels is shown to be
   limited to Israel (the exception being where individual Gentiles take the initiative in approaching Jesus), the Book of Acts
   shows that now, on the basis of the finished cross-work of Jesus
   Christ and on the basis of God's vindication of Jesus in the

---

25. Köstenberger and O'Brien, *Salvation to the Ends of the Earth*, Chap. 5.

resurrection, the gospel bursts forth and penetrates beyond its Jewish confines to the Gentile world, in fulfillment of the Abrahamic promise (Gen. 12:1–3; cf. Matt. 28:16–20); Paul will makes this most explicit when he says that there is "neither Jew nor Gentile" in Christ (Gal. 3:26–28).

In light of these observations, it becomes clear that on a canonical level the mission of the early church is shown in the book of Acts to be firmly grounded both in the Hebrew Scriptures and in Jesus' own mission. Thus the book of Acts provides a fitting continuation of the canonical story line moving from God's promises to Abraham, the father of the Jewish nation, to Jesus, Abraham's "seed" (Gal. 3:16), and through Jesus to all humanity, Jew and Gentile alike, through the instrumentality of Jesus' authorized and commissioned witnesses, the New Testament church.

EPISTLES, CHRIST, AND THE CHURCHES

The New Testament Epistles are living documents from the period of the early church's mission, providing a fascinating glimpse of the interaction between church-planting missionaries such as Paul and the churches he planted (or, in some cases, did not plant).[26] In many (if not most) cases, the book of Acts thus provides the canonical, historical, and logical foundation for our reading of the Epistles as it sets forth the early days and years of the church from its inception and its missionary setbacks and successes, following a geographical pattern from Jerusalem to Rome and featuring the missionary work of Peter, Paul, and their associates.

The way in which the book of Acts serves as an essential background to our reading of the New Testament Epistles (especially those of Paul) can be illustrated by the following chart:[27]

---

26. For a helpful survey of the relevant information, see the discussion under the heading "The Letters" in Goswell, "Order of the Books of the New Testament," 235–240.

27. Note that the listing of New Testament epistles is in the order corresponding to Acts, not necessarily in chronological order of writing. For a Pauline chronology, see Chapter 2.

4.1. ACTS AS BACKGROUND OF EPISTLES		
PASSAGE IN ACTS	**BACKGROUND EVENT**	**NEW TESTAMENT LETTER**
14; 16:6	Churches planted in Galatia	Galatians
15	Jerusalem Council	James
16:1–5	Paul and a disciple named Timothy	1–2 Timothy
16:11–40	Church planted in Philippi	Philippians
17:1–9	Church planted in Thessalonica	1–2 Thessalonians
18:1–17	Church planted in Corinth	1–2 Corinthians
19; 20:13–38	Church planted in Ephesus	Ephesians
28:30–31	Paul preaches the gospel in Rome	Prison Epistles

Beyond this, the book of Acts also features the ministry of Peter and John, who wrote 1–2 Peter and 1–3 John, respectively. Aquila or another member of the Pauline circle is a possible candidate for author of the book of Hebrews, though this is speculative.

With regard to a Pauline letter collection, there is some New Testament evidence that the Pauline corpus was formed very early, even while Paul's letters were still being written (2 Pet. 3:15–16).[28] Not only this, they were regarded on par with the Old Testament Scriptures, as were the Gospels (1 Tim. 5:18 possibly citing Luke 10:7 in conjunction with Deut. 24:5). There is also good reason to believe that Paul wrote 13 epistles included in the New Testament canon: Galatians, 1–2 Thessalonians, 1–2 Corinthians, Romans, the Prison Epistles (Ephesians, Philippians, Colossians, and Phi-

---

28. See, e.g., Jack Finegan, "The Original Form of the Pauline Collection," *HTR* 49 (1956): 85–103, esp. 88–90; David Trobisch, *Die Entstehung der Paulusbriefsammlung*, NTOA 10 (Freiburg: Universitätsverlag, 1989), 14–61.

lemon), and the Pastoral Epistles (1–2 Timothy, Titus), though not likely the book of Hebrews.

By Marcion's time, the Pauline corpus consisted of at least ten letters (including a letter to the Laodiceans, possibly Ephesians) and possibly 13 letters (including the Pastorals, whom Marcion may have rejected).[29] This is also confirmed by the papyrus manuscript 𝔓[46], which most dates to around A.D. 200. The Muratorian canon, also dated most likely to A.D. 180–200, lists 13 letters, and by the fourth century there is consensus that the Pauline corpus consists of 13 or 14 letters (depending on the authorship of Hebrews). With regard to order, Trobisch proposes that letters to congregations were placed before letters to individuals, and letters to the same church kept together.[30] Trobisch also suggests that Romans through Galatians may have been collected and arranged by Paul himself.[31] Alternatively, a close follower such as Timothy or Luke (cf. Col. 4:14; Phlm. 24; 2 Tim. 4:11) may have had a part in collecting Paul's letters. This would provide a further link between Paul and Luke.

While the book of Acts provides the foundation for our canonical reading of the New Testament Epistles, however, the latter go beyond a mere description of the progression of the mission of the early church. Each of the letters gives us an account of the problems and issues facing a particular church plus the New Testament writer's adjudication of these matters. This is perhaps most obvious in a letter such as 1 Corinthians, which, starting in chapter 7, deals with several matters the Corinthians apparently asked the apostle Paul to address (cf. 1 Cor. 7:1, 25; 8:1; 12:1; 15:1).

---

29. For the material in the present paragraph, see esp. Stanley E. Porter, "When and How Was the Pauline Canon Compiled? An Assessment of Theories," in *The Pauline Canon*, ed. Stanley E. Porter (Leiden/Boston: Brill, 2004), 95–127.

30. David Trobisch, *Paul's Letter Collection: Tracing the Origins* (Minneapolis: Augsburg Fortress, 1994), 52–54, 25, on which see the summary and critique in Porter, "Pauline Canon," 113–21. See also Brevard Childs, *The Church's Guide for Reading Paul: The Canonical Shaping of the Pauline Corpus* (Grand Rapids: Eerdmans, 2008), who proposed that the rest of the Pauline letter corpus ought to be read in light of Paul's mature teaching in the book of Romans. Childs also suggested that Romans and the Pastorals act as bookends, with the latter showing how the earlier letters should be read as Scripture (pp. 164–67).

31. Trobisch, *Paul's Letter Collection*, 54. See also E. R. Richards, *The Secretary in the Letters of Paul*, WUNT 2/42 (Tübingen: Mohr Siebeck, 1991), esp. 164–65, 187–88, with reference to 2 Timothy 4:13.

Let us remember at this point, however, that the occasional nature of the New Testament Epistles does not necessarily imply that the New Testament authors' adjudications of the various matters addressed are likewise of a merely temporary nature. To the contrary, because of their apostolic nature, many of these adjudications should be expected to have permanent relevance, at least on a principal level (though at times cultural factors may necessitate a transposition of the principle to one appropriate in today's culture).

For example, Timothy may have encountered difficulties with elders in the Ephesian church (cf., e.g., 1 Tim. 5:19–25, which speaks of "sinning elders" in v. 20 and warns against appointing church leaders hastily, v. 22), but this does not mean that the qualifications for church leaders in 1 Timothy 3 are likewise only of a temporary nature. More likely, they transcend the occasion at which they were given and are of permanent relevance for the church as inspired apostolic pronouncements. In other cases, such as 1 Corinthians 11:2–16, the principle (male headship, enunciated in v. 3) may be of abiding consequence while the cultural expression of it may be subject to change (i.e., female head coverings).

The New Testament Epistles also supply us with a more full-fledged theology of the implications of the work of Christ for the life of the believer, such as Paul's teaching of believers' union with Christ on an individual and his teaching on the church as the body of Christ on a corporate level. In addition, the Epistles also contain many other teachings which Paul wrestled to develop, including the nature of the resurrection body (1 Cor. 15:35–58), end-time events such as the rapture (1 Thess. 4:13–18), or the relationship between Gentiles and Israel on a salvation-historical scale (Romans 9–11). While at times Paul drew on Jesus' teaching, at other times Paul had to forge his own path in Spirit-led messianic application of the Hebrew Scriptures or other ways (cf. 1 Cor. 7:10, 12).

Thus, on a canonical level, the Epistles build on and yet go beyond the Gospels and the Book of Acts. In the Book of Acts, we read *about* Paul; in his Epistles, we hear *from* Paul directly. Conversely, in the Gospels, we hear *from* Jesus directly; in the Epistles, we hear *about* the ramifications of Jesus' work for believers. Both are necessary and complementary.[32] In the

---

32. Regarding the relationship between the "Paul of Acts" and the "Paul of the Epistles" see Köstenberger, "Diversity and Unity," 149–50 and the literature cited there; see also the section on alleged developments in Paul on pp. 151–52.

end, canonically speaking, the New Testament Epistles are a vital part of inspired Scripture and of authoritative divine revelation, communicated, as it were, through the apostolic writers dealing with real-life issues in the various churches under their care.[33]

Hermeneutically, while the book of Acts, as a historical narrative, tells us more overtly what *did* take place in the early church, the Epistles, as didactic material, focus more explicitly on what *should* happen in the church, both by way of direct pronouncement—e.g., "Forgive one another"—and case study or principle (e.g., exercising sensitivity toward others in the case of eating food offered to idols, 1 Corinthians 8; cf. Romans 14–15). This does not mean that every conceivable circumstance is dealt with in the Epistles. Rather, representative instances serve as illustrations of how the Spirit led the church through God's authorized representatives in dealing with various challenges and opportunities. Within these scriptural parameters, the church today is to develop discernment and mature judgment—"the mind of Christ"—so that it may understand what the will of God is in whatever circumstances it faces.

One final observation pertains to the contribution of the Epistles to the New Testament canon. Just as the Gospels make reference to the towering figure of Jesus and the book of Acts records the things Jesus continued to do from his exalted position through the church in the power of the Holy Spirit (Acts 1:1), in the Epistles, likewise, Christ is at the very center. Paul's letters in particular abound with references to "Christ," "Christ Jesus," or "the Lord Jesus Christ." David Wenham's comment is apt: "In short, for Paul Christianity is Christ."[34] The most basic early Christian confession was *Christos kyrios*, that is, "Christ is Lord" (e.g., Acts 2:36; Rom. 10:9; Phil. 2:11), and Paul taught that "there is but one Lord, Jesus Christ, through whom all things came and through whom we live" (1 Cor. 8:6). Paul also taught that Jesus himself, not church leaders, is the head of his church (Eph. 1:22; 4:15; 5:23; Col. 1:18) and that he should have supremacy in everything (Col. 1:18).

---

33. See also the important point by Richard B. Hays, *The Faith of Jesus Christ: The Narrative Substructure of Galatians 3:1–4:11*, 2d ed. (Grand Rapids: Eerdmans, 2002), 219–20, that there is a fundamental congruity of narrative structure between Paul's Epistles and the Gospels.
34. Wenham, "Unity and Diversity," 711, cited in Köstenberger, "Diversity and Unity," 156, n. 46.

Thus Christ is not only the presupposition of New Testament theology as Bultmann asserted but is at the very heart of the theology of the New Testament itself. There is no dichotomy between the Jesus of the Gospels and the Christ of the Epistles. Rather, there is essential unity between the Jesus who lived, died, and rose—the Jesus of the Gospels—and the Jesus of the gospel, the so-called "Christ of faith" in whom believers placed their trust.

APOCALYPSE AND THE REVELATION OF THE WORD

The Apocalypse, the final book of the New Testament canon and of the canon of Scripture altogether, provides the concluding bookend corresponding to the book of Genesis in the Old Testament. The first book in the Bible tells us about creation (Genesis 1–2), the last envisions a new creation (Revelation 21–22). The first book speaks of the fall of humanity (Genesis 3), the last of the curse being reversed, of sinful humanity and the devil and his minions being judged, and of a new humanity made up of the redeemed of all tribes, languages, and nations being restored (Revelation 4–5). The first book depicts the original state of humanity in an unbroken relationship with God, the last displays worship offered to God and to the Lamb, the Lord Jesus Christ.

As in the Old Testament (cf. Luke 24:25–27, 32, 44–49, quoted at the outset of this chapter), and as in the other portions of the New Testament canon, so also in the book of Revelation, Jesus is at the center—as the Lamb-turned-Lion (Revelation 4), as the Heavenly Warrior who defeats the Beast (Revelation 19), and as the End-time Judge (Revelation 20), Jesus utterly dominates the scene. On a canonical level, the Apocalypse presents the consummation of the age and the fulfillment of God's plan for humanity and the cosmos in Christ (cf. Eph. 1:10, which portrays God's purpose as "bring[ing] all things back together under one head [*anakephalaioō*], even Christ").

In continuity with the Epistles, the book of Revelation, too, includes seven epistles to the seven churches of Asia Minor (Revelation 2–3), including Ephesus, to which also one of Paul's letters is addressed. The concluding warning against adding to or taking away any words from the prophecy of the book extends at least to the book of Revelation in its entirety and very likely on a canonical level to the entire canon of Scripture.

Notably, it is the same Jesus who is depicted as crucified and risen in the Gospels, who is cast as fueling and engineering the mission of the early church in the book of Acts, and who is presented as the Lord and Head of the church in the Epistles, who is also the Returning Glorious Conqueror, Supreme Ruler, and King of the Apocalypse (see esp. Rev. 19:16). Jesus is shown as defeating all the forces of darkness and as inaugurating the eternal state in which there is no more curse, no more night, no more death, mourning, crying, or pain, for the old order of things will have passed away forever (Rev. 21:4; 22:3–4).

There is also no more temple, for God himself will live among his people. "They will be his people, and God himself will be with them and be their God" (Rev. 21:3). Not only will Eden be restored, but the end will be even better than the beginning, for Jesus, the incarnate, suffering, resurrected, and triumphant Savior will be worshiped and adored by God's people for all eternity.

On a salvation-historical (see the covenant theme, sounded in the just-cited Rev. 21:3) as well as on a literary and theological level, the Apocalypse thus provides a satisfying conclusion to the New Testament and biblical canon. As is all of Scripture, this conclusion is Christ-centered. It also takes up and satisfactorily resolves all the various tensions of Scripture, including believers' predicament of suffering persecution at the hands of the unrighteous and their cry for divine vindication. Theodicy, the vindication of God's righteous character and purposes, is thus at the heart of this final book of Scripture,[35] and the Apocalypse fleshes out in eschatological terms Paul's pronouncement that "God was reconciling the world to himself in Christ" (2 Cor. 5:19).

CONCLUSION

The overview of the Old and New Testament canon in this and the previous chapter provides a proper framework for biblical interpretation, in keeping with the important principle of interpreting the parts (i.e., individual passages) in light of the whole (the overarching teaching of Scripture). On the basis of these broad contours of the biblical landscape, we will focus on the special skills needed for interpreting the various genres of Scripture.

---

35. Grant R. Osborne, "Theodicy in the Apocalypse," *TrinJ* NS 14/1 (1993): 63–77.

GUIDELINES FOR INTERPRETING
THE NEW TESTAMENT CANON

1. Assign the passage you are studying to one of the following: Gospels/Acts, Epistles, or Revelation.

2. Understand the salvation-historical location of the book you are studying: in the Gospels, the earthly ministry of Jesus; in the book of Acts and the Epistles, the church age and the mission of the early church; in Revelation, the end times.

3. Be careful to observe how each of the respective portions of the New Testament canon complement and supplement one another and interpret them in proper relation to each other. For example, when studying Philippians, consult the account of the planting of the church of Philippi in the book of Acts.

4. Note any limitations that arise from the constraints of a given portion of the New Testament canon. For example, note how Jesus' pattern of training his disciples relates to Paul's teaching on the church as the body of Christ, made up of individual members with a unique set of spiritual gifts.

5. As relevant, carefully consider the New Testament use of the Old Testament (on which see more fully Chapter 15 below).

6. Note not only the historical progression of New Testament teaching but also the topical interconnection between passages on similar or related topics, in keeping with the Reformation principle that Scripture is its own interpreter.

KEY WORDS

Bultmannian: in conformity with the teachings of Rudolf Bultmann, a noted twentieth-century German theologian

Canonical Edition of the New Testament: the notion that the individual(s) responsible for the compilation of the books of the New Testament in a particular order shaped this document in a particular way

Eschatological: end-time

Eternal State: heaven

Farewell Discourse: final period of Jesus' instruction of his followers per John 13–17 or, more narrowly conceived, John 13:31–16:33

Hermeneutical: interpretive

Nomina sacra: contracted words for deity in early Greek New Testament manuscripts

Par excellence: the most perfect example

Parousia: Second Coming of the Lord Jesus Christ

Rapture: meeting between believers alive at the time of Christ's return and their risen Lord per 1 Thess. 4:13–18

Regula fidei: Latin, "rule of faith," i.e. the apostles' teaching as a standard for orthodox doctrine

Salvation-historical: events along the lines of God's unfolding plan of redemption

Theodicy: vindication of God's righteous character and purposes

STUDY QUESTIONS

1. Summarize how the Gospels, the Book of Acts, the Epistles, and the Apocalypse are the fulfillment of the Old Testament in the New with focus on the fulfillment of biblical prophecy in Christ.

2. What is the New Testament canon, and how did it come to be?

3. What do the Gospels contribute to the New Testament canon as a whole?

4. What does the book of Acts contribute to the New Testament canon as a whole?

5. What do the Epistles contribute to the New Testament canon as a whole?

6. What does the Apocalypse contribute to the New Testament canon as a whole?

7. Comment on the underlying theological unity in the New Testament amidst the diversity of the biblical writers in order to provide for yourself a general framework that can serve as a reference point for the interpretation of biblical passages.

ASSIGNMENTS

1. Discuss the use of Isaiah 61:1–2 in Luke 4:18–19, giving proper attention to both the original Old Testament context and the context in Luke. Show how the passage forms an integral part of the message of Isaiah and how the passage contributes to the theology of Luke.

2. Discuss how the book of Acts provides the basic framework for the New Testament Epistles. Provide a timeline which integrates events recorded in the book of Acts, the writing of New Testament letters, and other relevant information.

3. Identify at least three ways in which the book of Revelation culminates the message of the New Testament and of the Bible as a whole. Discuss each of these ways in detail and provide specific references from the book of Revelation to support your answer.

CHAPTER BIBLIOGRAPHY

Carson, D. A. *The Gagging of God: Christianity Confronts Pluralism.* Grand Rapids: Zondervan, 1996.

Goldsworthy, Graeme. *According to Plan: The Unfolding Revelation of God in the Bible.* Leicester, UK: Inter-Varsity, 1991.

Goswell, Greg. "The Order of the Books of the New Testament." *JETS* 53 (2010): 225–41.

Köstenberger, Andreas J. and Peter T. O'Brien. *Salvation to the Ends of the Earth: A Biblical Theology of Mission.* New Studies in Biblical Theology 11. Downers Grove: InterVarsity, 2001.

Köstenberger, Andreas J. "Diversity and Unity in the New Testament." Pp. 144–58 in *Biblical Theology: Retrospect & Prospect.* Edited by Scot J. Hafemann. Downers Grove: InterVarsity, 2002.

_____. "The Gospel for All Nations." Pp. 201–19 in *Faith Comes by Hearing: A Response to Inclusivism.* Edited by Robert A. Peterson and Christopher W. Morgan. Downers Grove: InterVarsity, 2008.

Porter, Stanley E., ed. *The Pauline Canon.* Leiden/Boston: Brill, 2004.

Schlatter, Adolf. *The History of the Christ: The Foundation of New Testament Theology.* Translated by Andreas J. Köstenberger. Grand Rapids: Baker, 1997.

_____. *The Theology of the Apostles: The Development of New Testament Theology.* Translated by Andreas J. Köstenberger. Grand Rapids: Baker, 1999.

Trobisch, David. *Paul's Letter Collection: Tracing the Origins.* Minneapolis: Augsburg Fortress, 1994.

_____. *The First Edition of the New Testament.* Oxford/New York: Oxford University Press, 2000.

Vanhoozer, Kevin J. *The Drama of Doctrine: A Canonical-Linguistic Approach to Christian Theology.* Louisville: Westminster John Knox, 2005.

UNIT 2: GENRE

CHAPTER 5 OBJECTIVES

1. To acquaint the student with the nature and modes of Old Testament narrative.

2. To enable the student to recognize the elements of Old Testament narrative.

3. To inform the student of stylistic approaches within Old Testament narrative.

4. To provide the student with a set of guides for interpreting Old Testament narrative.

CHAPTER 5 OUTLINE

A. Nature of Biblical Narrative
B. Modes of Old Testament Historical Narrative
   1. Stories
   2. Accounts
   3. Reports
C. Elements of Old Testament Historical Narrative
   1. External Elements
   2. Internal Elements
      a. Setting
      b. Plot
      c. Characterization
D. Narrative Style
   1. Repetition
   2. Highlighting
   3. Irony
   4. Satire
E. Sample Exegesis: 1 Kings 19
F. Guidelines for Interpreting Old Testament Narrative
G. Key Words
H. Study Questions
I. Assignments
J. Chapter Bibliography

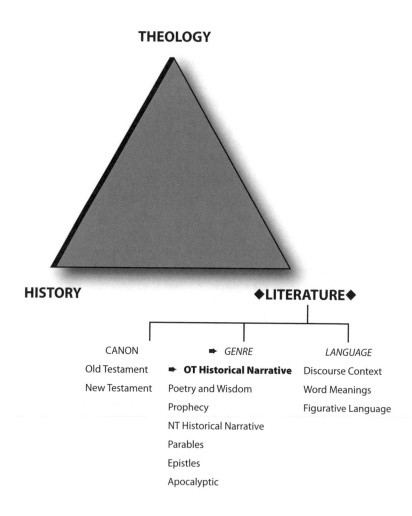

THEOLOGY

HISTORY   ◆LITERATURE◆

CANON   ➡ *GENRE*   *LANGUAGE*

Old Testament   ➡ **OT Historical Narrative**   Discourse Context

New Testament   Poetry and Wisdom   Word Meanings

                   Prophecy   Figurative Language

                   NT Historical Narrative

                   Parables

                   Epistles

                   Apocalyptic

Chapter 5

ENJOYING A GOOD STORY: OLD TESTAMENT HISTORICAL NARRATIVE

NATURE OF BIBLICAL NARRATIVE

NOW THAT WE HAVE DEVELOPED an appreciation of the overall canonical landscape—the theo-drama, "big story," or meta-narrative of Scripture—we are able to look around and familiarize ourselves with the various topographical features we encounter on our interpretive journey—the valleys, mountains, and plains, as it were. Applied to the interpretation of Scripture, these features—biblical genres or types of literature—are historical narrative, poetry and wisdom, and prophecy in the Old Testament, and historical narrative, parable, epistle, and apocalyptic in the New.

Thus our attention now turns to what Kevin Vanhoozer has called "the semantics of biblical literature," that is, the specific characteristics of any given genre of Scripture.[1] Some have compared interpreting types of literature such as narrative, epistle, or apocalyptic to playing various games such

---

1. Kevin J. Vanhoozer, "The Semantics of Biblical Literature: Truth and Scripture's Diverse Literary Forms," in *Hermeneutics, Authority, and Canon*, ed. D. A. Carson and John D. Woodbridge (Grand Rapids: Zondervan, 1986), 49–104.

as baseball, basketball, or soccer.[2] In each case, if you want to play the game, you must first acquaint yourself with the rules. Conversely, if you don't know the rules of a given game, you will most likely be lost and be unable to follow a game, much less participate in it.[3] It is similar with interpreting the various genres of Scripture: in order to pick up the fine nuances conveyed by the biblical text, we must learn the "rules" that guide the interpretation of that particular biblical genre.

The present chapter explores the first such genre found in Scripture, Old Testament narrative. Subsequent chapters explain the interpretation of wisdom and poetry (Chapter 6), prophecy (Chapter 7), New Testament narrative (the Gospels and Acts; Chapter 8), Jesus' parables (Chapter 9), the New Testament epistles (Chapter 10), and apocalyptic (the book of Revelation; Chapter 11). In each case, learning principles for interpreting a particular type of literature will be invaluable as we encounter various types of topographical features on our interpretive journey.

Narrative is a literary genre that builds its sentences and paragraphs around discourses, episodes, or scenes. Grasping the real nature of narrative is vital for accurate interpretation. The study of narrative units of the biblical text is of critical importance as well, since, as Grant Osborne points out, "Narrative studies recognize that meaning is found in a text as a whole rather than in isolated segments."[4] Narrative texts can appear in three different modes: story, account, and report. The ability to recognize the various ways a narrative can be presented is a necessary first step to its understanding.

Most often, narratives appear in dramatic form, that is, as *stories* that are presented by the biblical writer with a view toward driving home the significance of a given biblical event or series of events. In this regard,

---

2. The notion of "language games" was first popularized by the Austrian philosopher Ludwig Wittgenstein in his *Philosophical Investigations*, trans. G. E. M. Anscombe (Oxford: Blackwell, 1953).

3. I (Andreas Köstenberger) still remember watching my first game of baseball when I came from my native Austria to the United States. Having never learned the rules of baseball or even seen a game, you might as well have dropped me off on the surface of the moon!

4. Grant R. Osborne, *The Hermeneutical Spiral*, 2d ed. (Downers Grove: InterVarsity, 2006), 200. See also Bar-Efrat, "Some Observations on the Analysis of Structure in Biblical Narrative," *VT* 30 (1980): 156, who analyzes biblical narratives on four levels: the verbal level, the level of narrative technique, the level of the narrative world, and the level of conceptual content.

it is important to remember that these stories, in turn, typically contain historical *accounts* of speeches and dialogues that comprise the scenes or episodes which together make up the full story. Indeed, dialogues often form crucial points in a given narrative.[5] In addition, a story may contain one or several *reports.*

MODES OF OLD TESTAMENT HISTORICAL NARRATIVE

Stories

Much of the historical information in the Old Testament is contained in narratives that are told in story form. Thus we gather details of Israel's early beginnings in the stories of the patriarchs found in the book of Genesis. We learn of events in the early days of Israel's occupation of the Promised Land through the stories about the various judges. Information concerning the establishment of the monarchy is often related in the form of tales concerning the exploits of David in the books of Samuel, while many events in the periods of the united and divided monarchies are told in the form of stories. For example, we learn of Solomon's fabled wisdom through the stories recorded in 1 Kings 3 and 10:1–13. Conditions in the Northern Kingdom surface in the stories of the prophets Elijah and Elisha (1 Kings 17–19; 2 Kings 2–8; 13:14–21).

Although historical information may be presented in story form, this does not mean that the information is non-factual. Stories may be pure fiction or true stories of real people and real events. Certainly the stories of the Old Testament tell of real events. They deal "with real life and with real people. People are complex and so are the great stories about them."[6] Accordingly, the interpreter should not dismiss the great stories of the Old Testament as of secondary historical value. Rather, he or she should be alert to the fact that in many cases these stories carry the historical narrative along, even while helping the reader to see the true nature of conditions in the larger context. Thus they are important in their own

---

5. As Alter observes, "The biblical writers . . . are often less concerned with actions in themselves than with how individual character responds to actions or produces them; and direct speech is made the chief instrument for revealing the varied and at times nuanced relations of the personages to the actions in which they are implicated." Robert Alter, *The Art of Biblical Narrative* (New York: Basic Books, 1981), 66.
6. J. Scott Duvall and J. Daniel Hays, *Grasping God's Word*, 2d ed. (Grand Rapids: Zondervan, 2005), 320.

right. What is more, the interpreter needs to be alert to distinguishing stories from straight historical accounts and reports. Although many of the elements of narrative occur in the latter two types, they are especially prominent in stories.

One of the major ingredients in many stories contained in the Old Testament is embedded oral discourse. For example, much of the patriarchal story of Joseph's adventures hinge upon *speeches* and *dialogues*. Joseph's reporting of his two dreams provokes his brothers to taking him captive and selling him into slavery in Egypt. Details in Joseph's early life in Egypt likewise turn on speeches and dialogues. Thus in Genesis 39 the narrator gives details of Joseph's social life as the manager of Potiphar's household (vv. 1–6). In time, he is faced with the advances of Potiphar's wife. The ensuing dialogue reveals the nature of both characters involved: her lust and Joseph's purity:

> After a while his master's wife took notice of Joseph and said, "Come in bed with me." But he refused. "With me in charge," he told her, "my master does not concern himself with anything in the house; everything he owns he has entrusted to my care. No one is greater in this house than I am. My master has withheld nothing from me except you, because you are his wife. How then could I do such a wicked thing and sin against God?" (vv. 7–9)

The story turns and moves forward on Joseph's words and the next words of Potiphar's wife. Her speech to her husband then forces Potiphar's hand—he must send Joseph to prison.

While in prison, it is Joseph's discussions with his fellow inmates, the cupbearer and the baker, in which he interprets their dreams that eventually bring him before the Pharaoh. Pharaoh has had two dreams and there is no one to interpret them. The cupbearer, now restored to Pharaoh's favor in accordance with Joseph's interpretation of his dreams, informs Pharaoh of Joseph's ability. Consequently, Joseph is brought out of prison to interpret the dreams. Here once again, the crucial points are reported in speeches (Gen. 41:9–36). Likewise, Pharaoh's putting Joseph in charge of economic affairs in Egypt is also given in direct speech (vv. 37–41). With the speeches and discourses duly reported, the narrator returns to a narrative account of subsequent events during Joseph's stay in Egypt.

Although Joseph's story could have been told in straightforward narrative, the speeches and dialogues make not only for dramatic effect but also provide deeper understanding of the character of those involved. The author has so developed the story that those speeches and dialogues provide turning points for events in the surrounding narrative. For this reason it is crucial for the interpreter to pause and focus on the oral discourses within the larger narrative. In so doing, he or she will not only increase his or her understanding of the character of the persons involved in the story but be caught up in the flow and actions of the whole context. As Leland Ryken points out, "The focus of narrative interpretation is almost always on the dramatic scenes."[7]

Another frequent ingredient in biblical stories is *description*. Here the emphasis is on the background of the narrative or on the characters involved. This includes descriptions of the various aspects of the setting of the story and other contextual indicators tying in the story with the preceding and following narrative. In addition, biblical stories often involve *commentary* provided by the biblical writer. Here the narrator supplies parenthetical information in order to clarify a given element of the story or comments on the significance of a character's actions or a certain event. In introducing the story of the Levite and his concubine, for example, the narrator discloses that "in those days Israel had no king" (Judg. 19:1), making mention of the unsettled state of affairs in the land. Similarly, later on in the story he observes, "In those days Israel had no king; everyone did as he saw fit" (Judg. 21:25).

It is also of interest to note that all or several of these elements— speeches or dialogue, description, and commentary—may be found in a single context. Thus after Israel's miraculous crossing of the Red Sea, we read of the following incident (Exod. 15:22–24):

Description: Then Moses led Israel from the Red Sea and they went into the Desert of Shur. For three days they traveled in the desert without finding water.

Narrative: When they came to Marah, they could not drink the water because it was bitter.

Commentary: (That is why the place is called Marah.)

Narrative: So the people grumbled against Moses, saying, "What are we to drink?"

---

7. Leland Ryken, *Words of Delight* (Grand Rapids: Baker, 1987), 44.

Although not every narrative context will contain all of these story elements, it is important for the interpreter to recognize those that are there and interpret them correctly. We now turn to a consideration of accounts and reports before dealing with the external and internal elements of Old Testament historical narrative.[8]

Accounts

Large sections of Old Testament narrative are written as historical accounts, including the Pentateuch and the so-called historical books (Joshua–Esther). Using selected facts of past events as material for building his perception of reality, the author arranges these into a coherent written history. In the case of the biblical author, of course, he has the guidance and insight of the Holy Spirit in his choice of recorded events and oral tradition. Doubtless some of the author's material came from direct revelation.

Tremper Longman notes that the historical material as written is not only factual information but also theological and doxological (accomplished ultimately by God and to his praise), didactic (in order to teach proper response and conduct), as well as aesthetically constructed (written with a view to achieving a pleasing literary work).[9] The result is an informative narrative of real events designed to provoke a proper response on the part of the reader. Such a response may be expected, therefore, because, as Longman points out, biblical historical narrative is more than a mere catalogue of facts and a record of events. It is *theological history*—designedly so. One may take the book of Chronicles as an example: "The Chronicler's viewpoint reflects the perspective of God and the ideology of the Hebrew Bible, making Chronicles a theological commentary on Israelite history."[10] Jacob Licht adds that biblical history is essentially "all 'sacred' history, in the sense of being ultimately concerned with the ways

---

8. Although some have suggested the presence of epic in the biblical narratives of the exodus and the life of David, the case is not clear cut. That the Hebrews once told an epic centered on the exodus may be reflected in the ancient poetry found in Exodus 15:1–18 and Habakkuk 3:13–15, as well as in poetic fragments scattered throughout the Old Testament. For details see Richard D. Patterson and Michael E. Travers, "Contours of the Exodus Motif in Jesus' Earthly Ministry," *WTJ* 66 (2004): 25–47.
9. Tremper Longman III, *Literary Approaches to Biblical Interpretation* (Grand Rapids: Zondervan, 1987), 68–71.
10. Andrew E. Hill, *1 & 2 Chronicles*, NIVAC (Grand Rapids: Zondervan, 2003), 33.

of God to men. Some of God's deeds, however, are perceived as being realized through the ordinary working of human agents, such as kings and rebels."[11]

A representative example may be found in Joshua 24 where Joshua, having gathered the leadership and citizens of Israel to Shechem, delivered his farewell address. First, he reviewed seminal events in Israel's history, including the call of Abraham, the exodus and the crossing of the Red Sea, the wilderness wanderings, and the conquest of the Promised Land (vv. 1–13). The emphasis throughout is on God's sovereign and gracious leading and on his provision for his covenant people. All that occurred in Israel's past was superintended by God and ultimately to his praise. The account is recorded in four aesthetically designed sections (vv. 2–4, 5–7, 8–10, 11–13), complete with a metaphor (the hornet) describing the stinging defeat God allowed Israel to achieve against the various people of Canaan (v. 12).

After this, Joshua moves on from information to motivation. God's dealings with Israel should cause them to respond in faithfulness to the Lord who has shown himself faithful to his people.

> Now fear the LORD and serve him with all faithfulness. Throw away the gods your forefathers worshiped beyond the River and in Egypt, and serve the LORD. But if serving the LORD seems undesirable to you, then choose for yourselves this day whom you will serve, whether the gods your forefathers served beyond the River, or the gods of the Amorites, in whose land you are living. But as for me and my household, we will serve the LORD. (vv. 14–15)

The historical narrative proceeds to record that the people responded favorably to Joshua's challenge (vv. 16–24), after which he led them in an act of covenant renewal (vv. 25–27).

The details of this historical narrative are designed not only for the purpose of recording the proper response of the people in Joshua's day but should have a similar effect on the part of the readers of Holy Scripture (2 Tim. 3:16). Just as Israel was incapable of serving the Lord in her own strength (Josh. 24:19–20), so God's people of all ages must have a

---

11. Jacob Licht, *Storytelling in the Bible*, 2d ed. (Jerusalem: Magnes, 1986), 15.

genuine relationship with God that makes it possible for the Lord to live out his life through them to his glory and for their good. God alone must have first place in the believer's life (Deut. 6:4–5; Prov. 3:5–6; cf. Matt. 22:37–40).

In sum, biblical historical narrative is more than an accurate account of past events; it is a *selective presentation of the facts designed to present a theological evaluation of that record—one that will bring about a proper spiritual and ethical response on the part of its readers.*[12] The interpreter should therefore examine the historical accounts of the Bible with a view toward keeping all of this in balanced perspective.[13]

Reports

Biblical narratives may also contain a report that provides information of a historical nature. Scripture contains many such instances. For example, the men who were sent to spy out the land of Canaan returned with the following reported to Moses and the people:

> We went into the land to which you sent us, and it does flow with milk and honey! Here is its fruit. But the people who live there are powerful, and the cities are fortified and very large. We even saw descendents of Anak there. The Amalekites live in the Negev; the Hittites, Jebusites, and Amorites live in the hill country, and the Canaanites live near the sea and the Jordan. (Num. 13:27–29)

The Old Testament narratives are replete with various reports (e.g., 2 Chron. 34:14–18; 2 Sam. 20:18–23, 35–42). In the prophetic genre, we find a special type of report known as a *vocation report* telling of the prophet's call and commission to the ministry. The Old Testament also contains numerous *battle reports* (e.g., Gen. 14:1–12; Josh. 10:1–15; 1 Sam. 31:1–7; 2 Sam. 1:1–10; 1 Kgs. 22:29–38; 2 Kgs. 25:1–21; etc.). There are also *census*

---

12. For selectivity in biblical narrative see Meir Sternberg, *The Poetics of Biblical Narrative* (Bloomington: Indiana University Press, 1987), 186–229.

13. As we shall see in the chapter on prophecy below, historical narratives may also be found in the prophetic books. There, too, we shall examine some narratives that are unique to prophetic genre. It may be added that the understanding of historical narratives is important for the study of those biblical laws, which are encased within them. For details see Joe M. Sprinkle, "Law and Narrative in Exodus 19–24," *JETS* 47 (2004): 235–52.

reports (Num. 1:17–46; Num. 26:1–62; 2 Sam. 24:4–9), and various other types of reports (e.g., 1 Kings 6–7; Ezra 5:6–17).

Closely related to these narrative reports are *lists or rosters*, which at times appear embedded within an historical narrative. For example, after David's last words (2 Sam. 23:1–7) and before the account of David's decision to take a census of his fighting men (2 Sam. 24:1–2), there is a roster of David's mighty men together with reports of some of their exploits (2 Sam. 23:8–36). To be noted also are the several lists of the tribes of Israel (Gen. 35:23–26; Exod. 1:1–4) and various other lists (1 Chron. 6:31–47; 23:1–32; etc.).

Significant also are *vision reports*. While these appear most prominently in the prophetic genre, they are also found in narrative literature. Customarily such visions came during the night (e.g., Gen. 46:2; 2 Sam. 7:4; Job 7:13–14; 20:8; 33:15; cf. Dan. 7; Mic. 3:6), though not always so (e.g., Ezek. 8:1–3).[14] Vision reports take on special significance when they contain God's words of instruction to an individual (e.g., Gen. 15:1; 46:2; 2 Sam. 7:4) and are followed by reports of the addressees carrying out of the divine command. Vision reports thus not only contain factual information and the effect that the vision had upon its recipient but report key events that move the narrative forward.

ELEMENTS OF OLD TESTAMENT HISTORICAL NARRATIVE

External Elements

Literary analysis commonly distinguishes three external elements: author, narrator, and reader.[15] The author and reader are usually considered in the context of determining whether the real or implied author or reader is in view. The real author is the one who actually wrote the narrative or story. What we know of this person from the narrative or story is termed "the implied author." Thus we may not know the real author or all that he knows about the narrative, but we do know what he has written. From that we draw certain conclusions about the real author. As Longman

---

14. The time of some visions is not expressly given (e.g., Isa. 6:1; Ezek. 1:1; 40:2).
15. David Howard Jr., *An Introduction to the Old Testament Historical Books* (Chicago: Moody, 1993), 49–55.

expresses it, "*The implied author is the author as he or she would be constructed, based on inference from the text.*"[16]

By the reader is meant the actual readers of the narrative; the "implied reader" is the one or ones for whom the author has composed his work. The readers may be the original audience, hence identical with the implied readers, or any who actually read the text including contemporary readers. It is crucial for the interpreter to place himself or herself as much as possible in the world of the implied reader so that he or she may make the proper transfer of application to the contemporary world.

A third distinction has to do with the one telling the story (the narrator) and the narratee—the one to whom it is told. In some literary compositions, an author will create a narrator who then tells the story. In Old Testament narratives, however, the narrator is usually the same as the implied author. The narrator may also take part in the narrative. At times, events may be told in the first person, as in the case of portions of Nehemiah. In any case, the narrator is always omniscient, even to the point of being able to inform his readers as to what the characters in the narrative are thinking. For example, in the account of Ben Hadad's challenge to King Ahab of Israel, we learn that the Aramean king heard Ahab's proverbial reply to his challenge "while he and the kings were drinking in their tents" (1 Kgs. 20:12). The narrator also knows precisely the reasons for the fall of the Northern Kingdom (2 Kgs. 17:7–23). David Howard points out that "this omniscient and omnipresent narrator can tell us of the details of conversation when no one was present except for the protagonists. Examples of this are found everywhere in historical narratives."[17]

The narratee may also be a part of the narrative. This phenomenon is particularly common in Old Testament prophetic literature (e.g., large parts of Obadiah and Nahum) where foreign peoples, citizens, or cities are addressed. In such cases, a distinction exists between the narratee and the implied reader. Although the narratees are those addressed, the implied readers are the people of Israel and/or Judah. In standard Old Testament narrative, however, no difference exists between the implied reader and the narratee.

This distinction is important for the student to understand. For prophetic passages do occur within historical narratives. For example, in the

---

16. Longman, *Literary Approaches*, 84.
17. Howard, *Introduction*, 50.

account of Sennacherib's siege of Jerusalem Isaiah sends a message from the Lord to King Hezekiah (the primary implied reader) but which is addressed to the king of Assyria (the narratee). Note, for example, the Lord's message through Isaiah in 2 Kings 19:22:

> Who is it that you have insulted and blasphemed?
>   Against whom have you raised your voice
> and lifted your eyes in pride?
>   Against the Holy One of Israel!

Doubtless Sennacherib never read these words.[18]

In sum, in most cases of Old Testament narrative accounts and stories the implied author and the narrator are one and the same, and the implied reader and the narratee are identical. As we have seen, however, distinctions do sometimes occur.

Internal Elements

Three internal elements provide the dynamic for the narrative: setting, plot, and characterization. The *setting* may include matters of physical location, time, or the cultural background of the narrative. *Plot* has to do with the arrangement of details in the narrative, while *characterization* considers the spiritual, moral, and psychological makeup of the characters of the narrative, as well as their role in the story.

Before the interpreter begins his examination of the narrative, he or she must determine the limits or boundaries of the narrative. An important Semitic compositional technique is particularly helpful here. An author often arranges his material in such a way that at the end of the narrative he will return to a theme, subject, or words mentioned at the beginning. This technique is known by such names as "book-ending" or *inclusio*. In addition, J. T. Walsh points out that subunits in historical narrative accounts may be organized symmetrically as parallel sequences or in such a way that attention is called to the center of the account.[19]

---

18. It is interesting to note that within this divine oracle the Lord reveals that he knows Sennacherib's very thoughts (2 Kgs. 19:23–24).
19. See Jerome T. Walsh, *1 Kings*, Berit Olam (Collegeville, MN: Liturgical Press, 1996), xiv.

Parallel sequences (A B C, A' B' C') provide balance between the two subdivisions and stress the need for comparative examination of the details. First Kings 13:11–34 may serve as an example. The story has to do with the man of God and the old prophet, around whom the action proceeds. In part one, the old prophet (A) hears news of the man of God (v. 11); (B) speaks and has his son saddle his donkey (vv. 12–13); (C) finds the man of God and brings him back to his home (vv. 14–15); and (D) speaks God's message (vv. 20–22), which (E) is then fulfilled (vv. 23–24).

In part two the old prophet (A') hears news of the death of the man of God (v. 25); (B') speaks and has his sons saddle his donkey (vv. 26–27); (C') finds the man of God's body and brings it back home (vv. 28–30); and (D') confirms the Lord's message (vv. 31–32), which (E') serves as an example of the sin that will lead to the downfall of the dynasty of Jeroboam I (vv. 33–34).

Walsh suggests that historical accounts that are built around a central theme of a given narrative can be formed in one of two ways: concentric symmetry (A B C B' A' cf. 1 Kgs. 17:17–24) or chiastic symmetry (A B C C' B' A'; cf. 1 Kgs. 12:1–20).[20] Although both of Walsh's symmetrical patterns have been traditionally termed "chiasm," the single center structure forms a hinge to both halves of the subject. In some cases, it becomes the main emphasis of the subunit.

Setting

Understanding the setting of a given narrative can be crucial to its interpretation. Interpreters should take note of several factors and ask themselves questions such as: Is the *physical location* significant to the action of the story? Surely such is the case in the account of the Battle of Ta'anach between the forces of the Hebrews under Deborah and Barak and those of the Canaanites led by Sisera (Judges 4–5). Sisera picked a place for battle in the wide expanse of the eastern Esdraelon Plain that would favor his iron chariots (Judg. 4:12–13). But recent rains had left the battlefield soggy and his chariots bogged down in the mire, leaving them virtually helpless (Judg. 5:19–22). At that moment, Barak swept down with his forces from his vantage point on Mount Tabor and "the LORD routed Sisera and all his

---

20. Ibid.

chariots" (Judg. 4:15).[21] Here the setting not only contributes to the understanding of the account but adds vividness to it.

Time may also contribute to the dynamics of the narrative. Thus Jacob, who was already apprehensive regarding his meeting with Esau, finds himself alone at night. In the pitch darkness, he has a physical encounter with one who proves to be the Angel of the Lord (Gen. 32:22–24). The night setting doubtless made the encounter more frightening for Jacob. The careful reader will not miss the drama of it all. Time of day and atmospheric conditions likewise play a role in Joshua's victory over the Gibeonites (Josh. 10:12–14).

Knowledge of the *cultural background* is especially important because of the great distance in time and differences between ancient and modern societies. Thus an understanding of culture is crucial to the proper interpretation of events in the story of Ruth, including Ruth's meeting at night with Boaz on the threshing floor (chap. 3) and such customs as conducting business at the city gate, redemption of property, and the institution of Levirate marriage (chap. 4).[22]

Plot

By "plot" we mean the ordering of events in the story. Plot is concerned with the arrangement of details by which the story has a beginning, middle, and end. Each part of the story contributes to the fabric of the whole.[23] The plot in biblical stories usually revolves around a conflict or contest (physical, psychological, or spiritual) and suspense (curiosity, dread, anticipation, or mystery). It is important for the interpreter to come to grips with these elements and to see the interrelationships between them.

The court tales of Daniel 2–7 provide excellent examples. In each chapter, there is a clear beginning or setting to the story. Trouble develops which the hero alone is able to resolve, resulting usually in reward—all of which is a testimony to God's working through his servant(s). Chapter 5 is a case in point. The story begins with Belshazzar giving a grand banquet for his nobles,

---

21. For consideration of these events see Richard D. Patterson, "The Song of Deborah," in *Tradition and Testament: Essays in Honor of Charles Lee Feinberg*, ed. John S. and Paul D. Feinberg (Chicago: Moody, 1981), 123–60.
22. See further Donald A. Leggett, *The Levirate and Goel Institutions in the Old Testament* (Cherry Hill, NJ: Mack, 1974).
23. For details see G. W. Brandt, "Plot," in *Cassell's Encyclopaedia of Literature*, ed. S. H. Steinberg (London: Cassell & Co., 1953), 1.421–23.

during which they praise their gods while drinking from goblets taken from the temple in Jerusalem by Nebuchadnezzar II (vv. 1–4). A crisis develops when "the fingers of a human hand appeared and wrote on the plaster of the wall, near the lampstand in the royal palace" (v. 5). The phenomenon causes great panic among all who are present. Moreover, the hand has written something on the wall which none of Belshazzar's wise men can interpret (vv. 5–9). At this point, the story takes a decisive turn or what critics call "the crisis." The queen mother appears and suggests that Daniel be summoned (vv. 10–12) who then interprets the message on the wall (vv. 13–28). With the problem resolved, in an epilogue Daniel is rewarded and his interpretation of the words comes true in the fall of Babylon that very night (vv. 29–30).[24]

Narrative plots may also take the form of archetypal plot motifs. By archetypal plot, we mean features or experiences that are common to mankind. It is helpful for the interpreter to be able to recognize certain of these types. Among the many that could be catalogued in the Bible, we note the following: the *quest*, in which a hero endures many obstacles and trials before achieving his desired or appointed goal (e.g., David); *tragedy*, in which matters begin well but then take a turn for the worse until the difficulties are overcome and end in success (e.g., Daniel 3, 6); and the *journey*, in which the hero faces dangers as he moves from place to place but which contribute to his personal character growth (e.g., Abraham).[25]

Characterization

As the example in Daniel 5 demonstrates, "the close association between plot and character may be observed in the fact that it is the character who generates the action that makes up the plot."[26] Yet the reader seldom receives a detailed description of a character's full nature or personality. Literary critics often describe a character as being round, flat, or simply

---

24. Daniel's court tales consist of two types, a contest in which the hero alone is able to solve seemingly insoluble puzzles and a conflict in which the hero's purity and spirituality are tested.
25. It should be noted that archetypes may also include individuals with specific character traits such as heroes or villains. See Leland Ryken, *How to Read the Bible as Literature* (Grand Rapids: Zondervan, 1984), 187–93. One such interesting character is the trickster, a trait seen in the patriarch Jacob. For details, see Richard D. Patterson, "The Old Testament Use of an Archetype: The Trickster," *JETS* 42 (1999): 385–94.
26. Tremper Longman III, "Biblical Narrative," in *A Complete Literary Guide to the Bible*, ed. Leland Ryken and Tremper Longman III (Grand Rapids: Zondervan, 1993), 72.

an agent: "A round (or full-fledged) character has many traits. A round character appears complex, less predictable, and therefore more real. A flat character has only one trait and seems one-dimensional. An agent, finally, has no personality to speak of and simply moves the story along."[27]

For example, in the stories concerning Elijah and Ahab in 1 Kings 18–22, both Elijah and Ahab may be described as "round," while Jezebel is "flat," and others are mere agents (e.g., Obadiah). Yet what we can know of individuals in the biblical stories is only that which the narrator reveals him or her to be or by what that person does.[28]

More basically, a biblical character is usually identified as to whether he or she is the *protagonist*, the main character of the story (e.g., Elijah, Ruth); the *antagonist*, the one who opposes the protagonist (e.g., Ahab); or simply a foil, one who provides a clear contrast to someone in the story (e.g., Obadiah, Jezebel). Events can also serve as literary foils in a story, such as Jacob's trickery in contrast to Esau's early impropriety (Genesis 25, 27). David's love for the Lord serves as a foil for all the kings who follow him.

The ability to recognize and utilize the above narrative elements will not only give the interpreter added insight into the intricacies of Hebrew accounts and stories but will make his presentation of them more vivid and dramatic for his audience. Both biblical expositors and listeners or readers will thus be swept up in the dramatic effect. This can make the narrative more realistic. Biblical characters become not just long dead or idealized persons of a distant, very foreign culture but real persons who underwent experiences that are in some way common to all humankind.

NARRATIVE STYLE

Repetition

Biblical narratives are often filled with various types of repetition. Indeed, "Repetition is perhaps the most widespread and widely recognized stylistic feature of biblical narratives. We find seemingly endless catalogues

---

27 Longman, *Literary Approaches,* 91–92.
28 See further Ryken, *Words of Delight,* 74–81. It is important to keep in mind that behind the Old Testament narratives stands the real hero of Israel—God himself. This fact is not missed by Moses in his Victory Song in Exod. 15:1–18. As Duvall and Hays (*Grasping God's Word,* 322) point out, "Throughout most of the Old Testament narrative literature, *God is a central character.* God is not aloof in the Old Testament, speaking only in shadows through the narrator. He is a major player in the story."

of repeated actions, in which characters state that they or others intend to (or should) do something and then the narrator states that they did indeed do it."[29]

Repetition may include plays on sounds or roots, keywords, themes, motifs, repeated dialogue, or repeated action sequences.[30] Thus Abigail confirms that her husband Nabal is well named, for he is a fool (*nābāl*; 1 Sam. 25:25). The theme of the third day as a marker of some new spiritual emphasis is common to the Old Testament (e.g., Exod. 19:10–16). The covenant theme occurs throughout the pages of the Scriptures. For example, a key chain of covenants is found in the unconditional covenants, especially the covenants with Abraham and David as embedded in the new covenant, which is confirmed in Christ's blood. The exodus also forms a basic motif common to both Testaments.

A characteristic of Semitic narrative is the repetition of speeches or dialogue. For example, Rehoboam repeats verbatim the advice of his younger counselors (1 Kgs. 12:8–14). Action sequences are often repeated in groups of three. Joseph's life story is centered on three dreams. The Lord calls Samuel, who reports to Eli, three times before Eli realizes that God was speaking to the lad (1 Sam. 3:1–9). Israel repeatedly apostatized in the sight of the Lord (Judg. 3:7, 12; 4:1; 6:1; 10:6; 13:1). Coming to grips with the convention of repetition will often enable the interpreter to avoid critical suggestions that such cases constitute redactional influence.

Highlighting

The narrator often calls particular attention to some detail or character trait in the individual in the story. Thus Joseph's purity is underscored throughout the accounts of his life, as is David's having a heart for God, and Daniel's commitment to the Lord. Ahab is consistently portrayed as a selfish, even evil, person.

Irony

Irony has to do with the reversal of what is said or expected. Old Testament narratives are filled with many such instances.[31] For example, Job's

---

29. Howard, *Historical Books*, 56.
30. For details, see Alter, *Biblical Narrative*, 88–113; Licht, *Storytelling*, 51–95.
31. See further J. C. L. Gibson, *Language and Imagery in the Old Testament* (Sheffield: Almond, 1981), 18–20.

wife tells him, "Bless God and die" (Job 2:9). She really means, "Why not curse God and get it over with?" Indeed, although the Hebrew word literally means "bless," translators uniformly render the sense of the context, rendering the word as "curse." The expression is thus taken as a euphemism said in irony. In the book of Esther, Haman is hung on the gallows he had prepared for Mordecai!

There is also dramatic irony by which the narrator imparts to the reader a given piece of information that the characters in the narrative do not know. This phenomenon is common to both Testaments. For example, throughout the historical narratives in Kings we learn that the seeming changes in the political climate among the nations were not chance happenings but were regulated by God himself. Although David is moved to take a census of Israel, we learn that which David and his followers do not know; it is Satan who actually incited him to do so (1 Chron. 21:1). In 2 Samuel 24:1, however, we also learn that "the anger of the Lord burned against Israel and he incited David against them, saying, 'Go and take a census of Israel and Judah.'"[32] Thus the reader knows what none of the participants in the census knows: Satan, as permitted by God (cf. Job 1:12; 2:6), is the instigator behind David's decision to take a census.

Whenever the surface meaning of the text appears to be directly opposite to the context, we may suspect that the author intended the reader to understand that he is using irony.

Satire

Satire consists of an attempt to demonstrate through ridicule or rebuke the vice or folly of that which appears to be improper or ill-conceived. For example, in recounting the contest between David and Goliath, the narrator of Samuel exposes the giant's taunts as wrong-headed. What Goliath's gods and superior strength could not accomplish a young, ill-equipped shepherd boy could do, with God's help. Not only did the mighty warrior have a great fall from sling and stone, but he was decapitated by his own sword (1 Sam. 17:41–51)!

---

32. The seeming contradiction in the accounts is double edged. David's pride served as an easy avenue for Satan to tempt him to see just how great he was. The lack of genuine faithfulness among God's people would provide justifiable cause for God to allow Satan to pursue the temptation of David.

Ahab's classic retort to the taunts of the Aramean king Ben-hadad drips with satire: "Tell him: 'one who puts on his armor should not boast like one who takes it off'" (1 Kgs. 20:11). Ahab's reply suggests that Ben-hadad ought not to boast of victory while he is putting on his armor. He may not live to take it off! Another classic case is the familiar contest between Elijah and the prophets of Baal on Mount Carmel. At the height of the contest, when Baal has failed to respond to his prophets, Elijah taunts them by saying, "Surely he is a god! Perhaps he is deep in thought, or busy, or traveling. Maybe he is sleeping and must be awakened" (1 Kgs. 18:27).

SAMPLE EXEGESIS: 1 KINGS 19

Introduction

The account of Elijah's ministry in 1 Kings 19:1–18 is set within the long account of Elijah's ministry (1 Kings 17–19). This pericope serves to gather together additional details in bringing the full account to a close. The implied author (or narrator) writes the entire section to inform his readers of both the prophet's great moments of triumph and also of his shortcomings. Throughout the narrative, Elijah is portrayed as a fully human servant who succeeds only when God is in control of his life (e.g., 1 Kings 18). Composed in dramatic narrative, chapters 17–19 have a distinct literary structure built around the plot line concerning the story of Elijah's service of Yahweh:

1. Prologue: Elijah's call (17:1–6);

2. Development: Elijah at Zarephath (17:7–24);

3. Crisis: Elijah's message to King Ahab (18:1–19);

4. Climax: Elijah vs. the prophets of Baal and Asherah (18:20–46);

5. Denouement: Elijah's flight to Horeb (19:1–18); and

6. Epilogue: Elijah and the call of Elisha (19:19–21).

History

Elijah's prophetic ministry takes place in the days of the reign of Ahab, king of the northern kingdom (874–853 B.C.). It is an era of great spiritual drought typified in the conduct of Ahab and Queen Jezebel. First Kings 19:1–18 proceeds in a series of three short scenes: Jezebel's threat causes Elijah to flee (19:1–5a); although Elijah is discouraged to the point of wanting to die, he is sustained by an angel who tells him to go on further (19:5b–8); while at Mount Horeb, Yahweh first reproves and then restores his prophet (19:9–18).

Literature

As for characterization, Elijah is clearly the protagonist, while Jezebel serves as the antagonist. Indeed, her threats toward Elijah and his response demonstrate the fierceness of her personality. And no wonder, even Ahab was often intimidated and certainly corrupted by her. His marriage to Jezebel, a Sidonian princess, served only to bring further spiritual degeneration in Israel. Her consistently bad conduct and attitude thus make her to be viewed as a flat character.

Serving as a literary foil, the angel provides a striking contrast with Elijah as a servant of the Lord. The protagonist Elijah, while the presumed hero of the story, displays a far different side to his character than the reader has seen in the previous two chapters. Gone is the obedient servant of Yahweh who at God's direction was fed by ravens (17:1–6). Gone is the man of faith who saw to the widow's needs, including the resuscitation of her son (17:7–24). Gone, too, is the confident prophet who instructed Obadiah and the king himself (18:1–19) and who boldly and successfully confronted the prophets of Baal in Asherah (18:20–46).

Rather, it is a fearful and disillusioned Elijah who flees before the wrath of a vengeful and ruthless queen and in his despair wishes for death. Perhaps he had basked too long in the glow of the spectacular. In any case, he is seen to be one who has need of instruction, encouragement, and self-examination (19:1–5a). To his credit, in response to the divine instruction, correction, and divine recommissioning, Elijah (19:5b–18) returns to active service in the Lord's ministry (19:19–21).

Although the story line features Elijah throughout the denouement, in the ultimate sense it is Yahweh who is the true hero. It is he who again provides for the nourishment of his prophet (19:5b–9) and graciously admonishes and restores him to active duty (19:10–18). It is he who is sovereign over Elijah's journey to Horeb and the renewed opportunity to carry out the Lord's delegated work. It is the Lord, therefore, who is highlighted in such a way that he is both available for Elijah's needs and the one to whom Elijah must give an account.

Throughout chapter 19, the careful interpreter will find many opportunities to appreciate the author's skill in teaching by allusions. When studying this unit, he will be able to appreciate what the narrator intends his audience to understand. For example, he will recognize echoes of past events of Elijah's life and of Israel's forebears in the angel's nourishing of Elijah; in his 40 days' journey to Mount Horeb; his taking refuge in a cave during the Lord's personal dealing with him; and his threefold recommissioning to service. The earthquake and fire will recall similar phenomena at Mount Sinai. The strong contrast will be apparent between the Lord's spectacular answer to Elijah's petition on Mount Carmel and his speaking to him here in a "gentle whisper" (NIV). Nor will the careful interpreter fail to interact with a poignant datum in the dialogue between Elijah and the angel and his speaking with Yahweh.

Theology

With this data in hand, the student of Scripture will be able to understand the flow of the narrative more clearly and be in a position to make some pertinent applications to Christian living. At the very least, he or she will come to realize the most important spiritual lesson in this episode: living for God does not always take place in the world of the extraordinary. Rather, much of life's service for the Lord is carried on in the realm of the mundane realities of life. The believer's place is simply that of humble and obedient service to the Lord and his leading in the everyday occurrences of life.

GUIDELINES FOR INTERPRETING
OLD TESTAMENT HISTORICAL NARRATIVE

1. Determine the limits or boundaries of the narrative at hand, while recognizing its internal structural features.
2. Consider whether the narrative mode is direct, descriptive, dramatic, or commentary. Does the full context employ some combination of these?
3. Ask yourself whether the historical narrative functions basically as an account or report, or is it told in story form. Does more than one of these forms occur in the full context?
4. Come to grips with the respective roles of the author, reader, narrator, and narratee. Try to put yourself in the place of the narratee (or implied reader).
5. Examine the setting of the narrative. What do you learn from such features as geography, time, or culture within the narrative?
6. If the narrative is told in story form, look carefully for the flow of the story. Identify such features of the plot as its beginning, middle, denouement, resolution, and epilogue. Are there archetypal plot motifs present here? What biblical motifs and themes are resident in the full context?
7. In stories, identify the protagonist, antagonist, and what foils may be present.
8. Learn to appreciate the author's literary style, considering such features as dialogue, repetition, highlighting, irony, and satire.
9. Throughout the interpretive process employ sound exegetical procedures, noting the contributions of grammar, history, literary constraints, and theological emphases.
10. Drawing all of these data together, make a proper application to the contemporary situation. Ask how the narrative impacts the reader or hearer's spiritual life.

KEY WORDS

Account: presentation of history that includes theological interpretation

Antagonist: the person opposing the protagonist

Characterization: the depiction of major and minor figures in the narrative

External elements of narratives: features outside the narrative, such as author, narrator, and reader

Highlighting: the literary technique of drawing attention to a particular detail in the story

Internal elements of narrative: features of the narrative itself, including setting, plot, and characterization

Irony: a dramatic turn of events often involving reversal of expectations

Narrative: a literary genre that builds its sentences and paragraphs around discourses, episodes, or scenes

Plot: the arrangement of events in the story

Protagonist: the main character of a story

Report: a narrative providing historical information

Satire: an attempt to demonstrate through ridicule or rebuke the vice or folly of that which appears to be improper or ill-conceived

Setting: information as to the place, time, and circumstances of a given event

STUDY QUESTIONS

1. What is narrative, and what are the various modes of narrative?

2. What are some examples of Old Testament stories, accounts, and reports? Discuss how understanding these subgenres is significant for biblical interpretation.

3. What are the three external and three internal elements of biblical narrative? List and briefly describe each of these elements.

4. What are at least three characteristics of narrative style in biblical narrative?

5. How does the sample exegesis of 1 Kings 19 apply the various points made about the nature of narrative earlier in the chapter?

6. What are the guidelines for interpreting Old Testament historical narrative?

ASSIGNMENTS

1. Identify the basic modes of narrative. Apply this data to the narrative concerning Jacob in Genesis 32.

2. Discuss Esther 4 first as a story and then as an historical account. What results and values obtained in each case?

3. Daniel 6 has commonly been termed a "court tale." Accepting Daniel 6 as a valid historical account told in the format of a court tale, discuss such essential features as: historical setting (e.g., location, time, and cultural background), plot (including beginning, development, climax, and denouement), and characterization (identifying the protagonist, antagonist, and foil).

4. Discuss the use of repetition and highlighting in the following narratives:
    a. 2 Kings 1
    b. 2 Kings 2:1–18
    c. Acts 7

4. Discuss Job's use of irony in his reply to Zophar in Job 12:1–12.

5. Identify the element of irony in Jesus' parable of the rich fool in Luke 12:13–21.

CHAPTER BIBLIOGRAPHY

Alter, Robert. *The Art of Biblical Narrative.* New York: Basic Books, 1981.

Arnold, Bill T. and H. G. M. Williamson, eds. *Dictionary of the Old Testament Historical Books.* Downers Grove: InterVarsity, 2005.

Bar-Efrat, S. "Some Observations on the Analysis of Structure in Biblical Narrative." *VT* 30 (1980): 154–73.

Barton, John. *Reading the Old Testament; Method in Biblical Study.* Rev. and enl. ed. Louisville: Westminster John Knox, 1996.

Chisholm, Robert B. *From Exegesis to Exposition.* Grand Rapids: Baker, 1998.

Greidanus, Sidney. *Preaching Christ from Genesis.* Grand Rapids: Eerdmans, 2007.

Gunn, David M. and Danna Nolan Fewell. *Narrative in the Hebrew Bible.* Oxford: Oxford University Press, 1993.

Howard, David M. Jr. *An Introduction to the Old Testament Historical Books.* Chicago: Moody, 1993.

Licht, Jacob. *Storytelling in the Bible.* 2d ed. Jerusalem: Magnes, 1986.

Sternberg, Meir. *The Poetics of Biblical Narrative.* Bloomington: Indiana University Press, 1985.

Walsh, Jerome T. *Style and Structure in Biblical Hebrew Narrative.* Collegeville, MN: Liturgical Press, 2001.

CHAPTER 6 OBJECTIVES

1. To acquaint the student with the nature and characteristics of biblical poetry.

2. To acquaint the student with the chief structural patterns of biblical poetry.

3. To enable the student to recognize the major stylistic devices found in biblical poetry.

4. To acquaint the student with the nature and types of wisdom literature.

5. To suggest prominent biblical texts for the study of poetry and wisdom.

CHAPTER 6 OUTLINE

A. Nature and Characteristics of Biblical Poetry
   1. Parallelism
      a. Similar Parallelism
      b. Antithetic Parallelism
      c. Progressive Parallelism
   2. Terseness
   3. Concreteness
   4. Imagery
B. Poetry in the New Testament
C. Structural Devices in Biblical Poetry
   1. Building Blocks
   2. Structural Indicators
   3. Chiastic Structure
   4. Bifid Structure
D. Stylistic Devices in Biblical Poetry
E. Wisdom Literature
   1. The Nature of Wisdom
   2. Proverbs
   3. Ecclesiastes
   4. Job
   5. Wisdom Elsewhere in the Old Testament
   6. Wisdom in the New Testament
F. Sample Exegesis: The Book of Job
G. Guidelines for Interpreting Biblical Poetry
H. Guidelines for Interpreting Wisdom Literature
I. Key Words
J. Study Questions
K. Assignments
L. Chapter Bibliography

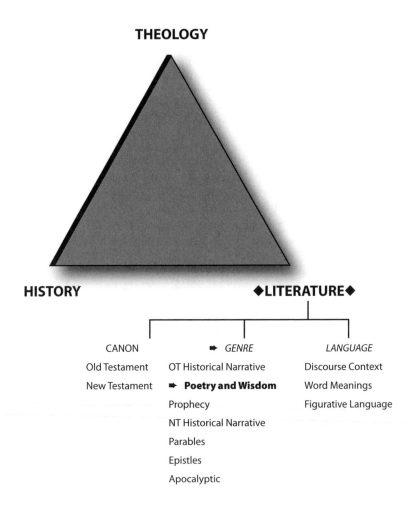

THEOLOGY

HISTORY   ◆LITERATURE◆

CANON   ➡ GENRE   LANGUAGE

Old Testament   OT Historical Narrative   Discourse Context

New Testament   ➡ **Poetry and Wisdom**   Word Meanings

                   Prophecy   Figurative Language

                   NT Historical Narrative

                   Parables

                   Epistles

                   Apocalyptic

Chapter 6

A WORD FROM THE WISE: POETRY AND WISDOM

NATURE AND CHARACTERISTICS OF POETRY

FOLLOWING OLD TESTAMENT NARRATIVE, THE next genre we encounter on our canonical journey through Scripture is that of poetry or wisdom. Although some have cast doubt on the accuracy of labeling any biblical text as poetry,[1] it is generally agreed that poetry does occur in the Bible. In addition to a host of positive features that distinguish poetry from prose,[2] certain prominent features that occur frequently in prose are rarely found in poetry. These include especially the definite article, the relative particle *'asher,* and the sign of the definite direct object (*'et*). Indeed, there is a paucity of connectives and prepositions in poetry. Granted the scholarly consensus concerning the parameters of biblical poetry, we will suggest guidelines for its interpretation.

Parallelism

In contrast to prose, which constructs its sentences and paragraphs around narrative discourse, episodes, or scenes, poetry is built around

---

1. E.g., James L. Kugel, *The Idea of Biblical Poetry* (New Haven: Yale University Press, 1981).
2. See, e.g., Wilfred G. E. Watson, *Classical Hebrew Poetry* (Sheffield: University of Sheffield, 1986), 44–62; Robert Lowth, *Lectures on the Sacred Poetry of the Hebrews* (Boston: Crocker & Brewster, 1829); Michael O'Connor, *Hebrew Verse Structure* (Winona Lake, IN: Eisenbrauns, 1980).

individual lines, which commonly feature the heightened use of imagery and figurative speech. Although the basic unit of thought remains the individual line, the most recurring feature of Hebrew poetry is repetition. This can be seen especially in the poet's use of parallelism, the practice of using similar language of approximately the same number of words and length, and containing a corresponding thought, phrase, or idea over succeeding lines. Parallelism may occur in various patterns and be used for different purposes.

Similar Parallelism

The most common use of parallelism is to provide a closeness of thought and expression over parallel lines. Yet even here we should guard against the idea that the poet is simply saying the same thing in two different ways. Thus Alter correctly observes that where similar parallelism does occur, there is a heightening or intensifying of meaning so as to "move from a standard term in the first verset to a more literary or highfalutin term in the second verset."[3] Note, for example, Psalm 19:1:

> The heavens declare the glory of God;
>> the skies proclaim the works of his hands.

In this example, the subject and verb of each line are clearly paralleled with nearly synonymous meaning, but the object in the second line moves beyond that of the first. The two lines display similar deliberately schematic features, yet there is a clear advance in the second. The combined effect of the two lines brings a new dynamic to the whole thought. Thus the heavens testify not only to the glory of God but to his creative work, here stated anthropomorphically as having been done by God's own hands.

Such instances could be greatly multiplied. Consider the following examples:

> If you have been trapped by what you said,
>> ensnared by the words of your mouth. (Prov. 6:2)

> For he founded it upon the seas
>> and established it upon the waters. (Ps. 24:2)

---

3. Robert Alter, *The Art of Biblical Poetry* (New York: Basic Books, 1985), 13.

In both cases, we detect a similarity of grammatical structure and phraseology, but there is a change of imagery. In the first example, the one putting up security for the other runs the danger of being trapped by words spoken from his very own mouth. In the second, the imagery of God's creative work involving the seas is transferred to that of water in motion. Consider also the following words from Psalm 46:7:

> The LORD Almighty is with us;
> the God of Jacob is our fortress.

The careful exegete will ask himself, "What similarities and advance do I find here?" This illustrates the essence of understanding poetry. Poetry calls for the interpreter to enter into the world and thinking of the poet. In so doing, he or she reflects on the poet's experiences and mood in order to discern the poet's meaning and reasons for his choice of imagery. In reflecting on Psalm 46:7, ideas and images such as God's presence, provision, and protection will come readily to mind as well as scriptural passages reflecting God's care for his own.

Some similar parallel structures are presented with an inversion of grammatical structure. We may call these *inverted similar parallelisms*. Note, for example, Psalm 78:10:

> They did not keep God's covenant
> and refused to live by his law.

Unfortunately, such cases are not always evident in English translations. Thus the Hebrew here would be better rendered:

> They did not keep God's covenant
> and in his law refused to walk.

By juxtaposing "covenant" and "law," the effect of the inversion in the parallel lines is to call attention to the seriousness of deliberate covenantal failure while changing the thought of personal conduct to that of the familiar biblical image of walking (cf. Gen. 17:1; Ezek. 18:9). In other passages, the movement from the first line to the second may involve (1) a change from a general location to a specific one (Ps. 78:43) or (2) from a personal name to one's patrilineage (Num. 23:18) or (3) from a personal name together with one's patrilineage to an individual's distinctive characteristic (Num. 24:3):

> The day he displayed his miraculous signs in Egypt,
>> his wondrous in the region of Zoan.
> Arise, Balak, and listen;
> '   hear me, son of Zippor.
> The oracle of Balaam son of Beor,
>> the oracle of one whose eye sees clearly.

All such examples may be listed under the general heading of *similar parallelism with epithet* in the second line.

Antithetic Parallelism

Rather than similarity of thought, some parallel lines may display a sharp contrast:

> Righteousness exalts a nation,
>> but sin is a disgrace to any people. (Prov. 14:34)

In addition to the just-noted simple parallelism over two lines, some contrast may be compounded over several lines. Note, for example, Isaiah 1:3:

> The ox knows his master,
>> the donkey his owner's manger,
> but Israel does not know,
>> my people do not understand.

The example contains poignant imagery. In contrast to dumb animals who recognize who their master is and where their daily provision comes from, God's people fail to understand that they belong to God and that everything they have is due to him.

Progressive Parallelism

With progressive parallelism, a succeeding line (or lines) supplements and/or completes the first line. Psalm 57:1 may serve as a representative example:

> Have mercy on me, O God,
>> have mercy on me,
>> for in you my soul takes refuge.

Here, the reason for the Psalmist's urgent cry is spelled out clearly in the closing line. We should note, however, that a causal particle is not always present in a parallel line. Consider Psalm 98:2:

> The LORD has made his salvation known
>> and revealed his righteousness to the nations.

Although there is a similarity of structure here, clearly the second line completes the thought of the first. The psalmist touches on two matters here: God's deliverance of his people, which in turn serves as a testimony of his righteousness to the surrounding people. That two groups are being considered is evident from the context, for the new song (v. 1) contains imagery of God's deliverance drawn from Exodus 15:11–12 (his right hand and his holy arm) while verse three commemorates God's covenant love and faithfulness toward Israel in his deliverance which the nations have clearly seen. Contextually, therefore, verse two displays a clear progression of thought that is only completed with both lines.

Special types of progressive parallelism may also be differentiated. In *staircase parallelism*, succeeding lines begin with similar phraseology leading to a completion of the thought in the first line.

> Sing to the LORD a new song;
>> sing to the LORD, all the earth.
> Sing to the LORD, praise his name;
>> proclaim his salvation day after day. (Ps. 96:1–2)

Here, the repeated call for singing God's praise leads to the celebration of his name (his established character and reputation) and is climaxed by the call to proclaim God's daily saving acts. Thus the new song of verse one is seen to be not only new in time with each day's passing but qualitatively new in accordance with God's continued blessings.

A type of staircasing is known as *terrace pattern parallelism*. In such instances, the progression is facilitated by repeating at the beginning of the second line the words or phraseology at the ending of the first. Note, for example, Psalm 96:12–13:

> Then all the trees of the forest will sing for joy;
>> they will sing before the LORD, for he comes,
>> he comes to judge the earth.

A variation of this arrangement is to omit one of the words or phrases so that a single element appears in one of the two lines but is to be understood in both. We can demonstrate this by comparing the words of Psalm 96:13 with those of Psalm 98:7–8:

> Let the rivers clap their hands,
>> let the mountains sing together for joy;
> let them sing before the LORD,
>> for he comes to judge the earth.

By comparing the phrase "for he comes" in Psalm 96:13 with that in Psalm 98:8 we can see that its single occurrence in the latter is intended to do double duty as a hinge connecting two parallel lines. We may term this type of parallelism *hinge terrace parallelism*.

Progression is at times indicated by utilizing a numerical sequence known as *ladder parallelism*. In these cases, the second line contains the next highest or corresponding digit. Consider the following two examples:

> There are three things that are too amazing for me,
>> four that I do not understand:
> The way of an eagle in the sky,
>> the way of a snake on a rock,
> the way of a ship on the high seas,
> and the way of a man with a maiden. (Prov. 30:18–19)

> Saul has slain his thousands,
>> and David his tens of thousands. (1 Sam. 18:7)

In both cases, the numerical sequence directs special attention to the elements indicated by the higher number. Where a literal number is intended, it is always the higher number, and the items under consideration are spelled out as in the Proverbs example. Where a literal number is not intended, no further details are given, as in the citation from 1 Samuel 18. In both cases, the numerical sequence not only attracts the hearer or reader's attention but also serves as an aid to memorization.

Progression may also be accomplished by the formal means of beginning each succeeding line or set of lines with the next successive letter of the Hebrew alphabet. Psalm 119 is a well-known case. Other psalms include Psalms 25, 34, 37, 111, 112, and 145. An incomplete alphabetic acrostic has often been noted in the combination of Psalms 9 and 10. Acrostics serve not only as stylistic and memory devices but invite the reader to consider the effect of the whole composition.

One other type of clear progression has traditionally been known as *emblematic parallelism*. Here, the parallelism is accomplished by way of a simile. Thus Psalm 103:15 states:

> As a father has compassion on his children,
> so the LORD has compassion on those who fear him.

Not only is God's love illustrated by comparing it to that of a human father but the comparison also invites an argument *a fortiori* (from the lesser to the greater; lit. "to the stronger"). If a father can have compassion on his children, how much more can God feel compassion for his own? The effect in Psalm 103:15 is to underscore the emphasis begun in verses 11–12. *A fortiori* arguments may of course also be stated in formal parallel fashion:

> If the righteous receive their due on earth,
> how much more the ungodly and the sinner! (Prov. 11:31)

Terseness

A second characteristic of Hebrew poetry is its terseness. Poets have a way of stating their thoughts so concisely that the result is a polished and succinct presentation free of unnecessary details. Consider the dramatic effect of Nahum's description of the attack against Nineveh:

> The crack of whips,
> the clatter of wheels,

galloping horses
   and jolting chariots!
Charging cavalry,
   flashing swords
   and glittering spears! (Nah. 3:2–3)

Note as well Moses' tribute to Yahweh in his victory song after Israel's deliverance through the waters of the Red Sea:

Yahweh is a man of war
   Yahweh is his name. (Exod. 15:3; Heb. text)

Here, we are presented in succinct fashion with the figure of the Lord as a conquering warrior with an established reputation as the sovereign God of all in the well-known theme of the Name.

Concreteness

A third feature of poetry is its concrete nature. As Michael Travers observes, poetry "allows the reader to see, taste, touch, smell, or hear the matters, which the poet portrays."[4] In this regard, the contrast between prose and poetry becomes pronounced. This may be seen in the dual accounts of the report of Sisera's death at the hands of Jael. The prose account details Sisera's flight from the Israelite army; his meeting with Jael and their conversation; Jael's killing of the now exhausted commander of the Canaanite army; and the subsequent arrival of Barak, the commander of the pursuing Israelites (Judg. 4:17–22). The poetic account, however, centers attention on Sisera's demise and reports with dramatic flair:

He asked for water, she gave him milk;
   in a bowl fit for nobles she brought him curdled milk.
Her hand reached for the tent peg,
   her right hand for the workman's hammer.
She stroke Sisera, she crushed his head,
   she shattered and pierced his temple.

---

4. Michael Travers, "Poetry," in *Dictionary for Theological Interpretation of the Bible*, ed. Kevin J. Vanhoozer (Grand Rapids: Baker, 2005), 595.

At her feet he sank,
　he fell; there he lay.
At her feet he sank, he fell;
　where he sank, there he fell—dead. (Judg. 5:25–27)

Here, one can almost see Jael as she takes the heavy iron tent stake, places it at sleeping Sisera's temple, and hammers it home. Jael has delivered the *coup mortel* to the mighty enemy commander who now lies dead at the feet of a simple Kenite wife. How the mighty have fallen!

Imagery

A fourth characteristic of poetry is its abundant use of imagery. Poets tend to think in images rather than abstractions. By using an image, a poet portrays reality or expresses it in more concrete terms that demand the interpreter's careful attention and interaction. As Tremper Longman observes, "Imagery is a concise way of writing, because an image conveys not only information but also evokes an emotional response."[5]

Imagery makes frequent use of figurative language. Here, words take on a sense other than their literal meaning. Thus two dissimilar things are brought together in a comparative way. By using figurative language, the poet not only makes his work more striking and colorful but also invites the reader to observe and meditate more closely on what he is saying. At the same time, the compressed language of figures makes for a conciseness of expression that is more easily remembered.

As we noted in Chapter 5, a host of figures occurs in biblical poetry.[6] Particularly plentiful are figures of comparison such as metaphor and simile. Thus the Song of Solomon is replete with imagery employing metaphor and simile. Note, for example, the following:

I am a rose of Sharon
　a lily of the valleys.

---

5. Tremper Longman III, "Psalms," in *A Complete Literary Guide to the Bible*, ed. Leland Ryken and Tremper Longman III (Grand Rapids: Zondervan, 1993), 251.
6. See also the extensive presentation in Roy B. Zuck, *Basic Bible Interpretation* (Wheaton: Victor, 1991), 143–68; E. W. Bullinger, *Figures of Speech Used in the Bible* (London: Eyre & Spottiswoode, 1898; repr. Grand Rapids: Baker, 1968).

Like a lily among thorns
    is my darling among the maidens (2:1–2).

Because many of these involved the person and work of God, it is important that the interpreter grasp the force of the figures involved. Consider the following:

The LORD is my shepherd. (Ps. 23:1)

As a shepherd looks after his scattered flock . . .,
    so will I look after my sheep. (Ezek. 34:12)

Hear us, O Shepherd of Israel. (Ps. 80:1)

In turn, God is likened by the use of metaphor, simile, and *hypocatastasis*. In a metaphor, a given object is identified as another: the Lord *is* a shepherd. By way of a simile, one object is likened to another: the Lord is (acts) *like* a shepherd. By means of *hypocatastasis*, one object is called another: "O shepherd," "you shepherd." In each instance, the poet creates a visual image of a shepherd and his sheep. As a shepherd tends his flock, so the Lord cares for his people.

Some comparisons are not so complimentary while nonetheless presenting vivid pictures. Consider the following:

Am I a dog that you come at me with sticks? (1 Sam. 17:43)

As a dog returns to its vomit,
    so a fool repeats his folly. (Prov. 26:11)

Dogs have surrounded me. (Ps. 22:16)

Here again, the careful observer will note the variation between the three figures mentioned above.

Anthropomorphisms ascribe human characteristics or qualities to God. Especially common are the various parts of the human body such as the face (Rev. 6:16), mouth (Isa. 1:20), tongue (Isa. 30:27), lips (Job 11:5), eyes (Ps. 33:18), ears (Ps. 71:2), feet (Ps. 18:9), hands (Isa. 64:8), arms (Isa.

51:5), fingers (Ps. 8:3), and heart (Jer. 32:41).[7] Anthropopathisms ascribe human emotions such as compassion to God:

> How can I give you up, Ephraim?
>> How can I hand you over, Israel?
> How can I treat you like Admah?
>> How can I make you like Zeboiim?
> My heart is changed within me;
>> all my compassion is aroused. (Hos. 11:8)

Similarly, God is often portrayed as repenting (Jer. 26:3) or relenting about performing a given action.

By the use of a zoomorphism, animal qualities are ascribed to God. Thus God's tender care of the believer may be likened to that of a bird, while his chastening power is compared to that of a lion:

> He will cover you with his feathers,
>> and under his wings you will find refuge. (Ps. 91:4)

> For I will be like a lion to Ephraim,
>> like a great lion to Judah.
> I will tear them to pieces and go away;
>> I will carry them off, with no one to rescue them. (Hos. 5:14)

The careful interpreter of God's Word will need to make the necessary comparative mental leap and visualize the poet's portrayal in these and the other figures detailed in Chapter 5. Coming to grips with the nature of the figures involved in context is crucial to proper interpretation. It can even be a means to avoiding improper theological conclusions. For instance, failure to recognize anthropomorphic descriptions of God could lead to viewing God in purely physical terms rather than as he is—an eternal, infinite, and perfect spirit (John 4:24).

7.　See Richard D. Patterson and Michael E. Travers, *Face to Face with God: Human Images of God in the Bible* (Richardson, TX: Biblical Studies Press, 2008).

POETRY IN THE NEW TESTAMENT

All the above examples have been taken from the Old Testament. Nevertheless, the principles involved are applicable in large measure where poetry exists in the New Testament. We will do well to remember that with the possible exception of Luke, the New Testament authors were all Jewish by background. When it came to poetry, therefore, they would likely think in terms of Old Testament precedents. This is easily missed in reading the New Testament, because our English translations often fail to present relevant passages as poetry.

For this reason the various parallel structures we have already noted can be encountered in the New Testament, whether (1) similar, (2) antithetic, or (3) progressive. Consider the following examples:

> (1) Ask and it will be given to you;
>> seek and you will find;
>> knock and the door will be opened to you. (Matt. 7:7)

> (2) Likewise every good tree bears good fruit,
>> but a bad tree bears bad fruit. (Matt. 7:17)

> (3) Blessed are the merciful,
>> for they will be shown mercy. (Matt. 5:7)

You will also find parallel structures such as (1) staircase parallelism, including (2) the terrace pattern, and (3) emblematic parallelism. Note the following examples:

> (1) Whoever welcomes this little child in my name
>> welcomes me;
> and whoever welcomes me
>> welcomes the One who sent me. (Luke. 9:48)

> (2) If anyone is to go into captivity,
>> into captivity he will go.
> If anyone is to be killed with the sword,
>> with the sword he will be killed. (Rev. 13:10)

(3) As the Father has sent me,
  I am sending you. (John 20:21)

Poetry may also be seen in the psalmic praises clustered around the nativity (Luke 1:47–55, 67–79), in many of the sayings of the New Testament (1 Tim. 3:16), and in its hymns and songs (Luke 2:14; Rev. 11:15; 15:3). Some passages are recorded as poetry in the New Testament (e.g., Phil. 2:5–11). It is of interest to note that it has often been suggested that one may detect here an earlier poetic saying around which Paul may have fashioned his full poem:

Being in the very nature of God,
  made himself nothing;
being found in appearance as a man,
  he humbled himself. (vv. 6–8)

New Testament poetry likewise features terseness and concreteness. Note the following examples:

(1) Everyone should be quick to listen, slow to speak
  and slow to become angry. (Jas. 1:19)

(2) You are like whitewashed tombs,
  which look beautiful on the outside
but on the inside are full of dead men's bones
  and everything unclean. (Matt. 23:27)

Imagery may be found throughout the pages of the New Testament, especially in the sayings of Jesus. Ryken observes concerning Jesus, "The leading poet of the New Testament is of course Jesus. In fact, Jesus is one of the world's most famous poets. His sermons and discourses are essentially poetic in style. Jesus' speech, for example, is saturated with metaphors and similes."[8] This may be seen in his discourses built around the "I am" sayings in John (6:25; 8:12; 9:5; 10:7, 11, 14; 11:25; 14:6; 15:1). Ryken correctly observes that Jesus "spoke in images rather than theological abstractions. . . . To understand the message

---

8. Leland Ryken, *Words of Life* (Grand Rapids: Baker, 1987), 102.

of Jesus in the Gospels, we need to apply all that we know about how poetry works."[9] Indeed, Jesus often taught in mind-engaging pictures.

By appreciating the poetic nature of relevant New Testament passages, the interpreter gains a new perspective. Even theological discourses become alive with new dramatic dimensions of structure, sight, sound, and stylistic sensitivity. Consider the effect of reading the familiar introduction to John's Gospel (1:1–18) as a predominantly poetic portion opening the Johannine account. In fact, "The prologue doubtless represents one of the most beautiful and carefully crafted poetic portions in the entire NT."[10] We note here only verses 1–5:[11]

> [1] In the beginning was the Word,
>   and the Word was with God,
>   and the Word was God.
> [2] He was with God in the beginning.
> [3] Through him all things were made,
>   and without him nothing was made
>   that has been made.
> [4] In him was life,
>   and that life was the light of men.
> [5] The light shines in the darkness,
>   but the darkness has not overcome it.

In light of our earlier discussion of poetic features and Semitic compositional techniques, what types of parallel structure do you see here? What compositional techniques are in evidence? What is the impact of such imagery as life, light, and darkness? How does an appreciation of terseness and concreteness help you to understand and feel more deeply the theological concepts that John is communicating? We suggest that in asking yourself questions such as these you will gain a new perspective and appreciation of the poetic skill with which John opened his Gospel.[12]

---

9. Ibid., 103.
10. Andreas J. Köstenberger, *John*, BECNT (Grand Rapids: Baker, 2004), 19–20.
11. Some have suggested that the prologue to John was drawn from an existing poem (whether written by John or another) into which John has inserted narrative material concerning the role of John the Baptist (vv. 6–8, 15). For details see David L. Barr, *New Testament Story* (Belmont, CA: Wadsworth, 1987), 242–43.
12. For consideration of the whole prologue, see Köstenberger, *John*, 19–50.

STRUCTURAL DEVICES IN BIBLICAL POETRY

Building Blocks

Quite obviously parallelism is both an essential feature of biblical poetry and also an important structural form. Here, however, we are thinking of the basic building blocks that comprise the full poem. Poetic structuring begins with the individual line known variously as a stitch (pronounced "stick"), verset, or colon. We shall adopt the term "colon" for our discussion.

A *monocolon* is an individual poetic line which does not combine closely with another colon.[13] It can be used to introduce a unit or a sub-unit of thought. Note, for example, Psalm 18:1: "I love you, O LORD, my strength." Here the psalmist's testimony of his love for God stands independently from the following poetic lines even though it colors all that he has to say throughout his psalm of praise to the Lord. Similarly, Psalm 11:1 begins with the psalmist's declaration of his love for God, which in turn is to be understood (though not structurally connected) in the rest of the psalm.

A monocolon can also be found at the close of a psalm. Thus Psalm 2 ends with a final single line of tribute to the Lord: "Blessed are all who take refuge in him" (Ps. 2:12). Occasionally, a monocolon functions as aposiopesis or sudden break in the flow of thought or structure. For example, in the midst of his description of eschatological military preparations Joel exclaims, "Bring down your warriors, O LORD!" (Joel 2:11) The individual line here serves not only as a sudden break in the description of events but constitutes an apostrophe or direct address to someone as though he were present. Not only people, but also things may be addressed as though they were present in form of an apostrophe: "O land, land, land, hear the word of the LORD!" (Jer. 22:29).

Parallel thought over two successive lines is commonly known as a *bicolon*. We have noticed such examples in the preceding discussions, for it is perhaps the most common of all poetic structural devices. It is especially present in wisdom poetry. Consider the following:

My mouth will speak words of wisdom;
    the utterance from my heart will give understanding. (Ps. 49:3)

---

13. For details, see Wilfred G. E. Watson, *Classical Hebrew Poetry* (Sheffield: University of Sheffield, 1986) 12.

> The fear of the LORD is the beginning of knowledge,
>> but fools despise wisdom and discipline. (Prov. 1:7)

A *tricolon* consists of three lines that form a distinct unit. It, too, is extremely common in biblical poetry. Although tricola may occur anywhere in a psalm (e.g., Ps. 10:9), they frequently stand at the head of a unit or subunit of poetry. Note the following examples:

> The LORD is my rock, my fortress and deliverer;
>> my God is my rock, in whom I take refuge.
> He is my shield and the horn of my salvation, my stronghold. (Ps. 18:2)

> Listen to my prayer, O God,
>> do not ignore my plea;
>> hear me and answer me. (Ps. 55:1–2a)

Tricola may also be found at the end of a unit or subunit. Psalm 16 ends with these words:

> You have made known to me the path of life;
>> you will fill me with joy in your presence,
>> with eternal pleasures at your right hand. (Ps. 16:11)

Psalm 18 concludes by saying,

> He gives his king great victories;
>> he shows unfailing kindness to his anointed,
>> to David and his descendants forever. (Ps. 18:50)

Bicola and tricola are at times interchanged to indicate structural boundaries of units or subunits of thought. In Habakkuk's two-part victory song (Hab. 3:1–7, 8–15), the transition between the two sections is effected by closing the first stage with a tricolon plus a bicolon and by initiating the second section with a bicolon plus a tricolon:

> The ancient mountains crumbled
>> and the age-old hills collapsed,

his ways are eternal.
I saw the tents of Cushan in distress,
    the dwellings of Midian in anguish. (vv. 6–7)
Were you angry with the rivers, O LORD?
    Was your wrath against the streams?
Did you rage against the sea
    when you rode with your horses
    under the wind and your victorious chariots? (v. 8)

Habakkuk not only combines his two poems by means of this structural patterning but also marks the change to the second poem by changing his sentence patterns to interrogatives.

Four-line cola (*tetracolon or quatrain*) and five-line cola (*pentacolon*) are rarer. Each, however, is attested. Psalm 114 is composed of four quatrains while Psalm 9:13–14 is structured by means of a pentacolon.

In poetry, the various line types are gathered together into larger units. Although different terminology is used among scholars, we adopt here the designations used by Watson who divides the full poem into successively smaller units known respectively as a *stanza* and a *strophe*.[14] Moving in the opposite direction from smallest to largest, the various cola discussed above may form a strophe. One or more strophes may constitute a stanza, and stanzas are combined to make up the full poem. Ideally, poems of some length consist of several stanzas, which are further subdivided into strophes consisting of one or more cola. Thus the above-mentioned psalm of Habakkuk (3:3–15) may be diagrammed as follows:

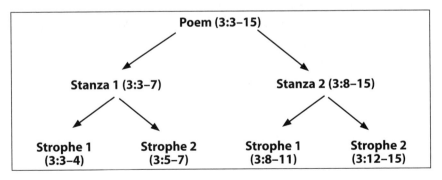

---

14. Ibid., 13–14.

The various strophes are composed of alternating bicola and tricola lines of poetry.

Structural Indicators

It is one thing to be aware of the building blocks of poetry; it is another to recognize them. In determining distinct subunits of a given poetic piece, such as a psalm, we should keep in mind the various compositional techniques mentioned in Chapter 5 which will be covered more fully in the following chapter in connection with the guidelines for interpreting prophecy. Here we note in particular *bookending* (or *inclusio*) and *stitching*, both of which are extremely common in biblical poetry.

Bookending entails the technique of returning at the end of a unit to a theme, subject, or word(s) mentioned at the beginning of that section. The result of the inclusio thus formed is to enclose the intervening material so as to form a distinctive section of thought, much as a collector places a series of similar books between two bookends. Poets at times employ bookending to enclose whole poems. Thus Psalm 103 begins and ends with a call, "Praise [lit. bless] the LORD, O my soul" (vv. 1, 22). Individual subunits may similarly be detected. For example, Nahum's prediction of the Lord's judgment against Nineveh is enclosed by the theme of wickedness (Nah. 1:11, 15). The psalmist condemns the folly of amassing wealth apart from godly living by employing words for riches (Ps. 49:16, 20).

Poets also made use of *stitching*. By stitching, we mean the author's practice of linking successive units or subunits of a poem by means of repeating a word, phrase, or idea. Whole psalms may be linked together in the canon by such means. For example, Psalm 135 picks up the emphases on praise and ministry in the house of the Lord expressed in Psalm 134 (cf. Ps. 134:1 with 135:1–2). In turn, Psalm 135 prepares the reader for Psalm 136 with its emphasis on God's goodness (cf. Ps. 135:3 with Ps. 136:1). Psalm 135 also serves as a hinge (a third compositional technique) between the two surrounding psalms.

Stitching between units of a poem is extremely common. We may take Psalm 146 as an example. Here the words "river" and "stream" of the second stanza (vv. 4–7) provide stitching to the theme of water (v. 3) in the first stanza (vv. 1–3). Likewise, the idea of God as a refuge and strength (v. 1) provides further stitching for the thought of God being with his people as a fortress (v. 7). In turn, stanzas two and three are stitched together by words such as "nations" (vv. 6, 10) and "fortress" (vv. 7, 11), and the thought of the Lord Almighty being "with us" (vv. 7, 11).

We noted above that Psalm 135 serves as a hinge (or bridge) psalm between Psalms 134 and 136. A single verse can also stand as an independent unit of thought which, though forming a transition between two sections, also partakes in some measure of the two it connects. Thus Zephaniah 3:8 picks up the theme of judgment/justice and the nations (vv. 1–7) and prepares the reader for the theme of the eschatological day in verses nine through twenty. Verse eight also links together the emphasis on the city of Jerusalem common to both the preceding and following sections (cf. vv. 1, 7, with 11, 16). Even the prophets could express themselves in finely structured poetry.

Several other structural indicators may also be noted. Introductory particles, words, or phrases often reflect the fact that the poet has moved on to a new topic or unit of thought. In Psalm 46, the transition from the poet's praise and confidence in God in the first two stanzas to a new emphasis is marked by his invitation to "come and see the works of the LORD" (v. 8). Such invitations are not uncommon (e.g., Ps. 34:11; 66:5, 16; Isa. 1:12). Similarly, transitions to new units of thought are accomplished in Psalm 17 by the psalmist's renewed call to hear and answer his prayer (v. 6) and his further plea for the Lord's deliverance, confident of God's action (v. 13). Also, poets often begin units by expressing the Lord's condemnation using words such as "woe" (e.g., Nah. 3:1; Hab. 2:6, 9, 12, 15; Zeph. 3:1).

A clear change of subject matter may also indicate a new poetic unit. Such is common enough in literature. By way of illustration, note the flow of thought in Psalm 18. David's praise to God for the Lord's answering his call for deliverance from great trouble (vv. 4–6) is followed by words drawn from the historical record of Israel's deliverance during the exodus event (vv. 7–15; cf. Exod. 15:14–16; Judg. 5:4b–5; Ps. 68:8–9; 77:16–18; 144:5–6; Hab. 3:8–15). David then returns to testifying of God's delivering him out of great distress (Ps. 18:16–18). The implication is that the same great power God used in liberating Israel has been exercised on David's behalf. Note that although there is a change of subject matter in successive units of thought, there is coherence in the overall portrayal. The interpreter therefore needs to look not only for the shifting emphases of thought and subject matter in successive sections but to discern how each part contributes to the total picture that the poet wishes to convey.

David's shift of subject matter in the second psalm is also illustrative of this fact. Here the psalmist turns his attention away from the prevailing rebellious attitude of the hostile powers of earth (vv. 1–3) to the Lord's reaction: he has installed his own king (vv. 4–6). The psalm then records that king's words concerning God's promise to him (vv. 7–9). This is followed by the psalmist's closing advice to the rebellious to surrender to God's declared plans for the governance of the earth through his Anointed One.

Grammatical change may also signal the start of a new unit. In Zephaniah 3, there is distinct verbal variation from God's rehearsal of his past dealings with Israel (vv. 6–7) to the above-mentioned hinge verse which contains an imperative (v. 8). This is then followed by appropriate verbs indicating God's future plans (vv. 9–20). Grammatical patterning also at times indicates change of subject matter. For example, Psalm 73 begins with the psalmist's opening statement of confidence in the Lord ("surely"; v. 1) and is followed by a statement of his past problem ("but as for me"; v. 2). The poet then states the cause of his problem: the success of the wicked, which includes expressions of their attitude and actions (introduced by the word "therefore"; vv. 6, 10). The poet's past problem is rounded out by means of another "surely" expressing his resultant feelings concerning their success despite their godless behavior (vv. 13–17). The latter parts of the psalm also show similar, though not identical, patterning (vv. 18–28).

Structural change may also include the use of the refrain. For example, consider these words in Psalm 42:5, 11:

Why are you downcast, O my soul?
　Why so disturbed within me?

Put your hope in God,
　for I will yet praise him,
　　my Savior and my God.

This twice-recurring refrain also appears in Psalm 43:5. Along with other data, this has suggested to many that originally the two psalms were one composition. Among other poetic refrains, we may note the following examples:

> Be exalted, O God, above the heavens;
>> let your glory be over all the earth. (Ps. 57:5, 11)

> O my Strength, I watch for you;
>> you, O God, are my fortress, my loving God. (Ps. 59:9; cf. v. 17)

Chiastic Structure

In *chiastic structure*, the second half of a composition takes up the same words, themes, or motifs as in the first half, but in reverse order. Often these two parts are united around a common core that can form the most prominent idea or intended emphasis of the author. The chiasm may cover two lines or three lines or even more. For example:

> A   Wait for the LORD;
>> B   be strong and take heart
>
> A' and wait for the LORD. (Ps. 27:14)

Whole compositions can also be written in form of a chiasm. Thus in Psalm 70, the psalmist's prayer for deliverance (vv. 1, 5) encloses a central core in which he asks for his enemies defeat (vv. 2–3) and God's blessing upon the righteous (v. 4).

One must avoid the temptation, however, to find chiastic structure almost everywhere. Some have gone to great lengths to reconstruct poetic pieces built around the slimmest of evidence such as a single word. To be sure, the A B A' pattern is attested even in the earliest literature of the ancient Near East, but this does not give precedent for ingeniously finding or creating a chiasm where it does not exist.

Bifid Structure

By *bifid structure*, we mean the poet's structuring of his material in two parts, each answering to the other in similar or corresponding fashion and in the same basic order. For example, in Psalm 135 the opening and closing calls to praise the Lord (vv. 1–2, 19–21) enclose a central section composed as a bifid. Verses 3–18 may be outlined as follows:

6.1. PSALM 135:3–18	
A. In his great goodness God has chosen Israel to be his people (3–12)	His unchanging nature guarantees his vindication of and compassion for his people (13–18)
1. Opening ascription of praise for God's goodness to his chosen people (3–4)	Opening declaration of God's fame and unchanging goodness (13–14).
2. Reminder of God's greatness over all gods/nature/peoples (5–12)	Rehearsal of God's greatness as compared with other gods and their idols (15–18)

Nahum's twofold prophecy of Nineveh's demise shows a pattern of theme, development, and application in each of its parts:

6.2. NAHUM'S TWOFOLD PROPHECY	
Nineveh's Doom Declared	*Nineveh's Doom Described*
Theme: 1:2	2:1–2
Development: 1:3–10	2:3–10; 3:1–7
Application: 1:11–15	2:11–13; 3:8–19

Likewise, Zephaniah can be understood as being written in bifid structure:

6.3. BIFID STRUCTURE OF ZEPHANIAH	
Pronouncements against the earth (1:2–3)	Pronouncements against the nations (2:4–15)
Pronouncements against Judah (1:4–6)	Pronouncements against Jerusalem (3:1–7)
Exhortation (1:7–13)	Exhortation (3:8)
Information (1:14–18)	Information (3:9–13)
Instructions (2:1–3)	Instructions (3:14–20)

Here again a note of caution is in order. The student should be careful not to suggest bifid structure unless the material clearly reflects the author's intended scheme.

STYLISTIC DEVICES IN BIBLICAL POETRY

In addition to characteristics such as terseness, concreteness, and the poet's skillful use of figures of speech and imagery, there are miscellaneous features of style. Two such devices are rhyme and rhythm. Unfortunately, unless one is dealing with the original text, rhyming is not always apparent in biblical translations. Too often we miss this nice touch of the literary artist. For example, consider Nahum 1:15:

> Celebrate your festivals, O Judah,
>> and fulfill your vows.

The parallel Hebrew words translated "festivals" and "vows" both end in -*ayik* but this is not apparent in our English translation. If one wished to reflect the sound form of the Masoretic Text, he could render the bicolon in question as follows:

> O Judah, observe your celebrations,
>> fulfill your sacred declarations.

When we think of rhyme, however, we must not consider the intricate patterns of western poetry. Most commonly Hebrew rhyming is a matter of repeated similar endings. Thus in Isaiah 33:22, the fourfold repetition of the personal plural pronominal suffix -*nû* forms a clear rhyming pattern, which is missed in translation.

Not to be forgotten also is the more common rhyming consisting of two-word patterns as in the well-known *tōhû wābōhû* (formless and empty, Gen. 1:2). Similar *assonance* is common enough. Note, for example, Nahum 2:10: *bûqāh ûměßûqāh ûměßullāqāh*. Here we see at work not only sound play (assonance) but *alliteration* in the repeated use of a restricted number of Hebrew letters. The effect of the whole may be represented as follows: "destroyed, despoiled, and denuded." Like assonance, so alliteration is very common in the Hebrew Old Testament. Both devices made for ease of memorization.

Another literary device of poetry is the use of synonyms in successive poetic lines. For example, note Habakkuk 3:8:

> Yahweh, were you angry with the rivers,
>   or was your wrath against the streams
>   or your fury against the sea?

Here, three sources of water are heaped up to call dramatic attention to the Lord's triumphs at the Red Sea and the Jordan River.

Admittedly, full-blown rhyming in whole stanzas or poems is rare if not virtually absent in the Old Testament (although they do occur in later Hebrew literature). So also is the use of rhythmic patterns despite many ingenious attempts to demonstrate various metrical patterns (which again do occur in later Hebrew literature). We are thinking here of patterns such as those that contain two beats, one long and one short: trochaic (/u), iambic (u /), or spondaic (uu), and those containing three beats: dactylic (/ uu), anapest (uu /), amphibrach (u / u), and tribrach (uuu).[15] Because the reader of modern translations seldom feels rhyme, assonance, and alliteration, the student who is unfamiliar with the original languages is dependent upon those commentaries that take the trouble to point out these features. To become familiar with them, however, is to appreciate more fully the poet's emphases, point of view, and literary skill.

Several other poetic devices are also worthy of passing mention. The poet will often use an unusual word order to draw attention to a particular item. Consider Psalm 63:8. Although not rendered adequately in English translations, the poet's great pleasure because of God's sustaining him is expressed in the placing of the direct object "me" as the first word in the parallel line of the bicolon (MT):

> My soul clings to you;
>   me your right hand upholds.

The effect is to underscore the intimate relationship between David and his Lord. A similar effect is felt in Jeremiah 2:13 where in succeeding lines Jeremiah rehearses the Lord's deep disappointment over his faithless

---

15. Note that / here represents an accented syllable and u an unaccented one.

people: "Surely my people have committed two evils; me they have forsaken." Not only is the direct object placed first in the clause for emphasis, but in the original text it is preceded immediately by "my people" as the final words in the previous clause. The effect is to juxtapose the words "my people" and "me."[16]

Another poetic device is *allusion*. Thus in his condemnation of the people's pursuit of the god Baal (Jer. 2:33) Jeremiah points out that the people have abandoned the true baal (= husband). The imagery of Yahweh as a husband versus the false god Baal forms an allusion which can be felt throughout the second and third chapters of Jeremiah (e.g., 2:2, 22; 3:14; see also Jer. 31:22). Allusion is common in both prose and poetry but is particularly efficient in poetry. Thus one can hear an allusion to Genesis 49:10 in Ezekiel's mournful dirge where the phrase "to whom it rightfully belongs" (Ezek. 21:27) is an echo of Jacob's blessing on Judah, which is usually translated simply as "Shiloh" (lit. "the one whose it is").

Still another poetic device is *ellipsis*, the deletion of a word present only in one parallel line of poetry even though it is to be understood in both. Consider the following examples:

Sound the trumpet in Gibeah,
> the horn in Ramah. (Hos. 5:8)

He shot arrows and scattered the enemies,
> bolts of lightning and routed them. (2 Sam. 22:15)

In both cases, the verb of the first parallel line is absent in the second line, though felt in both lines.

Other examples demonstrate yet another poetic device known as a ballast variant. In cases where a major variant in one line is not attested in the parallel line, one or more words tend to be longer than the counterpart in the other line. Note the following examples:

God came for Teman,
> the Holy One from Mount Para. (Hab. 3:3)

Balak brought me from Aram,

---

16. Note in the full verse the play on the idea of water in the repeated phrases and words: living water, cisterns, and broken cisterns that can hold no water.

the king of Moab from the eastern mountains. (Num. 23:7)

A familiar stylistic device is the use of *fixed word pairs.*[17] This entails the practice of utilizing standard pairs of words in succeeding parallel lines. Most commonly the words so employed are synonyms. Note the following examples:

Let all these rest on the head of Joseph,
on the brow [lit. pate] of the prince among his brothers. (Gen. 49:26)

On the day you stood aloof
when strangers carried off his wealth
and foreigners entered his gates. (Obad. 11)

In some cases, related activities are brought together as in the love-hate relationship:

Do not rebuke a mocker or he will hate you;
rebuke a wise man and he will love you. (Prov. 9:8)

Still others bring together a name, which is paralleled in the second line by an epithet. Note, for example, the following:

He swore an oath to the LORD
and made a vow to the Mighty One of Jacob. (Ps. 132:2)

A star will come out of Jacob;
a scepter will rise out of Israel. (Num. 24:17)

Although there are many examples of poetic devices in the Old Testament, the New Testament writers used some of these same devices to convey their thoughts. Thus Paul used rhyme and word pairs in the creedal hymn in 1 Timothy 3:16 and assonance and alliteration in his

---

17. For a consideration of the use of fixed word pairs in Northwest Semitic, see Mitchell Dahood, "Ugaritic-Hebrew Parallel Pairs," in *Ras Shamra Parallels*, Vol. 1, ed. Loren R. Fisher (Rome: Pontificium Institutum Biblicum, 1972), 71–382.

admonition in Philippians 4:4. Set word pairs and phrases are also found in the title "King of Kings and Lord of Lords" (1 Tim. 6:15; cf. Rev. 19:16). As with the Old Testament, the perceptive interpreter will identify poetic elements in the New Testament. In this regard, helpful information may be gained not only from special studies in New Testament literature but from newer translations, which often present pertinent passages in poetic format.

WISDOM LITERATURE

Nature of Wisdom

In approaching the literature traditionally termed as wisdom, the interpreter must first come to terms with its nature. Although the books of Job, Proverbs, and Ecclesiastes are commonly known as the books of wisdom, wisdom literature may be found in many places in both the Old Testament and New Testament. Accordingly, it is important to recognize wisdom as a genre and become acquainted with its chief characteristics.

One may gain insight into the biblical concept of wisdom by noting the words used to express wisdom. Among the many biblical terms are especially the following Hebrew words: *bīnâ* (insight), *haśkîl* (prudence), *tĕbunnâ* (understanding), and *tûšîyâ* (resourcefulness). Of central importance is the notion of the skill and expertise born of virtue to apply godly wisdom properly. This is expressed in both the Hebrew *hokmâ* and Greek *sophia* (wisdom). Common themes in wisdom literature such as genuine piety, morality, and proper thinking provide additional insight. Biblical wisdom "sought in the first place, to provide guidance for living by propounding rules of moral order and, in the second place, to explore the meaning of life through reflection, speculation, and debate."[18]

Although human wisdom that is traditional (e.g., Job 15:8–10) and/or purely humanistic wisdom (e.g., Isa. 29:14; 1 Cor. 1:20; 2:6) are acknowledged in the Bible, genuine wisdom is rooted in God, humanity's Creator (Job 28:25–28). True human wisdom finds its norm in the wisdom by

---

18. R. B. Y. Scott, *The Way of Wisdom in the Old Testament* (New York: Macmillan, 1971), 22.

which God created and orders his universe (Deut. 4:6; Prov. 8:22–31). It includes not only the accumulation of knowledge but above all the skill to discern how to apply the principles of godly wisdom to specific situations (e.g., 1 Kgs. 3:7–10, 16–28; cf. 27- Dan. 5:14). These include interaction with human institutions (cf. Matt. 19:1–12), whether legal or cultural standards, and with the created order, whether the world of creatures or the physical world (cf. Gen. 3:27–30; 1 Kgs. 4:29–34; Job 38–41; Prov. 3:19–24).

The roots of wisdom are in the fear of the Lord (Ps. 111:10; Prov. 1:7). This involves understanding God as the Creator who controls all things and consummates history (Ps. 104:24–32) and as the one with whom we all have to do (Eccl. 12:13–14). Where these principles are taught as keys to godly living, they belong to the genre of wisdom literature. All wisdom literature is basically instructional in nature, with the author attempting to impart wise observations on the meaning of life and the proper conduct necessary to enjoy life to the fullest.

Wisdom literature may appear in many types. It may involve precepts or instructions intended to give advice for living the successful and happy life. These are often delivered in the form of proverbs, at times expressed as the teaching of a father to a son or of a teacher to his students. Treatises or essays provide a discourse on the meaning of life. Wisdom may be expressed in the form of a disputation in which one takes up the merits or demerits of one's opponent. Some wisdom literature is pessimistic or devoted to a denunciation of the evils of society. Still other wisdom literature may occur as a lamentation due to the punishment society has incurred because of ungodly or immoral conduct. Much of wisdom literature is couched in imagery as figures of speech are designed to provoke thinking and reflection on the nature of its teaching. Literary devices such as satire, sarcasm, riddles, parables, and allegories are often found in wisdom literature as well.

Proverbs

When we think of wisdom literature, our minds are immediately drawn to the book of Proverbs. Proverbs are short memorable statements of the true state of things as perceived and learned by human observations over extended periods of experience. In terms of the biblical book of Proverbs, this refers to an apophthegm (a short, witty, and instructive saying) that has currency among those who fear the Lord.[19] The proverbial literature found here thus exists in short pithy statements, but it may be found in the more extended instructional saying as well. When reading Proverbs, the interpreter should also keep in mind the principles of poetry discussed earlier in the chapter.

Biblical proverbs may be categorized in various ways. Thus W. C. McKane classified the proverbs in chapters 10:1–22:16 and chapters 25–29 as to whether they deal with wisdom and life (A), society at large (B), or the individual (C).[20] Type A deals with general wisdom designed to give practical suggestions for a successful and harmonious life. Type B discloses behavior that has a distinct effect on society, while Type C features moral truths intended for personal piety and purity as standards for personal behavior. Although some overlap can be noted in McKane's classifications and his observations were limited to specific sections of the book, his suggestions do point to the various areas of need for living a life of wisdom in a great number of the proverbs.

Some proverbs may be classified as either descriptive or prescriptive. *Descriptive proverbs* may be presented as a portrait of a way of life:

> The sluggard says, "There is a lion in the road,
>> a fierce lion roaming the streets!"
> As a door turns on its hinges,
>> so a sluggard turns on his bed."
> The sluggard buries his hand in the dish;
>> he is too lazy to bring it back to his mouth.
> The sluggard is wiser in his own eyes,
>> than seven men who answer discreetly. (Prov. 26:13–16)

Sometimes proverbs such as these take the form of a short sketch such as a discussion on the exemplary ways of the ant.

> Go to the ant, you sluggard;
>> consider its ways and be wise!
> It has no commander,

---

19. Bruce Waltke, *The Book of Proverbs Chapters 1–15*, NICOT (Grand Rapids: Eerdmans, 2004), 56.
20. William McKane, *Proverbs: A New Approach*, OTL (Philadelphia: Westminster, 1970), *passim*.

no overseer or ruler,
    yet it stores its provision in summer
        and gathers its food at harvest. (Prov. 6:6–8)

Still other descriptive proverbs are extended into short narratives such as that of the adulterous woman (Prov. 7:6–23) or wisdom's preparing a feast (9:1–6).

The aim of *prescriptive proverbs* is motivational. Good standards and habits thus have their own reward:

The fear of the LORD is a fountain of life,
    turning a man from the snares of death. (Prov. 14:27)

Other proverbs may be viewed as comparative or contrastive. *Comparative proverbs* may be expressed as one thing being better than another or being likened to another. Note the following examples:

Better a dry crust with peace and quiet
    than a house full of feasting, with strife. Prov. 17:1)

Like one who seizes a dog by the ears
    is a passer-by who meddles in a quarrel not his own. (Prov. 26:17)

Such proverbs attempt to point out the superiority of one manner of living to another as well as suggesting the benefits of the superior way.

Contrastive proverbs likewise point to a better course of living but do so by presenting diametrically opposed settings. These may apply to the individual or corporate situations. Note the following:

Pride only breeds quarrels,
    but wisdom is found in those who take advice. (Prov. 13:10)

Righteousness exalts a nation,
    but sin is a disgrace to any people. (Prov. 14:34)

Conditional proverbs deal with the consequences of a person's actions. Consider the following:

If a man pays back evil for good,
> evil will never leave his house. (Prov. 17:13)

If a man digs a pit, he will fall into it;
> if a man rolls a stone, it will roll back on him. (Prov. 26:27)

In some cases, this type of proverb will contain an *a fortiori* argument (argument from the lesser to the greater).

If the righteous receive their due on earth,
> how much more the ungodly and the sinner! (Prov. 11:31)

Declarative proverbs are primarily designed to make a statement. Consider the following examples:

An unfriendly man pursues selfish ends;
> he defies all sound judgment. (Prov. 18:1)

Before his downfall a man's heart is proud.
> But humility comes before honor. (Prov. 18:12)

Although all proverbs provide insight into wise living, some may be specifically classified as *instructional proverbs*. These characteristically have a distinctive structure, which contains an imperative plus motivation and/or accompanying conditions:

A. Imperative
   1. Single: positive (3:9), negative (23:9)
   2. Double: positive (4:24), negative (22:24)
   3. Positive + negative (1:8; 3:1)
B. Motivation: reason(s) for the imperative(s)
   1. Via conclusion drawn from:
      a. Experience (23:20–21)
      b. Theological principle (3:11–12)
   2. Via consequential statement (3:2)
   3. Via behavioral description (1:16–17)
C. Attendant conditions (3:27–30)

Numerical proverbs are cast in the form of *staircase parallelism*, a feature we noted earlier in the chapter. As a further example, consider Proverbs 30:15–16:

> There are three things that are never satisfied,
>> four that never say, "Enough!"
> The grave, the barren womb,
>> land, which is never satisfied with water,
>> and fire, which never says, "Enough!"

This type of proverb usually contains wise observations on the way things appear to be, sometimes with a touch of satire as in the previously cited example from Proverbs 30:18–19. Other examples include Proverbs 6:6–11; 26:14–15; 30:21–23.

An interesting feature of biblical proverbs is that at times they appear to give directly contradictory advice or observations. For example, consider Proverbs 26:4–5:

> Do not answer a fool according to his folly,
>> or you will be like him yourself.
> Answer a fool according to his folly,
>> or he will be wise in his own eyes.

The contradiction may be more apparent than real, however. Thus in the above example, further reflection makes it clear that one is not to let the remarks of a fool go unchallenged but in answering him the respondent is not to stoop to his level by using unfit language or improper reasoning.

Short narrative passages also occur in the book of Proverbs. Although all of these are intended for wise reflection, their understanding varies in accordance with their purpose. Thus the autobiographical account concerning wisdom (chap. 8) is instructional in nature. So also are the contrasting instructional narratives concerning wisdom (9:1–12) and folly (9:13–18). Stories or vignettes may be intended as examples, whether positive (31:10–31) or negative (24:30–34). Because these are intended to motivate the hearer or reader to right conduct, they commonly conclude with a moral or lesson to be learned.

> Charm is deceptive and beauty is fleeting;
>   but a woman who fears the Lord is to be praised. (Prov. 31:30)

> A little sleep, a little slumber,
>   a little folding of the hands to rest—
> and poverty will come on you like a bandit
>   and scarcity like an armed man. (Prov. 24:33–34)

The perceptive interpreter has doubtless noticed that the various examples set out above are at times capable of being assigned to more than one class of proverb. Indeed, hard and fast distinctions are not always possible. Due to the popular nature of a proverb, it may often be viewed from more than one angle—perhaps even designedly so. It is therefore amenable to multiple insights that serve as guides for proper conduct and personal welfare.

The categories mentioned above do not necessarily exhaust all classes of proverbs. For example, the book of Proverbs also contains extended sayings (e.g., chaps. 30–31). These are usually intended for instruction or admonition. Yet the careful interpreter will find our general classifications to be helpful in interpreting the proverbial collection in general.

Ecclesiastes

The Book of Ecclesiastes speaks of the value of wisdom:

> Wisdom, like an inheritance, is a good thing
>   and benefits those who see the sun.
> Wisdom is a shelter
>   as money is a shelter,
> but the advantage of knowledge is this:
>   that wisdom preserves the life of its possessor. (Eccl. 7:11–12)[21]

The basic theme of the book is an autobiographical quest for the ultimate good and the real meaning of life.

In reading Ecclesiastes, interpreters will encounter many of the same literary devices that we have already presented in our previous discussions.

---

21. Tremper Longman III, *The Book of Ecclesiastes*, NICOT (Grand Rapids: Eerdmans, 1998), 17, calls Ecclesiastes a "framed wisdom autobiography."

Written for the most part as poetry, Ecclesiastes contains the usual features of poetry such as various types of parallelism as well as terseness, concreteness, figures of speech, and abundant imagery. Its pages are filled with literary features such as lyric poems (e.g., 3:1–8; 12:1–7) and proverbs (e.g., 7:1–2). An unusual feature of Ecclesiastes is the author's double approach in searching for ultimate reality. Along the way, we find both positive and negative attitudes as well as contrasting observations held in tension (e.g., 5:10–20). Thus, in 3:19–22 one may note a satirical tone in the author's negative conclusion, which is then followed by a more positive outlook.

> Man's fate is like that of the animals; the same fate awaits them both. As one dies, so dies the other. All have the same breath; man has no advantage over the animal. Everything is meaningless. All go to the same place; all come from dust, and to dust all return. Who knows if the spirit of man rises upward and the spirit of the animal goes down into the earth?
>
> So I saw that there is nothing better for a man than to enjoy his work, because that is his lot. For who can bring him to see what will happen after him?

This holding of negative and positive approaches is in keeping with the author's instructional goals (e.g., 12:9–10). As Ryken points out, "The writer of Ecclesiastes has set for himself the task of making us feel the emptiness of life under the sun and the attractiveness of a God-filled life that leads to contentment with one's earthly lot."[22]

Therefore, the perceptive interpreter must hold both negative and positive portions in tension until he or she is swept along in the flow of the author's thinking until the final conclusion (12:13–14). Premature judgment can easily lead to finding Ecclesiastes to be basically pessimistic and cause the interpreter to make an unwarranted application of a given text. Careful attention to both near and remote contexts is crucial for understanding the message of Ecclesiastes.

An added feature of Ecclesiastes is its abundant use of repetition such as the repeated emphasis upon meaninglessness and the phrase "under

---

22. Leland Ryken, "Ecclesiastes," in *A Complete Literary Guide to the* Bible, ed. Leland Ryken and Tremper Longman III (Grand Rapids: Zondervan, 1993), 271.

the sun." The inserting of repeated positive ideas may well supply a key to the author's designed structural division (e.g., 2:24–26; 5:18–20; 8:15–17; 11:9–12:8; 12:9–14). In short, rather than being overwhelmed by the shifting themes and observations of the author, the reminder that much of Ecclesiastes is poetry and awareness of the author's purpose and strategy will enable the interpreter to enjoy one of the richest literary masterpieces of wisdom literature ever written.

Job

Job is yet another important work in the corpus of biblical wisdom literature. In accordance with other biblical wisdom literature, Job examines the role of God in human affairs. Whereas the theme of Ecclesiastes centered on a search for the ultimate good, Job is concerned with the sufficiency of God. Can he be trusted for every situation in life?

Understanding the basic theme of Job is crucial to the book's interpretation. Although many have sought the basic genre of Job in theodicy—justifying the ways of God—or have held that the book is primarily concerned with why the righteous suffer, understanding the basic purpose of Job as a demonstration of the sufficiency of a sovereign God provides a balanced perspective on the book's message.

Like the Psalms, Proverbs, and the majority of Ecclesiastes, Job is written in poetry. Therefore, the interpreter will find that the conclusions we have reached thus far in the chapter will be largely applicable to the book of Job. Although many genres are present in the book, Job is chiefly an example of disputation literature: "Specifically, we hear the lengthy *disputation speeches* in which the speakers debate the cause of Job's suffering."[23] Along the way, Job not only carries on a dispute in dialoguing with his friends, but even complains against God (e.g., 10:2–3, 18; 19:7–12; 23:13–17; 30:19–23). To be noted also is Job's autobiographical account of his life prior to his testing (chaps. 29–30).

In the pages of Job, the reader encounters many literary devices. Of particular note are psalmic materials (e.g., 9:5–10; 12:13–28; 37:21–24), many proverbs (e.g., 5:6; 8:11; 12:11–12; etc.), biting satire (12:1–2; 17:10), and the abundant use of rhetorical questions. Recurring motifs (e.g., the

---

23. William W. Klein, Craig L. Blomberg, Robert L. Hubbard Jr., *Introduction to Biblical Interpretation*, rev. ed. (Nashville: Thomas Nelson, 2004), 393–94.

call/answer motif; 5:1; 13:22; 14:14–15; 19:26–27; 27:9–10) and themes such as righteousness and justice (about five dozen times), the problem of suffering, and the need for an intermediary (3:23–25; 5:2; 6:13; 9:32–33; 16:18–21; 19:25–26; 33:26–28) as well as the hope for immortality (14:14–15; 19:24–27) fill the pages of Job. Not to be overlooked is the wide-ranging use of imagery throughout the book, including mythopoeic language (language related to myth; e.g., 3:8; 5:7; 7:12; 9:8, 12–14; 18:13–19; 26:12).[24]

As befitting a piece of wisdom literature, the subject of wisdom figures prominently throughout the book, whether the traditional human quest for wisdom (e.g., 8:8–10; 12:12; 15:17–19), acquired specially revealed wisdom (e.g., 4:12–21; 33:14–22), wisdom instruction (32:13–22; 33:31–33), divine wisdom (38:36–41), or even a long treatise on the subject (chap. 28). Structurally, the book of Job is composed around Job's experiences in suffering. The book has a clear plot line beginning with a prologue dealing with Job's testing (chaps. 1–2). The plot develops around the examination of reasons for Job's condition by means of Job's lament (chap. 3) followed by a long section of dialogue in which Job enters into disputation with his three friends who have come ostensibly to comfort him (chaps. 4–27). A movement toward solving the problem of Job's suffering (denouement) begins with Job's speeches concerning his condition (chaps. 28–31) and is continued when a young man named Elihu enters into the discussion with Job (chaps. 32–37). The resolution comes with God's arrival and his revelation to Job of what it means to be God (chaps. 38–41), to which Job responds in repentance and is restored to a happy life before God (chap. 42).

The fact that Job is presented as a story points to the need for employing the features that make up a story such as setting, plot, and characterization. Only then will the interpreter gain a full appreciation of what the author is conveying. When all of this is taken into account, the interpreter will find Job to be not only a rich source of biblical truth with strong advice for godly living but also a literary masterpiece that is thoroughly enjoyable reading.

Wisdom Elsewhere in the Old Testament

Although certain Old Testament books are generally classified as belonging to the genre wisdom literature, examples of wisdom literature may

---

24. For further examples of the imagery in Job see "Job," in Ryken and Longman, *A Complete Literary Guide to the Bible*, 302.

be found throughout the pages of the Old Testament. Thus wisdom may be seen in the blessings of the patriarchs (e.g., Gen. 49:1–27). Wisdom may also be found in the historical books (e.g., Judg. 5:29–30; 14:14; 1 Sam. 10:12; 24:13; 2 Sam. 12:1–4; 1 Kgs. 3:16–28; 20:11; 2 Kgs. 14:9) and the prophetic books (e.g., Isa. 5:1–7; 10:15; 28:24–29; Hos. 7:8–10; Amos 3:3–8; 6:12).

Likewise, several of the psalms are appropriately designated as wisdom psalms (e.g., Psalms 1; 33; 49; 73). Such psalms exalt God-given wisdom as the key to successful living in the face of life's problems. Addressed to God, the tone of these psalms is declarative, hortatory, and reflective. Proverbs, figures of speech, and imagery as well as illustrations from life and nature are utilized in an effort to get the psalmist's hearers/listeners to heed his advice. Wisdom psalms feature themes such as righteousness versus wickedness, the importance of God's Word, the problem of why the wicked seem to prosper, and the importance of a trust in God that results in a faithful and obedient life. Note, for example, the psalmist's conclusions to an examination of the seeming prosperity of the wicked in Psalm 73:27–28:

> Those who are far from you will perish;
>> you destroy all who are unfaithful to you.
> But as for me, it is good to be near God.
>> I have made the Sovereign Lord my refuge;
>> I will tell of all your deeds.

The above examples suggest that the interpreter must be aware of noting and understanding the many occurrences of wisdom pieces throughout the Old Testament.

Wisdom in the New Testament

People in New Testament times were heirs of a long wisdom tradition. Jesus, of course, was the wise teacher par excellence. His sayings often contained wise observations about life and reality. Thus he contrasts earlier pronouncements and standards with newer, wiser ones (e.g., Matt. 5:21–48; Mark 2:15–17; 8:35–36). Note, for example, Matthew 5:38–42:

> You have heard that it was said, "Eye for eye, and tooth for tooth." But I tell you, do not resist an evil person. If someone strikes you on the right cheek, turn to him the other also. And if someone wants to sue you and

take your tunic, let them have your cloak as well. If someone forces you
to go one mile, go with him two miles. Give to the one who asks you, and
do not turn away from the one who wants to borrow from you.

Jesus' teachings (e.g., Matt. 5:13–14; 7:13–14, 18; 6:24; Luke 12:34) and
parables are often interlaced with proverbial material (e.g., Matt. 13:34–35;
Luke 14:11, 34; 18:14). Likewise, Jesus' "I am" metaphors speak the language of wisdom (John 6:48; 8:12; 10:7, 9, 11; 11:25; 14:6; 15:1).[25]

Wisdom literature may be noted in the teachings (e.g., Gal. 4:21–31;
6:7; 2 Tim. 2:11–13), parables, and aphorisms of the Epistles (e.g., 1 Cor.
15:33; Phil. 1:21; 1 Tim. 6:10). The book of James bears many of the marks
of wisdom (e.g., Jas. 1:17, 19, 22; 2:20–24; 4:13–17; 5:16b).[26] Particularly apropos is James' teaching concerning wisdom (3:13–17), which is concluded
with the words, "Who is wise and understanding among you? Let him
show it by his good life, by deeds done in the humility that comes from
wisdom" (Jas. 3:18). The above examples are but samples of the frequent
use of wisdom literature by the writers of the New Testament.

The careful interpreter must therefore be alert to the presence of
wisdom not only in the wisdom books of the Old Testament but throughout
the Scriptures. This is especially true of proverbial wisdom. Proverbs occur
in many places in the Bible. Leland Ryken underscores the high value of
proverbial literature saying, "Proverbial thinking enables us to master the
complexity of life by bringing human experience under the control of an
observation that explains it and unifies many similar experiences. Proverbs
are a way of organizing what we know to be true of life."[27]

SAMPLE EXEGESIS: THE BOOK OF JOB

Introduction

To show hermeneutical method, the book of Job, which is a source of

---

25. David L. Barr, *New Testament Story* (Belmont, CA: Wadsworth, 1987), 246, makes
    the interesting point that "wisdom had a long tradition in Israel before John wrote
    his prologue. Clearly he draws on them even though he speaks of Logos rather than
    Wisdom."
26. See further E. Baasland, "Der Jacobsbrief als neutestamentliche Weisheitsschrift,"
    ST 36 (1982): 119–39.
27. Ryken, *Words of Life*, 107.

both splendid poetry and a piece of wisdom literature as well as a grand example of storytelling, is a good example. If we first of all examine the entire account in order to ascertain the author's *basic purpose* and/or *central theme(s)*, it is readily apparent that this book deals with a number of issues such as the problems of pain and suffering, the problem of evil, the issues of justice and injustice, particularly divine justice, and the limitations of human wisdom. Yet none of these can be said to get at the underlying purpose, which is to demonstrate that the sovereign God is sufficient for all of life's circumstances. Accordingly, human beings are to maintain a proper reverence and trust in him who alone is perfect in his person and all that he does. Such a purpose is evident both in Job's name ("where is God?") and Job's final realization of who the Lord really is (42:1–6).

History

Specific details in the book of Job are illuminated in the usual manner associated with storytelling. Whatever its date, this wisdom story is set in the patriarchal period and reflects the usual social standards and practices of that era. Geographically, the action takes place in the land of Uz, best associated with the northern Arabian Peninsula and the land of Edom.

Literature

The *plot* features the usual prologue where the setting of Job is given, the principal characters involved are introduced, and Job's testing commences (chaps. 1–2). As indicated above, a hint of the central issue in the story is felt in Job's very name, which implies the availability and sufficiency of God to sustain Job during his testing. The plot is developed by featuring a dialogue between Job and three friends who discuss the reasons for Job's pitiable condition. In three rounds of discourses (chaps. 3–27) the discussion progresses from philosophical debate to defending God's actions and ultimately to outright accusation of Job concerning his sinfulness.

Denouement in the story is reached by Job's speech concerning his wisdom (chap. 28) and protestation of his innocence in the face of what he feels is God's questionable justice in his case (chaps. 29–31). When the younger Elihu joins the discussion, he gives not only a rehearsal and summation of the state of the debate but provides new direction by suggesting that Job's problem lies in maintaining his own righteousness while failing to acknowledge God's own essential integrity (chaps. 32–37).

The plot concerning Job's problem reaches its *resolution* in the divine speeches (chaps. 38–41) and Job's response to them (42:1–6). Rather than focusing on the issues of justice and righteousness, however, the divine speeches center on God's wise administration of the physical universe and animal world as well as his providential control of human history. By these, Job comes to realize both the magnanimity of God and his own finitude. In God's governing of all things in perfect harmony and equity, Job discovers the sufficiency he needs to give direction to his life. When he surrenders his will to God and rests in reverential trust in him, Job experiences a resolution to his problem and blessed restoration to the Lord's favor (42:1–17).

Characterization in the story is quite pronounced. God is seen as sovereign, just, and righteous and as the One who sets the limits to Job's horrendous test. Satan, true to his name, uses the occasion to find fault with God's perceived favoritism and partiality as much as an opportunity to put God's example of a righteous man (Job) to the test. Job's three friends also betray distinct qualities and approaches concerning Job and his condition. In Eliphaz, we see the rationalist who defends and applies traditional wisdom to Job's situation. Bildad behaves much like a self-appointed defense attorney for God's justice, while Zophar is more like an attorney appointed to prosecute Job. The younger Elihu, while polite toward his elders, is nonetheless impatient with them. Since they have failed to get to the root cause of Job's condition, he undertakes to do so. He both defends God's justice and proposes that Job has elevated himself to viewing himself as more righteous than God in his case.

Grasping this data, the interpreter can appreciate the basic lesson to be learned in the story of Job: the wise person will surrender to the sovereign, holy, and wise Lord of the universe and find him sufficient for all of life's needs. He must also remember to apply correctly the basic hermeneutical principles concerning poetry and wisdom literature at every stage of his or her examination of the text. For example, chapters 4 and 5 of Job contain the opening speech of Eliphaz, the most eloquent and perhaps most respected of the three friends. His remarks are filled with traditional wisdom (e.g., 4:7, 10–11). He claims to have been the recipient of special divinely given insight (4:12–16). Therefore, he feels even more secure in giving Job spiritual counsel (4:17–21).

Accordingly, in 5:1–7 Eliphaz provides instruction to Job. The interpreter is immediately confronted with the well-known call-answer motif, which often expresses the intimacy of fellowship the believer may enjoy with God (e.g., Isa. 65:20), including especially times of testing (e.g., Ps. 102:1–2). Another proverbial saying follows this:

> Resentment kills a fool,
>> And envy slays the simple. (5:2)

The verse is noteworthy for its similar parallelism (i.e., resentment// envy, fool//simple, kills//slays) and its declarative proverb. The interpreter of Scripture will need to take the data in these two verses into careful consideration in his or her exegesis of the passage.

In what follows (vv. 3–7), Eliphaz gives his advice to Job, telling him basically that in the changing vicissitudes of life people should expect trouble. Yet he should never exercise a bad attitude, for this only leads to further trouble both to himself and those around him. The careful interpreter will also take note of the phrase "sparks fly upward." The Hebrew term for "sparks" (lit. "sons of Resheph") may reflect a mythological allusion to the Canaanite god Resheph, the god of plague or pestilence. As a traditional saying, the term reinforces the fact that trouble is to be expected in this life, including natural or personal disasters.

With this data in hand, the interpreter is prepared for Eliphaz's personal advice and instruction, in which he suggests that Job should understand that he is being divinely disciplined (v. 18) and should appeal to God (vv. 8–9) and come to terms with him (vv. 20–26). If Job will but listen and apply Eliphaz's wise counsel, he will fare better.

Theology

A number of personal applications could be made on the basis of these chapters. At the very least, the interpreter can appreciate the wisdom of a great deal of that which Eliphaz has communicated. Yet he or she must realize the limits of traditional wisdom and that such practical and general wisdom cannot always be applied to specific situations. Eliphaz does not know the true cause of Job's troubles and so should have exercised caution in providing his advice. Comfort is often better than counsel. Nevertheless, his basic point is well taken and can be followed by all: if we see things from God's point of view and put our trust in him, we will find him sufficient in all of life's trials.

GUIDELINES FOR INTERPRETING BIBLICAL POETRY

1. Note the author's use of parallelism in accordance with the type employed.

2. In psalms and extended poetic pieces, read the entire passage.

3. Look for logical and formal structural devices.

4. Learn to appreciate the author's use of imagery and figures of speech.

5. Look for the author's unifying theme and consider carefully the flow of thought throughout the piece.

6. Using sound exegetical procedures relative to poetic medium, make proper application to the contemporary situation. Consider the impact of the author's emphases to the spiritual life of the reader or hearer.

GUIDELINES FOR INTERPRETING WISDOM LITERATURE

1. Determine the central purpose of any wisdom piece.

2. In Proverbs, note the type involved and the specific advice for godly living in its teaching.

3. Evaluate the general maxims of Proverbs in the light of the proverb's ancient setting as well as in comparison with other scriptural teachings.

4. Remember that proverbs are designed to be general guidelines and are not always applicable to every situation and circumstance.

5. Where instruction is the proverb's chief goal, take seriously the truths and moral standards it is teaching.

6. When interacting with Ecclesiastes, the interpreter should take careful note of both the positive and negative teachings of the book, balancing each in the light of the book's central purpose.

7. In Job, the interpreter must come to grips with the central message of the book and evaluate the contribution of each part to the book's ultimate purpose.

8. In Job, the interpreter should be careful to apply the rules of interpretation relative to storytelling such as setting, plot, and characterization. He should seek to determine what lessons are to be learned from the standpoint of each portion in the dialogue.

9. The interpreter should be alert to occurrences of wisdom throughout the pages of the Bible. Especially to be noted are the teachings of Jesus. One should pay close attention to the theological and moral truths embedded in his teachings as crucial for the development of Christian character and conduct.

10. In every wisdom piece of literature, determine the chief goal of the instruction. Be careful to evaluate it in the light of the total scriptural revelation in order that proper application of its truths and moral lessons may be applied properly to contemporary living.

KEY WORDS

A fortiori **argument:** argument from the lesser to the greater

Alliteration: subsequent words starting with the same letter

Allusion: the practice of invoking another passage by way of verbal or conceptual reference or echo

Antithetic parallelism: two poetic lines expressing sharp contrast

Anthropomorphism: ascription of human characteristics or qualities to God

Apophthegm: short, witty, and instructive saying

Assonance: see Alliteration

Bicolon: parallel thought over two successive lines of poetry

Bifid structure: the poet's structuring of his material in two parts, each answering to the other in similar or corresponding fashion and in the same basic order (e.g. Psalm 135; Nahum; Zephaniah)

Bookending: the technique of returning at the end of a unit to a theme, subject, or word(s) mentioned at the beginning of that section

Chiasm: a literary device in which the second half of a composition takes up the same words, themes, or motifs as in the first half, but in reverse order (A B B' A' pattern)

Concreteness: a feature of Hebrew poetry that involves a graphic description appealing to the reader's senses

Denouement: the final clarification or resolution of a narrative or dramatic plot

Ellipsis: the deletion of a word present only in one parallel line of poetry even though it is to be understood in both

Emblematic parallelism: two poetic lines showing progression of thought involving simile

Inclusio: see Bookending

Ladder parallelism: two or more poetic lines displaying progression in form of numerical sequence

Monocolon: an individual poetic line that does not combine closely with another line

Parallelism: the practice of using similar language to express corresponding thoughts in succeeding lines of poetry

Progressive parallelism: a succeeding line (or lines) supplements and/or completes the first line

Proverb: short memorable statement of the true state of things as perceived and learned by human observation over extended periods of experience

Similar parallelism: two poetic lines conveying closeness of thought and expression

Staircase parallelism: a thought stated in the first line is completed by a succeeding line beginning with similar phraseology

Stitching: an author's practice of linking successive units or subunits of a poem by means of repeating a word, phrase, or idea

Terrace pattern parallelism: type of staircase parallelism in which the beginning of the second line repeats the end of the first line

Terseness: feature of Hebrew poetry that involves succinctness of stating a point

Theodicy: vindicating the righteousness of God and his ways when called into question

Tricolon: three lines of poetry forming a distinct unit

Zoomorphism: ascription of animal qualities to God

STUDY QUESTIONS

1. What is the essence of Hebrew parallelism, and what are the three major kinds of parallelism found in the Old Testament poetic portions?

2. What are three other characteristics of Hebrew poetry?

3. What are some insights that may help you discern the structure of particular sections of Hebrew poetry?

4. What are at least two other features of style that will be helpful in interpreting biblical poetry?

5. What are the guidelines for interpreting biblical poetry?

ASSIGNMENTS

1. Identify the types of parallelism in the following Psalms:
    a. Psalm 1
    b. Psalm 96:1–3, 7–9, 11–13

2. Identify where applicable such poetic features as: repetition, terse-ness, concreteness, or imagery in the following passages:
    a. Nahum 1:2–6
    b. Habakkuk 3:8–15
    c. Zephaniah 3:14–16
    d. Luke 1:46–53

3. Consider Moses' song in Exodus 15:1–18 in terms of its building blocks and structural indicators. Which verses contain examples of the various types of colon structure? What stitching, hinging, and grammatical or literary variations are evidenced in the author's style?

4. Categorize the various types of Proverbs in Proverbs 26 as to whether they are primarily descriptive, prescriptive, contrastive, conditional, declarative, or instructional.

5. Wisdom sayings may be found in many places in the Old Testament. Consider carefully Qoheleth's teaching in Ecclesiastes 3:1–8 and then contrast it with the following texts.
    a. Job 15:30–35
    b. Psalm 37:37–40
    c. Hosea 13:12–13

CHAPTER BIBLIOGRAPHY

Alter, Robert. *The Art of Biblical Poetry.* New York: Basic Books, 1985.

Barr, David L. *New Testament Story.* Belmont, CA: Wadsworth, 1987.

Bullinger, E. W. *Figures of Speech Used in the Bible.* London: Eyre & Spottiswoode, 1898. Repr. Grand Rapids: Baker, 1968.

Bullock, C. Hassell. *An Introduction to the Poetic Books of the Old Testament.* Chicago: Moody, 1979.

Crenshaw, J. L. *Old Testament Wisdom: An Introduction.* Rev. ed. Louisville: Westminster John Knox, 1998.

Estes, Daniel J. *Handbook on the Wisdom Books and Psalms.* Grand Rapids: Baker, 2005.

Follis, Elaine R., ed. *Directions in Biblical Hebrew Poetry.* Sheffield: JSOT, 1987.

Gillingham, S. E. *The Poems and Psalms of the Hebrew Bible.* Oxford: Oxford University Press, 1994.

Greidanus, Sidney. *Preaching Christ from Ecclesiastes.* Grand Rapids: Eerdmans, 2010.

Kugel, James L. *The Idea of Biblical Poetry.* New Haven: Yale University Press, 1981.

Lowth, Robert. *Lectures on the Sacred Poetry of the Hebrews.* Boston: Crocker & Brewster, 1829.

McKane, William. *Proverbs.* Philadelphia: Westminster, 1970.

Murphy, R. E. *Wisdom Literature.* Grand Rapids: Eerdmans, 1982.

_____. *The Tree of Life.* 2d ed. Grand Rapids: Eerdmans, 1996

O'Connor, Michael. *Hebrew Verse Structure.* Winona Lake, IN: Eisenbrauns, 1980.

Scott, R. B. Y. *The Way of Wisdom.* New York: Macmillan, 1971.

Watson, Wilfred G. E. *Classical Hebrew Poetry.* Sheffield: University of Sheffield, 1986.

Whybray, R. N. *The Composition of the Book of Proverbs.* JSOT Supplement Series 168. Sheffield: JSOT, 1994.

CHAPTER 7 OBJECTIVES

1. To acquaint the student with the nature of the prophet and his role.

2. To enable the student to recognize the various subgenres within prophecy.

3. To suggest tools for determining the overall framework of a given book of prophecy as well as the make-up of individual units.

CHAPTER 7 OUTLINE

A. Nature of Prophecy
B. Subgenres of Prophecy
   1. Announcements of Judgment
      a. General Characteristics
      b. Woe Oracle
      c. Lament
      d. Covenant Lawsuit
   2. Salvation Oracles
      a. Promise of Deliverance
      b. Kingdom Oracles
      c. Apocalyptic
   3. Instructional Accounts
      a. Disputations
      b. Exhortation/Warning Speeches
      c. Satire
      d. Wisdom Sayings
      e. Prophetic Narratives
   4. Miscellaneous Subgenres
      a. Vision/Dream Reports
      b. Prophetic Hymns/Songs
      c. Prophetic Prayers
      d. Prophetic Letters
C. Prophecy Outside of the Old Testament Prophetic Books
   1. In the Old Testament
   2. In the New Testament
D. Sample Exegesis: The Book of Nahum
   1. Introduction
   2. History
   3. Literature
   4. Theology
E. Guidelines for Interpreting Prophecy
F. Key Words
G. Study Questions
H. Assignments
I. Chapter Bibliography

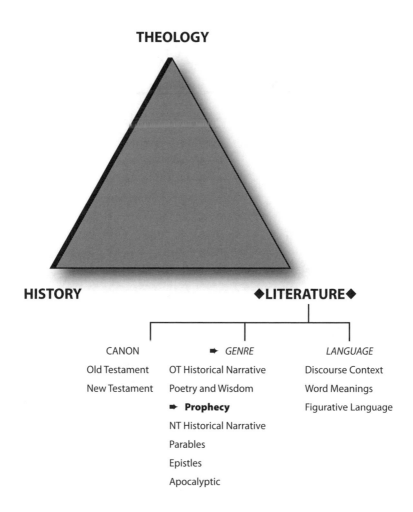

THEOLOGY

HISTORY

◆LITERATURE◆

CANON
Old Testament
New Testament

➡ *GENRE*
OT Historical Narrative
Poetry and Wisdom
➡ **Prophecy**
NT Historical Narrative
Parables
Epistles
Apocalyptic

LANGUAGE
Discourse Context
Word Meanings
Figurative Language

Chapter 7

BACK TO THE FUTURE: PROPHECY

NATURE OF PROPHECY

WE ARE MAKING GOOD PROGRESS in our interpretive journey through the canonical landscape. We have already gotten acquainted with sound principles for interpreting Old Testament historical narrative as well as poetry and wisdom literature. The last major portion of the Old Testament canon is made up of a total of almost a dozen and a half prophetic books: the four major prophets (Isaiah, Jeremiah/Lamentations, Ezekiel, and Daniel), and the twelve so-called "Minor Prophets" (Hosea, Joel, Amos, Obadiah, Jonah, Micah, Nahum, Habakkuk, Zephaniah, Haggai, Zechariah, and Malachi).

The understanding of prophecy, particularly the Old Testament prophetic books, seems at first sight a daunting task. The reader of English is at once confronted with a literature that has no direct parallels in his own language. Moreover, interpreters are introduced to a large and seemingly bewildering array of material to assimilate. They can encounter obscure messages concerning people and places with strange names and customs. They are called on to grapple with texts utilizing a rich kaleidoscope of literary figures, motifs, themes, and symbols.

Although the message the interpreter reads can be written in either prose or poetry, the fact that it was first delivered orally is reflected in the elevated and at times impassioned language. There is also an urgency of tone and theme to the message. Accordingly, some have gone so far as to say that prophecy is basically poetic. D. N. Freedman declares, "Most of these prophets were poets, and their oracles were delivered and have been preserved in poetic form."[1]

Perhaps this is only natural due to the fact that the biblical prophets were people called of God to proclaim his messages. As Robert Alter remarks, "Since poetry is our best human model of intricately rich communication, . . . it makes sense that divine speech should be represented as poetry."[2] Indeed, the most common word for "prophet" carries with it the sense of his call. Also, the common terms for his task emphasize his mission as a proclaimer of God's message. As noted, the prophet's message was originally delivered orally. Therefore, those of us who now read the inscripturated written messages are enjoined to attempt to *hear* as well as *read* what the prophet has said. This involves the exercise not only of the eye but of the ear and of the heart. This is because we have entered the ancient world of the spoken word. Some prophecies even have a setting that involves people and times that lie in the future from the vantage point of the prophet's own day, adding a further dimension and difficulty for the interpreter, who must look for the full meaning of the passage in a subsequent fulfillment. Some prophecies even seem to be filled with fantastic, otherworldly figures and images.

Although all of this presents many challenges to us as readers of prophecy, the realization that these prophets were real people sent by God to people in a real (albeit ancient) world gives us assurance that the understanding of their messages is a realizable goal. Indeed, the prophetic word was designed to be relevant to everyday life. Even more importantly, it was and is God's Word, which is designed to instruct people concerning his nature and standards for human conduct. Therefore, it has application for readers of every age. And herein lies the role of hermeneutics. Understanding and effectively communicating biblical prophecy are tasks that

---

1. David N. Freedman, "Pottery, Poetry and Prophecy: An Essay on Biblical Poetry," in *Pottery, Poetry, and Prophecy* (Winona Lake, IN: Eisenbrauns, 1980), 18.
2. Robert Alter, *The Art of Biblical Poetry* (New York: Basic Books, 1985), 141.

have their origin in a strategic grasp of the relevant principles related to interpreting this challenging, but rewarding genre of Scripture.

SUBGENRES OF PROPHECY

Many types and forms make up the genre of biblical prophecy. Great fluidity and some overlap exist. Therefore, the assigning of a specific subgenre label to a given portion of prophecy may lack absolute precision. In addition, a passage may include more than one type of subgenre and thus reflect more than one intention of the author. In every case, we must determine the basic subgenre on the basis of both form and the identification of the author's primary purpose in the full context. Comparison with other prophecies of a similar nature may also help. Such beginning steps in approaching a particular passage are necessary ones. For as Cotterell and Turner point out, "Our identification of what we take to be the genre to which a particular text belongs raises certain expectations about how the contents of the writing are to be understood."[3]

Most scholars, however, have agreed that the two most prominent subgenres of prophecy are those dealing with judgment and salvation. Because in our view prophecy consists basically of proclamation, we shall use the terms "announcements of judgment" and "salvation oracles."

Announcements of Judgment
General Characteristics

Announcements of judgment account for the preponderance of Old Testament prophecy. The pronouncing of judgment can also be embedded within other subgenres that we will consider. Formal announcements of judgment consist of two main elements:

1. *accusation*, stating the Lord's charges for which judgment must come
2. *announcement of a specific judgment* to be levied

---

3. Peter Cotterell and Max Turner, *Linguistics & Biblical Interpretation* (Downers Grove: InterVarsity, 1989), 99.

Amos 2:6–16 may serve as an example. Here the Lord lists the various charges he has against his people (vv. 6–12) and then warns them of impending doom to come (vv. 13–16). Announcements of judgment may also include a call to hear the word of the Lord (e.g., Amos 3:1; 5:1). Note the following example:

7.1. PROPHETIC ANNOUNCEMENT OF JUDGMENT	
Call	Hear this word
Accusation	You cows of Bashan on Mount Samaria, you women who oppress the poor and crush the needy and say to your husbands, "Bring us some drinks!"
Announcement	The Sovereign LORD has sworn by his holiness: "The time will surely come when you will be taken away with hooks, the last of you with fishhooks, you will each go straight out through breaks in the wall, and you will be cast out toward Harmon," declares the LORD. (Amos 4:1–3)

Other features can include a plea for repentance and the rewards of God's blessings for doing so. Thus the prophet Joel warned the people of his day that the present disastrous conditions in the land due to the locust plague were but a precursor to a more serious invasion of the land (1:1–2:11). He therefore called on the people to repent (2:12–14). Then, having further urged the people to call a formal ceremony of repentance and reconsecration to the Lord (vv. 15–17), he enumerated the resultant blessings of the Lord for doing so (vv. 18–27). Such themes appear abundantly throughout the prophets as they called God's people to vital religion in the face of God's threatened judgment. Duvall and Hays point out that prophetic messages "can be boiled down to three basic points, each of which is important to the message of the prophets:

1. You have broken the covenant; you had better repent!

2. No repentance? Then judgment!

3. Yet, there is hope beyond the judgment for a glorious, future restoration."[4]

The prophets also have messages of judgment for other nations as well. For example, note Nahum's denunciation of the Assyrian capital of Nineveh:

> Woe to the city of blood, full of lies,
>> full of plunder, never without victims!
> The crack of whips, the clatter of wheels,
>> galloping horses, and jolting chariots!
> Charging cavalry, flashing swords and glittering spears!
> Many casualties, piles of dead,
> bodies without number,
>> people stumbling over the corpses
> all because of the wanton lust of a harlot,
>> alluring the mistress of sorceries,
> who enslaved nations by her prostitution
>> and peoples by her witchcraft. (Nah. 3:1–4)

Nahum goes on to deliver the Lord's message of severe judgment against the city (vv. 5–7). Basically, the foreign nations are condemned for two reasons: (1) their treatment of God's people, a crime that constituted an attack against the Lord himself; and (2) their inhumane treatment of many nations (e.g., Isa. 14:12–17; Nah. 3:19).

Prophecies relative to the foreign nations are often gathered together in large collections (e.g., Isa. 13–23; Jer. 46–51; Ezek. 25–32; Amos 1:3–2:5; Zeph. 2:4–15). In some cases, these are arranged geographically in relation to the land of Israel. For example, Zephaniah's prophecies move from west of Judah (Philistia) to the east (Moab and Ammon), then south and north (Cush, Assyria). Ezekiel inverts Zephaniah's order, moving from east (Transjordan) to west (Philistia) and then north to south (Phoenicia, Egypt).

---

4. J. Scott Duvall and J. Daniel Hays, *Grasping God's Word*, 2d ed. (Grand Rapids: Zondervan, 2005), 373.

Woe Oracle

A specific type of an announcement of judgment involves the woe oracle. Woe oracles were traditionally made up of three elements:

1. invective (the pronouncement of woe)

2. threat (the details of coming judgment)

3. criticism (the reason for the coming judgment)

Typical examples may be found in Habakkuk 2:6–20. Note Habakkuk's opening taunt against the Chaldeans (or Neo-Babylonians):

7.2. WOE ORACLE	
Invective	Woe to him who piles up stolen goods and makes himself wealthy by extortion! How long must this go on?
Threat	Will not your debtors suddenly arise? Will they not wake up and make you tremble? Then you will become their victim.
Criticism	Because you have plundered many nations, the peoples who are left will plunder you. For you have shed man's blood; you have destroyed lands and cities and everyone in them. (Hab. 2:6–8)

These three elements need not occur in the same order in every case. Thus Micah announces woe to the evildoers of society (Mic. 2:1), supplies the criticism or reasons for which they must be judged (v. 2), and then announces the threatened judgment (vv. 3–5).

Lament

Another subgenre is the lament. Lament can be understood in two ways. On the one hand, it involves prayer to God (e.g. Psalm 22; Habakkuk 1–2). On the other hand, lament constitutes a statement of distress or mourning, with the latter type being the one further discussed here. In addition, laments are found not only in prophetic literature but also in the Psalms and wisdom literature such as the book of Job.

Amos 5:1–17 is clearly labeled as a lament (based on the Hebrew term *qinah*). Here the judgment of Israel is pronounced as though it had already happened—it is an accomplished fact (vv. 1–2). The threatened judgment is amplified with the prediction of how that judgment will play out (v. 3). There follows a long list of accusations against God's people for which their punishment must come, together with a plea for repentance (vv. 6–15). The prophet then returns to the prediction of judgment (vv. 16–17).

Another classic case of lament occurs in Ezekiel 19. Here the call to lament precedes a catalogue of accusations against Judah's leadership for which judgment had come. The judgment in this case is not repre sented as something certain to happen in the future but as a past reality resulting in the present misery. Nevertheless, the elements of accusation and announced judgment are still present even though the judgment is past.

Covenant Lawsuit

Another type of judgment speech is the covenant lawsuit, in which God summons his people to appear before him for covenant violations. Such announcements of judgment usually contain the summoning of witnesses, a list of the charges against the accused (or indictment), and an announcement of punishment (or sentencing). Micah 6:1–16 provides an excellent example. Here, the Lord initiates a case against his people, summoning the mountains to serve as a witness:

> Listen to what the LORD says:
> "Stand up, plead your case before the mountains;
>   let the hills hear what you have to say.
> Hear, O mountains, the LORD's accusation;
>   Listen, you everlasting foundations of the earth.
> For the LORD has a case against his people;
>   He is lodging a charge against Israel." (Mic. 6:1–2)

He then launches into a long list of charges against his people, in which he reminds them of his past goodness to them and calls attention to their present unfaithfulness (vv. 3–12). In so doing, he even includes a short imagined dialogue in which the people's projected response is given together with God's answer (vv. 6–7). A final divine sentence of judgment follows (vv. 13–15), accompanied by a concluding summation (v. 16):

> You have observed the statues of Omri
>> and all the practices of Ahab's house,
>> and you have followed their traditions.
> Therefore I will give you over to ruin
>> and your people to derision;
>> you will hear the scorn of the nations.

Salvation Oracles

The second most prominent subgenre of prophecy revolves around those prophecies that deal with God's saving work. You will note that in many of the cases cited here both judgment and salvation occur side by side. Moreover, a great many of these deal with Israel's projected final state.

Promise of Deliverance

Salvation prophecies customarily deal with God's deliverance after a time of experiencing his judgment. Frequently, you will detect a pattern of sin, judgment, repentance, and restoration. For example, Ezekiel informs his hearers that they have suffered the judgment of captivity and exile because of Israel's sin. Yet God will restore his people to their land and give them a new heart to serve the Lord (Ezek. 11:14–21).

Somewhat earlier, Jeremiah warned of the arrival of desperate circumstances (Jer. 16:1–9). God's coming chastisement would involve going into captivity because of the people's long-standing flirtation with various sinful practices (vv. 10–13). Nevertheless, there would come a time when their punishment would end and God would restore them to the Promised Land:

> "However, the days are coming," declares the LORD, "when men will no longer say, 'As surely as the LORD lives, who brought the Israelites up out of Egypt,' but they will say, 'As surely as the LORD lives, who brought the Israelites up out of the land of the north and out of the countries where he had banished them.' For I will restore them to the land I gave their forefathers." (vv. 14–15)

Here we see that the promise of deliverance/salvation is wedded to the motif of the new exodus (cf. Isa. 43:16–21; 48:20–21). It should be noted in passing that not only is the exodus motif a prominent one in the Old Testament but it culminates in a new, greater exodus. Such a promise may be found, as in the Jeremiah passage just cited, in many Old Testament prophecies as well as in numerous New Testament texts. "In most cases that contain a reference to the exodus experience it seems clear that the historical exodus from Egypt serves as an assurance of future exoduses. Often it is difficult to know whether a given text speaks of a future that is somewhat close at hand or to a far distant future or both (e.g., Isa. 52:4–13). Often the perspective is such that near and distant futures blend into one another (e.g., Isa. 61:1–3; Ezek. 20.32–38)."[5] Note for example, Jeremiah 16:14–15:

> "However the days are coming," declares the LORD," when men will no longer say, 'As surely as the LORD lives, who brought the Israelites up out of Egypt,' but they will say, 'As surely as the LORD lives who brought the Israelites up out of the land of the north and out of all the countries where he had banished them.' For I will restore them to the land I gave their forefathers."

Kingdom Oracles

A great many salvation oracles look to the distant or eschatological future, including those featuring the new exodus motif (e.g., Isa. 51:4–11; Jer. 23:3–8; Ezek. 37:18–20). We term such prophecies "kingdom oracles," for they deal with the establishment of Israel's final kingdom. Kingdom oracles not only tell of Israel's great future deliverance and return to the land but contain an announcement of universal judgment. These judgments often deal with the future in such a way that they predict a series of judgments. The last judgment completes the series and serves to prepare for the final era of blessing.

This judgment differs from other announcements of judgment in that it is universal in scope and features such dramatic details as cataclysmic phenomena in the natural world and widespread devastation on earth. Typical

---

5. Richard D. Patterson and Michael Travers, "Contours of the Exodus Motif in Jesus' Earthly Ministry," *WTJ* 66 (2004): 25–47.

of these is Joel 3:9–21. Here the prophet proclaims the need for the nation to prepare for war (vv. 9–11). It is no less than the time of God's great judgment on rebellious earthly forces (vv. 12–13). Through the clamor of war and natural upheaval God will deliver his people (vv. 14–17). He will then dwell in their midst and bring in everlasting peace and prosperity (vv. 18–21).

Other prophets give a similar picture of these great events. Zephaniah calls this era the great "day of the LORD" (Zeph. 1:14–18). It is a time for God's great judgment against this wicked world (Zeph. 3:8). He will initiate a final new exodus of his people, restore them to the land, bless them, and bring in everlasting happiness:

> "At that time I will gather you; at that time I will bring you home. I will give you honor and praise among all the peoples of the earth when I restore your fortunes before your very eyes," declares the LORD (Zeph. 3:20).

The careful student of prophecy can recognize kingdom oracles by the presence of both announcements of judgment and promises of salvation blended together in a future, universal setting. He can also recognize that at times details of the Lord's predicted judgment may have an anticipatory fulfillment somewhere within a series of God's future judgments without exhausting the full prediction. Because of this, God's people can find applications to various events in relation to the culmination of the full prophecy in the eschatological era. In any case, even though kingdom oracles apply primarily to the distant future, they provide an admonition to believers of all ages to live holy lives in anticipation of God's final consummation of earth's history.

Apocalyptic

Kingdom oracles have also been noted for their inclusion of dramatic events, which often record phenomena of a cosmic dimension accompanied by a sudden drastic divine intervention. In such cases, the text reads much like the apocalyptic literature that became so prominent in the period after the completion of the Old Testament.

John Collins put forward the classic definition of apocalyptic in defining apocalypse as "a genre of revelatory literature with a narrative framework, in which a revelation is mediated by an otherworldly being to a human percipient, disclosing a transcendent reality which is both temporal insofar as it envisages eschatological salvation, and spatial insofar as it involves another, supernatural world."[6] Among the many features of apocalyptic, five are especially prevalent:

1. This present world is evil and without hope and can be remedied only by sovereign divine intervention.

2. The issue of the ages is essentially a spiritual battle between good and evil.

3. The Lord's intervention will entail catastrophic events.

4. Following the time of God's universal judgment, a final new age of peace, prosperity, and righteousness will be ushered in.

Apocalyptic literature customarily is presented via visions of the future and contains graphic images, fantastic other-worldly settings and scenes, and an abundant use of symbols, such as the use of numbers, colors, and animals.[7]

Daniel (especially chapters 7–12) is commonly considered the apocalyptic book of the OT. Fully developed apocalypses, however, appeared after the Old Testament era. They were especially prominent from the second century B.C. to the early second century A.D. Unlike standard biblical prophecy, apocalypses were written in prose rather than poetry. By this time, their use of the special characteristics mentioned above enables us to think of apocalyptic as a distinct literary genre. Representative examples include 1 and 2 Enoch, 2 and 3 Baruch, 4 Ezra, and the New Testament book of Revelation.

We consider apocalyptic here because some have suggested that apocalyptic and apocalypses occur in the Old Testament. Frequently mentioned passages include Isaiah 24–27, Ezekiel 38–39, Daniel 7, Joel

---

6. John J. Collins, *The Apocalyptic Imagination* (New York: Crossroad, 1984), 4.

7. See further Leland Ryken, James C. Wilhoit, and Tremper Longman III, eds., "Apocalypse, Genre of," and "Apocalyptic Visions of the Future," in *Dictionary of Biblical Imagery* (Downers Grove: InterVarsity, 1998), 35–37 and 37–38; D. Brent Sandy, *Plowshares & Pruning Hooks* (Downers Grove: InterVarsity, 2002), 106–11.

2:28–32; 3:9–17, and Zechariah 1–6; 12–14.[8] Even a casual glance at several of these texts confirms that they contain some of the features found in classic apocalyptic literature. Old Testament prophecies betray a gradually increasing use of such features, especially toward the end of the Old Testament canon (e.g., Ezekiel 38–39; Daniel 7; Zechariah 1–6, 14). It is safe to conclude, therefore, that the apocalyptic genre, which was based upon Old Testament precedents and came into full bloom subsequent to the Old Testament era, was largely of Hebrew origin. It had its beginning in Old Testament kingdom oracles. Thus David Aune concludes:

> Prophecy appears to have gradually merged into apocalyptic. Most of the essential features of the kind of apocalyptic literature which flourished from 200 B.C. to A.D. 100 have roots in the prophetic literature of the sixth and fifth centuries B.C. Apocalyptic is therefore an inner-Jewish development.[9]

Because the Scriptures contain both a distinct apocalypse (the book of Revelation) and passages that utilize apocalyptic language both in the Old Testament (e.g., Daniel 7) and New Testament (e.g., Matthew 24), the student of prophecy needs to have a basic acquaintance with the nature and features of apocalyptic genre if he or she is to interpret the text correctly. We suggest the following guidelines:

1. Acquaint yourself with the characteristics of apocalyptic.

2. Note the setting of the passage both in its historical dimension and contextual orientation.

3. Distinguish carefully the use of symbols, themes, and figures of speech from their standard literal sense.

4. Determine the author's purpose in using apocalyptic features.

---

8. Note, however, that O. Palmer Robertson (*The Christ of the Prophets* [Phillipsburg, NJ: Presbyterian & Reformed, 2004], 446) terms such passages "cataclysmic prophecy."

9. David E. Aune, *Prophecy in Early Christianity and the Mediterranean World* (Grand Rapids: Eerdmans, 1983), 112.

5. As with other types of prophecy, try to place yourself in the oral setting of those who first heard the message. Approach it with your entire personality: "The reader must be attentive to the effect of the message not only on mind and eye but also on ear and heart."[10]

6. In teaching or preaching the passage to others, be sure to emphasize the spiritual content resident in its message, particularly in the ultimate resolution of the divine teleology it presents.

7 Above all, make the application of the passage relevant to the lives of those whom you are attempting to reach.

Instructional Accounts

You probably have noticed that in the two subgenres that we have considered there was often an element of instruction. Here again, we note that prophetic speeches are not always one-dimensional. God's prophet may weave two or more literary types together in achieving his purposes. Therefore, the student should not be surprised to find diverse types embedded within the basic type of prophecy that the prophet employs. We examine here those passages where instruction is clearly the main feature and general purpose of the context.

Disputation

We turn, first of all, to the disputation. The most common elements of disputation speeches are: declaration, discussion, and refutation. Of the several examples that could be cited (e.g., Ezekiel 18; Amos 3:3–8), perhaps Malachi is best known for using this literary device. Nearly the whole of his prophecy is presented as a disputation between the Lord and his people. Here, the dispute takes the form of an imagined dialogue between them. Note the following portion from the first chapter of Malachi:

---

10. Richard D. Patterson, "Old Testament Prophecy," in *A Complete Literary Guide to the Bible,* ed. Leland Ryken and Tremper Longman III (Grand Rapids: Zondervan, 1993), 298.

7.3. DISPUTATION	
Discussion	"A son honors his father and a servant his master. If I am a father, where is the honor due me? If I am a master, where is the respect due me?" says the LORD Almighty.
Declaration	"It is you, O priests, who show contempt for my name."
Refutation	"But you ask, 'How have we shown contempt for your name?'" (Mal. 1:6–7)

The passage goes on with discussion, refutation, and counter-refutation and is concluded with the lesson to be learned: only pure offerings are acceptable and honoring to God's great name. Note, for example, the Lord's words through his prophet in verse eleven:

> "My name will be great among the nations from the rising to the setting of the sun. In every place incense and pure offerings will be brought to my name, because my name will be great among the nations," says the LORD Almighty.

In this passage, Malachi's style is much like that of the classical Greco-Roman diatribe, which Aune describes as follows:

> The dialogical style of diatribes makes frequent use of imaginary opponents, hypothetical objections, and false conclusions. The questions and objections of the imaginary opponent and the teacher's responses oscillate between censure and persuasion.[11]

In keeping with his presentation, Malachi often utilizes uses a satiric tone to accomplish his objectives. We will have occasion to say more concerning satire in a later discussion.

Exhortation/Warning Speeches

We turn next to prophecy in which an exhortation toward repentance

---

11. David E. Aune, *The New Testament in Its Literary Environment* (Philadelphia: Westminster, 1989), 200.

or reform occurs. Here the hearers or readers are urged to follow the Lord and his standards. These instructional messages can be introduced with a call to hear the word of the Lord and contain motive, which encourages a favorable response. The motive may be positive (reward) or negative (warning of the consequences of the present lifestyle).

An example of the former case is Isaiah's message of exhortation to the exiles (Isa. 55:1–5):

7.4. POSITIVE EXHORTATION	
Call	Come all who are thirsty, come to the waters; And you who have no money, come buy and eat! Come, buy wine and milk without money and without cost
Exhortation	Why spend money on what is not bread, and your labor on what does not satisfy? Listen to me, and eat what is good, and your soul will delight in the richest of fare.
Call	Give ear and come to me; hear me, that your soul may live.
Motive	I will make an everlasting covenant with you; my faithful love promised to David. (Isa. 55:1–3)

The blessings attended to that covenant continue as added incentive in verses four and five.

Jeremiah 44:24–28 serves as an example of the negative response. Here, however, the exhortation is implied in the satire of verse twenty-five:

7.5. NEGATIVE EXHORTATION	
Call	Hear the word of the LORD, all you people of Judah in Egypt.
Exhortation	This is what the LORD Almighty, the God of Israel, says: "You and your wives have shown by your actions what you promised when you said: 'We will certainly carry out the vows we made to burn incense to and pour out drink offerings to the Queen of Heaven.'" Go ahead then, do what you promised! Keep your vows! But hear the word of the LORD, all Jews living in Egypt: "I swear by my great name," says the LORD, "that no one from Judah living anywhere in Egypt will ever again invoke my name or swear, 'As surely as the LORD lives.'" (Jer. 44:24–25)

The motive follows in a warning as to the tragic consequences of Israel's past worship practices. Worst of all, the Jewish exiles in Egypt would die with only a small remnant ever able to return to Judah (vv. 26–28).

Both reward and warning may be present in a single context. Typical of this is Jeremiah 7:2–7a:

7.6. REWARD AND WARNING EXHORTATION	
Call	Hear the word of the LORD, all you people of Judah who come through these gates to worship the LORD.
Exhortation	This is what the LORD Almighty, the God of Israel, says: "Reform your ways and your actions, and I will let you live in this place. Do not trust in deceptive words and say, 'This is the Temple of the LORD, the Temple of the LORD!'
Motive	If you really change your ways and your actions and deal with each other justly, if you do not oppress the alien, the fatherless or the widow and do not shed innocent blood in this place, and if you do not follow other gods to your own harm, then I will let you live in this place, in the land I gave your forefathers forever and ever."

The discourse that follows contains instructions concerning the objectionable nature of their present behavior (vv. 7b–11), together with the warning that Jerusalem could expect to fare no better than Shiloh. It, too, had once served as the dwelling place for God's name (vv. 12–15). God's presence there proved to be no guarantee of survival. Because of the people's sins, God's judgment had to come. Accordingly, the presence of the temple in Jerusalem should likewise be no mere good luck charm. The inhabitants of Jerusalem ought not to assume that they could carry on their abominable syncretistic worship and still expect to escape God's judgment.

The interpreter should also note that in these verses, prophetic instruction and judgment speeches are combined with disputation and satiric tone. The goal is to motivate the people toward genuine repentance and reformation. Such a mixture of literary devices is common enough in Old Testament prophecy (e.g., Isa. 42:18–25; Ezek. 18:25–32; Mic. 3:1–4). It may be added that instructional messages of exhortation or warning may be directed toward individuals, even kings (Jer. 22:1–6). Messages to false prophets (Jer. 29:20–23) or decadent priests (Amos 7:16–17) are delivered with strong words of warning. Here, the motivation toward reformation is only implied at best, for the individuals are so guilty that they appear doomed to judgment.

Satire

Satire can be thought of as containing four basic elements:

1. an object of attack—whether a particular thing, position, person, or the ills of society in general;

2. a satiric vehicle—ranging anywhere from a simple metaphor to a full-blown story;

3. a satiric tone—displaying the author's attitude toward the object of his attack; and

4. a satiric norm—a standard, whether stated or implied, by which the author's criticism is being applied.[12]

As we pointed out above, you can discern satiric elements in a great many of the prophetic messages. This is especially true of announcements of judgment and instructional accounts. Satire occurs in virtually every prophetic book. It is perhaps erroneous to speak of satire as a subgenre of prophecy. Most concede that formal satire originated with the Romans. Nevertheless, at least one scholar has suggested that formal satire can also be found in the biblical book of Jonah.[13] Whether or not Jonah may be viewed as the "greatest satiric masterpiece in the Bible," satire does figure prominently in the account of Jonah's spiritual odyssey (particularly, chaps. 1 and 4).[14]

No less than Jonah, Amos is replete with satire. The society that Amos condemns is "an evil society—a society that rejects the truth, lives in luxury, engages in exploitation, and perpetuates a corrupt judicial system. The attack takes the form of not only naming these vices but also

---

12. See "Satire," in Leland Ryken, James C. Wilhoit, and Tremper Longman III, eds., *Dictionary of Biblical Imagery* (Downers Grove: InterVarsity, 1998), 762.
13. Leland Ryken, *Words of Delight* (Grand Rapids: Baker, 1987), 337–40.
14. Ibid., 337.

predicting a coming judgment against them."[15] Amos' use of parody only adds to the satiric effect:

> The swift will not escape the strong will not muster their strength,
>> and the warrior will not save his life.
> The archer will not stand his ground,
>> the fleet footed soldier will not get away,
>> and the horseman will not save his life.
> Even the bravest warriors will flee naked on that day,"
>> declares the LORD. (Amos 2:14–16)

Amos even includes an obituary notice of the northern kingdom before its fall: "Fallen is virgin Israel, never to rise again, deserted in her own land, with no one to lift her up" (Amos 5:2).

Not to be forgotten also is Malachi's abundant use of satire throughout his disputation with an apostate society (e.g., 1:6–14; 2:7–9, 13–14, 17; 3:13–15). In each case, satire is most at home in contexts dealing with judgment. The widespread presence of satire in prophecy should alert biblical interpreters that they must come to grips with its purposes if they are to grasp the full force of the context.

Wisdom Sayings

Instruction may also take the form of proverbial wisdom. In criticizing Assyria's arrogance at thinking that it had been able to spread its power across the Near East by virtue of its own strength, Isaiah delivers God's judgment by way of a wise saying:

> Does the ax raise itself above him who swings it, or the saw boast against him who uses it? As if a rod were to wield him who lifts it up, or a club brandish him who is not wood! (Isa.10:15).

The Assyrian king needed to understand that his success came only through the power of Israel's God.

Jeremiah and Ezekiel chide their people for suggesting that their punishment is due to the sins of those who went before them rather than

---

15. Ibid., 335.

their own. For example, Ezekiel reports that the people were saying, "The fathers eat sour grapes, and the children's teeth are set on edge" (Ezek. 18:2). Apart from containing a proverbial wisdom component, the statement also drips with satire and irony. Hosea concludes his prophecy with a challenge to walk before God with words reminiscent of Proverbs 10:29:

> Who is wise? He will realize these things.
> Who is discerning? He will understand them.
> The ways of the LORD are right;
>> the righteous walk in them,
>> but the rebellious stumble in them. (Hos. 14:9)

Here, as in Jeremiah 21:8, we see a reflection of the familiar proverbial teaching of the two ways (cf. Prov. 4:14–19). The theme of the two ways became a well-known biblical motif (cf. Deut. 30:19; Psalm 1) and was also used by the sect at Qumran (e.g., 1 QS 3:20–22) and the early Christian church (e.g., *Didache* 1–6). Jesus also used this motif in his teaching concerning the nature of true life:

> Enter through the narrow gate. For wide is the gate and broad is the road that leads to destruction, and many enter through it. But small is the gate and narrow the road that leads to life, and only a few find it (Matt. 7:13–14).

The prophets often used such wise sayings in their admonitions. Thus they appear in exhortation or warning speeches to encourage God's people to righteous living and to impress on them the dangers of disobedience. The godless were warned of their certain judgment should they continue in their present course of action.

Prophetic Narratives

The prophetic books include several types of narrative accounts. These give details of the prophet's life and work. Two types have often been suggested. The first may be termed *vocation reports* (e.g., Jer. 1:4–19; Amos 7:14–17). These tell of the prophet's call and commission to the prophetic office. These serve to inform and assure their hearers that the prophets have an authentic role as God's ministers. The variation in the call of the

individual prophets can serve as a model for God's servants throughout
the ages as to the distinctive opportunities that are available to the Lord's
servants. A second type includes *biographical* (e.g., Jeremiah 26–29; 34–45)
and *autobiographical* (cf. Ezek. 24:15–27) details concerning the prophet's
life. They provide further instruction to God's servants as to what they
may face during their ministry.

Although traditionally not reckoned among the prophetic books, the
prophet Daniel obviously had the gift of prophecy. The first six chapters of the
book of Daniel give details of Daniel's being carried away captive and his life
at a foreign court. These court narratives are of two types: (1) the court contest—in which Daniel's wisdom is demonstrated as superior to the king's advi-
sors (chaps. 2, 4–5); and (2) the court conflict—in which Daniel's three friends
retain their spiritual purity in the face of formal opposition (chaps. 3, 6).[16]

Three other types of prophetic narratives may be noted. In some situations, a prophet is called upon to *dramatize his message via symbolic acts.*
For example, Isaiah went about naked and barefoot for three years to signify
the defeat of Egypt and Ethiopia (Isaiah 20); Jeremiah walked the streets of
Jerusalem with a yoke around his neck to symbolize the Babylonian conquest of the nations, including Judah (Jeremiah 27–28). Ezekiel performed
numerous symbolic acts (Ezek. 3:15; 4:1–17; 12:1–70), and Hosea was even
instructed to marry a prostitute as part of his prophetic calling (Hosea 1–3).

Occasionally, we meet the so-called *prophetic confessions* in which a
prophet acknowledges his or his people's sins. Thus Daniel prays:

> O LORD, the great and awesome God, who keeps his covenant of love
> with all who love him and obey his commands, we have sinned and
> done wrong. We have been wicked and have rebelled; we have turned
> away from your commands and laws. We have not listened to your ser-
> vants the prophets, who spoke in your name to our kings, our princes
> and our fathers, and to all the people of the land (Dan. 9:4–6).

Not to be forgotten are the *historical narratives telling of outstanding
public events* during the prophet's time of ministry (e.g., Isa. 36–39; Jer.
39–44; 52; Ezek. 24:1–2). In a sense, all of these prophetic narratives may

---

16. See Richard D. Patterson, "Holding on to Daniel's Court Tales," *JETS* 36 (1993):
445–54.

be viewed as subtypes of instructional accounts designed to provide spiritual instruction for God's servants.

Miscellaneous Subgenres
Vision/Dream Reports

Several other subgenres remain to be considered. Vision reports are instances in which the prophet receives God's message in a vision, which he in turn is to proclaim to his people. At least three types can be discerned.

1. We have noted previously that some kingdom oracles contain elements that partake strongly of the apocalypses that would become so prominent in the post Old Testament era. Here God's plans for his people and earth's future history are delivered in a vision that contains much symbolism and often fantastic imagery (e.g., Daniel 7).

2. Some vision reports deal with predictions of the less distant future (e.g., Daniel 8) and or give much needed instruction for God's people (e.g., Zechariah 1–6). On the basis of two visions, Amos warns the people of his day concerning the certainty of God's immanent judgment (Amos 7:1–6; 7:7–9). By a vision, Jeremiah understands the Lord's dealing with two groups of people. Like the difference between good and bad things, God will be with those who go into exile in Babylon but be against those who remain in the land (Jer. 42:7–12).

3. Isaiah (chap. 6) and Ezekiel (chaps. 1–3) both receive their calls to the prophetic ministry through a vision. Some vision reports feature the presence of angelic intermediaries (e.g., Dan. 8:13–27; Zechariah 2–6).

Prophetic Hymns/Songs

Whether prophecy was largely written in prose has been widely debated.[17] What is beyond dispute is that distinctive poetic pieces are found

---

17. See Freedman, *Pottery, Poetry, and Prophecy*, 17–18.

in the prophetic books (e.g., Isa. 5:1–2; 12:4–6; 42:10–12; 52:7–10; Jer. 20:13; 31:7; 33:11; Dan. 2:20–23; Amos 4:1–3; 5:8–9). Poetic songs could comprise extensive portions, such as an entire chapter (e.g., Isaiah 26; Habakkuk 3). Habakkuk even includes a long section apparently drawn from the epic literature telling of Israel's exodus from Egypt (Hab. 3:3–15).

Prophetic Prayers

The third chapter of Habakkuk is termed a prayer, and the subscription indicates that it has been set to music for liturgical purposes. You will also be able to identify several other prayers among the prophetic books (e.g., Isa. 37:14–20; 38:2; Jer. 32:16–25; Dan. 9:4–19; Jonah 2:1–9).

Prophetic Letters

In a few cases, we possess records of letters within the prophetic corpus (e.g., Jer. 29:24–28, 29–32). Such cases need to be interpreted in accordance with the normal principles of epistolary literature including careful regard to content and context.

PROPHECY OUTSIDE OF THE OLD TESTAMENT PROPHETIC BOOKS

In the Old Testament

Before moving on to list some specific principles for interpreting prophecy, we should point out that prophecy can be found in the Bible outside the books of the classical prophets. Indeed, in the Hebrew canon the books from Joshua to Kings are termed the Former Prophets. Accordingly, the interpreter may expect to find prophetic messages in the pages of these books. Here, we meet many prophets such as Nathan, Elijah, and Elisha. Nathan conveyed God's intention to David that the Lord would establish David's lineage as a royal dynasty in perpetuity (2 Samuel 7:11–16). Elijah and Elisha delivered many messages from the Lord, in addition to performing miraculous deeds.

Prophecy was known even before the Former Prophets.[18] Among the many examples that could be cited, we note just three. In blessing his sons,

---

18. Paul appears to view the whole of the Hebrew Scriptures as "prophetic writings" (Rom. 1:1–2; 16:25–26; cf. Dan. 9:10).

Jacob prophesied their future. Especially well known is his prediction that "the scepter will not depart from Judah, nor the ruler's staff from between his feet, until he comes to whom it belongs" (Gen. 49:10). Ezekiel, in turn, adapted this oracle in prophesying regarding the future ministry of the Messiah (Ezek. 21:27).

Within the oracles of Balaam found in Numbers 23 and 24 is the prophecy that "a star will come out of Jacob, a scepter will rise out of Israel" (Num. 24:17). This prophecy has been understood by Jewish and Christian scholars alike as having messianic implications (cf. Matt. 2:2; Luke 1:78; Rev. 22:16). In Deuteronomy 18, Moses delivered God's promise to raise up a prophet who would speak the very words of the Lord (Deut. 18:15–18). By this prophecy, Moses predicted the coming of a series of prophets culminating in the Messiah, the greatest of all prophets. The existence of these and other passages outside of the classical prophetic books (the so-called Latter Prophets) demonstrates that the interpreter should be not only aware of their existence but be prepared to interpret them in accordance with the normal subgenres and principles of prophecy.

In the New Testament

The literature of the New Testament mentions the existence and ministry of many prophets or persons engaging in prophetic ministry or conveying prophetic utterances. Examples include Elizabeth (Luke 1:41–45), Zechariah (Luke 1:67–69), Simeon (Luke 2:25–35), Anna (Luke 2:36–38), Agabus (Acts 11:27–28; 13:1; 21:10), Judas and Silas (Acts 15:32), and the daughters of Philip (Acts 21:9). Prophecy was considered an important gift in the early church (cf. 1 Cor. 12:28; Eph. 2:20; 3:5; 4:11). John the Baptist was recognized as a prophet by his contemporaries (Matt. 11:9; 14:5). Like the Old Testament prophets, he employed instructional prophecy, exhorting his hearer to repent and warning them of impending judgment should they fail to do so (Matt. 3:1–12).

Jesus was the prophet *par excellence* (Matt. 21:10–11; John 6:14; 7:40, 52; Acts 3:19–23), yet his speeches were not collected into a book of prophecies. The major theme in his prophetic pronouncements was his teaching concerning the kingdom, which he viewed as entailing both a present and a future dimension. With his presence among the people, the kingdom was now already here but in its full realization it was yet to come (Mark

1:15; 8:38; John 4:23; 5:24–29; 16:25–26, 32).[19] Jesus also put greater emphasis on the universality of the kingdom over against the strict exclusivity of Israel (Matt. 21:43–44; Luke 12:8–10; John 3:14–21). In this, we see the outworking of the age-old promise to Abraham (Gen. 12:3).

Another important aspect in Jesus' teaching pertained to life in the kingdom (Matt. 5:43–44; Luke 17:33; 22:26–27; John 4:23; 12:24–25). Jesus taught the need for essential righteousness, and thus the need for repentance (Matt. 5:20, 48; 6:33). Where repentance was lacking, judgment lay imminently in the future (Matt. 12:26–37). In such teachings, Jesus at times employed the familiar "woe formula" in announcing judgment. For example, in his warning to the cities of Chorazin, Bethsaida, and Capernaum he used the typical elements of invective, criticism, and threat (Matt. 11:21–24). Like the Old Testament prophets, Jesus' prophetic utterances included elements of forth-telling (present pronouncements) as well as a fore-telling (future predictions).

Similar to the message of the Old Testament prophets, Jesus' teaching concerning the kingdom at times focused on the coming of the future kingdom. Of particular importance in this regard is his Olivet Discourse (Matt. 24:3–44; Mark 13; Luke 21:7–33). In this discourse, the emphasis is on judgment blended with apocalyptic-type events such as cataclysmic disasters, worldwide war, terrible tribulation, and the glorious return of Christ. Although no precise salvation and end-time blessing is included here as in the Old Testament kingdom oracles, such features are found elsewhere in Jesus' teaching (e.g., Matt. 11:25–29; 19:28–29; 22:1–14; 25:21; Luke 22:29–30).

Among his announcements of judgment, Jesus also predicted the destruction of Jerusalem (Matt. 23:37–39; Luke 13:34–35). Not only will you find here the standard elements of judgment: address/call, accusation, and announcement, but in addition the prophecy has the form of a lament. This, of course, is another familiar subgenre of announcements of judgment. It should be noted that Jesus predicted his own suffering, death, and resurrection, as well as his return (e.g., Matt. 16:21–28; Mark 8:31–9:1; Luke 9:22–27). In these predictions, the interpreter may discern many Old Testament motifs such as the suffering Messiah, the third-day theme, the reality of resurrection, and the establishment of the final kingdom.

---

19. See here especially the classic work by George Eldon Ladd, *Jesus and the Kingdom: The Eschatology of Biblical Realism* (Waco, TX: Word, 1969).

Although he did not claim to be a prophet, the apostle Paul also exercised the prophetic gift.[20] Paul was certainly aware of the fact that he had the gift of prophecy (e.g., 1 Cor. 14:37–38; 2 Cor. 12:9). In a sense, Paul's whole ministry was much like that of the Old Testament prophets. Thus he, too, engaged in both forth-telling and fore-telling. With regard to the former, Paul's writings are closely related to the Old Testament instructional subgenres that emphasized exhortation or the giving of assurance. Thus Paul instructed the believers in Rome regarding the inclusion of Gentiles in God's plan of salvation (Rom. 11:25–26). At times, Paul issued warnings concerning the expected results of ungodly behavior (Gal. 5:21; 1 Thess. 4:2–8). This included Christians associating with those whose conduct was disruptive (2 Thess. 3:6). Paul also engaged in predictive prophecy, fore-telling matters such as his persecution and sufferings (1 Thess. 3:4), details regarding believers' future resurrection (1 Cor. 15:50–57), and the circumstances and conditions in the last days (1 Tim. 4:1–5; cf. 2 Tim. 3:1–9). Unlike the Old Testament kingdom oracles, Paul's emphasis does not center on the nation Israel.

The careful interpreter will recognize that whether in forth-telling or fore-telling, Paul's prophetic words contain a great deal of information and instruction, most of which is aimed at encouraging his fellow believers. Indeed, there is a strong hortatory element in Paul's prophetic speeches. We may add that much like the Old Testament autobiographical accounts, Paul often reports instances in which God revealed to him what lay before him in his future ministry (e.g., Acts 18:9–10; 23:11; 27:23–24).

Several distinctions between Old and New Testament prophecy remain. First, there is a more universal element in New Testament prophecy than in Old Testament prophecy.[21] We have observed this phenomenon in Jesus' teaching concerning the kingdom as well as in Paul's eschatological teachings. Second, although we have noted common elements between Old Testament prophetic genres and New Testament prophecy, the latter

---

20. Peter also displayed the prophetic gift at times. For example, filled with the Holy Spirit at Pentecost he cited several Old Testament passages as being applicable to the events at Pentecost. Instances of prophetic speech are found at various points in the book of Acts.

21. Though it should be noted that the Old Testament prophetic message frequently extends to the nations as well (e.g., Isa. 13–23; Jer. 46–51; Ezek. 25–32; Amos 1–2; Obadiah; Nahum) and the nations constitute a pervasive feature of the messianic and eschatological hope (e.g., Dan. 7:13–14).

tends to be far less structured. Third, outside of the ministry of Jesus, New Testament prophetic speeches are more difficult to identify than their Old Testament counterparts. Aune suggests three specific criteria for isolating cases of prophetic speech: (1) material that is distinctly attributed to a supernatural being; (2) predictive material that Paul could not have known by ordinary means; and (3) the presence of some specific identifying prophetic phrase.[22] Fourth, you should pay close attention to discerning those Old Testament predictions that find their realization in New Testament prophecy and events.

SAMPLE EXEGESIS: THE BOOK OF NAHUM

Introduction

By way of illustration, consider Nahum 3:14–19. This section completes Nahum's prophecy, which speaks of the judgment of Nineveh. Its genre is tied to its theme and structure. Composed in bifid (or two-part) structure, the first section deals with a declaration of Nineveh's doom (chap. 1). The second portion provides a description of that prophesied doom (2:1–3:19). Having pointed out that the God of justice will surely punish Nineveh (and the Assyrians; 2:1–2), Nahum presents a series of judgment oracles describing Nineveh's judgment (2:3–10; 3:1–7) and giving their ramifications for the Ninevites. The once proud city is hopelessly discredited (2:12–14) and totally defenseless (3:8–19).

Our passage provides a closing condemnation of Nineveh, written in biting satire. Accordingly, in approaching this section the interpreter is reminded to apply the rules of satire. As noted, the object of satirical attack is Nineveh. Nahum's prophetic message is leveled at the city by means of irony, simile, and metaphor. The satirical tone is thoroughly sarcastic, with an emphasis on Nineveh's punishment due to its cruelty toward others.

History

As for historical context, the emphasis on the collapse of Thebes in the near context (3:8–13), which can be accurately dated to 663 B.C., would appear to point to a recent event. Therefore, our passage is most meaningful to its original readers if understood to be set in the middle of the seventh

---

22. Aune, *Prophecy in Early Christianity and the Ancient Mediterranean World*, 247–48.

century B.C. Since the Assyrian civil war (648 B.C.) is not mentioned in Nahum's prophecy, a date around 655–650 B.C. would appear to be appropriate. This was the time when the Assyrian king Ashurbanipal was still conducting his military campaigns and the nation was at its height of strength. Meanwhile, Judah suffered greatly, both externally as a result of continued foreign pressure and internally due to the reign of its wicked king Manasseh (698/7–640 B.C.). For the beleaguered Southern Kingdom, that the humanly unthinkable would happen offered a ray of hope. The seemingly unchallengeable Assyrian aggressor would soon receive the judgment it deserved.

Literature

In this closing condemnation of the Assyrian Nineveh, Nahum uses several literary figures to portray its certain demise. In pure irony and graphic simile, Nahum tells the Ninevites to get ready for a coming siege, yet all of their preparations will do them no good. Their invader's fiery torches and swords will consume the city like a horde of devouring locusts (3:14–15a). In further irony composed of simile and metaphor, Nahum plays on the idea of locusts, reminding the Ninevites that Assyria had devoured others in increasing its own wealth. Moreover, their trusted guards would prove to be locust-like, for they would flee before the invader like locusts who fly off with the rising sun (3:15b–17). Nahum's witty sarcasm climaxes in verses 18–19. Nineveh's leadership will prove to be like inept shepherds who lie asleep while their sheep (the citizens) are scattered. In a closing figure, Nahum likens doomed Nineveh to a person with a mortal wound and predicts that all who hear of the city's fall will rejoice like those who clap their hands in approval over good news.

The setting of the prophecy and the facts of history combine to assure the reader that this unconditional prophecy is aimed at the near future. Indeed, proud Nineveh fell to Neo-Babylonian invaders in 612 B.C.

Theology

Theologically, our passage reminds us that God is sovereign over the earth's political history and will deal justly with all nations. Although God's people may need correction, he alone is their vindicator and hope. By way of application, this passage reminds believers that however difficult the times and situation they face, the Lord is nonetheless in control and will accomplish all things for his glory and humanity's good.

GUIDELINES FOR INTERPRETING PROPHECY

We have become aware that Scripture features a great variety of types of prophecy. We have seen that both literary mediums, prose and poetry, were utilized by the prophets. We have also observed that various genres often appear embedded in individual prophecies, such as narrative and wisdom literature. Accordingly, the hermeneutical principles we have learned concerning these genres need to be applied where they occur in prophetic passages. Not to be forgotten are also the customary exegetical constraints of grammar, historical and cultural backgrounds, literary devices, and theological truths. Above all, the interpreter must remember that the prophet's role was to communicate and proclaim the Lord's message to a specific people in a distinct time and place in history.

Obviously, today's reader does not have the advantage of actually hearing the prophets' speeches. Therefore, the interpreter must do his or her best to understand both the prophet's intention in delivering the message and the effect that it had on his hearers:

> To read prophecy, therefore, is to enter the world of the spoken word, a word that can be fully understood only by the exercise of the whole person. The reader must be attentive to the effect of the message not only on mind and eye but also on the ear and heart.[23]

On the positive side, we have the advantage of a completed canonical text that was intended to be understood and acted upon by generations subsequent to those who first heard the prophetic messages. In addition, in some cases we have before us the application a later writer of Scripture was led to make of a given prophetic speech.

Granted these general guidelines, what specific principles should we apply to a given passage of prophecy? What procedures

---

23. Richard D. Patterson, "Old Testament Prophecy," in *A Complete Literary Guide to the Bible*, ed. Leland Ryken and Tremper Longman III (Grand Rapids: Zondervan, 1993), 298.

and specific steps should we take in order to understand and then teach or preach a given passage of prophecy? We suggest the following principles.

1. As much as possible, the student of God's Word should strive to understand the nature and extent of the *context* in which the prophetic passage at hand is set. This includes the identification of *boundary markers*.[24] For shorter books such as some of the Minor Prophets, the interpreter can come to grips with the relation of the text he or she is considering to the full book of prophecy. For the larger prophetic books, however, this is impractical at best, although we should have at least a basic grasp of the contents of the entire book. One particular problem in dealing with longer prophetic books is that these tend to be collections of speeches whose boundaries are sometime difficult to determine. Here, of course, we will do well to consult dependable commentaries and books on biblical introduction.

Certain structural guidelines can also prove to be of help. For example, the prophet's individual messages may often be detected by distinctive headings or catchwords indicating the beginning of a prophecy. This is particularly useful in determining the limits of oracles in the larger prophetic collections (e.g., Jeremiah).[25]

Some knowledge of Semitic compositional techniques is also desirable. For example, the limits of a given section can often be detected by noting the author's use of "bookending" material, often called *inclusio* or envelope structure. In such cases, at the end of a unit the author returns to a theme, subject or words mentioned at the beginning of the section so as to form an *inclusio*. Thus Ezekiel's dumbness encloses the prophecies of chapters 3 through 24.

---

24. See the relevant discussion in the section on discourse analysis in chapter 12 of this volume.
25. See for example, Richard D. Patterson, "Of Bookends, Hinges, and Hooks: Literary Clues to the Arrangement of Jeremiah's Prophecies," *WTJ* 51 (1989): 109–31.

Likewise, the ministry of Jeremiah's scribe Baruch helps to determine the section boundaries of 36 to 45 in the book of Jeremiah.

A second compositional device involved the arranging of sections of material "on the basis of the association of ideas or words."[26] Such material has been called variously a link, catchword, stitchword, or hook. For example, material related to Jeremiah's conflict with Pashur, the chief Temple officer, is placed contiguously in Jeremiah chapters 20 and 21.

A third literary technique involved the placing of self-contained material in a central setting so as to bind together two adjacent literary units and thereby partake of both. Parunak refers to this technique as "hinging." In such cases, "the two larger units are joined together, not directly, but because each is joined to the hinge."[27] A hinge may be as small as a single verse (e.g., Zeph. 3:8) and as large as a whole chapter (e.g., Jeremiah 25; Daniel 7) or sequence of chapters (Ezekiel 25–32).

Determination as to the literary boundaries of the context will enable the student of prophecy both to isolate the full limits of a passage and to understand it in relation to the surrounding context as well as possibly the whole book. By so doing, he or she will be able to grasp more adequately the author's basic purpose or point of view in the target passage. He or she may then move on to the next preparatory step.

2.   Understanding to which *subgenre of prophecy* the passage in question belongs is vital. As we have seen, each subgenre has its own characteristics and elements. For this reason it is crucial for the interpreter to deal with a given passage in accordance with its subgenre or type. In so doing, he or she comes to grips with the nature of the text and gains further insight into the author's intention. For

---

26. U. Cassuto, *Biblical and Oriental Studies*, vol. 1 (Jerusalem: Magnes, 1973), 228.
27. H. Van Dyke Parunak, "Transitional Techniques in the Bible," *JBL* 102 (1983): 541.

the author certainly had a purpose in using that particular literary device.

3.   A third step toward proper interpretation deals with the *historical and cultural context* in which this speech was delivered. It is essential to know at least the era involved and if possible the historical setting. It is desirable also to know both when and why it was spoken, what was happening in Israel or Judah or both, and when applicable, what was taking place in the surrounding nations. For example, one should inquire as to just why Jonah was sent to Nineveh or why Jeremiah was called to deliver his messages to the people of Judah in such strong language. A solid understanding of the historical situations in Assyria and Babylon will enlighten the interpreter as to the thrust of such prophecies as Nahum, Habakkuk, and Zephaniah.

Matters of culture also play their part. The student of prophecy often needs to learn something of ancient Near Eastern culture in order to understand certain events and remarks in the prophets. For example, why did Amos describe the women of Israel as "cows of Bashan" (Amos 4:1)? What was the nature of the sinful practices at Bethel and Gilgal (Amos 4:4)? What did Amos mean by calling the northern kingdom "Virgin Israel" (Amos 5:2)? What customs or social practices lay behind the figure that Hosea uses concerning the baker's oven and the flat cake (Hos. 7:6–8)? What was the nature of the Molech worship that Jeremiah denounced (Jer. 32:35)? Often, the proper understanding of an ancient culture is a necessary step toward the proper application by the interpreter to contemporary society. If he or she is to make a proper application of a situation in a biblical text to a modern one, the interpreter will need some knowledge of the ancient culture. His or her application will only be as accurate as his or her grasp of the culture of the biblical text with which he or she is dealing.

4.   It is now time to take the fourth step, which is the *careful exegesis of the passage at hand.* This means the accurate use of lexicography and syntax. If the interpreter does not read the Hebrew, Aramaic, or

Greek of the original text, he or she is attempting to interpret, it is essential that he or she consult reliable grammars, lexicons, word studies, and commentaries that will enable him or her to make proper decisions as to the meaning of the passage.[28]

5. A fifth step involves a further appreciation of the *literary constraints* of the passage. We have already spoken of the need to recognize the subgenre of a given passage and to apply its principles and of the need to determine the boundaries of the section. Here we refer to the need of understanding the prophet's frequent use of literary figures, motifs, symbols, and antecedent biblical themes. Hosea, for example, is a rich source of figurative language. Among the many images that occur in his prophecy are those of Israel the unfaithful wife (chaps. 1–3), God as the jealous (2:2–13) or forgiving (3:1–5) husband, or God as the caring, concerned father of Israel his son (11:1–3). Spiritually insensitive Israel is likened to an unturned pancake seemingly unaware of the fire that threatens to burn it (7:8) or is compared to a silly dove flitting from one foreign power to another to find security instead of trusting in God (7:11). Such language can be found in great abundance in the prophetic speeches, for it allowed the hearers to better understand the spiritual principles and lessons the prophet sought to impart.

Not to be forgotten also is the need to recognize cases in which a prophet applies a previous text (e.g., Hosea's application of Mosaic Law, 4:2–3) or adapts a previous text to a new setting and fills it with new emphases. For example, note Zephaniah's use of Joel 2:1–11 in Zephaniah 1:14–18 and Ezekiel's adaptation of Zephaniah 3:3–4 in Ezekiel 22:25–28.[29]

---

28. A helpful place to become aware of common interpretative mistakes is D. A. Carson, *Exegetical Fallacies*, 2d ed. (Grand Rapids: Baker, 1996); see also Robert B. Chisholm Jr., *From Exegesis to Exposition* (Grand Rapids: Baker, 1998) and the discussion of exegetical fallacies in chapter 13 of the present volume.

29. For a good discussion of the subject of inner biblical exegesis see Michael Fishbane, *Biblical Interpretation in Ancient Israel* (Oxford: Clarendon, 1988);

6. As a sixth step, the student should be sensitive to the *theological context*. Here, you should pay particular attention to the theological perspective of the prophet, including theological teachings established prior to the prophet's time. That the prophets were familiar with texts loaded with theological truth is evident in that (a) each of the Ten Commandments is found in the prophetic writings; and (b) each of the three main previously established covenants—Abrahamic, Mosaic, and Davidic—is referenced with some frequency. In fact, in one instance all three are brought together and the prophet envisions their culmination in the great new covenant (Ezek. 37:24–28).[30] The interpreter needs to understand what theological truths the prophet held and what perspective he sought to communicate. Above all, the interpreter must be cautious not to bring his or her own preconceived theology to a given text. As Grant Osborne wisely cautions, "Do not impose your theological system on the text. . . . a system that has become rigid can lead the interpreter to thrust the text in a direction it does not wish to go and thereby can seriously hamper the search for truth."[31]

7. Another necessary step is to determine whether or not the prophet is speaking *predictively*. If so, the interpreter must endeavor to understand to which era the prophet is referring, whether in the near or distant future. Moreover, he or she must ask whether the prophecy has been fulfilled or not. Most of the predictive prophecies actually deal with the immediate or not too distant future. We have already become acquainted with prophecies related to the foreign nations when considering the announcements of judgment. These are ordinarily conceived as referring to that which will take

Text and Texture (New York: Schocken Books, 1979); Walter C. Kaiser Jr., *Toward An Exegetical Theology* (Grand Rapids: Baker, 1981), 161–62.

30. Cf. Jeremiah 31:31–34. A good discussion of the role of Mosaic Law and covenant in the prophetic books may be found in Robertson, *Christ of the Prophets*).

31. Grant R. Osborne, *The Hermeneutical Spiral*, 2d ed. (Downers Grove: InterVarsity, 2006), 274.

place rather soon (e.g., Obadiah's prophecy concerning Edom). Note, for example, the following prophecies concerning Assyria:

> O king of Assyria, your shepherds slumber;
>   your nobles lie down to rest.
> Your people are scattered on the mountains
>   with no one to gather them.
> Nothing can heal your wound;
>   your injury is fatal. (Nah. 3:18–19)

> This is the carefree city
>   that lived in safety.
> She said to herself,
>   "I am, and there is none besides me."
> What a ruin she has become;
>   a lair for wild beasts!
> All who pass by her scoff
>   and shake their fists. (Zeph. 2:15)

The case for Israel and Judah is much the same, should no repentance come:

> The people of Samaria must bear their guilt,
>   because they have rebelled against their God.
> They will fall by the sword;
>   their little ones will be dashed to the ground,
>   their pregnant women ripped open. (Hos. 13:16)

> This is what the LORD says:
> "Stand at the crossroads and look;
>   ask for the ancient paths,
> ask for where the good way is, and walk in it,
>   and you will find rest for your souls.
> But you said, 'we will not walk in it.' . . .
>   Hear, O earth:

I am bringing disaster on this people,
    the fruit of their schemes,
because they have not listened to my words
    and have rejected my law." (Jer. 6:16, 19)

Even kings were warned of their future judgment (Jer. 22:1–30). We know that all of these predictive prophecies have taken place and thus been fulfilled. For we have the established facts of the biblical record and secular history to confirm this. We know that Hosea's prophecy was fulfilled because Samaria fell in 722 B.C. Jeremiah's prophecy was fulfilled with the fall of Jerusalem in 586 B.C. The last king of Israel went into captivity in Assyria (cf. Amos 7:9 with 2 Kgs. 17:3–4), and all of the prophecies concerning the kings of Judah were literally fulfilled (cf. Jeremiah 22 with 2 Kgs. 24:1–25:7). When we have such data, it is easy to declare a prophecy fulfilled. Be careful, however, not to find supposed fulfillments in historical circumstances that go beyond the constraints of sound exegesis. It is all too easy and common to read current events, as some do, in a sensationalist way that oversteps the biblical context.

The interpreter needs to be aware of another problem that at times makes the determination of a prophecy's fulfillment difficult. A prophecy may be merely conditional even if no "if clause" appears in the context. For example, Jonah prophesied the "overturning" of Nineveh within forty days (Jonah 3:4). He announced no conditions for escaping the threatened judgment. Yet Nineveh was spared due to its repentance (Jonah 3:5–12). Certainly, had the people not repented, Nineveh would have been destroyed, and Jonah would have been happy (Jonah 4:1–3). Apparently, however, Jonah missed the point. Nineveh *was* "overturned," but not like Sodom and Gomorrah (Gen. 19:25–28; Deut. 29:23[22]); its "overturning" consisted in the transformation of its people and society. Here, the recognition of the range of meanings in the Hebrew word allows the prophecy to be seen as fulfilled in a conditional manner—either the destruction of the city or the complete change of society.

Other conditional prophecies are not so easily discerned, however. For example, Ezekiel prophesied the destruction of Tyre by Nebuchadnezzar (Ezek. 26:7–21). It was not Nebuchadnezzar, however, who destroyed both mainland and island Tyre (332 B.C.). Nevertheless, it is true that Nebuchadnezzar did lay siege to Tyre for some thirteen years (586–573 B.C.) without actually completely taking the city. The point is that a God-given opportunity was there for Nebuchadnezzar to fulfill the prophecy. Should he not do so, the task would be left to others. As it was, Nebuchadnezzar became the initiator of a long series of judgments against Tyre (Ezek. 26:3). We might add that in such cases of prophecies that seem to lack precise fulfillment, both the sovereignty and the compassion of God need to be kept in mind (cf. Jonah 4:2). Thus the fulfillment of a prophecy at times includes an element of human responsibility, issuing a call to compliance with God's Word on the part of those who must give an account of their actions.

The apparent delay in the fulfillment of Ezekiel's prophecy concerning Tyre points to the fact that prophecies that seem to be imminent may in fact come true hundreds of years later (cf. 1 Kgs. 13:1–3 with 2 Kgs. 23:15–16). In other cases, the seeming delay is in fact connected with a series of events that will find eventual total fulfillment. Prophecies concerning the day of the Lord are a case in point. Thus Zephaniah (1:14–18) predicted that the "day of the LORD is near" (v. 14). Judgment was at hand. Nevertheless, in the description following Zephaniah's pronouncement the prophet portrays conditions that apply to a more universal judgment. Some of the prophecy was fulfilled in Jerusalem's fall in 586 B.C.; another part was fulfilled in the destruction of Jerusalem in A.D. 70; still further fulfillment awaits the end times (cf. Zech. 14:1–2).

Similarly, Joel refers to the day of the Lord in the locust plague (Joel 1:15), the Assyrian invasion (Joel 2:1–11), and the eschatological future—all of which are described as "near" or "at hand." Each historical fulfillment of the day of the Lord thus serves as a reminder and herald of the fact that there is coming a great day of the Lord in connection with events that will take place at Christ's second coming (Matt. 24:15–31; Rev. 6:17; 16:14).

The prophets therefore had "telescoped" vision, seeing the present age and near future, while predicting events that would occur only in a coming age. Some phrase such as "in that day" or "in the last or latter days" often help the interpreter to identify that future era (cf. Isa. 2:2; 11:10–11; 24:21; Jer. 23:5; 31:31; Joel 2:28; 3:1). Even here, you should allow for the possibility that the prophesied event may find a partial fulfillment without its realization being completely exhausted. For example, Joel prophesied concerning events associated with the coming future age (Joel 2:28–32 [3:1–5]), which Peter indicated were fulfilled on the day of Pentecost (Acts 2:14–21). Yet it is just as apparent that the events described in Acts 2:14–21 do not exhaust all the details specified in Joel's prophecy:

I will show wonders in the heavens and on earth,
  blood and fire and billows of smoke.
The sun will be turned to darkness
  and the moon to blood
  before the coming of the great and
dreadful day of the LORD.
And everyone who calls
  on the name of the LORD will be saved;
for on Mount Zion and in Jerusalem
  there will be deliverance,
  as the LORD has said,
among the survivors
  whom the LORD calls. (Joel 2:30–31 [3:3–4])[32]

Although it is true that Joel is using traditional imagery here, the persistence of this imagery in eschatological contexts reveals that something extraordinary involving natural phenomena will occur

---

32. For a study of the imagery in this passage, see Richard D. Patterson, "Wonders in the Heavens and on Earth: Apocalyptic Imagery in the Old Testament," *JETS* 43 (2000): 385–403.

in that future age. Therefore, Peter's use of Joel's prophecy indicates that this prophecy had a fulfillment at Pentecost but that its fulfillment was not exhausted by that event. Prophecies of this sort are therefore viewed as "fulfillments without [final] consummation."[33]

Peter's use of Joel's prophecy points to yet another area of concern: the relation of Old Testament prophecy to New Testament fulfillment. Were all such Old Testament prophecies literally fulfilled or simply in the process of final fulfillment? We have seen that Peter's citing of Joel's prophecy is an instance of the latter. On the other hand, something of the former may be seen in connection with Jesus' ministry (e.g., cf. Isa. 42:1–4 with Matt. 12:17–21; Isa. 61:1–2 with Luke 4:18–19). In many contexts, however, the New Testament citation goes beyond that of the Old Testament text and finds a new, broader setting.

Matthew's exegesis of various Old Testament passages in his various "fulfillment quotations" (especially in Matthew 1–4) is illustrative of a method of exegesis that can be abundantly documented in the New Testament (e.g., cf. Matt. 26:31 with Zech. 13:7; Acts 15:16–17 with Amos 9:11–12; and Heb. 8:8–12 with Jer. 31:31–34). That the "fulfillments" of such Old Testament passages in connection with God's teleological purposes were so understood by Spirit-filled writers of the New Testament, however, does not allow those of us who have not been called to be inspired instruments of the divine revelation to construe unwarranted associations of prophecies to supposed fulfillments in contemporary events. Any such proposed fulfillments should be viewed as tentative at best.

8.   All of this leads to a final step: seek valid *applications* of the prophetic text to the modern church. The proper identification of points of contemporary application will depend on careful adherence to the preceding steps. In all cases, the interpreter should remember that although biblical prophecies were written long ago and to a specific

---

33. For an explanation of this terminology see R. T. France, *Jesus and the Old Testament* (London: Tyndale, 1971), 160–62.

people in a distinct culture, they nonetheless have value for succeeding generations. As do all other genres of the Scriptures, prophecy carries with it biblical themes and principles that are informative and important for the Christian understanding of God and thus for godly character and conduct: "All Scripture is God-breathed and is useful for teaching, rebuking, correcting and training in righteousness, so that the man of God may be thoroughly equipped for every good work" (2 Tim. 3:16–17).

By way of summation, the student should be alert to the following principles as a guide to interpreting Old Testament prophecy:

1. Select and determine the boundaries of the prophecy.

2. Understand the specific type of subgenre to which the passage belongs and apply its rules carefully. In the case of the New Testament, care must be taken not to force Old Testament subgenres onto the New Testament context. As we have seen, New Testament prophecy is far less structured than its Old Testament counterpart.

3. Investigate the historical and cultural contexts of the passage. For the New Testament, this involves correctly assessing both the relevant Old Testament and extrabiblical data.

4. Interpret the passage carefully in accordance with sound grammatical exegesis.

5. Observe the literary features of the passage, considering the prophet's use of figurative language, imagery, motifs, themes, and symbols. Try to determine the meaning or emphasis that the figure is conveying.

6. Be sensitive to the theological truths conveyed by the passage. Note whether the prophet is building on previously revealed theological principles or is presenting new truths. Keep in mind

that Jesus' prophetic perspective was especially concerned with the Kingdom of God.

7. Determine whether the prophecy applies to the prophet's day or to a future time or both. Keep in mind the distinction between forth-telling and fore-telling. Prophets were usually concerned primarily (though not necessarily exclusively) with conditions in their own day.

8. Determine whether the prophecy's future orientation looks to the near, short term, or to the more distant future, whether to the New Testament era or to the end of the age. Also seek to ascertain whether the prophecy as given was conditional or unconditional in nature.

9. In the case of the New Testament, remember that some prophecies were fulfilled in part but their fulfillment not exhausted in the New Testament era. Determine also whether the prophecy has been literally fulfilled or whether the New Testament writer was applying the prophecy in a non-literal manner.

10. Make judicious application of the prophecy to the modern situation. Be careful to ask how the prophecy impacts your spiritual life or the spiritual condition of your church or the church as a whole.

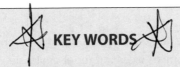

KEY WORDS

Announcement of judgment: a prophetic oracle involving the stating of an accusation and the a pronouncement of the ensuing judgment

Apocalypse: a genre of literature with a narrative framework in which a revelation is mediated by an otherworldly being to a human recipient, disclosing a transcendent reality which is both temporal and spatial

Apocalyptic: a world view anticipating God's climactic and cataclysmic intervention in human history at the end of time

Covenant lawsuit: a type of prophetic judgment speech in which God summons his people to appear before him for covenant violations

Disputation: a literary device that deals with a given topic by way of presenting different sides of an argument, often involving declaration, discussion, and refutation

Exhortation speech: an instructional message in which the recipients are urged to follow the Lord and his standards

Instructional account: various forms of prophetic material, including disputation and exhortation speeches, satire, or wisdom sayings

Lament: a special type of a prophetic announcement of judgment similar to the woe oracle in which the prophet deplores the state of affairs among God's people

Prophetic narrative: an account of the prophet's calling, life, and work

Salvation oracle: prophecy that deals with God's saving work, such as a promise of deliverance, a kingdom oracle, or apocalyptic

Satire: an attempt to demonstrate through ridicule or rebuke the vice or folly of that which appears to be improper or ill-conceived

Vision or dream report: instance in which a prophet receives God's message in a vision, which he in turn is to proclaim to his people

Woe oracle: a special type of a prophetic announcement of judgment that involves (1) invective (the pronouncement of woe); (2) threat (the details of coming judgment); and (3) criticism (the reason for the coming judgment)

STUDY QUESTIONS

1. What was the essential task of Old Testament prophets?

2. What are the two major types of prophetic subgenres in Scripture?
   Judgement /Salvation

3. What are the two major elements of announcements of judgment?
   accusation / announcement

4. What are particular forms of announcements of judgment?
   Woe /Lament / Covenant lawsuit

5. What are particular forms of salvation oracles?
   Kingdom /

6. What is the definition of apocalyptic and its major elements?
   Pages 328-329

7. When did apocalyptic appear, and what are possible apocalyptic passages in the Old Testament?
   2nd century BC - 2nd century AD / Daniel

8. What are the guidelines for interpreting apocalyptic?
   Pages 330 - 331

9. What are various subgenres of prophetic instructional accounts and other subgenres? *Disputation / Exhortation / Satire Wisdom / Narratives*

10. What are examples of prophecy outside the prophetic books in the Old and New Testament?

11. What are the guidelines for interpreting prophecy?
    Pages 346 -358

ASSIGNMENTS

1. Evaluate Hosea 4:1–6 as an announcement of judgment, which also contains elements of covenant violation.

2. Point out the typical prophetic elements of an announcement of judgment against foreign nations in Isaiah 10:8–19. Discuss the force of the prophecy as introduced in terms of a woe oracle.

3. Discuss the typical prophetic features of salvation contained in the kingdom oracle of Jeremiah 31:31–40.

4. Read carefully Isaiah 24. Which verses contain features of apocalyptic genre?

5. By comparing Peter's address on Pentecost (Acts 2:14–36), evaluate Joel 2:28–32 as an example of a prophecy that is fulfilled but not completely exhausted. What basic genre is best assigned to Joel's prophecy?

6. Compare Isaiah 5:1–7 and 27:2–6 as prophetic songs. What overriding generic distinctions may be seen in the basic message and tone of each passage?

7. Identify the following prophecies as to whether they are to be classified as (1) disputation; (2) exhortation; (3) satire; or (4) wisdom sayings
   a. Isaiah 44:13–20
   b. Jeremiah 9:23–24
   c. Jeremiah 10:23
   d. Ezekiel 18:10–20
   e. Hosea 6:1–3
   f. Joel 2:12–14
   g. Malachi 2:10–14

8. By understanding the words of Nathan to David in 2 Samuel 7:11–16 as an example of prophecy, compare Nathan's message with that of Ezekiel in Ezekiel 37:22–28. What prophetic genre(s) is (are) best assigned to the respective passages?

9. Evaluate Luke 17:20–37 as an example of the present and future aspects of the Lord's kingdom. What basic prophetic genres are present in Jesus' words?

10. 11 Thessalonians 4 has been cited as an example of Paul's exercise of the prophetic gift (cf. 1 Cor. 14.37–38). What prophetic genre may be seen in Paul's message to the Thessalonian Christians?

CHAPTER BIBLIOGRAPHY

Aune, David E. *Prophecy in Early Christianity and the Ancient World.* Grand Rapids: Eerdmans, 1983.

Armerding, Carl E. and W. Ward Gasque, eds. *Dreams, Visions and Oracles.* Grand Rapids: Baker, 1977.

Bullock, C. Hassell. *An Introduction to the Old Testament Prophetic Books.* Chicago: Moody, 1986.

Collins, John J. *The Apocalyptic Imagination.* New York: Crossroads, 1984.

Heschel, Abraham. *The Prophets.* New York: Harper & Row, 1962.

Hughes, Philip Edgcumbe. *Interpreting Prophecy.* Grand Rapids: Eerdmans, 1976.

Patterson, Richard D. "Old Testament Prophecy." Pp. 296–309 in *A Complete Literary Guide to the Bible.* Edited by Leland Ryken and Tremper Longman III. Grand Rapids: Zondervan, 1993.

Payne, J. Barton. *Encyclopedia of Biblical Prophecy.* New York: Harper & Row, 1973.

Sandy, D. Brent. *Plowshares & Pruning Hooks.* Downers Grove: InterVarsity, 2002.

Sawyer, John F. A. *Prophecy and the Biblical Prophets.* Rev. ed. Oxford: Oxford University Press, 1993.

Smith, Gary V. *The Prophets as Preachers.* Nashville: B&H, 1994.

Tucker, Gene M. "Prophecy and the Prophetic Literature." In *The Hebrew Bible and Its Modern Interpreters.* Edited by Douglas A. Knight and Gene M. Tucker. Chico: Scholars Press, 1985.

Van Gemeren, Willem A. *Interpreting the Prophetic Word.* Grand Rapids: Zondervan, 1990.

Walvoord, John F. *The Prophecy Knowledge Handbook.* Wheaton: Scripture Press, 1990.

Westermann, Claus. *Basic Forms of Prophetic Speech.* Cambridge: Latterworth, 1967.

CHAPTER 8 OBJECTIVES

1. To acquaint the student with the nature, genre, and origins of the Gospels.

2. To discuss general hermeneutical principles related to the Gospels and Acts.

3. To delineate the overall structure and theology of the Gospels and Acts.

4. To provide the student with a set of guidelines for interpreting the Gospels and Acts.

CHAPTER 8 OUTLINE

A. Nature of the Gospels
B. Genre of the Gospels
C. Origins of the Gospels
   1. Why Four Gospels?
   2. Critical Study of the Gospels
   3. John and the Synoptics
   4. The Historical Reliability of the Gospels
D. General Hermeneutical Principles
   1. Characteristics of the Gospels
   2. Historical Context
   3. Literary Context
      a. External Elements
         i. Author
         ii. Narrator
         iii. Reader
      b. Internal Elements
         i. Setting
         ii. Plot
         iii. Characterization
         iv. Style
         v. Narrative Time
   4. Chronology/Arrangement
      a. Matthew
      b. Mark
      c. Luke/Acts
      d. John
   5. Structure
      a. Matthew
      b. Mark
      c. Luke-Acts
      d. John

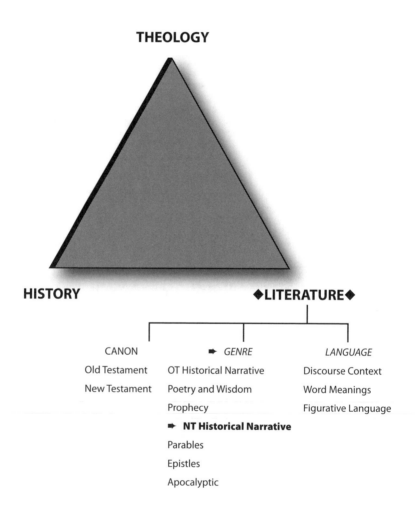

THEOLOGY

HISTORY   **◆LITERATURE◆**

CANON   ➡ *GENRE*   *LANGUAGE*

Old Testament   OT Historical Narrative   Discourse Context

New Testament   Poetry and Wisdom   Word Meanings

                    Prophecy   Figurative Language

                    ➡ **NT Historical Narrative**

                    Parables

                    Epistles

                    Apocalyptic

CHAPTER 8

HEARING THE GOOD NEWS: NEW TESTAMENT HISTORICAL NARRATIVE (GOSPELS & ACTS)

NATURE OF THE GOSPELS

AS WE CONTINUE TO TRAVEL through the canonical landscape, we now cross the threshold from the Old to the New Testament. The Gospels make up the first four books of the New Testament, bearing the titles "The Gospel according to Matthew, Mark, Luke, and John," respectively. While these titles were attached to these documents by the early church, most likely in the decades following the composition of the Gospels by the original authors, only Mark uses this self-designation in the text of his Gospel (Mark 1:1). Originally, the word "Gospel"—which literally means "good news," from the Greek prefix *eu-*, "good," and the noun *angelion*, "news" or "message"—was used for oral, rather than written, proclamation.

Since the Gospels are narratives that focus on the earthly life and ministry of Jesus, all four Gospels share common characteristics in both form and content. For this reason, they are generally put in the same literary genre. Luke is unique in that his Gospel is part of a two-volume work that consists of the Gospel and the book of Acts. The importance of Luke-Acts is further underscored by the fact that in terms of length, Luke's writings make up a quarter of the entire New Testament corpus.[1] In what follows, we will take a close look at the nature, genre, and origins of the Gospels. We will also develop an acquaintance with the pertinent hermeneutical principles and close with a sample exegesis and guidelines for interpreting the Gospels and Acts.

GENRE OF THE GOSPELS AND ACTS

One of the major issues in Gospels studies is the genre of the four canonical Gospels. Not only do these works display similarities with other early Christian writings, they also reflect aspects of their Greco-Roman literary setting. As early as 1915, C. W. Votaw found similarities between the Gospels and popular biographical literature of the Greco-Roman era. He suggested that the Gospels be put in the category of "Greco-Roman biography" (*bios*). In 1923, K. L. Schmidt argued against this classification, suggesting instead that the Gospels should be classified as popular writings rather than as literary works. He proposed that the Gospels should not be viewed as resembling Greco-Roman literature but as comprising a distinct literary form and hence as constituting a new literary genre altogether (as works *sui generis*, "one of a kind").[2] Since then, the Gospels have been variously categorized as biographies of Jesus, memoirs of the apostles, aretalogies (strings of "I am" statements), comedies, tragedies, or theological biography. While Schmidt's proposal remained popular for a considerable amount of time, the genre most commonly proposed today is that of Greco-Roman biography.[3]

Indeed, a comparison between the particular characteristics and features of the Gospels and Acts on the one hand and Greco-Roman literature on the other reveals numerous similarities. For instance, the formal preface of Luke (Luke 1:1–4; cf. Acts 1:1) closely resembles the introductions of Greco-Roman literary works. There are also similarities in thematic emphasis and content. Popular Greco-Roman biographies tended

---

1. Andreas J. Köstenberger, L. Scott Kellum, and Charles L. Quarles, *The Cradle, the Cross, and the Crown: An Introduction to the New Testament* (Nashville: B&H, 2009), 256.

2. D. A. Carson and Douglas J. Moo, *An Introduction to the New Testament*, rev. ed. (Grand Rapids: Zondervan, 2005), 113, citing K. L. Schmidt, "Die Stellung der Evangelien in der allgemeinen Literaturgeschichte," 59–60.

3. Cf. Richard A. Burridge, *What Are the Gospels?*, SNTSMS 70 (Cambridge: Cambridge University Press, 1992; 2d ed. Grand Rapids: Eerdmans, 2004).

to promote a particular hero or important person. Similarly, the Gospels may be said to promote a "hero," Jesus Christ, setting forth his deeds and activities and presenting him as the Savior of humanity. The inclusion of a vindication scene, in the case of the Gospels Jesus' post-resurrection appearances, was also a common device in Greco-Roman literature.[4] In addition, we find literary similarities such as the use of genealogies (Matt. 1:1–16; Luke 3:23–38) and chronologies (Luke 2:1–2; 3:1–2). Finally, in terms of narrative technique, the anecdotal style shows close affinities with Greco-Roman literary techniques.[5] These and other similar characteristics and features may indicate that the Gospels and Acts belong to the genre of Greco-Roman biography.[6]

Despite these similarities, however, there are sufficient differences to suggest that the canonical Gospels constitute a unique genre. A common objection to classifying the Gospels as biography relates to the lack of comprehensive biographical detail regarding Jesus. The absence of a consistent chronological order in the four Gospels is noted as well. While each of the four Gospels devotes considerable space to the final days of Jesus' life, we know little of the events prior to the inception of his ministry. Only Matthew and Luke include the birth narrative (Matt. 1:1–25; Luke 2:1–20); only Matthew recounts the flight to Egypt and the subsequent return to Nazareth during Jesus' childhood (Matt. 2:13–23); and only Luke records the temple incident during Jesus' twelfth year (Luke 2:41–51). Apart from these accounts, little is known about Jesus' early life, and neither Mark nor John has any additional information about Jesus' childhood or early adulthood. However, Greco-Roman biographies likewise did not necessarily provide complete biographical details. Only those segments that were viewed as pertinent to the telling of a given story were included.[7]

There are, however, other significant differences that distinguish the Gospels from Greco-Roman biographies. Of the four Gospels, only Luke has a formal literary preface (though John's introduction is highly literary in nature as well). Moreover, unlike their Greco-Roman counterparts, all

---

4. *Dictionary of Jesus and the Gospels,* ed. Joel B. Green, Scot McKnight, and I. Howard Marshall (Downers Grove: interVarsity, 1992), 278.
5. Ibid., 279.
6. For a discussion of the genre of John's Gospel, see Andreas J. Köstenberger, *A Theology of John's Gospel and Letters,* BTNT (Grand Rapids: Zondervan, 2009), 104–24.
7. William W. Klein, Craig L. Blomberg, and Robert L. Hubbard Jr., *Introduction to Biblical Interpretation,* rev. ed. (Nashville: Thomas Nelson, 2004), 400.

the Gospels are formally anonymous. Another important difference lies in the evangelists' intended audience. All the Gospels as well as the book of Acts were written for a Christian audience. For this reason, these works served a different purpose than the literature of the day and were intended to achieve a different response from the readers. After all, no ordinary hero could compare with Jesus Christ.

In light of these similarities and differences, it seems preferable to view the Gospels and Acts as a subgenre of historical narrative. Like the Old Testament historical narratives, the Gospels and Acts do not merely report facts. The evangelists carefully selected and arranged material that most effectively conveyed God's message. They used a Christ-centered approach that presented a theologically motivated account of the life and work of Jesus and significant events in the life of the early church. Their accounts represent God's saving activity in history and demand a faith response from the readers. In their presentation, the Gospels and Acts reflect a close connection with the literary forms, vocabulary, and themes of Old Testament historical narrative.[8]

The literary style of all four Gospels and the book of Acts, for example, is very similar to that of Old Testament historical narratives. Luke, in particular, displays a Septuagintal style that reveals the influence of the Hebrew Scriptures and reflects self-conscious patterning of his account after Old Testament models.[9] John, likewise, from his opening introduction features salvation-historical points of reference in presenting his Gospel. Also, all four Gospels as well as Acts feature numerous direct Old Testament quotations and allusions.[10] In many cases, these are used in contexts indicating the fulfillment of prophecy. Matthew, for instance, cites Isaiah 7:14, indicating the fulfillment of Isaiah's prophecy that a virgin would be with child and give birth to a son (Matt. 1:22–23).[11]

---

8. For instance, the extended metaphor of the shepherd and the flock (John 10:1–18) is characteristic of the shepherd imagery used in many portions of the Old Testament. For additional examples, see the *Dictionary of Biblical Imagery*, ed. Leland Ryken, James C. Wilhoit, and Tremper Longman III (Downers Grove: InterVarsity, 1998).

9. For example, compare the Lucan birth narrative of Jesus in Luke 2 with the birth narrative of Samuel in 1 Samuel 1–2.

10. See especially the rich compendium by G. K. Beale and D. A. Carson, eds., *Commentary on the New Testament Use of the Old Testament* (Grand Rapids: Baker, 2007).

11. This literary style is also prominent in Acts, particularly in the speeches. The outpouring of the Holy Spirit at Pentecost as recorded in Acts 2, as explained by Peter's

The four modes of narrative identified earlier in this volume are all present in the Gospels and Acts (i.e., reporting of events, dramatic mode, pure description, and commentary).[12] The account of the birth of Jesus (Matt. 1:18–19) emphasizes both *setting and character*:

> *Setting:* "This is how the birth of Jesus Christ came about: His mother Mary was pledged to be married to Joseph, but before they came together, she was found to be with child through the Holy Spirit."

> *Character:* "Because Joseph her husband was a righteous man and did not want to expose her to public disgrace, he had in mind to divorce her quietly."

Like the Old Testament historical narratives, the Gospels and Acts have their fair share of *dialogue.* The speeches and dialogues in the narrative provide dramatic effect and a deeper understanding of the characters involved. For instance, the conversations between Jesus and the Jewish authorities in John are a window into their unbelief and rejection of his revelation (John 8:48–51):

> *The Jews:* The Jews answered him, "Aren't we right in saying that you are a Samaritan and demon-possessed?"

> *Jesus:* "I am not possessed by a demon," said Jesus, "but I honor my Father and you dishonor me. I am not seeking glory for myself; but there is one who seeks it, and he is the judge. I tell you the truth, if anyone keeps my word, he will never see death."

There are also numerous instances of *explicit commentary.* In Mark's account of the raising of Jairus's daughter (5:21–43), the evangelist inserts the explanatory statement, "She was twelve years old." In the earlier

---

ensuing speech at that time, are presented by Luke as the fulfillment of the prophecy in Joel 2:28–32.

12.   See the discussion of Old Testament historical narrative in Chapter 5 above.

example given of the use of chronologies, Luke inserts an editorial comment (indicated in the NIV by parentheses):

> In those days Caesar Augustus issued a decree that a census should be taken of the entire Roman world. (*This was the first census that took place while Quirinius was governor of Syria.*) (Luke 2:1–2)

Reports, such as that of the Samaritan woman to her townspeople, and visions and dreams are also evident. After her conversation with Jesus, the Samaritan woman returns to her town and reports, "Come see a man who told me everything I ever did. Could this be the Christ?" (John 4:29). We find the record of Paul's vision of the man of Macedonia recorded in Acts 16:9–10:

> During the night, Paul had a vision of a man of Macedonia standing and begging him, "Come over to Macedonia and help us." After Paul had seen the vision, we got ready at once to leave for Macedonia, concluding that God had called us to preach the gospel to them.

These and numerous other characteristics found in Old Testament historical narratives can be identified in the Gospels. Larry Hurtado notes that a "writing can be associated with a particular genre only to the degree that all characteristics of the writing can be understood adequately in terms of the features of the genre."[13] For this reason, rather than suggesting that the Gospels and Acts constitute a new genre altogether or are to be identified with Greco-Roman popular biography, it seems best to understand them as belonging to the genre of historical narrative. This requires the interpreter to be familiar with the features of Old Testament historical narrative discussed in Chapter 5 above.

ORIGINS OF THE GOSPELS

Why Four Gospels?

While the Gospels are very similar in content and tone, it is clear that they are not identical. The differences raise the issue of why four canonical

---

13. *DJG* 276.

Gospels were needed to tell the story of Jesus. The issue also has implications for the Gospels' historical reliability and has caused some to question the integrity of the Gospel accounts. In the days of the early church, the diversity found in the four Gospels led to attempts to reconcile these differences. The second-century church father Tatian combined all four Gospels in his *Diatessaron* (Grk. "through four"), the first known harmony of the Gospels. Later, Augustine wrote a treatise entitled *The Harmony of the Gospels.*

Why, then, did the early church see fit to include four Gospels in the Christian canon? Gordon Fee and Douglas Stuart propose that one of the reasons for the need for multiple canonical Gospels is a simple and pragmatic one. Each Gospel was originally written to address the concerns of a particular community or group of believers, and since such concerns differed, the Gospels could not for that reason be identical.[14] Hence, there arose the need for several different Gospels serving Christian communities in various geographical locations. At the same time, all four canonical Gospels were intended for a broad readership not limited to a particular locale.[15]

The question of the diversity of the Gospels for interpretation cannot be overstated. While the four Gospels all focus on the story of Jesus, each Gospel has a unique contribution to make, so that what emerges is a composite, multi-faceted picture of Jesus. The cumulative effect resulting from reading all four Gospels is that readers attain a more comprehensive understanding of the story of Jesus as a whole than if they were only reading one of these Gospels. For instance, reading the Gospel of John on its own apart from the Synoptic Gospels may lead to the conclusion that Jesus never taught in parables or performed exorcisms; however, when we read Matthew, Mark, and Luke, we learn that much of Jesus' teaching was given in parables and that Jesus performed a fair share of exorcisms. Reading Mark's Gospel on its own—a much shorter account—for its part may raise questions about gaps in the story of Jesus. For example, unlike Matthew or Luke, Mark does not begin with a birth narrative, but having established that the Gospel is about Jesus Christ the Son of God (Mark

---

14. Gordon D. Fee and Douglas Stuart, *How to Read the Bible for All Its Worth*, 3d ed. (Grand Rapids: Zondervan, 2003), 129.
15. See Richard Bauckham, ed., *The Gospels for All Christians: Rethinking the Gospel Audiences* (Grand Rapids: Eerdmans, 1998).

1:1) Mark immediately moves on to an account of Jesus' baptism (Mark 1:9–11). Here, the more extensive accounts provided by Matthew and Luke fill in some of the gaps in Mark's shorter presentation.

Understanding that each evangelist had his own unique purpose in writing his Gospel and that the needs of the readers differed, the perceptive interpreter will be careful to read each Gospel in its own right ("vertically") while paying careful attention to the distinctive story line and theological emphasis of the respective Gospel. At the same time, the other Gospels should not be ignored because they serve to enhance the overall understanding of the story of Jesus; thus you should also read across all four Gospels ("horizontally"). Not only do the Gospels share the same overall genre in continuity with Old Testament historical narrative, all four Gospels have as their primary subject the life, death, and resurrection of Jesus Christ and the training of his followers, the new messianic community.

The Critical Study of the Gospels

At the end of the eighteenth century, J. J. Griesbach assigned the term "Synoptic" to the first three Gospels.[16] He had noted the similarities among the first three canonical Gospels in their presentation of the ministry of Jesus. This was evident in their structure, content, and tone. The similarities between the Gospels are not superficial but extend even to wording, order of pericopes (small, self-contained narrative units), parenthetical material, and biblical quotations. An excellent example of this phenomenon is provided by the Beatitudes recorded in Matthew 5:3–12 and Luke 6:20b–23:

What is interesting in comparing the Matthean and Lucan presentation of the Beatitudes is not only the degree of verbal agreement but also the differences in adaptation (which some attribute to Matthew's and Luke's use of a common source, "Q," which comes from *Quelle*, the German word for source). While Matthew features eight beatitudes, Luke limits himself to four; yet unlike Matthew, Luke follows up his four beatitudes with four corresponding woes (Luke 6:24–26). In addition, Luke uses the more personal second person address ("you") rather than the third person as does Matthew, and he has Jesus pronounce a blessing on

---

16. The term "Synoptic" is derived from the Greek word *synopsis*, which means "seeing together." See further Carson and Moo, *Introduction*, 77.

those who are "poor" (Luke 6:20) rather than on those who are "poor in spirit" (Matt. 5:3). Clearly, this is not the place to adjudicate all these similarities and differences in detail; for this the reader is referred to the standard commentaries.[17]

8.1. COMPARISON OF THE TWO BEATITUDE ACCOUNTS	
Matthew 5:3–12	**Luke 6:20b–23**
Blessed are the poor in spirit,	Blessed are you who are poor,
for theirs is the kingdom of heaven.	for yours is the kingdom of God.
Blessed are those who mourn,	
for they will be comforted.	
Blessed are the meek,	
for they will inherit the earth.	
Blessed are those who hunger and thirst	Blessed are you who hunger now,
for righteousness,	
for they will be filled	for you will be satisfied
	Blessed are you who weep now, for you will laugh.
Blessed are the merciful, for they will obtain mercy.	
Blessed are the pure in heart, for they will see God.	
Blessed are the peacemakers, for they will be called sons of God.	
Blessed are those who are persecuted	
because of righteousness,	
for theirs is the kingdom of heaven.	
Blessed are you when men revile you	Blessed are you when men hate you, and
And persecute you and utter	when they exclude you and insult you
All kinds of evil against you falsely	and reject your name as evil
on my account	because of the Son of Man.
Rejoice and be glad,	Rejoice in that day and leap for joy,
for your reward is great in heaven,	because great is your reward in heaven.
for so men persecuted the prophets	For that is how their fathers treated the
who were before you.	false prophets.

---

17. See the commentaries on Matthew and Luke listed in the Appendix to this volume.

In any case, while alternative explanations may be offered, the similarities in presentation especially among the three Synoptic Gospels are best explained on the assumption of some kind of literary interdependence.[18] This likelihood of literary interdependence is further underscored by remarkable similarities in various biblical quotations found in the Synoptics. For instance, note that Matthew, Mark, and Luke all feature joint citations of Malachi 3:1 and Isaiah 40:3 (Matt. 3:3; Mark 1:2–3; Luke 3:4). This is particularly striking since all three Gospels differ from both the Hebrew and the Greek Old Testament. The same can be said with regard to similarities in editorial or parenthetical material.

Apart from this high degree of similarity, the Gospels also exhibit many differences. This raises a number of questions: Were the evangelists dependent on a common oral source? Did they have access to a common pool of written material? Are they literarily dependent on one another in some way? These and other questions have troubled scholars for centuries. How are we to account for the similarities and differences between the Gospels?

Over the last two centuries, there have been three major approaches to this problem of Gospel origins and development: *form criticism*, which focuses on the period of oral transmission; *source criticism*, which explains how the different literary units were compiled; and *redaction criticism*, which highlights the literary and theological contributions of the individual Gospel writers.[19] More recently, the eyewitness character of the Gospels has been asserted as a counterbalance as well.[20]

The great similarities, particularly in the wording of the Greek text, seem to suggest that the three Gospel writers were dependent on each other to a considerable extent. In addition to these similarities, there are also many differences. Various proposals have been made to explain this relationship between the Synoptic Gospels. Historically, we can identify at least three major theories of interdependence. These are the Augustinian Proposal (order of writing: Matthew, Mark, Luke), the Griesbach

---

18. See the detailed presentation in Köstenberger, Kellum, and Quarles, *Cradle, the Cross, and the Crown*, 158–75.
19. The scope of the present work permits only a brief overview. For more detailed treatments, see standard dictionaries and reference works and the brief overview in Köstenberger, Kellum, and Quarles, *Cradle, the Cross, and the Crown*, 173–75.
20. Richard Bauckham, *Jesus and the Eyewitnesses: The Gospels as Eyewitness Testimony* (Grand Rapids: Eerdmans, 2006).

Hypothesis (Matthew, Luke, Mark), and the Two-Document Hypothesis (Mark and "Q" used by Matthew and Luke).[21]

John and the Synoptics

The nature of the relationship between John and the Synoptics is difficult to determine.[22] Proposals range from mutual independence to varying degrees of mutual interdependence. The blocks of material that are common to John and the Synoptics are limited to the feeding of the five thousand, the anointing, and the passion narrative. In addition, John features extended discourses, such as Jesus' encounters with Nicodemus and the Samaritan woman (John 3–4) or the "Farewell Discourse" in John 13–17. Also included are several startling "signs" of Jesus, most notably the raising of Lazarus (John 11).

The inclusion of selected "signs" of Jesus as well as of large blocks of discourse material has led to the proposal that John drew on two primary sources, a "Signs Source" and a "Discourse Source."[23] Among other things, scholars pointed to the initial numbering of "signs" in John 2:11 and 4:54 as evidence for a "signs source" used and adapted by the fourth evangelist. However, the fact that subsequent "signs" are not numbered does not inspire confidence in the theory. More likely, the references to the "first" and "second" signs mark these two events as a literary *inclusio* designating the "Cana cycle" in John 2–4 as Jesus' initial ministry circuit in the Gospel.[24] Little more is to be said in favor of the existence of a "Discourse Source." In fact, as one scholar aptly put it, in light of the similarity of style throughout the Gospel, if John used sources in composing his Gospel, he appears to

---

21. The Four-Document Hypothesis holds that in addition to using Mark and Q, Matthew and Luke also used sources unique to them (labeled "M" and "L"). For fuller treatments, see Carson and Moo, *Introduction*, 92–103; and Köstenberger, Kellum, and Quarles, *Cradle, the Cross, and the Crown*, 158–75.
22. For a detailed discussion, see Köstenberger, *Theology of John's Gospel and Letters*, 550–63.
23. See Rudolf Bultmann, *Das Evangelium des Johannes*, 2d ed. (Göttingen: Vandenhoeck & Ruprecht, 1941; ET: *The Gospel of John* [Philadelphia: Westminster, 1971]); Robert T. Fortna, *The Gospel of Signs* (Cambridge: Cambridge University Press, 1970); idem, *The Fourth Gospel and Its Predecessors* (Philadelphia: Fortress, 1988); and idem, "Jesus Tradition in the Signs Gospel," in Robert T. Fortna and Tom Thatcher, eds., *Jesus in Johannine Tradition* (Louisville: Westminster John Knox, 2001), 199–208.
24. See Andreas J. Köstenberger, *John*, BECNT (Grand Rapids: Baker, 2004), 89–90.

have written them all himself![25] Indeed, it is possible that in his Gospel John incorporated material previously used in his preaching and teaching ministry. One important theme in the first major part of John's Gospel (John 1–12) is the presence or absence of faith, which may provide a common thread uniting the material.

While it seems precarious to isolate sources underlying John's Gospel, one thing seems reasonably certain: the degree of difference between John and the Synoptic Gospels suggests that John probably wrote his Gospel independently of the other three, although it is likely that he was aware of their existence. The latter is suggested by several unselfconscious references that appear to betray awareness of Synoptic tradition if not the Synoptic Gospels themselves:

1. the reference to Andrew as "Simon Peter's brother" in John 1:40;

2. the aside in John 3:24, "(This was before John [the Baptist] was put in prison)";

3. the reference to Jesus' saying in John 4:44 that a prophet is not without honor except in his own county (cf. Matt. 13:57; Mark 6:4; Luke 4:24);

4. the reference to "the village of Mary and her sister Martha" in John 11:1–2 (cf. Luke 10:38–42); and

5. the reference to "the Twelve" in John 6:67, 71, even though they were not previously mentioned in John's Gospel.[26]

---

25. See especially Eugen Ruckstuhl and Peter Dschulnigg, *Stilkritik und Verfasserfrage im Johannesevangelium: Die johanneischen Sprachmerkmale auf dem Hintergrund des Neuen Testaments und des zeitgenössischen hellenistischen Schrifttums*, NTOA 17 (Göttingen: Vandenhoeck & Ruprecht, 1991); and more recently L. Scott Kellum, *The Unity of the Farewell Discourse: The Literary Integrity of John 13.31–16.33*, JSNTSup 256 (London: T&T Clark, 2004).

26. See Andreas J. Köstenberger, *Encountering John* (Grand Rapids: Eerdmans, 1999), 36–37; see also Richard Bauckham, "John for Readers of Mark," in Bauckham, ed., *Gospels for All Christians*, 147–71.

These pieces of evidence, together with an underlying pattern of "interlocking traditions" (i.e., mutually explanatory material),[27] suggest that John wrote his Gospel with an awareness of the Synoptic Gospels while pursuing his own unique purposes and agenda. Having said this, the relationship between John's Gospel and the other canonical Gospels is of course considerably more complex than can be discussed here. If you are interested in pursuing this issue further, you may want to read the more extensive treatment of this issue in *A Theology of John's Gospel and Letters*.[28]

Historical Reliability of the Gospels

Another issue that arises in the study of the Gospels relates to the tensions resulting from different versions of certain events in the different Gospels and the alleged "fabrications" that surface at some points. Critical scholars have suggested that large blocks of the Gospel material lack historical credibility. Thus, the Gospel records of the words and deeds of Jesus are judged to be unreliable. This skepticism has grave implications for the interpretation of the Gospels.

For instance, the different chronologies of Jesus' temptations in Matthew 4 and Luke 4 raise questions about the historical credibility of their respective narratives. Both accounts are placed by the evangelists after the episode of Jesus' baptism. Both Gospels indicate that Jesus was tempted three times by the devil. However, Matthew and Luke differ in their placement of the second and third temptations, respectively. In Matthew's account, the scene of the second is the temple and that of the third is a mountain where the devil promises to give Jesus all the world's kingdoms if he falls down and worships him. In Luke's account, however, the two locations are reversed so that the Jerusalem temple is now the scene of the final temptation. As noted above, each evangelist had a specific purpose in composing his Gospel and this is reflected in the way he arranged his material. It is important for the interpreter to understand that the placement of material in a certain order most likely reflects a particular theological concern on part of a given evangelist rather than impugning his reliability as an evangelist.

---

27. See D. A. Carson, *The Gospel according to John*, PNTC (Grand Rapids: Eerdmans, 1991), 258–59.
28. Köstenberger, *Theology of John's Gospel and Letters*, 550–63.

Rather than doubt the credibility of the Gospels and Acts, the judicious interpreter therefore will evaluate these documents with an understanding of the conventions of their day. Students of the Gospels ought not to force modern conventions onto the Gospels but must understand that the use of paraphrase and the telescoping of events were legitimate devices in ancient historiography. In addition, given that there were four different writers involved one cannot expect them to feature identical translations from the original Greek and Aramaic nor should one expect a given event to be recounted in an identical fashion.[29] Moreover, there is sufficient agreement in the relating of accounts and the placement of events to engender confidence in the evangelists' credibility. Consequently, any approach to the interpretation of the Gospels must begin with the presumption that the Gospels are historically accurate and reliable.[30]

GENERAL HERMENEUTICAL PRINCIPLES

Characteristics of the Gospels

Grant Osborne notes that the "interpretation of narrative has two tasks: poetics, which studies the artistic dimension or the way the text is constructed by the author; and meaning, which recreates the message that the author is communicating."[31] Both poetics and meaning can be understood from a study of the following major characteristics of the Gospels:

1. historical context;
2. literary context;
3. structure; and
4. chronology and arrangement.

These four elements provide us with a crucial interpretive tool for understanding the message of the Gospels and Acts.

---

29. See Craig L. Blomberg, *The Historical Reliability of the Gospels*, 2d ed. (Downers Grove: InterVarsity, 2007).
30. This reverses the unfortunate common practice among critical scholars who put the burden of proof on the Gospels who are assumed to be historically unreliable unless proven otherwise. See the discussion in Köstenberger, Kellum, and Quarles, *Cradle, the Cross, and the Crown*, 143–58.
31. Osborne, *Hermeneutical Spiral*, 203.

We have noted previously that the Gospels and Acts are narratives that tell the story of the life, death, and resurrection of Jesus Christ and the training of his followers, the new messianic community. This shared subject necessarily means that the Gospels share certain material in common and concur in placing primary emphasis on the significance of Jesus. In telling this story, the evangelists used certain literary techniques. In recent years, narrative criticism has gained popularity and various scholars have applied this method to study the Gospels. Its advantage lies in the fact that it views the text as a literary whole and avoids fragmenting the text into unrelated units. Thus the Gospels are read as integrated narratives with all the various component parts contributing to the overall story. The major drawback of this approach is that it tends to downplay the historical element. Thus Osborne rightly cautions that narrative criticism "should never be done by itself but should be combined with source and redaction criticism, which will act as a corrective to its ahistorical tendencies and to the excesses of its stress on the text as a final product rather than as a developing unit."[32]

For this reason, it is crucial to remember that while the literary elements of a narrative are important, the theological and historical elements must also be given their proper place in the interpretive task (the hermeneutical triad). In telling the story of Jesus and the early church, the evangelists wrote from a particular historical perspective and were theologically motivated to highlight the significance of Jesus. But in doing so, they used the literary forms and conventions of their day. Our task as interpreters is to study the text before us with these three elements—history, language, and theology—always in mind.

Historical Context

Historical context provides us with vital background information necessary for understanding the purpose of a given text and aids in reconstructing the particular situations that generated the need for it. For instance, the footwashing scene of John 13 brings to the fore the importance of understanding cultural practices during the time of Jesus. Footwashing was a task customarily done by non-Jewish slaves and never by a superior to his inferior. In taking on this menial stance, Jesus provides an example of true service, the kind he expected of all his followers.

---

32. Ibid., 200.

Without the understanding that this task was considered too de-meaning for disciples or even Jewish slaves, the significance of Jesus' action would be lost or at least much less apparent.[33] The areas that yield the most useful data for reconstructing historical context include geography, politics, economics, military and war, cultural practices, and religious customs. Bible dictionaries, encyclopedias, atlases, and so on are valuable resources for uncovering this data.[34] In addition, allusions to Old Testament and Second Temple literature, as well as Qumran, rabbinic, and Hellenistic parallels should not be ignored.[35]

The historical context of the Gospels operates on two levels: the *Sitz im Leben Jesu* (the life setting in Jesus' day) and the *Sitz im Leben der Kirche* (the life setting of the church at the time of composition). Because the Gospels are about Jesus, they record events that happened during his earthly life (the *Sitz im Leben Jesu*). This means that his sayings, miracles, and signs were generated by a particular historical context. As these stories and sayings were passed on from community to community, the original context surrounding most of them gradually receded into the background. At the same time, the Gospels were written by the evangelists at a later date and adapted for a different historical context (the *Sitz im Leben der Kirche*). Since the Gospels are formally anonymous, it is not an easy task to recover the historical contexts of the evangelists. This creates difficulty in interpretation. A good rule of thumb as one reads the four Gospels is to find out whether Jesus' audience for a given teaching were his close disciples, the larger crowds, or his opponents.[36]

At this point, knowledge of the redactional patterns of the Gospels proves useful. Used with caution, the findings of redaction criticism may provide insights into the different life settings of the various evangelists in these early Christian communities.[37] For instance, Mark's emphasis on the disciples' fear and misunderstanding is most likely intended to reassure and encourage a Gentile Christian audience, possibly in Rome, at a time when

---

33. See Köstenberger, *John,* 403–5.
34. See the resources listed in the Appendix at the end of this volume.
35. See Osborne, *Hermeneutical Spiral,* 127–39. For a general framework of the history, literature, and theology of the Second Temple period, see Köstenberger, Kellum, and Quarles, *Cradle, the Cross, and the Crown,* chap. 2.
36. Fee and Stuart, *How to Read the Bible,* 133.
37. See the brief survey in Köstenberger, Kellum, and Quarles, *Cradle, the Cross, and the Crown,* 174–75.

imperial persecution against Christians intensified.[38] Luke wrote, at least in part, to defend Christianity against Jewish charges that the movement was politically subversive, which (among other things) explains his extensive account of Paul's trials before various Roman officials in the final chapters of the book of Acts. With this, we move on to a consideration of the second major aspect of Gospels study, the exploration of the literary context.

Lliterary Context

Klein, Blomberg, and Hubbard note that "[a] basic principle of biblical hermeneutics is that *the intended meaning of any passage is the meaning that is consistent with the sense of the literary context in which it occurs.*"[39] The literary context refers to the place of a given pericope in the context of any one of the Gospels. The material that comes before and after it forms its literary context. Fee and Stuart refer to the principle (already briefly touched on above) of reading the Gospels *vertically* and *horizontally*.[40] This means that in cases where a similar incident is recorded in all four Gospels or in the Synoptics, the first step is to determine what the passage means in the context of the Gospel in which it is found (the "vertical" reading). Only after this is done is it appropriate to compare a given textual unit with parallels in the other Gospels (the "horizontal" reading). Note, for instance, the literary contexts within which the four evangelists chose to fit their feeding accounts in the following horizontal comparison:

8.2. LITERARY CONTEXT OF THE FEEDING ACCOUNTS IN THE GOSPELS			
Matthew	**Mark**	**Luke**	**John**
14:1–12	6:14–31	9:1–9	5:31–47
John the Baptist beheaded	John the Baptist beheaded	Jesus sends out the twelve	Testimonies about Jesus
14:13–2	16:32–44	9:10–17	6:1–15
Feeding account	Feeding account	Feeding account	Feeding account
14:22–36	6:45–56	9:18–27	6:16–24
Jesus walks on water	Jesus walks on water	Peter's confession of Christ	Jesus walks on water

---

38. Klein, Blomberg, and Hubbard, *Biblical Interpretation,* 406.
39. Ibid., 214 (emphasis original).
40. Fee and Stuart, *How to Read the Bible,* 133–39.

Whereas Matthew and Mark include the passage on John the Baptist's beheading just prior to the feeding incident, Luke and John feature the sending out of the twelve and testimonies about Jesus, respectively. Matthew, Mark, and John place the incident of Jesus walking on the water after their accounts, while Luke chooses to follow up the feeding narrative with Peter's confession of Jesus as the Messiah. Each of the accounts, while relating the same incident, must be interpreted in light of their literary contexts, always keeping in mind the author's purpose as far as it can be determined. After this, it is appropriate to consult the other three Gospels. This is best done by consulting a synopsis or harmony of the Gospels. In so doing, one should always keep in mind the following:

There were three principles at work in the composition of the gospels: selectivity, arrangement and adaptation. On the one hand the evangelists selected those narratives and teachings that suited their purposes (Jn 21:25). At the same time the evangelists and their churches had special interests that also caused them to arrange and adapt what was selected.[41]

The value of context is that it provides the flow of thought and the accurate meaning of words and delineates correct relationships among units.[42]

As we proceed to a study of Gospel narratives in their literary dimension, it will be important to understand how the agents of communication (external elements) as well as the actual features of the narrative (internal elements) function in the genre of historical narrative. The *external elements* of a narrative include the author, the narrator, and the reader. The *internal elements* include the setting, plot, characterization, style, and narrative time.

External Elements

Author

The *real author* is the one who actually wrote the text. As noted previously, the readers never see the real author, only what he has written. The *persona* that he creates of himself in the text is what is referred to as the

---

41. Ibid., 141.
42. For further discussion of this see Klein, Blomberg, and Hubbard, *Biblical Interpretation*, 214–16.

implied author. The implied author is therefore a literary figure. R. Alan Culpepper notes, "Unlike the narrator, the implied author has no voice and never communicates directly with the reader."[43] It is only on the basis of inferences from the text that the interpreter is able to reconstruct the theological concerns and emphases that the implied author has chosen to make known.

For instance, we may infer from Luke's two-volume account that the implied author is concerned to demonstrate the continuity of God's plan and to highlight God's interest in the socially disadvantaged. Since what is made known by the implied author can never constitute the entirety of who the real author is, the two are always distinct. While we generally focus on the implied author in interpreting a narrative, it is important to keep in mind that the presence of the real author grounds the narrative historically and keeps us focused on the intended meaning of the text.[44]

Narrator

The narrator, like the implied author, is also a literary figure or a rhetorical device created by the author to tell the story and to interpret the significance of the narrative. In terms of communication, the narrator stands at a level above the text and the characters within the story. The narratee is the one to whom the story is told, and in certain cases may even be part of the narrative. A possible example is Theophilus in Luke 1:1–4 and Acts 1:1.

Although the narrators of the Gospels and Acts are not represented as characters in the story, their presence is obvious. For instance, in the extended introduction of John 1:1–18 it is the voice of the narrator who proclaims the entrance of the divine Word into the world. Narrators may use either the first or third person to tell their story. In the Gospels and Acts, the narrative is generally in the third person. However, in certain portions of Acts, the "we speeches," the narrator reverts to the first person. Consider Acts 20:5, for example:

---

43. R. Alan Culpepper, *The Anatomy of the Fourth Gospel: A Study in Literary Design* (Philadelphia: Fortress, 1983), 15.
44. Osborne, *Hermeneutical Spiral*, 204.

These men went on ahead and waited for *us* at Troas. But *we* sailed from Philippi after the Feast of Unleavened Bread, and five days later joined the others at Troas, where *we* stayed seven days.

Narrators use different expositional modes to tell their story. The expositional mode of the narrator of John's Gospel, for instance, is chronological, preliminary, and concentrated.[45] Numerous scholars have noted that the Johannine introduction previews themes that are subsequently developed as the narrative unfolds in a chronological manner. The narrator allows his readers to share in his omniscience by providing crucial information at the beginning of the narrative. The more straightforward a narration is in terms of how much the reader is allowed to know, and when, the more reliable the narrator appears. The narrator of John's Gospel is an omniscient figure whose stature steadily increases as the narrative progresses.

Because the narrators in the Gospels and Acts represent the point of view of the authors, they serve as the voice of the implied authors. Yet while the narrator and the implied author may not always be distinguished, they are always distinct. As interpreters, we will do well to maintain this distinction because it forces us to look at the seams and editorial asides of the text as important indicators of its meaning.[46] These markers, which briefly suspend narrative time, provide insights into the writer's scale of values, his ideology, and point of view. They take the form of information (e.g., description), comments, explication, or a value judgment from the writer.[47] Distinguishing editorial comments from narration is not always an easy task. Note, for instance, the example given earlier of Mark's account of the raising of Jairus' daughter (Mark 5:41–43). The text in parenthesis indicates Mark's editorial comments:

He took her by the hand and said to her, "*Talitha koum!*" (which means, "Little girl, I say to you, get up!"). Immediately the girl stood up and walked around (she was twelve years old.)

---

45. Culpepper, *Anatomy*, 19.
46. Osborne, *Hermeneutical Spiral*, 204.
47. J. P. Fokkelman, *Reading Biblical Narrative: An Introductory Guide* (Louisville: Westminster, 1999), 69.

The first comment, in which the author provides the reader with a translation of Jesus' words, is easy to identify because of the phrase "which means." The second remark is more difficult to discern in the absence of explicit textual markers. Nevertheless, the perceptive interpreter will observe that the evangelist here added the girl's age, increasing the reader's confidence in the trustworthiness of the narrator and his narrative. The overall impact of this kind of commentary is that it allows the reader to develop increasing confidence in the narrator's competence and reliability as he or she is guided through the story.[48]

The value of distinguishing between narrative and commentary becomes clear in the following example. John 3:1–15 relays Jesus' conversation with Nicodemus (with 2:23–25 serving as an introduction), and 3:16–21 contains the evangelist's exposition or commentary. Rather than read the whole as one section of narrative, the recognition that verses 16–21 serve as a commentary on Jesus' previously reported conversation between Jesus and Nicodemus allows the reader to understand that the latter verses contain the explanation provided by the evangelist rather than being part of Jesus' words to Nicodemus.[49]

An important aspect of any narrative is *point of view.* Osborne defines point of view as follows: "The point of view is the perspective taken by various characters or aspects in the narrative. Most frequently, it is connected with the narrator, who interacts with the action within the story in various ways and so produces the effect that the story is to have on the reader."[50] There are at least five dimensions of this phenomenon.

Psychological dimension. This is related to what the narrator knows concerning the thoughts, feelings, and motivations of the characters. It may be limited or omniscient (in a literary rather than theological sense). How much the reader is allowed to share in this omniscience is left to the discretion of the narrator. In the case of the Gospels and Acts, the narratives reflect an omniscient perspective, providing information that is otherwise unknowable. For instance, in Mark 14:72 the evangelist reveals to the reader Peter's inner thoughts and the reason for his distress:

48. David Rhoads and Donald Michie, *Mark as Story: An Introduction to the Narrative of a Gospel* (Philadelphia: Fortress, 1982), 39.
49. See Köstenberger, *John,* 113–14.
50. See Osborne, *Hermeneutical Spiral,* 204; Culpepper, *Anatomy,* 21–33.

Immediately the rooster crowed the second time. *Then Peter remembered the word Jesus had spoken to him:* "Before the rooster crows twice you will disown me three times." And he broke down and wept.

Evaluative or ideological dimension. This is concerned with the question of right or wrong in the narrative. While it is reflected at three levels—the author, the narrator, and the characters themselves—it is the narrator's point of view that guides the readers' response to the narrative. This perspective, in turn, reinforces the notion of the reliability of the narrator. The narrator may sometimes support the evaluative point of view of a character or characters in the story. In other instances, he may reject it; in yet others, he may choose to remain neutral, allowing the readers to render their own judgment. With respect to characters, the ideological mentality that a character possesses is displayed as the narrative unfolds. Rhoads and Michie comment that in Mark there are only two basic ideological points of view: that of Jesus and most minor characters (reflecting the thoughts of God) and that of his opponents (reflecting a merely human perspective).[51]

Spatial dimension. This refers to the geographical location from which the narrator relates his story. The narrators in the Gospels and Acts are omnipresent, moving effortlessly from place to place and relaying their story from different vantage points.

Temporal dimension. This refers to the location in time that the narrator adopts when telling his story. He may tell his account retrospectively, subsequent to the occurrence of a given event, or as the event is taking place. All four evangelists tell their story from a retrospective or post-resurrection perspective. Critical scholars have often sought to drive a wedge between the "historical Jesus" on the one hand and the "Christ of faith" on the other. A careful reading of the Gospels shows, however, that the evangelists were well aware of the possible impact of their current situation on their presentation of Jesus' story and that they were perfectly capable to write an accurate historical account without imposing their later perspective onto the time of Jesus.[52]

---

51. Rhoads and Michie, *Mark as Story*, 44.
52. For a perceptive treatment of this issue in the case of John's Gospel, see D. A. Carson, "Understanding Misunderstandings in the Fourth Gospel," *TynBul* 33 (1982): 59–81.

Phraseological dimension. This relates to the dialogue or speeches in a narrative. The narrator allows the reader to listen in on conversations of which the other characters in the story are unaware. As an example, Osborne cites the private dialogue between Festus and Agrippa regarding Paul's innocence (Acts 26:31–32).[53]

Reader

The reader is the actual reader of the narrative. This is a label that properly applies to a contemporary reader. The *implied* reader is the one or ones for whom the author composed his work. It is necessary to understand this distinction, because while the original readers of the text are no longer alive, the message was originally intended for them. Understanding this original context permits the interpreter to gain more insight into the original purpose of the author. This is always an important goal of interpretation.

Internal Elements

Setting

The setting of a narrative includes such factors as the *physical location*, *time*, and *cultural background* in which the narrator tells his story. In some instances, the *physical location* plays an important role in the interpretation of the events unfolding in the narrative. For instance, Mark 6:45–52 describes a scene where Jesus asks his disciples to go on ahead of him to Bethsaida by boat. Then, "About the fourth watch of the night he went out to them, walking *on the lake*" (v. 48). Mark also notes that Jesus stills the wind (v. 51), thus drawing the reader into a deeper understanding of Jesus' power over nature. The fact that the evangelist places this account immediately after the miracle of the loaves serves to further highlight Jesus' authority. Osborne notes that the story of the two disciples on the road to Emmaus in Luke 24:13–35 is set in a geographical framework with Jerusalem serving as the focal point signifying both their discouragement and their victory.[54] One should also note the different patterns of movement

---

See also Eugene Lemcio, *The Past of Jesus in the Gospels*, SNTSMS 68 (Cambridge: Cambridge University Press, 2005).
53. Osborne, *Hermeneutical Spiral*, 206.
54. Ibid., 209.

reflected in the four records of Jesus' ministry as well as in the narrative depicting the extension of the church in the book of Acts.

The *time* within which the narrator sets his story may also play a significant role. After the footwashing scene and Jesus' prediction of his betrayal (John 13:1–30), the author ominously adds, "And it was *night*." While a straightforward reading understands this statement to refer to night in a literal sense (which is doubtless part of the authorially intended meaning), a deeper meaning is almost certainly in view as well: "The present reference in all likelihood also conveys the notion of spiritual darkness entered by the betrayer (cf. Luke 22:53: 'this is your hour—when darkness reigns')."[55] Therefore, with this indicator of time, the dramatic intensity of the narrative is heightened and the reader is drawn more deeply into the narrative, recognizing that a malevolent spiritual element, in the person of Satan (cf. John 13:2, 27), is at work.

The *cultural background* also provides important clues for interpreting the narrative. Again, you will do well to consult reliable study Bibles and the relevant commentary literature.

Plot

As noted earlier, "plot" refers to the arrangement of events in a story and revolves around *conflict* (physical, psychological or spiritual) and *suspense* (curiosity, dread, anticipation or mystery). Plot is not confined to the larger narrative alone but also extends to the smaller units that make up the narrative. It takes on a different shape in the hands of each of the evangelists because while all may be relating the same story, their authorial purpose is different and hence the interaction between the characters is portrayed differently. Osborne observes, "The interplay of opponents and the interaction between major and minor characters are the clearest possible guidelines to the meaning of a passage."[56] For instance, as noted in an earlier example, the manner in which Mark's plot develops consistently emphasizes the disciples' failure to understand Jesus' messianic identity. Matthew's plot, on the other hand, while mentioning these same instances, unfolds in a manner that does not draw sustained attention to their lack of insight.

---

55. Köstenberger, *John*, 418.
56. Osborne, *Hermeneutical Spiral*, 208.

An understanding of the plot also includes the awareness that the evangelists chose to sequence their events in the order that best reflected their theological emphases. While many of the same events and sayings appear in all four Gospels, their immediate context in the narrative is an indicator of the plot. Culpepper's comment is apropos:[57]

> The plot therefore interprets events by placing them in a sequence, a context, a narrative world, which defines their meaning. The events are then secondary to the story or message which gives them meaning. Where each evangelist chose to begin and end his gospel and which conflicts receive the most attention tell a great deal about their plots.

Recognizing that unlike the Synoptics John presents the temple incident as occurring early in Jesus' ministry is very helpful for the interpreter (John 2:12–16; cf. Matt. 21:12–17; Mark 11:15–19; Luke 19:45–46). In John's plot, Jesus' authority and power are asserted early in the narrative. In the Synoptics, this recognition unfolds more gradually.[58]

Characterization

As mentioned, literary critics generally identify three kinds of characters: round, flat, and agent. An interpreter must seek to understand how the narrator develops his characters because these personages and their interactions determine how the plot develops. Jesus is a flat character because unlike other characters he does not grow. What grows, however, is people's perception of him. The character in a narrative is either the protagonist or the antagonist. In the four Gospels, the protagonist is Jesus. The antagonists may oppose the protagonist, as in the case of the Jewish authorities, or may serve as a foil to highlight a contrast, such as Nicodemus or the Samaritan woman (John 2:23–3:21; 4:1–42). In this case, the contrasts painted by the narrator provide the reader with an interpretive tool for understanding the message of the evangelists.

In some cases, the narrators in the Gospels and Acts portray the same characters in different ways. Perhaps the most striking example is their representation of the Jews. In the Synoptic Gospels, the term "the Jews" is

---

57. Culpepper, *Anatomy*, 185.
58. See the discussion in Köstenberger, *John*, 111.

a straightforward term, generally referring to those of Jewish descent. In John, however, the expression typically takes on a different connotation. It is frequently used to refer to the hostile Jewish authorities and ultimately represents those non-messianic Jews who reject Jesus as Messiah. Another example is the distinctive way in which John the Baptist is portrayed in the four Gospels. While the Synoptics depict him as a prophet, the fourth evangelist never refers to John as a prophet but consistently describes him as a witness to Jesus (John 1:6–8, 15; 5:33).

Style

One of the primary tasks of interpretation is to identify the stylistic devices that contribute to a narrative's literary artistry. The most common literary devices in the Gospels and Acts include dialogue, repetition, irony, misunderstandings, and symbolism. Without a proper understanding of the nature and function of these devices it is often virtually impossible to uncover the authorial intent behind the narrative.[59]

Dialogue. All four Gospels and Acts display numerous instances in which the narrator uses dialogue to develop the narrative. Dialogue gives the reader insight into the character of the one speaking and heightens drama, particularly in scenes where confrontation is prominent. The dialogues in the Synoptics reveal that Jesus preferred to teach in a style that was filled with aphorisms and parables. In John, however, this style is not as immediately apparent as both Jesus and his opponents speak in the Johannine idiom. This is particularly evident when one compares the style of John's Gospel to that of his epistles. A study of the four Gospels reveals that John has longer discourses, which contributes to his more meditative and reflective style.[60]

Repetition. It was noted earlier that repetition is perhaps the most widespread and widely recognized stylistic feature of biblical narratives. All four Gospels and Acts employ use repetition in their narratives. Repetition extends to words, sequence of words, themes, imagery, signs, and scenes. Repetition is also achieved through *inclusio* and other structural devices such as chiasms. While repetition may seem tedious by modern

---

59. For a thorough study of Johannine style and literary devices, see Köstenberger, *Theology of John's Gospel and Letters*, 130–67.
60. See the discussion in ibid., 115–18.

literary standards, this stylistic device served a very important purpose. It was always used to emphasize or clarify a point.

For instance, in John's Gospel Jesus repeatedly performed signs, both miraculous (e.g., John 2:1–11) and non-miraculous (e.g., John 2:14–22).[61] Judaism held that signs were an affirmation of God's presence and hence the evangelist's inclusion of these repeated signs testifies to the fact that Jesus was not only a divine prophet (John 6:14; 7:40) but also the God-sent Messiah (John 7:31; 20:30–31).

Rather than regard repetition as a monotonous phenomenon, the interpreter should keep in mind that "even though a writer may repeat a string of words without any change, their sense and function cannot remain unaltered as the context has changed: they have moved along the linear axis, and in the meantime all sorts of developments have taken place."[62]

Irony. Irony is reflected in both words and events and is easily identified in situations where the surface meaning of the text appears to contradict the context. Note, for example, the irony of Caiaphas' words at a meeting of the Sanhedrin in John 11:49b–50: "You know nothing at all! You do not realize that it is better for you that one man die for the people than that the whole nation perish." Jesus did indeed die for the nation—even for the whole world—but the Jewish nation still perished. The irony would be all too apparent to John's readers, for whom the Gospel was written in all likelihood more than a decade after the temple's destruction in the year 70.[63]

Misunderstanding. The four Gospels provide numerous instances of misunderstandings, particularly in Jesus' conversations with the minor characters in the narrative. This aspect of narrative has already been noted in the Gospel of Mark. John also provides us with numerous examples of misunderstandings.[64] Nicodemus understood Jesus' statement about the new birth in a literal rather than spiritual manner (John 3:4). The Samaritan woman assumes that Jesus, in referring to living water, is speaking of literal water (John 4:15). In both instances, Jesus is shown to utter a statement that is promptly misunderstood by the other party. This opens up

---

61. See ibid., 323–35.
62. Fokkelman, *Reading Biblical Narrative,* 121.
63. On Johannine irony, see Köstenberger, *Theology of John's Gospel and Letters,* 150–55.
64. Ibid., 141–45.

the opportunity for further dialogue and explanation as well as clarification of the statement's theological significance.

Symbols. Mark Stibbe defines a symbol as a link which connects two levels of meaning in a story.[65] The Gospels and Acts are replete with symbols, connecting concrete images with abstract meanings. The seven "I am" statements of Jesus are a representative example of the use of this stylistic device. In the last of these statements, Jesus asserts, "I am the true vine" (John 15:1). The Old Testament frequently uses the vineyard or vine as a symbol for Israel, God's covenant people. Through this symbol, Jesus presents himself as the ultimate contrast to unfaithful Israel. In this case, the author's intent is not to cause the reader to focus on the vine as such; his emphasis is rather on the notion of intimacy conveyed by the organic, vital connection between the branches and the vine.

Narrative Time

Narrative time is dependent on three factors: order, duration, and frequency of events in the narrative.[66] *Order* refers to the sequence of events as presented in the narrative. While the order is generally linear in the Gospels and Acts, there are certain situations in which anachronisms occur (events that have either happened in the past or that will happen in the future but are evoked in the present context). For instance, in John 1:19–51, the narrator uses numerous analepses (flashbacks), prolepses (previews), mixed analepses, and mixed prolepses, which create a distinction between the sequence of the narrative and the sequence of the story.[67] Anachronisms function to heighten dramatic intensity, fill gaps in the story, and enhance narrative flow.

An instance where an analepsis is used to good effect is found in Mark 6:14–29. In this account, the narrator relates Herod's fearful reaction to the news about the miraculous activities taking place because of Jesus' influence. Knowing that he himself had ordered the execution of John the Baptist, he concludes that John has come back to life in Jesus. Having

---

65. Mark W. G. Stibbe, *John as Storyteller: Narrative Criticism and the Fourth Gospel* (Cambridge: Cambridge University Press, 1992), 19; see also Köstenberger, *Theology of John's Gospel and Letters,* 155–67.
66. The following categories are largely dependent on Culpepper, *Anatomy,* 53–74.
67. See ibid., 54–57.

last featured John in prison as narrated in Mark 1:14, the narrator now provides the readers with information related to his death in a flashback (Mark 6:17–19). Without this scene, the reader would be left with a gap in the narrative (for a similar, though not identical, dynamic see John 3:24).

Duration refers to the relationship between the length of the narrative and the story. There is a difference between *story time*, the passage of time covered by the events as recorded by the evangelists, and *narrative time*, the level of time in the narrative. At times, story and narrative time may correspond but for the most part they remain distinct. There are some instances, however, where they may appear to be one and the same. In his analysis of the plot of John 11:1–44, Stibbe notes that the first phase of the Lazarus story (John 11:1–16) takes place over a period of several days. In the rest of the story (John 11:17–44), narrative time is slowed down dramatically, giving the impression that the story and the narrative time are one and the same. The action takes place over a matter of minutes, which may almost give the appearance of creating a temporal imbalance between the two sections.[68]

Frequency refers to the number of times an event is narrated. In historical narrative, as mentioned, repetition is a frequently used stylistic device. For instance, in the book of Acts, the Holy Spirit comes repeatedly on different people at different times but in the same manner. Similarly, repetition in all four Gospels is evident in the repeated teachings, callings, miracles, parables, signs, healings, exorcisms, and other events that are recorded.

Chronology and Arrangement

The chronology and arrangement of the four Gospels and Acts also provides us with an important interpretive tool for understanding the message conveyed by the four evangelists. In some situations, a Gospel may reflect a chronological as well as a topical arrangement. The two are not necessarily mutually exclusive. In other instances, the same event may be narrated in the context of differing chronological presentations.

Matthew

The arrangement of Matthew's Gospel shows clear evidence of redactional activity for stylistic, theological, and thematic reasons. Matthew's

---

68. Mark W. G. Stibbe, *John* (New York: Routledge, 1994), 84.

Gospel is structured thematically around five discourses found in chapters 5–7; 10:5–42; 13:1–52; 18:1–35; and 24–25. They are identified by the concluding transitional markers that more or less conform to the following formula: "When Jesus had finished saying these things . . ." (Matt. 7:28; 11:1; 13:53; 19:1; 26:1). In certain instances, Matthew chose not to arrange his material in a chronological manner because apparently his authorial purpose was better served by a thematic approach.

Mark

Overall, Mark presents Jesus' ministry along a geographical pattern from Galilee to Jerusalem. The watershed or turning point in the narrative is marked by Peter's confession of Jesus as Messiah at the midway point of the Markan narrative (Mark 8:29). While Mark largely follows a chronological approach, there are times when his Gospel is arranged thematically. For instance, in chapters 4–5 Mark demonstrates Jesus' authority over four different entities: (1) nature (Mark 4:35–41); (2) demons (Mark 5:1–20); (3) death (Mark 5:21–24, 35–43); and (4) sickness (Mark 5:35–43).

Luke/Acts

Luke's Gospel is organized around a geographical motif with an emphasis on Jerusalem. Among other places, this focus on Jerusalem is evident in the temptation scene where, as mentioned, Luke reverses the order of the temptations recorded in Matthew in order to be able to conclude with the temptation involving the Jerusalem temple. At the heart of Luke's narrative is the extended Lucan "travel narrative" which shows Jesus journeying toward Jerusalem on his "way to the cross" for the better part of ten chapters in the Gospel (Luke 9:51–19:27). After narrating Jesus' passion in Jerusalem at the end of his Gospel, Luke's second volume, the book of Acts, takes its point of departure from Jerusalem. From there the gospel moves outward to Judea, Samaria, and finally to the Gentile nations (Acts 1:8). This movement is also characteristic of Paul's mission and is shown to fulfill Old Testament prediction (Acts 13:47 citing Isa. 49:6; Acts 28:26–27 citing Isa. 6:9–10).

John

The pattern of John's Gospel is chronological.[69] As will be seen further

---

69. See the chart in Köstenberger, *John*, 11–13.

below, John arranges his material around his presentation of seven messianic signs of Jesus, revealing him as "the Christ" and "the Son of God" (John 20:30–31). These messianic signs, spanning from John 2 to 11, are part and parcel of Jesus' ministry to the Jews. They are designed to convince the Jewish people that Jesus is the messianic Son sent by God the Father. Though crucified, Jesus was nonetheless God in the flesh and the Savior of the world. The second half of John's Gospel anticipates Jesus' exaltation with God and shows Jesus preparing his new messianic community—the Twelve minus Judas—for their mission subsequent to Jesus' crucifixion, resurrection, and ascension (his "glorification").[70]

Structure

The principle of selectivity, arrangement, and adaptation applies also to structure. The evangelists chose to organize their accounts differently, both at the macro- and the micro-level. An understanding of how the evangelists chose to structure their message is important because it provides the reader with clues about the ideological focus of the author. Fokkelman notes that before one can identify the ideological focus of the author, or even where a judgment has been incorporated, the plot and the structure must first be clarified.[71] Structure, therefore, provides us with an interpretive tool for understanding the message of the author. At the micro-level, there are different planes of structure that delineate the pericopes. Note, for instance, the example below from John's Gospel:

In what follows, we will discuss the basic structure of each of the four Gospels and discuss the major theological themes found in Matthew, Mark, Luke, and John.[72] We reiterate that with regard to structure, in keeping with our "hermeneutic of perception," what we are after is not our own outline of a given book but rather the author's literary structure and presentation. You will best be able to discern this structure by paying close attention to the transitional phrases, literary *inclusios*, and other textual markers found in these documents.

---

70. For a more detailed discussion of John's structure, see Köstenberger, *Theology of John's Gospel and Letters*, 167–70.
71. Fokkelman, *Reading Biblical Narrative*, 149.
72. For more detailed presentations, the reader is referred to the specialized commentary literature. See also Köstenberger, Kellum, and Quarles, *Cradle, the Cross, and the Crown*, Chapters 4–8.

8.3. STRUCTURE IN JOHN 1–12

Level 1
(Major
units)
5:1–10:42

Level 2
(Subunits)   Cana cycle (1:19–4:54)

First week in Jesus'
ministry (1:19–2:11)

Level 3
(Pericope)
(1:19–2:11)

John the Baptist
(1:19–34)

Jesus (1:35–51)

First sign (2:1–11)

Transitional phrase:
"after this" (2:12)

Ministry in Jerusalem,
Judea, Samaria, to
Gentiles (2:13–4:54)

Festival cycle (5:1–10:42)

The climactic sign (Lazarus) and
conclusion (11–12)   [Transitional phrase: "after this" (11:7, 11)]

Matthew

As mentioned, the structure of Matthew's Gospel centers on the five major discourses presenting the content of Jesus' teaching in chapters 5–7; 10:5–42; 13:1–52; 18:1–35; and 24–25. Each of these discourses is set off from the adjacent narrative portions by concluding phrases that read roughly as follows: "When Jesus had finished saying these things . . ." (Matt. 7:28; 11:1; 13:53; 19:1; 26:1).

In keeping with numerical symbolism (five "books of Jesus" corresponding to the five books of Moses, the Pentateuch), Jesus is presented as the "new Moses" (note that the first discourse is the Sermon on the Mount in Matthew 5–7 which relates Jesus' teaching to that of Moses). Note the pattern of narration that oscillates between narrative and discourse:

The most significant theological theme in Matthew's Gospel is that *Jesus is the Messiah* predicted in the Hebrew Scriptures. This fulfillment is highlighted especially in Matthew 1–4 in form of several "fulfillment quotations."[73] At the very beginning, Matthew presents Jesus as the son of David and the son of Abraham (Matt. 1:1–18). Jesus is also the new Moses, who in his "inaugural address" in the Gospel, the Sermon on the Mount, ascends a mountain and instructs his followers in his new Law (chaps. 5–7). Another major Matthean motif is that of the kingdom of God, which forms the subject of several series of parables (chaps. 13, 18, 25).

---

73. See, e.g., Matthew 1:22–23 citing Isaiah 7:14; 8:8, 10; Matthew 2:5–6 citing Micah 5:2; Matthew 2:15 citing Hosea 11:1; Matthew 2:18 citing Jeremiah 31:15.

Mark

Mark presents Jesus' ministry first in Galilee and then in Jerusalem. The major turning point in the Gospel is Peter's confession of Jesus in 8:26–27. Throughout the Gospel, Mark features selected references to Jesus as Son of God peaking with the centurion's confession in 15:39. The basic structure of Mark's Gospel presents itself as follows:

I.   INTRODUCTION (1:1–18)
II. JESUS' MINISTRY IN GALILEE (1:16–8:26)
    A. First Part of Galilean Ministry (1:16–3:12)
    B. Second Part of Galilean Ministry (3:13–5:43)
    C. Third Part of Galilean ministry (6:1–8:26)
III. THE WAY TO THE CROSS (8:27–16:8)
    A. The Way of Suffering and Glory (8:27–10:52)
    B. Final Ministry in Jerusalem (11:1–13:37)
    C. The Passion and the Empty Tomb (14:1–16:8)

The preeminent theological theme in Mark's Gospel is that *Jesus is the miracle-working, authoritative Son of God.* Strategic references to Jesus as the Son of God are found at the following locations in Mark's Gospel (the respective person or persons uttering the statement are indicated in the chart below):

8.4. STRATEGIC REFERENCES TO JESUS AS THE SON OF GOD IN MARK								
I. Introduction			II. Galilean ministry			III. The way to the cross		
1:1	1:11	3:33	5:7	9:7	12:6	13:32	14:61	15:39
Mark	God	Demons	Demons	God	Jesus	Jesus	Caiaphas	Centurion

The chart indicates that this theme forms the all-inclusive bookend of the Markan narrative. The evangelist frames his narrative in terms of Jesus being the Son of God in the opening verse and the climactic reference in 15:39 features the Roman centurion—no coincidence, since Mark's audience was the church in Rome—uttering the final reference to Jesus as Son of God in the Gospel.

In between, Jesus is declared by the heavenly voice to be the Son of God at his baptism (1:1) and at the Transfiguration (9:7). Apart from Jesus' two self-references (12:6; 13:32) and Caiaphas' question at Jesus' trial (14:61), the only other characters in Mark's Gospel who acknowledge Jesus as Son of God are demons (though see Peter's confession of Jesus as the Messiah in 8:29, which, however, is at once revealed as lacking full understanding, 8:31–33). Remarkably, demons are the only ones to acknowledge Jesus as God throughout his entire Galilean ministry narrated in 1:16–8:26.

This indicates that in Mark's Gospel, no one—other than God and Jesus, and demons!—understands that Jesus is the Son of God prior to the crucifixion. This, in turn, works hand in hand with two other major Markan themes, the so-called *"messianic secret"* and the *"discipleship failure"* motif. Another important Markan topic is the *kingdom of God*, which is proclaimed by Jesus (1:15), featured in several parables (4:11, 26, 30), and addressed in the form of entrance requirements (9:47; 10:14–15, 23–25; 11:10; 12:34; see also 9:1; 14:25; 15:43).

Luke/Acts

Luke/Acts is a two-volume work (Acts 1:1) centered on Jesus' journey to Jerusalem issuing in his crucifixion (vol. 1, Gospel of Luke) and on the church's spread from Jerusalem to the ends of the earth (vol. 2, book of Acts; see Acts 1:8). In his preface, Luke frankly acknowledges his reliance on a variety of sources in compiling his account (Luke 1:1–4). In fact, his overall chronology is similar to Mark's and Matthew's in that it first records various rounds of Jesus' ministry in Galilee and subsequently presents Jesus' journey to Jerusalem. In Luke's narrative, however, this so-called "travel narrative" is considerably more extensive and includes much material unique to Luke (9:51–19:27).

I.   INTRODUCTION (1:1–4:13)
    A. Preface (1:1–4)
    B. Jesus' and the Baptist's Birth and Jesus' Boyhood (1:5–2:52)
II.   JESUS' GALILEAN MINISTRY (4:14–9:50)
    A. First Part of Galilean Ministry (4:14–7:50)
    B. Second Part of (8:1–39)
    C. Third Part of Galilean Ministry and Withdrawal (8:40–9:50)

III. JESUS' JOURNEY TO JERUSALEM AND HIS PASSION
      (9:51–24:53)
      A. The Lucan Travel Narrative (9:51–19:27)
      B. Final Ministry in Jerusalem (19:28–22:38)
      C. Jesus' Crucifixion, Resurrection, and Ascension
         (22:39–24:53)

In contrast to Matthew who presents Jesus first and foremost as the
Jewish Messiah, Luke's Gospel focuses on Jesus as *"the son of Adam, the
son of God"* (Luke 3:37). Throughout the Gospel, Jesus is shown to engage
in fellowship with people viewed as "sinners" by the Jewish religious establishment. He is presented as *a friend of sinners* and as a *compassionate
healer,* who is guided by a concern for those who are socially disenfranchised and of low status, including the poor, the Gentiles, women, and
children. Perhaps Jesus' mission according to Luke is best summarized by
Jesus' statement in Luke 19:10, "For the Son of Man came to seek and to
save what was lost."

The book of Acts, as mentioned, narrates the *spread of the gospel from
Jerusalem all the way to the ends of the earth* (Acts 1:8). Jesus, through the
Holy Spirit, is shown to lead the church as it bears *bold witness to the resurrection* and *overcomes a variety of external and internal obstacles.* This includes legal challenges before Roman government officials, which remain
unproven and inconclusive, amounting to a vindication of Christianity as
"not guilty" of the political charges brought against it. In the end, nothing
is shown to stop the irresistible spread of the gospel on its march to the
capital of the Roman Empire, and the book concludes with reference to
Paul's free and unhindered proclamation of the good news there (Acts
28:15–31).

I.   FOUNDATIONS FOR THE CHURCH AND ITS MISSION
      (1:1–2:41)
      A. Preface (1:1–5)
      B. Jerusalem: Waiting for the Spirit (1:6–26)
      C. Pentecost: The Church is Born (2:1–41)
II.   THE CHURCH IN JERUSALEM (2:42–6:7)
      A. The Early Church (2:42–47)
      B. A Miracle and its Aftermath (3:1–4:31)

As mentioned, the book of Acts continues and completes Luke's two-volume work. While Jesus in volume 1 (the Gospel) is presented as the Crucified and Risen One, he appears in volume 2 (the book of Acts) as the One Exalted to God's right hand who directs the church's mission through the person of the Holy Spirit (Acts 1:1; see also the logic underlying Peter's Pentecost sermon in Acts 2). Peter in the first half and Paul in the second half of the book are the key figures who advance the gospel following a geographical pattern from Jerusalem and Judea to Samaria and to the Gentile world.

John

John's Gospel is carefully structured as is evident from the outline below. The Gospel breaks down symmetrically into a corresponding introduction and epilogue and two equal halves. The introduction sets the entire Gospel in perspective as Jesus is presented as *the pre-existent Word* that was *made flesh* and definitively revealed God the Father. The remainder of the narrative is thus to be read as *Jesus' revelation of God in word and deed* (including the cross). The first major half sets forth *seven selected signs of Jesus*, startling works that display his messianic status to the Jewish people. The second half first presents Jesus' *cleansing and instruction of his new messianic community* and subsequently narrates his *passion and resurrection appearances*. In the purpose statement, John affirms that all those who believe in Jesus will have eternal life in him.

I. INTRODUCTION: THE WORD MADE FLESH (1:1–18)
II. THE BOOK OF SIGNS: THE SIGNS OF THE MESSIAH (1:19–12:50)
  A. The Forerunner, Jesus' Inaugural Signs & Representative Conversations (1:19–4:54)
  B. Additional Signs amidst Mounting Unbelief (5–10)
  C. Final Passover: The Climactic Sign and Other Events (11:1–12:50)
III. THE BOOK OF EXALTATION: THE NEW MESSIANIC COMMUNITY (13–20)
  A. The Cleansing and Instruction of the New Covenant Community (13–17)
  B. The Passion Narrative (18–19)
  C. Jesus' Resurrection, Appearances, and Commissioning of Disciples (20:1–29)
  D. Purpose Statement (20:30–31)
IV. EPILOGUE: COMPLEMENTARY ROLES OF PETER AND BELOVED DISCIPLE (21)
  A. Jesus' Third Appearance, to Seven Disciples in Galilee (21:1–14)
  B. Jesus and Peter (21:15–19)
  C. Jesus and the Disciple Jesus Loved (21:20–25)

The introduction presents Jesus as the pre-existent Word through whom God created the world and who, made flesh, made known the Father (see esp. 1:1, 14, 18). The entire subsequent Gospel narrative, both Jesus' works and his words, are thus cast in terms of revelation of God, including the cross where God's love for the world was made manifest and salvation was made available for those who believe. Virtually all the major theological themes of John's Gospel are featured in the purpose statement in 20:30–31: (1) Jesus' signs; (2) the need to believe that Jesus is the Messiah and the Son of God; and (3) eternal life for those who place their trust in him.

SAMPLE EXEGESIS: MARK 15:33–41

History

In studying Mark 15:33–41, the first step is to gain a basic understanding of the *historical setting* and *major theological emphases* of Mark's Gospel. The Gospel of Mark is a fast-paced story, a "Gospel" about Jesus (1:1; cf. 1:14, 15; 8:35; 10:29; 13:10; 14:19) that is most likely informed by Peter's preaching.[74] Like the other Gospels, Mark focuses his attention squarely on the person and work of Christ.

Ancient tradition has always attributed this Gospel to Mark, with the earliest and most important attestation of Markan authorship being that of Papias, bishop of Hierapolis in Phrygia in Asia Minor.[75] The most probable identification of this Mark is the John Mark referred to in 1 Peter 5:13; Acts 12:12, 25; 13:13; 15:37–39; and in the Pauline corpus in Philemon 24; Colossians 4:10; and 2 Timothy 4:11. While this is not certain, Mark may be the young man referred to at the end of the Gospel who fled from the scene of Jesus' arrest, leaving his linen garment behind (14:51–52).[76]

This Gospel was probably written in the years before the final siege of Jerusalem and the destruction of the temple. Although internal evidence

---

74. Peter's sermon in Acts 10:34–43 provides the reader with a brief summary of the basic structure of the narrative common to all four canonical Gospels.

75. Papias' five-volume work *Interpretation of the Lord's Sayings* (c. A.D. 120/30) was cited by Eusebius in the early 300s (*Hist. Eccl.* 3.39).

76. For a discussion of this Markan pericope see Bauckham, *Jesus and the Eyewitnesses*, 184–87 (with reference to Gerd Theissen's theory of "protective anonymity") and 197–201, who speculates the young man may have been Lazarus (!).

is scanty, what little there is points to an origin and destination in Rome. The universal character of this Gospel has been noted by many, and while this makes it difficult to pinpoint a specific audience for Mark's Gospel, a non-Jewish destination is supported by the use of Aramaic terms and expressions as well as the explanation of Jewish laws and customs, numerous Latinisms, the mention of Rufus, and a Roman method of reckoning time.[77]

Literature

The opening statement, "The beginning of the gospel of Jesus Messiah Christ, Son of God" (1:1), indicates that Mark's purpose is bound up with the demonstration that Jesus is the Son of God (1:1). Later in the Gospel, persons as diverse as God (1:11; 9:7), demons (1:25; 3:11–12; 5:7), Jesus himself (12:6; 14:61), and the Roman centurion (15:39), concur. Indeed, of the four Gospels, it is Mark who most methodically displays the authority of Jesus' miracle-working power over the realms of nature, sickness, death, and the supernatural (4:35–5:43).

Having discerned Mark's overall purpose, the next step is to determine the *boundaries of the pericope* being studied based on the structure and arrangement of the entire narrative. Mark's Gospel consists of two main sections that portray Jesus as both the Messiah (1:1–8:26) and the Suffering Servant (8:27–16:8), with Peter's confession of Jesus as the Messiah as the major turning point in the narrative (8:27–30). In the second half, Mark focuses on Jesus' teaching regarding his impending suffering and death. That the events of the cross are of great significance to Mark is revealed by the space devoted to them by the evangelist.

The last major section of this second half (14:1–16:8) begins with accounts of the anointing and the institution of the Lord's Supper. Jesus' trial before the Sanhedrin (14:53–65) provides a harsh contrast with this intimate scene. It is at the height of this trial that Jesus identifies himself as the Christ, the Son of the Blessed One, but refrains from answering Pilate's question as to whether he is the king of the Jews, presumably owing to the term's political overtones (15:2). Thus the reader is led to understand that Jesus is the Messiah in keeping with Jewish Old Testament expectations but not a king in Roman political terms (cf. John 18:36).

---

77. For a thorough discussion of introductory matters for Mark's Gospel, see Köstenberger, Kellum, and Quarles, *Cradle, the Cross, and the Crown*, chap. 5.

The present text begins at 15:33, commencing a section that details the account of Jesus' last moments and ends with the evangelist's record of Jesus' final breath. The section therefore logically ends at 15:41 with a listing of the women who had been with Jesus and had supported him during his ministry. This forms a natural conclusion to the life and earthly ministry of Jesus. Since what comes before this section is a recounting of the actual crucifixion and what follows is the account of his burial, 15:33–41 naturally emerges as a narrative unit.

Having identified the boundaries of the pericope, the next step is to identify its *vertical and horizontal literary contexts*. The recounting of the final hours of Jesus' life is usually referred to as the "passion narrative." It probably circulated as a written tradition about Jesus' life and teaching. As in Mark, the parallel accounts (Matt. 27:45–56; Luke 23:44–49; John 19:28–30) are all preceded by a depiction of the crucifixion of Jesus and followed by a portrayal of the burial of Jesus. Thus, there is no evidence for particular Markan redaction.

After this it is necessary, in light of the particular characteristics of the *genre* of Mark, namely historical narrative, to identify how the *external elements* function in the narrative. In general, the evangelist frames his narrative in terms of Jesus being the Son of God in the opening verse and the climactic reference in 15:39 featuring the Roman centurion. This *inclusio* serves to highlight Mark's purpose with the Roman centurion uttering the final reference to Jesus as Son of God in the Gospel. The narrator provides an explanatory comment at 15:34, a translation from Aramaic to Greek.

Next comes an identification of the *internal elements* and how they function in the narrative, such as the setting, plot, characterization, literary style, and narrative time. The narrative takes place within shifting geographical locales, encompassing Galilee and the surrounding regions, and finally comes to a dramatic close in Jerusalem. The events of the present passage take place in Jerusalem at a place the narrator identifies as Golgotha, "the place of the skull." This was the place where Roman executions by crucifixion were carried out. Throughout the present pericope, Jesus is hanging on the cross.

The plot is centered on the "gospel about Jesus Christ, the Son of God" (1:1) and, as with many plots, the development involves conflict. However, as Rhoads and Michie note, "Although Jesus is the immediate cause of the conflicts, the story shows that God is the ultimate origin of many of the actions and events of the story."[78] A corollary to this conflict motif is the question of Jesus' identity, which is complicated by the messianic secret and discipleship failure motifs. This is significant because it is in this pericope that Jesus' true identity is finally revealed.

The Gospel as a whole is set in an unspecified time frame between Jesus' baptism and crucifixion. This compactness may seem to suggest that the events occurred within a one-year period, especially since only one Passover is mentioned. However, as Guelich notes, "Though seeking to provide the reader with a connected narrative, the evangelist makes no claim about either the extent of the chronology or the completeness of his story."[79] Mark 15:33–41 is marked by the evangelist's introduction of these events as occurring during the day, beginning during the sixth hour and culminating in the ninth hour with Jesus' death. The supernatural darkening of the whole earth conveys the spiritual reality of Jesus' victory over evil and serves as a sign of the coming judgment.[80]

If there were *important words* requiring special study or problematic *grammatical and/or syntactical issues*, this would be the place to note them. Since there are none that contribute significantly to the understanding of this pericope, the interpreter is in a position to *draw all the findings together* and to summarize the meaning of the pericope. The evangelist frames his narrative portraying Jesus as the Son of God with the climactic reference in 15:39 featuring the Roman centurion. The theme of Jesus as the Suffering Servant featured in the book of Isaiah culminates in this section with Jesus' cry, "My God, my God, why have you forsaken me?" (15:34), a quotation from Psalm 22:1.

The fact that it is not a Jew but a Gentile who confesses Jesus at the end of Mark is highly significant for the Gospel's narrative thrust. Mark's audience was the church in Rome, and it is only appropriate that the final reference to Jesus as Son of God in the Gospel should be uttered by a Roman. This signifies the transfer of allegiance from the Roman emperor to the true Son of God. At the same time, it is certainly no coincidence that a Christological confession by a Gentile (cf. Peter's "Jewish" confession at 8:29) is not issued until *after* Jesus' death. Thus, with the Roman centurion

---

78.   Rhoads and Michie, *Mark as Story*, 74.
79.   Robert A. Guelich, *Mark 1–8:26*, WBC 34A (Dallas: Word, 1989), xxv.
80.   James A. Brooks, *Mark*, NAC 23 (Nashville: B&H, 1991), 260.

as the key identification figure for his Roman audience, Mark brings the "Son of God" motif to an appropriate culmination in this pericope.

Theology

The last step is the *application* of the passage to the interpreter's contemporary situation. Indeed, for readers today, this proclamation of Jesus as Son of God by a non-Jew is significant. It not only reveals that Jesus is the one in whom salvation is to be found, it demonstrates that there is no longer any ethnic barrier that separates individuals from God. Any such obstacle has been removed by Jesus through the cross. All who desire to do so can today profess by faith that Jesus is truly the Son of God and receive entry into God's kingdom.

GUIDELINES FOR INTERPRETING
THE GOSPELS AND ACTS

1.   Before you begin working on your target text, have a general understanding of the background issues related to the book you are studying. Identify the theological emphases and themes, not only of the author, but of the particular book. Make sure you understand the purpose of the book.

2.   Based on the structure and arrangement of the entire narrative, determine the boundaries of the pericope or text under study. Keep in mind that the author's own literary structure and pre-sentation provide guidelines for this process. Ensure that you correctly identify transitional phrases, literary inclusions, and various other textual markers found.

3.   Identify the literary context of your passage, first vertically, in its own setting and then horizontally, comparing it with parallel accounts if any. Keep in mind the redactional patterns of each evangelist.

4.   In light of the particular characteristics of the genre of the Gospels and Acts, identify how the external elements function in the narrative. The external elements of a narrative include the author, the narrator, and the reader. Assume the mind-set of the implied reader. In this step you should also clarify issues related to expositional mode, narration vs. commentary, and point of view.

5.   Identify the internal elements and how they function in the narrative. These include the setting, plot, characterization, literary style, and narrative time. Do any of these elements contribute significantly to the interpretation of your target text?

6. Take note of the historical-cultural context. Keep in mind that the Gospels have two levels: the life setting in Jesus' day and the life setting of the church at the time of composition. What is the contribution of features such as geography, politics, economics, military and war, cultural and religious customs?

7. Keep in mind that the entire interpretive process should be based on sound exegetical procedures. Take note of the meaning of significant words and the contribution of grammar and syntax.

8. Draw all your findings together and summarize the meaning of your pericope or text. Ensure that this is consistent with authorial intent.

9. Finally, following the appropriate guidelines for this last step, apply this passage to the contemporary situation.

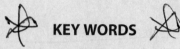

KEY WORDS

Aretalogy: string of "I am" statements

Augustinian proposal: theory that Matthew wrote first, then Mark using Matthew, then Luke using both Matthew and Mark

Chreia: pronouncement story

Diatessaron: Grk. "through four"; first parallel presentation ("harmony") of the four canonical Gospels Matthew, Mark, Luke, and John by the second-century Church Father Tatian

Form criticism: study of the Gospels that focuses on the period of oral transmission

Four-Source hypothesis: modification of the Two-Source hypothesis by B. H. Streeter, which adds "M" and "L" for material unique to Matthew and Luke as sources

Griesbach hypothesis: theory popularized by J. J. Griesbach that Matthew wrote first, then Luke using Matthew, then Mark using both Matthew and Luke

Horizontal reading: comparison of the presentations of a given event by the different Gospels

Implied author: persona created in text by real author

Markan priority: theory that Mark was the first to write his Gospel

Matthean priority: theory that Matthew was the first to write his Gospel

Narrator: person telling the story

Q: hypothetical document containing material common to Matthew and Luke (from the German word *Quelle*, meaning source)

Real author: actual writer of a given document

Synoptic Gospels: Grk. "seeing together"; common designation for Matthew, Mark, and Luke owing to the similarities between these Gospels

Two-Document hypothesis: theory that Mark (written first) and "Q" served as the 2 sources for Matthew and Luke

Vertical reading: initial study of a given incident in the Gospel in which it is narrated

STUDY QUESTIONS

1. What are the various proposals for genre of the Gospels and what are some similarities and dissimilarities?

2. Why are there four Gospels in our canon?
   Reach different audiences

3. What are methods scholars have used to try to account for differences among the Gospels?

4. What is the relationship between John and the Synoptics?

5. What are the external and internal elements of Gospel narratives?

6. What is the chronological arrangement and what are the structure and themes of each of the four canonical Gospels?

7. What are the guidelines for interpreting the Gospels and Acts?

ASSIGNMENTS

1. Using a Harmony of the Gospels, compare the accounts of Jesus' feeding of the 5,000 in all four Gospels. Note similarities and differences in wording and presentation and develop a hypothesis of Gospel relationships based on the observations from your study of this pericope.

2. Identify ways in which Luke structures and presents the history of the early church in the book of Acts. Read through the entire book and take notes as to Luke's narrative technique and skill, then group similar passages together and provide a list of categories of literary devices used.

3. Analyze the account of Jesus' healing of the paralytic in Mark 2:1–12. Identify the setting, plot, characters, and other stylistic features in this pericope and discuss how an analysis along these lines enhances your understanding of the deeper spiritual meaning and message of this passage in Mark's Gospel.

4. Discuss what is commonly called "the Synoptic problem." Why, do you think, are there four Gospels in the New Testament canon? Do you agree that the differences among the Gospels present a "problem" for the student of Scripture? How should we account for the "problem" of differences in presentation and how can the "problem" be solved? Support your answer with specific passages in the Gospels.

5. Discuss the structure of Matthew's Gospel by providing clues left by the First Evangelist that indicate the literary plan he intended. Then discuss the theological significance of the structure of Matthew's Gospel. How does an understanding of the literary plan underlying the Gospel help us to understand Matthew's theology in a deeper way?

CHAPTER BIBLIOGRAPHY

Alter, Robert. *The Art of Biblical Narrative*. New York: Basic Books, 1981.

Bauckham, Richard, ed. *The Gospels for All Christians*. Grand Rapids: Eerdmans, 1998.

_____. *Jesus and the Eyewitnesses*. Grand Rapids: Eerdmans, 2006.

Blomberg, Craig L. *The Historical Reliability of the Gospels*. 2d ed. Downers Grove: InterVarsity, 2007.

Burridge, Richard A. *What are Are the Gospels?* SNTS Monograph Series 70. 2d ed. Cambridge: Cambridge University Press, 2004.

Carson, D. A. *The Gospel according to John*. Grand Rapids: Eerdmans, 1991.

Culpepper, R. Alan. *The Anatomy of the Fourth Gospel*. Philadelphia: Fortress, 1983.

Dunn, James D. G. *Jesus Remembered*. Grand Rapids: Eerdmans, 2003.

Fokkelman, J. P. *Reading Biblical Narrative: An Introductory Guide*. Louisville: Westminster, 1999.

Fee, Gordon D. and Douglas Stuart. *How to Read the Bible for all Its Worth*. 3d ed. Grand Rapids: Zondervan, 2003.

Green, Joel B. Scot McKnight, and I. Howard Marshall, eds. *Dictionary of Jesus and the Gospels*. Downers Grove: InterVarsity, 1992.

Kellum, L. Scott. *The Unity of the Farewell Discourse: The Literary Integrity of John 13.31–16.33*. JSNTSup 256. London: T&T Clark, 2004.

Klein, W. William, Craig L. Blomberg, and Robert L. Hubbard Jr Pp. 399–418 in *Introduction to Biblical Interpretation*. Rev. ed. Nashville: Thomas Nelson, 2004.

Köstenberger, Andreas J. *Encountering John*. Grand Rapids: Eerdmans, 1999.

_____. *John*. Baker Exegetical Commentary on the New Testament. Grand Rapids: Baker, 2004.

_____. *A Theology of John's Gospel and Letters: The Word, the Christ, the Son of God*. BTNT. Grand Rapids: Zondervan, 2009.

Köstenberger, Andreas J., L. Scott Kellum, and Charles L. Quarles. *The Cradle, the Cross, and the Crown: An Introduction to the New Testament*. Nashville: B&H, 2009.

Osborne, Grant R. *The Hermeneutical Spiral*. 2d ed. Downers Grove: InterVarsity, 2006.

Rhoads, David and Donald Michie. *Mark as Story: An Introduction to the Narrative of a Gospel*. Philadelphia: Fortress, 1982.

Ryken, Leland, James C. Wilhoit, and Tremper Longman III, eds. *Dictionary of Biblical Imagery*. Downers Grove: InterVarsity, 1998.

Stibbe, Mark W. G. *John as Storyteller: Narrative Criticism and the Fourth Gospel*. Cambridge: Cambridge University Press, 1992.

CHAPTER 9 OBJECTIVES

1. To impart a basic knowledge of the style of Jesus' teaching including parables.

2. To provide a set of guidelines for interpreting Jesus' parables.

CHAPTER 9 OUTLINE

A. Style of Jesus' Teaching
B. Parables of Jesus
   1. Definition and Purpose of Parables
      a. Definition of Parable
      b. Purpose of Parables
   2. History of Interpretation of Parables
      a. Early Church Fathers (100–500)
      b. Middle Ages (500–1500)
      c. Reformation (1500–1800)
      d. Modern Period (1800–Present)
   3. Toward a Proper Interpretation of Parables
   4. Jesus' Parables in the Synoptic Gospels
   5. Jewish Background and Parallels
   6. Salvation History and the *Sitz im Leben Jesu*
   7. Characteristics of Parables
C. Guidelines for Interpreting the Parables
D. Key Words
E. Study Questions
F. Assignments
G. Chapter Bibliography

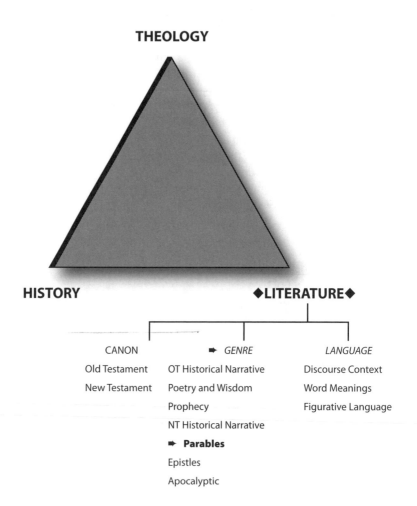

THEOLOGY

HISTORY

◆LITERATURE◆

CANON	➡ *GENRE*	*LANGUAGE*
Old Testament	OT Historical Narrative	Discourse Context
New Testament	Poetry and Wisdom	Word Meanings
	Prophecy	Figurative Language
	NT Historical Narrative
	➡ **Parables**
	Epistles
	Apocalyptic

Chapter 9

CALLING FOR DISCERNMENT: PARABLES

STYLE OF JESUS' TEACHING

BEFORE WE MOVE ON TO a consideration of the next major corpus in the New Testament—the epistles—it will be important to take some extra time to look at a fairly subtle genre represented in the canonical Gospels, that of parable. Our study of Jesus' parables, in turn, is best set within the larger framework of Jesus' teaching as a whole. At least in my experience, preachers often struggle with interpreting parables, in part because they tend to treat them as historical narratives or because they unduly spiritualize every element of a given parable. In the present chapter, we hope to set forth principles that will help students of Scripture steer clear of either extreme and to develop growing sensitivity to this attractive yet at times treacherous feature of the biblical landscape.

A look at any of the Gospels reveals that Jesus engaged in extensive teaching activity. In order to understand what Jesus taught, it is important to understand how he taught, while at the same time recognizing that the how is simply a medium for the message and not the message itself. His teaching method reflects his familiarity with and indebtedness to the wisdom tradition of the Old Testament. This can be clearly seen in the beatitudes, admonitions, parables, and his longer discourses. Approximately one third of Jesus' teaching is given in form of parables.

Before we turn to a study of parables, it should be noted that Jesus also taught in a variety of other ways. The fact that Jesus was not confined to one style or method of teaching made his teaching even more effective. Robert Stein identifies the following forms and techniques used by Jesus in his teaching:[1]

Overstatement. Overstatement involves the exaggeration of a point or the heightening of a truth in order to capture the attention of one's audience. This technique was not unique to Jesus; it was a general characteristic of Semitic speech. Its aim was to communicate to the listeners the need to get rid of sinful attitudes and behavior in their lives. In these statements, it is the meaning underlying the actual words that needs to be discerned if one wants to understand the essential message (Matt. 5:29–30; Luke 14:26).

Hyperbole. The use of hyperbole is closely related to overstatement, and it is sometimes difficult to differentiate the two. The difference lies in the fact that the degree of exaggeration is more pronounced in the case of hyperbole and the fact that, unlike with regard to overstatement, a literal fulfillment or portrayal is impossible (Matt. 23:23–24; 7:3–5; Mark 10:24b–25).

Pun. A pun is a play on words in which one word may have more than one meaning or two like-sounding words (homonyms) may be intentionally used to suggest two or more different meanings. Often the reader misses the use of puns by Jesus. While they are obvious in the original language (Aramaic or sometimes the written Greek), Bible translations are not always able to transmit them intact. Note, for instance, the following pun in Matthew 23:23–24, originally spoken by Jesus in Aramaic: "You blind guides! You strain out a gnat (*galma*) but swallow a camel (*gamla*)." Another well-known example is that of the Greek text of Matthew 16:18 and Jesus' reference to Peter (*Petros*) as a rock (*petra*).

Simile. A simile is a figure of speech that compares two things that are essentially like each other. It uses connectives such as "like," "as," or "than" or a verb such as "seems." In its simplest form, a simile identifies a single correspondence between two items in a sentence.[2] When extended

---

1. Robert H. Stein, *The Method and Message of Jesus' Teachings* (Philadelphia: Westminster, 1978), 7–33.
2. William W. Klein, Craig L. Blomberg, and Robert L. Hubbard, *Introduction to Biblical Interpretation*, (Nashville: Nelson, 2004), 305.

into a picture, it is known as a similitude. When expanded into a story, it becomes a story parable (e.g., Matt. 10:16; 12:40; Luke 17:6; 13:34).

Metaphor. A metaphor, like a simile, also compares two things that are essentially different, but that share one thing in common.[3] Like similes, they may also occur in series and in extended form (Matt. 9:37–38; Mark 8:15; 9:49–50; Luke 13:31–32).

Proverb. A proverb is a succinct, pithy statement that conveys truth in a memorable manner. In his use of proverbs, Jesus displayed his continuity with Israel's wisdom tradition. In a broad sense, this category also includes maxims and aphorisms (Matt. 26:52; Mark 6:4; Luke 9:62).

Riddle. A riddle is a simple statement with a hidden meaning which the hearer must uncover. As in the case of proverbs, Jesus' use of riddles finds its antecedent in Old Testament usage. A commonly-cited example of a riddle in the Bible is Samson's riddle in Judges 14:14 (see also Matt. 11:12; Mark 14:58; Luke 13:32b–33).

Paradox. A paradox is a statement that appears to be contradictory. These sayings must be interpreted in light of the values and beliefs of Jesus' contemporaries (Matt. 23:27–28; Mark 10:43–44).

A *fortiori* statement. An a fortiori statement, arguing from the lesser to the greater, is a type of argument "in which the conclusion follows with even greater logical necessity than the already accepted fact or conclusion previously given" (Matt. 6:28–30; 7:9–11; 10:25).[4]

Irony. Narrowly conceived, irony is a literary device that intends a statement to be understood in a manner that is opposite its literal meaning. It is often placed in a context in which there is a feigned sense of ignorance. The most basic definition of irony recognizes that this device contrasts appearance and reality (possible examples include Matt. 16:2–3; Luke 12:16–20).

Questions. Jesus frequently used questions to make a point and to impress a truth more effectively upon his listeners (Mark 8:27–32). His preferred questioning style involved the use of rhetorical questions which were intended to produce an effect in his hearers (16; Mark 3:23; Luke 15:8). He also employed used the device of counter-question, particularly in hostile situations (Mark 3:1–4; 11:27–33).

---

3. Ibid., 308.
4. Stein, *Message and Method of Jesus' Teachings*, 20.

Parabolic or figurative actions. In some instances, Jesus used non-verbal teaching techniques in which the action itself made a specific point. In such cases, though a verbal commentary may have followed, this was not necessary for the lesson to be understood (Mark 3:14–19; Luke 19:1–6).

Poetry. The Gospels reflect a number of instances in which the sayings of Jesus are mediated through poetry.[5] There are numerous examples of poetry in the sayings of Jesus in the Gospels (Matt. 7:7–8; Mark 3:24–25; Luke 6:27–28).

Stein helpfully notes that the "form or vehicle that Jesus used to convey his message is clearly not the language of twentieth century science but rather the metaphorical, exaggerating, impressionistic language of a culture that loved to tell stories."[6] With this, we turn to a discussion of the most commonly used form of teaching in Jesus' ministry, namely parables.

PARABLES OF JESUS

Definition and Purpose of Parables
Definition of Parable

A parable is a short narrative that demands a response from the hearer. With regard to genre, parables are true-to-life or realistic stories. They differ from historical narrative in that they are not true stories, though they are told with verisimilitude. Parables are not historical narratives. At the same time, parables do not include fanciful elements as do fables, legends, or other mythical stories. Since they are not historical narratives, the characters and the story are created for the purpose of teaching a particular spiritual lesson. For instance, there probably was no historical innkeeper or "good Samaritan." Although most focus on the story parables, there are a variety of other forms as well. This is often obscured by the fact that the English word "parable" is often more narrowly construed than the Hebrew *mašal* or the Greek *parabolē*.

In keeping with the genre's Semitic origin, there is a range spanning from extended similes (e.g., "the kingdom of heaven is like a merchant

---

5. Stein's identification of these forms is based on Hebrew parallelism: see ibid., 27–32.
6. Ibid., 32.

looking for fine pearls"; Matt. 13:45) to full-orbed story parables. This spectrum from short and simple to more extensive and complex can be diagrammed as follows:

9.1. EXTENDED FIGURE OF SPEECH TO FULL PARABLE			
Short Simile or Metaphor			**Long Allegory**
Similitude	Short parable	Story parable/ example story	Allegorical parable
Matt. 13:33	Luke 17:7–10	Luke 15:11–32	Mark 12:1 12 pars.

The various forms of parables found in Scripture should therefore be understood along the continuum depicted above, with the understanding that the distinctions between these categories are often fluid. Grant Osborne suggests that although similitudes and short parables are similar in that they stress comparisons, a similitude is more straightforward and uses the present tense while a parable is indirect, shaped in narrative form, and uses the past tense.[7] A possible example of a similitude is the parable of the yeast in the dough (Matt. 13:33; Luke 13:20–21).

There are many examples of story parables in the Gospels. One that is familiar to many readers is the parable of the Good Samaritan (Luke 10:25–37), which is a story with a plot and active interaction of characters.[8]

Perhaps the most difficult distinction to be made is that between parables and allegories. Allegories are a series of related metaphors.[9] An easily identifiable allegory in the Gospels is that of the sower in which Jesus himself identifies the seed and the soil as representing the Word of God and a person, respectively (Matt. 13:2–23; Mark 4:1–20; Luke 8:4–15). Some do not view allegory as a literary form but as a literary device. While many scholars today distinguish between parable and allegory by suggesting that unlike allegories parables never have symbolic significance and are characterized by just one point, this may not be strictly the case.

---

7. Osborne, *Hermeneutical Spiral*, 293.
8. See Fee and Stuart, *How to Read the Bible*, 151–52.
9. *Dictionary of Jesus and the Gospels*, ed. by J. B. Green and S. McKnight (Downers Grove: InterVarsity, 1992), 593.

A case in point is the parable of the Royal Wedding Feast in which many of the details in the story are representative of something else (Matt. 22:1–14). The king refers to God, the servants to the prophets, and the son to Christ.[10] Another example of an allegorical parable is that of the Wicked Tenants (Matt. 21:33–44; Mark 12:1–11; Luke 20:9–18). However, it should be noted that not all concur regarding this classification. Fee and Stuart note that although a parable may in some cases resemble an allegory, as in the example of the Wicked Tenants, they are not allegories. This is because the two have differing functions.[11]

An example story is a narrative that is used to emphasize a positive or negative trait through the use of a character that serves as either a positive or a negative example. According to Snodgrass, there are only four of these in the canonical Gospels and all are found in Luke (the Good Samaritan, the Rich Fool, the Rich Man and Lazarus, and the Pharisee and the Tax Collector).[12]

Fee and Stuart observe that unlike most parabolic sayings, Jesus' story parables "do not serve to illustrate Jesus' prosaic teaching with word pictures. Nor are they told to serve as vehicles for revealing truth—although they end up clearly doing that. Rather the story parables function as a means of calling forth a response on the part of the hearer."[13] Thus, not only do they convey Jesus' message, they are themselves the message.

Purpose of Parables

Parables serve a didactic purpose. They are designed to teach a particular spiritual or moral lesson to a particular audience. In this sense, they are similar to fables. However, the means by which they teach the lesson is different. Jesus himself commented on the purpose of his parables in Mark 4:10–12, the Parable of the Sower (parallels Matt. 13:10–15; Luke 8:9–10). When asked by the disciples why he used parables, Jesus responded with the words of Isaiah 6:9–10:

> so that "they may be ever seeing but never perceiving,
> and ever hearing but never understanding;
> otherwise they might turn and be forgiven!"

---

10. Osborne, *Hermeneutical Spiral*, 236.
11. Fee and Stuart, *How to Read the Bible*, 152.
12. DJG 593.
13. Fee and Stuart, *How to Read the Bible*, 153.

This seems to suggest that Jesus' parables were spiritually appraised in such a way that precluded understanding by those who rejected his messianic claim and proclamation of the kingdom of God.

The key to understanding Jesus' statement is to be found in the context. Note that this parable is told in response to the phenomenon of Jewish unbelief and rejection. Jesus' use of an Old Testament text that stresses the same motif clarifies that his particular emphasis is on unbelief. The unbelieving reception of Jesus by the Jews parallels the unbelief with which the people of Isaiah's day received his message. Thus, the Parable of the Sower emphasizes the fact that the lack of people's response to Jesus' words was in continuity with how people responded to God's message in Old Testament times.

At other times, Jesus used parables in order to challenge individuals to respond to his message or to instruct them in some other way (e.g., Matt. 24:32–25:46; Luke 7:40–43; 10).[14] Osborne's statement encapsulates the purpose of parables well:

> It seems clear that Jesus did indeed have a larger purpose in using the parable form. Parables are an "encounter mechanism" and function differently depending on the audience. . . . The parables encounter, interpret and invite the listener/reader to participate in Jesus' new world vision of the kingdom. They are a "speech-event" that never allows us to remain neutral; they grasp our attention and force us to interact with the presence of the kingdom in Jesus, either positively (those "around" Jesus in Mark 4:10–12) or negatively (those "outside").[15]

Understood as "encounter mechanism," the purpose of Jesus' parables was not limited to instruction but also served to engage his hearers' value system, priorities, and way of thinking. When Jesus told a given parable, he aimed not merely at imparting information but sought to effect a change in people's perception and a reversal in their values and world view. In essence, parables were Jesus' preferred teaching tool for producing in his listeners a proper alignment with God's values which characterized the kingdom Jesus had come to inaugurate and proclaim.

---

14. Osborne, *Hermeneutical Spiral*, 294.
15. Ibid., 294–95

History of Interpretation of Parables

Before looking at Jesus' parables in further detail, it will be helpful to survey briefly the history of parable interpretation. The fact that the Gospels are documents operating on the level of Jesus' original context as well as that of the evangelists makes it necessary to develop a certain amount of hermeneutical sophistication in order to do justice to the complex challenges posed by the parables found in the Gospels. As we will see, there has not been a consensus throughout the history of the church as to how parables ought to be interpreted. For this reason, it will be instructive to survey the different approaches used during the course of the history of interpretation on our way to developing an informed approach on how to interpret parables today.

Early Church Fathers (100–500)

During the patristic period, an allegorical method of interpreting Scripture began to emerge. Parables were treated as spiritual treasure troves which served as vehicles to communicate a deeper spiritual truth. This meant that practically every detail of a parable was believed to have spiritual significance and hence had to be reinterpreted in order to communicate this deeper spiritual meaning. This technique was refined during the time of Origen of Alexandria (A.D. 185–254) who is generally acknowledged to have elevated this approach to a "science." Origen believed that Scripture was imbued with a threefold sense which corresponded to Paul's definition of the human being as consisting of body, soul, and spirit (1 Thess. 5:23). For Origen, the "body" was the literal sense of the text; the "soul" was the moral or tropological sense of the text; and the "spirit," the spiritual sense of the text.[16] A commonly cited example of this approach as applied by Augustine, although first allegorized by Origen, is the parable of the Good Samaritan.[17]

While this kind of interpretation might seem far-fetched by modern standards, interpretations such as these were perfectly acceptable during the time of the early church fathers. Craig Blomberg notes the following with regard to their penchant toward allegorization: "The church fathers wished to derive additional meaning from the text beyond that which a

---

16. Ibid., 46.
17. Cited in Fee and Stuart, *How to Read the Bible*, 150.

more straightforward reading would elicit, especially in narratives where there seemed to be few explicit lessons or where character's actions seemed morally suspect."[18] For the interpreters of the early church, there seemed to be no doubt that Jesus' teaching contained a high proportion of allegories.

9.2. ALLEGORIZED GOOD SAMARITAN PARABLE

Scripture Text	Allegorical Interpretation
A man was going down from Jerusalem to Jericho	Adam
Jerusalem	the heavenly city of peace, from which Adam fell
Jericho	the moon, signifying Adam's mortality
Robbers	the devil and his angels
Stripped him	of his immortality
Beat him	by persuading him to sin
Leaving him half dead	as a man he lives, but he died spiritually; therefore he is half dead
The priest and Levite	the priesthood and ministry of the Old Testament
The Samarian	is said to mean Guardian; therefore Christ himself is meant
Bandaged his wounds	binding the restraint of sin
Oil	comfort of good hope
Wine	exhortation to work with a fervent spirit
Donkey ("beast")	the flesh of Christ's incarnation
Inn	the church
The next day	after the resurrection
Two silver coins	promise of this life and the life to come
Innkeeper	Paul

Middle Ages (500–1500)

This practice of allegorizing not only continued unabated throughout the Middle Ages, it further intensified. In addition to Origen's threefold sense of Scripture (literal, moral, and spiritual) was added one other element—the anagogical. This fourfold sense incorporated the element of the

---

18. Blomberg, *Interpreting the Parables*, 30.

heavenly or eschatological significance of Scripture.[19] When applied, for instance, to the term "Jerusalem," the following interpretation was derived: literally, Jerusalem referred to a specific city in Judea; morally, it referred to the human soul; spiritually, it referred to the church; and anagogically, it referred to the heavenly abode of the saints.[20]

Reformation (1500–1800)

Although Chrysostom and Aquinas, in the patristic and medieval periods respectively, had tried to curb the tendency to allegorize, their efforts failed to meet with much success. In fact, they were unable to avoid allegorizing in their own exegesis.[21] With the Reformation came new developments and approaches to Scripture. Martin Luther (1483–1546), a major proponent of the literal and grammatical interpretation of Scripture, strongly opposed the fourfold sense of biblical interpretation. In his opinion, the allegorizers were "clerical jugglers performing monkey tricks," and Origen's exegesis worth "less than dirt."[22] Calvin expressed a similar distaste for the allegorical method. Unfortunately, while sound in theory, both Luther and Calvin often followed the approach of the allegorizers in their own interpretation of parables.

Hence the method of treating parables as thoroughgoing allegories continued to thrive in the church. Unfortunately, however, the allegorical approach was often subjective, yielding diverse interpretations for the same parable and tending to be arbitrary and at times anachronistic.[23] For instance, not only was the prodigal's robe in the Parable of the Prodigal Son seen to represent immortality, other suggestions included sinlessness, spiritual gifts, the imputation of Christ's righteousness, or the sanctity of the soul.[24]

Modern Period (1800–Present)

It is in the modern period that this allegorical approach to the interpretation of parables received its greatest challenge. The forerunner of this

---

19. Stein, *Method and Message of Jesus' Teachings*, 49.
20. Ibid.
21. Blomberg, *Interpreting the Parables*, 31.
22. Stein, *Method and Message of Jesus' Teachings*, 49.
23. Klein, Blomberg, and Hubbard, *Introduction to Biblical Interpretation*, 411.
24. Blomberg, *Interpreting the Parables*, 16.

change was the New Testament scholar Adolf Jülicher. In his two-volume work *Die Gleichnisreden Jesu* (1888, 1889), he proposed that the parables contained a single picture and taught a single point.[25] From his analysis of parables, he concluded that Jesus neither used allegories nor allegorical traits in his parables and that the presence of such traits was to be attributed to the evangelists. For Jülicher, the parables were to be understood as one-point comparisons between the image and the idea being expressed and hence had no need for interpretation. The point of the parable was usually a general religious maxim. The important distinction for him was that the parables were extended similes, whereas allegories were extended metaphors.[26] From this point on, all subsequent approaches were to be influenced in one way or the other by his thesis.

Building on Jülicher's perspective, C. H. Dodd, in *The Parables of the Kingdom* (1935), argued that the parables must be situated within the life and teaching of Jesus, primarily his preaching of the kingdom. For Dodd, Jesus' message was to be understood as realized eschatology: the kingdom had already arrived. Hence, parables involving harvest imagery were not about a coming end time but about the time of Jesus' earthly ministry.[27]

At the same time as these developments took place, form criticism was on the rise. This proved providential for Jülicher's proposal. Rudolf Bultmann, while formulating his "laws of transmission," gave impetus to the proposal that simple parables evolved into complex allegories as they were told and retold. Joachim Jeremias refined and elaborated these laws.[28] Jeremias, in *Die Gleichnisse Jesu* (1947), building his theory of parable interpretation on the foundations of both Jülicher and Dodd, also argued that the parables made only one point and that allegorical details were later church embellishments or additions. To reconstruct Jesus' original parables these had to be removed. Unfortunately, however, this approach is itself problematic.[29]

Klyne Snodgrass noted that in this process, the context in the Gospels, such as the introductions, conclusions, and any interpretive comments, were generally considered secondary. The resultant "de-allegorized" forms closely resemble the versions of the parables in the Gospel of Thomas, a

---

25. Osborne, *Hermeneutical Spiral*, 250.
26. DJG 591–92.
27. Ibid., 592.
28. Blomberg, Interpreting the Parables, 33.
29. Osborne, *Hermeneutical Spiral*, 293.

collection of sayings of Jesus dating probably from the second century. Parable studies were dominated by Dodd and Jeremias from 1935 to roughly 1970. In fact, Jeremias's book on the parables continues be influential to this day.[30]

With the rise of redaction criticism came the emphasis on studying the parables individually, with the focus being on a given evangelist's reworking of the parable. Thus, there developed a shift of interest from that of Jesus to that of the evangelist.[31] In addition, dissatisfied with the historical approach employed used by Dodd and Jeremias, different groups with varying emphases on existentialist, structuralist, and literary approaches came to the fore. The "new hermeneutic" of E. Fuchs and E. Jüngel viewed the parables as "language events" that conveyed Jesus' self-understanding of his existence in a way that was intelligible to the listeners, pointing to a certain reality.[32] Blomberg notes that the "new hermeneutic" emphasizes that attempting to interpret a narrative in a non-narrative manner by breaking down the details into points is not only impossible; it also violates the original meaning.[33]

Following the emergence of the "new hermeneutic," two schools of thought that emphasized the perspective of the reader had an immense impact on parable research: "aesthetic critics" (Stein's term) and structuralists. Modern interpreters such as G. V. Jones, A. N. Wilder, and D. O. Via all view the parables as aesthetic works and hence focus on their artistic and existential character. Others, such as Kenneth Bailey, who seek to interpret the parables in light of the Palestinian mind-set, focus on their rhetorical structure.[34] Aesthetic critics, in seeking to understand the communicative power of the parable, apply literary paradigms from the ancient world, such as tragedy or comedy, to parables.[35]

Structuralists, whose influence on parable studies was felt mainly between 1970 and 1980, aim to discern the "codes" of the text, determine grids, and map the "deeper structures" of meaning behind the surface parable.[36] For them, meaning can be found only by a study of the deep

---

30. DJG 592.
31. Osborne, *Hermeneutical Spiral*, 309.
32. DJG 592.
33. Blomberg, *Interpreting the Parables*, 23.
34. DJG 592.
35. Osborne, *Hermeneutical Spiral*, 309.
36. Ibid.

structures of the text. The emphasis, for both structuralists and aesthetic critics, is on "the autonomous and polyvalent nature of the parables. Thus the original meaning of the parable is not a goal and in fact is perceived to be a detriment to the power of the parable to address us today in new and significant ways."[37] While they are to be commended for seeking more than the historical aspects of the parables, these approaches still tend to "de-allegorize" the parables as well as remove all interpretive additions.

One major problem with the one-point approach and the denial of allegorical elements in Jesus' parables is that the Gospels themselves strongly attest to the presence of allegory at the earliest stage of Jesus' teaching. Note, for instance, the following parables with multiple lessons: the Parable of the Sower (Mark 4:3–9 pars.); the Tares (Matt. 13:24–30); the Net (Matt. 13:47–50); and possibly the Allegory of the Vine and the Branches (John 15:1–8). Osborne's word of caution is worth noting: "only the context may decide which details provide local color without spiritual significance (part of the story world) or have individual theological meaning themselves (meant to be contextualized)."[38]

Literary criticism, especially theorists practicing a reader-response approach, has also proved to be very influential in parable studies. The difficulty with these approaches, however, is that interpretations are often highly subjective, and in the absence of clear criteria for valid interpretation of parables one is left with a plurality of readings that are mutually contradictory. Other approaches that are gaining popularity today are interpretations based on comparisons of the parables of Jewish with early rabbinic parables. Most notable in this field are P. Fiebig, A. Feldman, and more recently David Flusser, a Jewish New Testament scholar. The conclusions of these scholars have challenged the findings of Jülicher and Jeremias as well as those of reader-response approaches and of New Testament scholarship in general.[39]

Toward a Proper Interpretation of Parables

Given this history, how should we view parables in order to bring out their intended meaning as accurately as possible? Most importantly, the

---

37. Ibid., 310.
38. Ibid., 293.
39. Ibid.

parables should be viewed as authentic. Although critical scholarship has put forth arguments discarding the authenticity of the parables of Jesus in the Gospels, the evidence set forth is hardly convincing. One key example is the Jesus Seminar, whose Red Letter edition of the parables of Jesus is color-coded to indicate the level of confidence in the authenticity of the various parables. This group aims to demonstrate that Jesus said those words, or something similar; did not speak these words but expressed similar ideas; or the ideas are from a later time.[40] Even for those who regard the parables as having been supplemented by the early church, there is reason for confidence in the parables' ability to provide some of the most authentic and reliable teaching from Jesus.[41] One of the "proofs" of this authenticity is the closeness in language and content to other attested sayings of Jesus.[42]

In addition, while not falling back on the pattern of extreme allegorization and subjectivity that dominated the interpretation of the church for so long, it is clear that the parables may be more allegorical in character than is generally acknowledged. As Blomberg notes, "allegorizing one detail does not commit an interpreter to allegorizing all of the details."[43] The fact that Jesus himself used allegory should also give us confidence in our interpretations. However, one should allegorize only if the text points to the presence of allegorization by the author. On the basis of the literary and the historical contexts, the interpreter should learn to distinguish between "local color" and details that are meant to convey allegorical significance.[44] Parables are human interest stories with a spiritual lesson attached to them, but usually they are not allegories.

Finally, parables generally make more than one point. One should not confine a parable to one point if it is evident that more than one truth is being conveyed. Recent parable studies have come to the conclusion that approximately two thirds of Jesus' stories are triadic in structure. That is, they represent three main characters or groups of characters: a master figure (king, master, father, shepherd) and two contrasting subordinates

---

40. *The Five Gospels*, ed. Robert W. Funk, Roy W. Hoover, and the Jesus Seminar (San Francisco: Harper, 1996), ix-x). See the discussion in DJG 596.
41. For specific evidence, see DJG 596.
42. Stein, *Method and Message of Jesus' Teachings*, 45.
43. Blomberg, *Interpreting the Parables*, 20–21.
44. Osborne, *Hermeneutical Spiral*, 305.

(servants, sons, sheep). The implication of this is that the perspectives of the main characters reflect different parts of the overall meaning of the parable.[45] For instance, the Parable of the Good Samaritan conveys the following three truths: "from the example of the priest and Levite comes the principle that religious status or legalistic casuistry does not excuse lovelessness; from the Samaritan we learn that we must show compassion to those in need; from the man in the ditch emerges the lesson that even an enemy is a neighbor."[46]

Apart from the one-point approach, the historical approach popularized by Jeremias should also be approached with caution. As Osborne notes, "it can denigrate the narrative dimensions of the parable and lead to a radical dichotomy between the 'situation' in Jesus' life and the use of the parable by the individual evangelists."[47] The aesthetic and literary approaches are also not hermeneutically sound by themselves because they neglect the historical dimension surrounding parables. An approach that in keeping with the hermeneutical triad seeks to balance the historical, literary, and theological dimensions in parable interpretation is the most appropriate. With this, we turn to a survey of the specific parables of Jesus recounted in the Synoptic Gospels.

Jesus' Parables in the Synoptic Gospels

While parables abound in the Synoptic Gospels (especially Matthew and Luke), there are no parables in a more narrow sense in John's Gospel (though see the parabolic element in John 9:39–41 and the symbolic discourses in John 10:1–5 and 15:1–8). The parables in the Synoptic Gospels are frequently arranged thematically to highlight certain theological emphases.[48] Note, for instance, the surrounding contexts of the Parable of the Wicked Tenants, a parable found in all three Synoptic Gospels. Whereas Mark and Luke place their version of the parable in the context of Jesus' authority, Matthew accentuates more keenly Israel's rejection.

---

45. Klein, Blomberg, and Hubbard, *Introduction to Biblical Interpretation*, 413; Blomberg, Interpreting the Parables, 171.
46. Klein, Blomberg, and Hubbard, *Introduction to Biblical Interpretation*, 414.
47. Osborne, *Hermeneutical Spiral*, 302.
48. The following information on the distribution of parables in the Synoptics is largely derived from DJG 596–98.

9.3. SYNOPTIC COMPARISON OF THE PARABLE OF THE WICKED TENANTS		
MARK	**MATTHEW**	**LUKE**
Mark 11:27–33	Matthew 21:28–32	Luke 20:1–18
The authority of Jesus questioned	The parable of the two sons	The authority of Jesus questioned
Mark 12:1–12	Matthew 21:33–46	Luke 20:9–19
The wicked tenants	The wicked tenants	The wicked tenants
Mark 12:13–17	Matthew 22:1–14	Luke 20:20–26
Paying taxes to Caesar	The parable of wedding banquet	Paying taxes to Caesar

It is more than likely that Jesus retold some of these parables and this may explain the different variations encountered. At the same time, one should keep in mind that the evangelists themselves may have reshaped some of the parables to suit their theological interests.

Most of Matthew's parables are found in three of his five discourses in Matthew 12–13, 18, and 24–25. In conformity with his overall theological thrust, Matthew groups the kingdom parables in Matthew 13; parables on his "ecclesiastical discourse" in Matthew 18:10–14, 21–35; those on Israel's rejection in Matthew 21:28–22:14; and seven more related to the end times in Matthew 24:32–25:46. At least twelve parables are unique to Matthew. With regard to story parables, Mark has the fewest, featuring only four, with three of these in chapter 4 (the Sower; the Secretly Growing Seed; and the Mustard Seed) and one in chapter 12 (the Wicked Tenants). Matthew and Luke have all these except for the Secretly Growing Seed and also share the parables of the Leaven and the Lost Sheep. Luke places most of his parables in his travel narrative (Luke 9:51–19:27). At least fifteen parables are unique to him.

Jewish Background and Parallels

Jesus did not invent the parable teaching form. The background of parables is found in the wisdom tradition of Israel (Heb. *mašal*; Grk. *parabolē*). Mašal has broad usage encompassing forms as diverse as "saying," "proverb," "wisdom saying," or "mocking song." While commonly associated with teachers of wisdom (1 Kgs. 4:32; Prov. 26:7, 9; Eccl. 12:9), its most general usage is in describing a popular saying or maxim whose origins have been lost in antiquity (cf. 1 Sam. 24:4). Osborne notes that from its more popular meaning of proverb, it came to be used as a technical term for wisdom teaching until eventually it was taken to encompass a wide range of terms including prophetic proverbs, parables, riddles, and symbolic action.[49]

Salvation History and the Sitz im Leben Jesu

An important interpretive issue with regard to parables has to do with understanding the life situation of Jesus. You should ask the question: "Is there anything significant about the particular juncture in Jesus' ministry in which the parable was told?" In order to answer this question, you must understand Jesus' ministry in terms of its place in salvation history Whereas God is active in all of history in general, his redemptive activity in the history recorded in Scripture is unique. This "salvation history" is intimately tied up with God's revelation of himself. As George Ladd points out, "[W]hile God is the Lord of all history, in one series of events God has revealed himself as he has nowhere else done. German theologians have coined the useful term Heilsgeschichte ('history of salvation') to designate this stream of revelatory history."[50] Of great significance is his ultimate self-revelation through his Son Jesus Christ.

Hence, the Parable of the Sower (Mark 4:1–9, 13–20; Matt. 13:1–9, 18–23; Luke 8:4–8, 11–15) which describes the reception of a seed by four different kinds of soils anticipates the rejection that Jesus would eventually face. Whereas all four soils received the same seed, only one bore fruit. This parable demonstrates, among other things, that although obedience in faith is the right response to the revelation that has come in Jesus Christ, not all who hear will respond positively. In the Matthean context, the parable concludes with the following words: "He who has ears, let him hear." This reflects the fact that the parable "has to do with receptivity. It amounts to an appeal to hear positively and to respond appropriately (cf. v 43)."[51] All three evangelists place this parable in contexts in which the Jewish leaders express their rejection of Jesus and his message. Thus, this parable serves the purpose of explaining to the hearers—particularly

---

49. Osborne, *Hermeneutical Spiral*, 292.
50. George Eldon Ladd, *A Theology of the New Testament* (Grand Rapids: Eerdmans, 1974), 22.
51. Donald A. Hagner, "Matthew's Parables of the Kingdom," in *The Challenge of Jesus' Parables*, ed. Richard N. Longenecker (Grand Rapids: Eerdmans, 2000), 104.

Jesus' disciples who by this time were surely wondering why people's response to Jesus was not more positive—why people did not respond in larger numbers to Jesus and his message.

Likewise, the allegorical Parable of the Wicked Tenants must be understood from a pre-Christian vantage point (Mark 12:1–11; Matt. 21:33–44; Luke 20:9–19). The owner of the vineyard represents God; the first group of tenants represents Israel's leaders; and the second, those who replace this original, corrupt group.[52] Both God's patience and his judgment on these wicked people come to the fore in this parable. The focus in the parable is on the son, who is symbolic of Jesus himself. Arising from a context in which Jesus' authority is in question this parable exposes the eventual rejection of Jesus by the Jews and anticipates his death. Thus, "as the wicked tenants rejected the landowner's son and therefore were punished and lost the vineyard to other tenants, so also Israel has rejected Jesus, the Son of God."[53] This comes into sharper focus from a post-resurrection perspective.

Characteristics of Parables

In order to interpret parables effectively, it is important to recognize that parables have certain defining characteristics. Identifying these characteristics and understanding what role they play in the parable is crucial for correct interpretation. Osborne identifies the following ten characteristics of parables:[54]

Earthiness: Almost all the parables are told within a setting in which the images in the parables are supported by earthy details. Understanding these details is crucial to understanding the parable itself.

Conciseness: Unlike complex narratives that have numerous characters and a detailed plot, parables are simple and uncomplicated.

Major and minor points: This is one of the issues in parable research that has yet to be settled. Many modern interpreters tend to emphasize a "one-point" approach. However, most parables have one major point as well as one or more secondary points.

52. Blomberg, *Interpreting the Parables*, 248.
53. Allan W. Martens, "'Produce Fruit Worthy of Repentance': Parables of Judgment against the Jewish Religious Leaders and the Nation," in *Challenge of Jesus' Parables*, 162.
54. Osborne, *Hermeneutical Spiral*, 296–302. The following discussion is based largely on Osborne's treatment.

Repetition: In telling his parables, Jesus sometimes used repetition to stress the climax or the major point. An example is the twofold confession of the prodigal son.

Conclusion: In most instances, Jesus used a terse dictum to conclude a parable (note, for instance, Luke 12:21: "This is how it will be with anyone who stores up things for himself but is not rich toward God"). In others, he used the technique of questions or even interpreted the parable himself. Whereas the conclusion generally provides the main point, it may in some instances apply to the broader situation.

Listener-relatedness: The main purpose of parables is to elicit a response from the listener, either positive or negative.

Reversal of expectation: Parables frequently contain unexpected elements that force the hearer to reconsider a course of action or an attitude. They frequently promote norms that run counter to those listening. Without an understanding of the historical context, it is impossible to grasp this reversal. For instance, "good Samaritan" was considered an oxymoron in Jesus' day, for Jewish relations with Samaritans were strained (cf. John 4:9). Only by understanding the hatred that existed between the Jews and the Samaritans of Jesus' times can one begin to understand the point of the parable.

Kingdom-centered eschatology: The thread that ties the parables together is the kingdom of God. They reflect the reality of the kingdom as present as well as future since the kingdom is an expression used for God's power and rule. At the same time, they are christological in focus since they center on Jesus Christ as the one who brings this kingdom into being.

Kingdom ethics: Since the kingdom is present and not just future, there is a demand for higher ethical standards. This has important implications for discipleship. It is reflected especially in the Sermon on the Mount and the illustrations found there.

God and salvation: The parables reflect the fact that God, in all the guises in which he is represented (king, father, landowner, employer, judge), is a gracious God who offers forgiveness and salvation. All that is required is repentance and a positive response to his offer.

GUIDELINES FOR INTERPRETING THE PARABLES

One of the contributions of the "new hermeneutic" has been the emphasis on the aesthetic dimension of parables and the reminder that parables are intended to evoke a response within the listeners. It is this emphasis that has led to the argument that a parable should not be interpreted but be presented to the reader. With this perspective has come the useful proposal that parables should be translated into today's context, an approach that effectively communicates the imagery and narrative form of the parable. Note, for instance, the impact on a modern reader of a contemporization of the Good Samaritan given by Fee and Stuart in which the priest is represented by a local bishop, the Levite by a Kiwanis Club president, and the Samaritan by an atheist.[55]

While their concern is valid, it is not the case that interpreting a parable by placing it in its historical perspective and translating it in propositional terms necessarily "destroys" it. Since the modern reader is so far removed from the original historical context, some steps are necessary to bridge the gap and to allow us to experience what the original hearers heard and felt. The following guidelines are designed to help the interpreter do precisely that, without destroying the original intent and form of the parable.[56] Since the parables share certain characteristics with narratives, the principles for interpreting narratives may be consulted with profit as well, as long as it is kept in mind that parables are not historical narratives.

1. Determine the structure of the parable. Make note of plot development, literary style, and narrative flow, taking care to follow the author's literary structure and presentation. Ensure that you correctly identify transitional phrases, literary inclusions, and various other textual markers. Note the crucial pointers that constrain the purpose of the parable. For instance, in the story of the Good Samaritan, the purpose is indicated by the initial

---

55. Fee and Stuart, *How to Read the Bible*, 160–61.
56. These guidelines are adapted from Osborne, *Hermeneutical Spiral*, 302–8; Fee and Stuart, How to Read the Bible, 153–60.

question by Jesus' audience: "But he wanted to justify himself, so he asked Jesus, 'And who is my neighbor?'" (Luke 10:29). The issue therefore is the question of who is one's neighbor, contra Jewish narrow definitions and the questioner's effort to justify himself.

2. Determine the literary context of the parable. This should be done first vertically in its own setting and then horizontally, comparing it with parallel accounts if available. How does this fit into the theological emphasis of the particular evangelist? For instance, the parable of the Prodigal Son is part of a trilogy of lost things in Luke 15, the other two being the parables of the Lost Sheep and the Lost Coin. This has significant ramifications for interpretation.

3. Establish the historical context in order to understand the earthy details. Note other aspects of the setting that may contribute to an understanding of the parable: geography, politics, economics, military and war, cultural and religious customs. What are the nature and circumstances of both the listeners of Jesus' time and the evangelists? Always keep in mind the two-level nature of the parables. Remember that the original contexts of many of the parables were not preserved in transmission.

4. Make careful note of the points of reference, that is, those items with which the hearer is to identify, and the climax of the narrative (such as the welcoming reaction of the father in the prodigal son parable). What shifts occur after this point? Include the introductions and the conclusions in your analysis. Most often, it is in the conclusion that the reader is confronted with the necessity to make a decision. Avoid placing too much emphasis on the points of reference; the point of the parable is found in the response elicited by the parable.

5. <u>Determine the main point of the parable as well as any secondary points.</u> For instance, the main point of the parable of the Prodigal Son has to do with the younger brother. But there is also a secondary point: the elder brother with his negative and resentful attitude that fails to reflect joy at the restoration of his brother. Avoid placing too much significance on surrounding details and allegorize only if the text warrants it. In this regard, it is more likely that rather than represent God (as some propose), the human father in this parable is displaying the divine characteristics of forgiveness and compassion?

6. <u>Determine the original intent of the parable.</u> What is the function of this parable in terms of Jesus' kingdom teaching and the message of the evangelists? What theological message does it convey? Ensure that you clarify any doctrine with other parts of Scripture.

7. Keep in mind that the entire interpretive process should be based on sound exegetical procedures. Take note of the meaning of significant words and the contribution of grammar and syntax.

8. Draw all your findings together and summarize the meaning of your parable. Ensure that this is consistent with authorial intent.

9. Apply the central truth(s) of this parable to the contemporary situation. As you do so, identify points of contact between the original context of Jesus' hearers and the first readers of the Gospels and your own situation. Once you have discerned the essential dynamics at work, try to locate comparable dynamics in your own life or in the life of believers today.

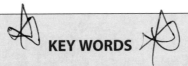

KEY WORDS

Allegory: series of related metaphors

Hyperbole: a form of overstatement in which literal fulfillment or portrayal is impossible

Parable: true-to-life or realistic story told in form of an extended simile, short story, or allegory to teach a spiritual lesson

Paradox: a statement that appears to be contradictory

Pun: a play on words in which one word may have more than one meaning, or two similar-sounding words may be intentionally used to suggest two or more different meanings

Riddle: a simple statement with a hidden meaning which the hearer must uncover

Simile: a figure of speech that compares two things that are essentially like each other

Similitude: extended simile

Sitz im Leben: the life setting of a given literary unit in history (e.g. of a parable)

Sitz im Leben der Kirche: the life setting of the church at the time of composition

Sitz im Leben Jesu: the life setting of a story or parable in Jesus' day

STUDY QUESTIONS

1. What is a definition of "parable" and how do parables differ from his-
    torical narratives?

2. What is the spectrum of parables found in the Gospels?

    Overstatement, Pun, Simile, Riddle, Proverb

3. What are some of the major characteristics of parables?

4. What are the guidelines to interpreting parables?

ASSIGNMENTS

1. Provide an interpretation of the Parable of the Sower in Matthew 13:1–23. Explain the nature of the four different kinds of soil and the theological implications of Jesus' teaching for believers today. Show also how this parable is situated within its Matthean context, both its immediate context (chapter 13) and its place in the Gospel as a whole.

2. Keeping in mind the classification of various types of parables provided in the course text, classify the Parable of the Tenants in Mark 12:1–12. Provide a basic interpretation of the parable and discuss its significance within the plot and theological message of Mark's Gospel.

3. In the course of the history of interpretation, the Parable of the Good Samaritan in Luke 10:25–37 has been interpreted in a variety of ways. Discuss some of the ways in which the Parable of the Good Samaritan has been interpreted and provide your own interpretation including an assessment of its setting, plot, characterization, peak, and theological message. Discuss also how the genre of parable enhances Jesus' message in the present pericope.

4. Discuss Jesus' three parables on "lost things" in Luke 15, focusing on the Parable of the Prodigal Son. Identify the historical setting of the parable and show how it organically fits within Luke's Gospel and theological message. Provide a reflection on why Luke might have chosen to record this parable (as well as the Parable of the Good Samaritan in Luke 10) when neither of these parables is found in any of the other Gospels.

CHAPTER BIBLIOGRAPHY

Blomberg, Craig L. *Interpreting the Parables.* Downers Grove:
   InterVarsity, 1990.

Fee, Gordon D. and Douglas Stuart. Pp. 149–62 in *How to Read the
   Bible for all Its Worth.* 3d ed. Grand Rapids: Zondervan, 2003.

Klein, W. William, Craig L. Blomberg, and Robert L. Hubbard Jr.
   Pp. 411–15 in *Introduction to Biblical Interpretation.* Rev. ed.
   Nashville: Thomas Nelson, 2004.

Köstenberger, Andreas J. "Jesus the Good Shepherd Who Will Also
   Bring Other Sheep (John 10:16): The Old Testament Background
   of a Familiar Metaphor." *Bulletin for Biblical Research* 12 (2002):
   67–96.

Ladd, George Eldon. *A Theology of the New Testament.* Rev. ed.
   Grand Rapids: Eerdmans, 1993.

Longenecker, Richard N., ed. *The Challenge of Jesus' Parables.* Grand
   Rapids: Eerdmans, 2000.

Osborne, Grant R. Chapter 12 in *The Hermeneutical Spiral.* 2d ed.
   Downers Grove: InterVarsity, 2006.

Snodgrass, Klyne. "Parable." Pp. 591–601 in *Dictionary of Jesus and
   the Gospels.* Downers Grove: InterVarsity, 1992.

_____. *Stories with Intent: A Comprehensive Guide to the
   Parables of Jesus.* Grand Rapids: Eerdmans, 2008.

Stein, Robert H. *The Method and Message of Jesus' Teachings.*
   Philadelphia: Westminster, 1978.

_____. *An Introduction to the Parables of Jesus.* Philadelphia:
   Westminster, 1981.

Wilson, Gerald. "משׁל." Pp. 1134–36 in *New International Dictionary
   of Old Testament Theology and Exegesis.* Vol. 2. Edited by Willem
   A. VanGemeren. Grand Rapids: Zondervan, 1997.

CHAPTER 10 OBJECTIVES

1. To acquaint the student with the genre of the New Testament epistles by reference to ancient epistolary conventions.

2. To present and evaluate the application of rhetorical criticism to the study of the epistles.

3. To introduce special issues pertaining to individual New Testament letters.

4. To discuss general hermeneutical issues related to the epistles.

5. To provide the student with a set of guidelines for interpreting the epistles.

CHAPTER 10 OUTLINE

A. New Testament Epistles and Ancient Epistolography
   1. Introduction
   2. Opening
   3. Body
   4. Closing
   5. Types of Letters
   6. Letter-Writing
   7. Pseudonymity and Allonymity
   8. Conclusion
B. New Testament Epistles and Rhetorical Criticism
   1. Introduction: Rhetorical Species and Proofs
   2. Written Versus Oral Communication in Antiquity
   3. Conclusion
C. Pauline Epistles
   1. Paul's Use of the Old Testament
   2. Paul's Use of Christian Traditions:
      a. Creeds/Hymns
      b. Domestic Codes
      c. Slogans
      d. Vice and Virtue Lists
D. General Epistles
   1. Hebrews
      a. Oral Nature of Hebrews
      b. Literary Structure of Hebrews
      c. Atypical Feature: The Lack of a Formal Epistolary Introduction
   2. James
      a. Jewish-Christian Nature of James
      b. Jesus as a Source
   3. Jude and the Petrine Epistles
      a. Relationship between Jude and 2 Peter
      b. Alleged Pseudonymity of 2 Peter

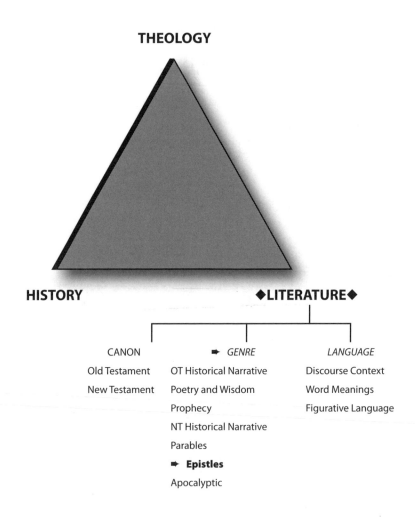

THEOLOGY

HISTORY

◆LITERATURE◆

CANON | ➡ GENRE | LANGUAGE
Old Testament | OT Historical Narrative | Discourse Context
New Testament | Poetry and Wisdom | Word Meanings
 | Prophecy | Figurative Language
 | NT Historical Narrative |
 | Parables |
 | ➡ **Epistles** |
 | Apocalyptic |

Chapter 10

GOING BY THE LETTER: EPISTLES

THE NEW TESTAMENT EPISTLES
AND ANCIENT EPISTOLOGRAPHY

Introduction

A S WE CONTINUE OUR INTERPRETIVE journey through the canonical landscape, two more important genres found in the New Testament remain: epistle and apocalyptic. Epistles constitute the subject of the present chapter; the following chapter will be devoted to a study of apocalyptic. As we turn to an investigation of the epistolary genre, it is hard to exaggerate the importance of the New Testament letters. It is here that we find the bulk of the New Testament instruction as to how we should live our lives as believers today. Especially in Paul's letters, we find the most vital teaching with regard to our union with Christ, concerning the church as the body of Christ, and pertaining to how Christians should conduct themselves as they live their lives in the light of Christ's return. This explains why many preachers spend a considerable amount of time expounding the epistles and why the present chapter is one of the most thorough of the entire volume.

Although epistles make up a considerably larger portion of the New Testament, several letters are also embedded in various books of the Old Testament. These include several found in narrative and prophetic literature, many of them quite short (2 Sam. 11:14–15; 1 Kgs. 21:9–10; 2 Kgs. 5:6; 10:2–3, 6; 19:10–13 [= Isa 37:10–13]; 2 Chron. 2:11–15; 21:12–15; Neh. 6:6–7;

Ezra 4–5; Jer. 29:4–23, 26–28).[1] Official letters were dispatched to report various military or other matters to a king or other superior (e.g. 1 Kgs. 5:8–9; 2 Chron. 2:3–15). As in the case of New Testament epistles, these letters typically consisted of an opening, a body, and a closing. Openings and closings were fairly stereotypical while there was a wide range of options for the body of the letter depending on the nature of the matter to be conveyed.

Readers of the New Testament will quickly discover that the majority of the books making up the New Testament (21 out of 27 books) have the superscript "Epistle."[2] This designation, though not part of the original documents themselves, nonetheless identifies correctly the genre of these writings as epistles (Grk. *epistolai*). In fact, the designation "epistle" can be found in several of the New Testament letters (e.g., Rom. 16:22; 2 Cor. 7:8; Col. 4:16; 1 Thess. 5:27; 2 Thess. 3:14; 2 Pet. 3:1). It was Paul's custom to write to his churches in letter form (2 Thess. 3:17). His opponents acknowledged that he wrote "weighty and forceful" letters (Grk. epistolai; 2 Cor. 10:10), and Peter referred to Paul's letters as "hard to understand" (2 Pet. 3:16).

In the early twentieth century, Adolf Deissmann sought to make a distinction between "letters" and "epistles," arguing that Paul's writings fall under the category of letters.[3] In his view, letters were occasional writings addressing specific situations while epistles were literary compositions intended for posterity. Deissmann's view, however, is rightly doubted today since Paul's letters are clearly both occasional and literary in nature.4 The weakness of Deissmann's theory primarily resulted from an unduly close identification of Paul's letters with the papyri or private Hellenistic letters as distinct from public or official letters.

---

1. See Grant R. Osborne, *The Hermeneutical Spiral: A Comprehensive Introduction to Biblical Interpretation*, rev. and exp. ed. (Downers Grove: InterVarsity, 2006), 312–14.
2. An excellent treatment of epistles is found in D. A. Carson and Douglas J. Moo, *An Introduction to the New Testament*, 2d ed. (Grand Rapids: Zondervan, 2005), 331–54.
3. Adolf Deissmann, *Light from the Ancient East: The New Testament Illustrated by Recently Discovered Texts of the Graeco-Roman World* (London: Hodder & Stoughton, 1927), 228–41.
4. See the critiques by Stanley K. Stowers, *Letter Writing in Greco-Roman Antiquity, Library of Early Christianity* (Philadelphia: Westminster, 1986), 18–19; Thomas R. Schreiner, *Interpreting the Pauline Epistles, Guides to New Testament Exegesis* (Grand Rapids: Baker, 1990), 23–25; and Carson and Moo, *Introduction to the New Testament*, 333–34.

More recently, M. Luther Stirewalt Jr. set forth the theory that Paul "fashioned the logistics for his communications after the examples offered by official correspondence."[5] In support of his thesis, he offers an array of support: (1) both Paul's letters and ancient official correspondence were delivered and addressed to a constituted body and read before that assembly; (2) in both cases, carriers delivered oral messages and answered inquiries related to the letter's content; (3) both were intended to emphasize the writer's official position in the community; (4) the co-senders were legal witnesses; and (5) in both cases, the recipients were multiple rather than individual. In spite of these similarities, Stirewalt rightly states that, "It must be said that neither in form, nor function, nor style can Paul's letters be contained in one category. . . . The Pauline letters arose in a unique epistolary setting."[6]

Since Paul is the author of the vast majority of the letters included in the New Testament—13 out of 21—our discussion of ancient epistolography will make reference mostly to his letters, though the insights gained concerning Paul's letters pertain to the other New Testament letters as well. After the discussion of epistolography with special focus on Paul's writings, we will address the other letters included in the New Testament.

Opening

The similarities between Paul's letters and ancient epistles are most clearly seen in the opening and closing sections of the letter. Typically, the ancient letters opened with an identification of the sender and the addressee, followed by a salutation or greeting (e.g., "Paul to Timothy, greetings"; cf. Acts 15:23; Jas. 1:1), and adding the element of prayer, which could contain a health wish (cf. 3 John 2) and/or a prayer to the gods on behalf of the addressee. It is important to observe how the writers of the New Testament letters, particularly Paul, followed these conventions and how they deviated from them, because the similarities and differences provide indications as

---

5. M. Luther Stirewalt Jr., *Paul, the Letter Writer* (Grand Rapids: Eerdmans, 2003), 1. See pp. 1–30 for what follows. See also chapter 2 in Hans-Josef Klauck, *Ancient Letters and the New Testament: A Guide to Content and Exegesis* (Waco, TX: Baylor University, 2006).
6. Stirewalt, *Paul, the Letter Writer*, 26.

to the occasion and circumstances surrounding the writing of a given New Testament letter.[7]

Most of the New Testament letters identify in their opening section the sender. In addition, co-senders are mentioned in most of Paul's letters (except for Romans, Ephesians, and the Pastorals). These co-senders were not necessarily co-writers but were mentioned for various other reasons, such as to let the congregation know the whereabouts of the people with whom they were acquainted or to establish the authority of the carrier of a given letter.

Apart from the sender, the New Testament epistles customarily mention the addressee. Most New Testament letters were sent to Christian communities. The designations used for the reader likewise have interpretive significance. In his first letter to the Corinthians, for instance, Paul adds "all those everywhere who call on the name of our Lord Jesus Christ—their Lord and ours" (1 Cor. 1:2), most likely in order to remind his readers that they are not an isolated body of believers. In using the expression "the church of God in Corinth" (1 Cor. 1:2), Paul may be communicating the fact that the church belonged to God and not to Paul or Apollos.

The opening section of a Pauline letter also contains distinctive features in its salutation or greeting. A typical Hellenistic greeting was chairein ("greetings"; see Acts 15:23). Paul Christianized the term by changing the greeting to *charis* ("grace"). He also added the greeting that was usually present in the Aramaic or Hebrew letters (shalom meaning "peace"), which in Greek is *eirēnē*. The inclusion of both a Greek and Hebrew type of greeting may indicate the fact that Paul was writing to a mixed audience including both Jews and Gentiles, and thus suggesting that both groups had equal standing before God (cf. Gal. 3:28–29).

The prayer section in the Hellenistic letters addressed to the gods was likewise Christianized and presented in the form of a thanksgiving. Thus the occasion for the thanksgiving was no longer favor with the gods but salvation by Jesus Christ. This section also alerts the readers to central themes that the author will develop in the body of the letter.[8] For instance,

---

7. For details see Schreiner, *Interpreting the Pauline Epistles.*
8. See P. Schubert, *Form and Function of Pauline Thanksgivings* (Berlin: Töpelmann, 1939); P. T. O'Brien, *Introductory Thanksgivings in the Letters of Paul* (Leiden: Brill, 1977); and G. P. Wiles, *Paul's Intercessory Prayers: The Significance of the Intercessory*

in his first letter to the Corinthians, Paul reminds them of spiritual gifts and blessings they possessed as a result of God's generous grace, gifts that gave rise to problems in the Corinthian church (1:4–9; cf. chaps. 12–14).[9] Of Paul's letters, only Galatians and Titus lack a thanksgiving section, in the case of Galatians most likely because of the urgency of the matter at hand.

Body

While the opening and the closing of Paul's letters reflect certain similarities with ancient Hellenistic letters, such similarities are less recognizable in the body of his letters. This may be due again to Paul's freedom in adopting and adapting the conventional forms in light of the exigencies that determined the writing of his letters. According to Doty, "in the body sections of the longer letters, at least, Paul had more inclination to strike out on his own and to be least bound by epistolary structures," similar to the letter-essays of his day that had no formal structures.[10] Ancient letters were fairly stereotypical, closely following epistolary conventions, while Paul's letters do not seem to conform to any one literary pattern and structure.[11]

We will discuss the rhetorical structure of the Pauline epistles in more detail below; for now it will be sufficient to note that no consensus has been reached on the structure of Paul's letters. While Paul's letters exhibit a considerable degree of diversity, the body of his letters often begins with typical phrases, including: (1) a disclosure formula by which he seeks to inform the addressees about a certain subject—"I do not want you to be unaware" (Rom. 1:13; cf. 2 Cor. 1:18; Phil. 1:12; 1 Thess. 2:1); (2) a request formula which in Philemon is strikingly extended by Greek standards—"I appeal (*parakaleō*) to you" (1 Cor. 1:10; cf. 2 Thess. 2:1); or (3) an expression of astonishment—"I am astonished that you are so quickly deserting the one who called you" (Gal. 1:6).

Prayer Passages in the Letters of St. Paul (London: Cambridge University Press, 1974).

9. See the essays in Karl P. Donfried and Johannes Beutler, eds., *The Thessalonians Debate: Methodological Discord or Methodological Synthesis?* (Grand Rapids: Eerdmans, 2000).

10. Ibid., 44.

11. Ibid., 12–13.

Closing

The apostle Paul typically included several items in the closing of his letters, apparently in no particular order, except for the benediction which always came at the end (Romans is an exception).[12] Among the items Paul includes in the closing of his letters are: prayers (Rom. 15:33, 16:25–27; 1 Thess. 5:23; 2 Thess. 3:16); commendations of fellow workers (Rom. 16:1–2; 1 Cor. 16:10–12); prayer requests (Rom. 15:30–32; Col. 4:2–4; Eph. 6:18–20; 1 Thess. 5:25); greetings (Rom. 16:3–16, 21–23; 1 Cor. 16:19–21); final instructions and exhortations (Gal. 6:11–17; Col. 4:16–18a); references to a "holy kiss" (1 Cor. 16:20b; 2 Cor. 13:12a; 1 Thess. 5:26); autographed greetings (1 Cor. 16:21; Gal. 6:11; Phlm 16); and a grace benediction (Rom. 16:20b; 1 Cor. 16:23–24; Col. 4:18b).

As might be expected, Paul Christianized the typical formula for closing a Hellenistic letter of the day with the word "farewell" (Errōsthe or Errōso as in Acts 15:29) by using the word *charis*. Likewise, we do not find in Paul's letters the wish for good health of the recipients which was typical of the Hellenistic letters, a formula that came to function as bidding farewell. Instead, Paul replaced such a wish with a benediction or doxology, which served as functional substitutes and had a similar effect.[13] Thus Paul's letters are less bound by the conventional formulas of closing characteristic of Hellenistic letters.

Types of letter

We have already mentioned the broad categories of private and official letters. Apart from these, there are other more specific types of letters in antiquity. Demetrius and Proclus or Libanius are the only ones who have transmitted these or in whose name letter handbooks have been transmitted. In his *Typoi epistolikoi* (Epistolary Types) Demetrius differentiates between 21 types of letters, while Proclus in his Peri epistolimaiou charakteros (Concerning the Epistolary Type) discusses 41 types. Among them are letters of friendship, introduction, blame, reproach, consolation, criticism, censure, praise, interrogation, accusation, apology, and gratitude. According to William Doty, however, these guides do not seem to have

---

12. For details see Schreiner, *Interpreting the Pauline Epistles*.
13. See William G. Doty, *Letters in Primitive Christianity, Guides to Biblical Scholarship*, New Testament Series (Philadelphia: Fortress, 1973), 39.

had much influence on the actual writing of letters.[14] Even so, it is worth mentioning here some of the features of the various types of ancient letters, since many of these are also present in Paul's letters.

First, according to Demetrius (citing Artemon who in turn had edited Aristotle's letter), "A letter ought to be written in the same manner as a dialogue, a letter being regarded by him as one of the two sides of a dialogue,"[15] though an exact imitation is not always desirable especially when it comes to ornamentation. Demetrius preferred the plain, carefree speech (*lalikon*) rather than the elevated style (*logoeides*), being thus modeled on the everyday speech of educated individuals. In this regard, the letter should not be too long, nor should the writer include frequent breaks in sentence structure, thus imitating conversation. One could thus almost speak of spoken letters. In our discussion of the rhetorical features of Paul's letters below, we will see that traits of oral presentation are present in his letters and that we get a sense at times that Paul is preaching as if he were with his readers in person.[16]

Second, letters were intended to be expressions of friendship or of one's friendly feelings (*pholophronesis*) and were thus to be written more carefully than a dialogue since they formed a sort of literary present to their recipient and "a picture of his [i.e. writer's] own soul."[17]

The third feature is that of *parousia* or "presence." A letter was intended to revive the existence of a friendship when the correspondents were physically separated. Proclus (Concerning the Epistolary Type 2) states that a letter writer should write "to someone not present as if he were present." Paul likewise wrote letters usually as substitute communication. This is not to say that Paul always preferred bodily presence, for in some cases he deemed the writing of a letter as more expedient. For example, a personal visit to Corinth ended in disaster (2 Cor. 12:20–21) while Paul's use of an envoy (i.e. Titus; 2 Cor. 7:5–16) and a painful letter (2 Cor. 2:4) proved to be more effective.[18]

---

14. For more information on the types and the two ancient writings, see Doty, *Letters in Primitive Christianity*, 8–24.
15. See his *Peri hermeneias* (*On Style*).
16. See Paul Achtemeier, "Omne verbum sonat: The New Testament and the Oral Environment of Late Western Antiquity," *JBL* 109 (1990): 19, who states that the New Testament writings are "oral to the core."
17. Demetrius, *On Style*, 227.
18. See Margaret Mitchell, "New Testament Envoys in the Context of Greco-Roman Diplomatic and Epistolary Conventions: The Example of Timothy and Titus," *JBL*

Finally, fourth, we may identify several specific types of letters that are found in the New Testament.[19] One type is that of diatribe, which includes a series of questions and answers and which characterizes parts of Paul's Epistle to the Romans (see sample exegesis below). Another epistolary subgenre is that of the apologetic letter of self-commendation, which was a well-known form of rhetorical self-defense (see especially 2 Corinthians 10–13). Yet another type of letter is that containing paraenesis or exhortation, a frequent feature in Paul's and other New Testament letters. After preparing his readers to receive his exhortation by commending them for their faith, godly example, or some other Christian virtue, the letter writer proceeded to the business at hand, whether the existence of divisions in the church, people's lack of humility, or some other problem or issue. Then there is the letter of introduction or commendation, which is exemplified particularly in Philemon.

Letter-Writing

Of importance here is the use of secretaries or amanuenses and dispatchers or carriers since Paul used both of these in the writing of his letters.[20] There are three ways in which a secretary might have been used: (1) word-by-word dictation; (2) dictation of the sense of the message, leaving the formulation of the material to the secretary; and (3) instruction of a secretary to write in one's name, without indication of specific contents.[21] It is beyond dispute that Paul used secretaries (see Rom. 16:22; 1 Cor. 16:21; 2 Thess. 3:17; Phlm 19). In any case, Paul, before sending a given letter, doubtless made sure that what was written was exactly what

---

111 (1992): 641–42. She concludes that "the letter (and envoy, in some cases) was not an inadequate substitute for the more desirable Pauline physical presence, but was in fact deemed by him a superior way to deal with a given situation." See also E. Randolph Richards, *Paul and First-Century Letter Writing: Secretaries, Composition and Collection* (Downers Grove: InterVarsity, 2004), 15–16.

19. See William W. Klein, Craig L. Blomberg, and Robert L. Hubbard, Jr., *Introduction to Biblical Interpretation*, rev. and exp. ed. (Nashville: Nelson, 2004), 430–31, plus the literature cited there.

20. For details on these two aspects of letter writing as well as the tools used see Stirewalt, *Paul, the Letter Writer*, 2–12. See also the excellent, concise treatment in Carson and Moo, *Introduction to the New Testament*, 334–35; and Klauck, *Ancient Letters and the New Testament*, chap. 2, who rightly believes that the rudimentary writing tools played a factor in the shape and style of the ancient epistle.

21. Doty, *Letters in Primitive Christianity*, 40.

he intended to communicate, proof being his signature written with his own hand (e.g., Gal. 6:11).

The dispatchers or carriers of letters were very important. In antiquity, private letters were often entrusted for delivery to strangers passing through or stumbled upon in the marketplace.[22] The only way a sender could exercise any control over the delivery of a letter was by sending his own servant, which implied some measure of wealth and social status. The writers of (official) letters would often send the real message by word because of the insecurity of the postal system and owing to political intrigue. Regardless of the system of delivery, the oral aspect of private letters was present, given several factors such as (1) that greetings at times were to be shared with others; (2) the possibility that the recipient was illiterate and thus the letter needed to be read aloud and before an assembled family, making the arrival of a correspondence a social event; and (3) the fact that letter carriers often waited for a reply before returning to the original writer. The oral aspect of official letters was also due to the general distrust of the written word and to the need for carriers to answer inquiries related to the letter's contents.

Paul's letters display the same characteristics when it comes to their delivery. In contrast to the dispatch of private letters through hired carriers or slaves or the chance of journeying of friends or strangers, Paul had trusted colleagues (e.g., his co-senders) who carried his letters and were invested with authority from Paul to interpret his letters upon arrival and to read out loud the content of his letters (Eph. 6:21–22; Col. 4:7–8; 1 Thess. 5:27).[23] The carriers were thus his surrogates, his personal representatives.[24] In light of these factors in the writing of a letter, one can easily see why the mention and the selection of the carriers of his letters were important for Paul.

Pseudonymity and Allonymity

Given the use of secretaries and carriers, one is confronted with the issue of pseudonymity and allonymity.[25] Pseudonymity refers to a writing

---

22. For details on what follows see Stirewalt, *Paul, the Letter Writer*, 2–44.
23. Ibid., 45–46.
24. Stirewalt, *Paul, the Letter Writer*, 43, claims that co-senders functioned as witnesses in Jewish societies who could at any time authenticate a letter, its origin, and content.
25. See esp. the excellent and very thorough treatment by Carson and Moo, *Introduction to the New Testament*, 337–50. For a thorough discussion of pseudonymity that

in which a later follower attributes his own work to his revered teacher in order to perpetuate that person's teachings and influence.[26] Among the letters alleged to have been written by someone other than Paul are his correspondence with Timothy and Titus in the Pastoral Epistles. One reason why some commentators claim pseudonymity for the Pastoral Epistles is the distinctive vocabulary we find in these letters in comparison to the commonly acknowledged Pauline writings (such as Romans or Galatians). But this argument based on stylistic differences is of limited value when one takes into account the type of recipients for the Pastoral Epistles (i.e. individuals) in comparison with the recipients of Paul's other letters (i.e. public, with the possible exception of Philemon). Another argument is that the Pastoral Epistles present a well-structured church organization based on a hierarchical model, a sort of "early Catholicism," which supposedly proves a second-century date. This argument, however, does not take sufficiently into consideration the fact that the appointing of elders and deacons was already a practice found in the church long before the writing of the Pastoral Epistles (Acts 14:23; 15:2; 20:28–31; 21:18). Most likely, Paul wrote the Pastoral Epistles sensing an urgency to leave behind a clearly defined body of doctrine as he was nearing the end of his life.

In the end, pseudonymity is a historical matter. How is the alleged pseudonymity of the Pastorals or other New Testament epistles supported from first-century usage and practice? The answer is, not very well at all. First, while pseudonymous writings in other genres (such as Gospels or apocalypses) were not uncommon, pseudonymous letters were exceedingly rare, if not completely unknown, apparently because letters in their very essence constitute a person-to-person or person-to-group communication. Second, in the apostolic era, far from a prevailing acceptance of pseudonymous epistles, there was actually considerable concern that letters might be forged (see, e.g., 2 Thess. 2:2). In the second century, Tertullian (*Bapt.* 17) reports that an Asian presbyter was removed from office

---

still repays careful reading see Donald Guthrie, *New Testament Introduction,* 4th ed. (Downers Grove: InterVarsity, 1990), 1011–28.

26. Cf. Andreas J. Köstenberger, "1 Timothy," in *Expositor's Bible Commentary (rev. ed.; Grand Rapids: Zondervan, 2006),* 492–94. See esp. Terry L. Wilder, "Pseudonymity and the New Testament," in *Interpreting the New Testament: Essays on Methods and Issues,* ed. D. A. Black and D. S. Dockery (Nashville: B&H, 2001), 296–335; and Thomas R. Schreiner, *1, 2 Peter and Jude,* NAC 37 (Nashville: B&H, 2003), 270–74.

for forging a letter in Paul's name. Serapion in A.D. 211 distinguished between apostolic writings and those that "falsely bear their name" (pseudepigrapha; cited in Eusebius, *Eccl. Hist.* 6.12.3).[27]

Another difficulty with the supposed pseudonymous authorship of
certain ones of Paul's letters (as well as Peter's; see the discussion below)
is that this theory requires the assumption that scores of incidental details in Paul's, Timothy's, and Titus' life were invented by the alleged later
pseudonymous author, all supposedly without deceptive intent. However,
it is unclear what purpose such large-scale fabrication of fictional details
would serve. Finally, if pseudonymity is found not to be an acceptable
theory for the writing of the Pastoral Epistles since it was most likely not
an accepted practice, some have claimed allonymity or allepigraphy, a me-
diating position, which holds that a later author edited what Paul wrote
but attributed the writing to Paul or another person without intent to deceive.[28] However, this view is problematic as well. A better hypothesis is
frequently that the author (such as Paul) used an amanuensis, which may
account for the distinct vocabulary, a practice attested in his other letters,
as we have seen.

Conclusion

Paul was part of a culture that used letters for different purposes, anywhere from private correspondence intended to maintain friendship to
official correspondence intended to establish authority. Paul inevitably
followed some of the epistolographic conventions as is evident especially
in the introduction and conclusion of his letters. But even here, we see
Paul not only adopting but also adapting some of the forms in order to
fit them to his purpose for writing. At times, he Christianized the secular

---

27. See the stimulating work of L. R. Donelson, *Pseudepigraphy and Ethical Argument
    in the Pastoral Epistles* (Tübingen: Mohr, 1986), who rightly states that, "No one ever
    seems to have accepted a document as religiously and philosophically prescriptive
    which was known to be forged. I do not know a single example. . . . We are forced to
    admit that in Christian circles pseudonymity was considered a dishonorable device
    and, if discovered, the document was rejected and the author, if known, was excori-
    ated" (pp. 11, 16).
28. See, e.g., I. Howard Marshall, *The Pastoral Epistles*, ICC (Edinburgh: T&T Clark,
    1999), 63–66, 79–84; J. D. G. Dunn, *The Living Word* (London: SCM, 1987), 82; and
    idem, "Pseudepigraphy," in *Dictionary of the Later New Testament and Its Develop-
    ment*, ed. Ralph P. Martin and Peter H. Davids (Downers Grove: InterVarsity, 1997),
    977–84.

terms and format while at other times he left out certain conventional phrases because of the exigencies that prompted him to write. Thus, we can see in Paul a level of freedom in structuring his letters, not bound to any one form. Even when we compare his letters with one another, we find that they display a natural diversity.

In content, many of Paul's epistles deal with complex relationships among Christians rather than with cultivating friendly relations with outsiders. While the subject of his letters is more akin to official correspondence (e.g., establishing his authority as in Galatians), Paul sought to bring his addressees into richer experiences of the new-found relationship with Christ, not merely to move them to submission to his authority or to maintain friendly relations. Therefore, a student of Paul's epistles will be wise to analyze each letter on its own terms, noting each detail in its introduction and conclusion in order to determine the purpose for writing and studying its contents in order to find out what clues it offers to the situation that gave rise to the writing of the particular letter. In determining the purpose for writing, we may get some help from rhetorical criticism, our next subject of discussion.

NEW TESTAMENT EPISTLES AND RHETORICAL CRITICISM
Introduction: Rhetorical Species and Proofs

Rhetoric, simply stated, is the art of persuasion. An orator was considered successful to the extent to which he was able to persuade his audience to adopt his viewpoint. Regarding the aim of persuasion, according to classical tradition, a speech falls into one of the three species of rhetoric: forensic, deliberative, and epideictic.[29] This is not to say that any one speech cannot be a combination of two or all three of these types since one speech can employ topoi (characteristics) from different genres. Nevertheless, one type usually dominates, since any speech seeks to accomplish primarily one purpose.

In this respect, forensic or judicial speech defends or accuses someone regarding past actions by seeking to prove that one's actions were just or

---

29. See G. W. Hansen, "Rhetorical Criticism," in *Dictionary of Paul and His Letters*, ed. Gerald F. Hawthorne, Ralph P. Martin, and Daniel G. Reid (Downers Grove: Inter-Varsity, 1993), 822–23.

unjust. Deliberative speech exhorts or dissuades the audience regarding future actions by seeking to show the expediency or lack thereof of one's future actions. Epideictic discourse affirms communal values by praise or blame in order to affect a present evaluation. Epideictic rhetoric thus seeks to appeal to the social values of honor and shame by asking the question of the praiseworthiness of one's actions.

Any orator in ancient times would use three accepted proofs to persuade his audience of a desired end: ethos, pathos, and logos or apodeixis.[30] The first element, ethos, is the aspect in a speech that establishes the speaker's good character and credibility. The second component, pathos, refers to the effort of appealing to the emotions of the hearer. The third factor, logos, is the furnishing of clear, persuasive proof, a process of reasoning that moves the argument from what is certain to what the orator seeks to prove.

This succinct presentation of ancient rhetoric raises the following set of questions. Do the rules for oral communication apply to written texts as well? If so, the follow-up question is: Did Paul and the writers of the other New Testament epistles structure their letters according to the rhetorical genres? This leads to a third, related question: Should we as interpreters of the New Testament letters use rhetorical criticism for the study of the New Testament letters, drawing on the available knowledge of ancient Greco-Roman rhetorical conventions? It is to this related set of issue that we now turn.

Written Versus Oral Communication in Antiquity

In order to determine whether Paul structured his letters according to the three elements of rhetoric discussed above, we must first answer the question regarding the similarities and differences between written and oral forms of communication. It is widely recognized that in the ancient world there was a preference for extemporaneous orators over written forms of communication. The reason for this was the spontaneity,

---

30. See Aristotle's discussion of these in his *Rhetorica* 1.2.4. For a detailed discussion of proof in Aristotle as applied to 2 Corinthians 10–13 see Mario M. DiCicco, *Paul's Use of Ethos, Pathos, and Logos in 2 Corinthians 10–13*, Mellen Biblical Press Series 31 (Lewiston, NY: Mellen, 1995), 36–77, 113–64, and 188–241.

adaptability, flexibility, and improvisation required by those who spoke extemporaneously.[31]

Nevertheless, it was popular for rhetors to write speeches intended for oral delivery either by the author or another reader since the written speeches were for the ear and not for the eye. In this regard, we have already mentioned that Paul intended his letters to be read out loud to his addressees so that they functioned as "long-distance oral communication."[32] This is attested by the functional similarity between 1 Thessalonians 4:9; 5:1; and 1:8c where the verb "to speak" (*laleō*) is interchangeable with the verb "to write" (*graphō*).

Consequently, one may argue that since Paul wrote his letters as ancient rhetoricians composed speeches (i.e., for oral delivery), the same rules apply to both and therefore analysis of Paul's letters through the lens of rhetorical criticism seems legitimate.[33] This type of reasoning has led to a trend among many New Testament commentary writers to classify each New Testament letter according to the three rhetorical genres and then to outline these using terms from the handbooks on classical rhetoric.

For instance, in Hans-Dieter Betz's opinion Galatians is an example of forensic rhetoric since Paul seeks to defend his authority and the authority of his gospel.[34] As a result, Betz outlines Galatians as follows:

1. Epistolary Prescript (1:1–5)

2. *Exordium* (1:6–11)

3. *Narratio* (1:12–2:14)

4. *Propositio* (2:15–21)

---

31. See further Corin Mihaila, *The Paul-Apollos Relationship and Paul's Stance toward Greco-Roman Rhetoric: An Exegetical and Socio-Historical Study of 1 Corinthians 1–4*, LNT (Edinburgh: T&T Clark, 2009).

32. For details see Richard F. Ward, "Pauline Voice and Presence as Strategic Communication," *Semeia* 65 (1995): 95–107; Pieter J. J. Botha, "The Verbal Art of the Pauline Letters: Rhetoric, Performance and Presence," in *Rhetoric and the New Testament: Essays from the 1992 Heidelberg Conference*, ed. S. Porter and T. Olbricht, JSNTSup 90 (Sheffield: *JSOT*, 1993), 409–28; and Raymond F. Collins, "'I Command that This Letter Be Read': Writing as a Manner of Speaking," in *Thessalonians Debate*, 319–39.

33. See, e.g., Frank W. Hughes, "The Rhetoric of Letters," in *Thessalonians Debate*, 198.

34. Hans-Dieter Betz, *Galatians*, Hermeneia (Philadelphia: Fortress, 1979).

5. *Probatio* (3:1–4:31)

6. *Exhortatio* (5:1–6:10)

7. Epistolary Postscript or *Peroratio* (6:11–18)

The Latin terms correspond to the seven parts described in the classical rhetorical handbooks: (1) an opening greeting or epistolary prescript, including mention of the author and addressees; (2) the *exordium* or introduction, which defines the character of the speaker and the central issue(s) addressed; (3) the *narratio* or presentation, which lays out the events related to the central issue; (4) the *propositio*, a set of propositions which summarize the central thesis or theses to be proved; (5) the *probatio* or confirmation, which sets forth logical arguments in support of the thesis/theses; (6) the *exhortatio* or refutation, which refutes the opponents' arguments; and (7) the *peroratio* or conclusion, which serves as an epistolary postscript and recapitulates the basic points and seeks to evoke a favorable response.

There is, however, no agreement on the rhetorical genre into which Galatians (and for that matter, any other Pauline letter) should fit.[35] For example, George Kennedy classifies Galatians as deliberative since Paul seeks to exhort his readers to be true to the gospel and to dissuade them from accepting the false gospel of the Judaizers, while Richard Longenecker sees Galatians as a mixture of the forensic and deliberative kinds of rhetoric.[36]

Apart from the lack of consensus on how we should classify Paul's letters rhetorically, there is also the problem that the assumption of the legitimacy of applying rhetorical criticism to the study of the Pauline letters has no theoretical basis. In other words, ancient rhetorical categories described in the handbooks were meant for speeches, both oral and written, and not for the writing of letters.[37] It was only in the fourth century A.D.

---

35. For other examples and references see Hansen, "Rhetorical Criticism," 823.

36. George A. Kennedy, *New Testament Interpretation through Rhetorical Criticism* (Chapel Hill: University of North Carolina, 1984); and Richard N. Longenecker, *Galatians*, WBC 41 (Dallas: Word, 1990).

37. For what follows see Jeffrey A. D. Weima, "What Does Aristotle Have to Do with Paul? An Evaluation of Rhetorical Criticism," *CTJ* 32 (1997): 458–68; idem, "Ancient Rhetorical Analysis and Discourse Analysis of the Pauline Corpus," 249–74; Stanley

(i.e., Julius Victor, *Ars Rhetorica 27*) that epistolary theory became part of rhetorical theory.[38] Thus, Jeffrey Reed points out that

> there appears to be a general principle that letters displaying rhetorical influence lack many of the optional epistolary formulas found in the personal letters (e.g., prayer, thanksgiving, disclosure formulas, closing greetings)—an observable difference between literary and personal letters. Conversely, letters replete with epistolary formulas lack full-blown rhetorical conventions. In sum, the rhetorical and epistolary genres may have been betrothed, but were never wed.[39]

The implications of these kinds of observations for the interpretation of New Testament letters are obvious: the application of rhetorical criticism to the study of Paul's letters and those of the other New Testament writers is of doubtful merit.

Conclusion

We cannot show that Paul's letters constitute examples of ancient speeches since they follow clearly the epistolographic categories (with much freedom). Thus, rhetorical categories seem to have had only a minor influence on the New Testament epistolary literature. At the most, there are some functional similarities between epistolary and rhetorical categories (e.g., influence at the level of style). What is less clear is that there are formal similarities that justify the application of rhetorical criticism to the study of Paul's epistles.[40]

E. Porter, "Paul as Epistolographer and Rhetorician?" in *The Rhetorical Interpretation of Scripture: Essays from the 1996 Malibu Conference,* ed. Stanley Porter and Dennis L. Stamps, JSNTSup 180 (Sheffield: Sheffield Academic Press, 1997), 222–48; see also Jeffrey T. Reed, "Using Ancient Rhetorical Categories to Interpret Paul's Letters: A Question of Genre," in *Rhetoric and the New Testament,* 292–324; Stanley E. Porter, "The Theoretical Justification for Application of Rhetorical Categories to Pauline Epistolary Literature," in ibid., 100–22; idem, "Paul of Tarsus and His Letters," in *Handbook of Classical Rhetoric in the Hellenistic Period 330 B.C.–A.D. 400* (Leiden: Brill, 1997), 531–85; Reed, "The Epistle," in ibid., 171–93; and Peter T. O'Brien, *The Letter to the Ephesians,* PNTC (Grand Rapids: Eerdmans, 1999), 73–82.

38. See R. Dean Anderson Jr., *Ancient Rhetorical Theory and Paul,* Contributions to Biblical Exegesis and Theology 18 (Kampen: Kok Pharos, 1996; rev. ed. 1999), 121–27.

39. For examples see Reed, "The Epistle," 186–90.

40. See David E. Aune, *The New Testament in its Literary Environment, Library of Early Christianity* 8 (Philadelphia: Westminster, 1987), 49, 159, 203; Charles A.

PAULINE EPISTLES

In this section of the chapter, we will deal with special issues in the letters of the New Testament. We will treat the Pauline letters as a body of literature and not address individual writings, except for illustrative purposes. In the case of the other New Testament letters, we will point out issues that are pertinent to each of them as they affect interpretation.[41]

Paul's Use of the Old Testament[42]

One highly significant feature of Paul's letters is his extensive use of the Old Testament in constructing his arguments. We find quotations, paraphrases, and allusions in every Pauline letter with the exception of Philemon. These are introduced with the formula "it is written" or with some other introductory phrase. In addition, Paul's letters reflect Old Testament themes, structures, and theology. In fact, one could say that the Old Testament provided the framework and foundation for Paul's theology, Paul's view of the function of the Law as temporary and fulfilled in Jesus notwithstanding.[43]

When studying Paul's quotations of the Old Testament, we must take into consideration the text type that he used: Hebrew, Aramaic, or Greek.[44] Of more than 100 quotations, more than 60 of these quotations agree with the Greek version of the Old Testament (i.e., the LXX), though many of these agree with both the LXX and the Hebrew (Masoretic [MT]) text (e.g. Rom. 2:6; 3:4, 13, 18; etc.). Several quotations agree with the LXX, but not with the MT (e.g. Rom. 2:24; 3:14; etc.). A small number agree with

---

Wanamaker, "Epistolary vs. Rhetorical Analysis: Is a Synthesis Possible?" *in Thessalonians Debate*, 255–86 (esp. 283).

41. On Pauline chronology, see chapter 2 above. Only the most salient topics can be treated below. For other matters pertaining to the interpretation of Paul's letters such as the question of development in Pauline thought, see Andreas J. Köstenberger "Diversity and Unity in the New Testament," in *Biblical Theology: Retrospect & Prospect*, ed. Scott J. Hafemann (Downers Grove: InterVarsity, 2002), 144–58 (with further bibliographical references).

42. Cf. M. Silva, "Old Testament in Paul," in *Dictionary of Paul and His Letters*, 630–42; Craig A. Evans, "The Function of the Old Testament in the New," in *Introducing New Testament Interpretation, Guides to New Testament Exegesis* (Grand Rapids: Baker, 1989), 162–95; and idem, "New Testament Use of the Old Testament," in *New Dictionary of Biblical Theology*, ed. T. Desmond Alexander and Brian S. Rosner (Downers Grove: InterVarsity, 2001), 72–80.

43. For different views on the Law and the Gospel, see Wayne G. Strickland et al., *Five Views on Law and Gospel* (Grand Rapids: Zondervan, 1996).

44. For a chart of the citations from different text-types, see Silva, "Old Testament in Paul," 631.

the MT and against the LXX (Rom. 1:17; 11:4, 35; etc.). A larger number of others differ from both (e.g. Rom. 3:10–12, 15–17; etc.).

In light of this diversity, we may conclude that Paul felt no compulsion to follow a certain pattern in quoting the Old Testament or to reproduce a text type exactly, though when the argument required it he paid close attention to details.[45] In exegeting Paul's quotations of the Old Testament, there are several questions we must answer in order to determine their function in Paul's context more accurately.[46]

1. What Old Testament text(s) is (are) being cited? Is it just one or a combination? If it is a combination, what is the contribution of each text?

2. Which text type is being followed (Hebrew, Greek, or Aramaic)? What does each version of the citation mean? How does the version that the New Testament has followed contribute to the meaning of the citation?

3. Is the Old Testament citation part of a wider tradition or theology in the Old Testament? If it is, the citation may be alluding to a context much wider than the specific passage from which it has been taken.

4. How did various Jewish and Christian groups and interpreters understand the passage in question? And in what ways does the New Testament citation agree or disagree with the interpretations found in the versions and other ancient exegeses?

5. How does the function of the citation compare to the function of other citations in the New Testament writing under consideration?

6. Finally, what contribution does the citation make to the argument of the New Testament passage in which it is found?

---

45. For a helpful discussion of the textual problems, see ibid., 632–33.
46. Cf. Evans, "Function of the Old Testament in the New," 170.

We may take as example the quotation in 1 Corinthians 2:16. In quoting Isaiah 40:13a MT ("Who has known the spirit of the Lord?"), Paul changes the word "spirit" to the word "mind" in 1 Corinthians 2:16 just as the LXX does. The reason becomes apparent when we understand that the context of Paul's use of Isaiah 40:13a is a discussion of the Spirit as the means by which one comes to the knowledge of the mystery of the gospel. Thus having the mind of Christ really means possessing his Spirit.[47]

When it comes to allusions and echoes, it becomes much harder to identify where Paul relies on the Old Testament text, theme, or theology.[48] We will take one example from the letter to the Philippians. In Philippians 1:19 ("what has happened to me will turn out for my deliverance"), Paul follows the LXX of Job 13:16. As Richard Hays points out, while Paul's words are intelligible without reference to Job, an understanding of the context in Job helps us appreciate Paul's message more fully.[49] For example, Paul's citation of Job identifies him with the righteous sufferer who, like Job, will be vindicated by God before his interlocutors and rivals.

The greatest interpretive challenge may be to understand how Paul exegeted a particular Old Testament text or arrived at a certain interpretation of a given passage. What may aid us in understanding Paul's exegetical style is to look at the Jewish hermeneutical methods that most likely affected Paul. Apart from the use of the LXX, it is reasonable to think that Paul also learned from the targumic tradition (i.e., the Aramaic paraphrase of the Hebrew Bible used in synagogue liturgy), as in Ephesians 4:8, where Paul used the verb "gave" as in the Targums instead of "took" as in both the LXX and the MT of Psalm 68:18.[50] Another hermeneutical parallel exists with the Qumran exegesis known as *pesher* (i.e., verse-by-verse

---

47. For a thorough analysis of the quotations in 1 Corinthians 1–3, see H. H. Drake Williams III, *The Wisdom of the Wise: The Presence and Function of Scripture within 1 Cor 1:18–3:23*, Arbeiten zur Geschichte des Antiken Judentums und des Urchristentums 49 (Leiden: Brill, 2001).

48. See especially Richard B. Hays, *Echoes of Scripture in the Letters of Paul* (New Haven: Yale University Press, 1989), who also provides criteria for identifying echoes (pp. 14–24). See also Christopher D. Stanley, *Arguing with Scripture: The Rhetoric of Quotations in the Letters of Paul* (New York: T&T Clark, 2004); and James W. Aageson, "Written Also for Our Sake: Paul's Use of Scripture in the Four Major Epistles, with a Study of 1 Corinthians 10," in *Hearing the Old Testament in the New Testament*, ed. Stanley E. Porter (Grand Rapids: Eerdmans, 2006), 152–81.

49. Hays, *Echoes*, 21–23.

50. Cf. Silva, "Old Testament in Paul," 635.

interpretation), in particular its eschatological orientation. But even here, the comparison is limited given the fact that Paul believed that with Christ the age to come had already arrived (cf. 1 Cor. 10:11).

More likely is an affinity with the rabbinic exegesis called midrash, which generally means "interpretation" or "commentary." This should not be viewed as different or contradictory to the peshat, which is the plain or obvious meaning, but midrash, while including this meaning, at the same time transcends it. Early midrash is recognized by the seven rules (middoth) attributed to the famous first-century rabbi Hillel.[51] We will mention here the three most often found in Paul. The first rule is *qal wa-homer* ("light and heavy"), an argument from the lesser to the greater, that is, what applies in a less important case will certainly apply in a more important one (e.g., Rom. 5:10).

The second rule is *gezera shawah* ("rule of equivalence"), a method that states that passages that share similar vocabulary clarify each other (e.g., Rom. 4:7–10; 11:7–10). This is similar to the Reformation principle of Scripture interpreting Scripture and the parallel passage apparatus in many of today's Study Bibles.

The third rule is *kelal upherat* ("general and particular"), where a general principle may be deduced from a specific passage and vice versa (e.g., Rom. 13:8–10). But even these parallels must be drawn with great caution. Paul was surely immersed in Jewish culture and therefore most probably made use of its exegetical methods. However, the precise nature of Paul's dependence continues to be debated, since Rabbinic Judaism (from which we derive most data) developed only subsequent to the first century. Moreover, some of the Jewish hermeneutical rules are general logical principles of arguing, such as the *qal wahomer* rule, which reflects the general a fortiori ("from the lesser to the greater") argument used in different cultures.

Paul's use and interpretation of the Old Testament may at times be difficult to understand in light of our modern grammatical-historical exegesis. But what may seem to us strange interpretation may have represented conventional hermeneutical procedure to Paul's contemporaries. This is why Paul's interpretation of the Old Testament had considerable

---

51. See Richard Longenecker, *Biblical Exegesis in the Apostolic Period*, 2d ed. (Grand Rapids: Eerdmans, 1999), 20. See the whole chapter for details on early Jewish exegesis that may have influenced Paul's exegetical method when dealing with the Old Testament.

apologetic power and convinced many Jews to believe in Jesus as the fulfillment of Old Testament prophecy as Paul interpreted it. Paul, like his contemporaries, sought to bring a verse or a concept from the Old Testament into a new historical and theological context, which involved some levels of shift in meaning and yet remained faithful to the message in its original context.

Paul's Use of Christian Traditions
Creeds or Hymns

In constructing his arguments in his letters, Paul made use of different Christian traditions.[52] Among the most discussed are creeds or hymns. Creeds are usually contained in hymns, and therefore our focus here will be on the latter.[53] It is usually possible to detect a hymn by the presence of strophes and/or rhythm, which marks the intrusion of poetic style into prose material. In this regard, these passages can be identified as traditional preexistent material, because they contain terminology uncommon to the Pauline letters as well as information that goes beyond the need of the immediate context. This is true particularly when it comes to major christological hymns (see esp. Phil. 2:6–11; Col. 1:15–20).

A quick look at Philippians 2:6–11 will help us to recognize some of the important aspects of Paul's use of traditional material. The text falls into two stanzas that describe the condescension vv. 6–8) and exaltation (vv. 9–11) of Jesus. Each of these, in turn, subdivides into three strophes of three lines each, each line containing three stressed syllables. This symmetry shows that Paul most likely borrowed the tradition from its liturgical context with its emphasis on creed/doctrine, especially since the

---

52. Cf. M. B. Thompson, "Tradition," in *Dictionary of Paul and His Letters*, 944; Klein, Blomberg, and Hubbard, *Introduction to Biblical Interpretation*, 435–38; and R. P. Martin, *New Testament Foundations*, 2 vols. (Exeter: Paternoster; Grand Rapids: Eerdmans, 1978), 2.248–75.

53. It is hard to distinguish between the creedal formulations and hymnic material. Perhaps the distinction is in the length as Rudolf Bultmann argued on stylistic grounds in his "Bekenntnis- und Liedfragmente im ersten Petrusbrief," *ConNT* 11 (1949): 1–14. Among the creeds that are separate from hymns, an important instance is 1 Corinthians 15:3–5, where Paul explicitly uses the introductory verbs "received" (*parelabon*) and "handed on" (*paredōka*). For more examples and ways of identifying creeds see R. P. Martin, "Creed," in *Dictionary of Paul and His Letters*, 190–92. For more on hymns in general as well as examples see R. P. Martin, "Hymns, Hymn Fragments, Songs, Spiritual Songs," in ibid., 419–23.

passage goes beyond the paraenetic purpose of the immediate context: to exhort the Christians to humility for the sake of unity by giving the example of Christ. Even though it does not contribute much to his message, Paul leaves untouched the added information on Christ's exaltation, but he does include the phrase "even death on a cross" (at the end of v. 8) in order to emphasize the theological center of his preaching (cf. 1 Cor. 2:2).[54]

Domestic Codes

Another example of Paul's use of Christian tradition is the *domestic/social/household codes*.[55] Household codes deal with reciprocal responsibilities between the members of the household: husband/wife; parents/children; and master/slave. The household codes are found in the later letters of Paul (Eph. 5:22–6:9; Col. 3:18–4:1; Titus 2:1–10; cf. Rom. 13:1–7). Usually, these codes are identifiable by the presence of verbs conveying the notion of submission or obedience (*hypotassō* and *hypakouō*) in the instructions Paul gives to individuals. While for us today such instructions of submission seem outdated given our culture's emphasis on the equality of individuals not only in essence but also in function, in Paul's day they most likely offered a clear alternative to the authoritarian-based society, since these instructions seem to place value on the submissive part in the relationship. Thus Paul's use of these codes had not only the purpose of regulating the social relationships within the church, but they also had an apologetic purpose—to show that Christianity was not subversive (1 Tim. 3:7, Titus 2:5, 8, 10; 3:10)—as well as a missionary/evangelistic purpose in a hostile world (1 Thess. 4:12).[56]

Slogans

The book of 1 Corinthians presents us with yet another example of traditional material: *slogans*.[57] First Corinthians is unique among the Pau-

---

54. For an in-depth study of this hymn see R. P. Martin, *A Hymn of Christ: Philippians 2:5–11 in Recent Interpretation and in the Setting of Early Christian Worship* (Downers Grove: InterVarsity, 1997).

55. See P. H. Towner, "Households and Household Codes," in *Dictionary of Paul and His Letters*, 417–19, for more details as well as examples in Paul.

56. See J. E. Crouch, *The Origin and Intention of the Colossian Haustafeln* (Göttingen: Vandenhoeck & Ruprecht, 1972); and E. Best, "The Haustafel in Ephesians," *IBS* 16 (1994): 146–60.

57. For an in-depth study of slogans see Paul Charles Siebenmann, "The Question of Slogans in 1 Corinthians" (Ph.D. diss., Baylor University, 1997). See also Klein, Blomberg, and Hubbard, *Introduction to Biblical Interpretation*, 436–37.

line letters because it is clearly an epistle written in response to questions raised by the Corinthians (chaps. 7–16) in a letter that they sent through a carrier as well as Paul's discussion of congregational issues reported by the members of Chloe's household (chaps. 1–6). The topics addressed by Paul in response to the questions raised by the Corinthians are usually marked by the phrase *peri de* ("now about" in 1 Cor. 7:1, 25; 8:1; 12:1; 16:1, 12).[58] In discussing these topics, Paul usually quotes Corinthian slogans.

One such slogan is found in 1 Corinthians 6:12: "Everything is permissible for me" (cf. 1 Cor. 10:23). Many recent translations rightly put quotation marks around these words in order to show that they are slogans and not Paul's own words. Paul uses this slogan in a context in which he discusses sexual sins among which incest that was taking place in the Corinthian body. While Paul initially agrees with the Corinthian saying, he introduces qualifications by using the contrastive conjunction *de* ("but"). Thus, as Anthony Thiselton translates, the Corinthian church members have "liberty to do all things"—but not everything is helpful. "Liberty to do anything"—but I will not let anything take liberties with me.[59]

It is thus important to differentiate between Paul's own words and the Corinthian slogans borrowed from the surrounding pagan culture so as not to develop a false theology from statements which Paul himself qualifies. As one may expect, slogans are typically short and concisely worded. Other likely slogans in 1 Corinthians are found in 6:13 ("Food for the stomach and the stomach for food"); 7:1 ("It is good for a man not to marry"); and 8:1 ("We all possess 'knowledge'").

Vice and Virtue Lists

The last example of preexistent material incorporated by Paul into his letters is the vice and virtue lists. The general purpose of including such lists in his letters is to point out the distinctiveness of the Christian community in contrast to the larger pagan society that condoned especially

---

58. For the functions of the conjunction *de* in 1 Corinthians see Kathleen Callow, "The Disappearing de, in 1 Corinthians," in *Linguistics and New Testament Interpretation. Essays on Discourse Analysis*, ed. David Alan Black (Nashville: B&H, 1992), 183–93. See also Margaret M. Mitchell, "Concerning peri. de, in 1 Cor," *NovT* 321 (1989): 229–56.
59. Anthony C. Thiselton, *The First Epistle to the Corinthians: A Commentary on the Greek Text* (Grand Rapids: Eerdmans, 2000), 458.

sexual sins. Specifically, the lists have at least five functions.[60] First, these lists depict the depravity of unbelievers. In Romans 1:29–31, for instance, Paul describes the immorality of the Gentiles, though in chapter 2 he accuses the Jews of practicing the same sins. In 1 Corinthians 5:9–11, he lists sexual sins for the purpose of exhorting the believers to dissociate themselves from any Christian who still practices such sins, like the man in the Corinthian congregation involved in incest. Second, and most importantly, Paul lists vices and virtues in order to encourage the believers to avoid the vices and practice the virtues (e.g., Gal. 5:19–23). Third, in writing to Timothy, Paul lists vices in order for Timothy to clearly distinguish between true and false teachers (e.g., 1 Tim. 1:3–11; 6:4–5). By contrast, fourth, Paul lists virtues that are required of the church leaders (e.g., 1 Tim. 3:2–13). Lastly, Paul lists vices in his advice to Timothy in order to warn him of the sinful behavior of the people in the last times (2 Tim. 3:2–5).

You can find parallels of these lists, both of virtues and vices, in both Hellenistic Judaism and Greek literature. At the same time, you should be careful not to overinterpret the vice list as being necessarily an exact depiction of the sins of the community Paul is writing to, though certainly some were characteristic.[61]

GENERAL EPISTLES

Hebrews
Oral Nature of Hebrews

Hebrews is an unusual document, because it combines oral and written features.[62] On the one hand, the document was known and circulated in the days of the early church in written form and at the end of the

---

60. For details see Klein, Blomberg, and Hubbard, *Introduction to Biblical Interpretation*, 438; and especially C. G. Kruse, "Virtues and Vices," in *Dictionary of Paul and His Letters*, 962–63, whom we follow here.

61. One important aspect of the issue here is that of "mirror-reading"—how much of Paul's (negative) statements can be interpreted as responses to the theology and practice of his readers. For guidelines and a test case of mirror-reading see John Barclay, "Mirror-Reading a Polemical Letter: Galatians as a Test Case," *JSNT* 31 (1987): 73–93.

62. Regarding the authorship of Hebrews and other relevant information, see chapter 16 in Andreas J. Köstenberger, L. Scott Kellum, and Charles L. Quarles, *The Cradle, the Cross, and the Crown: An Introduction to the New Testament* (Nashville: B&H, 2009).

letter the author mentions that he has written to his readers briefly (Heb. 13:22).

On the other hand, there are also clear indications of the oral nature of the letter, which may suggest that it originated as a series of sermons that only later was written down and sent as a letter. One such indication may be the lack of formal epistolary introduction (on which see below). Also, the author himself calls his communication a "word of exhortation" (Heb. 13:22; *logos tēs paraklēseōs),* a phrase found elsewhere in the New Testament only in Acts 13:15 where synagogue officials invited Paul and Barnabas to give a "word of exhortation to the people." Here and elsewhere, the phrase functioned as "an idiomatic designation for the homily or edifying discourse that followed the public reading from the designated portion of Scripture in the Hellenistic synagogues."[63] Thus, it appears that the author of Hebrews conceived of his communication primarily as a sermon of exhortation. Some even contend that this composition is "the only example of a completely preserved homily" from this period, to which a prescript was added when it was put down in a written form.[64]

There are other aspects of the writing that indicate the essentially oral character of the epistle. The most important is the author's repeated use of the word "speak" (*lalein;* Heb. 5:11; 6:9; 8:1; 13:6). As mentioned above, New Testament letters were intended to be read aloud and therefore have oral features. The same is true with Hebrews. The author's use of the word "speak" clearly indicates that his letter is intended to be one end of a verbal communication. William Lane rightly observes, "The writer assumes a conversational tone in order to diminish the sense of geographical distance that separates him from his audience and makes writing necessary. He conceives of his work as speech. By referring to 'speaking' and 'listening,' he is able to establish a sense of presence with his audience."[65] In Hebrews 5:11, he indicates that he wished to convey ("speak") to them deeper things but he is hindered from doing this because they have literally become "dull in the ears." This expression points to the oral nature of the communication intended for the ear, not the eye. Also, the phrase

---

63. William L. Lane, *Hebrews,* WBC (Dallas: Word, 1991), 2.568, citing 1 Maccabees 10:24; 2 Maccabees 7:24; 15:8–11; and 1 Timothy 4:13.

64. Ibid., lxix, quoting H. Thyen, *Der Stil der jüdisch-hellenistischen Homilie,* FRLANT 47 (Göttingen: Vandenhoeck & Ruprecht, 1955), 10.

65. Lane, *Hebrews,* lxxiv.

"many words" (*logos polus*) is indicative of a lengthy speech (cf. Acts 15:32, 20:2) which in the present instance the speaker does not have the time to deliver.[66]

Apart from the lexical evidence, there are also rhetorical devices used by the author that point to its oral nature. We have already registered a word of caution concerning the use of rhetorical criticism in analyzing letters, but here we are referring to the stylistic features of a speech, both oral and written. These stylistic features are part of any speech that seeks to convey a message to the audience clearly and to make a lasting impact on their minds and hearts.[67] The author of Hebrews uses stylistic devices such as diatribe and rhythm that reflect the letter's oral character.[68] Diatribe is a technique for anticipating objections to an argument, raising them in the form of questions, and then answering them. It is a technique that is rather harsh and therefore used only with an audience that has more than a superficial relationship with the speaker since it intends to shame the student into a consideration of the truth. It is certainly a technique found in letters (such as Romans; see the Sample Exegesis below) but is most effective in an oral presentation.[69] The author of Hebrews uses this technique of asking rhetorical questions in several places. The most pertinent to our study is 3:16–18. Here the author uses the triple rhetorical question format which he answers with three more questions in order to warn against rebellion and unbelief and to point out the serious consequences as illustrated in the generation that perished in the wilderness.

---

66. See Paul Ellingworth, *The Epistle to the Hebrews: A Commentary on the Greek Text*, NIGTC (Grand Rapids: Eerdmans, 1993), 299, for references in classical literature to similar phrases indicating orations.

67. It is doubtful whether the New Testament authors used the techniques described in the rhetorical handbooks of the time in order to persuade, since Paul clearly indicates in 1 Corinthians 2:1–5 that he intentionally refrained from worldly eloquence and "persuasive words of wisdom" in his preaching. See Mihaila, *Paul-Apollos Relationship*; see also Bruce W. Winter, *Philo and Paul among the Sophists: Alexandrian and Corinthian Responses to a Julio-Claudian Movement* (Cambridge: Cambridge University Press, 1997; 2d ed. Grand Rapids: Eerdmans, 2002); and Duane Litfin, *St. Paul's Theology of Proclamation: 1 Corinthians 1–4 and Greco-Roman Rhetoric*, SNTSMS 79 (Cambridge: Cambridge University Press, 1994).

68. For details see Andrew H. Trotter, Jr., *Interpreting the Epistle to the Hebrews*, Guides to New Testament Exegesis 6 (Grand Rapids: Baker, 1997), 66–75.

69. See Stanley Kent Stowers, *The Diatribe and Paul's Letter to the Romans*, SBLDS 57 (Chico, CA: Scholars Press, 1981).

Rhythm is usually found in poetical compositions, but the author of Hebrews uses it extensively in his writing, thus demonstrating some familiarity with the Hebrew poetry besides the Greco-Roman rhetorical style. One of the most famous instances of the use of rhythm in Hebrews is the first four verses of the book as they appear in the original, with its alliteration with the letter "p," assonance, as well as a chiastic structure.[70] Here is how the letter opens: (1) *Polymerōs kai* (2) *polytropōs* (3) *palai ho theos lalēsas tois* (4) *patrasin en tois* (5) *prophētais* (Heb. 1:1). As you can see, all the relevant words ("at many times," "in various ways," "in the past," "fathers," "prophets") are alliterated (beginning with the Greek letter "p") to aid memorization and to increase memorability. The texture of the text is so refined that we cannot avoid the conclusion that the author of Hebrews has taken great pains in making an impression on the ear of his readers. The oral style of his communication is not, however, employed just for the sake of aesthetic beauty but concords with his high christological message contained in these verses. Style does not overshadow the content but brings it to the forefront, so that the medium enhances the poignancy of the message.

In light of all these features, the conclusion is unavoidable that the letter of Hebrews has a distinctively oral character. We may thus speak of the letter as a "sermon that changed its name."[71]

Literary Structure of Hebrews

Determining the structure of a book or its flow of argument is important for the interpretation of that book. The interpretation of each part is dependent on our understanding of the overall message. When it comes to Hebrews, however, apart from the uncertainty surrounding the issues of authorship and literary genre, discussion and debate have focused also on the literary structure of the letter.[72] Some emphasize the formal aspects, while others stress the content of the book. Recently, Steve Stanley has rightly acknowledged that a proper outline of Hebrews should take

---

70. For a detailed analysis of these verses with close attention paid to stylistic features, see David Alan Black, "Literary Artistry in the Epistle to the Hebrews," *Filologia Neotestamentaria* 7/13 (1994): 43–51.

71. Trotter, *Interpreting the Epistle to the Hebrews*, 62.

72. For a detailed presentation and evaluation of different proposals for the literary structure of Hebrews see Lane, *Hebrews*, lxxxv–xcviii; and Elingworth, *Hebrews*, 50–58.

into consideration both aspects (i.e., rhetorical elements and content) as well as the literary genre, with the understanding that content is critical in determining the literary structure.[73]

When seeking to determine the outline of the Epistle to the Hebrews, we should keep in mind several prominent topics in the book. The outline, for instance, should reflect the important place that the warning passages have in the flow of the argument (i.e., Heb. 2:1–4; 3:7–19; 5:11–6:12; 10:19–39; 12:14–29). Likewise, chapter eleven, with its "Hall of Fame of Heroes of the Faith," should be given its due. Neither should one neglect the argument centering on the superiority of Christ or the author's repeated use of the phrase "greater than." Another relevant feature is the distinction between the doctrinal and the paraenetic or ethical sections of the book. The author moves back and forth between doctrine and exhortation. He accomplishes this not, as Paul does in some of his letter, by dividing the letter into two parts, a doctrinal and an ethical one (see, e.g., Ephesians 1–3 and 4–6). Rather, his organization of material and the connection between units is signaled by way of "hook-words," such as the subject of faith that is predominant in several different sections of the book (see also the hook-word "Melchizedek" connecting 5:10 with 7:1). One must also pay close attention to transitional and summarizing elements such as in 8:1, "The point of what we are saying is this" (the dream of every exegete and listener to a sermon!), which serves the purpose of summarizing what has been said thus far and of transitioning to the next unit.

George Guthrie has been one of the first to take into consideration all these aspects and has followed a text-linguistic approach in delineating the structure of Hebrews.[74] Space does not permit us to reproduce a detailed outline of the book. The macrostructure of the Epistle to the Hebrews presents itself as follows:

Introduction: God Has Spoken to Us in a Son (1:1–4)

I. The Son Is Superior (1:5–4:13)

---

73. Steve Stanley, "The Structure of Hebrews from Three Perspectives (Genre, Rhetoric, Content)," *Tyn Bul* 45 (1994): 245–71.
74. See George H. Guthrie, *Hebrews*, NIVAC (Grand Rapids: Zondervan, 1998), 39.

Atypical Features: The Lack of a Formal Epistolary Introduction

We have already seen the oral nature of the letter to the Hebrews. We have also mentioned the fact that Hebrews is also a written document. But is it a letter just like the other letters of the New Testament? There are pieces of evidence that point in both directions. The conclusion includes the conventional greeting or health wish (13:24) and a final "grace" benediction (13:25). Moreover, the letter is found among the Pauline corpus in the earliest manuscripts (e.g., in $\mathfrak{P}^{46}$ between Romans and 1 Corinthians) and has the typical superscript for a letter "To the Hebrews" like all the other New Testament letters. Thus its association with the epistolary genre seems to support the notion that the writing was considered an epistle.

Yet while the composition has an epistolary conclusion, it has no opening salutation. The writer identifies neither himself nor the addressees. He offers no prayer for grace and peace and no expression of thanksgiving or blessing. He starts directly with the proposition to be proven. In other words, the book starts more like a sermon. Nevertheless, despite the distinctively oral character of the composition, we are led to conclude that the composition, in its present form, is a letter. It has always been known as a letter and has come down to us in the form of a letter. The lack of the formal epistolary introduction may be due to the fact that the author did not consider it fitting for the high Christological message expressed in the first four verses.

James
Jewish-Christian Nature of James

Doubtless James is a Jewish writing in the sense that it has its roots in Judaism and the Old Testament. For instance, James chooses Old Testament examples of faith such as Abraham (2:23), Rahab (2:25), Job (Job 5:11), and Elijah (5:17–18) rather than Jesus as Peter does in his first letter (1 Pet. 2:21). Second, James demonstrates familiarity with some of the concepts of first-century Judaism such as *gehenna* (3:6). He is aware of rabbinic theological and psychological anthropology such as the belief in the *yesarim*, the two impulses within each one of us (1:14). In his advice for believers to be concerned for widows and orphans (1:27), he shows familiarity with the prophetic notion of justice.[75] No wonder that in the nineteenth century it was suggested that James originated as a Jewish writing and was later Christianized by the double interpolation of "Jesus Christ" (1:1; 2:1).[76] Despite the fact that the interpolation theory does not find any manuscript support, the issue of the non-Christian writing of James still remains in light of the fact that James makes no mention of the important events in the earthly life of Jesus such as his miracles, death, and resurrection. Therefore Johnson rightly states that, "If 'Christian' means 'Christocentric,' James fails the test."[77]

Despite its lack of direct references to and mention of Jesus, James does use Jesus as a source for his teaching, as we will see later. But evidence for the letter's Christian nature can be gathered also from noting the topical parallelism between James and the other writings of the New Testament. Luke Timothy Johnson observes, "[James] uses a language that finds its home only within a developing Christina *argot*. By this I mean terms and expressions that may be attested occasionally in the LXX or in the other Jewish literature, but never with the frequency or intensity or in the same complex combinations as can be found with the New Testament writings themselves."[78]

We will give several examples, beginning with the lexical evidence. One of the surest signs of James' essentially Christian character, according to Dibelius, is the absolute use of the word *onoma* ("name") in 2:7.[79] Although its use is attested in the LXX (e.g., Exod. 20:7, 24), it is a specifically Christian designation used in reference to the power of the resurrected Jesus (e.g., Acts 5:40, 41; 9:14–15, 21). Likewise, the self-designation of James as *doulos* ("servant") parallels not only the use in the LXX by leaders such as Joshua (Josh. 24:30) and David (Ps. 88:4) but

---

75. For such examples and others see David Nystrom, *James*, NIVAC (Grand Rapids: Zondervan, 1997), 16–17.
76. See Luke Timothy Johnson, *The Letter of James: A New Translation with Introduction and Commentary*, AB 37A (Random House, 1995), 48, with reference to L. Massebieau and F. Spitta. The argument below essentially follows Johnson.
77. Ibid., 49.
78. See ibid. For a thorough listing of parallels see ibid., 48–58.
79. Martin Dibelius, *James*, Hermeneia (Augsburg: Fortress, 1976), 23.

the term is used extensively by Christian leaders such as Paul (e.g., Rom. 1:1–2) and Peter (2 Pet. 1:1). Though James does not mention "hope," he does discuss at length the other two Christian virtues: faith (2:14–26) and love (2:8; cf. 1 Thess. 1:2–3; 1 Cor. 13:13; 1 Pet. 1:3–9). Another distinctively Christian feature of James is his use of eschatological language. He talks about "the Lord's coming" in 5:7–8, a phrase never found in the LXX but a common phraseology for the return of Jesus (e.g., Matt. 24:3, 27, 37, 39; 1 Cor. 15:23; 1 John 2:28).

Apart from the lexical evidence, and more importantly the combination of terms that identifies the letter as having a distinctly Christian character within the Jewish literature of the first century, there is also thematic parallelism with other New Testament writings. For instance, both James 4:8–10 and 1 Peter 5:5–6 talk about "submission" and "lowliness of attitude" and cite Proverbs 3:34 (LXX), though the target of their instruction is different. Therefore we conclude that James is just as Christian a writing as the other New Testament documents (though its Jewish Christian nature is unmistakable).

Jesus as a Source

The Christian nature of the letter of James can best be seen in James' dependence on Jesus' words. A remarkable feature of the epistle of James is that he borrows extensively from the teachings of Jesus, especially as expounded on in the Gospel of Matthew (e.g., the Beatitudes). In fact, James' dependence on Jesus is not matched by any other New Testament author. This is remarkable in light of the fact that James does not quote Jesus (except in 5:12; cf. Matt. 5:33–37) and, even more strikingly, uses the name of Jesus only twice (1:1; 2:1).

Despite James' lack of reference to Jesus' deeds, he does show interest in Jesus' words. For James, then, "'the faith of Jesus' means living before God in a manner shaped by the words of Jesus, and above all by his declaration that loving the neighbor as oneself is the royal law."[80] Thus, his method is to "weave Jesus' teaching into the very fabric of his own instruction."[81]

---

80. Luke Timothy Johnson, *The Letter of James*, NIBC 12 (Nashville: Abingdon, 1998), 180.
81. Douglas J. Moo, *The Letter of James*, PNTC (Grand Rapids: Eerdmans, 200), 7. For a thorough comparison of James and Jesus see Johnson, *Letter of James*, 48ff.

The parallelism between James and Jesus can be seen both at the linguistic and the thematic level. The topics he discusses in his letter as well as the approach, interpretation, and emphasis he gives to them resonate with Jesus' teachings and emphasis. It appears that James was so immersed in the teachings of Jesus that he subconsciously replicated them in his letter.

Here is a sample of the striking linguistic parallels between James and Jesus:[82]

- believers are to rejoice in trials (1:2; cf. Matt. 5:12);

- believers are called to be perfect/complete (1:4; cf. Matt. 5:48);

- believers are encouraged to ask God, for God loves to give (1:5; cf. Matt. 7:7);

- believers should expect testing and be prepared to endure it, after which they will receive a reward (1:12; cf. Matt. 24:13);

- believers are not to be angry (1:20; cf. Matt. 5:22);

- actions are the proof of true faith (2:14; cf. Matt. 7:16–19);

- the poor are blessed (2:5; cf. Luke 6:20);

- the rich are warned (2:6–7; cf. Matt. 19:23–24);

- believers are not to slander (4:11; cf. Matt. 5:22);

- believers are not to judge (4:12; cf. Matt. 7:1);

- the humble are praised (3:13; cf. Matt. 5:3).

---

82. Cf. Nystrom, *James*, 17–18. For a complete listing of the possibilities see D. B. Deppe, *The Sayings of Jesus in the Epistle of James* (Chelsea, MI: Brookcrafters, 1989); see also P. J. Hartin, *James and the Sayings of Jesus*, JSNT 47 (Sheffield: JSOT, 1991). See also Johnson, *James*, 55–57.

At the thematic level, the similarities are particularly seen in the shared theology of prayer with Matthew.[83] There is thus no doubt that Jesus was a significant source for James and his teaching, both lexically and thematically.[84]

Jude and Petrine Epistles
Relationship between Jude and 2 Peter

A cursory reading of Jude and 2 Peter will bring to light the close resemblance between the two. In light of the many similarities in terminology between the two letters, scholars have wondered whether there is any kind of literary relationship between the two or if each author independently used a common source. In fact, a comparison between Jude 4–19 and 2 Peter 2:1–3:3 yields a considerable number of parallels.[85]

The following four hypotheses have been posited:[86] (1) Peter used Jude; (2) Jude used Peter; (3) both independently used a common source; and (4) common authorship. Until the nineteenth century, the predominant view was that Jude used 2 Peter as a source,[87] but more recently a consensus has emerged that 2 Peter used Jude.[88] The third view is also possible in view of the lack of precise verbal links between the two, although literary dependence is preferred as a simpler hypothesis.[89]

---

83. For details see R. Cooper, "Prayer: A Study in Matthew and James," *Encounter* 29 (1968): 268–77.

84. For other important hermeneutical challenges in interpreting James, including the identification of its genre and the difficulty of outlining James, see chapter 17 in Köstenberger, Kellum, and Quarles, *Cradle, the Cross, and the Crown.*

85. For a detailed study of these parallels see Köstenberger, Kellum, and Quarles, *Cradle, the Cross, and the Crown*, chapter 18.

86. For details see Richard J. Bauckham, *Jude, 2 Peter*, WBC 50 (Dallas: Word, 1983), 141.

87. Martin Luther, "Sermons on the Epistle of St. Jude," in *The Catholic Epistles*, ed. J. Pelikan and W. A. Hansen, *LW* 30 (St. Louis: Concordia, 1967 [1523]), 203. See also more recently Douglas J. Moo, *2 Peter, Jude*, NIVAC (Grand Rapids: Zondervan, 1996), 18.

88. So already Adolf Schlatter, *The Theology of the Apostles*, trans. Andreas J. Köstenberger (Grand Rapids: Baker, 1999), 103, n. 54, and the majority of contemporary commentators. Douglas J. Rowston, "The Most Neglected Book in the New Testament," *NTS* 21 (1975): 563, rightly states: "It is much easier to assume that Jude is the original."

89. See Bo Reicke, *The Epistles of James, Peter and Jude*, AB 37 (Garden City, NY: Doubleday, 1964), 189–90; and Michael Green, *2 Peter and Jude*, TNTC, rev. ed. (Leicester/Grand Rapids: InterVarsity, 1987), 58–64. See also R. L. Webb, "2 Peter," in *Dictionary of the Later New Testament and Its Developments*, 611–21, though he

The more likely view is that Jude was written prior to 2 Peter and served as a source. This can be illustrated by the way in which these writings use Jewish apocryphal literature. Jude includes three such quotations or allusions: (1) to *The Assumption of Moses* in verse 9; (2) to *1 Enoch* in verses 14–15; and (3) to an otherwise unattested saying of the apostles in verse 18. All three quotations are lacking in 2 Peter. It seems more likely that Peter avoided reference to these apocryphal works than that Jude added these references on the assumption of Petrine priority.[90]

In addition to these remarkable verbal similarities, the two texts display a rather striking similarity in terms of the sequential development of the argument. In particular, Jude and Peter concur in their basic structure: angels—Sodom and Gomorrah—[archangel Michael]—Balaam. Beyond this, Peter (on the assumption that Jude served as his source) replaced his two negative examples, Cain and Korah, with two positive figures, Noah and Lot. While the similarity in structure could also be accounted for on the basis of a common source, it seems more probable that Peter used Jude directly and adapted his epistle to his own situation. If so, it is particularly conspicuous that Peter reworked Jude's letter in such a way that the sequence of his examples is in proper Old Testament chronological order while Jude uses a topical arrangement.

Despite the similarities between the two works and their interdependence, we should not assume that they are similar in purpose. Just like the chronicler used the material in 1 and 2 Kings and yet pursued a different purpose and the Gospel writers most likely used Mark but had different audiences and purposes, so Peter's use of Jude must not be interpreted as indicating lack of distinctiveness. Both writings must be studied for what each contributes to the teaching and theology of the Bible.

Alleged Pseudonymity of 2 Peter

The Petrine authorship of 2 Peter has been contested by many recent

---

acknowledges that recent works in redaction and rhetorical criticism have strengthened the position that Jude served as a source for 2 Peter. The fourth view, according to Bauckham, *2 Peter*, 141, is implausible because of differences in style and background.

90. Perhaps in order to compensate, Peter supplements Jude's Epistle with the biblical examples of Noah (2 Pet. 2:5) and Lot (2 Pet. 2:7–9) and provides a more thorough presentation of Balaam (2 Pet. 2:15–16).

commentators.[91] There are several alleged pieces of evidence against authorship by Peter. First, some argue that the language used is un-Petrine, displaying a preference for Hellenistic terminology and featuring many unusual terms. Given its elaborate Greek style, detractors argue, a Galilean fisherman could not have written in this style. A comparison between the language of 1 and 2 Peter also is alleged to reveal a difference in language, with the author of 2 Peter using many unusual words. Even if the author mentions the first letter (2 Pet. 3:1), this is no proof, it is argued, that the same author wrote both, since the author of 2 Peter otherwise shows disregard for 1 Peter. That Peter was not the author is supposed to be strengthened by the fact that there is a lack of specifically Petrine material, indicating that the pseudonymous author was confident in his own writing ability.

The linguistic argument, however, is an argument from silence; we cannot know what Peter could or could not have written. Also, it is hard to see how a pseudepigraphical author could have written the Transfiguration episode mentioned in 2 Peter 1:16–18 with any credibility. Moreover, the use of a secretary or amanuensis could account for the difference in style between the two Petrine writings. We have argued earlier in this chapter that a secretary could have used his own words to express Peter's thoughts. We do not know how much freedom Peter allowed his secretaries. Finally, the difference in style could be explained in part by the fact that the two Petrine letters addressed different situations and therefore required emphases and terminology.

But the evidence that apparently rules out composition during Peter's lifetime is that of literary genre and date. According to Richard Bauckham, "either of these might be fatal for any degree of Petrine authorship. Together they must be regarded as entirely conclusive against Petrine authorship."[92] It is claimed that the unknown author desired to write an apostolic "testament" and that "Peter" was the natural pseudonym in a letter from the church at Rome, since Peter exercised a leadership role

---

91. See Bauckham, *2 Peter*, 159–62. Even Schlatter, *Theology of the Apostles*, 356, who defended the authenticity of every epistle of the New Testament, had doubts about 2 Peter. Among the recent defenders of the Petrine authorship of 2 Peter are Michael J. Kruger, "The Authenticity of 2 Peter," *JETS* 42 (1999): 645–71 and Moo, *2 Peter, Jude*, 21–26. For an excellent survey and evaluation of arguments see Schreiner, *2 Peter*, 255–85.

92. Bauckham, *2 Peter*, 159.

there. It is claimed that someone wrote this testament in Peter's name because the crisis caused by the false teachers required an authoritative word
of an apostle. But this is not as strong an argument as some assume. The
presence of testimonial elements in the letter does not necessarily make it
a testament, at least not a testament like others.[93] Moreover, a testament
does not have to be pseudonymous. Peter could have written it at the end
of his life. But the most devastating argument against the testament genre
is the fact that there is no evidence that the early church accepted 2 Peter
while recognizing its pseudepigraphical character as a "transparent fiction" of Peter's testament.[94]

Two more arguments are strongly against the pseudonymity of 2
Peter. First, in spite of the doubts that many early writings express concerning the authenticity of 2 Peter, the ones that accept Petrine authorship outweigh those that do not. For instance, Origen (third century
A.D.) acknowledges that 2 Peter was a disputed letter but believes that
Peter wrote it.[95] Although Eusebius (*Eccl. Hist.* 6.25.11) rejects authenticity, he notes that the majority accepted it. The fact is, 2 Peter ended up
being included in the canon while other works falsely attributed to Peter
were rejected. Second, as mentioned in the section on pseudonymity and
allonymity, claiming authorship for a letter written by someone else is
a deceitful practice and does not comport with the character and message of the biblical writings.[96] Therefore, in spite of arguments against
the Petrine authorship of 2 Peter, there are weightier reasons for Petrine
authorship.

Johannine Epistles
Oral Nature of 1 John

We will discuss shortly the question of the genre of 1 John and the
fact that the letter lacks a formal epistolary introduction and conclusion.
This has led some to suggest that 1 John is a general treatise, perhaps a
pamphlet, a brochure, or an encyclical. Other commentators classify the

---

93. J. H. Neyrey, *2 Peter, Jude*, AB (Garden City: Doubleday, 1993), 112, rightly notes that
letters containing testaments are rare.
94. Cf. Schreiner, *2 Peter*, 274.
95. Cf. Kruger, "Authenticity of 2 Peter," 649–50.
96. See Calvin, *Catholic Epistles*, 363: "It would have been a fiction unworthy of a min-
ister of Christ, to have personated another individual."

document as a homily, given its strong hortatory style.[97] The designation of "homily" points to the suggestion that the letter has an oral character. Evidence for this is the author's reference to traditional material. The author frequently appeals to what his audience has known "from the beginning" (1 John 2:13, 24; etc.). Like Hebrews, 1 John also functions as a word of exhortation (1 John 2:7–11), though the phrase itself does not appear in the letter. Raymond Brown, however, is correct when he states that, "Even if there is some truth in this suggestion and even if some of the material in 1 John was once orally proclaimed, the author's stress on *writing* throughout 1 John makes the ordinary meaning of 'homily' somewhat inappropriate."[98] There are clear indicators within the book that it is a written document. Most importantly, the author states 13 times that he is *writing*. Thus we are dealing with a literary document. All these factors, however, "do not preclude its having been experienced orally or aurally by its first readers," since letters were read aloud.[99]

Literary Structure of 1 John

There is a lack of consensus on the literary structure of 1 John. The proposals fall into three categories: a division into (1) two; (2) three; or (3) multiple parts.[100] Those who advocate a twofold division argue that this is required for two reasons. First, the two declarations that John makes in the Gospel (i.e., "God is light," 1 John 1:5; and "God is love," 1 John 4:6) are keys to the structure of his epistle. Second, the similarities between John's Gospel and 1 John allegedly point to the Gospel as the structural model for the Epistle.[101] Those who hold to a multiple-part structure do so on the

---

97. C. H. Dodd, *The Johannine Epistles*, MNTC (London: Hodder & Stoughton, 1946), xxi, considers 1 John as "an informal track or homily"; and I. H. Marshall, *The Epistles of John*, NICNT (Grand Rapids: Eerdmans, 1978), 14 refers to it as "a written sermon or pastoral address." See the different suggestions for genre in Colin G. Kruse, *The Letters of John*, PNTC (Grand Rapids: Eerdmans, 2000), 28.

98. Raymond Brown, *The Epistles of John*: Translated with Introduction, Notes, and Commentary, AB 30 (Garden City, NY: Doubleday, 1982), 90.

99. C. Clifton Black, *The First, Second, and Third Letters of John*, New Interpreter's Bible 12 (Nashville: Abingdon, 1999), 370.

100. For a chart with all the proposals see L. Scott Kellum, "On the Semantic Structure of 1 John: A Modest Proposal," *Faith & Mission* 23/1 (Fall 2005): 36–38. Kellum also proposes a fourth category he calls "interrelated paragraphs."

101. See Brown, *Epistles of John*, 122–29; Stephen S. Smalley, *1, 2, 3 John*, WBC 51 (Dallas: Word, 1984), xxxii; and Gary M. Burge, *The Letters of John*, NIVAC (Grand Rapids: Zondervan, 1996), 43.

basis of the argument that there is no developing argument throughout the letter and no logical plan that the author is following.[102] Most scholars, however, divide the letter into three parts, a structure that we will follow here, based on grammatical and semantic indicators. Such a structure takes into consideration both the form and the content.

> Prologue: The Word of Life Witnessed (1:1–4)
> I.   The Departure of the False Teachers (1:5–2:27)
> II. The Proper Conduct of God's Children (2:28–3:24)
> III. The Proper Beliefs of God's Children (4:1–5:12)
>   Epilogue: The Confidence of Those Who Walk in God's Light and Love (5:13–21)

Atypical Feature: The Lack of a Formal Epistolary Introduction in 1 John

While we can say that 2 and 3 John fit the criteria for ancient letters, 1 John is an altogether different matter. Second and 3 John contain the conventional introduction and conclusion. Both are addressed specifically to a local church or a network of house churches (i.e., "the chosen lady and her children"; cf. 2 John 1) and to an individual (i.e. "Gaius"; cf. 3 John 1). The mention of the author ("the elder") and the addressees is followed by a greeting or a prayer for their well-being. Both letters also contain in their closing sections elements seen in the Pauline letters, such as an expression of the wish to visit soon and to communicate in person ("face to face") and a greeting. In this sense, these two letters resemble closely the personal type of ancient letters, especially given their reduced length. They fit easily on a single sheet. And they also clearly indicate that these letters are (inadequate but for the time being necessary) substitutes for the author's physical presence. In this sense, 2 and 3 John are probably closer to the ancient personal/private letter form than any of Paul's epistles, with the possible exception of Philemon.[103]

First John, however, is different. It lacks the opening address and greeting and the closing greeting. Among the New Testament writings,

---

102. See Kruse, *Letters of John*, 32; and Marshall, *Epistles of John*, 26.
103. For details see John Painter, *1, 2, and 3 John*, SacPag 18 (Collegeville, MN: Liturgical Press, 2002), 37–39, though he seems to maintain a sharp distinction between (private) letters and (official) epistles, as we have seen with Deissmann. For a discussion of 2 and 3 John in light of epistolary format see Brown, *Epistles of John*, 788–95.

the letter to the Hebrews comes closest to the form of 1 John, since it lacks the formal introduction. And just as we mentioned in our discussion of Hebrews, so here the genre of 1 John has been a matter of debate. Its resemblance to Hebrews could very well point to the fact that 1 John initially was a sermon that was then written down and sent to a specific community of believers, though we have seen the weaknesses of such a hypothesis. It also resembles the Epistle of James in that it does not contain a formal closing. But no other letter in the New Testament omits both the epistolary introduction and closing as 1 John does.

At least two things, however, are clear. First, despite the lack of formal epistolary introduction and conclusion, 1 John addresses a specific situation. We find a reference to schism in the community (1 John 2:19) as well as to the doctrinal and ethical reasons for such a schism (e.g., christological matters and lack of love, respectively). The lack of a conventional epistolary framework could be owing to the fact that the letter was meant for a network of churches. Second, the question of genre becomes somewhat secondary when we speak of the three Johannine writings jointly. The convention is to speak of the three together and designate them by the title "Johannine Epistles." This is the title that appears in the most important Greek manuscript such as the fourth-century Codices Vaticanus and Sinaiticus and the fifth-century Codex Alexandrinus, and that is listed in the Muratorian canon.[104]

First John is thus a letter, though an unusual one, in light of the fact that it does not follow epistolary conventions in several respects. More specifically, as mentioned, 1 John does not include the typical epistolary framework.

GENERAL HERMENEUTICAL ISSUES

Occasionality and Normativity

One of the basic characteristic of letters is that they are occasional or situational. This means that they were written to address situations and offer solutions to problems related to the author or (most often) to the

---

104. See the detailed presentation of the evidence in the early church and manuscripts in Brown, *Epistles of John*, 4–13.

readers(s). The ethical instructions that are offered in the New Testament letters in response to some of the problems that were faced by the audiences are thus situation-specific.

We can illustrate this by reference to 1 Corinthians, one of the most occasional letters in the New Testament. We have already noted that Paul organizes his material according to topics, which are answers to questions raised by the Corinthians in a letter (chaps. 7–16) and responses Paul gives to some of the problems in the Corinthian congregation he heard about from a report (chaps. 1–6). Among the topics he discusses in this letter is that of meat associated with idols in chapters 8–10, a topic introduced by the phrase "now concerning." It is obvious that in the idolatrous culture of Paul's day, when temples dedicated to pagan deities abounded and immorality was associated with sacrifices, people who turned from their pagan worship to the true God were wondering whether practices in which they had engaged while in their state of unbelief were compatible with their new life in Christ or not. One such issue was the meat associated with idol worship. There was a lack of consensus among the Corinthian Christians as to whether they should continue to consume such meat, the result being that some were being a stumbling block to others by the way in which they related to this issue. So Paul had to offer a solution to the specific issue. Examples such as this indicate what makes 1 Corinthians and the other New Testament letters situation-specific.

Faced with such specific situations that are time- and culture-bound, the interpreter has the responsibility to *reconstruct as precisely as he can the original situation* that gave rise to the problem which Paul addressed by looking into the social, historical, and cultural contexts of Corinthian Christianity. Without such information we will be in danger of misunderstanding what was at issue in the Corinthian church. But once we understand the original situation, the task of interpretation has just begun, for we are now faced with the question of its applicability and normativity for us. The question is whether a situational issue like the meat associated with idols has anything to teach Christians today who are not faced with debates surrounding pagan temple worship. Does 1 Corinthians 10–12 contain any binding principles for us today? Are Paul's instructions on meat associated idols normative for us?

Put in more general terms, how do we distinguish between what is purely occasional and what is normative? Why, for instance, should the prohibition of stealing be normative for us today (e.g., Eph. 4:28) and wearing something on one's head be non-binding for women (1 Cor. 11:2–16)? The issue is further complicated in cases where part of the original context cannot be easily reconstructed. For instance, who are the original readers of Hebrews and what were the reasons that prompted the author to write his letter? What was the heresy confronting the audience of 1 John? The difficulty of reconstructing the original situation thus complicates the question of normativity.

Another corollary to the issue of a situation-specific letter is that of *constructing a biblical and systematic theology for today*. Since the letters are occasional, they were not meant to be exhaustive dictionaries of Christian doctrine. So even if we can extract normative principles for us today from a particular letter, we should beware of not thinking that what a letter teaches on a certain topic is all we need to know about that topic. In other words, we should not conclude too much from one letter. For instance, if we only had James, we might be led into thinking that works justify the one who believes. But Romans gives us the other side of the issue with its emphasis on justification by faith. For this reason, if we want to have a more complete and balanced view of a given issue, we must read all the letters—in fact, the entire New Testament and all of Scripture—that address situations that deal with similar or related problems.

Another aspect of which the interpreter must be aware when trying to determine the normative principle embedded in a text is the *distinction between primary and secondary issues* in a text. Most of the time, normativity is connected with the main topic discussed in the text rather than with secondary issues. In other words, the interpreter must be careful not to extract a principle or build a theology from a context in which the issue is not addressed as the primary topic. In building a theology, we must go to those passages that clearly touch on the issue and avoid drawing principles from obscure passages.[105] This constitutes a general hermeneutical principle of avoiding teaching the right doctrine from the wrong text.

---

105. For examples of this see Andreas J. Köstenberger and David A. Croteau, "'Will a Man Rob God?' (Malachi 3:8): A Study of Tithing in the Old and New Testaments," *BBR* 16 (2006): 53–77; and "Reconstructing a Biblical Model for Giving: A Discussion of Relevant Systematic Issues and New Testament Principles," *BBR* 16 (2006): 237–60 and the cautions registered with regard to interpreting the references to tithing in Malachi, Matthew, or Hebrews.

For now, it will suffice to state that the letters of the New Testament are occasional and that they address specific situations. At the same time, there is clear evidence that the authors believed that what they were communicating was normative at least for the original readers. What is more, in light of the fact that their instructions are always based on theological convictions, it is inevitable to conclude that the teachings offered to the churches facing certain circumstances are *applicable to any church or individual facing similar situations* throughout the ages. But what about teachings that are responding to circumstances that we might never face, such as meat associated with idols? Are there any normative principles to be drawn from such teachings? Our belief in the divine inspiration and authority of Scripture compels us to give an affirmative answer. Even in passages where the author deals with issues that are specific to a place, time, and culture, he offers general abiding principles.

For instance, in Paul's response to the issue raised by the Corinthians concerning meat sacrificed to idols, he discusses the issue of the believer's freedom and rights. Thus, in chapter 9, in what seems like a parenthesis, he offers the solution to the dispute by way of personal example: the giving up of his rights for the sake of winning others to Christ. While we may never be faced with the question of whether or not we can eat from meat associated with idols (though missionaries in some cultures will be), we are certainly faced all the time with the issue of how we may win our neighbor for Christ and not be a stumbling block to him.

In conclusion, the New Testament letters are *both occasional and normative* at the same time. The way we determine the normativity of a passage is by looking closely at the occasion of the writing and its social, cultural, and, historical contexts and then trying to find the general principles that are transferable to us today. In so doing, we must ask ourselves questions such as: Is the topic from which we are drawing the principle the main one in the text? Is it clearly taught? What other passage(s) must we study to corroborate the teaching in order to get as complete a picture as possible concerning the entire biblical counsel on the topic? When answering such questions, we should guard ourselves from drawing out principles that are not in the text or not corroborated by the rest of Scripture.

Other Issues in Interpreting Epistles

There are many other relevant issues in interpreting the New Testament epistolary literature. Having outlined the most pertinent issue, namely that of the occasional and normative nature of New Testament epistles, it will suffice to summarize briefly what Duvall and Hays call the "interpretative journey" in their book *Grasping God's Word* and what Klein, Blomberg, and Hubbard in their work *Introduction to Biblical Interpretation* call "the four-step methodology for legitimate application."[106] Essentially, the interpretive task, when reading the New Testament epistles as well as other biblical books, includes the following four elements:

1. *Original Application:* What did the text mean to the original audience? In order to discover the meaning and application to the original audience one must get as much information on the cultural, social, and historical background as possible. Another important element in determining the meaning for the original audience is looking at the literary context. Context is determinative for meaning, and without an understanding of the picture of the whole we will be in danger of misinterpreting the parts. We must make sure that we do not impose onto a passage a meaning that is not dictated by the context. For this, we must look at the grammatical and semantic connections and constructions.

2. *Specificity of Original Application:* What are the differences and similarities between the biblical audience and us? As already mentioned, if the situation faced by the original audience and our own circumstances are similar, the principles are transferable without modification or generalization. But in many cases, where letters are written to answer specific situations most churches today do not face (e.g., meat associated with idols), we must identify the differences between our situation and that of the original audience.

3. *Broad Principles:* What is the theological principle in the text? Once we determined the meaning of the passage for the

---

106. J. Scott Duvall and J. Daniel Hays, *Grasping God's Word*, 2d ed. (Grand Rapids: Zondervan, 2005), 19–27; Klein, Blomberg, and Hubbard, *Introduction to Biblical Interpretation*, 482–503.

original audience and noted the similarities between our situation and that of the original audience, it is time to draw out general principles. These must be reflected in the text studied but at the same time not bound to the text and its situation. Thus they must be specific enough to apply to the situation in the text but general enough not to be bound to its time and culture. In this sense, these principles must correspond to the teaching of the rest of Scripture.

4. *Contemporary Application:* How should we apply the principles in our lives today? The application can take different forms, depending on the specific situation faced by the contemporary audience. Thus, with E. D. Hirsch, we contend that we must differentiate between meaning and significance. While the text has one meaning (i.e., the original meaning), this meaning can be applied in different ways depending on the situation. In order to apply correctly the general principles discovered in the text, however, we must be careful to apply them to contemporary situations that are equivalent to the original situation.

SAMPLE EXEGESIS: ROMANS 7:14–25

Introduction

Romans 7:13–25 truly has been a *crux interpretum* (a hard-to-interpret-passage) for biblical interpreters. Typically, it has been assumed that the switch to the first person singular in verse 13 indicates that Paul is speaking here of his own experience by way of personal testimony. This seems undeniable in the climactic verse of the unit, verse 24, when Paul exclaims, "What a wretched man I am! Who will rescue me from this body of death?" For this reason most of the discussion surrounding this section has revolved around the question—assuming the autobiographical nature of the passage—whether Paul is here describing the period prior to his conversion (pre-conversion) or subsequent to his conversion (post-conversion).

Unfortunately, however, neither scenario coheres very well with what Paul says in his other letters about his pre-Christian past and about his life subsequent to his radical conversion on the road to Damascus. Before

Paul's encounter with the risen Christ which is narrated in Acts 9, there is not a shred of evidence for the struggle Paul describes in Romans 7:13–25 of desperately trying to do what is good while finding himself to be bound by his sinful nature. To the contrary, Paul is presented as utterly confident of the righteousness of his cause of persecuting the Christians. So what about his experience after his conversion? Again, we see nothing in Paul's letters that suggests the kind of struggle described in 7:13–25. Paul immediately turned to Christ, preached the gospel, and had to be removed by some fellow believers in order to save Paul's life. Later, Paul shows great courage and persistence in preaching the gospel far and wide. In his letters, he writes about believers being seated in the heavenly realms in Christ (Col. 3:1) and of living a new life in the Spirit (e.g., Romans 8). Notice also that not once is the Holy Spirit mentioned in 7:13–25. If this passage is describing the life of a believer, this is a curious omission, especially since Paul says in the following chapter that if anyone does not have the Spirit, he is not even a Christian! How, then, can he be said here to describe Paul's experience after his Christian conversion? This is hard to fathom.

History

Historically, Paul wrote his letter to the Romans toward the end of his second missionary journey, most likely from Corinth, in the mid-50s A.D.. While earlier in his ministry he had defended the gospel against opponents who argued that Gentile converts must continue to obey the Jewish law (the Judaizers), this issue was settled at the Jerusalem Council Acts 15). More recently, Paul's attention was devoted to planting churches that underscored the oneness of both Jews and Gentiles in the church. As a symbol of this unity, Paul had collected an offering collected by Gentile churches to assist the church in Jerusalem. When Paul wrote Romans, he hoped to be on his way to Spain (15:28), though in fact he was arrested when delivering the collection to the church in Jerusalem and ended up in Rome, not as a free man, but under Roman custody.

Literature

What is the purpose of Paul's letter to the Romans? A careful, repeated reading of the epistle suggests that Paul's purpose hinges primarily on a pastoral concern that drives him to address the Roman congregation: that of Jewish-Gentile unity. It is this concern that leads him to show that the gospel "is the power of God that brings salvation to everyone who believes: first to the Jew, then to the Gentile" (1:16). Why? "For in the gospel the righteousness of God is revealed—a righteousness that is from faith[fulness] to faith, just as it is written [in the book of Habakkuk]: 'The righteous will live by faith'" (1:17; our translation).

It is this concern that also leads Paul to emphasize that both Jews and Gentiles—that is, all people—are sinners (1:18–3:20) and that justification is only by faith in the finished work of Christ (3:21–5:21). Importantly, this justification by faith alone is a gracious provision by God and is effected "apart from law" (3:21), as Paul states provocatively, in a move that was sure to raise the eyebrows of law-observing Jews. Apart from law? This was not the way in which the Jews had learned to live lives pleasing to God in the period subsequent to the giving of the Law at Sinai through Moses. We will return to this point, which is addressed in chapters 6–8, in which our passage is found, shortly below. It is also Paul's pastoral concern for Jewish-Gentile unity that leads him to write his treatment in chapters 9–11, desiring to level the playing field once again between Jews and Gentiles.

According to Paul, God's plan encompasses both, and neither group must feel superior to the other. In fact, Paul spent much of the years surrounding the writing of the letter to the Romans collecting an offering among the Gentile churches for the Jewish famine-stricken mother church in Jerusalem. Upon delivering the gift, he was promptly arrested and spent the next few years in Roman custody. Yet for Paul, Jewish-Gentile unity was of more than symbolic value—as he elaborates in Ephesians 2:11–22, it was "Exhibit 1" in his preaching of the gospel. In Christ, the dividing wall between Jews and Gentiles had been torn down, and both groups were now part of the new people of God. Perhaps most memorable are Paul's words in Galatians 3:26–28: "You are *all* sons of God through faith in Christ Jesus . . . . There is neither Jew nor Greek, . . ., for *you are all one in Christ Jesus.*" Hence rather than serving as an excursus or digression from Paul's major purpose for writing Romans as is sometimes thought, chapters 9–11 serve as the climax of Paul's entire letter, just as Paul's demonstration that "all have sinned" in 1:18–3:20 (see 3:23) should be understood within the framework of Jewish-Gentile unity: because both Jews (yes, even Jews) and Gentiles are sinners and in need of salvation through Christ, there is no room for boasting: salvation does not come through observing the law but through faith alone. This proved to be a truth that was hard to accept for many Jews: "Since they did not know the righteousness that comes from God and sought to establish their own, they did not submit to God's righteousness" (10:3).

This, third, was yet another aspect of Paul's pastoral concern for Jewish-Gentile unity: the demonstration that all of God's purposes were faithful, righteous, and true. As Paul writes in 9:6, "It is not as though God's Word had failed." Some alleged that Israel's failure to believe in the Messiah (Jesus) meant that God had not kept his promises to his covenant people Israel. But Paul, like David driven by a passion to vindicate God's honor, shows that God, in his wisdom, is sovereign even over Israel's unbelief and that he will yet keep his promises to Israel so that in the end, "all Israel will be saved" (11:26). The Reformers had it half-right when they focused on Romans' message on the justification of man by faith. But, rightly understood, Paul's ultimate focus is not the justification of *man*, but the justification of *God*. "Let God be true, and every man a liar" (3:4).

Now that we have established the overall framework for interpreting 7:13–25—Paul's concern for Jewish-Gentile unity and his desire to vindicate the righteousness of God and his purposes—a look at the more *immediate context* of our passage is in order. As we have seen, prior to chapters 6–7 we find the preface in 1:16–17; the demonstration that both Jews and Gentiles are sinners in 1:18–3:20; and the presentation of justification by faith in Christ alone in 3:21–5:21. It appears that chapter 8 picks up where 5:21 leaves off, talking about the new life in the Spirit, and then chapters 9–11, as mentioned, demonstrate that God delicately balances his concerns for Jews and Gentiles as he brings salvation history to an end, followed by practical exhortations in chapters 12–16. As a look at chapters 6–7 indicates, these chapters are punctuated by a series of rhetorical questions, all of which focus on the role of the law, and all of which are answered by a resounding "By no means!" What this means is that these are not questions to which Paul does not know the answer, but questions that Paul raises for the purpose of supplying the correct answer. He was anticipating objections, or better yet, taking the opportunity to address real, actual objections or misrepresentations of his gospel message. Here, then, is the series of questions and answers in Paul's "Q & A"—or, to use more technical language, in *diatribe* format—in chapters 6–7:

Question: What shall we say, then? Shall we go on sinning so that grace may increase? (6:1)

Answer: By no means! We died to sin; how can we live in it any longer? (6:2)

Question: What then? Shall we sin because we are not under law but under grace? (6:15)

Answer: By no means! Don't you know that when you offer your-selves to someone to obey him as slaves, you are slaves to the one whom you obey . . . ? (6:16)
(Illustration in 7:1–6.)

Question: What shall we say, then? Is the law sin? (7:7)

Answer: Certainly not! Indeed I would not have known what sin was except through the law (7:7)

Question: Did that which is good, then, become death to me? (7:13)

Answer: By no means! But in order that sin might be recognized as sin, it produced death in me through what was good, so that through the commandment sin might become utterly sinful (7:13)

Theology

In light of the fact that the role of the Law is clearly the sustained main subject in chapters 6–7, we must understand 7:13–25 within the context of Paul's discussion of the role of the Law. Paul's treatment of universal sin and justification by faith apart from the Law in chapters 1–5 should have settled the issue once for all. But before moving on to a treatment of life in the Spirit in chapter 8, Paul takes one more opportunity to address the role of the Law for those who remained yet unconvinced. How could something so good—the Law—which had been given by God himself be set aside? Keeping the Law had become a way of life for many Jews and was clearly commanded by God up until Christ. Why would now, in Christ, a different "law" take effect, as Paul's gospel proclaimed (see 10:4: "Christ is the end of the law")?

As Paul develops in 7:14–25, the reason is, short and simple, our sinful nature, sin that has taken up residence inside of us, a "law" (v. 23: the law of sin) that wages war against the external, righteous requirements stipulated in God's law. In this war, sin always triumphs, which is why Paul at the end of the chapter concedes defeat in man's titanic struggle against sin: sin, you have the victory, and the law, good as it is, is not sufficiently powerful to help man overcome the indwelling sin. So does Paul speak about his own personal experience, then? As mentioned, this seems un-likely. More likely, especially in light of the abundant rhetorical features found in these chapters, is Paul's use of the rhetorical "I," a feature found elsewhere in Paul's writings (see esp. 1 Cor. 13:1–3). Rather than speaking about himself, whether prior or subsequent to his conversion, Paul speaks about a fictional character, a Jew, who tries as hard as he can to keep the law but finds that the sin inside of him is stronger.[107] Trying to keep the law will always lead to death. Life comes only through trusting in what Christ has done for us on the cross. Justification is by faith, apart from the law.

---

107. I hasten to add that the interpretation presented above is just one of several possible understandings of this difficult passage. For alternative views, see the commentary literature on Romans listed in the appendix to this volume.

GUIDELINES FOR INTERPRETING EPISTLES[108]

1. Find out as much as possible about the situation behind the writing of the letter. Corroborate the information found in the text with background information (i.e., historical, social, and cultural setting).

2. Discern the major parts of the letter (introduction, body, and conclusion) and their constitutive elements.

3. Look for the conventional elements that the letter-writer included and left out, especially in the introduction and conclusion. It is in these parts of the letter, especially in the introduction, that we can discern the major problem(s) that occasioned the writing of the letter.

4. Determine the structure and argument of the epistle by paying close attention to grammatical, semantic, and rhetorical elements. Above all, it is important for the structure to correspond as closely as possible to the flow of the argument.

5. Interpret each passage in light of the message of the letter as a whole. In other words, always interpret a passage in light of its larger literary context.

6. Seek to discern what is purely occasional and what normative principles can be drawn out from the specific situation the writer is addressing. The normativity of a teaching is usually imbedded in the theological basis for the writer's ethical teaching.

---

108. See also Osborne, *Hermeneutical Spiral*, 319–22.

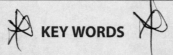

KEY WORDS

Allonymity or allepigraphy: the theory that a later author edited what the original author wrote while attributing the writing to the original author or writing in another person's name without intent to deceive

Amanuensis: scribe or secretary who wrote down the message of the author of an epistle, whether by way of word-by-word dictation or by filling out the sense of a missive

Crux interpretum: a passage that is difficult to interpret

Deliberative speech: exhorts or dissuades the audience regarding future actions by seeking to show the expediency or lack thereof of one's future actions

Diatribe: a technique for anticipating objections to an argument, raising them in the form of questions and then answering them (e.g. Romans 6–7)

Disclosure formula: indication that author wants to inform his readers about a given subject (e.g. "I do not want you to be ignorant")

Epideictic discourse: affirms communal values by praise or blame in order to affect a present evaluation

Exhortatio: refutation of the opponents' arguments

Exordium: introduction defining the character of the speaker and the central issue(s) addressed

Forensic or judicial speech: defends or accuses someone regarding past actions by seeking to prove that one's actions were just or unjust

Gezera shawah: rule of equivalence, that is, the principle of Scripture interpreting Scripture

Haustafel: household code delineating the responsibilities of the various members of the ancient household such as wives and husbands, children and parents, slaves and masters

Midrash: Jewish commentary-style interpretation or exposition of a religious text

Mirror-reading: the (often doubtful) interpretive practice of inferring the circumstances surrounding the writing of a given text from explicit statements made in the text

Narratio: unit presenting the events related to the central issue

Paraenesis: exhortation

Pesher: Jewish verse-by-verse commentary

Peroratio: recapitulation of the basic points aimed at evoking a sympathetic response.

Probatio: confirmation setting forth logical arguments.

Positio: a summary of the central thesis or theses to be proved.

Pseudonymity: a writing in which a later follower attributes his own work to his revered teacher in order to perpetuate that person's teachings and influence.

Qal wahomer: argument from the lesser to the greater (lit. "light and heavy").

Quod erat demonstrandum: Latin for "that which needed to be demonstrated."

Targum: the Aramaic paraphrase of the Hebrew Bible used in the synagogue liturgy.

STUDY QUESTIONS

1. What are the three major divisions of an epistle and important components of each?

2. What are the main arguments for and against pseudonymity and allonymity?

3. How do you define and evaluate rhetorical criticism?

4. What are the major contours of a chronology of Paul's life and ministry?

5. How does Paul use the Old Testament?

6. Was Paul the follower of Jesus or the founder of Christianity? Support your answer.

7. What are some of the special issues in interpreting New Testament epistles?

8. What are the guidelines for interpreting epistles?

ASSIGNMENTS

1. Engage in a comprehensive study of the openings of all 21 letters included in the New Testament, both the 13 letters written by Paul and those written by others. Note the elements contained the various introductions and compare and contrast the letter openings, noting any features that in your judgment are theologically significant.

2. Do the same with the letter closings. Identify each of the 21 letter closings and provide a basic, initial study comparing and contrasting these closings. Discuss also what light these closings shed on the nature of the letter under consideration.

3. Discuss the theory of the pseudonymity of several of the letters included in the New Testament. In your view, if there were any pseudonymous letters in the New Testament, would this affect the notions of the divine inspiration of Scripture and of biblical inerrancy? Why or why not? What is the evidence for pseudonymous letters in the New Testament and elsewhere, and how do you assess the argument that the Pastorals and 2 Peter are pseudonymous?

4. Identify various lines of evidence that support the argument that the Letter to the Hebrews originated as a series of orally delivered messages.

5. Provide an inductive comparative study of the contents of Jude 4–19 and 2 Peter 2:1–3:3. Discuss possible scenarios which account for the similarities in content and indicate your preferred scenario and reasons why.

6. What are features of the letter of James that point to its Jewish Christian nature? Discuss why it is important to recognize the Jewish Christian nature of James in interpreting the book and in making proper application for contemporary believers.

7. In light of the discussion of the occasionality of the New Testament epistles and the issue of normativity for believers of all ages, provide a list of principles that can aid the interpreter in making proper application of a given epistolary passage to his or her personal life or the church today.

CHAPTER BIBLIOGRAPHY

Alexander, "Chronology of Paul." Pp. 115–23 in *Dictionary of Paul and His Letters*. Edited by Gerald F. Hawthorne, Ralph P. Martin, Daniel G. Reid. Downers Grove: InterVarsity, 1993.

Anderson, R. Dean Jr. *Ancient Rhetorical Theory and Paul*, Contributions to Biblical Exegesis and Theology 18. Kampen: Kok Pharos, 1996; rev. ed. 1999.

Aune, David E. *The New Testament in its Its Literary Environment*. Library of Early Christianity 8. Philadelphia: Westminster, 1987.

Botha, J. J. "The Verbal Art of the Pauline Letters: Rhetoric, Performance and Presence." Pp. 409–28 in *Rhetoric and the New Testament: Essays from the 1992 Heidelberg Conference*. Edited by S. Porter and T. Olbricht, JSNT Supplement Series 90. Sheffield: JSOT, 1993.

Carson, D. A. and Douglas J. Moo. "New Testament Letters." Pp. 331–54 in *An Introduction to the New Testament*. 2d ed. Grand Rapids: Zondervan, 2005.

Deissmann, Adolf. *Light from the Ancient East: The New Testament Illustrated by Recently Discovered Texts of the Graeco-Roman World*. London: Hodder & Stoughton, 1927.

Donelson, L. R. *Pseudepigraphy and Ethical Argument in the Pastoral Epistles*. Tubingen: Mohr, 1986.

Donfried, Karl P. and Johannes Beutler, eds. *The Thessalonians Debate: Methodological Discord or Methodological Synthesis?* Grand Rapids: Eerdmans, 2000.

Doty, William G. *Letters in Primitive Christianity*. Guides to Biblical Scholarship, New Testament Series. Philadelphia: Fortress, 1973.

Dunn, J. D. G. "Pseudepigraphy." Pp. 977–84 in *Dictionary of the Later New Testament and Its Development*. Edited by Ralph P. Martin and Peter H. Davids. Downers Grove: InterVarsity, 1997.

Evans, Craig A. "New Testament Use of the Old Testament." Pp. 72–80 in *New Dictionary of Biblical Theology*. Edited by T. Desmond Alexander and Brian S. Rosner. Downers Grove: InterVarsity, 2001.

Guthrie, Donald. Pp. 1011–28 in *New Testament Introduction*. 4th ed.
    Downers Grove: InterVarsity, 1990.

Hansen, G. W. "Rhetorical Criticism." Pp. 822–23 in *Dictionary of Paul
    and His Letters*. Edited by Gerald F. Hawthorne, Ralph P. Martin,
    Daniel G. Reid. Downers Grove: InterVarsity, 1993.

Hays, Richard B. *Echoes of Scripture in the Letters of Paul*. New Haven:
    Yale University Press, 1989.

Kennedy, G. A. *New Testament Interpretation through Rhetorical
    Criticism*. Chapel Hill: University of North Carolina, 1984.

Klauck, Hans-Josef. *Ancient Letters and the New Testament: A Guide to
    Content and Exegesis*. Waco: Baylor University, 2006.

Klein, W. William, Craig L. Blomberg, and Robert L. Hubbard Jr
    Pp. 426–40 in *Introduction to Biblical Interpretation*. Rev. ed.
    Nashville: Thomas Nelson, 2004.

Köstenberger, Andreas J. "1 Timothy." Pp. 492–94 in *Expositor's Bible
    Commentary*. Rev ed. Vol. 12. Grand Rapids: Zondervan, 2006.

_____. "Diversity and Unity in the New Testament." Pp. 144–
    58 in *Biblical Theology: Retrospect & Prospect*. Edited by Scott J.
    Hafemann. Downers Grove, InterVarsity, 2002.

Köstenberger, Andreas J., L. Scott Kellum, and Charles L. Quarles.
    *The Cradle, the Cross, and the Crown: An Introduction to the New
    Testament*. Nashville: B&H, 2009.

Longenecker, Richard. *Biblical Exegesis in the Apostolic Period*. 2d ed.
    Grand Rapids: Eerdmans, 1999.

Mihaila, Corin. *The Paul-Apollos Relationship and Paul's Stance toward
    Greco-Roman Rhetoric: An Exegetical and Socio-Historical Study
    of 1 Corinthians 1–4*. New Testament Library. Edinburgh: T&T
    Clark, 2009.

Murphy-O'Connor, Jerome. *Paul: A Critical Life*. Oxford: Clarendon,
    1996.

O'Brien, P. T. *Introductory Thanksgivings in the Letters of Paul*. Leiden:
    Brill, 1977.

Porter, Stanley E. "The Theoretical Justification for Application of
    Rhetorical Categories to Pauline Epistolary Literature." Pp.
    100–22 in *Rhetoric and the New Testament: Essays from the 1992*

Heidelberg Conference. Edited by Stanley E. Porter and Thomas
H. Olbricht. JSNT Supplement Series 90. Sheffield: JSOT, 1993.
_____. "Ancient Rhetorical Analysis and Discourse Analysis
of the Pauline Corpus." Pp. 249–74 in *The Rhetorical Analysis
of Scripture: Essays from the 1995 London Conference*. Edited by
Stanley E. Porter and Thomas H. Olbricht, JSNT Supplement
Series 146. Sheffield: Sheffield Academic Press, 1997.
_____. "Paul of Tarsus and His Letters." In *Handbook of
Classical Rhetoric in the Hellenistic Period 330 B.C.–A.D. 400*, 533–
85. Leiden: Brill, 1997.
Reed, Jeffrey T. "Using Ancient Rhetorical Categories to Interpret
Paul's Letters: A Question of Genre." Pp. 292–324 in *Rhetoric
and the New Testament*. Edited by S. E. Porter and T. H. Olbricht.
JSNT Supplement Series 90. Sheffield: Sheffield Academic Press,
1993.
_____. "The Epistle." Pp. 171–93 in *Handbook of Classical
Rhetoric in the Hellenistic Period 330 B.C.–A.D. 400*. Leiden: Brill,
1997.
Richards, E. Randolph. *Paul and First-Century Letter Writing:
Secretaries, Composition and Collection*. Downers Grove:
InterVarsity, 2004.
Schreiner, Thomas R. *Interpreting the Pauline Epistles*. Guides to New
Testament Exegesis. Grand Rapids: Baker, 1990.
Schubert, P. *Form and Function of Pauline Thanksgivings*. Berlin:
Töpelmann, 1939.
Stanley, Christopher D. *Arguing with Scripture: The Rhetoric of
Quotations in the Letters of Paul*. New York: T&T Clark, 2004.
Stowers, Stanley K. *Letter Writing in Greco-Roman Antiquity*. Library
of Early Christianity. Philadelphia: Westminster, 1986.
Stirewalt, M. Luther Jr. *Paul, the Letter Writer*. Grand Rapids:
Eerdmans, 2003.
Wenham, David. "Appendix: Unity and Diversity in the New
Testament." Pp. 684–719 in George Eldon Ladd, *A Theology of
the New Testament*.

_____. *Paul: Follower of Jesus or Founder of Christianity?* Grand Rapids: Eerdmans, 1995.

Wilder, Terry L. "Pseudonymity and the New Testament." Pp. 296–335 in *Interpreting the New Testament: Essays on Methods and Issues*. Edited by D. A. Black and D. S. Dockery. Nashville: B&H, 2001.

Wiles, G. P. *Paul's Intercessory Prayers: The Significance of the Intercessory Prayer Passages in the Letters of St. Paul*. London: Cambridge University Press, 1974.

CHAPTER 11 OBJECTIVES

1. To acquaint the student with the most important characteristics of apocalyptic literature and to sketch the most significant issues with which the interpreter is faced when seeking to understand the Book of Revelation.

2. To equip the student with knowledge of the most important historical background information, literary features, and theological issues involved in interpreting Revelation.

CHAPTER 11 OUTLINE

A. Introduction and Definition of Apocalyptic
   1. Introduction
   2. Definition of Apocalyptic
B. Major Interpretative Approaches to the Study of the Book of Revelation
   1. Preterist
   2. Historicist
   3. Idealist
   4. Futurist
C. Historical Background
   1. Type of Persecution
   2. Emperor Cult
   3. "Nero *Redivivus* Myth"
D. Literary Aspects
   1. General Literary Features
      a. Genre
      b. Setting
      c. Narrative Framework
      d. Characterization
      e. Minor Transition Markers
      f. Series of Sevens and Relationship between the Sevens
      g. Interludes
   2. Special Literary Features
      a. Assessing and Interpreting Old Testament Allusions
      b. Types of Figurative Language
      c. Symbolic Nature of Revelation
      d. Interpreting Symbols in Revelation
   3. Structure
      a. Outline #1
      b. Outline #2
E. Sample Exegesis: Revelation 11:1–13
   1. History
   2. Literature
   3. Theology

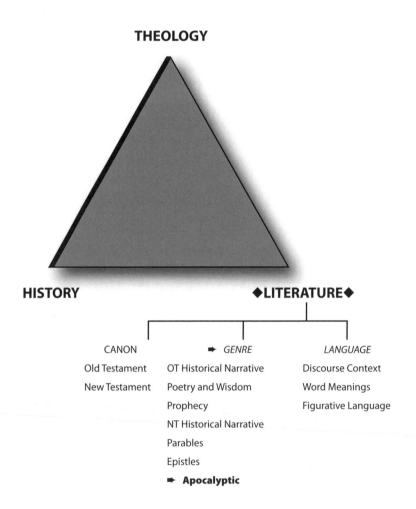

THEOLOGY

HISTORY ◆**LITERATURE**◆

CANON   ➡ *GENRE*   *LANGUAGE*

Old Testament   OT Historical Narrative   Discourse Context

New Testament   Poetry and Wisdom   Word Meanings

     Prophecy   Figurative Language

     NT Historical Narrative

     Parables

     Epistles

     ➡ **Apocalyptic**

Chapter 11

VISIONS OF THE END:
APOCALYPTIC (REVELATION)

INTRODUCTION AND DEFINITION OF APOCALYPTIC

Introduction

A T LONG LAST, WE HAVE arrived at the final leg of our canonical journey. Having encountered Old Testament narrative, poetry and wisdom, prophecy, as well as New Testament narrative (Gospels and Acts), parables, and epistles, we must climb one final mountain: the tricky but exceedingly rewarding genre of apocalyptic. On this arduous journey, only well-prepared climbers will scale the heights, and challenges abound. In the following pages, we will first develop a definition of apocalyptic and survey the major approaches to interpreting Revelation. After this, we will discuss important historical background matters such as the "Nero *redivivus* myth" or the emperor cult and various relevant literary aspects that have a bearing on the interpretation of the book of Revelation. We will close with a sample exegesis of Revelation 11:1–13 and a list of interpretive guidelines for interpreting New Testament apocalyptic.

While there is no book in the Old Testament that is apocalyptic in its entirety, as mentioned in the chapter on prophecy, apocalyptic is a significant component of the Old Testament prophetic literature (e.g., Isaiah 24–27; Ezekiel 38–39; Daniel 7; Joel 2:28–32; 3:9–17; and Zechariah 1–6,

12–14). Together with promises of deliverance and kingdom oracles, we identified Old Testament apocalyptic as a subset of salvation oracles. At the same time, we noted that fully developed apocalypses did not appear until after the Old Testament era. This kind of literature flourished during the Second Temple period, especially between 200 B.C. and A.D. 200.

In terms of salvation-historical development, the arrival of Jesus the Messiah "in the fullness of time" indicated that certain eschatological expectations had come to fruition. Jesus announced the nearness and even (partial) arrival of God's kingdom (Mark 1:15; Luke 11:20). The presence of God's kingdom suggests the eschatological fulfillment of the prophetic promises regarding the son of David, the restoration of Israel, and the renewal of creation. Jesus inaugurated the end times with his resurrection followed by the outpouring of the Holy Spirit, but believers still expect a time of final consummation at the end of the age. This time between the ages is commonly viewed as the "already and not yet" of God's eschatological fulfillment. In this regard, the New Testament shares affinities with an apocalyptic worldview.

For this reason, we should not be surprised to find apocalyptic portions in various places of the New Testament. The Olivet discourse (Matt. 24:1–31; Mark 13; Luke 21:5–32), also known as "the little apocalypse," comprises Jesus' apocalyptic expectations in the Synoptic Gospels. Apocalyptic language and images appear scattered throughout the New Testament letters. The book of Hebrews, for example, exhibits an apocalyptic worldview, contrasting the temporary earthly institutions with eternal heavenly realities. Second Peter 3 also represents eschatological expectations expressed in terms of apocalyptic imagery (i.e., the earth and all the elements being consumed by fire).

In this chapter, we will provide you with a more thorough definition of apocalyptic and deal with major interpretive issues raised by the book of Revelation such as identifying and interpreting Old Testament allusions and dealing with figurative and symbolic language. We will also discuss important matters of historical-cultural background that have a bearing on interpreting Revelation, such as the imperial cult or the "Nero *redivivus* myth." After this, we will assess the genre of Revelation and conclude with a discussion of several general and special literary features of the book, including the question of the structure of Revelation.

Definition of Apocalyptic

In seeking to define "apocalyptic," we will do well to revisit and further extend the discussion of apocalyptic in chapter 7 on prophecy. The very word "apocalypse" conjures up a myriad of images. Scholars typically distinguish between (1) "apocalypse"; (2) "apocalyptic"; and (3) "apocalypticism."[1] "Apocalypse" refers to a particular genre of literature written between approximately 200 B.C. and A.D. 200.[2] The adjective "apocalyptic" is used when describing either the literary genre or the worldview. "Apocalypticism," finally, denotes a worldview, ideology, or theology merging the eschatological aims of particular groups into a cosmic and political arena.[3]

The development of the definition for the apocalyptic genre has a long complex history.[4] Early studies identified formal features such as pseudonymity, visionary accounts, and historical reviews as well as exhibiting a content expressing a doctrine of two ages, pessimism and hope, universalism, and imminent expectation of the end.[5] In 1979, John J. Collins, in conjunction with a group of scholars, developed the following classic definition:

> "Apocalypse" is a genre of revelatory literature with a narrative framework, in which a revelation is mediated by an otherworldly being to a human recipient, disclosing a transcendent reality which is both temporal, insofar as it envisages eschatological salvation, and spatial, insofar as it involves another, supernatural world.[6]

---

1. Paul D. Hanson, *Dawn of Apocalyptic* (Philadelphia: Fortress, 1975), xi; John J. Collins, *The Apocalyptic Imagination*, 2d ed. (Grand Rapids: Eerdmans, 1998), 2.
2. Collins, *Apocalyptic Imagination*, 21; Morton Smith, "On the History of *Apokalyptō* and *Apokalypsis*," in *Apocalypticism in the Mediterranean World and the Near East: Proceedings of the International Colloquium on Apocalypticism*, ed. David Hellholm (Tübingen: Mohr Siebeck, 1983), 9–20.
3. Klaus Koch, *The Rediscovery of Apocalyptic*, trans. Margaret Kohl (Naperville, IL: Alec R. Allenson, 1972), 28–33.
4. See the survey by David Mathewson, "Revelation in Recent Genre Criticism: Some Implications for Interpretation," *TJ* 13 NS (1992): 193–213.
5. Philipp Vielhauer, "Apocalypses and Related Subjects," in *New Testament Apocrypha II*, ed. Edgar Hennecke and Wilhelm Schneemelcher (Philadelphia: Westminster, 1965), 583–94. See also Koch, *Rediscovery of Apocalyptic*, 23–28.
6. John J. Collins, "Introduction: Towards the Morphology of a Genre," *Semeia* 14 (1979): 9.

This definition emphasized the *form* as a narrative framework involving an otherworldly mediator and the *content* as containing both temporal (eschatological salvation) and spatial (supernatural world) elements. The definition, however, lacked any reference to the *function* of an apocalypse. For this reason, a subsequent study group, led by Adela Yarbro Collins, David Hellholm, and David E. Aune, added an amendment in 1986 which stated that an apocalypse is "intended to interpret present, earthly circumstances in light of the supernatural world and of the future, and to influence the understanding and behavior of the audience by means of divine authority."[7]

This amended definition of the apocalyptic genre, then, pertains to its form, content, and function.[8] The apocalyptic genre exhibits several *formal* features including visionary accounts, otherworldly mediators, and symbolic language. The apocalyptic genre also expresses *content* depicting temporal and spatial realities as a way to emphasize the heavenly realities and devalue earthly circumstances. Finally, the apocalyptic genre *functions* to encourage piety and faithfulness in the midst of suffering or during times of crisis (whether real or perceived).

These definitions broadly encompass all canonical, extrabiblical, rabbinical, and sectarian examples of apocalyptic literature. Not all apocalyptic writings necessarily exhibit every genre characteristic discussed in the above definition.[9] This warrants the need to posit a scaled-down assessment of essential elements attributed to the apocalyptic genre. The first essential element is that an apocalypse comprises a *visionary or revelatory means of communication*. Apocalyptic literature must reveal some heavenly or spiritual reality through the agency of a seer or prophet. Usually, the vision is autobiographical and expressed in a narrative framework. In addition, apocalyptic communication frequently employs the use of divine or angelic intermediaries as guides and interpreters. Embedded within this revelatory communication are prophetic exhortations for desired behaviors, choices,

---

7. Adela Yarbro Collins, "Introduction: Early Christian Apocalypticism," *Semeia* 36 (1986): 7.
8. Lars Hartman, "Survey of the Problem of Apocalyptic Genre," in *Apocalypticism in the Mediterranean World and the Near East*, 332–36. So David E. Aune, "The Apocalypse of John and the Problem of Genre," *Semeia* 36 (1986): 65–96.
9. Collins, *Apocalyptic Imagination*, 5–9. For example, although Revelation is written in a narrative framework recounting an otherworldly journey, it is not pseudonymous, because the author identifies himself as "John" (1:1, 4, 9; 22:8) rather than as a revered historical character such as Enoch.

and responses from the recipients. Non-essential elements include pseud-onymity and historical reviews (written in predictive form).

Second, apocalyptic literature is saturated with *symbolic, figurative, and metaphorical language.* Symbols and other figures constitute the common stock of apocalyptic writing. Human and angelic beings and even animals serve as symbolic representations of spiritual truths. Symbolic imagery may express historical, contemporary, or future events in cosmic terms. By using metaphors when describing cosmic scenarios, the author invests both current and anticipated earthly events with symbolic meaning.[10]

A final element essential to the apocalyptic genre is the *dualism between earthly and heavenly realities,* usually steeped in eschatological significance. Earthly situations are depicted as temporary and transitory in light of the eternal realities of the spiritual world. This heavenly perspective dramati-cally contrasts the worldly scenarios facing the recipients. Although some scholars downplay the eschatological nature of the visions, apocalyptic lit-erature provides a provocative and effective vehicle for communicating end-time expectations.[11] The belief that God is sovereign over history permeates most apocalyptic writings, including the idea that he will radically intervene in the near future to consummate his plans for all creation.

MAJOR INTERPRETATIVE APPROACHES TO THE STUDY OF THE BOOK OF REVELATION

How you read the book of Revelation will largely depend on your ap-proach to understanding the areas of history, symbolism, and eschatology. Interpreters differ in their view of the relationship between John's vision

---

10. G. B. Caird, *The Language and Imagery of the Bible* (Grand Rapids: Eerdmans, 1997), 256.

11. "Eschatology" is a slippery term with a broad range of meaning. For example, Caird, *Language and Imagery of the Bible,* 243–56, identifies seven senses of eschatology; cf. idem, *New Testament Theology,* ed. L. D. Hurst (Oxford: Oxford University Press, 1995), 243–67. See also I. Howard Marshall, "Slippery Words, 1: Eschatology," *Expository Times* 89 (1978): 264–69; idem, "A New Understanding of the Present and the Future: Paul and Eschatology," in *Road from Damascus: The Impact of Paul's Conversion on His Life, Thought, and Ministry,* ed. Richard N. Longenecker (Grand Rapids: Eerdmans, 1997), 43–61; idem, "Is Apocalyptic the Mother of Christian The-ology?," in *Tradition and Interpretation in the New Testament: Essays in Honor of E. Earle Ellis for his 60th Birthday,* ed. Gerald F. Hawthorne and Otto Betz (Grand Rapids: Eerdmans, 1987), 33–42. In its most basic sense, eschatology pertains to the future consummation of God's dealings with humanity.

and history. Does the book of Revelation reflect past, present, or purely future events, or does the book feature events future to John but historical to modern readers? The way you answers these questions will significantly influence how you interprets the book.

No one doubts that Revelation is saturated with symbolism, but not all agree on what those symbols mean. Do they have literal referents or literary ones? Literal interpretations produce remarkably divergent meanings from those who follow more literary approaches. Finally, your eschatological perspective becomes the theological lenses which influence how you answer the historical questions and how you interpret the book's symbols. The history of interpretation has produced four basic interpretative schools of thought for approaching this complex work.[12]

Preterist

The preterist position approaches the relationship of history and the Apocalypse from the vantage point that the events prophesied were fulfilled in the first century.[13] One school of preterism interprets the book of Revelation as a message of judgment against apostate Israel for rejecting Christ by prophesying the destruction of Jerusalem in A.D. 70.[14] Other preterist interpreters see the Roman Empire and the situation of Christians as the focus of John's vision prophesying the fall of Rome.[15] The primary virtue of this approach is that it takes seriously the historical circumstances of the first-century audience of Revelation. On the negative side, the preterist position unduly diminishes the more remote future fulfillment of biblical prophecy.

Historicist

The historicist approach represented the most popular interpretive approach for the book of Revelation during the Middle Ages and

---

12. For a more detailed discussion, see Andreas J. Köstenberger, L. Scott Kellum, and Charles L. Quarles, *The Cradle, the Cross, and the Crown: An Introduction to the New Testament* (Nashville: B&H, 2009), chapter 20. See also C. Marvin Pate, *Reading Revelation: A Comparison of Four Interpretive Translations of the Apocalypse* (Grand Rapids: Kregel, 2009).
13. The term "preterist" comes from the Latin *praeteritus* meaning "gone by."
14. See Kenneth L. Gentry, "A Preterist View of Revelation," in *Four Views on the Book of Revelation*, ed. C. Marvin Pate (Grand Rapids: Zondervan, 1998), 37–92.
15. On the types of preterists see G. K. Beale, *The Book of Revelation*, NIGTC (Grand Rapids: Eerdmans, 1999), 44–45; and Osborne, *Revelation*, 19–20.

throughout the Reformation.[16] The historicists viewed John's vision as forecasting the course of history in Western Europe with particular emphasis on popes, kings, and wars.[17] Thus Martin Luther, John Calvin, and other Reformers equated the Vatican with the harlot Babylon that corrupted and persecuted the true church.[18] While this approach has been largely abandoned, one may detect modern variations in readings of Revelation as if it were being fulfilled through current events on the world's stage.[19] A historicist approach is inadequate owing to its narrow focuses on Western history and its insufficient consideration of the first-century historical context of the churches to which the book of Revelation is addressed.[20]

Idealist

The idealist, timeless, or symbolic approach sets aside the historical question altogether by positing that Revelation is not about events in the space-time continuum but rather symbolically portrays the spiritual and timeless nature of the battle between good and evil.[21] Thus the vision and its symbolism are loosed from their historical moorings so that they represent a universal message to all believers about God's defeat of Satan and the spiritual victory of faith in Christ as the church contends with a world ruled by wicked potentates. Variations of this view are found in Origen, Dionysius, and Augustine.

On the positive side, this approach accounts for the symbolic nature of John's vision and underscores its universal relevance for believers throughout history. Negatively, the view does not adequately address the historical nature of Revelation. John writes to real churches facing specific circumstances. The allusions to the imperial cult, the Nero *redux* myth, and other first-century events indicate that the book's meaning is grounded in history. Also, this approach does not adequately explain the church's expectation of the consummation of God's plan in history with the return of Christ.

---

16. Carson and Moo, *Introduction to the New Testament*, 720.
17. Mounce, *Book of Revelation*, 42.
18. Ibid.
19. Osborne, *Revelation*, 19.
20. Beale, *Book of Revelation*, 46.
21. See Sam Hamstra Jr., "An Idealist View of Revelation," in *Four Views*, 95–131.

Futurist

The fourth major approach for interpreting Revelation contends that chapters 4–22 refer to future events. Early Christian writers such as Justin Martyr, Irenaeus, Tertullian, and Hippolytus held to a futuristic interpretation known as *chiliasm*.[22] In modern times, the futurist position enjoys pride of place among most evangelical Christians. Not all futurists, however, agree as to how Revelation portrays the unfolding of future events, taking one of two basic forms: dispensational and modified or moderate futurism.[23]

The hermeneutical hallmark of classic dispensationalism is a commitment to the literal interpretation of prophetic Scripture,[24] a principle often expressed with the dictum, "When the plain sense of Scripture makes common sense, seek no other sense."[25] This hermeneutical approach has resulted in a particular theological system that makes a strict and consistent distinction between Israel and the church and contends that Revelation focuses on the future of ethnic Israel.[26]

Since the term "church" does not occur after Revelation 4:1, dispensationalists contend that God will rapture the church at the beginning of the tribulation in order to be able to deal with Israel. Thus, the tribulation and Christ's millennial reign have nothing to do with the church. Progressive dispensationalism, on the other hand, believes that the various dispensations overlap and that Jesus already began his reign as the Davidic king at the resurrection, his millennial reign constituting the complete fulfillment for Israel.[27]

---

22. Isbon T. Beckwith, *The Apocalypse of John: Studies in Introduction with A Critical and Exegetical Commentary* (London: MacMillan, 1919; repr. Grand Rapids: Baker, 1967), 318–34. Cf. Mounce, *Book of Revelation*, 39.
23. For the title "modified futurism" see Beale, *Book of Revelation*, 47; for the title "moderate futurism" see George Eldon Ladd, *A Theology of the New Testament*, rev. ed. (Grand Rapids: Eerdmans, 1993), 673.
24. C. Marvin Pate, "Introduction to Revelation," in *Four Views*, 29.
25. David L. Cooper, "An Exposition of the Book of Revelation: The Great Parenthesis," *Biblical Research Monthly* (May 1954): 84; quoted in Tim LaHaye, *Revelation Unveiled* (Grand Rapids: Zondervan, 1999), 17.
26. Charles C. Ryrie, *Dispensationalism* (Chicago: Moody, 1995), 85, who asserts that the words "church" and "Israel" are always kept distinct in the New Testament, maintaining that this distinction is the result of "a consistent use of literal, normal, or plain method of interpretation without the addition of any other principle that will attempt to give respectability to some preconceived conclusions."
27. Blaising and Bock, *Progressive Dispensationalism*, 22. See also Robert L. Saucy, *The Case for Progressive Dispensationalism* (Grand Rapids: Zondervan, 1993).

A second form of a futurist approach, modified or moderate futurism, is commonly associated with historical premillennialism because of its affinities with the *chiliasm* of the early church.[28] The view is similar to dispensationalism in that it affirms a thousand-year reign of Christ on earth but it departs from the dispensational insistence on a strict literalism, the rigorous distinction between Israel and the church, the chronology of end-time events, and the belief in a pretribulational rapture.

While dispensationalists argue that the second coming of Christ will involve a *secret* return for the church prior to the tribulation followed by his *visible* return after seven years, modified futurists affirm *only one* return of Christ to earth allowing the church to persevere through the tribulation.[29] This is largely due to the inauguration of the new covenant making all believers in Jesus the spiritual descendants of Abraham and therefore covenant members of the people of God—true Israel.[30]

Modified futurism and historical premillennialism are appealing because they enable interpreters to maintain the future orientation of John's vision while avoiding the literalism of dispensationalism that limits the applicability of Revelation for today's church. In addition, there are various eclectic approaches that combine elements of each of the above-discussed positions in order to capitalize on the perceived strengths of given arguments while avoiding their weaknesses.

HISTORICAL BACKGROUND

There are several important background features that aid in interpreting the book of Revelation. The most relevant are the type of persecution faced by the readers, the imperial cult, and the "Nero *redivivus* myth."[31]

Type of Persecution

For generations, tradition has maintained that the churches suffered from monstrous persecution at the hands of the tyrant Domitian who

---

28. Wayne Grudem, *Systematic Theology: An Introduction to Biblical Doctrine* (Grand Rapids: Zondervan, 2000), 1111.
29. Osborne, *Revelation*, 21.
30. Beale, *Book of Revelation*, 47.
31. For a discussion of these and other historical background issues, see Köstenberger, Kellum, and Quarles, *Cradle, the Cross, and the Crown*, 815–22.

mandated obeisance throughout the Roman Empire.[32] Until the late twentieth century, many scholars accepted Domitian as the second great persecutor of the church (Eusebius, *Eccl. Hist. 4.26.9*). Recent scholarship has
altered this traditional view of Domitian by demonstrating the paucity of
evidence supporting an official imperial persecution against Christians
during his reign.[33] In the wake of this reevaluation, scholars have sought
to reconstruct the historical situation in terms of possible social crises,
real or perceived, that left the churches in the dilemma of capitulating
to socio-cultural pressures or clinging to their faith in Christ.[34] Believers
in Asia Minor, however, did not merely imagine this crisis because they
lived with the genuine threat of unjust treatment due to their faith in
Christ.

John indicates that he was on Patmos owing to persecution related to his
Christian witness (1:9) and associates his suffering with what the believers in
Asia Minor will experience (6:9; 12:17; 20:4). He was on Patmos because of "the
word of God and the testimony of Jesus" (1:9). This phrase occurs regularly
throughout the book of Revelation in connection with persecution.[35] This
reading is supported by John's self-identification as a fellow participant with
the churches in their hardships (1:9). The letters to the seven churches reveal
various situations ranging from spiritual lethargy to external opposition.
The Christians in Ephesus were commended for enduring hardships because
of the name of Christ (2:3). The exact nature of their suffering, however, remains elusive. At least some of the hardships may have derived from internal
conflicts with the Nicolaitans (2:6), but this does not rule out external opposition from non-Christian sources.

Conflict in Smyrna apparently arose from the Jewish community (2:9).
Their suffering relates to unspecified tribulations, poverty, and slander from
Jews. The forensic nature of this slander is confirmed by the reference to fu-
ture imprisonment (2:10). Jewish hostilities against Christians in the form of

---

32. E.g., John A. T. Robinson, *Redating the New Testament* (London: SCM, 1976), 230–31.
33. The most significant contribution on these lines is Leonard L. Thompson, *The Book
of Revelation: Apocalypse and Empire* (New York: Oxford University Press, 1990),
95–115.
34. Fiorenza, *Book of Revelation*, 187–99; Adela Yarbro Collins, *Crisis and Catharsis: The
Power of the Apocalypse* (Philadelphia: Westminster, 1984), 84–110; idem, "Persecution and Vengeance in the Book of Revelation," in *Apocalypticism in the Mediterranean World and the Near East*, 729–49.
35. See 6:9; 12:17; 20:4 (cf. 13:7–10).

legal denunciation commonly occurred in the early church.[36] The situation for Christians in Smyrna also paralleled conditions in Philadelphia (3:8–9). In both cities, believers were few in number and poor but faced intentional, religious, and legal opposition from Jews who sought to decimate their number. In at least one case, this opposition escalated to the point of martyrdom of one Antipas in the city of Pergamum (2:13).

The remaining visions either reflect or expect a time of intense persecution as believers engage in a spiritual battle with the forces of Satan (chaps. 12–13). The scenes depicted in Revelation 13:1–18 evoke images of forced participation in the imperial cult. That the hostility envisioned relates to a Roman threat is seen in the identification of Babylon as Rome (17:9). Throughout the vision, Christians are encouraged to remain faithful and endure patiently because one day God will vindicate them through judgment and renewal (20:4). While it is unlikely that believers in Asia Minor were currently experiencing this level of persecution, they lived at a time and in an environment that fostered hostility toward those who maintained exclusive religious devotion to Jesus Christ.

Emperor Cult

Another important background datum is the cult of the emperor. The imperial cult existed as part of Asia Minor's religious climate ever since the time of Augustus.[37] Pergamum hosted the very first temple dedicated to Augustus and Roma for the entire province of Asia beginning in 29 B.C. and remained active well past the reign of Hadrian.[38] The cult's political

---

36. See Matthew 27:22–23; Mark 15:12–14; Luke 23:20–23; John 19:6–7, 14–15; Acts 13:5–12, 50; etc. For examples of general Jewish hostility against Christians see Acts 7:1–8:3; 9:1–9; Galatians 1:13–14; 1 Thessalonians 2:14–16. See also *The Martyrdom of Polycarp* (Rev. 12:2–3; 13:1), Justin Martyr (*Dial.* 16.4; 47.4; 93.4; 95.4; 96.2; 108.3;110.5; 131.2; 133.6; 137.2), Tertullian (*Scorp.* 10.10; *Haer.* 26.6), and Eusebius (*Eccl. Hist.* 5.16.12).

37. For more on the rise and history of the imperial cult see John Ferguson, *The Religions of the Roman Empire* (London: Thames and Hudson, 1970), 88–98; Duncan Fishwick, *The Imperial Cult in the Latin West: Studies in the Ruler Cult of the Western Provinces of the Roman Empire*, EROER 108/2 (Leiden: Brill, 1991); Philip A. Harland, "Imperial Cults within Local Cultural Life: Associations in Roman Asia," *ZAG* 17 (2003): 85–107.

38. Steven J. Friesen, *Imperial Cults and the Apocalypse of John: Reading Revelation in the Ruins* (Oxford: Oxford University Press, 2001), 25, 27.

purpose was to express just how grateful and loyal the provinces were to the emperor.[39]

The cult used religious conventions for political purposes. From its inception, the emperor along with the goddess Roma was worshipped and honored for their benevolence toward the provinces. During the reign of Tiberius, the cities of Sardis and Smyrna competed for the right to host a second provincial imperial cult in Asia, which was won by Smyrna in A.D. 26.[40] Then, during the reign of Domitian, the city of Ephesus erected an unprecedented third imperial temple in Asia Minor (A.D. 89/90).[41] Some estimate that there were more than 80 smaller localized imperial temples in over 60 cities in Asia Minor.[42] These cities and their citizens ensured the success of the imperial cult due to their enthusiastic participation in worshipping the divine Caesar.[43]

The imperial cult, however, was much more than a mere political tool; it had an important religious dimension as well. Participants actually worshipped the emperor as divine.[44] Inscriptional evidence demonstrates that the emperors Augustus and Gaius were considered gods.[45] The use of the term *theos*, though rare, attests to the fact that worshipers esteemed emperors by elevating them to a status high above regular mortals.[46] The cult employed all the trappings and paraphernalia of rituals common to other religious practices. Images of the emperor or his family members greeted worshippers in the form of massive statues.[47] Adherents offered prayers to these statues and even carried smaller

39. Nicolaus of Damascus, *Die Fragmente der griechischen Historiker*, ed. F. Jacoby, 90 F 125; quoted in S. R. F. Price, *Rituals and Power: The Roman Imperial Cult in Asia Minor* (Cambridge: Cambridge University Press, 1984), 1.
40. Friesen, *Imperial Cults*, 36–38. Cf. Tacitus, *Ann.* 4.15; 55–66.
41. Friesen, *Imperial Cults*, 44–46.
42. Price, *Rituals and Power*, 135.
43. Bert Jan Lietaert Peerbolte, "To Worship the Beast: The Revelation to John and the Imperial Cult in Asia Minor," in *Zwischen den Reichen: Neues Testament und Römische Herrschaft*, ed. Klaus Berger, TANZ 36 (Tübingen: A. Francke, 2002), 245–48.
44. On the religious nature of the imperial cult see H. W. Pleket, "An Aspect of the Emperor Cult: Imperial Mysteries," *HTR* 58 (1965): 331–47; Fergus Millar, "Imperial Cult and the Persecutions," 145–75; Harland, "Imperial Cults within Local Cultural Life," 87–90, 93–103.
45. Friesen, *Imperial Cults*, 31, 39.
46. Harland, "Honours and Worship," 328–29; Steven J. Friesen, *Twice Neokoros: Ephesus, Asia and the Cult of the Flavian Imperial Family* (Leiden: Brill, 1993), 146.
47. Price, *Rituals and Power*, 170–206. See also Friesen, *Imperial Cults*, 50. He notes that archaeologists have discovered the remains of a colossal statue of either Domitian or Titus. Based on the size of the head, left forearm, and left big toe, this statue most have towered above worshippers.

pocket-sized statues of imperial figures.[48] Those who lived in a polytheistic culture easily adopted the imperial cult into their pantheon.

Domitian's religious devotion is beyond dispute and evidenced by the numerous temples that he constructed or renovated. In keeping with the Flavian tradition, he worshipped Jupiter and throughout his reign was portrayed as Jupiter's "warrior vice-regent."[49] The temple to Domitian in Ephesus represented the pinnacle of the imperial cult's popularity in Asia Minor during his reign. Here, worshippers would perform obeisance to Domitian and other members of the Flavian family. The colossal statue of Domitian, between twenty-two and twenty-six feet tall, was not only awe-inspiring but an object of worship.[50] Thus, the second beast (13:11–15) that erects an image of the first beast and mandates everyone to worship it may correspond to the high priest of Domitian's imperial cult in Ephesus.[51]

References to the imperial cult in the Apocalypse can are unmistakable. Allusions to it occur frequently in the latter half of the second vision (13:4, 15–16; 14:9–11; 15:2; 16:2; cf. 20:4). John envisions a time when the imperial cult escalates to a point of universal mandatory participation. Significantly, the term *proskyneō* ("worship") is used in direct connection with the beast (13:4, 8, 12, 15); it was also a term commonly employed in the imperial cult.[52] Thus, Christians abhorred the imperial cult as idolatry which was doubly evil due to the political ramifications associated with it.

"Nero Redivivus Myth"

Another piece of important background information for interpreting Revelation is the "Nero *redivivus* myth." Shortly after Nero committed suicide on June 9, A.D. 68, Roman historians recount how a belief emerged throughout the empire that Nero had not actually died but was going to return with the Parthian army (Suetonius, *Nero* 49.3). Even after his death, many people decorated Nero's statue "as if he were still alive and would shortly return and deal destruction to his enemies" (Suetonius, *Nero* 57.1). The fact that very few saw Nero's corpse, coupled with uncertainty regarding the location of his tomb,

---

48. Fergus Millar, "Imperial Cult and the Persecutions," 147–48. Millar notes that some statues had a legal function.
49. Brian W. Jones, *The Emperor Domitian* (New York: Routledge, 1992), 99.
50. Price,, *Rituals and Power*, 187.
51. Ibid., 196–98.
52. Dio Cassius, *Hist.* 59.24.4; Philo, *Leg.* 116; David E. Aune, *Revelation 6–16*, WBC 52b (Nashville: Thomas Nelson, 1998), 741.

gave credence to this belief, which was further nourished and reinforced by at least three pretenders.[53]

The Nero *redivivus* myth surfaced in several apocalyptic Jewish and Christian writings toward the end of the first century.[54] The Christian apocalypses, likewise, associate Nero with Beliar and cast him as the paradigmatic persecutor of the church (e.g., *Ascen. Isa.* 4:2–4 [end of first century A.D.]). These writings indicate that toward the end of the first century, two distinct traditions developed regarding Nero's supposed return.[55] One stems from the idea that Nero never died and that he was going to return with the Parthian army to conquer Rome. The other envisions a demonically empowered Nero-like figure that will attack God's people.[56]

The book of Revelation, according to many commentators, reflects an awareness of the return of Nero legend.[57] Revelation 13 describes how the dragon gives rise to the beast and endows him with authority. In Revelation 13:3, one of the beast's heads receives a fatal head wound but is miraculously resuscitated. As a result, the entire world worships him as he proceeds to slaughter faithful Christians (13:4–10). Although Nero is not mentioned by name, the language in Revelation13:1–7 suggests that John may have adapted the form of the Nero myth that alludes to the enemy of God's people in Daniel 7:2–25.[58]

In addition, Revelation 17:10–12 reflects parallels with the other form of the Nero *redux* myth depicting Nero's attack on Rome. John's portrayal differs radically from the other expectations of Nero's return, because in the Apocalypse the beast actually rises from the dead (*redivivus*), whereas all the other examples assume Nero never died (*redux*). The reason John departs from the usual tradition is that in his vision the beast mimics Christ who died and rose again and will return to conquer the world's kingdoms.

53. P. A. Gallivan, "The False Neros: A Reexamination," *Historia* 22 (1973): 364–65; Albert Earl Pappano, "The False Neros," *CJ* 32 (1937): 385–92; Aune, *Revelation 6–16*, 738–39; Bauckham, *Climax of Prophecy*, 412–14.
54. *Sib. Or.* 3.63–74; 4.119–24, 138–39; 5.28–34, 93–110, 137–54, 214–27, 361–80. Cf. Bauckham, *Climax of Prophecy*, 411–20; Aune, *Revelation 6–16*, 739.
55. Bauckham, *Climax of Prophecy*, 423.
56. Ibid., 424–28. Bauckham demonstrates that this apocalyptic tradition is rooted in a reading of Daniel 7.
57. E.g. Beale, *Book of Revelation*, 17–18; Aune, *Revelation 6–16*, 737–40; Osborne, *Revelation*, 496.
58. Bauckham, *Climax of Prophecy*, 424–29.

LITERARY ASPECTS

Continuing the study of the book of Revelation along the lines of the hermeneutical triad, history, literature, and theology, it is vital to engage in a thorough investigation of the various literary aspects of the book. This will entail a study of the general and special literary features of Revelation.[59]

General Literary Features
Genre

The book of Revelation constitutes one of the most unique biblical books, not only because it represents the concluding work of inspired revelation, but also because it is the only apocalyptic book of the New Testament. Revelation exhibits elements consistent with the genres of apocalyptic, prophecy, and epistle.[60] Some have maintained that the first word of the book, *apokalypsis*, suggests an immediate genre classification, especially given the use of apocalyptic language and imagery throughout the Apocalypse. A more accurate genre designation, however, occurs in 1:3 and 22:7, 10, 18–19 (cf. 11:16; 19:10) where John identifies the book as a *prophēteia* ("prophecy"). This close association between apocalypse and prophecy is natural because the apocalyptic genre originated from and remained under the rubric of Old Testament prophecy. Apocalyptic writings derived from prophetic oracles, and therefore the lines of demarcation separating these genres are somewhat fluid. What is more, Revelation is addressed to specific congregations and thus also has certain epistolary features.

For these reasons, Revelation constitutes a mixed genre. The book falls into the overall genre of prophecy but corresponds to apocalyptic writings in many respects. George Ladd correctly argued for the designation of "prophetic-apocalyptic."[61] Elisabeth Schüssler Fiorenza, likewise, contended that the dichotomy between apocalyptic and prophecy cannot be sustained with regard to the book of Revelation but that elements of both

---

59. See the discussion of external and internal elements in chapter 5 on Old Testament historical narrative above. See also the treatment of the literary context of the Gospels in chapter 8.

60. D. A. Carson and Douglas J. Moo, *An Introduction to the New Testament*, 2d ed. (Grand Rapids: Zondervan, 2005), 713, with reference to Beasley-Murray, *Revelation*, 12.

61. George Eldon Ladd, "Why Not Prophetic-Apocalyptic?," *JBL* 76 (1957): 192–200.

are present.[62] The best overall assessment regarding the genre of Revelation is that the book constitutes "a prophecy cast in an apocalyptic mold written down in a letter form."[63]

Setting

In addition to the historical setting, you should take careful note of the visionary setting of the book. Understanding that the book of Revelation presents a series of visions John saw will be vitally important in interpreting the book correctly and in understanding its structure. The book opens with John banished to the rocky isle of Patmos in the Aegean Sea (1:9b). There, he received his vision on the Lord's Day (1:10). John used the phrase "in the Spirit" to indicate the means of his vision, and this phrase occurs four times to signal a new vision (1:9; 4:2; 17:3; 21:10). In the first vision, John sees the exalted Christ standing among his churches and delivering messages to each of the seven churches (chaps. 1–3).

The setting changes, however, with the introduction to the second vision (4:1–2) when John is transported from the barren isle of Patmos to the heavenly throne room of God. This is followed by three series of sevens (involving numerical symbolism, the number seven conveying the notion of completeness and perfection): the breaking of the seven seals; the sounding of the seven trumpets; and the pouring out of the seven bowls. At the heart of each of these three series of sevens is God's judgment of the world which proves his righteous character and also serves as a vindication of believers who suffered persecution on account of their faith. Although the scenes in chapters 6–16 alternate between heaven and earth, John remains before the throne of God, giving him a heavenly vantage point.

In 17:3, John is transported in the Spirit from heaven into a desert in order to witness the judgment of "Babylon," signifying the perversion and corruption of the world apart from God, depicted as a seductive and lewd prostitute (Babylon had taken Old Testament Israel into exile and served as a common cipher of godless world empires in Second Temple Jewish literature).

---

62. Elisabeth Schüssler Fiorenza, *The Book of Revelation: Justice and Judgment* (Philadelphia: Fortress, 1985), 133–56.
63. D. A. Carson, Douglas J. Moo, and Leon Morris, *An Introduction to the New Testament* (Grand Rapids: Zondervan, 1992), 479.

After "Babylon" is judged and destroyed, John is once again transported in the Spirit to a great and high mountain (21:10). From this lofty
height, John sees the New Jerusalem as a heavenly bride descending to
earth where God will dwell with his people for all eternity.

Narrative Framework

Revelation represents an intricately woven literary masterpiece intended to convey a unified message.[64] The book has a clearly delineated
prologue (1:1–8) and epilogue (22:6–21). As mentioned, it is divided into
four visions marked by the phrase "in the Spirit" (1:9; 4:2; 17:3; 21:10), and
several series of sevens pervade the book (2:1–3:22; 6:1–8:1; 8:2 11.19, 15:1–
16:21). In a "tale of two cities," the harlot city of Babylon (chaps. 17–18) is
contrasted with the bride city of the New Jerusalem (chaps. 21–22).

The book of Revelation tells a story complete with characters, a variety of settings, a plot, and a climax. The narrative dynamic of Revelation
centers on the opening of several heavenly scrolls. The first scroll contains
Christ's prophetic message to the seven churches of Asia Minor at the
time of writing (1:9–3:22). The bulk of the Apocalypse (4:1–22:5) revolves
around the unveiling of the contents of the heavenly scroll by the slain
Lamb of God, Jesus Christ. The seven seals are opened (5:1–8:1), followed
by the seven trumpets announcing divine judgment (8:2–11:19), and a detailed description of the open scroll (12:1–22:5). The open scroll features
several apocalyptic figures, including the woman and the dragon, the
beasts from the sea and the earth, the Lamb, and the 144,000. At last, the
seven bowls of judgment are poured out, and the judgment of the world
and the victory of Christ ensue.

As mentioned, Revelation consists of four separate interrelated visions
introduced by the phrase "in the Spirit." Tenney noted how "[e]ach occurrence of this phrase locates the seer in a different place."[65] The phrase
indicates a shift of setting from Patmos (1:9) to the heavenly throne room

---

64. Bauckham, *Climax of Prophecy*, 3–22. See also Leonard L. Thompson, "The Literary
Unity of the Book of Revelation," in *Mappings of the Biblical Terrain: The Bible as
Text*, ed. Vincent L. Tollers and John Maier (Lewisburg, PA: Bucknell University
Press, 1990), 347–63; James L. Resseguie, *Revelation Unsealed: A Narrative Critical
Approach to John's Apocalypse*, Biblical Interpretation Series 32 (Leiden: Brill, 1998);
Dal Lee, *The Narrative Asides in the Book of Revelation* (Lanham, MD: University
Press of America, 2002).

65. Merrill C. Tenney, *Interpreting Revelation* (Grand Rapids: Eerdmans, 1957), 33.

(4:1–2) into a desert (17:3) and finally to a high mountain (21:10). Moreover, the phrase "I will show you" occurs three times (4:1; 17:1; 21:9) in close proximity to "in the Spirit" (4:2; 17:3; 21:10), suggesting that these two phrases are used in conjunction with each other to signal major structural transitions.[66] Interestingly, 4:1–2 also contains one of the three occurrences of the phrase "what must take place" (1:1; 4:1; 22:6), which stresses the future prophetic nature of 4:1–22:4.

Characterization

At the heart of the characterization of the book is the Lord Jesus Christ who is presented as risen and glorious, as the source of revelation regarding the state of the seven churches (chaps. 1–3) as well as regarding the final judgment (chaps. 4–18), and as the one who returns triumphantly at the end of time to establish his kingdom (chaps. 19–22). It is in this Christ that the other major themes in the book of Revelation find their integrative center.

John also features prominently in the book as the author and narrator. He identifies himself three times in the beginning and once at the end as the author (1:1c, 4a, 9a; 22:8a). The use of the first person, then, signals that John is the one narrating, seeing, and hearing the contents recorded unless it is attributed to another figure (i.e., Christ in 1:17–18; 2–3). The function of the first person is that it brings the narrative closer to the reader by conveying direct witness to the truth. In 1:1c, John testifies as an eyewitness to the veracity of the message handed to him by God. You can detect the eyewitness nature of the account by frequent references to seeing and hearing but also by John's active participation in events at various junctures of the vision (e.g., 1:17; 5:4; 10:8–11; 11:1; 19:10; 22:8–9). Thus John, as the narrator, guides the reader through all he saw, heard, and experienced.

Angels, both elect and evil, appear as significant characters throughout the book. Angelic beings come in all different shapes, sizes, and colors ranging from the four living creatures (4:4), to the colossal angel straddling earth and sea (10:1), to Satan as a great red dragon (12:3), to the locust demons ascending forth from the great abyss (9:2–11), and even demonic spirits that resemble frogs (16:13–14). Elect angels function as mediators of

---

66. Beale, *Book of Revelation*, 110.

divine messages to the churches (2:1, 8, 12, 18; 3:1, 7, 14), to the inhabitants of heaven (5:2; 14:15) and earth (8:13; 14:6–11). They continuously worship God declaring his worthiness and justice (5:11–12; 16:5). They function as the agents that carry out God's decrees, which involve the judgment of humanity (8:1–6; 15:1) as well as the protection of believers (7:1–3). They engage in war against Satan and the evil angels (12:7–9).

The *believers in the seven churches* are a final set of characters that are important to recognize when interpreting the book of Revelation. The book was written to the believers in the seven churches of Asia Minor, suggesting not only that they are the intended audience but that they serve as implicit characters as the people of God. They are addressed in the prologue and epilogue as "the one who reads" (1:3; 22:19), "those who hear" (1:3; 22:18), and those within the "seven churches" (1:4; 20; 22:16). They are also identified by a number of other terms to associate them with all Christian believers.[67]

Minor Transition Markers

As you attempt to interpret a given passage in the book of Revelation and try to locate boundary markers for a given set of textual units, you will want to be sensitive to minor transition markers. Discerning these will help you identify correctly the microstructure and the macrostructure of the book. Minor visionary transitions within any one of the four visions featured in the book are often signaled by references to "seeing" or "hearing." The phrase "and I saw," in particular, acts as a marker within a given vision, signaling a minor transition. It demonstrates a progression within the narrative but does not necessarily introduce a new vision if the location of the seer remains the same.[68] The effect of this narration would be like listening to someone excitedly share what he or she saw while sitting in a theater watching a play or movie, creating a flow similar to "I saw this and then I saw that, oh, and then I saw and heard such and such." While the phrase "in the Spirit" indicates the beginning of a new vision, therefore, the phrase "and I saw" conveys the series of images John sees in a given vision, similar to watching a movie or a play.

---

67. These terms include "servants," "a kingdom and priests," "brothers," "those who keep the words or commandments," "those who overcome," and "the saints."
68. Osborne, *Revelation*, 223. See also Lee, *Narrative Asides*, 142–47.

Series of Sevens and Relationship between the Sevens

Another significant structuring device is a series of sevens specifically enumerated as such. Within these series of sevens, schemes vary from six, seven, and eight septets. Although John demonstrates a proclivity for explicitly arranging his material into groups of sevens, only three or four septets are explicitly numbered.[69] As mentioned, the number seven carries significant symbolic weight, indicating perfection or completion. Apart from the explicitly numbered septets, however, the effort to identify additional unnumbered series of sevens is precarious and often contrived.

The nature of the relationship between the seven seals, trumpets, and bowls has long confounded interpreters. There are three primary theories: (1) chronological succession; (2) recapitulation; and (3) telescopic progression. *Chronological succession* argues that the series of septets occur in strict chronological order without any overlap. The strength of this view is its simplicity. On the downside, however, such an approach does not sufficiently account for the many areas of overlap between the septets. *Recapitulation* holds that the each septet represents an intensification and closer look at the same material. In other words, the trumpets cover the same occurrences as the seals, and the bowls signify the same period as the seals and trumpets. While recapitulation allows for an intensification of severity with each successive septet and offers a viable explanation for the apparent overlap, it does not adequately account for the dissimilarities between each series of septets.

The *telescopic theory* (also known as "dove-tailing") maintains that the seventh seal contains the seven trumpets and the seventh trumpet comprises the seven bowls. It attempts to demonstrate the interconnectedness and overlap between the series of septets but also to account for the progression evident in each new septet. A progressive telescopic theory seems to offer the most satisfying explanation for the literary relationship between the septets. However, caution against too strict an application of these theories is warranted, because the Apocalypse exhibits both repetition and progression in the unfolding series of judgments revealed in the

---

69. 2:1–3:22; 6:1–8:1; 8:2–11:19; 15:1–16:21. See Andrew E. Steinmann, "The Tripartite Structure of the Sixth Seal, the Sixth Trumpet, and the Sixth Bowl of John's Apocalypse (Rev 6:12–7:17; 9:13–11:14; 16:12–16)," *JETS* 35 (1992): 69–79. See also Bauckham, *Climax of Prophecy*, 9–11.

septets which culminate in the consummation of God's judgment and the establishment of his kingdom on earth.[70]

Interludes

John incorporates several interludes interspersed throughout the seals, trumpets, and bowls. The first two emerge between the breaking of the sixth and seventh seals (7:1–17) and between the blowing of the sixth and seventh trumpets (10:1–11:14). These interludes appear in the narrative for theological reasons. They are bound to the preceding sections and provide answers for questions that the audience might be asking. The sixth seal (6:12–16) unleashes devastating catastrophes causing the earth's inhabitants to flee into caves praying to die. In their terror, they cry out concerning the wrath of God and the lamb, asking, "Who can stand?" The succeeding narrative (7:1–17) answers this question by depicting the protective sealing and salvation of God's people who are standing before the throne.[71]

A similar pattern occurs when the fifth and sixth trumpets unleash horrible and devastating plagues upon the earth's inhabitants. Their response indicates a failure to repent from their sins. The succeeding narrative (10:1–11:14) not only provides justification for the plagues but also depicts the people of God in their role as prophetic witnesses before the nations. These interludes enable the hearers to identify their role within the narrative first as protected and then as prophetic witnesses. The purpose of the interludes, then, is to challenge the churches to remain faithful and to endure opposition because God will protect them and use them as witnesses.

The third interlude differs from the first two in that it occurs at the end of the seventh trumpet and precedes the introduction of the seven bowls. Revelation 12 represents a dramatic shift in the flow of John's vision narrative; it is introduced by the statement "A great and wondrous sign appeared in heaven" (12:1) followed by "Then another sign appeared in heaven" (12:3) and later with "I saw in heaven another great and marvelous sign" (15:1). As in John's Gospel, "sign" in the Apocalypse most

---

70. See Beale, *Book of Revelation*, 121–26.
71. Beale, ibid., 405, offers the best treatment of the relationship between the question in 6:17 and chapter 7.

likely points to something more significant than a given miracle itself.[72] Thus this third interlude, in form of a "signs narrative," occurs prior to the final outpouring of God's judgments.

As with other interludes, the signs narrative focuses on the role of the people of God concomitant with the series of judgments. The first interlude illustrates the protection and ultimate salvation of believers (7:1–17). The second interlude pictures their role as God's final prophetic witnesses (10:1–11:14). This third interlude (12:1–15:4) portrays believers as engaged in a holy war against Satan. Although the precise microstructure of this interlude proves elusive, the narrative falls into three natural divisions: (1) holy war in heaven (chap. 12); (2) holy war on earth (chap. 13); and (3) believers' vindication followed by the judgment of unbelievers (chap. 14). Amid the scenes of this cosmic spiritual warfare, John makes the purpose of this interlude explicit by interjecting calls for encouragement (12:10–12), patient endurance (13:9–10), and believers' ultimate vindication (14:6–13). Revelation 12:1–15:4 also provides the basis and justification for the severe and final nature of the judgments brought upon the inhabitants of the earth.

Special Literary Features
Assessing and Interpreting Old Testament Allusions

Because the issue of assessing Old Testament allusions remains rife with difficulties, we will need to probe this topic in some detail.[73] Stanley Porter has isolated three problematic issues related to the scholarly study of the use of the Old Testament in the New. "The first," according to Porter, "is that there is persistent confusion over terminology, including what appears to be confusion over echo, allusion and quotation or citation."[74] The second difficulty he posits is with the audience-oriented or reader-re-

---

72. See Osborne, *Revelation*, 456. For an analysis of the use of *sēmeion* in John's Gospel see Andreas J. Köstenberger, *Studies on John and Gender*, Studies in Biblical Literature 38 (New York: Lang, 2001), 99–116.

73. As the discussion in this section is of necessity fairly technical, beginning students of Scripture should feel free to skip this portion for the time being and return to it at a later time.

74. Stanley E. Porter, "The Use of the Old Testament in the New Testament: A Brief Comment on Method and Terminology," in *Early Christian Interpretation of the Scriptures of Israel: Investigations and Proposals*, ed. Craig A. Evans and James A. Sanders (Sheffield: Sheffield Academic Press, 1997), 92.

sponse approach to the use of the Old Testament. "The reasonable solution would appear to be to adopt the author-centered approach," he argues, "in which each set of words is assessed on its own merits."[75] The third issue revolves around the question of what is intended by such analyses of the use of the Old Testament. The issues identified by Porter provide us with the framework for identifying allusions in Revelation.

To begin with, we will need to define some basic terms, namely "intertextuality," "allusion," and "echo."[76] Intertextuality was first introduced by Julia Kristeva, building on the work of Bakhtin. Kristeva used the term *intertextualité* to suggest a dialogical relationship between texts broadly conceived of as a system of codes or signs.[77] The concept made its way into the field of biblical studies with the publication of Richard Hays's *Echoes of Scripture in the Letters of Paul*.[78] Hays maintained that the phenomenon of intertextuality, that is, the imbedding of fragments of an earlier text within a later one, played a significant role in Israel's scriptural tradition.[79] However, the problem is that the term has been used in many different ways, so that many today are wary of using it at all.

Nevertheless, in a broad sense, "intertextuality" still serves as a helpful umbrella term for the complex set of interrelationships that exist between texts. In distinction from allusions, intertextuality represents the rubric of all interaction between texts in general, whereas allusions represent the specific occurrences of an intentional appropriation of an earlier text for a particular purpose.[80]

Allusion, then, occurs when an author incorporates the language, imagery, and themes of another text without direct citation. Allusions are distinct from formal citations in that there is no introductory formula but

---

75. Ibid.
76. Hays, *Echoes of Scripture*, 23. See also Richard B. Hays, Stefan Alkier, and Leroy A. Huizenga, eds., *Reading the Bible Intertextually* (Waco, TX: Baylor University Press, 2009).
77. Julia Kristeva, *Desire and Language: A Semiotic Approach to Literature and Art*, trans. Leon S. Roudiez (New York: Columbia University Press, 1980). See Steve Moyise, "Intertextuality and the Study of the Old Testament in the New Testament," in *The Old Testament in the New Testament: Essays in Honour of J. L. North*, ed. Steve Moyise, JSNTSup 189 (Sheffield: Sheffield Academic Press, 2000), 14–15.
78. Hays, *Echoes of Scripture*, 14–24. See also Sipke Draisma, ed., *Intertextuality in Biblical Writings: Essays in Honour of Bas van Iersel* (Kampen: Kok, 1989).
79. Ibid., 14. So Michael Fishbane, *Biblical Interpretation in Ancient Israel* (Oxford: Clarendon, 1984).
80. Sommer, *A Prophet Reads Scriptures*, 8.

the phrases are woven into the text and are often less precise in wording.[81] Nevertheless, allusions still represent an intertextual reference.[82] Allusions include both verbal and thematic parallels to words and themes.[83] Authorial intention serves as the crucial criterion for distinguishing between allusions and echoes.[84]

Richard Hays's explication of an echo remains the standard treatment on the subject. Hays specifies the force of an echo as follows: "Allusive echo functions to suggest to the reader that texts B should be understood in light of a broad interplay with text A, encompassing aspects of A beyond those explicitly echoed."[85] In order for echoes to exist, one must embrace "the notion that every text embodies the interplay of other texts and so exists as a node within a larger literary and interpretive network."[86] Texts behave like echo chambers, so that even a word or phrase "may easily carry rumors of its resounding cave."[87] Therefore, echoes are "faint traces of texts that are probably quite unconscious but emerge from minds soaked in the scriptural heritage of Israel."[88]

Second, this methodology adheres to a hermeneutic that locates textual meaning in authorial intention.[89] The almost continuous allusion to the Old Testament in the book of Revelation is not a haphazard phenomenon but reflects a "pattern of disciplined and deliberate *allusion* to specific Old Testament texts."[90] The debate surrounding Revelation centers on

---

81. Moyise, "Intertextuality," 18.

82. Hays, *Echoes of Scripture*, 29. David Mathewson, "Assessing Old Testament Allusions in the Book of Revelation," *EvQ* 75 (2003): 322.

83. Ian Paul, "The Use of the Old Testament in Revelation 12," in *Old Testament in the New Testament*, 261.

84. Beale, *Use of Daniel*, 306–9.

85. Hays, *Echoes of Scripture*, 20. Cf. John Hollander, *The Figure of Echo: A Mode of Allusion in Milton and After* (Berkeley: University of California Press, 1981).

86. Richard B. Hays and Joel B. Green, "The Use of the Old Testament by New Testament Writers," in *Hearing the New Testament: Strategies for Interpretation*, ed. Joel B. Green (Grand Rapids: Eerdmans, 1995), 228.

87. Hollander, *Figure of Echo*, 95; quoted in Mathewson, "Assessing Old Testament Allusions," 320–21.

88. Moyise, "Intertextuality," 18–19.

89. E. D. Hirsch, *Validity in Interpretation* (New Haven: Yale University Press, 1967), 1–23; Kevin J. Vanhoozer, *Is There a Meaning in This Text?* (Grand Rapids: Zondervan, 1998), 201–65. For a helpful critique of postmodern hermeneutics, see D. A. Carson, *The Gagging of God: Christianity Confronts Pluralism* (Grand Rapids: Zondervan, 1996), 93–137.

90. Bauckham, *Climax of Prophecy*, x–xi.

the question whether or not John used the Old Testament as a "servant" (a source to appropriate freely) or "master" (an authoritative guide) or somewhere in between.[91]

A possible way forward is to propose a distinction between levels of authorially intended meaning. When interpreting a text and its appropriation of another text, the issue of meaning is complicated by the presence of two or more authors. The distinction proposed is between the authorially intended meaning of the surface/primary text and the source/subtext. The interpreter of Revelation is ultimately concerned with what John intended the allusion to mean rather than with the original intent of the Old Testament writer.[92] This is not a distinction in kind (pitting the texts against one other) but in degree (giving precedence to the new context).

It is also important to remember the exegetical practices underlying much of Jewish and Christian literature.[93] What may appear to be lack of regard for the Old Testament context may upon closer inspection reveal careful exegesis. In any case, the primary goal for our present purposes is to interpret the intended meaning of the text of Revelation.

Third, before we will be able to answer the question of what is intended by the author's use of the Old Testament, we will need to develop criteria for identifying allusions.[94] In doing so, you can place all potential refer-

---

91. Barnabas Lindars, "The Place of the OT in the Formulation of NT Theology," *New Testament Studies* 23 (1976): 66, concludes that the Old Testament never serves as master. See also the interchanges between Jon Paulien, "Dreading the Whirlwind Intertextuality and the use of the Old Testament in Revelation," *AUSS* 39 (2001): 5–22; G. K. Beale, "A Response to Jon Paulien on the Use of the Old Testament in Revelation," *AUSS* 39 (2001): 23–34; Steve Moyise, "Authorial Intention and the Book of Revelation," *AUSS* 39 (2001): 35–40; idem, "The Old Testament in the New: A Reply to Greg Beale," *IBS* 21 (1999): 54–58; Beale, "Questions of Authorial Intent, Epistemology, and Presuppositions and Their Bearing on the Study of the Old Testament in the New: A Rejoinder to Steve Moyise," *IBS* 21 (1999): 152–80; and Moyise, "Does the Author of Revelation Misappropriate the Scriptures?" *AUSS* 40 (2002): 3–21.

92. Stephen Pattemore, *The People of God in the Apocalypse: Discourse, Structure, and Exegesis*, SNTSMS 128, ed. Richard Bauckham (Cambridge: Cambridge University Press, 2004), 36–43.

93. Longenecker, *Biblical Exegesis in the Apostolic Period*.

94. Jon Paulien, "Elusive Allusions: The Problematic Use of the Old Testament in Revelation," *Biblical Research* 33 (1988): 37–53; idem, "Criteria and the Assessment of Allusions to the Old Testament in the Book of Revelation," in *Studies in the Book of Revelation*, ed. Steve Moyise (Edinburgh: T&T Clark, 2001), 113–29; Paul, "Use of the Old Testament in Revelation 12," 257–62; Mathewson, "Assessing Old Testament Allusions," 319; Beale, *Book of Revelation*, 77–86; Moyise, *Old Testament in the Book of Revelation*, 11–23.

ences along a sliding scale of three categories: (1) embedded allusion; (2) implied allusion; and (3) incidental allusion. These categories are weighted according to the probability of an actual, intentional Old Testament allusion. The analogy of a sliding scale is appropriate because some cases may cover a range of possibilities.[95] The primary key to determining the presence of an allusion is authorial intention. The more likely an author intentionally evoked an Old Testament subtext, the more weight of probability it is accorded. The more weight an allusion has, the more impact it should have on the interpretation and theology of the text.

Embedded allusions consist of what are typically identified as clear, probable, and direct allusions.[96] Embedded allusions represent cases where allusions are assessed with a high degree of probability. Implied allusions constitute cases where the potential allusion is identified as indirect or demonstrated through logical necessity and therefore is relegated to a moderate degree of probability. This classification corresponds to the categories of "possible allusion" and "influence."[97] Incidental allusions pertain to minor or subordinate cases of low probability for an intended allusion. Echoes are typically relegated to this category.

Incorporating the insights of the literature on the subject, we will now proceed to posit the following five criteria for identifying and classifying allusions. In the chart below, we have placed allusions along the sliding scale of probability in one of the heuristic categories based on how many

---

95. Mathewson, "Assessing Old Testament Allusions," 322. Cf. Hays, *Echoes of Scripture*, 29.

96. Beale, *Book of Revelation*, 78, defines a clear allusion as one in which "the wording is almost identical to the OT source, shares some common core meaning, and could not likely have come from anywhere else." Regarding probable allusions, Beale explains, "Though the wording is not as close, it still contains an idea or wording that is uniquely traceable to the OT passage" (ibid.). According to Paulien, "Elusive Allusions," 40–41, a direct allusion occurs when the author was consciously referring to previous literature.

97. Beale, *Book of Revelation*, 78, defines possible allusions as ones in which "the language is only generally similar to the purported source, echoing either its wording or concepts." Sommer, *A Prophet Reads Scripture*, 14–15, borrows the concept of "influence" from literary criticism and explains that the "study of influence often accompanies the study of literary tradition: as writers continue adopting themes, topics, genres, and styles from their precursors, patterns of theme and topic develop which constitute a tradition investigated by literary historians." Sommer differentiates between "allusion" (positing a relationship between particular sets of lines in texts) and "influence" (incorporating a much broader phenomenon of relations between authors, whole works, and traditions).

of the criteria they match. Allusions we deem as fitting four or five of the criteria are identified on the scale as embedded allusions. If the potential allusion only matches three or four criteria, it is ranked as an implied allusion. In cases where a possible allusion matches fewer than three criteria, it should be classified as an incidental allusion.

10.1. SLIDING SCALE OF ALLUSION PROBABILITY							
Embedded		Implied				Incidental	
Clear Allusion	Probable Allusion	Structural Allusion	Thematic Allusion	Typological Allusion	Conceptual Allusion	Loud Echo	Soft Echo

Each category is also divided into additional degrees of probability. Embedded allusions may be divided into clear and probable allusions. Implied allusions are ranked according to the degree of correspondence with an Old Testament text. These rankings include structural, thematic, typological, and conceptual similarities. Incidental allusions are subdivided into loud and soft echoes.[98] Loud echoes may meet two of the criteria and thus may indicate conscious choice on part of the author. A soft echo matches only one criterion and most likely is the result of an unconscious use of Old Testament language.[99]

---

98. Hays, *Echoes of Scripture*, 23, posits that the "volume of intertextual echo varies in accordance with the semantic distance between the source and the reflecting surface."

99. Ibid. Hays further explains, "As we move farther away from overt citation, the source recedes into the discursive distance, the intertextual relations become less determinate, and the demand placed on the reader's listening powers grows greater. As we near the vanishing point of the echo, it inevitably becomes difficult to decide whether we are really hearing an echo at all, or whether we are only conjuring things out of murmurings of our own imaginations."

The first of the five criteria is that of *linguistic parallels.* Linguistic parallels represent the most crucial and visible of the criteria. Without linguistic parallels, allusions cannot be identified with confidence. They may be detected through lexical, syntactical, and structural indicators or markers.[100] *Lexical* indicators are verbal links between words in the primary text and a subtext. Comparing the Greek wording of Revelation with various versions of the Old Testament elucidates the validity of the supposed connections.[101] *Syntactical* indicators refer to grammatical phenomena that may signal shifts in the text to alert the reader to an Old Testament allusion.[102] Finally, *structural* indicators relate to instances when the patterns, ordering, and chronology of the primary text may be appropriated in the structure of a given text.[103]

Theological significance constitutes the second criterion. This criterion refers to the impact of the potential allusion on the reading of the text. This assumes that the allusion serves a theological rather than merely literary purpose. If the potential Old Testament reference does not contain any theologically significant dimension that accounts for its inclusion in the new context, its designation as an allusion remains in doubt. Theological significance is determined by a number of indicators. If the Old Testament passage is heavily theological in that it expresses something about God or other theological concepts (e.g., redemption, covenant, faith, sin, judgment), it may indicate continuity, revision, replacement, or a polemic in the new context.[104] Other theological indicators include themes, typology, analogical use, universalization, fulfillment, inversion, stylistic use, and salvation history.[105]

The third criterion is that of *contextual consistency.* Contextual consistency pertains to the correspondence between the potential allusion and its consistency with the original Old Testament context. Does John

---

100. Paulien, "Elusive Allusions," 41–43.
101. See Paul, "Use of the Old Testament in Revelation 12," 275–76.
102. Beale, *Book of Revelation,* 100–103, persuasively argued that solecisms in Revelation may be intentional grammatical irregularities as a means of indicating dependence on the Old Testament. Cf. Bauckham, *Climax of Prophecy,* 286, who observed, "Unusual and difficult phrases in Revelation frequently turn out to be Old Testament allusions."
103. Paulien, "Elusive Allusions," 43. For example, several significant studies have demonstrated Revelation's structural dependence on Ezekiel, Isaiah, and Daniel.
104. Sommer, *A Prophet Reads Scripture,* 25–29.
105. Beale, *Book of Revelation,* 86–96.

demonstrate sensitivity to the original context of the Old Testament passage to which he is alluding? This question is distinct from how he actually uses the Old Testament allusion. The criterion relates to the very nature of an allusion as a means to evoke an earlier text.[106] An intended allusion summons a specific Old Testament passage to the mind of the reader or hearer. This establishes a link between author and audience by appealing to shared knowledge. In cases such as these, the knowledge of the Old Testament passage plays a significant part in understanding how it is used in Revelation. The more Revelation coheres with the context of a given Old Testament passage, the greater the probability for the allusion.[107]

The fourth criterion relates to the *transitivity* of the allusion from the author to the audience. Transitivity denotes the ability of the audience to grasp and comprehend the allusion and its source text. Is the alluded text something to which the original readers or hearers had access or with which they possessed a measure of familiarity? If they did not, a measure of doubt is cast upon whether or not the author would have alluded to something that would have been foreign to his audience. Although this criterion is fairly subjective and requires a modicum of conjecture, two aspects aid in adjudicating the transitivity of an allusion.

First is the aspect of *availability*. Was the source text available to the recipients? The question of dating helps to minimize the danger of anachronism. It is naturally impossible to allude to a document not yet in existence at the time of writing. Another question related to availability is the geographical distribution of the source text (e.g., the Old Testament would have had greater geographical distribution than Egyptian magical texts). The second aspect is *shared knowledge*. Did the recipients share the same "presupposition pools"?[108] Did they have the same Scriptures as the author? To be sure, John intended his vision to be passed to the seven churches in Asia, but he most likely envisioned that they be read and inter-

---

106. Bauckham, *Climax of Prophecy*, xi, writes, "Allusions are meant to recall the Old Testament context, which thereby becomes part of the meaning the Apocalypse conveys, and to build up, sometimes by a network of allusion to the same Old Testament passage in various parts of the Apocalypse, an interpretation of whole passages of Old Testament prophecy."

107. Mathewson, "Assessing Old Testament Allusions," 316–17. See also Beale, *Book of Revelation*, 79–80, who cites the example of 4:2–9.

108. Peter Cotterell and Max Turner, *Linguistics and Biblical Interpretation* (Downers Grove: InterVarsity, 1989), 90–97.

preted through prophets who would have been trained in interpreting the images and in explaining the meaning of the Old Testament allusions.[109]

The fifth criterion pertains to the *exegetical tradition* of an Old Testament text. This criterion examines the tradition of how the text of a potential Old Testament allusion has been interpreted in both inner- and extrabiblical exegesis. Tracing the interpretive history of a particular Old Testament passage enables you to identify certain traits of similarity and dissimilarity that may illuminate the potentiality of the allusion in Revelation. If other writings quote, cite, or allude to an Old Testament passage in a manner comparable to Revelation, this bolsters the probability of the allusion. Innerbiblical exegesis tracks the (re)interpretation of earlier Old Testament writings in later Old Testament documents.[110] The phenomenon of innerbiblical exegesis represents a valid, substantial, and significant contribution to the study of intertextuality.

Extrabiblical exegesis, on the other hand, examines how Old Testament passages were interpreted in non-canonical Jewish writings. Craig Evans describes this analysis succinctly as follows:

> To determine how a New Testament writer has understood the Old Testament passage being quoted or alluded to, it is necessary to reconstruct as closely as possible the first-century exegetical-theological discussion surrounding the OT passage in question. How was the Old Testament passage understood by early Christians and Jews? To answer this question, every occurrence of the passage should be examined. This involves study of the ancient versions themselves (MT, LXX, Targum) and citations of the passage elsewhere in the New Testament, Old Testament, apocrypha, pseudepigrapha, Qumran, Josephus, Philo, and early rabbinic sources. Some of these sources will prove to be utterly irrelevant; others may significantly clarify the New Testament writer's exegesis.[111]

---

109. David E. Aune, "The Prophetic Circle of John of Patmos and the Exegesis of Revelation 22.16," *JSNT* 37 (1989): 103–16; Bauckham, *Climax of Prophecy*, 85–91.

110. Michael Fishbane, "Revelation and Tradition: Aspects of Inner-Biblical Exegesis," *JBL* 9 (1980): 359, discusses the range of innerbiblical exegesis, as concerned with the legal, homiletic and prophetic matrices through which later prophets and writers amended, replaced, revised, and rearticulated the Sinaitic revelation given by God.

111. Craig A. Evans, "The Old Testament in the New," in *The Face of New Testament Studies: A Survey of Recent Research*, ed. Scot McKnight and Grant R. Osborne (Grand

As a criterion, however, our purpose at this point is not to determine how a New Testament writer understood the Old Testament but to adjudicate the plausibility that a given New Testament text contains an Old Testament allusion. It would have been possible for John to allude to an Old Testament text that had previously escaped the attention of canonical or non-canonical writers, which is why this criterion cannot stand on its own in our attempt to establish the probability of an allusion.

These five criteria serve as heuristic tools for adjudicating the probability of a potential allusion. In doing so, we should be careful to distinguish between the identification of allusions and their interpretation.[112] Once you have successfully identified and classified a given allusion, you can proceed to interpret it. As Mathewson correctly observed, "The discussion surrounding the use of the Old Testament in Revelation needs to move beyond classifying and substantiating allusions based on perceived authorial intention and interpretive confidence in identifying them, to focusing on the interpretive and theological significance of a given allusion or echo in Revelation."[113]

The task of determining how John used the Old Testament allusion is challenging but also very rewarding. To date, G. K. Beale has contributed the most comprehensive analysis of the different ways in which John used the Old Testament in the book of Revelation.[114] We can identify seven categories of usage: (1) *fulfillment of prophecy*: an Old Testament prophecy is presented as directly or indirectly fulfilled in John's vision; (2) *analogical use*: an Old Testament text is compared to an area such as judgment, persecution, false teachings, divine protection, etc.; (3) *indirect Old Testament typological prophecies*: parts of historical narratives (e.g., the plagues of the Exodus) are presented in an escalated or universalized manner involving a

---

Rapids: Eerdmans, 2004), 134. Cf. idem, *Noncanonical Writings and New Testament Interpretation* (Peabody, MA: Hendrickson, 1992), 1–8; Richard Bauckham, "The Relevance of Extra-Canonical Jewish Texts to New Testament Study," in *Hearing the New Testament*, 94–95.

112. This is done in order to heed the corrective critique of Stanley Porter who observes that others who have set forth criteria often confuse the difference between identification and interpretation. See Porter, "Use of the Old Testament in the New Testament," 81–83.

113. Mathewson, "Assessing Old Testament Allusions," 319.

114. Beale, *John's Use of the Old Testament in Revelation*, 60–128. See also G. K. Beale and Sean M. McDonough, "Revelation," in *Commentary on the New Testament Use of the Old Testament*, ed. G. K. Beale and D. A. Carson (Grand Rapids: Baker, 2007), 1085–87.

climax of salvation history; (4) *inverted* or *ironic use of the Old Testament:* the Old Testament promise is applied to the church rather than Israel or universalized to include all nations; (5) *use of Old Testament themes:* passages that develop or continue important concepts that run throughout the Old Testament (e.g., creation and new creation, covenant, exodus, holy war); (6) *use of Old Testament as a literary prototype or model:* instances where the Old Testament influences the structure and language of significant portions of John's vision; (7) *stylistic use of Old Testament language:* observable by the numerous grammatical incongruities in the Greek language (called "solecisms") that result from the appropriation of the Hebrew text. These seven categories of John's use of the Old Testament provide a basic framework for interpreting the meaning of the allusions in the book of Revelation.

Types of Figurative Language

As will be discussed in more detail in the chapter on of figurative language below, figures of speech serve as devices of comparison. By using analogical language, figures of speech lead the reader from the known to the unknown, in the present case, future events. Thus, their use helps alleviate the difficulty of communicating a subject—the end times—that defies mere propositional or descriptive language.

As do all forms of human communication, figurative language operates within a particular context. In the case of Revelation, this context is essentially made up by Old Testament prophetic-apocalyptic portions. Since Revelation depicts *a series of real visions* experienced by the seer, John, it is only natural that this individual, steeped in the world of Old Testament depictions of the end, saw these visions *in terms reminiscent of these passages*. At the same time, this does not mean that his portrayal of these visions *slavishly* follows the original Old Testament context. Thus, Revelation ought to be interpreted not merely in literary terms as if the seer operated exclusively on a literary level, performing a series of cut-and-paste operations in working with various Old Testament antecedent passages.

Rather, these texts constitute *points of departure* that guided the seer in experiencing these visions but did not *limit* him in describing what he saw. Thus, the interpreter's work is not done once he or she has identified one or several possible Old Testament texts to which a given passage in Revelation may allude. In the end, it is the interpreter's goal to understand the visions depicted in Revelation *on their own terms* and to identify the real-life historical referents which form the point of reference for the various symbols and figures in a given passage in Revelation.

Symbolic Nature of Revelation

The book of Revelation presents the reader with a vast number of captivating images: the glorified Christ, the heavenly throne and those surrounding it, a slain lamb with seven horns and seven eyes, a woman crowned with twelve stars, a red dragon, a seven-headed beast, a great prostitute, and a host of awe-inspiring angelic beings. These highly symbolic images make Revelation a truly unique book and one that is highly controversial and frequently misunderstood. It is undeniable that the Apocalypse contains a legion of symbolic and metaphorical images, but interpretive approaches divide sharply as to how these symbols should be interpreted. Two major divergent hermeneutical positions have emerged in this regard: (1) primarily literal and secondarily symbolic; or (2) primarily symbolic and secondarily literal.[115]

The first approach advocates interpreting Revelation primarily in a literal manner unless it is impossible to do so. This view is encapsulated in the hermeneutical dictum "When the plain sense of Scripture makes common sense, seek no other sense." While recognizing the presence of symbols, this view holds that we should identify a given term as symbolic only when it does not make sense to take it literally (e.g., Jesus does not have a literal sword protruding from his mouth).[116] Thus Tim LaHaye contends, "[T]ake every word at its primary, ordinary, usual, literal meaning unless the facts of the immediate text, studied in the light of related passages and axiomatic and fundamental truths, clearly indicate otherwise."[117] Interpreters such as these argue that non-literal interpretations result in an unchecked polyvalence based on human imagination.[118]

Many of those favoring literal interpretation maintain that the figures of speech (i.e., symbols) result from John attempting to describe future objects and scenarios from the limited framework of his ancient conceptions and language. The goal for interpreting these symbols, then, is to identify the one-to-one correspondence between his image and a modern

---

115. At this point, the reader is referred to the discussion on the nature of figurative language in chapter 14 below, which lays the foundation for the treatment below.

116. John F. Walvoord, "The Theological Context of Premillennialism," *Bib Sac* 150 (October-December 1993): 390; Zuck, *Basic Bible Interpretation*, 146.

117. LaHaye, *Revelation Unveiled*, 17.

118. John F. Walvoord, *The Revelation of Jesus Christ* (Chicago: Moody, 1966), 30; Ryrie, *Dispensationalism*, 29.

parallel. On the positive side, this approach takes the text at face value, avoids reducing it to an extended allegory, and often produces a simple, straightforward interpretation. However, while the approach may work when interpreting narrative or texts, its application to highly figurative genres such as apocalyptic falls short.

What could be wrong with interpreting apocalyptic literature such as Revelation literally? The main problem with such an approach is that it inadequately considers that the literary genre of a given text establishes the rules for how it should be interpreted. Meaning is intrinsically bound up with genre.[119] It follows that genre provides a context assigned by the author to communicate meaning. We have already shown that the genre of Revelation is prophetic-apocalyptic. The apocalyptic genre, by definition, is highly symbolic and not intended to be interpreted in a literal manner. For this reason, a rigid literal interpretation or literalism may actually obscure the author's intended meaning rather than expose it. Kevin Vanhoozer correctly poses a distinction between the literal sense and literalism.[120] If the interpreter is concerned with authorial intention, the literal sense must not be reduced merely to letters, *langue*, or locutions. Vanhoozer contends that "literalistic reading is less than fully 'literal'—that it is insufficiently and only 'thinly' literal—insofar as it ignores the role of authorial intentions and communicative acts."[121] What Vanhoozer means by this is that the literal—but not the "literalistic"— sense is what the author intended to convey by a given text; this, in turn, is especially true for figurative and symbolic language. In other words, if Revelation is prophetic-apocalyptic in nature, ascribing literalism to its numbers, proper nouns, and other images may actually prevent a proper understanding of John's intended meaning.[122] A more profitable hermeneutical approach is to reverse the interpretive order by placing the symbolic in the foreground while shifting the literal into the background. Thus, rather than positing the dictum "When the literal makes sense, seek no other sense," we suggest that a better maxim in interpreting apocalyptic is "Start out with the assumption that a given statement or image is figurative rather than literal."

---

119. Hirsch, *Validity in Interpretation*, 236.
120. Vanhoozer, *Is There a Meaning in This Text?*, 310.
121. Ibid., 311.
122. Carson, *Exegetical Fallacies*, 90.

G. K. Beale makes a strong case for the primacy of the symbolic over straight one-to-one literal correspondence.[123] He argues that *sēmainō* in Revelation 1:1 conveys the idea of "communication by symbols,"[124] noting that the normal usage of *sēmainō* in Scripture implies some type of "symbolic communication."[125] Since Revelation is a symbolic means of communication, the literal approach for interpreting the "plain sense" of the image may actually distort the intending meaning of the text. Beale maintains, "Of course, some parts are not symbolic, but the essence of the book is figurative. Where there is lack of clarity about whether something is symbolic, the scales of judgment should be titled in the direction of a nonliteral analysis."[126] For reasons such as these, the symbolic plane should be considered primary while care should be taken not to reduce the meaning of symbols to something exclusively spiritual.

Interpreting Symbols in Revelation

How, then, should you interpret the symbolic language in the book of Revelation? The symbols of Revelation, although enigmatic, are intended to reveal meaning rather than conceal it. The interpreter's task is to determine how a given symbol functions in its context and what it signifies. To grasp the meaning of a symbol, you must recognize both the mental or conceptual idea and the image it represents.[127] Visionary accounts represent a genre of biblical literature that employs the full arsenal of figurative language—similes, metaphors, and symbols—intended to communicate through the medium of symbolic images that burst with meaning. Symbols represent a type of metaphor in which a visual or linguistic sign (i.e., vehicle) of a known object or concept is used to express an unknown object or concept (i.e., tenor).[128]

The symbols in the Apocalypse derive from John's visual experience as a means to express *in* words what cannot be necessarily expressed *with* words. As Edith Humphrey observes, "Visions are, after all, visions, and to 'decode' them into a proposition or method is to change not only the form

---

123. Beale, *Book of Revelation*, 50–55.
124. Ibid., 52.
125. Ibid., 51. See the discussion of the allusion to Daniel 2:28–30 (LXX) in Revelation 1:1.
126. Ibid., 52.
127. Osborne, *Hermeneutical Spiral*, 283.
128. Ian Paul, "The Book of Revelation: Image, Symbol and Metaphor," in *Studies in the Book of Revelation*, ed. Steve Moyise (Edinburgh: T&T Clark, 2001), 135. See chapter 14 on figurative language below.

but also the meaning.[129] This is rather unlike a historical narrative where the primary theological meaning corresponds rather straightforwardly to the events narrated. The symbolism in Revelation dominates in such a way that the passage expresses directly the theological significance and only indirectly points to the underlying event.[130] John communicates through symbolic imagery so as to recreate the details of his vision but the symbols point beyond the text to spiritual, theological, and also physical realities.

Determining the denotation of a symbol is muddled by the possibility of polyvalence (multiple meanings). While some symbols potentially trigger a plethora of connotations, we recommend the judicious use of the following interpretive steps to arrive at the most probable intended meaning for a given symbol.

1. *Recognize the symbolic imagery associated with the description of people and beings, colors, numbers, institutions, places, and events.* The first step is to recognize the presence of symbolic imagery in the text. This seems simple enough, but all too often interpreters fail to recognize that almost everything in Revelation resonates with symbolic connotations. Think of Revelation as an impressionistic painting instead of a video recording of the future world. John paints verbal pictures depicting the contents of his vision replete with symbolic hues and shades. His descriptions are intended to evoke a sense of wonder, awe, and worship as well as to communicate prophetic eschatological expectations. This implies that most descriptions of people or beings, colors, numbers, institutions, places, and events carry a metaphorical or symbolic connotation. This is especially true if a person, number, color, or anything else recurs throughout the book. For example, the number seven not only occurs explicitly but also implicitly with the sevenfold repetition of certain words or phrases. The symbolic weight of the number seven as representative of completion or perfection can hardly be overstated. Much of the imagery in the Apocalypse, however, is merely designed to heighten the coloring of the picture by adding vividness and movement to its scenes. For this reason, a careful reading of the text will avoid making everything a

129. Edith M. Humphrey, *And I Turned to See the Voice: The Rhetoric of Vision in the New Testament* (Grand Rapids: Baker, 2007), 21.
130. Vern S. Poythress, "Genre and Hermeneutics in Rev 20:1–6," *JETS* 36 (1993): 42.

symbol for something else. Therefore, read Revelation with an informed sensitivity to the symbolic nature of its language and imagery.

2. Look for interpretations of those symbols within the vision. The second step is to look for an interpretation of symbols within the context of the vision narrative. Many times, the intended meaning of a symbol is explicitly provided by John or a heavenly being. These are fairly easy to identify because of the formula: *symbol + "is this" "these are" "which are" = identification.* The following list provides a brief summary of some of the occurrences of self-interpreted symbols in Revelation:

While these self-interpreted symbols help to narrow the range of referents for a given symbol, they also create a whole new set of questions. At times, they interpret the symbol with another symbol. The seven lamps represent the seven spirits of God, and the seven spirits of God figuratively represent the Holy Spirit. The two witnesses are identified as two olive trees and two lampstands. The olive trees and lampstands are symbolic representations borrowed from Zechariah 4 and seem to denote the Spirit-empowered people of God. Although the interpretation of a symbol with a symbol can be potentially confusing, it helpfully limits the intended meaning of a symbol in the text. Once the referent is identified within the text, it typically becomes the fixed meaning for that particular symbol in Revelation.

10.2. SELF-INTERPRETED SYMBOLS IN REVELATION:			
Reference	Symbol	Interpretive Signal	Symbol Identified
1:20	seven stars	"[they] are" (*eisin*)	the angels of the seven churches
1:20	seven lampstands	"[they] are" (*eisin*)	the seven churches
4:5	seven lamps before the throne	"these are" (*ha eisin*)	the seven spirits of God
5:6	seven horns and seven eyes of the Lamb	"which are" (*hoi eisin*)	the seven spirits of God sent out into all the earth
5:8	golden bowls full of incense	"which are" (*hai eisin*)	the prayers of the saints

7:13–14	the multitude in white robes	"these are" (*houtoi eisin*)	the saints who have come out of the great tribulation
11:4	the two olive trees and the two lampstands that stand before the Lord of the earth	"these are" (*houtoi eisin*)	the two witnesses
14:4	the 144,000	"these are" (*houtoi eisin*)	those who did not defile themselves with women and kept themselves pure
17:9	the seven heads of the beast	"[they] are" (*eisin*)	seven hills (Rome) and also seven kings (emperors?)
19:8	fine linen, bright and clean	"stands for" (*gar...estin*)	the righteous acts of the saints

3. Determine if the symbol stems from an allusion to the Old Testament. A third step for adjudicating the meaning of a symbol relates to the use of the Old Testament. The entire text of John's vision(s) is saturated with allusions to the Old Testament. John frequently uses the language and imagery of the Old Testament to provide his readers with a framework for understanding the significance of what he saw. This does not imply that John was performing an exegesis of the Old Testament, but rather that he borrowed the wording, images, themes, and eschatological expectations from the Old Testament. These allusions are pressed into the service of the textual imagery. The interpreter must first determine if the text alludes to an Old Testament subtext. After the allusion is verified, the interpreter should seek to understand the meaning of the Old Testament passage in its context. Next, you need to compare carefully the similarities and differences between the Old Testament and its allusion in Revelation. Once you have compared the texts, you will be able to see how John ascribes a particular meaning to the Old Testament language and imagery by using and reworking it into the account of his vision.

For example, in Revelation 11:4, John states that these two witnesses are the two olive trees and two lampstands that stand before the Lord of the Earth. The positive statement "these are" (*houtoi eisin*) followed by the two plural nouns with the article suggest that John expected his readers to figure out their identity. This verse constitutes a direct allusion to Zechariah 4:1–14 regarding Joshua (the post-exilic high priest) and Zerubbabel (the post-exilic Davidic descendent). Zechariah sees one lampstand with seven lamps sitting upon it and seven oil channels keeping the lamps supplied with olive oil. An olive tree stood flanked on the left and right side of the lampstand. The trees provided the olives to keep the bowl of the lampstand supplied with oil. The interpreting angel explicated the meaning of the image: it is the Holy Spirit who accomplishes the task of rebuilding the temple. Zechariah inquires as to the exact identity of the two olive trees and discovers that they are the two anointed ones (Zerubbabel and Joshua) who serve the Lord of all the earth. Despite the obvious lexical parallels between Zechariah 4:1–14 and Revelation 11:4, John diverges from Zechariah's vision in that he sees two lampstands instead of one. John also equates the trees *with* the lampstands, while in Zechariah they are kept distinct. This suggests that John modified the imagery rather than merely patterning his vision after Zechariah's. The alteration from one lampstand to two comprises the most striking difference between Revelation 11:4 and Zechariah 4:2. The reason for this shift is probably that lampstands are used in the Apocalypse to denote the churches (1:20).

4. Compare the symbol with other apocalyptic writings to see if it is a common symbol with a relatively standard meaning. John primarily uses Old Testament imagery, but he occasionally employs imagery belonging to the common stock of apocalyptic writings. Some images have no parallels in the text of the biblical canon. In these cases, a comparative reading of other apocalyptic texts and Jewish writings may shed light on Revelation. Before consulting these texts, a few caveats are in order. First, the existence of any parallels between Revelation and these writings does not necessitate, demand, or imply any form of literary dependence on the part of Revelation. What it does indicate is that the authors of these writings all had access to certain traditions circulating independently of the apocalypses existing in either oral or written form.[131]

Second, most of these are not exact parallels in that they rarely share identical wording. When examining a potential apocalyptic parallel, it is important to observe the distinctions and understand how the variations

---

131. Bauckham, *Climax of Prophecy*, 88–91.

affect the symbol's meaning in the text. Third, the date of a given writing deserves serious consideration because if the other apocalyptic work post-dates Revelation the symbolic parallel may derive from Revelation, indicate a shared tradition, or be unrelated. Nevertheless, this may provide a glimpse into the tradition history of the imagery by seeing how other writings employed similar imagery. An awareness of these traditional apocalyptic images can help us clarify some of the symbolic imagery in Revelation, especially in cases where Old Testament parallels are lacking.

Richard Bauckham demonstrates the exegetical and hermeneutical value of this comparative analysis by examining four images in the book of Revelation. These are the blood up to the horses bridle (14:20b); the completion of the number of martyrs (6:9–11); the giving up of the dead (20:13); and the silence in heaven (8:1).[132] The interpretation of these symbols in Revelation is possible without the additional parallels in apocalyptic literature. These parallels, however, help establish a more nuanced and stable understanding of this imagery. One would expect some overlap of imagery and concepts in writings from a common genre.

5. Look for any possible connections between the symbol and the cultural-historical context. The fifth step looks beyond the text in an attempt to set the imagery within the cultural and historical context of first-century Asia Minor. Two thousand years of history separate modern readers of Revelation from the social, cultural, and political environment of the original recipients. Some of the confusion regarding the imagery of the Apocalypse derives directly from the fact that John wrote to people that all shared a common understanding of their surrounding culture within the Roman Empire. Images of beasts, kings, and cities wielding enormous military and political power over its citizens may seem strange and foreign to the modern reader living in America. The readers of John's vision in Asia Minor, however, would have resonated with the cultural connotations associated with these images. This would be equivalent to someone writing in the year 2011 referring to the "smoke ascending from the twin towers." People would instantly recall the dreadful events of September 11, 2001 and think of the terrorist attack on the World Trade Center. Fast-forward 2,000 years

---

132. Ibid., 38–83.

into the future. Someone in China reads the reference to "twin towers" and may completely miss the allusion to these events. A historically informed reading of the text will often clear up the haze of a given set of symbols. The mark of the beast in Revelation 13:18 provides an example of how some symbols are wedded to the historical context.

6. *Consult treatments of the symbol in scholarly commentaries and other works*. The sixth step is to see how scholars have interpreted the symbols. This step may actually occur in tandem with steps one through five. The complex nature of symbolism requires the mature insights of seasoned experts who have devoted serious time studying the text of Revelation. Keep in mind, however, that serious time and study does not guarantee that a given interpretation is plausible or probable. Avoid depending on any one commentator. Each scholar brings his or her own set of presuppositions to the text that may produce radically differing interpretations. One commentator may say that a symbol has a multiple range of meanings and another may posit a very particular referent with astounding confidence. While scholars may not have all the answers, they have certainly thought through the issues, and their years of reading the text will more often than not provide a very helpful understanding of the meaning of Revelation's imagery.

7. *Remain humble in your conclusions.* Interpreting Revelation requires humility and an openness to return to the text again and again. Once you have thoroughly studied the text, avoid thinking that you have now unlocked all the mysteries of the Apocalypse. Make studying the book of Revelation a lifetime pursuit. Repeat steps one through six on a regular basis. This will prevent you from falling into the temptation of thinking that you alone have the right interpretation of this mysterious and complex book. No one other than God has the final answer on the meaning of Revelation. While this is sobering, it will keep you humble and encourage you to keep studying God's Word.

Structure

While certain areas of agreement exist, there is no broad consensus on the outline of the Revelation. As a help and general guideline, we will present two possible outlines. This is not to preclude your own work with the text but is intended to serve as an initial framework from which you may want to proceed. The first outline, per the discussion above, focuses on the four visions "in the Spirit" depicted in the book. The second outline seeks to capture the narrative dynamic centering on the opening of the heavenly scroll which, as mentioned, is one of the major narrative peaks of the story of the book.

Outline #1

I.   Prologue (1:1–8)

II. Vision One (Patmos): The Glorified Christ and His Message to the Churches (1:9–3:22)
     A. The Inaugural Vision of Jesus Christ (1:9–20)
     B. The Messages to the Seven Churches of Asia Minor (2:1–3:22)

III. Vision Two (Heaven): The Divine Court Proceedings and the Trial of the Nations (4:1–16:21)
     A. Transition from Patmos to Heaven (4:1–2)
     B. Worship around the Throne (4:3–11)
     C. The Divine Courtroom (5:1–14)
     D. Preliminary Investigative Judgments (6:1–17)
     E. First Interlude: The Protective Sealing of God's People (7:1–17)
     F. Eschatological Investigative Judgments (8:1–9:21)
     G. Second Interlude: God's People as Prophetic Witnesses (10:1–11:19)
     H. Third Interlude: The Signs Narrative/God's People in Holy War (12:1–15:1)
     I. Final Investigative Judgments: The Third Woe/Seven Bowls (16:1–21)

IV. Vision Three (Desert): The Destruction of Babylon and the Return of Christ (17:1–21:8)
     A. Transition: "Come, I Will Show You the Punishment of the Great Prostitute" (17:1–2)
     B. The Prostitute City Babylon Described (17:3–6)
     C. The Prostitute City Babylon as Rome (17:7–18)
     D. The Trial and Sentencing of Babylon (18:1–24)
     E. The Heavenly Celebration of Babylon's Destruction (19:1–10)
     F. The Divine Warrior and the Final Tribunal (19:11–20:15)

G. The Renewal of Creation and the Arrival of the New
   Jerusalem (21:1–8)

V.   Vision Four (Mountain): Believers' Reward and the Renewal of
     Creation (21:9–22:5)

   A. Transition: "Come, I Will Show You the Bride" (21:9–10)

   B. The Description of the New Jerusalem Descending from
      Heaven (21:11–27)

   C. The Paradise of God: The Renewal of Creation (22:1–5)

VI. Epilogue (22:6–21)

Outline #2

I.   Prologue: Opening Remarks and Doxology (1:1–8)

II.   The Seven Letter Scroll (1:9–3:22)

   A. Preparation: Christ among the Seven Churches (1:9–20)

   B. Letters to the Seven Churches (2:1–3:22)

III. The Heavenly Scroll (4:1–22:5)

   A. Preparation: Heavenly Worship (4:1–11)

   B. The Seven Seals Opened (5:1–8:1)

   C. The Seven Trumpets: Heralding the Opening of the Scroll
      (8:2–11:19)

   D. The Open Scroll (12:1–22:5)

IV. Epilogue: Closing Remarks and Benediction (22:6–21)

SAMPLE EXEGESIS: REVELATION 11:1–13

Revelation 11:1–13 contains the separate but interrelated visionary accounts of the temple measuring (Rev. 11:1–2) followed by the ministry of
the two witnesses (Rev. 11:3–13). These two accounts represent one of the
most challenging passages to interpret in Revelation.[133] The different interpretations essentially boil down to whether or not the referents in the
vision are literal (i.e., a literal temple in Jerusalem and two literal prophets
witnessing in Jerusalem) or symbolic (i.e., the temple represents the people
of God/church in the midst of worship and persecution and the two witnesses represent the church in a prophetic role). The following sample

---

133. Grant Osborne notes that Rev. 11:3–13 is one of the most debated passages in the
    book. Osborne, *Revelation*, 417.

exegesis will examine both of these issues in light of the hermeneutical triad.

History

Concerning the temple in Rev. 11:1–2, scholars have postulated four possible explanations for the reference to the temple. First, preterist interpreters assert that this clearly presupposes that the temple in Jerusalem is still standing. Second, other scholars suggest that Rev. 11:1–2 was written prior to A.D. 70 but was included in a later redaction during the reign of Domitian. A third option, common to dispensationalist interpreters, views this as a future third temple that will be built in Jerusalem during the tribulation. The fourth option views the temple reference as symbolic, rendering a literal temple still standing in Jerusalem at the time of composition unnecessary. The first and third options represent the simplest and most natural explanations of the text, but the text itself may not support a literal referent for the temple.

Revelation, due to its genre, frequently employs figurative language and symbols. There are no reasons to suppose that Rev. 11:1–2 should be interpreted any differently from the rest of the vision. John becomes an active participant who is given a reed and instructed to perform a symbolic prophetic action by measuring the temple. Measuring, in the OT, was sometimes used to connote destruction (2 Sam. 8:2; Isa. 28:16–17; 34:11; Lam. 2:8; Amos 7:7–9) but also implied divine protection (Jer. 31:38–40; Zech. 1:16; 2:1–2; Ezek. 40:1–6; 42:20). Ezekiel 40–48 and Zech. 2:1–2 are typically identified as the specific backdrop for this text, but Dan 8:11–14 also casts an important shadow on this passage. John is instructed to measure the temple/sanctuary of God, the altar, and the worshippers, but to exclude/cast out the outer court because it was given to the Gentiles along with the holy city to trample for forty-two months. The image is of the holy place (containing the holy of holies), the innermost court of the biblical temple (court of the priests), and the altar of incense together with those worshipping in the sanctuary.

The terms used for the temple favor a non-literal usage. John's language regarding the temple could just as easily denote a heavenly or symbolic temple as it could a literal temple. The word used for temple, *naos*, refers specifically to the temple sanctuary rather than the entire temple complex (*hieron*). John uses *naos* throughout Revelation to refer to the heavenly temple (Rev. 3:12; 7:15; 11:19; 14:15, 17; 15:5, 6, 8; 16:1, 17). Likewise, the term translated as "altar" frequently occurs denoting the heavenly altar of incense (Rev. 6:9; 8:3, 5; 9:13;

14:18; 16:7). Since the typical usage of temple language refers to spiritual realities instead of earthly institutions, it seems likely that the temple in Rev. 11:1-2
may symbolically represent the people of God. In addition, the outer-court and
"holy city" also may be understood as references to the people of God.[134] The
image of the church as symbolically denoting the temple is supported by the
association of the church as the temple of the Holy Spirit (1 Cor. 3:16–17; 6:10; 2
Cor. 5:15; Eph. 2:21–22; 1 Pet. 2:5; Rev. 3:12).

Literature

Concordant to this three and a half year period, God will give his two
witnesses to prophesy for 1,260 days (Rev. 11:3–13). Rather than viewing
this historically, the time frame is more literary in nature and corresponds
to the times, time, and half a time of Dan. 7:25 and 12:7 denoting an intense but limited period of suffering. The word "witness" (*martysin*), in this
context, appears to have the same meaning as "prophet" (cf. Rev. 11:10).[135]
That God gives his two witnesses corresponds to the judicial requirement
of two witnesses in any legal case (Num. 35:30; Deut. 17:6; 19:15).

The prophetic ministry of the two witnesses is expressed not only
in their commission but also in their description. The phrase "they will
prophesy" not only represents their prophetic commission but also connects it with John's commission in Rev. 10:11. The witnesses, then, are commissioned to proclaim a message of impending judgment against many
peoples, nations, languages, and kings. Failure to repent of their idolatry,
wickedness, and bloodshed will certainly incur God's wrath. This prophetic activity ensures that all the people of earth will know exactly why
these judgments are befalling them. Even their attire of sackcloth highlights their prophetic message of judgment by evoking familiar OT images
related to times of individual and national mourning and repentance.[136]

Their prophetic message is affirmed by supernatural displays of power
reminiscent of Moses and Elijah. During the days appointed for them to
prophesy they are divinely protected from any physical harm. If someone
attempts to harm them, fire issues forth from the mouth of the witnesses
and consumes their enemies. This is similar to the occasion when Elijah

---

134. Beale, *Book of Revelation*, 568–71.
135. Aune, *Revelation 6–16*, 610.
136. 1 Kgs. 20:31-32; 21:27; 1 Chron. 21:16; Neh. 9:1; Isa. 22:12; 32:11; 58:5; Jer. 4:8; 6:26;
   48:37; Jon. 3:5-8; Mt. 11:21; Lk. 10:13

called down fire upon his opponents in 2 Kings 1:9–16. Their commission to prophesy grants them the authority to prevent rain like Elijah and to turn water into to blood like Moses. They also have the ability to inflict any kind additional plagues on the earth. Both witnesses apparently share these abilities equally since no distinction is made regarding which witness can perform which miracle. These supernatural displays of power validate their testimony and verify them as true prophets speaking on Christ's behalf.

Theology

An attempt at identifying these two witnesses largely depends on whether or not they are representative of two individuals or a group of people. The most natural explanation is to identify them as the eschatological return of Moses and Elijah or at least two future individuals like them. The clear allusion to the ministries of Elijah and Moses coupled with the Jewish expectation of their return lends credibility to this view (Deut. 18:18; Mal. 4:5–6; cf. Sir. 48:10) Jewish tradition posited the expectation of the eschatological return of figures like Moses, Elijah, and Enoch. Since the witnesses are presented as two eschatological prophets it is possible that John envisioned two future Christian prophets coming in the spirit and power of Israel's two greatest prophets.[137] However, John offers a clue to identification in Rev. 11:4.

In Revelation 11:4, John states that these two witnesses are the two olive trees and two lampstands that stand before the Lord of the Earth. The positive assertion that "these are" followed by the two plural nouns with the article suggest that John expected his readers to figure out their identity. This verse constitutes a direct allusion to Zechariah 4:1–14 regarding Joshua (the post-exilic high priest) and Zerubbabel (the postexilic Davidic descendant). Zechariah sees one lampstand with seven lamps sitting upon it and seven oil channels keeping the lamps supplied with olive oil. He also sees to olive trees flanked on the left and right side of the lampstand. Zechariah inquires as to the exact identity of the two olive trees and discovers that they are the two anointed ones (Zerubbabel and Joshua) who serve the Lord of all the earth. Despite the obvious lexical parallels between Zechariah 4:1–14 and Revelation 11:4, John diverges from Zechariah's vision in that he sees two lampstands instead of one. John also equates the trees with the lampstands, but in Zechariah they are kept distinct. This suggests John

---

137. Osborne, *Revelation*, 418.

modified the imagery so as not to equate his vision as simply a rehashing of Zechariah's.

The alteration from one lampstand into two comprises the most striking difference between Revelation 11:4 and Zechariah. 4:2. The reason for this shift probably rests with the fact that the symbol of lampstands in the Apocalypse is clearly used to denote the churches (Rev. 1:20). If John intended to use "lampstand" to denote any other entity or individual he fails to make this usage explicit. John probably does not intend to equate the witnesses with all the churches since he restricts their number to only two out of seven. The use of two also reinforces the notion of the church as a witness giving legal testimony. One plausible solution is to equate these two lampstands with the churches in Smyrna and Philadelphia. Both churches were commended for their faithfulness and endurance despite persecution and hardships. These are the only two churches free from any accusations from Christ. They may represent the churches who faithfully maintain their witness of Christ in the midst of persecution.

Despite the combined challenges of interpreting this passage along with the abundance of competing interpretations, it is possible to arrive at a possible understanding of the text that does justice to the symbolic nature of the visionary images, the abundant use of OT allusions, and the overall message of the book. John writes to encourage weary and persecuted Christians to remain faithful to Christ by depicted them as the protected but persecuted holy people of God who are commissioned as prophetic witnesses to pagan nations.

GUIDELINES FOR INTERPRETING APOCALYPTIC LITERATURE

1. Locate the historical setting of the book of Revelation.

2. Distinguish between intertextuality, inner-biblical exegesis, allusion, and echo.

3. Identify the type of allusion, whether embedded, implied, or incidental.

4. Identify the specific Old Testament passage(s) invoked in a given passage in Revelation.

5. Identify the plot and development of the book of Revelation and relate the specific passage to the overall plot.

6. Identify the major characters and their role in the narrative.

7. Identify the major theological themes in the book of Revelation.

8. Identify the way in which a given theological theme finds its culmination in Revelation.

9. Determine principles for godly living in view of the culmination of Christ's kingdom at his return.

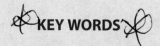

KEY WORDS

Allusion: an authorially intended reference to a preceding text of Scripture involving verbal or, at a minimum, conceptual similarity

Apocalypse: a genre of revelatory literature, written between approximately 200 B.C. and A.D. 200, depicting the end times in highly symbolic language and imagery

Apocalyptic: an adjective used when describing either the literary genre or the worldview

Apocalypticism: denotes a worldview, ideology, or theology merging the eschatological aims of particular groups into a cosmic and political arena

Eclectic approach: interpretation of Revelation combining insights from the preterist, historicist, idealist, and futurist approaches

Emperor cult: the mandated, enforced worship of the Roman emperor as deity

Eschaton: the end times

Futurist approach: interpretation of Revelation as primarily depicting future events

Historicist approach: interpretation of Revelation as forecasting the course of history in Western Europe

Idealist approach: interpretation of Revelation focusing on the symbolic portrayal of spiritual and timeless truths regarding the end times

Inaugurated eschatology: aspects of the end times that have already begun to be a present reality in the lives of believers

Interlude: a literary feature interspersing additional material into a given unit

Intertextuality: relationship between texts

Millennium: the 1,000-year reign of Christ at the end of time depicted in Revelation 20

Nero *redivivus* myth: the belief that the Roman emperor Nero (A.D. 54–68) did not truly die but was still alive and would return

Preterist approach: interpretation of Revelation that focuses on the book's message to its contemporary, first-century readers

Progressive dispensationalism: belief that the various eras of salvation history (dispensations) progressively overlap in keeping with the "already/not yet" tension of inaugurated eschatology

Prophetic-apocalyptic: the likely genre of the book of Revelation, combining prophetic and apocalyptic features

Theodicy: the justification of God's righteous purposes, particularly in judgment of rebellious people

Transitivity: the ability of the audience to grasp and comprehend an allusion and its source text

STUDY QUESTIONS

1. What is apocalyptic? Provide a basic definition and a commentary explaining the component parts of your definition.

2. What are at least three major important background features of the book of Revelation? Provide some basic information of each.

3. What is the genre of Revelation?

4. What is the plot and structure of the book of Revelation? Discuss with special emphasis to the phrase "in the Spirit" and the role of the various scrolls in the unfolding narrative.

5. What are some major criteria for identifying Old Testament allusions in the book of Revelation?

6. What are two special literary features in Revelation?

7. What are the four major approaches to the book of Revelation? Which approach do you prefer?

8. What is one major theological theme in Revelation, and what is its significance for interpreting the book as a whole?

9. What are the guidelines for interpreting apocalyptic literature?

ASSIGNMENTS

1. Provide a basic definition of apocalyptic and show how the book of Revelation is similar or different from other exemplars of Second Temple apocalyptic literature. For each component part of your definition, give a brief commentary explaining the feature and provide relevant scriptural references to support your presentation.

2. How does the apocalyptic genre differ from historical narrative? How should one approach the book of Revelation with regard to interpreting its abundant symbolism? Should one expect references to be literal unless literal interpretation does not make sense, or should one expect references to be symbolic?

3. Assess the historical character of the book of Revelation. What is asserted by the author of the book with regard to the historical events that are portrayed in the book? How does understanding the original historical setting help in understanding the message of the book?

4. Who are the 144,000 mentioned in Revelation 7? What are the major views regarding their identity, and how are these views informed by the larger theological systems of a given school of interpretation? Who do you think are the 144,000, and how do you support your view by a close contextual exegesis of the passage?

5. Discuss the basic structure and major theological themes in the book of Revelation.

CHAPTER BIBLIOGRAPHY

Aune, David E. *Revelation*. 3 vols. Word Biblical Commentary 52.
    Nashville: Thomas Nelson, 1997, 1998.
_____. "The Apocalypse of John and the Problem of Genre."
    Semeia 36 (1986): 65–96.
Barr, David. *New Testament Story: An Introduction*. Belmont, CA:
    Wadsworth, 1987.
Bauckham, Richard. *The Climax of Prophecy: Studies on the Book of
    Revelation*. London: T&T Clark, 1993.
_____. *The Theology of the Book of Revelation*. Cambridge:
    Cambridge University Press, 1993.
Beagley, Alan J. *The "Sitz im Leben" of the Apocalypse, with Particular
    Reference to the Role of the Church's Enemies*. Beihefte zur
    neutestamentlichen Wissenschaft 50. Berlin: de Gruyter, 1987.
Beale, G. K. *The Book of Revelation*. New International Greek
    Testament Commentary. Grand Rapids: Eerdmans, 1999.
Blaising, Craig A. and Darrell L. Bock. *Progressive Dispensationalism*.
    Grand Rapids: Baker, 1993.
Charles, R. H. *The Revelation of St. John*. International Critical
    Commentary. 2 vols. New York: Scribner's, 1920.
Collins, Adela Yarbro. *Crisis and Catharsis: The Power of the
    Apocalypse*. Philadelphia: Westminster, 1984.
Collins, John J. "Introduction: Towards the Morphology of a Genre."
    Semeia 14 (1979): 1–20.
Farrer, Austin M. *The Revelation of St. John the Divine*. Oxford: Oxford
    University Press, 1964.
Ford, J. Massyngberde. *Revelation*. Anchor Bible 38. New York:
    Doubleday, 1975.
Hemer, Colin J. *The Letters to the Seven Churches of Asia in Their Local
    Setting*. JSNT Supplement 11. Sheffield: JSOT, 1986.
Johnson, Alan F. "Revelation." Pp. 571–789 in *The Expositor's Bible
    Commentary*. Rev. ed. Vol. 13: *Hebrews–Revelation*. Grand
    Rapids: Zondervan, 2005.

Koester, Craig R. "On the Verge of the Millennium: A History of the Interpretation of Revelation." *Word and World* 15 (1995): 128–36.

Köstenberger, Andreas J., L. Scott Kellum, and Charles L. Quarles. Chapter 20 in *The Cradle, the Cross, and the Crown: An Introduction to the New Testament*. Nashville: B&H, 2009.

Kovacs, Judith and Christopher Rowland. *Revelation: The Apocalypse of Jesus Christ*. BBC. Oxford: Blackwell, 2004.

Ladd, George Eldon. *A Commentary on the Revelation of John*. Grand Rapids: Eerdmans, 1972.

Maier, Gerhard. *Die Johannesoffenbarung und die Kirche*. Wissenschaftliche Untersuchungen zum Neuen Testament 25. Tübingen: Mohr Siebeck, 1981.

Michaels, J. Ramsey. *Revelation*. IVP New Testament Commentary 20. Downers Grove: InterVarsity, 1997.

Mounce, Robert H. *The Book of Revelation*. Rev. ed. New International Commentary on the New Testament. Grand Rapids: Eerdmans, 1997.

Osborne, Grant R. *Revelation*. Baker Exegetical Commentary on the New Testament. Grand Rapids: Baker, 2002.

Pate, C. Marvin, ed. *Four Views on the Book of Revelation*. Grand Rapids: Zondervan, 1998.

Porter, Stanley E. "The Language of the Apocalypse in Recent Discussion." *New Testament Studies* (1989): 582–603.

Sandy, D. Brent. *Plowshares and Pruning Hooks: Rethinking the Language of Biblical Prophecy and Apocalyptic*. Downers Grove: InterVarsity, 2002.

Smalley, Stephen S. *The Revelation to John*. Downers Grove: InterVarsity, 2005.

_____. *Thunder and Love: John's Revelation and John's Community*. Milton Keynes, UK: Word, 1994.

Wainwright, Arthur W. *Mysterious Apocalypse: Interpreting the Book of Revelation*. Nashville: Abingdon, 1993.

Wilson, Mark. *Charts on the Book of Revelation: Literary, Historical, and Theological Perspectives*. Grand Rapids: Kregel, 2007.

UNIT 3: LANGUAGE

CHAPTER 12 OBJECTIVES

1. To acquaint the student with some of the basic characteristics of biblical Greek and Hebrew.

2. To address important grammatical and syntactical matters pertaining to the study of Scripture.

3. To introduce the student to the analysis of biblical discourse.

4. To impress upon the student the importance of interpreting smaller exegetical units in light of a book's overall structure.

5. To present the student with a simple method for outlining the structure of a biblical book or interpretive unit.

CHAPTER 12 OUTLINE

A. Defining the Terms: Grammar, Syntax, and Discourse
   1. Discourse
   2. Other Definitions
B. Grammatical Foundations: Basics of Biblical Greek and Hebrew
   1. Introduction
   2. Basic Characteristics of New Testament Greek
      a. Verbal System
      b. The Greek Article
      c. The Genitive Case
      d. The Greek Participle
C. Word Order and Sentence Structure: Basics of Greek Syntax
   1. Word Order
   2. Larger Syntactical Features
   3. Sentence Structure
      a. Asyndeton
      b. Parenthesis
      c. Anacoluthon
D. Discourse Analysis: Overview of Method
   1. Major Steps in Discourse Analysis
      a. Boundary Features
      b. Cohesion
      c. Relations
      d. Prominence
      e. Situation
   2. Sample Discourse Analysis: John 2:1–11
E. Discourse Analysis: Specific Examples
   1. Discerning the Macrostructure: Level #1
   2. Discerning the Macrostructure: Level #2
   3. Discerning the Microstructure: Level #3
   4. Discerning the Microstructure: Level #4
F. Discourse Analysis: Tracing the Thought Flow
G. Guidelines for Outlining a Biblical Book or Interpretive Unit
H. Key Words
I. Study Questions
J. Assignments
K. Chapter Bibliography

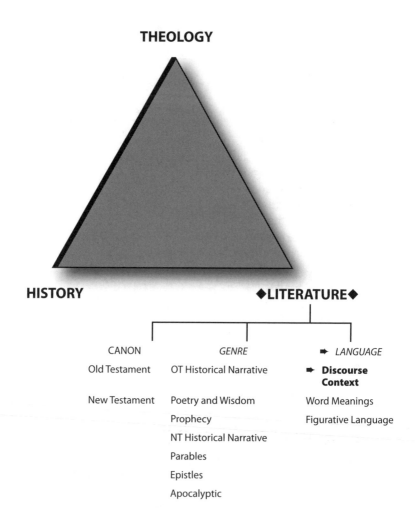

THEOLOGY

HISTORY   ◆LITERATURE◆

CANON	GENRE	➡ LANGUAGE
Old Testament	OT Historical Narrative	➡ **Discourse Context**
New Testament	Poetry and Wisdom	Word Meanings
	Prophecy	Figurative Language
	NT Historical Narrative	
	Parables	
	Epistles	
	Apocalyptic	

Chapter 12

THE IMPORTANCE OF CONTEXT:
GRAMMAR, SYNTAX, AND DISCOURSE

DEFINING THE TERMS: GRAMMAR, SYNTAX, AND DISCOURSE

NOW THAT WE HAVE SURVEYED the canonical landscape and acquainted ourselves with the various types of literature found in Scripture, we will move from the "semantics of biblical *literature*" to the "semantics of biblical *language*."[1] Continuing to follow the principle of interpreting the parts in light of the whole, we will now attempt to come to terms with three important phenomena of the language of Scripture: (1) the discourse level of the biblical text; (2) word meanings and the sentence level of Scripture; and (3) figurative language.

In this chapter, we will deal with syntax and the vital role of context in interpretation; in the next chapter, we will discuss linguistics and semantics primarily as they relate to words. Syntax may be defined as the relationships of words to one another. Importantly, the proper textual unit at which meaning is to be discerned is not the individual word, the phrase,

---

1. "Semantics of biblical language" is the title of James Barr's famous book, *The Semantics of Biblical Language* (London: SCM, 1961). We have mentioned the title "semantics of biblical literature" (used by Kevin Vanhoozer, in obvious allusion to James Barr's seminal work) at the outset of our discussion of the various genres of Scripture in chapter 5 above.

or even the sentence, but the larger discourse, that is, the paragraph level and ultimately the entire document of which a given word, phrase, or sentence is a part. This simple insight, amply confirmed by recent linguistic research, has the potential of revolutionizing your study of the biblical text.[2]

Before moving on to the discussion, it will be helpful to define three major terms: (1) grammar; (2) syntax; and (3) discourse. There is no sharp distinction in definition and usage between the terms "grammar" and "syntax." If any distinction can be made at all, it may be said that *grammar* denotes specific features of syntax, such as a certain kind of genitive or participle (form), while *syntax* refers more broadly to relationships between words in the larger scheme of discourses and sentence structures. A distinction exists also between semantics (the subject of the next chapter) and syntax. *Semantics* is concerned with the meaning of *individual words* (based on the recognition that word meaning is to be discerned in context), while *syntax* is concerned with *the relationship between words*.

In the following discussion of the basics of biblical Greek and Hebrew, we will discuss several foundational areas of grammar that affect biblical interpretation, such as the verbal system, the article, the genitive, or the Greek participle. After providing an overview of Greek sentence structure, we will move on to discover the approach to Scripture called "discourse analysis." After giving an overall survey of the method, we will look at several specific examples of a discourse-oriented model of biblical interpretation. This model is based on the realization that hermeneutics should be concerned not merely with word study (semantics), grammar, and syntax but with the larger discourse unit, the fabric out of which biblical texts are spun.

Discourse

Before delving into the subject, it will be helpful to define several key terms, most importantly that of discourse itself. What is discourse? Essentially, *discourse* may be defined as any coherent sequence of phrases or sentences, whether a narrative, logical argument, or poetic portion of

---

2. For a helpful treatment see George H. Guthrie, "Discourse Analysis," in *Interpreting the New Testament*, ed. David Alan Black and David S. Dockery (Nashville: B&H, 2001), 253–71, with further bibliography on pp. 268–69.

text.[3] To be coherent and intelligible, all forms of extended human discourse must possess certain features that provide them with boundary markers, cohesion, prominence, relations, and situatedness. As will be seen, this is accomplished by a variety of linguistic means, such as initiatory phrases, topics or themes, logical connections, and a myriad of other linguistic, grammatical, and syntactical features.

An example of the relevance of discerning the boundaries of biblical discourse for interpretation is John's account of Jesus' encounter with Nicodemus. The chapter division would suggest that the account commences with John 3:1. More likely, however, the unit starts with 2:23–25, which serves both as a conclusion to the temple clearing in 2:13–22 and as an introduction to the Nicodemus narrative. This is suggested by several verbal tail-end hooks (on which see further below) which are found in both 2:23–25 and 3:1–2, including references to Jesus' signs and references to people who witnessed Jesus' signs in Jerusalem to whom Jesus would not entrust himself and Nicodemus as a "man of the Pharisees."

Therefore, rather than understanding Jesus' encounter with Nicodemus as merely a face-off between two prominent rabbis, we see that in John's theology Nicodemus is presented as a prototype of a person who witnessed Jesus' teaching and signs but who did not truly understand Jesus' identity as Messiah and Son of God. Thus an understanding of the features of biblical discourse, and in the present case a proper identification of discourse boundaries, is absolutely essential to a proper and full-fledged interpretation of a given textual unit.

Other Definitions

To aid in the understanding of the discussion below and to clarify the terminology used, it will be beneficial to define several other important syntactical terms as well.[4] The first such term is that of "phrase," which may be defined as any meaningful word cluster that lacks a verb form, such as a prepositional phrase plus an article plus a noun (e.g., Grk. εἰς τόν

---

3. Cf. Richard J. Erickson, *A Beginner's Guide to New Testament Exegesis* (Downers Grove: InterVarsity, 2005), 71, who defines discourse as "any complete, self-contained act of communication." Peter Cotterell and Max Turner, *Linguistics & Biblical Interpretation* (Downers Grove: InterVarsity, 1989), 230, similarly define discourse as "any coherent sequence of strings, any coherent stretch of language."
4. Cf. Erickson, *Beginner's Guide*, 71–74.

οἶκον [*eis ton oikon*], "into the house"). Typically, prepositional phrases modify (i.e., explain or give additional information regarding) the main verb in a given clause or sentence. In the above example, "into the house" may modify "he went" (ἐλθέν, *elthen*), indicating *where* a given person went. Phrases are thus part of what makes up a larger discourse.

Two more definitions will be helpful, those for "clause" and "sentence." A "clause" is any meaningful cluster of words that includes a verb, while a "sentence" is any complete thought expressed in form of one or several independent clauses. An example of a clause would be, "because he loved us." An example of a sentence would be, "Jesus died because he loved us." Notice the difference here. The former example is a coherent thought but not a complete one; the latter is both. Hence the notion of "sentence" comprises and includes that of "clause." Clauses may be dependent or independent clauses, the latter of which are sentences, while the former will be part of a sentence but not constitute a sentence.[5]

At the very outset, it is also important to note that *literary genre* itself, be it narrative, poetry, or parable, provides an important parameter for the discourse type of a given portion of text. We devoted the entire previous section of the present volume to a discussion of the interpretation of specific biblical genres. For now it will be sufficient to point out that there are four major types of genre: (1) exposition (development of an argument; e.g., "therefore"); (2) exhortation (command); (3) narration (recounting sequence of past events; e.g., "then"); and (4) procedure (explanation of how something is to be done).[6] Most of the examples later on in this chapter will be drawn from biblical narrative or epistolary material.

GRAMMATICAL FOUNDATIONS: BASICS OF BIBLICAL GREEK AND HEBREW

Except for a few short portions written in Aramaic, the language of the Old Testament is Hebrew. The entire New Testament was penned in

---

5. For a helpful survey of Greek clauses see Daniel B. Wallace, *Greek beyond the Basics* (Grand Rapids: Zondervan, 1996), 656–65; idem, *The Basics of New Testament Syntax* (Grand Rapids: Zondervan, 2000), 286–92, who under "Adverbial Clauses" lists Cause, Comparison, Concession, Condition, Complementary, Location, Manner/Means, Purpose, Result, and Time.
6. Richard A. Young, *Intermediate New Testament Greek* (Nashville: B&H, 1994), 248–51.

Greek. While we would highly recommend for you to acquire knowledge of these languages if at all possible, such knowledge will not be required for following the presentation in the present volume. Nevertheless, it will be helpful to provide a brief synopsis of the character and nature of biblical Greek and Hebrew to enable you to understand more accurately the task of biblical interpretation.

At the very outset, it is worth remembering that all the major doctrines related to Scripture, such as its inerrancy or infallibility, its inspiration, and its authority, are defined with reference to the Bible in its original languages. No translation—not even the King James Version!—can legitimately lay claim to being infallible or inerrant in every instance (though the best English translations available are on the whole highly accurate).[7] The ultimate reference point of the interpreter must always remain the original text.[8] This underscores the need for good commentaries and reference tools.

Introduction

In contrast to the New Testament which came into being over the span of just a few decades, the Old Testament was written over a long period of time. This presents challenges for interpretation in that the vocabulary is considerably larger than that of the New Testament and historical circumstances changed over time. Comparative linguistics is important as well, since there is a large number of so-called *hapax legomena*, that is, words occurring only once in the entire Old Testament. In all these cases, it is profitable to consult usage in other ancient Near Eastern languages in order to find help in discerning word meanings.

The New Testament was written by a fairly small number of individuals—the four evangelists, plus Paul, Peter, James, Jude, and the author of Hebrews—in a reasonably short span of time, probably no more than

---

7. For a treatment of many of the relevant issues see Andreas J. Köstenberger, L. Scott Kellum, and Charles L. Quarles, *The Cradle, the Cross, and the Crown: An Introduction to the New Testament* (Nashville: B&H, 2009), chapter 1.
8. This raises the issue of textual criticism, that is, the determination of the most likely original reading of a given biblical passage. For a helpful presentation of the history, methods, and results of textual criticism, see Paul D. Wegner, *A Student's Guide to Textual Criticism of the Bible* (Downers Grove: InterVarsity, 2006). For treatments of textual issues in specific New Testament passages, see Bruce M. Metzger, *A Textual Commentary on the Greek New Testament*, 2d ed. (New York: United Bible Societies, 1994).

a half-century from about A.D. 45 to 95. Rather than write in their native Hebrew or Aramaic, these Palestinian Jews (with the possible exceptions of Luke and the author of Hebrews) composed their writings in the *lingua franca* of the day, so-called *koinē* or "common" Greek, that is, the Greek spoken by everyday persons all over the Roman Empire.

There is thus no special "Holy Spirit" Greek. Rather, the Greek of the New Testament is the same as that spoken in ordinary language and found in everyday documents, such as papyri recording business transactions, personal letters, and the like.[9] Because there is no sharp distinction between biblical and non-biblical Greek, it will often be profitable to study the use of a given word outside of the New Testament in order to shed light on its biblical usage. This is true especially where a given expression occurs only once or highly infrequently in the New Testament. One pertinent example is the occurrence of the rare verb αὐθεντέω (*authenteō*, "to have authority") in 1 Timothy 2:12.[10]

This also means that the various biblical genres, most notably historical narrative, epistles, and apocalyptic, all have parallels in non-biblical material.[11] Once again, it will be helpful to be aware of the characteristics of these genres in the non-biblical world, though, to be sure, "parallelomania" will need to be avoided.[12] In previous chapters, we already explored several of these issues more fully, including the question of whether or not Greco-Roman biography constitutes the genre of the canonical Gospels; the extent to which the New Testament epistles and their various rhetorical features are indebted to epistolary literature outside the Bible; and how the book of Revelation compares to extant Second Temple apocalypses.

Let us also remember that every biblical writer has his own particular idiolect or style, which extends to choice of vocabulary (semantics) as well

---

9. See the seminal work by Adolf Deissmann, *Light from the Ancient East*, trans. Lionel R. M. Strachan (London: Hodder & Stoughton, 1911); and the pathbreaking reference work by James Hope Moulton and George Milligan, *The Vocabulary of the New Testament* (Grand Rapids: Eerdmans, 1930). See also several of the essays collected in Stanley E. Porter, ed., *The Language of the New Testament: Classic Essays*, JSNTSup 60 (Sheffield: JSOT, 1991).
10. See the essays by H. Scott Baldwin and Andreas J. Köstenberger in *Women in the Church*, ed. Andreas J. Köstenberger and Thomas R. Schreiner, 2d ed. (Grand Rapids: Baker, 2005).
11. See James H. Charlesworth, ed., *The Old Testament Pseudepigrapha*, 2 vols. (Garden City, NY: Doubleday, 1983, 1985).
12. See the following chapter.

as syntax and other linguistic features. The apostle John, for example, characteristically uses inter-sentence conjunctions (οὖν, δέ, καί, *oun, de, kai,* and asyndeton) in a way that differs from the Synoptic Gospels.[13] Paul's stacking of clauses by the frequent use of participles (e.g., Eph. 1:3–14) is another example of personal style characteristics in the New Testament. The important implication of this observation is that interpretation should be author-specific and sensitive to personal style rather than proceed on the assumption that all biblical authors employ the exact same syntax and other linguistic features.

Basic Characteristics of New Testament Greek

With regard to some basic characteristics of the Greek language (particularly in comparison with, and contrast to, English), Greek is, first of all, an *inflected* language.[14] This means that New Testament Greek features noun and verb endings that provide information as to whether a person serves as the subject or the object, specify the person performing an action, and so on. This is different from English where, as mentioned, the sentences "Dog bites man" and "Man bites dog" are distinguished only by word order. It also means that word order can be more flexible and be sued for emphasis, as the following example of a transliterated Greek sentence demonstrates (our translation):

διὰ τοῦτο οὖν μᾶλλον ἐζήτουν αὐτὸν οἱ Ἰουδαῖοι ἀποκτεῖναι, ὅτι οὐ μόνον ἔλυεν τὸ σάββατον ἀλλὰ καὶ πατέρα ἴδιον ἔλεγεν τὸν θεόν, ἴσον ἑαυτὸν ποιῶν τῷ θεῷ.

Therefore, then, rather were seeking him the Jews to kill, because not only he was breaking the Sabbath, but also father his own he was saying God equal himself he was making to God.

In the sample from John 5:18, the word ἐζήτουν (*ezētoun*), "seeking," is emphasized by being placed earlier in the sentence, as are the phrases πατέρα ἴδιον (*patera idion*), "his own father," and "himself equal." The

---

13. Stephen H. Levinsohn, *Discourse Features of New Testament Greek*, rev. ed. (Dallas: SIL, 2000), 81–89; Vern S. Poythress, "The Use of the Intersentence Conjunctions *de, oun, kai,* and Asyndeton in the Gospel of John," *NovT* 26 (1984): 312–40.
14. Biblical Hebrew is an inflected language as well.

fact that these finer points cannot be gleaned from English translations underscores the value of knowing biblical Greek. Exegetically, knowing Greek syntax and word order in the above example enables the interpreter to understand even more fully that in the evangelist's account special emphasis is placed on the plot to kill Jesus and on the perceived preposterous nature of Jesus' claimed equality with God.

Verbal System

Another important characteristic of the Greek language is its *verbal system*.[15] Scholars specializing in Greek grammar advocate various theories as to how the Greek verbal system actually works. Most likely, the use of verbs in the Greek involved a significant subjective element. In other words, whether an author such as Mark chose, say, the perfect or imperfect tense had as much to do with his own perception of a given action (called "aspect") as it did with the way in which the action actually took place (called *Aktionsart*, or "kind of action").[16]

According to verbal aspect theory, a theory that stresses the importance of "aspect," that is, a writer's choice to portray a given action from a particular vantage point, the Greek tense called "aorist" (which has no exact equivalent in English) is used as a default tense to carry on a given narrative. Other tenses, such as the present, imperfect, or perfect tense, are used where the writer intends to foreground (i.e., emphasize) particular events that form part of the overall course of action. So we can understand this better, let's take a quick look at the anointing pericope (narrative unit) in John 12:1–8.[17]

John narrates Jesus' coming to Bethany in verse 1 and the giving of a dinner in his honor in verse 2 in the aorist. He gives special emphasis to Martha's serving and to Lazarus' presence at the dinner, for both of which he uses the imperfect (v. 2). Mary's actions, the taking of the perfume, her anointing of Jesus, and her wetting of his feet with her hair are all recounted in the aorist default tense (v. 3). The introduction of Judas in verse 4 draws attention by the use of the present tense for speaking and "about

---

15. For a helpful survey of the debate see Stanley E. Porter and D. A. Carson, eds., *Biblical Greek Language and Linguistics*, JSNTSS 80 (Sheffield: JSOT, 1993), 18–82.
16. A work that incorporates advances in Greek verbal aspect theory is Stanley E. Porter, *Idioms of the Greek New Testament* (Sheffield: JSOT, 1992).
17. For a fuller treatment see Andreas J. Köstenberger, "A Comparison of the Pericopae of Jesus' Anointing," in *Studies on John and Gender*, Studies in Biblical Literature 38 (New York: Peter Lang, 2001), 49–63.

to betray" (compare the use of the aorist for speaking later on in v. 6). In verse 6, John consistently characterizes the betrayer in the more prominent imperfect. This includes mention of his lack of concern for the poor, his identity as a thief, and his habitual stealing from the communal money bag. Jesus' response, finally, employs two present tense verbs with regard to people always "having" the poor but not always "having" him (v. 8).

What light does this brief analysis of the use of Greek verbs in John 12:1–8 shed on the interpretation of this passage? First of all, it confirms that the setting and the ensuing actions are deftly and swiftly narrated by the use of the aorist tense. Second, we learn what the evangelist sought to stress in his depiction of the event. Perhaps surprisingly, it is not so much Mary's action as it is Judas's objection that is the focus of attention. This becomes clear when one realizes that Mary's actions are recounted by aorist verbs while references to Judas involve verbs in more prominent tense forms. Note also that only one verse (v. 3) is devoted to Mary while five (vv. 4–8) are dealing with Judas' objection. Especially when we compare John's way of telling the story with the parallel accounts in Matthew and Mark (which focus on Mary), we realize that John sought to draw attention to the fact that Judas' objection foreshadowed his betrayal of Jesus in the next chapter.

For John, the anointing thus primarily served as an event where the identity of the betrayer was revealed. This, in turn, is apparent from the way in which John chose particular verb tenses to convey the various actions that form part of the narrative unit. To recap, the actions that took place at the anointing were one and the same. What is different, however, is *the way in which the various evangelists chose to portray these actions*. These differing ways of portraying one and the same scene are entirely legitimate, since, as we have learned, language involves a significant subjective element, extending to personal style, characteristic syntax, and even the way in which actions are portrayed by particular kinds of tenses.

Formally speaking, the distinction between aspect and *Aktionsart* (kind of action) is also observed in the verbal system of biblical Hebrew.[18] Aspect or the shape of the action, whether complete (perfective) or incomplete (non-perfective) is expressed by way of conjugations as determined

---

18. Though it should be noted that the field is in considerable ferment on this point at the moment.

through various prefixes and suffixes. *Aktionsart, the kind of situation or type of action* (e.g., repeated, causative, etc.) is expressed in its stems by which the root idea is modified by way of various affixed vowels and consonants. Tense is not formally marked in biblical Hebrew but is expressed in a variety of ways which can be discerned only from particular usage in a given context.

For example, in the narrative account of earth's creation we are told, "Thus the heavens and the earth were completed in all their vast array" (Gen. 2:1). The verbal phrase "were completed" indicates the process by which God's creative work was brought to an end (non-perfective verbal conjugation). This summary statement also indicates that God's work was "made complete" (indicated by the verbal stem). The passive voice in the verb indicates that the work of the six days of creation was completed prior to God's resting on the seventh day (Gen. 2:2).

The Greek Article

Another topic calling for discussion is the *Greek article,* a subject on which preachers (as well as cults) often go astray. Again, there is no perfect correspondence between Greek and English in this regard. Unlike English, Greek does not have an indefinite article ("a," "an"). While English only has one generic definite article, "the," Greek has three, one for each gender, masculine, feminine, and neuter. Remember, however, that a distinction must be made between grammatical and biological gender.[19]

In similar fashion, Hebrew also has a definite article (though not marked for gender) but no indefinite article. The definite article was used in a variety of ways. Most commonly, it indicates a distinct reference or particular identity (e.g., "the adversary": i.e., Satan, Job 1:6; "the land": Deut. 6:10). Often the article calls attention to that which was definite in the mind of the author or narrator, even though such definiteness has no correspondence in English. For example, in 1 Samuel 10:25, Samuel's scroll is marked with a definite article in the Hebrew text to indicate the particular scroll on which Samuel's words were written, even though the scroll itself was previously randomly chosen. Accordingly, the English versions properly translate the noun as "a scroll." Particular reference may also be made to that which was mentioned previously (anaphoric use). Note, for

---

19. See further the following chapter.

example, that in Genesis 1:3–4 "the light" (v. 4) harks back to the previous reference to "light" in verse 3 (see also Job 1:1, where the NIV translates "the man" as "this man"). The student should note that definiteness may also be indicated in a variety of ways other than by the definite article in biblical Hebrew.

The presence of the definite article in Greek often, but not always, indicates that a specific person or object [20] Another important function of the article is to mark a noun as abstract or generic. Examples of the former are nouns such as "truth" or "righteousness" (ἡ ἀλήθεια, *hē alētheia* and ἡ δικαιοσύνη, *hē dikaiosynē*, respectively in Greek, but simply "truth" and "righteousness" in English). Examples of the latter are proper nouns (names or titles) such as "God" or "Jesus" (ὁ θεός, *ho theos* and ὁ Ἰησοῦ, *ho Iēsous* in the Greek, but simply "God" and "Jesus" in English).

The important implication for this less-than-perfect equivalence between the uses of the article in Greek and English is that the absence of the article does not necessarily mean a word is indefinite; nor does the presence of the article invariably mark a noun as definite. Thus the interpreter who seeks to fit the Greek article into the pattern of the article's usage in English attempts the equivalent of fitting a square peg into a round hole. The picture is considerably more complex, and other factors must be considered to arrive at a judicious assessment of the function and role of a particular instance of the article (or its absence) in a given passage and context.

The classic example of this is the absence of the Greek definite article in John 1:1 ("In the beginning was the Word, and the Word was with God, and the Word was God"), which has been taken by groups such as the Jehovah's Witnesses as evidence that Jesus was not truly God but merely "a" god.[21] However, as we will be reminded in the next chapter, a little knowledge can be dangerous, and in the present case leads to a serious misunderstanding and distortion of the biblical teaching regarding the divinity of Christ.

---

20. For a thorough treatment of the Greek article, see Wallace, *Greek beyond the Basics*, 206–90, who under the category "individualizing article" distinguishes between as many as eight different uses of the article. Also helpful is the same author's abridgement *Basics of New Testament Syntax*, 93–128.
21. See esp. Wallace, *Greek Grammar beyond the Basics*, 266–69; abridged in *Basics of New Testament Syntax*, 119–20.

In fact, Colwell's rule (refined by McGaughy) indicates that in Greek syntax it is common for a definite nominative predicate noun preceding a finite verb to be without the article, so that it is illegitimate to infer indefiniteness from the lack of the article in John 1:1. Rather, omitting the article in the case of the predicate nominative ("God") serves to distinguish between the subject ("the Word") and the predicate nominative ("God") rather than marking the former as definite and the latter as indefinite. For this reason it is best to understand the anarthrous (non-articular) expression "God" as indicating the quality or essential nature of the Word: it (or he) was God in every sense that God the Father was God.[22]

Another feature of Greek grammar pertaining to the article is that it is often omitted in prepositional phrases (e.g., ἐν συναγωγῇ, *en synagogē*, "in the synagogue," John 6:59). However, once again this does not mean that the anarthrous (article-less) noun is indefinite. We could give additional examples, but the point is clear: we must be cautious when dealing with interpretive issues related to the Greek article and avoid simplistic solutions. Beyond this, it is always a good idea to consult a reliable commentary based on the original Greek or Hebrew text or in some cases a study Bible or other reference work.

The Genitive Case

A third item of syntax in Greek that has posed problems for interpreters is the *genitive case*.[23] Are believers to be constrained by their love *for* Christ or by the love *of* Christ (i.e., Christ's love; 2 Cor. 5:14)? Greek syntax (i.e., the genitive case of the noun "Christ" modifying "love") allows for either construal of the meaning of this phrase. Clearly, the message is different depending on which is the proper interpretation of the passage. Yet

---

22. For a fuller treatment of John 1:1, see Andreas J. Köstenberger, *John*, BECNT (Grand Rapids: Baker, 2004), 28–29, with further reference to the work of Colwell, McGaughy, Wallace, and Hartley. Similarly, in Hebrew non-verbal clauses/sentences where classification is the prominent purpose, predicate nouns and adjectives most commonly precede their corresponding substantives. For example, note the following translations as given in accordance with the Hebrew order: "Spies are you" (Gen. 42:9) and "Great is his mercy" (1 Chron. 21:13). Where a particular identification or previous mention is involved, however, the article will appear and the order will be subject-predicate. For example, note 2 Samuel 12:7: "You are the man."

23. See Wallace, *Greek Grammar beyond the Basics*, 72–136; idem, *Basics of New Testament Syntax*, 41–64.

the Greek is inconclusive here. Context must decide, and in our judgment the more likely rendering is "Christ's love compels us" (so, e.g., the NIV).[24]

Another interesting type of usage for the Greek genitive case is the Semitic-style genitive, patterned after the Hebrew construct state in which two related nouns are strung together in a way that the second of the two modifies the first in a genitival manner.[25] An example of this is 1 Peter 1:14 where reference is made to (literally) "children of obedience." This is explainable as a reflection of Semitic style, but in English, what are "children of obedience"? This is hardly proper English usage. The answer: "children of obedience" are nothing other than obedient children!

The Greek Participle

One last example of an important Greek syntactical feature must suffice for our present purposes, namely the Greek *participle*.[26] Participles are verbal nouns (such as ὁ πιστεύων [*ho pisteuōn*], "the one who believes," i.e., "the believer,"), which may be used in three different ways: (1) as a substantive or noun; (2) as an adjective; and (3) adverbially. An example of a substantival use would be "one who believes" or "the believer." An adjectival use would look like this: "the *believing* disciple." Most important is the third, adverbial, use in the Greek, which can have a large number of possible nuances: temporal, manner, means, cause, condition, concession, purpose, result, or attendant circumstance.

What adverbial participles have in common is that they modify (i.e., give more information about) a verb. For example, in Philippians 2:7, Paul says that Jesus "made himself nothing" (ἑαυτὸν, ἐκένωσεν, the main verb of the clause) *taking* (λαβών, *labōn*, adverbial participle) the form of a

---

24. Wallace, *Basics of New Testament Syntax*, 59, cites 2 Corinthians 5:14 as a possible example of the plenary genitive, in which case *both* subjective and objective ideas are present. Similarly, among the many uses of the Hebrew genitive case one may note that some genitives may be understood as subjective or objective. Thus the Hebrew word order in Psalm 73:28 reads: "The nearness of God is my good." Does the genitive relationship indicate that the believer's good is to be near God (objective genitive) or that God's nearness is the believer's good (subjective genitive)? Note the following English translations: "But as for me, it is good to be near God" (NIV); "But as for me, God's presence is my good" (HCSB).

25. Wallace, *Greek Grammar beyond the Basics*, 86–88; idem, *Basics of New Testament Syntax*, 48, calls this "Attributive Genitive (Hebrew Genitive, Genitive of Quality)," citing, e.g., Romans 6:6 ("body of sin" = "sinful body").

26. See Wallace, *Greek Grammar beyond the Basics*, 612–55; idem, *Basics of New Testament Syntax*, 266–85.

servant. The participle "taking" answers the question "How?" How did Jesus humble himself? The answer: by taking on the form of a servant. It is important to note here that in the Greek original all that is found is the participle. Discerning the precise force, nuance, or connotation—whether the participle is temporal, causal, conditional, and so on—is left to the interpreter or translator. Knowing this helps explain different renderings of individual participles in different English translations.

One example of the use of the Greek participle that is exegetically significant is found in Matthew 28:19–20—the "Great Commission." In this passage, Jesus, after assuring his followers of his complete authority in verse 18, tells them, "Therefore go and make disciples of all nations, baptizing them . . ., and teaching them . . ." In the Greek, the main command is "to make disciples" (μαθητεύσατε, *mathēteusate*), which is modified by two participles, "baptizing" (βαπτίζοντες, *baptizontes*) and "teaching" (διδάσκοντες, *didaskontes*). The way in which the latter are subordinated to the main command suggests that baptizing and teaching is the characteristic *mode* of making disciples (participles of manner). The verb "go" is a participle as well and, in conjunction with the command "make disciples," takes on an imperatival force as well ("go!"), though the main emphasis rests on the command to make disciples. Wherever Jesus' followers might go, be it near or far, they are to make disciples of Jesus by baptizing and teaching them.[27]

Examples for each of these important syntactical issues—verb tenses, the Greek article, the genitive case, and the Greek participle—could be multiplied. In fact, some distinguish between as many as thirty or so different types of usage for the genitive case alone! Perhaps we should adapt the Athenian example of coining a generic type of genitive that can serve as a catch-all category in case we have failed to identify all the different kinds of usage, on the pattern of their building of an altar to "an unknown God" (Acts 17:23)! In fact, this has already been done: witness the category of the "general genitive."

---

27. For a fuller discussion and analysis of Matthew 28:18–20 see Andreas J. Köstenberger and Peter T. O'Brien, *Salvation to the Ends of the Earth*, NSBT 11 (Downers Grove: InterVarsity, 2001), 101–6, esp. 103–4 (incl. p. 104, n. 66). The same grammatical construction featuring the Greek word *poreuomai*, "to go," is found in Matthew elsewhere in five other places: Matthew 2:8; 9:13; 10:7; 11:4; and 28:7.

We trust that the discussion of some of the most egregious instances in biblical literature where grammar and syntax matter in interpretation has provided a general sense of the importance of this subject. This is not merely an obtuse, irrelevant area of study. Grammar and syntax are critical factors in interpretation, and, like it or not, anyone who takes Scripture seriously must learn to wrestle with the various grammatical and syntactical issues raised by the words and phrases found in the Bible. This, too, is required for the one who aspires to be a worker who needs not to be ashamed but who accurately handles the word of truth.

WORD ORDER AND SENTENCE STRUCTURE: BASICS OF GREEK SYNTAX

Word Order

Since, as mentioned, Greek (like Hebrew) is an inflected language, word order is more fluid than, for example, in English. Nevertheless, we are able to discern certain patterns. While a comprehensive treatment of Greek syntax is beyond the scope of the present volume, and readers are referred to standard Greek grammars, a brief survey of important features of Greek sentence structure will be helpful especially in aiding us to discern emphasis. In Greek, emphasis is conveyed, among other things, by fronting a given word or phrase or clause, that is, by placing it earlier in the sentence than normal word order would require. If nothing else, the following discussion will alert the reader to the complexity of Greek sentence structure, a realization that should lead to humility in dealing with these phenomena.[28]

One typical pattern is that of a *conjunction*, followed immediately by the finite *verb*, and then the *subject*, one or several *objects*, and other parts of the sentence (such as supplementary participles, etc.). An example of this is Luke 1:12: καὶ ἐταράχθη Ζαχαρίας ἰδών, *kai etarachthē Zacharias idōn* (lit., "And [conjunction] was troubled [finite verb] Zachariah [subject] seeing [participle]"; emphasis is conveyed, e.g., in Luke 1:67: "And

---

28. For the following material see F. Blass and A. Debrunner, *A Greek Grammar of the New Testament and Other Early Christian Literature*, trans. and ed. Robert W. Funk (Chicago/London: University of Chicago Press, 1961), §§471–484.

Zechariah . . ."). Also, *vocatives* are typically at the beginning, indicating which person or group is addressed by a given statement or command (e.g., 1 John 2:1, 7, 18; 4:1, 7; though see John 14:9 where "Philip" is not found until later in the sentence). Likewise, subordinate conjunctions typically (though not invariably) are found at the beginning of a dependent clause (examples are numerous; but see John 1:19; 4:18; 1 Cor. 15:36; 2 Cor. 2:4).

With regard to the position of *nouns, adjectives, and adverbs,* the following patterns apply: (1) adjectives usually (though not always) follow nouns; (2) adverbs which further define adjectives follow them. All things being equal, elements in the sentence that belong together are kept together, such as articletive adjective(s). At times, however, other expressions intervene. For example, Mark 5:30, in the original Greek, reads as follows: ἐν ἑαυτῷ τὴν ἐξ αὐτοῦ δύναμιν ἐξελθοῦσαν, *en heautō tēn ex autou dynamin exelthousan* (lit., "[At once Jesus realized] the-from-him-power had gone out"). The insertion of the phrase "from him" (ἐξ αὐτοῦ/ ex autou) between the article ἐν/tēn and the noun δύναμιν underscores the close relationship between the two expressions, as in "the indwelling power" (see also Heb. 6:7).

Larger Syntactical Features

Larger syntactical issues in the Greek New Testament are raised by the presence of a variety of devices indicating incompletion or fullness of expression.[29] *Ellipsis* represents a feature by which an incomplete idea requires the reader to supply a missing element which is self-evident (e.g., 2 Cor. 5:13: "If we are out of our mind, [it is] for the sake of God").

Zeugma is a special type of ellipsis in which a different verb is to be supplied, that is, one verb occurs with two subjects or objects while suiting only one. An obvious example is 1 Timothy 4:3: "They [i.e., the false teachers] forbid people to marry [and order them] to abstain from certain foods." Another New Testament instance of this phenomenon is 1 Corinthians 3:2: "I gave you milk to drink, not solid food [to eat]."

---

29. Osborne, *Hermeneutical Spiral*, 121–30, in his chapter on syntax includes both traditionally conceived figures of speech (such as metaphors and similes) and what might more properly be considered features of Greek sentence structure (such as ellipsis or pleonasm) under the heading "Figures of Speech."

Aposiopesis is the breaking off of a speech or statement owing to strong emotion, modesty, or other reasons. New Testament examples include passages such as John 1:22 ("Who are you? [Give us an answer] to take back to those who sent us") and Luke 13:9 ("If it bears fruit next year [it should be allowed to grow]. If not, then cut it down").

Brachylogy is "the omission, for the sake of brevity, of an element which is not necessary for the grammatical structure but for the thought" (BDF §483). A typical example involves the putting of a purpose clause ἵνα, *hina*) at the beginning of a sentence prior to the main clause in order to preface it with the abbreviated form of a train of thought (e.g., Matt. 9:6; John 1:22; 9:36; 2 Cor. 10:9).

Hendiadys represents an arrangement of two or more expressions that essentially convey the same idea. Hence, an element of redundancy is present. New Testament examples include the reference to "kingdom and glory" in 1 Thessalonians 2:12 or to the "blessed hope and glorious appearing" in Titus 2:13. At other times, however, two ideas may be distinct and thus may not be found to truly represent this form of expression.[30]

Pleonasm, finally, is a form of redundancy by which a previously expressed idea is repeated as a way of speaking (not for emphasis; the interpreter is cautioned not to jump to false conclusions here). This feature frequently involves the use of the Greek word πάλιν, *palin* ("again"; e.g., John 4:54; Acts 10:15; Gal. 1:17). Another frequent example is the phrase "he answered and said" or the phrase "the household master of the house" (Luke 22:11).

Many modern translations eliminate this kind of redundancy in English (e.g., NIV: "the owner of the house"). Note also that a prepositional verbal prefix is often coupled with the same preposition being used in a prepositional phrase (e.g., Luke 1:76: προπορεύσῃ, *proporeusē*; "he went before [twice, as a verbal prefix and as a preposition] his face").

Sentence Structure

As you may know, the original Greek manuscripts of the New

---

30. Examples of this may be the reference to "grace and truth" in John 1:17 or to teaching and exercising authority in 1 Timothy 2:12, on which see Andreas J. Köstenberger, *John*, 47–48, and *1–2 Timothy, Titus*, 517, respectively.

Testament do not include punctuation such as periods, commas, colons, or semicolons. These were added by later critical editions of the New Testament, as were spaces between words (in the original manuscripts, Greek words run together). Nevertheless, divisions between units are discernible in places such as Luke's elegantly-crafted prologue (Luke 1:1–4; see also Acts 15:24–26; John 13:1–5; Heb. 1:1–3).

There are two main types of style in the Greek New Testament: (1) a running style which is characterized by an unconnected (asyndetic, paratactic) sentence structure; and (2) a compact style in which the initial sentence is expanded by way of a participial phrase, a relative clause, a dependent clause, or some other similar construction. The former is largely characteristic of the Gospels, particularly Mark (but also John). The latter is found Paul's writings, particularly in Ephesians and Colossians.[31]

Asyndeton

An example of *asyndeton* (the absence of connectives) involving adjectives is 2 Timothy 4:2: "in season [and] out of season" (εὐκαίρως ἀκαίρως, *eukairōs akairōs*). Asyndeton also occurs in lengthy enumerations such as John 5:3: "a great number of disabled people—the blind, the lame, the paralyzed" (see also 1 Cor. 3:12; 1 Tim. 1:10; 2 Tim. 3:2; 1 Pet. 4:3). Asyndeton is also found when two or more verbs as juxtaposed rather one being subordinated to the other. An example of this construction is Matthew 5:24: "Go, first be reconciled" (see also Matt. 9:30; 24:6; Matt. 26:46 = Mark 14:12; Mark 2:11; 4:39).

On a larger discourse level, asyndeton between clauses and sentences is a common feature in the Gospels (e.g., Matt. 5:3–17; John 1:23, 28, 37–39, 41–42; 3:6–8). There are also many examples of rhetorical asyndeton in Paul's writings (e.g., 1 Cor. 7:18, 21, 27; 2 Cor. 11:23–28). Finally, asyndeton is also found between paragraphs and larger discourse units, especially in James, 1 John, and some of Paul's writings (e.g., Rom. 9:1), but not in Hebrews.

Parenthesis

Regular sentence structure may be interrupted by either *parenthesis*

---

31. For the following material see esp. BDF §§458–471. A distinction should be made between sentence structure (which is dealt with in the present chapter on syntax) and figures of speech (which are discussed in the following chapter).

(the interjection of an independent additional thought) or *anacoluthon* (an incomplete thought). The need for either device arises when a writer finds it necessary to accommodate an afterthought or chooses to interject an additional piece of information that temporarily interrupts the flow of thought in a given passage. For example, John's Gospel features numerous asides or parentheses, informing the reader of translations, geographical or topographical locations, or other helpful pieces of information (e.g., John 1:38, 41; 9:7). In the book of Acts, an example of parenthesis is Acts 5:14, which interrupts the flow of Acts 5:13 and the narration of the result in Acts 5:15.

Anacoluthon

Anacoluthon refers to a sentence structure that includes an incomplete thought. This may involve instances where "a preceding case is assimilated by attraction to a following relative clause which required an antecedent" (BDF §466; e.g., Acts 7:40; 2 Cor. 12:17). It also includes pendent nominatives (e.g., Matt. 10:11) and expressions following an introductory participle (e.g., John 7:38: "Whoever believes in me [introductory participle], as the Scripture has said, *streams of living water will flow from within him*").

More complicated are instances where anacoluthon occurs after an intervening clause of sentence. In those cases, after interjecting a thought, rather than resume the sentence structure of the original sentence, the author starts a new sentence with its own syntactical construction and does not complete the initial thought and thus does not follow smoothly from it. An example of this is Galatians 2:6: "As for those who seemed to be important—whatever they were makes no difference to me; God does not judge by external appearance—[γάρ "for"; Grk. *gar*] those men added nothing to my message" (see also Tertullus' speech in Acts 24:5–6). Other instances of anacoluthon involve the use of a participle in place of a finite verb (e.g., 1 Pet. 3:7, 9).[32]

DISCOURSE ANALYSIS: OVERVIEW OF METHOD

Are you ready to go deeper in your study of Scripture? If so, you may want to get acquainted with a relatively new method that holds considerable promise for biblical interpretation—discourse analysis. The purpose

---

32. For a discussion of anacoluthon see BDF §§ 466–470.

of discourse analysis is the accurate discernment of the authorial intention expressed in a given text.[33] The following overview of this method is based on the recognition that biblical interpretation should be conducted on the level of discourse rather than on the sentence or paragraph level.

As anyone perusing the literature on the subject will soon discover, there is considerable diversity in the specific method of discourse analysis adopted by different authors or groups (such as individuals associated with the Summer Institute of Linguistics [SIL]). There is also a certain amount of variance with regard to specific terminology (e.g., some call discourse analysis "semantic structure analysis"; others subsume it under narrative criticism).

The purpose of the following overview is not to privilege any one of these methods but rather to pinpoint the underlying textual features that form the basis for biblical interpretation and that must be properly discerned and understood by the interpreter. We hope that you will be persuaded of the relevance, even necessity, of analyzing biblical discourse—regardless of genre (though this is particularly relevant in epistolary material)—and incorporate the insights presented below in your method for personal Bible study. Beyond this, we have already taken up narrative and rhetorical analysis in the chapters on Gospels and epistles above.

Properly understood and implemented, discourse analysis has the potential to revolutionize the study of Scripture in that it shifts the emphasis from the work of the interpreter in breaking up units from his or her own vantage point to a careful analysis of the features of the biblical text itself. By providing the interpretive tools associated with discourse analysis (used in the present chapter in a non-technical sense, that is, as the analysis of discourse apart from one specific method), we seek to equip the Bible student, teacher, and preacher to develop confidence and skill in tracing the concrete makeup and contours of the biblical text and to teach and preach it accordingly.

---

33. Helpful resources include Joel B. Green, "Discourse Analysis and New Testament Interpretation," in *Hearing the New Testament: Strategies for Interpretation*, ed. Joel B. Green (Grand Rapids: Eerdmans, 1995), 175–96; Cotterell and Turner, *Linguistics and Biblical Interpretation*, 230–56; Johannes P. Louw, "Discourse Analysis and the Greek New Testament," *BT* 24 (1973): 108–18; and L. Scott Kellum, *The Unity of the Farewell Discourse*, JSNTS 256 (London/New York: T&T Clark, 2004), 138–49.

Major Steps in Discourse Analysis

In the following discussion, we will treat the following five aspects of discourse analysis: (1) boundary features; (2) cohesion; (3) relations; (4) prominence; and (5) situation. There is a certain logical flow to this sequence. At the outset, *boundary features* deal with isolating the beginning and end point of a given textual unit. *Cohesion* is concerned with features that weave together the fabric of a textual unit and constitute it as a coherent whole. *Relations* deal with the logic of the thought flow of a given passage, be it by indicating cause, purpose, result, or another coordinating or subordinating relation. *Prominence* seeks to discern emphasis, whether on the micro-level of an individual sentence or phrase or on the macro-level of the larger discourse of narrative (peak). *Situation*, finally, focuses on the way in which linguistic expression is part of the larger phenomenon of a speaker's or writer's embeddedness in a given culture, which has important historical, social, and cultural implications.

Boundary Features

A necessary first step is to screen the text for particular *boundary features* that set it off from the preceding and successive textual units. Some distinguish here between episodes, units, paragraphs, propositional clusters, and propositions. The identification of boundary features is critical for the proper delineation of a text for preaching or teaching and is thus of immense practical importance. Major boundary features include:

1. Initial markers, such as orienters ("I do not want you to be ignorant," 1 Cor. 10:1; "I praise you," 1 Cor. 11:2; "I want to remind you," 1 Cor. 15:1; "Finally," Phil. 3:1; 4:8), conjunctions, vocatives ("Dear children": 1 John 2:1, 12; "Dear friends," Jude 3, 17, 20), deictic indicators (such as adverbs of time or space; "After this he went down to Capernaum," John 2:12), topic statements ("Now about," 1 Cor. 7:1, 25; 8:1; 12:1), rhetorical questions introducing a new topic (Rom. 6:1–3, 15; 7:1, 7, 13), and changes in characters or setting (John 4:1–4).

2. Final markers, such as summary statements (Matt. 4:23–25; Acts 2:41; 9:31; Heb. 11:39–40), doxologies (Rom. 11:33–36; Eph. 3:20–21), colophons ("Amen" or "Goodbye"), or tail-head links

(mention of a topic at the end of a section to be developed in the following unit; e.g. the mention of "salvation" in Heb. 1:14, which becomes the basis for subsequent exhortation, see Heb. 2:3).

3. Literary devices such as *inclusio* (John 2:11 and 4:54), chiasm (John 1:1–18), or other textual features such as changes in subject, object, or topic (e.g. the transition from icebreaker in Phlm. 4–7 to the business at hand in Phlm. 8–22); changes in time, setting, and participants (e.g., Matt. 5:1; 8:1, 5, 14, 16; 17:1); conjunctions or changes in verbal tense, mood, or aspect (shift from indicatives to imperatives from Phlm. 8–16 to Phlm. 17–22 or from Jude 3–16 to 17–23).

4. Repeated units (whether terms, phrases, clauses, sentences, or syntactical structures; e.g., Matt. 7:28; 11:1; 13:53; 19:1; 26:1; of significant structural import is the phrase, "I was in the Spirit" or a similar expression, occurring in Rev. 1:10; 4:2; 17:3; and 21:10, by which the book of Revelation divides into four major visions).[34]

Cohesion

A second important discourse feature is that of *cohesion*. Cohesion is provided by various lexical, thematic, or syntactical devices that make up the glue that holds a discourse together. As George Guthrie observes, "Cohesion is that quality of a text that gives it unity."[35] A text may be given cohesion by certain formal features (such as the alliterated five words starting with the Greek letter "p" in Heb. 1:1); semantic features (i.e., related word meanings in a given textual unit; e.g., 1 Tim. 5:3–16 on widows, or the "wealth and poverty" theme in Luke-Acts); or a text's pragmatic effect on its readers or hearers. Richard Young distinguishes four kinds of cohesion:

---

34. See the chapter on apocalyptic literature in the present volume. See also Young, *Intermediate New Testament Greek*, 253–54.
35. Guthrie, "Discourse Analysis," 258.

1. Grammatical cohesion (e.g., subject-verb agreement);

2. Lexical cohesion (the use of the same or similar words, e.g. Jas. 1:2–5);

3. Relational cohesion (conjunctions, relative pronouns and clauses, participles);

4. Referential cohesion (links between a given text and other textual units in a piece of writing), particularly anaphora (e.g., "thus," referring back to a previous clause or unit).[36]

Relations

A third major feature of discourses is that of *relations*, that is, various ways in which statements or propositions are conjoined in a given text.[37] We can discern the following major types of relations in biblical discourse:

1. Addition relations or coordination characterized by equal prominence (e.g., "So he went to her, took her hand and helped her up," Mark 1:31): these may be successive or sequential (i.e., chronological), simultaneous, or non-temporal.

2. Support relations characterized by unequal prominence: this may take the form of orientation (e.g., "After John was put in prison, Jesus went into Galilee," Mark 1:14); logic (be it reason-result, means-result, means-purpose, grounds-conclusion, condition-consequence, or concession-contra-expectation); or clarification (whether by way of restatement or expansion).

Peter Cotterell and Max Turner provide the following helpful detailed list of possible relations whereby the first category constitutes an additional relation and the other categories two through four represent various forms of support relations:

---

36. Young, *Intermediate New Testament Greek*, 254–55.
37. See Cotterell and Turner, *Linguistics and Biblical Interpretation*, chapter 7, esp. 236–40.

1. Coordination
   a. sequential ("and")
   b. alternating ("or")
   c. comparison ("as")
2. Argumentation or Discourse Deixis
   a. result ("so that")
   b. purpose ("in order that")
   c. manner or means ("by doing")
   d. reason or inference ("because," "for," "therefore")
   e. concession ("although")
   f. conclusion ("now," "then")
3. Orientation or Circumstantial Deixis
   a. personal or social ("we," "sir," etc.)
   b. circumstances (e.g. "as he was passing by")
   c. location ("at the temple," "nearby," etc.)
4. Clarification or Elaboration ("that is," etc.)

Prominence

A fourth discourse feature is that of *prominence* or emphasis. This refers to the observable phenomenon that certain aspects of a given discourse will stand out more than others, marking a point, theme, or plot. While readers are often oblivious to this dimension, it is nonetheless critical. In fact, if all features of a discourse were equally prominent, it would be virtually unintelligible, similar to a white bird in a blizzard or a black cat in a tunnel.

There are two kinds of prominence. *Natural* prominence relates to elements pertaining to the plot structure of a given pericope (its backbone). An example of this would be the reference to Jesus' performance of his "first sign" in John 2:11. *Marked* prominence is conveyed by a variety of elements, such as word order, morphemes (e.g., intensifying word forms), various grammatical features, figures of speech, repetition, orienters, rhetorical questions, anaphora, discourse proportion (i.e., relative length), asyndeton (lack of a conjunction at the beginning of a sentence), and personal names.

On a larger scale, coherent units in a certain discourse share a given topic, gradually progressing to a climax or *peak*, particularly in narrative discourse. As Robert Longacre states, "The peak in a hortatory discourse is its final and most effective attempt to influence someone else's conduct."[38] For example, the Johannine farewell discourse, which extends from John 13:31 to 16:33, peaks at 15:1–8, Jesus' symbolic discourse on the vine and the branches.[39] Cotterell and Turner discuss the phenomenon of delayed peaking and note that a change of participants, locus, or pace (such as rapid closure) may ensue after the peak has been reached.[40] An example of the latter is Jesus' raising of Lazarus in John 11:43–44, after which the narrative ends almost immediately. A typical discourse structure may include a title, stage, pre-peak episodes, the peak, post-peak episodes, and closure.[41]

Situation

One final element is called _situation_, the real-life setting which is studied by a variety of disciplines, including pragmatics, speech act theory, and sociolinguistics. This field of study analyzes the non-linguistic features of discourse such as social environment or shared knowledge, which is relevant particularly for biblical instances of interpersonal communication or dialogue.[42] One relevant example here is that of _implicature_, that is, implicit yet necessary information for understanding a given discourse. In fact, much remains unsaid or unexplained because of a "presupposition pool" that is shared between the author and his readers (or, in the case of oral communication, between a speaker and his listeners).[43]

The value of including this dimension in our analysis of discourse stems from the recognition that texts and their linguistic and literary aspects are part of a larger relational framework, which, in turn, is firmly embedded in a historical, social, political, economic, and general cultural framework. For this reason it would be both artificial and highly reductionistic to limit our study of the biblical text in a narrow

---

38. Robert E. Longacre, "Discourse Peak as a Zone of Turbulence," in Jessica R. Wirth, ed., _Beyond the Sentence: Discourse and Sentential Form_ (Ann Arbor: Karoma, 1985), 84.
39. Cf. Kellum, _Unity of the Farewell Discourse_, 193–93, 203–4; see also pp. 145–46 for general comments on peak.
40. Cotterell and Turner, _Linguistics & Biblical Interpretation_, 245–47.
41. Ibid., 247–48; see the analysis of the narrative of the rape of Tamar on pp. 248–53.
42. See esp. the helpful chapter "The Special Case of Conversation" in Cotterell and Turner, _Linguistics & Biblical Interpretation_, chapter 8, including the excellent analysis of Jesus' interchange with Nicodemus on pp. 278–87.
43. See ibid., 257–59.

manner to textual phenomena without recognizing that there are connotations to be discerned, underlying presuppositions to be made explicit, and the socio-linguistic and relational dimensions of language to be recognized.

To be sure, we must be careful not to confuse reading the text with reading between the lines of the text. The text must remain the final point of reference for biblical interpretation. Nevertheless, it is in the nature of human communication, both written and oral, that assumptions sometimes remain unstated and need to be supplied by the reader or interpreter. When Paul writes, "Don't you remember that when I was with you I used to tell you these things?" (2 Thess. 2:5), one only wishes that one had been privy to the previous teaching received by the Thessalonians. In 1 Corinthians, Paul most likely cites sayings common in the Corinthian church in order to address them (e.g., 1 Cor. 7:1: "It is good for a man not to marry").

For this reason it is part of the interpreter's role to unearth the implicit assumptions underlying a given text as part of the interpretive task. It also will be helpful to recognize that in many cultures, including first-century Palestinian Judaism, communication was frequently indirect, so that one must not cling to the surface meaning of a given phrase but seek to discern the underlying actual purpose or intended message of a given statement. An example of this is Nicodemus' opening gambit when visiting Jesus by night. Rather than taking his polite pleasantries at face value, it may be better to understand Nicodemus' words as a tacit inquiry as to the nature of Jesus' teaching (John 3:1–2; cf. 1:19, 22).

Sample Discourse Analysis: John 2:1–11

As mentioned, discourse analysis does not only pay attention to what might be called micro-elements of discourse such as the words denoting coordination, argumentation, orientation, or clarification above, it also seeks to discern larger features or the *macro-structure* of discourses. These are discourse boundaries, whether initiatory markers, transitional devices, or concluding sequences, and various features of the internal structure of discourse, such as setting or staging, peaking, and closure.

John 2:1–11 may serve as an example. The *discourse boundaries* are set by the introductory phrase "On the third day" in verse 1 on the one hand and by the concluding statement of the pericope in verse 11 ("This, the first of his [the NIV has "miraculous," but the Greek simply has σημέιων, *sēmeion*] signs, Jesus performed at Cana in Galilee. He thus revealed his glory, and his disciples put their faith in him"). We should also note that verse 12 serves as a transitional statement between the pericopes narrated in verses 1–11 and verses 13–22, respectively. The *initiatory marker*, as mentioned, is the phrase "On the third day." This phrase, in turn, follows on the heels of repeated previous references to "the next day" (John 1:29, 35, 43).

The *concluding sequence*, as mentioned, is found in verse 11, where John makes reference to this being "the first of [the] signs" Jesus performed in Cana of Galilee (see the corresponding reference to "the second sign" in Cana in John 4:54, a literary *inclusio*). The features of the *internal structure* of the discourse in John 2:1–11 include a large variety of elements. The *setting* is provided in verses 1 and 2. The *peak* gradually builds from verse 3 until it is finally reached in verse 10, with suspense created in verses 7–9.

In keeping with the presentation of the different types of syntactical elements presented above, John 2:1–11 includes a large number of references ensuring the reader's orientation. The various persons are identified: Jesus' mother (v. 1), Jesus and his disciples (v. 2), the servants (v. 5), the master of the banquet (v. 8), and the bridegroom (v. 9). A variety of social or status implications are found in the text as well, such as the probable shame associated with people running out of wine at a wedding (v. 3).

Time markers place the event "on the third day" (v. 1), presumably from the last reference to "the next day" in John 1:43. Hence the present event concludes the narration of the first week of Jesus' public ministry, an important discourse structuring device hinging on time (1:35–2:11). On the other end of the discourse, the boundary is marked by the expression "after this" and the reference to Jesus staying in Capernaum "for a few days" (2:12).

The location is described, first, as Cana in Galilee (v. 1). Later, the action unfolds "nearby" where six stone water jars were placed (v. 6). Still later, the master of the banquet is shown to call the bridegroom aside (v. 9), indicating the private nature of the interchange. The private nature of previous interchanges is also implied with regard to Jesus and his mother (vv. 3–4), Jesus' mother and the servants (v. 5), and Jesus and the servants (vv. 7–8), respectively.

The above discussion on studying a given textual unit on the larger discourse level has demonstrated that meaning resides not on the individual word level, or even on the sentence level, but on the level of larger discourse units. The syntactical relationships sustained between a given unit and the previous and subsequent units (initiatory markers and closure) and the various internal discourse features (such as peak) are vital to a full and accurate understanding of the authorial intention expressed in the biblical text. It remains to illustrate the validity of these insights on a fuller and more detailed scale.

DISCOURSE ANALYSIS: SPECIFIC EXAMPLES

The various books of Scripture all can be looked at in terms of their macrostructure and their microstructure. *Macrostructure* refers to the breakdown of literary units on a larger scale. *Microstructure* means the arrangement of a smaller section of Scripture. In the next chapter, we will elaborate on the importance of interpreting the parts in light of the whole in greater detail. In the present unit we will gain some practice and experience in discerning the patterns underlying a book's macrostructure and microstructure to do just that.

Discerning the Macrostructure: Level #1

The first step in interpreting and learning to communicate the contents of a given book of the Bible is to discern the "big picture," that is, the macrostructure of the book. Take John's Gospel, for example. On a basic level, it is clear that the macrostructure presents itself as follows:

12.1. MACROSTRUCTURE OF JOHN			
1:1–18	1:19–12:50	13:1–20:31	21:1–15
Introduction	Book of Signs	Book of Exaltation	Epilogue

How do we know this is the book's macrostructure? In large part, we do so from internal clues left by the author. This includes various structuring devices, such as transitions, openings, conclusions, and the like. It also includes literary devices such as chiasm (an "ABB'A'" pattern), *inclusios*, and so on. Identifying the structure of a given biblical passage is often significant for interpretation since the literary layout is one of the authorially intended vehicles for communicating meaning and a particular theological message. The *medium* (structure, words) and the *message* thus work hand in hand in the way language and literature work, and we must be concerned with *both* (not just the latter) if we want to arrive at an accurate and full-orbed understanding of the text.

In John's Gospel, for example, the transitional phrase "now this" makes clear that 1:19 marks the beginning of the actual Gospel narrative. The first half of the book then presents Jesus' performance of several startling "signs" as proofs of his messiahship to the Jewish people. The conclusion of Part One is found in 12:37–50, which provides a closing indictment of Jewish unbelief and sets the stage for Jesus' preparation of his new messianic community in Part Two.

The opening of John 13 represents a carefully crafted literary introduction, not just to the ensuing footwashing scene, but to the remainder of the Gospel as a whole, focusing on Jesus' perfect love for his followers (see esp. v. 1). This marks the cross as the climactic demonstration of Jesus' love for humanity, in keeping with the programmatic statement in John 3:16 that God so loved the world that he sent his one and only Son. Part Two concludes with a purpose statement in 20:30 31.

The epilogue in chapter 21 is set off by the transitional phrases "afterward" and "again." Its major purpose is to draw together some of the themes—most notably, the relationship between Peter and the "disciple Jesus loved"—from the body of the Gospel. The Gospel concludes with an authenticating statement by its author and the customary affirmation that there were many more things that could have been included in the particular book (21:24–25).

This, then, is the macrostructure of John's Gospel. It cannot be stressed enough at this point that what the perceptive interpreter is after in discerning a given book's macrostructure (remember the "hermeneutic of perception") is not his own clever (or not so clever) alliterative devices in outlining a book but rather the structure *intended by the biblical author* as it can be reconstructed from the various literary clues described above that were left by the author in the text.

Discerning the Macrostructure: Level #2

On the next level of depth and thoroughness, and still on the level of macrostructure, the two major parts of the Gospel can be broken down further still into smaller pericope or narrative units. Along these lines, John 1:19–2:11 marks the first week of Jesus' ministry, punctuated by several references to "the next day" (1:29, 35, 43; 2:1: "On the third day"). At the same time, chapters 2 through 4 constitute the "Cana cycle," set off by the *inclusio* in 2:11 and 4:54 ("first sign," "second sign" in Cana).

The "Festival cycle," which features Jesus appearing at various Jewish festivals and presents him as the fulfillment of the underlying symbolism of these feasts, comprises chapters 5 through 10. At the end of chapter 10, we find a literary *inclusio* referring to John the Baptist (who, on a historical level, is long dead; 10:40–42), which sets off this from the following unit. Chapters 11 and 12 constitute a bridge section narrating the conclusion of Jesus' public ministry and his performance of the climactic sign, the raising of Lazarus.[44]

Part Two of John's Gospel is built around two major units, Jesus' farewell discourse (chaps. 13–17) and his death, burial, and resurrection (chaps. 18–20). Within these sections, we can discern the following structure. John 13:1–30, narrating the footwashing and Judas' betrayal, constitutes the preamble to the farewell discourse proper, which occupies 13:31–16:33 and is followed by Jesus' final prayer (chap. 17). The passion narrative in chapters 18–20 follows the familiar contours.

The second half of John's Gospel is connected to the epilogue through two of Jesus' resurrection appearances in chapter 20 (vv. 19–23 and vv. 24–29, respectively) and a third such appearance in chapter 21 (vv. 1–14; see esp. v. 14). The final special commissioning of Peter corresponds to his earlier denials and complements the commissioning of the Eleven in 20:21–23. The juxtaposed presentation of Peter and the "disciple Jesus loved" continues the pattern of parallel characterization of these two figures in John.[45]

The extended macrostructure of John's Gospel, including second-level headings, presents itself therefore as follows:

---

44. For a more in-depth presentation see Köstenberger, *John*, 52.
45. See the chart in Köstenberger, *John*, 599. Locations where these two characters are featured jointly include the upper room (John 13:23–24), the high priest's courtyard (18:15–16), the empty tomb (20:2–9), and the Sea of Galilee (21:15–23).

12.2. EXTENDED MACROSTRUCTURE OF JOHN		
John	**Level #1**	**Level #2**
1:1–18	Introduction	
1:19–12:50	The Book of Signs	
	1:19–51	John the Baptist and Jesus
	2–4	The "Cana Cycle"
	5–10	The "Festival Cycle"
	11–12	Bridge: Climactic Sign, Concluding Indictment
13:1–20:31	The Book of Exaltation	
	13–17	The Farewell Discourse

		13:1–30	Preamble
		13:31–16:33	Discourse Proper
		17	Final Prayer
	18–20	The Passion Narrative	
		18:1–19:37	Arrest, Trial, and Crucifixion of Jesus
		19:38–42	Burial of Jesus
		20 [including vv. 30–31]	Empty Tomb, Appearances, Commissioning
21:1–25	Epilogue		

Discerning the Microstructure: Level #3

Now that we have discerned the two levels of macrostructure in John's Gospel, we are ready to look at the two levels of microstructure of a particular narrative unit. John 9 may serve as an example. It will be helpful initially to break the passage down into subunits and then to break each of these units down into even smaller sections. A look at the transitions reveals that chapter 9 is only loosely connected to chapter 8, which ends with a reference to Jesus slipping away from the temple grounds. On the other end, one notes the lack of overt transition between chapters 9 and 10 (though note the phrase "I tell you the truth" in 10:1), which suggests that 9:1–10:21 is to be treated as a narrative unit. This is convincingly underscored by the *inclusio* referring to the opening of the eyes of the blind in 10:21.

The unit is thus best understood as reflecting the following microstructure:

12.3. EXTENDED MICROSTRUCTURE OF JOHN: LEVEL #3	
9:1–12	The Healing of the Man Born Blind
9:13–17	The First Interrogation of the Formerly Blind Man
9:18–23	The Interrogation of the Man's Parents
9:24–34	The Second Interrogation of the Formerly Blind Man
9:35–41	The Pharisees' Spiritual Blindness
10:1–21	The Good Shepherd and His Flock

Discerning the Microstructure: Level #4

One final level of microstructure remains. Our example, again, is from John's Gospel, specifically, the unit narrating the healing in 9:1–12. Clearly, the narration unfolds from the actual setting (v. 1), to the disciples' question which raises a theological dilemma (v. 2), to Jesus' response highlighting his messianic ministry (vv. 3–5), to the healing (vv. 6–7), to the mixed response of the man's neighbors to the healing (vv. 8–12). An important contextual link is the reference to Jesus as "the light of the world" in 9:5 which harks back to 8:12. Also, the evangelist translates Siloam as "Sent" (9:7), presumably to designate Jesus as the Sent One.

12.4. EXTENDED MICROSTRUCTURE OF JOHN: LEVEL #4	
9:1	Setting ("As he went along")
9:2	The Disciples' Question ("Rabbi, who sinned . . .?")
9:3–5	Jesus' Response ("Neither this man nor his parents sinned, . . .")
9:6–7	The Healing ("Having said this")
9:8–12	The Neighbors' Response ("His neighbors and those who had formerly seen him begging . . .")

The expressions cited in the parentheses above make clear that John uses various means of indicating discourse boundaries, such as initial markers or orienters (v. 1, "As he went along"), questions (v. 2,

"Rabbi, who sinned?") and answers (v. 3), or orienters halfway through the unit (v. 6, "Having said this"). The additional relations detailed in verses 6–7 ("he spit on the ground, made some mud with the saliva, and put it on the man's eyes") build toward the preliminary climax or peak at the end of verse 7, "So the man went and washed, and came home seeing."

Interestingly, up to this point the main point of objection—the fact that the healing had taken place on a Sabbath (cf. 5:1–15, esp. v. 9)—is suppressed by the evangelist until the next narrative unit (cf. v. 14), which introduces Jesus' major protagonists, the Pharisees (v. 13). Thus 9:1–12 is focused on the remarkable nature of the actual healing, while the following unit, 9:13–34, focuses on the Pharisees' bone of contention, Jesus' alleged breaking of the Sabbath in performing the miracle. John 9:13–34, fittingly, climaxes in the final verse of the unit, verse 34, with the reference to the formerly blind man's expulsion from the synagogue.

By way of tail-hook, the mention of the casting out of the blind man in the last verse of the previous unit (v. 34) and the first verse of the following unit (v. 35), the evangelist both sets boundaries and provides cohesion for his narrative. This is further underscored by the fact that Jesus, who had been silent in the narrative since the healing in verse 11, now resurfaces as a character in verses 35–41 (see the comments on the reintroduction of a character below).

Finally, 10:1 picks up seamlessly where 9:41 leaves off, introduced by Jesus' authoritative pronouncement, "Truly, truly, I say to you . . ." The unit 10:1–21 comes to a close with an *inclusio* referencing the healing of the blind man in 10:21. The content of 10:1–18, of course, is Jesus' "Good Shepherd" discourse, in which he contrasts himself with the Pharisees, the major forces pursuing the formerly blind man's expulsion from the synagogue in the previous chapter. By contrast, while the Pharisees are blind guides (9:39–41), Jesus is the "good shepherd" of the sheep.

After discerning the microstructure of 9:1–10:21 and delineating this as the proper narrative unit, it will be helpful to locate its place in the macro-structure of the book. Per the above discussion, the unit is part of the "Festival cycle" that makes up chapters 5–10 and narrates Jesus' messianic signs. In fact, the healing of the man born blind is the sixth such sign, and the last sign included in the "Festival cycle." Only the raising of Lazarus is still to follow.

The healing of the man born blind thus serves as the foil for the Pharisees' spiritual blindness to be revealed, similar to the anointing revealing the antagonism of Judas later on (see the comments on the account of Jesus' anointing by Mary in 12:1–8 above). The Pharisees' wrongheaded spiritual leadership and their expulsion of the healed man from the synagogue are contrasted with Jesus, the "good shepherd," who does not cast out anyone who comes to him (cf. 6:37). The healed man, finally, is the paradigmatic disciple who progresses all the way from blindness and spiritual ignorance to worship (9:38).

As we have seen, breaking down a given unit in Scripture both in terms of macrostructure and microstructure is absolutely essential for interpretation and yields rich insights that could not have been gained apart from locating the part within the larger discourse context. Anyone teaching on or preaching from John 9 will be able to follow the above-outlined procedure and develop confidence in his or her ability to understand the literary plan and theological message of a portion of Scripture and communicate it with the authority vested in God's Word itself.

DISCOURSE ANALYSIS: TRACING THE THOUGHT FLOW

Armed with an understanding of the theoretical foundations of discourse analysis and equipped with some of the most important categories in our interpretive toolbox, we conclude this chapter with a thought flow analysis of a wonderful portion of Scripture, Ephesians 5:15–6:18. A diagram of this passage will serve as a point of reference for the following brief presentation of the major discourse features of this text. Note that in the following diagram indentation conveys conceptual (and normally grammatical) subordination. Important discourse features are noted in the margin. The diagram was prepared on the basis of the Greek text but is reproduced here in English translation.[46]

---

46. The NIV breaks up a very long sentence in the Greek into several shorter English sentences. In the above translation, we have restored several Greek participles in order to show the pattern of syntactical subordination in these verses.

12.5. DIAGRAM OF EPHESIANS 5:15–6:18

Transition	15 Be very careful, **then**, how you live—
Contrast [neg./pos.]	*not* as unwise *but* as wise,
Manner	16 making the most of every opportunity
Reason	**because** the days are evil.
Inference	17 **Therefore** do *not* be foolish,
Contrast [neg./pos.]	*but* understand what the Lord's will is
Command [neg]. Contrast [neg./pos.]	18 Do *not* get drunk on wine,
Elaboration	which leads to debauchery.
Command [pos.]	*Instead*, be filled with the Spirit,
Result	19 speaking to one another with psalms, hymns and spiritual songs,
Result	singing and making music in your heart to the Lord,
Result	20 always giving thanks to God the Father for everything,
	in the name of our Lord Jesus Christ,
Result	21 submitting to one another out of reverence for Christ,
Command	22 wives, to your own husbands
Comparison	*as* to the Lord.
Reason	23 **because** the husband is the head of the wife
Comparison	*as* Christ is the head of the church,
Elaboration	his body, of which he is the Savior:
Conclusion/ Repetition (cf. v. 22)	24 **now** *as* the church submits to Christ,
Comparison	*so* also wives should submit to their husbands in everything.
Command	25 Husbands, love your wives,
Comparison	*just as* Christ loved the church and gave himself up for her
Purpose	26 to make her holy,
Manner	cleansing her by the washing with water through the word,
Purpose	27 and to present her to himself as a radiant church, without stain or wrinkle or any other blemish, but holy and blameless.
Comparison	28 In this same way, husbands ought to love their wives as their own bodies.

Analogy	He who loves his wife loves
	himself.
Elaboration	29–32 ...
Summary	33 However, each one of you also must love
	his wife
Comparison	as he loves himself,
	and the wife must respect her husband.
Command	6:1 Children, obey your parents
	in the Lord,
	for this is right...
Elaboration	2–3 ...
Command	4 Fathers, do not exasperate your children;
Contrast	instead, bring them up in the training
	and instruction of the Lord.
Command	5 Slaves, obey your earthly masters with respect and
	fear, and with sincerity of heart,
Comparison	just as you would obey Christ.
Elaboration	6–8 ...
Command	9 And masters, treat your slaves in the same way. .
Transition/ Command	10 Finally, be strong in the Lord and in his mighty power ...

The above example shows how a proper apprehension of the structure, logic, and flow of a given passage will lead to a fruitful exploration of the biblical message in context. It is important to remember that this flow is part of the author's intended meaning just as much as is the meaning of individual words. While we believe in the verbal inspiration of Scripture, this does not mean that meaning resides in a string of isolated words. Rather, syntax connects these words within the larger context of discourse.

The following are just a few examples of the type of fruitful exploration that can flow from a careful analysis of the structure and flow of a biblical text. First, 5:15–6:20 builds on the previous comments on living in a manner worthy of one's calling in 4:1–5:14, which in turns builds on the doctrinal section in chapters 1–3.[47] The theme of the current unit is the importance of wise, Spirit-filled living in these present evil times. In

---

47. Cf. Cotterell and Turner, *Linguistics & Biblical Interpretation*, 243, with reference to M. Barth.

the New Testament era, wise living is Spirit-filled living, and Spirit-filled living extends both to corporate worship and to personal relationships.

Paul's characteristic syntax and style include devices such as commands (5:18, 22, 25; 6:1, 4, 5, 9, 10), contrast ("not . . . but"; 5:15, 17, 18), manner (5:16, 26), result (5:19, 20, 21), purpose (5:26, 27), reason ("because," "for"; 5:16, 23), comparison ("as . . . so"; 5:16, 22, 23, 24, 25, 28, 33; 6:5), repetition and summary ("now," compare 5:24 with 5:22), and elaboration (5:29–32; 6:2–3, 6–8). Logically, the flow of argument starts with the assertion of the need for wise living as a result of Paul's previous comments (v. 15), supported with reference to the evil times in which believers live (v. 16); wise living is then defined as understanding the Lord's will (v. 17), which in turn is further developed as being filled with the Spirit (v. 18).

Under this head command, believers are exhorted corporately as a result of Spirit-filling to engage in grateful worship (vv. 19–20) and to practice proper submission in their relationships with others (5:21–6:9). This is extended to marriage (wife-husband; 5:21–33); parenting (child-parent; 6:1–4); and work (servant-master; 6:5–9; cf. 1 Pet. 2:11–3:22). The global command "Put on the full armor of God" concludes this emphasis on wise, circumspect, and Spirit-filled living (6:10–18). In this way, we have interpreted the parts in light of the whole, that is, the larger discourse unit, and have accurately discerned the thought flow of the biblical writer.

GUIDELINES FOR OUTLINING A BIBLICAL BOOK OR INTERPRETIVE UNIT

1. Discern the macrostructure: break down a book into its largest constituent units.

2. Discern the second level of macrostructure, discerning the sub-units of the broadest outline of the book.

3. Determine the microstructure of a chosen narrative unit.

4. Determine the microstructure of one or several portions of the narrative unit.

5. Interpret this narrative unit in the context of the book as a whole.

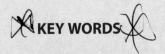

KEY WORDS

Aktionsart: German for "kind of action"

Anaphora: pronouns and other terms referring back to a previous clause or textual unit

Aposiopesis: the breaking off of a speech or statement owing to strong emotion, modesty, or other reasons

Aspect: a writer's choice to present a given action from a particular vantage point

Asyndeton: lack of a conjunction at the beginning of a sentence

Brachylogy: the omission, for the sake of brevity, of an element which is not necessary for the grammatical structure but for the thought

Chiasm: ABB'A' pattern

Clause: any meaningful cluster of words that includes a verb

Closure: the concluding statement in a given discourse unit

Cohesion: the glue that holds a discourse together

Discourse: any coherent sequence of phrases or sentences, whether a narrative, logical argument, or poetic portion of text

Discourse analysis: a study of a textual unit for the purpose of discerning various features of the text such as boundary markers, cohesion, prominence, relations, and situatedness

Discourse boundary: the opening and closing phrases or devices marking the beginning and end of a given discourse unit

Ellipsis: a feature by which an incomplete idea requires the reader to supply a missing element which is self-evident

Grammar: specific features of syntax, such as a certain kind of genitive or participle (form)

Hapax legomenon (pl. hapax legomena): a word occurring only once in the Old or New Testament

Hendiadys: an arrangement of two or more expressions that essentially convey the same idea

Implicature: implicit yet necessary information for understanding a given discourse

Inclusio: the occurrence of a given word or phrase at the beginning and at the end of a discourse unit for the purpose of marking this portion of material as a textual unit

Orienter: an initial marker indicating a boundary feature in a given discourse

Parataxis: unconnected juxtaposition of sentence units or clauses

Peaking: the height of action reached in a particular discourse unit

Pericope: narrative unit

Phrase: any meaningful word cluster that lacks a verb form

Pleonasm: a form of redundancy by which a previously expressed idea is repeated as a way of speaking

Prominence: elements in a discourse that stand out, be it by way of natural or marked prominence

Relations: various ways in which statements or propositions are conjoined in a given text

Semantics: concerned with the meaning of individual words based on the recognition that word meaning is to be discerned in context

Sentence: any complete thought expressed in form of one or several independent clauses

Situation: the real life-setting of a given discourse

Staging: the presentation of setting of a given action or event

Syntax: refers more broadly to relationships between words in the larger scheme of discourses and sentence structures

Tail-head link: mention of a topic at the end of a section to be developed in the following unit

Thought flow: discourse structure as conveyed by various discourse features per discourse analysis

Zeugma: a special type of ellipsis in which a different verb is to be supplied

STUDY QUESTIONS

1. What are some of the basics of Greek and Hebrew?

2. Why is knowledge of the basics of Greek and Hebrew important for biblical interpretation?

3. What is discourse analysis? Include major steps and examples for discerning the macrostructure and microstructure and tracing the thought flow of biblical passages.

4. What are the guidelines for outlining a biblical book?

ASSIGNMENTS

1. Perform a basic discourse analysis of the entire book of Philippians. Identify the boundary features and give attention to factors such as cohesion, relations, prominence, and situation. Conclude your analysis with a detailed outline of Philippians.

2. Perform a discourse analysis of the Old Testament book of Esther. Again, identify the major boundary markers and pay close attention to other relevant features of the text. In particular, identify the peak of the narrative and sketch both the macrostructure and microstructure of the book.

3. Review the material on discourse analysis in the course text. List and define the major terms and apply them to the study of a given text which you are currently studying. Discuss the value of discourse analysis for biblical study and identify any remaining questions or concerns you have with this method.

CHAPTER BIBLIOGRAPHY

Andersen, Francis I. *The Hebrew Verbless Clause in the Pentateuch.* Journal of Biblical Literature Monograph 14. Nashville: Abingdon, 1970.

Barr, James. *The Semantics of Biblical Language.* Oxford: SCM, 1983.

Bergsträsser, Gotthelf, *Introduction to the Semitic Languages.* Translated by Peter T. Daniels. Winona Lake: Eisenbrauns, 1983.

Blass, F. and A. Debrunner. *A Greek Grammar of the New Testament and Other Early Christian Literature.* Translated and edited by Robert W. Funk. Chicago: University of Chicago Press, 1961.

Cotterell, Peter and Max Turner. *Linguistics & Biblical Interpretation.* Downers Grove: InterVarsity, 1989.

Dooley, Robert H. and Stephen H. Levinsohn. *Analyzing Discourse: A Manual of Basic Concepts.* Dallas: SIL, 2001.

Erickson, Richard J. *A Beginner's Guide to New Testament Exegesis.* Downers Grove: InterVarsity, 2005.

Goetze, Albrecht. "The So-called Intensive of the Semitic Languages." *JAOS* 62 (1942): 1–8.

Green, Joel B. "Discourse Analysis and New Testament Interpretation." Pp. 175–96 in *Hearing the New Testament: Strategies for Interpretation.* Edited by Joel B. Green. Grand Rapids: Eerdmans, 1995.

Guthrie, George H. *The Structure of Hebrews: A Text-linguistic Analysis.* Leiden: Brill, 1994.

Kellum, L. Scott. *The Unity of the Farewell Discourse.* London/New York: T & T Clark, 2004.

Kutscher, Eduard Y. *A History of the Hebrew Language.* Edited by Raphael Kutscher. Jerusalem: Magnes, 1982.

Larson, Mildred L. *Meaning-Based Translation: A Guide to Cross-Language Equivalence.* 2d ed. Dallas: SIL, 1998.

Levinsohn, Stephen H. *Discourse Features of New Testament Greek.* Rev. ed. Dallas: SIL, 2000.

Longacre, Robert. *Grammar of Discourse.* 2d ed. New York: Plenum, 1996.

McFall, Leslie. *The Enigma of the Hebrew Verbal System.* Sheffield: Almond, 1982.

Moscati, Sabatino. *An Introduction to the Comparative Grammar of the Semitic Languages.* Wiesbaden: Harrassowitz, 1964.

Muraoka, T. *Emphatic Words and Structures in Biblical Hebrew.* Leiden: Brill, 1985.

Osborne, Grant R. *The Hermeneutical Spiral.* 2d ed. Downers Grove: InterVarsity, 2006.

Porter, Stanley E. and D. A. Carson, eds. *Biblical Greek Language and Linguistics.* JSNTSup 80. Sheffield: JSOT, 1993.

_____. *Discourse Analysis and Other Topics in Biblical Greek.* JSNTSup 113. Sheffield: Sheffield Academic Press, 1995.

Porter, Stanley E. *The Language of the New Testament: Classic Essays.* JSNTSup 60. Sheffield: JSOT, 1991.

_____. *Idioms of the Greek New Testament.* Sheffield: JSOT, 1992.

VanGemeren, Willem A., ed. *New International Dictionary of Old Testament Theology & Exegesis.* 5 vols. Grand Rapids: Zondervan, 1997.

Wallace, Daniel B. *Greek Grammar beyond the Basics.* Grand Rapids: Zondervan, 1996.

_____. *The Basics of New Testament Syntax.* Grand Rapids: Zondervan, 2000.

Waltke, Bruce K. and M. O'Connor. *An Introduction to Biblical Hebrew Syntax.* Winona Lake: Eisenbrauns, 1990.

Wegner, Paul D. *A Student's Guide to Textual Criticism of the Bible.* Downers Grove: InterVarsity, 2006.

Young, Richard A. *Intermediate New Testament Greek.* Nashville: B&H, 1994.

CHAPTER 13 OBJECTIVES

1. To acquaint the student with the elementary principles involved in studying a given language, in particular the biblical languages.

2. To introduce the student to the science of determining word meanings.

3. To impress upon the student the importance of context and larger discourse units in biblical interpretation.

4. To present the student with a representative list of exegetical fallacies in order to guard him or her against the dangers of improper interpretation.

5. To equip the student with a sound method of studying individual words of Scripture as part of the larger goal of developing a proper method of interpretation.

CHAPTER 13 OUTLINE

A. Linguistics: The Nature of the Study of Languages
B. Semantics: The Science of Determining Word Meanings
C. Context and Discourse: Interpreting the Parts in Light of the Whole
D. From Word Study to Semantic Field Study: A More Excellent Way
E. Exegetical Fallacies: Pitfalls to Avoid in Determining Word Meanings
    1. Fallacy #1: The Etymological or Root Fallacy
    2. Fallacy #2: Misuse of Subsequent or Previous Meaning (Semantic Anachronism or Obsolescence)
    3. Fallacy #3: Appeal to Unknown or Unlikely Meanings or Background Material
    4. Fallacy #4: Improper Construals of Greek or Hebrew Grammar or Syntax
    5. Fallacy #5: Improper Appeal to Alleged Parallels
    6. Fallacy #6: Improper Linkage of Language and Mentality
    7. Fallacy #7: False Assumptions about Technical Meaning
    8. Fallacy #8: Improper Distinctions Made Regarding Synonyms
    9. Fallacy #9: Selective or Prejudicial Use of Evidence
    10. Fallacy #10: Unwarranted Semantic Disjunctions or Restrictions (Including Illegitimate Totality Transfer)
    11. Fallacy #11: Unwarranted Neglect of Distinctive Characteristics or Personal Style
    12. Fallacy #12: Unwarranted Linking of Sense and Reference
F. Conclusion
G. Guidelines for Determining Word Meanings in Scripture
H. Key Words
I. Study Questions
J. Assignments
K. Chapter Bibliography

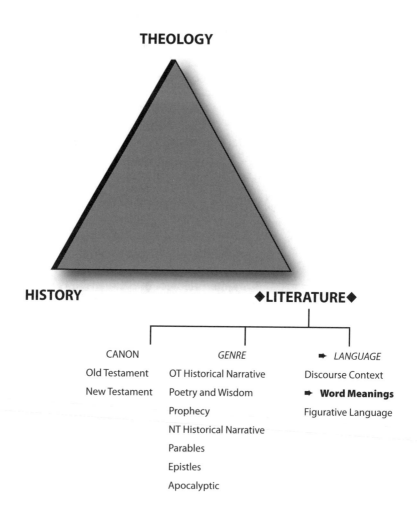

THEOLOGY

HISTORY

◆LITERATURE◆

CANON

Old Testament

New Testament

GENRE

OT Historical Narrative

Poetry and Wisdom

Prophecy

NT Historical Narrative

Parables

Epistles

Apocalyptic

➡ LANGUAGE

Discourse Context

➡ **Word Meanings**

Figurative Language

Chapter 13

THE MEANING OF WORDS: LINGUISTICS, SEMANTICS, AND EXEGETICAL FALLACIES

LINGUISTICS: THE NATURE OF THE STUDY OF LANGUAGES

SOME INTERPRET SCRIPTURE AS IF word meaning were found on the level of individual words whose meaning can simply be looked up in a dictionary or be gleaned from a study of parallel passages in Scripture. While this may at times prove adequate, we have seen in the previous chapter that, understood more properly, word meaning is in fact determined by the use of a word in context, that is, on the larger discourse level. It remains now for us to apply this crucial insight to our specific word study methodology.

At the very outset, it is worth remembering that language, and the various literary forms and genres in which it finds expression in Scripture, is part of history and culture. That is, the linguistic forms in which Scripture has come down to us—in the original Greek, Hebrew, and Aramaic—are a reflection of the historical-cultural world in which God chose to reveal himself to his people in both Testaments.

In fact, the failure to appreciate that we are dealing here with *language*, which by its very nature is subjective and varied in style and often eludes being reduced to a simple formula or rigid dictionary definitions, hinders much of common biblical interpretation. What is language? In short, language is *convention*. It is the arbitrary assigning of a certain sequence of letters or symbols to a particular object or action. There is no reason why the object we know as "apple" should be designated by the successive letters "a," "p," "p," "l," and "e," other than that at one point in the past a language user or a group of language users determined to call this particular fruit by that particular name.

To be sure, once this usage had attained common acceptance, it became the standard, and new language users (such as children or non-native speakers) were taught that 🍎 means "apple." The important lesson for us at this point is that there is nothing sacred, or absolute, about 🍎 being an "apple." Language is a human convention, and as such is subject to change or modification. Words have a history and can take on new meanings over time or acquire additional connotations.

All that has been said thus far (and much more could and will be said below) already makes clear that language is not a hard science like mathematics or quantum physics but rather a "soft," rather subjective and malleable affair. Perhaps this is why theologians and others who deal with religious absolutes and theological certainties have frequently had such a difficult time adjusting to the challenges presented with interpreting biblical texts. Unless we become students of language and literature *as well as* theology we will always be limited in our ability to "accurately handle the word of truth."

SEMANTICS: THE SCIENCE OF DETERMINING WORD MEANINGS

As we have seen, *linguistics* is the field of research devoted to a study of the nature of language. A related field of study is the area of *semantics*, the science of determining word meanings.[1] Ever since the seminal contributions of the French philologist Ferdinand de Saussure in the early 1900s and subsequently the Austrian philosopher Ludwig Wittgenstein, it has been increasingly understood that language is an intricately interwoven fabric in which, in de Saussure's words, *"tout se tient"* ("everything holds together"). For this reason de Saussure spoke of "associative fields" or systems of paradigmatic relations between words.

---

1. For a helpful treatment see J. P. Louw, *Semantics of New Testament Greek* (Atlanta: Scholars Press, 1982).

John Lyons provides a helpful articulation of the seminal insights of de Saussure and others:

> People often think of the meaning of words as if each of them had an independent and separate existence. But . . . no word can be fully understood independently of other words that are related to it and delimit its sense. Looked at from a semantic point of view, the lexical structure of a language—the structure of its vocabulary—is best regarded as a large and intricate network of sense-relations; it is like a huge, multidimensional, spider's web, in which each strand is one such relation and each knot in the web is a different lexeme.[2]

In his *General Course in Linguistics*, de Saussure distinguished between two linguistic phenomena: *langue* and *parole*, whereby the former constitutes the language system in its entirety and the latter specific words chosen by the language user for the sake of written or oral communication.[3] In essence, de Saussure's point was that a given language user, in construing particular utterances or discourses, draws on his general knowledge of a certain language system (e.g., English), made up of its stock of vocabulary and syntactical options. Wittgenstein, in positing the notion of "language games," made a similar point, showing that language users have a variety of options in accordance with the parameters of a given linguistic system at large.[4]

Applied to the field of biblical studies, Paul, for example, when wanting to say that Jesus died for our sins, had several linguistic options available to him in keeping with the Greek language in which he was writing. Should he say that "Jesus died *anti* us," that is, "in our place" or "instead of us"? Or should he choose the wording "Jesus died *hyper* us," that is, "for our sake"? The options may be partially overlapping, but they are nonetheless distinct. Which word best encapsulates Paul's intended meaning? This process illustrates de Saussure's model well. Paul's Greek vocabulary, in the present instance comprising prepositions conveying the notion of "for" or "in the place of," corresponds to language viewed as a

---

2. John Lyons, *Language, Meaning and Context* (London: Fontana [Collins], 1981), 75.
3. Ferdinand de Saussure, *General Course in Linguistics* (New York: McGraw-Hill, 1966 [1915]).
4. Ludwig Wittgenstein, *Philosophical Investigations*, trans. G. E. M. Anscombe (New York: Macmillan, 1953).

whole (*langue*), while his specific chosen wording (e.g., *hyper*) represents his actual words (*parole*).

The important implications of this kind of theory for the study of biblical words may not be immediately obvious, but they are significant nonetheless. Rather than study merely the specific word a biblical writer, such as Paul, was using in a particular instance, biblical interpreters, in applying de Saussure's insights, will do well to study also other words Paul may have used in a given passage but chose not to use. This will be justified especially where Paul does use alternative or similar expressions elsewhere in his writings. This will result in a more realistic, more relevant, and richer picture of the message and meaning of a given text of Scripture. Since our underlying hermeneutical purpose is the determination of authorially intended meaning, and authors have a number of linguistic options to convey a particular proportion or meaning, the larger linguistic system must be taken into account.

CONTEXT AND DISCOURSE: INTERPRETING THE PARTS IN LIGHT OF THE WHOLE

What is the proper relationship between words and context in the study of biblical concepts? Many older treatments tend to detect meanings in biblical words that are actually supplied by the context in which those words are used. However, it is important to distinguish between information supplied by the context in which a word occurs and the component of meaning contributed by the word itself. As Grant Osborne observes, "Meaning is determined on the basis of the congruence of two factors, semantic field . . . and context."[5]

Among these two factors, context must have priority. Moisés Silva notes, "[A]mong the diverse meanings a word possesses, the only one that will emerge into consciousness is the one determined by the context."[6] Anthony Thiselton concurs: "Any meaningful linguistic unit . . . has meaning in context."[7] J. P. Louw and Eugene Nida, too, make reference to the basic principle of semantic analysis "that differences in meaning are marked by

---

5. Grant R. Osborne, *The Hermeneutical Spiral* (Downers Grove: InterVarsity, 1991), 414.
6. Moisés Silva, *Biblical Words and Their Meaning* (Grand Rapids: Zondervan, 1983), 139.
7. Anthony C. Thiselton, "Semantics and New Testament Interpretation," in *New Testament Interpretation*, ed. I. Howard Marshall (Grand Rapids: Eerdmans, 1977), 75.

context, either textual or extratextual. . . . Since any differences of meaning are marked by context, it follows that the correct meaning of any term is that which fits the context best."[8]

Nevertheless, the fact that context must be given priority does not warrant the neglect of the other factor relevant for determining a term's meaning, namely, semantic field. The semantic field provides the word options available to the writer, the assumption being that a writer chose the word employed to communicate a meaning or nuance not provided by a different word. The following guidelines will be helpful here: (1) semantic field (i.e., terminology) and context are both important for the study of a biblical concept; (2) context has priority over semantic field; (3) if the second point is kept in mind, semantic field seems to be a very appropriate starting point to guide one to at least some of the most relevant context which need to be considered in one's study of a concept. Thus terminology (in the present case, biblical terminology) will serve as a guide to most of the relevant contexts where a given word or group of words is found.

As mentioned above, therefore, rather than narrowly focusing on words in isolation, resulting in reductionism, part of the solution is an expansion of one's focus beyond *words* to *concepts*. Thus Osborne cautions against "the failure to consider the concept as well as the word, that is, the other ways the biblical writers could say the same thing."[9] Indeed, "We dare never study only occurrences of the particular term if our purpose is to trace the theology behind a word or phrase. . . . None of us ever uses the exact same words to describe our thoughts. Rather, we use synonyms and other phrases to depict our ideas. Therefore a truly complete picture must cluster semantically related terms and phrases."[10]

These insights with regard to semantic fields and biblical concepts, in turn, should be viewed within the larger framework of biblical discourses. In their important work *Linguistics and Biblical Interpretation*, Peter Cotterell and Max Turner draw the vital distinction between *lexical* and

---

8. Johannes P. Louw and Eugene A. Nida, *Greek-English Lexicon of the New Testament Based on Semantic Domains*, 2 vols. (New York: United Bible Societies, 1988, 1989), 1.xvi.

9. Grant R. Osborne, *The Hermeneutical Spiral*, 2d ed. (Downers Grove: InterVarsity, 2006), 92.

10. Ibid., 92–93.

discourse concepts.[11] The example provided by Cotterell and Turner is that of "Uncle George's old red bike," which later in a given discourse may be simply called "the bike." However, in the context of the discourse at large, "the bike" is not just any bike, but rather "Uncle George's old red bike." Or to use a biblical example, when reference is made in Revelation 13:1 to "the dragon" who stood on the shore of the sea, reference to the larger discourse unit of which the verse is a part leads the interpreter to the fuller reference to "the great dragon, . . . that ancient serpent called the devil, or Satan, who leads the whole world astray" (Rev. 12:9). The lesson is clear: biblical concepts must be understood and interpreted within the context of the larger discourse of which they are a part.

FROM WORD STUDY TO SEMANTIC FIELD STUDY: A MORE EXCELLENT WAY

The old-fashioned notion of "word studies" has in recent years been increasingly replaced by the more refined approach of what has been called a "semantic field study." By "semantic field" we mean a particular set of words that are linguistically related, be it by synonymy, antonymy, or some other association of meaning. Groundbreaking in this regard was the *Greek-English Dictionary Based on Semantic Domains* compiled by Johannes P. Louw and Eugene A. Nida under the auspices of the United Bible Societies (1988, 1989).[12] Initially prepared as a resource for Bible translators, the innovative approach used by this dictionary has pointed the way forward to a more accurate and faithful appraisal of word meanings in both Testaments, particularly the New Testament.

In this dictionary, the vocabulary of the New Testament is grouped into a total of 93 semantic domains, which in turn are divided into two or more sub-domains each. For example, you might want to conduct a study of possessions in the New Testament. If so, you would want to include an analysis of several words related to wealth and poverty, be it nouns, verbs,

---

11. Peter Cotterell and Max Turner, *Linguistics and Biblical Interpretation* (Downers Grove: InterVarsity, 1989), 151.

12. Louw and Nida, *Greek-English Lexicon.* Though no corresponding work exists at present for the Old Testament, there is a growing interest in such a work. A search of Hebrew semantic/lexical projects on the internet reveals several data base projects currently underway. (United Bible Societies is working on an OT counterpart titled *Semantic Dictionary of Biblical Hebrew,* edited by Reiner de Bois. I'm not sure when it will be released. See http://sdbh.org.)

adjectives, or adverbs, such as "rich," "poor," "wealth," "poverty," and so on, of course in the original Greek. Most of these terms are found together in Louw and Nida's domain 57, "Possess, Transfer, Exchange," which is divided into as many as 21 sub-domains.

Assume that your focus is on a study of wealth and poverty in the Gospel of Luke, a New Testament book where this theme is particularly prominent. Perhaps the ace for you to turn in order to locate specific instances of "wealth and poverty" vocabulary in the Gospel of Luke is *The Book Study Concordance*, which organizes the vocabulary of the New Testament book by book.[13] This enables you to survey the vocabulary of any one New Testament book much more quickly than by the use of a conventional concordance. By way of scanning the English glosses even those interpreters who do not know New Testament Greek are able to delineate the contours of the Lucan theology of wealth and poverty.

The (partial) results present themselves as follows (references are to the Gospel of Luke):

13.1. SEMANTIC FIELD STUDY OF WEALTH AND POVERTY IN THE GOSPEL OF LUKE	
πτωχός (*ptōchos*, "**poor**")	
4:18	anointed me to proclaim good news to the poor
6:20	Blessed are you who are poor
7:22	the poor have good news preached to them, etc.
πλούσιος (*plousios*, "**rich**")	
6:24	But woe to you who are rich
12:16	The land of a rich man produced plentifully
14:12	When you give a dinner or a banquet, do not invite your . . . rich neighbors, etc.
πλουτέω (*plouteō*, "**be rich**")	
1:53	he has filled the hungry . . ., and the rich he has sent empty away
12:21	So is the one who lays up treasure for himself and is not rich toward God
πλοῦτος (*ploutos*, "**wealth, riches**")	
8:14	choked by the cares and riches and pleasures of life

---

13. Andreas J. Köstenberger and Raymond P. Bouchoc, *The Book Study Concordance* (Nashville: B & H, 2003).

A quick glance at passages show that wealth and poverty is indeed an important theme in Luke's Gospel. A semantic field study, rather than a series of isolated word studies, is better able to provide the interpreter with a full-orbed understanding of Luke's theology of wealth and poverty. It is not our purpose here to develop this theology further. The above listing of passages merely provides us with the relevant data from which this important Lucan theme can be profitably studied.

The value of semantic field studies for the Old Testament can be illustrated in a study of the word "kill" in the command "You shall not kill" (Deut. 5:17; רָצָה, [rěṣāḥ]). The more recent translations of the Old Testament read "You shall not *murder.*" This change of wording is, in part, based on the recognition that the English word "kill" is more general than is the Hebrew, which comes into sharper focus when one compares it with other Hebrew words used of taking life.[14]

EXEGETICAL FALLACIES: PITFALLS TO AVOID
IN DETERMINING WORD MEANINGS

Now that we have laid out a responsible procedure for conducting semantic field studies, it will be helpful to take a look at several common exegetical fallacies, in particular fallacies that relate to determining word meanings. This is an important subject, because, as mentioned in the introduction, the biblical interpreter is ultimately accountable to God and charged with handling the word of truth accurately. This, in turn, involves discerning the meaning of individual words in context.

At this point it is worth remembering that our hermeneutic is founded on the two bedrock principles of (1) the integrity of Scripture (including its verbal inspiration); and (2) the importance of determining the meaning intended by the original author (rather than supplying a meaning of our own). Giving utmost care to the study of each individual word of Scripture flows directly from these two bedrock principles (though it must be said that this does not entail a rigid, atomistic approach to word study that fails to consider contextual meaning).[15]

---

14. Regarding helpful tools for word studies and semantic field studies and other original language biblical research, see chapter 16 below.
15. See especially Kevin Vanhoozer, "Lost in Interpretation? Truth, Scripture, and Hermeneutics," in *Whatever Happened to Truth?*, ed. Andreas J. Köstenberger

It has been said that a little knowledge is dangerous. This is nowhere truer than when it comes to the knowledge of biblical languages. Many a preacher has been known to parade his command of the Greek or Hebrew language before his congregation and to make confident assertions that would have made competent linguists or informed biblical scholars cringe. We therefore turn our attention now to the matter of exegetical fallacies related to the meaning of words.[16]

Fallacy #1: The Etymological or Root Fallacy

We all have heard people say, "You know, the word X originally meant such-and-such," with the implication that knowing this original meaning of a given expression is significant for interpreting the meaning of the word in a later instance. But while this may at times be the case, it is not invariably so, and in many cases will be downright fallacious. To use an example from the English, the word "nice" comes from Latin *nescius*, which means "ignorant." How does knowing that the term underlying the word "nice" originally meant "ignorant" help the contemporary reader understand the use of the word in a particular written text (or oral communication)? The answer is, only does it not help, drawing on the root meaning of the word can be rather confusing and lead to wrong and unfounded conclusions, in some cases even bizarre or humorous ones. For example, "butterfly" does not mean "butter" + "fly," nor does "pineapple" mean "pine" plus "apple"![17]

This caution pertains also to conclusions drawn from the meaning of two or more component parts of a given expression. Among the common examples in this area is the Greek word ὑπηρέτης (*hypēretēs*) which is properly translated "servants" in many English translations of 1 Corinthians 4:1. However, some have pointed to the fact that, taken by itself, the preposition ὑπό (*hypo*) means "under," and the word ερέτης (*eretēs*) means "rower"; hence, ὑπηρέτης (*hypēretēs*) means "under-rower," as in "one who

---

(Wheaton: Crossway, 2005), 93–129; and his earlier treatment, "The Semantics of Biblical Literature: Truth and Scripture's Diverse Literary Forms," in *Hermeneutics, Authority, and Canon*, ed. D. A. Carson and John D. Woodbridge (Grand Rapids: Zondervan, 1986), 49–104.

16. For helpful treatments of exegetical word fallacies see D. A. Carson, *Exegetical Fallacies*, 2d ed. (Grand Rapids: Baker, 1996), chapter 1 and Osborne, *Hermeneutical Spiral*, chapter 3.

17. Cf. Johannes P. Louw, *Semantics of New Testament Greek* (Atlanta: Scholars Press, 1982), 27.

is part of a crew rowing a boat." The all-important question, however, is: Was Paul consciously drawing on rowing imagery when writing to Corinthians? Or had the original metaphor been lost as a connotation that would have resonated in the writer's and readers' minds? If the latter (and in the present instance, there is good evidence that it had), it is fallacious to claim that Paul invoked an illustration from the realm of rowing in 1 Corinthians 4:1. It may be tempting for the preacher to suggest this, and hard to pass up an opportunity to impress the audience with one's knowledge of the original Greek, but such temptations must nonetheless be firmly resisted, for our quest for truth must override points made on flimsy linguistic foundations. Contextually, it appears that ὑπηρέτης (hyperetēs) used in 1 Corinthians 4:1 is a virtual synonym of διάκονος (diakonos), "servant."[18]

A further pitfall in this regard can be illustrated as follows. In several instances, Jesus is called μονογενής (monogenēs) in John's Gospel (John 1:14, 18; 3:14, 18). Many have claimed that the best understanding of this word is that Jesus is the "only-begotten" Son of God. Even on the premise that the sum of a word's parts makes up the meaning of the word as a whole, however (which we have shown to be fallacious), the problem in the present instance is that μονογενής (monogenēs) is derived not from μονο (monos, "only") + γενναω (gennaō, "beget" or "give birth"), which would add up to "only-begotten," but from μονός (monos, "only") + γενος (genos, "kind"). Thus μονογενής (monogenēs), based on the meaning of its component parts, more properly means "the only one of a kind" (i.e., unique), not "only begotten." This is confirmed by the usage of the word in the Greek Septuagint (e.g., Judg. 11:34) and other New Testament passages (e.g., Luke 7:12; 8:42; 9:38), where the term is applied to only children who by virtue of being such were considered unique and particularly precious to their parents.[19]

In short, then, we must avoid the etymological or root fallacy and study the contextual meaning of a given word in a biblical passage. Rather than focusing on *diachronic* study (the use of a given word "over time"), the emphasis should lie on *synchronic* study (the use of a word "at the

---

18. See ibid., 26–27, followed by Carson, *Exegetical Fallacies*, 29–30.
19. For a fuller treatment see Andreas J. Köstenberger, *John*, BECNT (Grand Rapids: Baker, 2004), 42–44.

same time" as the word under consideration). This way we will compare apples to apples rather than to oranges, will build our linguistic work on more proper foundations, and will more likely arrive at accurate conclusions with regard to the meaning of a particular biblical word in its proper context.

Fallacy #2: Misuse of Subsequent or Previous Meaning (Semantic Anachronism or Obsolescence)

As mentioned, language is a matter of convention, and words have a history. The relevance of these observations has already been shown with regard to the "root fallacy" above. It is also an issue related to the present set of fallacies. *Semantic anachronism* may be defined as the reading of a later use of a word back into earlier literature.

It may seem compelling to many preachers and people in the congregation that God loves a "hilarious" giver (2 Cor. 9:7), because the Greek word underlying "hilarious" is ἱλαρόν *(hilaron)*, but this conclusion is also certainly wrong, because "hilarious" is a later connotation taken on by the word in subsequent English usage. At the time of the writing of New Testament, the Greek word meant "cheerful" (NIV), not "hilarious," and the preacher should be content to leave it at that. No playing of laughing tapes during offertory, please!

Likewise, while it is true that the Greek word underlying "miracle" in the New Testament is *dynamis*, this does not mean that Jesus' miracles were "dynamite"! "Dynamite" is a later linguistic development that should not be read back into earlier usage. This would be committing the fallacy of semantic anachronism. Or, is Paul telling Romans 12:1 to render "logical worship" because the word modifying "worship" is Grk. λογικὴν *(logikēn)*, this improperly assumes that λογικὴν *(logikēn)* = "logical," which may or may not actually be the case. "Spiritual" or "reasonable" (orig. [changed in 2010 version]) is therefore a better translation. Another example of such a fallacy is the use of the word "bishop" to translate Greek ἐπίσκοπος *(episkopos)*. "Overseer" [e.g. 1 Tim. 3:2 NIV]) is better; "bishop" carries unwelcome connotations of the later development of a three-tiered monarchical episcopate.

And are we really God's "poem" merely because the Greek word underlying "workmanship" in Ephesians 2:10 is ποίημα *(poiēma)*, the word from which we get "poem" in the English language? Hardly. More properly understood, ποίημα *(poiēma)* is related to the Greek verb ποιέω *(poieō)*, which means "do" or "make," so that ποίημα *(poiēma)* denotes the work of one's hands more generally, as in "workmanship" or "product," not necessarily the work of a poet, as in "poetry." Finally, when Jude urges his readers to contend for the faith" (Jude 3), does the fact that the Greek word ἐπαγωνίζομαι *(epagōnizomai)* is used to denote the word "contend" in this passage mean that we should "agonize over" our faith? This is hardly the case. We could give more examples, but the point is clear enough.

A related fallacy is that of *semantic obsolescence*, in which case the interpreter assigns to a word in a given biblical passage a meaning that the word in question had at an earlier point in the development of the language but that is no longer within the live, semantic range of the word. In other words, this meaning is semantically obsolete.[20] A possible example is the meaning "to kiss" for the word φιλέω *(phileō)*, which is quite common early on but seems to be largely obsolete in the New Testament.[21] A New Testament instance where obsolescence can be detected with regard to a type of grammatical form is the almost complete loss of the superlative sense in most superlative forms.[22] The important interpretive implication is that most superlatives should be understood to carry "elative" force, that is, convey simple comparison or even mere emphasis.[23]

---

20. Carson, *Exegetical Fallacies*, 56, cites as an example of semantic obsolescence the Greek word μάρτυς meaning "martyr," but this is itself fallacious, since it is not the case that the meaning "martyr" had become obsolete by the time of the New Testament, but that it had not yet appeared! Thus this is actually an instance of semantic anachronism, not obsolescence.
21. See the observation registered by W. Feneberg, "φιλέω," in Horst Balz and Gerhard Schneider, ed., *Exegetical Dictionary of the New Testament* (Grand Rapids: Eerdmans, 1990), 3.425 (with references to further bibliography): "Why, in sharp contrast to secular usage, does φιλέω phileō recede so noticeably in the LXX (15 occurrences, vs. 266 of ἀγαπάω) and (doubtless dependent on this) also in the NT (25 occurrences vs. 143)?" See also the thorough survey by G. Stählin, "φιλέω κτλ.," in Gerhard Kittel and Gerhard Friedrich, eds., *Theological Dictionary of the New Testament*, trans. Geoffrey W. Bromiley (Grand Rapids: Eerdmans, 1974), 9.113–71.
22. See F. Blass, A. Debrunner, trans. by R. Funk, *A Greek Grammar of the New Testament and Other Early Christian Literature* (Chicago: University of Chicago Press, 1961), 1, n. 2.
23. For a full discussion and numerous New Testament examples, see ibid., §60, pp. 32–33. E.g., ἥδιστα in 2 Corinthians 12:9 means "all the more gladly," not "gladdest"; in 2 Corinthians 12:15, the same word is to be rendered "very gladly."

Or, conversely, interpreters may assign a particular meaning to a word that it took on at a later point in its semantic development but that it did not yet possess at the time period from which the text stems. An example of this latter fallacy is the imposition of the notion of martyrdom onto the New Testament instances of the μάρτυς (*martys*) word group (with the possible exception of certain instances of this word group in the book of Revelation). Another example is the translation, "On this rock I will build my *church*," of Matthew 16:18, even though "church" may anachronistically suggest the New Testament doctrine of the church as the body of Christ that was developed only subsequently by Paul. More properly, Jesus spoke of establishing his new messianic "community" (the more likely meaning of the term ἐκκλησία (*ekklēsia*) in the present example).[24]

Fallacy #3: Appeal to Unknown or Unlikely Meanings or Background Material

The appeal to unknown or unlikely meanings or background material is one of the most common fallacies in biblical interpretation and preaching. One of the most serious negative consequences of this practice is that the actual explicit message of the text is set aside in favor of an alleged construal of background or word meaning, which substitutes the message intended by the given interpreter for that intended by the biblical author and ultimately God himself as the author of Scripture. In light of the above comments made about the importance of context, we must be careful in our use of lexical or background information so that we give preference to the connotation that is most likely in keeping with the surrounding and later context rather than resort to dubious extratextual pieces of information. As Louw and Nida aptly note, "the correct meaning of any term is that which fits the context best."[25]

Perhaps one of the most egregious examples of the present fallacy in biblical scholarship of which I am aware is the argument by Catherine and Richard Kroeger that the term αὐθεντέω (*authenteō*), commonly

---

24. Note that the expression occurs only twice in all of the Gospels, here and in Matthew 18:18, which makes clear that "church" had not yet become a technical term in Jesus' day. See further the fallacy related to false assumptions about technical meaning below.

25. Louw and Nida, *Greek-English Lexicon*, 1.xvi.

translated "to have authority," in 1 Timothy 2:12 should be translated as "to proclaim oneself the author of man."[26] The Kroegers posited this previously unknown meaning on the basis of an alleged teaching in Ephesus at the time of writing, according to which women claimed that God created the woman first, and then the man, rather than the other way round. If so, Paul's prohibition against women occupying authoritative offices over men in the church would be recast as a prohibition for women to claim, wrongly, that God made, first Eve, and then Adam.[27] The problem with this interpretation is that it lacks complete textual support, which is why few, if any, scholars have adopted this rendering.

Fallacy #4: Improper Construals of Greek or Hebrew Grammar or Syntax

In any given language, there are certain rules of proper word order, grammar, and syntax that, while capable of being broken, nonetheless are required for proper expression in that particular language. To cite an example in English, "Car kills man" means something quite different than "Man kills car," though the words are exactly the same. Word order makes all the difference. Or someone may say, "I is Andrew." We may still understand that the person's name is Andrew, but clearly the person is using improper grammar (in the present case, the third rather than the first person singular of the verb "to be").

The same principle applies in the biblical languages, Greek, Hebrew, and Aramaic. Properly understood, these fairly hard and fast rules of Greek or Hebrew grammar and syntax (as well a certain semantic range, which means that certain words will be outside this range) can be the interpreter's best friend, for these rules set proper boundaries for correct or incorrect interpretation. The problem comes only where someone is either ignorant of what constitutes proper grammar in a biblical language underlying a particular text or where such a person willfully sets aside these rules in order to advance his or her own preferred interpretation

---

26. Richard and Catherine Clark Kroeger, *I Suffet Not a Woman* (Grand Rapids: Baker, 1992).
27. Incidentally, it is interesting to note that the well-known Hebrew scholar and feminist Phyllis Trible recently suggested just that—though this does not prove that the interpretation of 1 Timothy 2:12 advanced by the Kroegers is accurate! See Phyllis Trible, "Wrestling with Scripture," *BAR* 32/2 (March/April 2006): 49–50.

even though it violates common usage with regard to semantic range, grammar, or syntax.[28]

Let's look at a few examples of this fallacy. The first comes from Genesis 1:2. Many have attempted to show that Genesis 1:2 forms a parenthetical observation to Genesis 1:1 (e.g., the translation in the Anchor Bible of Gen. 1:1–3). Others have suggested that there is a gap between Genesis 1:1 and 1:2, so that a long period of time existed after the original creation, allowing for the fall of Satan and his hosts. Genesis 1:2 then becomes a subsequent recreation because of what the earth had become: "formless and empty."

The former view illegitimately assumes an unlikely grammatical structure, because the Hebrew verbal phrase here contains a perfect rather than the normal imperfect tense in a special construction denoting verbal sequence. The latter view would also demand an imperfect verb tense and call for a different construction with "formless and empty" if the meaning "became" were to be distinctly clear. Appeal to Isaiah's remarks that the Lord did not create the earth "to be empty, but formed it to be inhabited" (Isa. 45:18) likewise fails to substantiate the case for the gap theory, for Isaiah simply emphasizes the Lord's purpose in creating the earth rather than the process of his activity in doing so.

It is best simply to view verse 1 as a sovereign God's original creation and verse 2 as the opening conditions from which God proceeded in his further creative and fashioning work with regard to planet earth. The Hebrew construction in verse 2 (*waw* + the perfect) is thus best viewed as conveying anticipatory emphasis. Having spoken of the universe, the text now moves on to consider the earth: "Now as for the earth."

A New Testament example comes from John 2:20, a verse in which translations commonly render the Greek original as indicating that the temple had been under construction "for 46 years." This seems to make good sense in that Jesus then would be saying that he can tear down and rebuild the temple in three days rather than the 46 years that it had already taken to do so in his day. The problem with this, however, is that the expression "46 years" in the Greek is in the dative rather than accusative case. Yet it is the accusative that would need to be used (an "accusative of

---

28. With regard to semantic range, see the example of the alleged meaning of αὐθεντέω in 1 Timothy 2:12, "to proclaim oneself the author of man," discussed above.

time") if the above-cited interpretation were valid. On the former reading, the dative suggests, not duration *of* time ("for 46 years") but location *in* time: "at [a point] 46 years [ago]." Therefore what is most likely in view is the beginning of reconstruction of the temple 46 years ago in the past (location), not the extended period of reconstruction (duration) of the temple.[29]

Fallacy #5: Improper Appeal to Alleged Parallels

Another very common fallacy is the improper appeal to alleged parallels, whether semantic or conceptual. Regarding the latter, Samuel Sandmel has written a well-known essay opposing what he calls "parallelomania," that is, the urge felt by some scholars to adduce parallels of questionable value.[30] Often it appears that interpreters feel they can simply *assume* that a given passage constitutes an actual parallel without demonstration. Yet it must be stated unequivocally that simply quoting a similar-sounding passage and asserting that this is a "parallel" does not amount to and must never take the place of an argument supported by evidence.

During the heyday of the history-of-religions school, for example, it was common practice to explain virtually every feature of Christianity by appeal to other religions, particular the so-called "mystery religions." Scholars explained baptism in connection with secret initiation rites in those cults, and likened the Lord's Supper to sacred ritual meals. Similarly, they interpreted Old Testament legal observance and worship in light of other ancient Near Eastern religions. Somehow, it was always other religions that had a claim to originality, except for Christianity, which was always assumed to borrow its ideas from other religions![31]

Caution is always called for when we adduce a given parallel, because we must never assume that even the predominant usage of a given word or image prevails in each and every case. It is highly precarious simply to take the most frequently attested lexical meaning of an expression from a dictionary and to assume it obtains in a particular instance. There is no

---

29. See Köstenberger, *John*, 109–10. Note that this rendering has been added as a footnote to the ESV.
30. Samuel Sandmel, "Parallelomania," *JBL* 81 (1962): 2–13.
31. See the sidebar on mystery religious and the history-of-religions approach in Andreas J. Köstenberger, L. Scott Kellum, and Charles L. Quarles, *The Cradle, the Cross, and the Crown: An Introduction to the New Testament* (Nashville: B&H, 2009), 88.

substitute for contextual interpretation, and what we said about determinative role of context for word meanings above applies here as well.

For example, 1 Timothy 2:15 is commonly rendered, "But women will be saved through childbearing." Saved by childbearing? This sounds very un-Pauline, for according to the apostle, salvation is by grace through faith, not works (e.g., Rom. 3:21–28; Eph. 2:8–9). Some have sought to alleviate this difficulty by arguing that future salvation *on the last day* is in view here, but it is hard to see how merely transferring the point in time of salvation from the present to the future takes care of the problem.[32]

A better solution involves a close look at the meaning of the Greek word underlying "saved," σῴζω/sōzō. While the expression connotes religious salvation in most instances in Paul's writings, in its non-biblical usage the word refers more broadly to rescue or deliverance from any kind of danger. In the New Testament epistles, this "danger" from which people are said to be delivered is normally sin and eternal death. However, the sense "rescue from danger" is still found in the New Testament in the several uses of the word διασῴζω/diasōzō in the book of Acts in conjunction with Paul's shipwreck (Acts 27:43-44; 28:1, 4; cf. 23:24, which speaks of Paul being "taken safely" to Governor Felix). The Gospels use σῴζω/sōzō differently as well. There, the word refers to a person getting well or whole as a result of being healed by Jesus (e.g., Mark 5:23, 28, 34; 6:56; note that these people do not always experience religious salvation as well). In light of these semantic data and in light of the difficulty of translating σῴζω (sōzō) with its common Pauline meaning, the question arises if there is an alternative way of rendering the term in 1 Timothy 2:15.

In fact, there is. Later in the same epistle, Paul urges Timothy to pay close attention to how he lives and to the content of his teaching, so that he may "preserve" or "ensure salvation" (NASB) for both himself and his hearers (1 Tim. 4:16). Clearly in this instance Timothy will not literally "save" himself or those who listen to him. Rather, Paul's concern is for the *spiritual preservation* of those under Timothy's care, the danger lurking in

---

32. Thomas R. Schreiner, "An Interpretation of 1 Timothy 2:9–15: A Dialogue with Scholarship," in *Women in the Church*, ed. Andreas J. Köstenberger and Thomas R. Schreiner, 2d ed. (Grand Rapids: Baker, 2005), 115–20. See also Philip B. Payne, *Man and Woman, One in Christ: An Exegetical and Theological Study of Paul's Letters* (Grand Rapids: Zondervan, 2009), 417–41, who argues for women's salvation through "*the* Childbirth," i.e. Mary's giving birth to Jesus the Messiah.

the form of the false teachers who sought to lead believers astray. Likewise, in 1 Timothy 2:15 Paul's probable intended meaning is not that women will literally be *saved* by childbearing (or even by "the" Childbearing of Mary) but that they will be *preserved* by adhering to their God-ordained role of motherhood (a figure of speech called synecdoche).[33] The lesson, therefore, as mentioned, is this: one must never assume that the predominant meaning of a given word (in the present case, "save" for σῴζω/*sōzō*) will certainly prevail in a particular passage. The actual meaning of the word will be indicated by the respective context.

The same principle obtains when it comes to the use of common metaphors, such as sheep or infants. Many things may be said about either of these metaphors, but not all characteristics may be the point of a biblical writer's illustration. Since "sheep" is also a good illustration of another fallacy called "illegitimate totality transfer," we will discuss this example below, but a brief look at the way in which infants are used to illustrate spiritual truths in the New Testament will make the issue clear. In places such as Hebrews 5:12–13, the readers are chastised by the author who says that these believers are like babies who "need milk, not solid food! Anyone who lives on milk, being still an infant, is not acquainted with the teaching about righteousness." Conversely, "solid food is for the mature, who by constant use have trained themselves to distinguish good from evil" (Heb. 5:14). Clearly, babies are used as a negative example here. Believers ought to grow up. But consider 1 Peter 2:1–3. In context (1 Pet. 1:23), Peter wrote that believers have been born again to new life. As those who have been reborn spiritually, Peter proceeds to exhort the recipients of his letter, "Like newborn babies, crave pure spiritual milk, so that by it you may grow in your salvation, now that you have tasted that the Lord is good." Strikingly, here babies are used in a diametrically opposite fashion, as good examples of something the biblical author wants his readers to emulate. This means that we must not assume that a given type of illustration is used in the same way in every instance. Again, context must decide.

---

33. See Andreas J. Köstenberger, "Ascertaining Women's God-Ordained Roles: An Interpretation of 1 Timothy 2:15," *Bulletin of Biblical Research* 7 (1997): 107–44; idem, "Saved through Childbearing? A Fresh Look at 1 Timothy 2:15 Points to Protection from Satan's Deception," *CBMW News* 2/4 (1997): 1–6; and the interchange with Ben Witherington posted at www.biblicalfoundations.org.

On a verbal level, the same principle applies. In English, "gift" means a present given to or a special ability possessed by a person. In German, "Gift" means poison. Context must decide—in this case, which language is in play? Depending on the language in which you are operating, you are advised to accept a gift in English but *not* in German! In our study of the Bible, too, we must beware of assuming too quickly that an *apparent* parallel is a *genuine* parallel. Again, merely quoting a similar-sounding passage and assuming without further substantiation that it will be self-evident to others that the alleged "parallel" explains the use of a given word in a certain passage is inadequate. Beware of "parallelomania" and recognize the all-important role of context in interpretation.

Fallacy #6: Improper Linkage of Language and Mentality

Conventional wisdom has it that Hebrew thought was concrete while Greek thought was abstract. This leads to corresponding assertions in the interpretation of specific biblical passages. Truth, for example, is said to be conveyed in the sense of a person's faithfulness in the Old Testament (in keeping with Hebrew thought) while the term is said to convey the notion of correspondence to reality in the New Testament (corresponding to the Greek way of thinking). This would be a nice theory if it were true; the problem is that the evidence does not bear this out, whether on a general or on a specific level.[34]

On a specific level, to continue with our example of the concept of, and words for, "truth" for the moment, both the Old and the New Testament feature both types of usage, "truth" in the sense of faithfulness and in the sense of correspondence to reality. In both Testaments, statements are said to be true (i.e., they correspond to reality), and in both Testaments truth is conveyed in personal terms, by people—or God—keeping his word and proving to be faithful (as suggested by the English word "fidelity" or the expression of one remaining "true" to his word).

On a general level, too, it has been shown convincingly that generalizations with regard to language use and word meanings on the basis of the mentality of peoples cannot be sustained.[35] Are all French people

---

34. See James Barr, *The Semantics of Biblical Language* (London: SCM, 1961), chapter 7.
35. See especially the trenchant critique of works such as Thorleif Boman's *Hebrew Thought Compared with Greek* in Barr, *Semantics of Biblical Language*, esp. 46–79.

gourmets? Are all Germans perfectionists? The list could go on and on. Yet the claim persists, as a representative work has it, that "the Hebrew thought in pictures, and consequently his nouns are concrete and vivid. There is no such thing as neuter gender, for the Semite everything is alive."[36] Yet we must not confuse grammatical and biological gender or hold that there is a necessary correspondence between the two. Do Germans believe girls are neuter because of the gender of "das Mädchen"? Did Greeks think sin was a uniquely or distinctively female trait because "sin," ἡ ἁμαρτία (hē hamartia), is feminine in grammatical gender? If so, they must have thought "truth" was a feminine trait as well, since the Greek word for truth, ἡ αληθεία (hē alētheia), is likewise feminine in gender. Examples such as these illustrate that linking language to mentality is fraught with problems and is best avoided altogether.

Fallacy #7: False Assumptions about Technical Meaning

We have already made reference to Matthew 16:18, which is commonly translated as, "On this rock I will build my *church.*" In light of the fact that the Greek word underlying "church," ἐκκλεσία (ekklēsia), only occurs one other time in all the Gospels combined (Matt. 18:17), we suggested that the translation "church" may be misleading since it suggests, erroneously, that this term had already become a technical term in Jesus' day when in fact it did so only in the days of the apostle Paul who developed the notion of the church as the body of Christ. For this reason we proposed that "community" may better convey the sense of Jesus' statement in Matthew 16:18.[37]

Another possible instance where a technical meaning may be wrongly surmised is the New Testament doctrine of sanctification.[38] The student of systematic theology would tend to assume that "sanctification" refers to the process of Christian growth following a person's conversion. It is often

---

For a good summary of the debate, see Silva, *Biblical Words and their Meaning,* 17–32.

36. Norman L. Geisler and William E. Nix, *A General Introduction to the Bible* (Chicago: Moody, 1968), 219.

37. Perhaps the reason why translation committees are slow to embrace this is that the conventional rendering is so deeply entrenched in our collective psyche that an alternative rendering, even if more accurate, would take some getting used to. But this is no good reason not to translate more accurately.

38. See especially the excellent study by David Peterson, *Possessed by God*, NSBT 1 (Leicester: Apollos, 1995).

assumed that justification (a person being declared righteous on the basis of Christ's substitutionary cross-death) occurs at the time of conversion, while sanctification is a process that takes place subsequent to this event. However, as a study of the instances of "sanctification" terminology (especially the ἁγιάζω (hagiazō), "set apart," word group) makes clear, according to the New Testament people are not only justified but also "set apart" ("sanctified") at the point of conversion (e.g., 1 Cor. 1:2; 6:11). For this reason the neat distinction between justification and sanctification in our systematics textbooks collapses. Both justification *and* sanctification take place at conversion, and the New Testament terminology for what we call "sanctification" is that of Christian growth (e.g., 2 Pet. 3:18)

Fallacy #8: Improper Distinctions Made Regarding Synonyms

One very common fallacious assumption in biblical interpretation is the notion that every difference in wording is theologically motivated. This assumption is fallacious because it fails to consider alternative possibilities such as that two or more different words which are roughly synonymous may be used owing to stylistic variation or other factors. This fallacy, in turn, is linked to another improper hermeneutical practice, that is, the unwarranted linking of sense and reference (see further below). The classic example is the use of two different verbs for "love" in John 21:15–17, αγαπάω (agapaō) and φιλέω (phileō).[39] The state of affairs can be laid out as follows:[40]

13.2. TWO DIFFERENT VERBS FOR "LOVE" IN JOHN 21:15–17	
v. 15	Jesus to Peter: "Simon son of John, do you love (ἀγαπάω, *agapaō*) me more than these?"
v. 15	Peter to Jesus: "Yes, Lord, you know that I love (φιλέω, *phileō*) you."
v. 16	Jesus to Peter: "Simon son of John, do you love (ἀγαπάω, *agapaō*) me?"
v. 16	Peter to Jesus: "Yes, Lord, you know that I love (φιλέω, *phileō*) you."
v. 17	Jesus to Peter: "Simon son of Johyou love (φιλέω, *phileō*) me?"
v. 17	Peter to Jesus: "Lord, you know everything. You know that I love (φιλέω, *phileō*) you."

---

39. See the discussion in Carson, *Exegetical Fallacies*, 51–53.
40. Our own translation. The original NIV inserts the word "truly" (which has no equivalent in the Greek) in verses 15 and 16 (rendering αγαπάω with "truly love") in order to bring out the meaning of the passage.

The standard explanation of the use of verbs for "love" in this passage is that the first two times Jesus uses ἀγαπάω (*agapaō*) to denote a divine form of love, while Peter only pledges a human form of love. The third time around, we are told, Jesus lowered himself to Peter's standard and used the "human" word for love, φιλέω (*phileō*), rather than the "divine" one, αγαπάω (*agapaō*) seems to be a very satisfying explanation of the data that only has one problem: it does not comport with the linguistic evidence from John's Gospel. D. A. Carson and others have shown, both ἀγαπάω (*agapaō*) and φιλέω (*phileō*) are used in John with reference to both divine and human love and function interchangeably in the Gospel![41] This means that the underlying semantic distinction between the two words for "love" in John 21:15–17 is illegitimate. Another explanation must be found. Most likely the two words are synonyms that are used alternatively for the sake of stylistic variation. This is strongly suggested by the presence of two other sets of synonyms for common words in the same passage: γινώσκω (*ginōskō*) and οἶδα (*oida*) for "to know," and expressions such as "feed my lambs" or "tend my sheep."

Or take the use of the Greek word for "receive," δέχομαι (*dechomai*), in 1 Thessalonians 1:6. In a recent sermon, the preacher made the point that the use of this particular word for "receiving" in the present passage, rather than the other Greek word for "receiving," λαμβάνω [*lambanō*], is significant, because it means that the Thessalonians did not merely "take" the word (as would be indicated by λαμβάνω (*lambanō*), they truly "received" it. However, once again, there is little support for making such a distinction between these two Greek words. More likely, they are virtual synonyms that are used with no discernible distinction in meaning. For this reason students and teachers of the Word should take care lest they find distinctions in their interpretation of biblical words even where the original authors did not intend to make such a distinction.

Fallacy #9: Selective or Prejudicial Use of Evidence

Virtually every one of us at one time or other has been guilty of selective or prejudicial use of evidence.[42] By this we mean the practice of citing

---

41. Cf., e.g., John 3:35 and 5:20 (the Father loves the Son) or John 11:5 and 36 (Jesus loves Lazarus). D. A. Carson, *The Gospel according to John* (Grand Rapids: Eerdmans, 1991), 676–77.

42. For a helpful discussion and some examples, see Carson, *Exegetical Fallacies*, 93–94.

only the evidence that can be adduced in favor of a person's viewpoint while countervailing evidence is omitted or suppressed. Not only is this practice fallacious from a standpoint of thoroughness of research and presentation, it is also ethically suspect if not dishonest. Awhile back one researcher asked the other, "How is your research going?" To which the other person replied: "Great! I'm finding a lot of people who agree with my conclusions."

If this is your definition of research, it has to change, for whatever the above-stated procedure is, it is certainly *not* research. Research means the unearthing of *all* of the evidence, whether it agrees with one's own findings or not. Everything else is merely a matter of prooftexting or deduction, and while some may dress up their findings as research, unless they present the evidence in an even-handed, thoroughgoing manner, their arguments will likely fail to convince, because it will quickly become transparent that theirs is an exercise in dogmatism likely to convince only those already converted.

As mentioned, biblical interpretation, properly understood, requires a commitment to listening and perception of what is there. Proper procedure demands that the various alternatives be set forth and pros and cons be weighed before the interpreter settles on the interpretation that accounts best for all the data under consideration. This will flow from an honest search for truth that is willing to hold one's own predetermined notions in abeyance and to be seriously engaged by the data of the biblical text. In the end, this will also most likely convince others of a given view.

Fallacy #10: Unwarranted Semantic Disjunctions or Restrictions (Including Illegitimate Totality Transfer)

As in many other areas of life, so also in the realm of biblical interpretation, simplistic "either-or" alternatives are often suspect. An example of this "disjunctive fallacy" is the insistence by some that the Greek word κεφαλή (*kephalē*), translated "head," in Ephesians 5:23 means "source" rather than conveying the notion of authority, when contextual study shows that *both* senses are present: the husband is to be a source of nourishment and encouragement to his wife, *and* he is put in charge of his wife as Christ is over the church as the head is over the body (Eph. 5:23–30).[43]

---

43. See Thomas R. Schreiner, "Women in Ministry," in *Two Views on Women in Ministry*, ed. James R. Beck and Craig L. Blomberg (Grand Rapids: Zondervan, 2001),

Also in this category falls the unwarranted restriction of a semantic field, that is, the insistence that a word can only mean one thing when there is in fact a semantic range (i.e., a multiplicity of potential meanings). This problem may arise with a too narrowly conceived notion of formal equivalence, leading to the insistence that every instance of a given Greek or Hebrew word be translated with the same English word. However, this insufficiently accounts for the possibility—and often reality—that a word's semantic range in Greek or Hebrew on the one hand and in English on the other may differ. If so, it is not only legitimate but even imperative to render the same Greek or Hebrew word with a variety of English words. While this may make it harder to see from the English translation where the same word was used in the original, the practice of finding context-appropriate renderings will prove to be more accurate and faithful to the meaning intended by the original authors.

The opposite of the unwarranted restriction of the semantic field is the unwarranted adoption of an expanded semantic field, a fallacy that has also been called "illegitimate totality transfer." In this fallacy a word's entire semantic range is improperly considered to be part of the term's meaning in a specific context when, in fact, only one of the several possible meanings obtain in that particular instance. This is the fallacy at least suggested, if not committed, by the "Amplified Version."

A case in point is the biblical use of the shepherd metaphor.[44] Many a preacher, when expounding on the meaning of a particular passage involving a reference to sheep, has imported all the characteristics of sheep, even though not all of these may be in play in that particular case. To be sure, Isaiah 53:6 says, "We all, like sheep, have gone astray," but is this the point of Jesus' statement, "My sheep listen to my voice; I know them, and they follow me" (John 10:27)? This is hardly so. In the former case, it is sheep's waywardness that is the point of the biblical illustration; in the latter instance, it is sheep's need for a shepherd and their following of his voice. Both are characteristics of sheep, but one is invoked in the

---

212–13; Andreas J. Köstenberger, "Head," in *The New Interpreter's Dictionary of the Bible*, vol. 2, ed. Pheme Perkins et al. (Nashville: Abingdon, 2007), 754–55.

44. For useful treatments, see Derek Tidball, *Skilful Shepherds: Explorations in pastoral theology* (2d ed.; Leicester, UK: Inter-Varsity, 1997); and Timothy S. Laniak, *Shepherds After My Own Heart: Pastoral Traditions and Leadership in the Bible* (NSBT; Downers Grove: InterVarsity, 2006).

former passage and the other in the latter. The fallacy of illegitimate totality transfer unduly lumps all the characteristics of sheep together and wrongly claims that all of these are relevant every time an illustration involving sheep is used.

Or take Jesus' reference to salt in his statement, "You are the salt of the earth" (Matt. 5:13). We have all heard sermons where the various characteristics of salt are mentioned at this point: salt is a preservative, salt provides seasoning, and so on. Did Jesus intend to invoke all of these attributes in the present passage? Maybe so, but this must be established on contextual grounds rather than be assumed merely on the basis that salt is mentioned.

Fallacy #11: Unwarranted Neglect of Distinctive Characteristics or Personal Style

As mentioned, language is convention, and as such inevitably involves a subjective element. This includes matters such as personal style, preference, and distinctive vocabulary, and even theology. Hence we must beware of the notion that "righteousness" must mean exactly the same in Matthew or Paul, or that the relationship between faith and works is construed in exactly the same way in Paul and James (compare and contrast the use of Gen. 15:6 in Gal. 3:6 and Jas. 2:23).

In terms of the interpretation of specific biblical passages, one example where this comes into play is John 1:17, where the evangelist writes that "the law was given through Moses; grace and truth came through Jesus Christ." In light of the fact that in Paul's writings a distinction is regularly made between observance of the law (which is unable to lead to salvation) and faith in Christ, some have construed John's message here in similar terms. In fact, some even inserted the adversative conjunction "but" between the two phrases (e.g., NLT: "For the law was given through Moses, *but* God's unfailing love and faithfulness came through Jesus Christ"), even though the word is absent from the Greek. However, as a contextual study of John 1:17 shows, both with regard to the immediate context and the context of the theology of the entire Gospel, the Pauline law-gospel distinction is not present in John. Instead, John 1:17 presents Jesus as the climactic fulfillment of earlier manifestations of God's grace, *including* the law. For this reason, John 1:17, rather than constituting a negative reference to the law (conveying its inability to provide salvation, cf. Rom. 3:21; Gal. 2:17–21; 3:23–25), presents the law in positive terms: it, too, was God's gracious provision, albeit one that was preliminary to his ultimate provision of grace and truth in Jesus Christ.[45]

Or take instances of the Greek word σάρξ (*sarx*), "flesh," for example. In Paul, the term frequently serves as a synonym for "sinful nature," that is, it carries a negative connotation. In other passages, however, "flesh" is used neutrally to refer to humanity, without intended reference to human sinfulness (e.g., 1 Pet. 1:24–25 citing Isa. 40:6–8). In light of the personal style characteristics and distinctive vocabulary and usage of individual biblical writers, the interpreter must take care to allow for the context of Scripture to guide his or her study and to avoid a "one-size-fits-all" approach when it comes to word meanings or biblical concepts.

Fallacy #12: Unwarranted Linking of Sense and Reference

While the fallacy of an illegitimate linking of sense and reference is more subtle than some of the others and requires a bit of explanation, it is a fallacy nonetheless. For this reason it is worthwhile to understand the dynamics underlying this misuse. If *sense* is the actual meaning of a word in a specific context and *reference* is the object to which the word is referring, it is important to realize that part of a word's meaning in a given passage is supplied not by the word itself but by other words in its immediate context. The important implication of this realization is that it is improper to construe a word's lexical meaning on the basis of its contextual meaning as if the two were identical. They are not.

Take Paul's repeated reference to Timothy as his "coworker" (συνεργός [*synergos*]; Rom. 16:21; 1 Thess. 3:2; also Titus: 2 Cor. 8:3; Epaphroditus: Phil. 2:25) as an example. Apart from being Paul's coworker, Timothy also was an apostolic delegate and what some might call a "senior pastor." Does the fact that Timothy, as Paul's "coworker," was also a senior pastor imply that the meaning for "coworker" includes "senior pastor"? This does not necessarily follow. Timothy was both, and so is a shared referent of both terms, but this still allows for the possibility that there may be others who were Paul's coworkers but not senior pastors. Ignoring this important fact would be to confuse sense (i.e., the contextual meaning) and referent (the object to which a given term is referring).

---

45. See Köstenberger, *John*, 47–48.

For this reason it is fallacious to argue, as some have done, from the fact that Euodia and Syntyche in Philippians 4:2 are referred to as Paul's "coworkers" that this implies that they also served as pastors since this was true of Timothy. As we have seen, this follows neither logically nor is this conclusion linguistically sound or otherwise defensible. Whether or not these two women were pastors must be established on other grounds—such as Paul's teaching on women serving as pastors—not on the basis of the meaning of the word "coworker" alone.[46]

As James Barr has shown in *The Semantics of Biblical Language*, the failure to distinguish between sense and referent is endemic to the work of many theologians, including even respected reference works such as the massive ten-volume *Theological Dictionary of the New Testament*.[47] As Barr has demonstrated, much of what is listed under the rubric of specific Greek *words* flows in fact from the study of biblical *concepts* conveyed through various contexts. The reason why this is fallacious is because by listing a given entry under a particular word the editors misleadingly suggest that aspects of the contextual meaning of a given word reside in the lexical meaning of the word itself rather than being contributed by the context.

A case in point is the article on verbs of "sending" by K. H. Rengstorf.[48] On the basis of various contextual factors, Rengstorf argues that the two Greek verbs ἀποστέλλω (*apostellō*) and πέμπω (*pempō*) are distinct in meaning. In fact, Rengstorf construes an entire semantic profile on the basis of his study of the various contexts in which these two verbs are used. As it turns out, however, Rengstorf, like many other contributors to the dictionary, illegitimately intermingles sense and reference and thus arrives at fallacious conclusions with regard to the meaning of Greek

---

46. See Andreas J. Köstenberger, "Women in the Pauline Mission," in *The Gospel to the Nations*, ed. Peter Bolt and Mark Thompson (Leicester: Apollos, 2000), 225–26, 232–33. Note also that, in a close parallel to Philippians 4:3 ("*contended* at my side for the sake of the gospel"), the verb συναθλέω in Philippians 1:27 is applied to all believers, so that it is at least equally plausible to align Euodia and Syntyche with the rest of the congregation as it is to put them on par with Timothy. After all, it is hardly possible that all believers in that church served as pastors!

47. Barr, *Semantics of Biblical Language*, chapter 8.

48. Karl-Heinz Rengstorf, "ἀποστέλλω, etc.," *TDNT* 1.398–446. See the thorough evaluation of Rengstorf's thesis in Andreas J. Köstenberger, *The Missions of Jesus and the Disciples according to the Fourth Gospel* (Grand Rapids: Eerdmans, 1998), 99–102.

"sending" verbs. More likely, the words are virtual synonyms and are used interchangeably for the sake of stylistic variation and several other factors.[49]

CONCLUSION

In the chapter on historical-cultural background, we sought to reconstruct a responsible historical framework for our study of Scripture and dealt with interpretive challenges arising from the cultural embeddedness of biblical revelation (the first element of the hermeneutical triad).

In the present chapter, we built on this chapter by considering an important dimension of the second aspect of the hermeneutical triad, literature. Drawing on the findings of recent linguistic research, we attempted to establish sound procedures in determining word meanings, involving the more sophisticated use of a "semantic field study" approach.

To round out our discussion, we concluded the chapter with a discussion of several commonly committed exegetical fallacies, warning signs, as it were, that must be heeded by the skilled interpreter, lest he or she fall prey to a variety of questionable methods in the lexical study of words in Scripture.

---

49. See Andreas J. Köstenberger, "The Two Johannine Verbs for Sending: A Study of John's Use of Words with Reference to General Linguistic Theory," in *Linguistics and the New Testament: Critical Junctures*, ed. Stanley E. Porter and D. A. Carson. JSNTSup 168. Studies in New Testament Greek 5 (Sheffield: Sheffield Academic Press, 1999), 125–43, esp. 131–34. As I point out, in order to sustain his thesis Rengstorf finds himself compelled to argue that a writer such as Luke, who uses the two "sending" verbs interchangeably, was insufficiently aware of such a distinction! However, rather than charging a writer as sophisticated as Luke with linguistic incompetence, it seems more appropriate to urge Rengstorf to reconsider the validity of his theory.

GUIDELINES FOR DETERMINING WORD MEANINGS IN SCRIPTURE

1. Select the word or words to be studied. This should be a word that is significant for the interpretation of a given biblical passage.

2. Make sure you study a given Greek or Hebrew term or set of terms, not the English one. This is important since, depending on the particular translation, a given Greek or Hebrew word will be rendered by several different English words and vice versa. What we want to study is what a given word means in the original rather than in English. This is possible even for those who have not studied Greek or Hebrew through the use of New Testament tools such as Louw and Nida's *Greek-English Lexicon* and *The Book Study Concordance*.

Old Testament word studies have traditionally relied on a general knowledge of English synonyms and antonyms to find related English words and then worked back to the Hebrew (or Aramaic). Electronic resources improve on this process by giving the student access to the Hebrew lexicons without the formal study of the original languages. The standard Brown, Driver, and Briggs lexicon provides words that are "||" (in parallelism with) and "opp." ("opposite") the target word, yielding possible synonyms and antonyms.[50] In the digitized Old Testament texts of Bible study software programs, the student can usually access these Old Testament words in BDB with a click of the mouse. Another type of electronic resource is the reverse interlinear. For example, the Logos ESVRI[51] has a Bible Word Study feature that will give a cluster of Hebrew words also translated "murder," the ESV's translation for רָצָח (rĕṣāḥ) in Deuteronomy 5:17.

---

50. The original work by Francis Brown, S. R. Driver, and Charles A. Briggs (Oxford: Clarendon, 1901) now appears in several updated editions.
51. Chip McDaniel and C. John Collins, *The ESV English-Hebrew Reverse Interlinear Old Testament* (Logos Research Systems, 2006, 2009).

Clicking on these other Hebrew words brings up representative biblical passages and locates the discussion in the Hebrew lexicon.

3. If studying, for example, the different words for "love" in the Gospel of John, both nouns and verbs, and perhaps also adjectives and adverbs, identify the specific words by looking up the word "love" in the index volume (vol. 2) of Louw-Nida. Then locate the specific semantic domain (#25) in vol. 1 of Louw-Nida and determine which Greek words fall under this rubric.

4. Armed with this information, go to *The Book Study Concordance* and look up each of these Greek words under the respective heading. This will supply you with all the relevant data for your study (or at least the vast majority of relevant data).

5. Conduct a contextual study of all the relevant passages. In practical terms, one should start with passages for the target word. Lexicons and concordances can provide a quick overview of the semantic ranges for related words or can provide material for a more exhaustive (and sometimes exhausting) study.

6. Categorize the passages according to types of usage (i.e., word meanings). This will yield the semantic range of the word or words. In terms of Deuteronomy 5:17, an examination of all the uses of the verb רָצַח (rĕṣāḥ) reveals that it is never used for the war or the killing of animals—other Hebrew words denote these—suggesting that the command should not be used to support pacifism or a vegetarian diet. It is usually found in a context of interpersonal killing (whether intentional or accidental) in the context of a community.

7. In light of this semantic range, return to your base passage and see how it fits within the overall semantic profile of your word and what it contributes to the overall theology or concept or theme in question. This is the process that led more recent

translations to render Deuteronomy 5:17 as "murder." Given the two nuances in the majority of uses for רָצַח (rĕṣāḥ) , it seems for some interpreters that God would not command a person not to have an accident.

KEY WORDS

Connotation: the meaning added to the lexical meaning or denotation by the context

Denotation: the "dictionary" definition of a word apart from a particular context

Diachronic: the study of language "over time"

Etymology: the root (i.e. original) meaning of a word

Illegitimate totality transfer: the improper assumption that a word in a given context means everything the word can mean in a variety of different contexts

Lexis or lexical meaning: a word's meaning as listed in a dictionary

Linguistics: the study of the nature of language

Parallelomania: the adducing of parallels of questionable value

Reference: the linguistic procedure by which a word points to an extra-textual object

Referent: the object to which a word points

Semantic anachronism: the imposition of the later meaning of a word onto earlier uses

Semantic field: a group of words that are related in meaning

Semantic field study: the study of the meaning of a word and related words

Semantic obsolescence: rendering a word with a meaning it once possessed but that has since fallen into disuse

Semantic range: the variety of meanings of which a word is capable in different contexts

Semantics: the science of determining meaning

Sense: the meaning of a word in context including the word's connotation

Synchronic: the study of language "together with" (i.e. at the same) time

STUDY QUESTIONS

1. What is the definition of important key words listed at the beginning of the chapter?

2. Why is semantics important in biblical interpretation?

3. What is the relationship between word meaning and context?

4. What are three major exegetical fallacies? Provide a definition and give at least one example.

5. What is a sound step-by-step method of studying individual words of Scripture?

6. What are at least two important resources for word studies?

ASSIGNMENTS

1. Engage in a close study of the "warning passage" in Hebrews 6:1–8. Identify at least three words requiring careful study. Then, using *The Book Study Concordance* or another Greek concordance, list all New Testament occurrences of each of these words and proceed to delineate a range of meaning. Use the findings of these individual word studies to shed light on the interpretation of this difficult passage.

2. After having read the section on exegetical fallacies, reflect on sermons you have heard, or preached yourself, or other biblical teaching you have received or imparted, which fell prone to a given exegetical fallacy. List each of these and demonstrate their fallacious nature in light of the discussion in the course text.

CHAPTER BIBLIOGRAPHY

Barr, James. *The Semantics of Biblical Language.* London: SCM, 1961.

Black, David Alan. *Linguistics for Students of New Testament Greek: A Survey of Basic Concepts and Applications.* 2d ed. Grand Rapids: Baker, 2000.

Black, David Alan and David S. Dockery, eds. *Interpreting the New Testament: Essays on Methods and Issues.* Nashville: B&H, 2001.

Carson, D. A. *Exegetical Fallacies.* 2d ed. Grand Rapids: Baker, 1996.

Cotterell, Peter and Max Turner. *Linguistics and Biblical Interpretation.* Downers Grove: InterVarsity, 1989.

Köstenberger, Andreas J. and Raymond P. Bouchoc. *The Book Study Concordance.* Nashville: B&H, 2003.

Lee, John A. L. *A History of New Testament Lexicography.* Studies in Biblical Greek. New York: Peter Lang, 2003.

Louw, Johannes P. and Eugene A. Nida. *A Greek-English Lexicon of the New Testament Based on Semantic Domains.* 2 vols. New York: United Bible Societies, 1988, 1989.

Louw, J. P. *Semantics of New Testament Greek.* Atlanta: Scholars Press, 1982.

Osborne, Grant R. *The Hermeneutical Spiral: A Comprehensive Introduction to Biblical Interpretation.* 2d ed. Downers Grove: InterVarsity, 2006.

Silva, Moisés. *Biblical Words and their Meaning.* Grand Rapids: Zondervan, 1983.

CHAPTER 14 OBJECTIVES

1. To acquaint the student with the nature and characteristics of figures of speech.

2. To enable the student to recognize the various figures of speech in the Bible.

3. To acquaint the student with some of the primary figures of speech in the Bible.

4. To provide the student with principles by which he can interpret the various figures of speech appropriately.

5. To suggest ways in which figures of speech contribute to meaning in the biblical texts.

CHAPTER 14 OUTLINE

A. Nature and Characteristics of Figures of Speech
    1. Introduction
    2. How Figures of Speech Work
    3. Figures of Speech and Meaning
    4. Figures of Speech and Contexts
    5. Figures of Speech and the Inexpressible
B. Issues in Interpreting Figures of Speech in the Bible
    1. Figures of Speech and Literal Meaning
    2. Vehicle and Tenor in Meaning
    3. Connotations and Denotations
    4. Active Participation by the Reader
    5. Context
    6. Figures of Speech and Contexts
    7. Figures of Speech and Propositional Explanations
C. Types of Figures of Speech in the Bible
    1. Anthropomorphism
    2. Euphemism
    3. Hypocatastasis
    4. Image
    5. Metaphor
    6. Metonymy
D. Sample Exegesis: Psalm 18
    1. History
    2. Language
    3. Theology
E. Guidelines for Interpreting Figures of Speech in the Bible
F. Key Words
G. Study Questions
H. Assignments
I. Chapter Bibliography

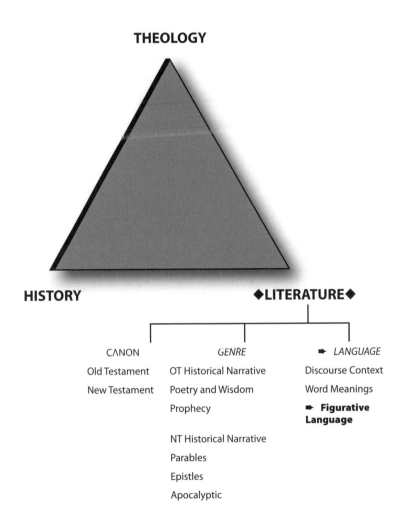

THEOLOGY

HISTORY

◆LITERATURE◆

CANON

Old Testament

New Testament

GENRE

OT Historical Narrative

Poetry and Wisdom

Prophecy

NT Historical Narrative

Parables

Epistles

Apocalyptic

➡ LANGUAGE

Discourse Context

Word Meanings

➡ **Figurative Language**

Chapter 14

A WAY OF SPEAKING: INTERPRETING
FIGURATIVE LANGUAGE

NATURE AND CHARACTERISTICS
OF FIGURES OF SPEECH

Introduction

NOW THAT WE HAVE EXPLORED the importance of context on the discourse level and discussed the various issues associated with determining word meanings, we turn to one final topic related to biblical language. In the present chapter, we will seek to enhance our appreciation for figurative language in the Bible and to develop greater skill in recognizing various figures of speech and in interpreting them appropriately. This will deepen our understanding of various genres of Scripture that were already discussed above, most prominently poetry and wisdom, as well as prophecy and apocalyptic, and portions in historical narrative.

The Bible, in both the Old and the New Testament, is replete with figures of speech. Most readers subconsciously recognize many such figures in their reading of Scripture, because they are often intuitively self-evident. Difficulties may arise when a figure of speech is more subtle, such as in the case of portions of the book of Revelation, or when different theological traditions disagree as to whether a particular expression is figurative, as in the matter of the "bread" and the "wine" in the Lord's Supper, Communion, or Eucharist.

To appreciate the complexity of biblical figures of speech, one needs to go no further than to E. W. Bullinger's groundbreaking 1898 volume, *Figures of Speech Used in the Bible: Explained and Illustrated*. Bullinger states that there are some 200 different types of figures of speech in the Bible, and he points out that no other "branch of Bible study can be more important, or offer greater promise of substantial reward" than a study of its figures of speech.[1] If we want to read the Bible well, we must learn to interpret its figurative language. In our quest to acquire the necessary expertise, we will first look at how figures of speech work. Next, we will turn to a study of various issues involved in interpreting figurative language in Scripture. Finally, we will get acquainted with specific types of figurative speech in the Bible and conclude with a sample exegesis of Psalm 18.

How Figures of Speech Work

How do figures of speech work? In its simplest form, a figure of speech is a device of comparison. More precisely, a figure of speech is a use of language in which there is a comparison, either stated or implied, between two terms. Ian Paul states that all figures of speech "share the same basic feature whereby two terms are brought together that have different, apparently distinct ranges of meaning to express something new."[2] The challenge figures of speech present relates to the way in which such comparisons function and how they are to be interpreted.

Figures of speech have two "terms," or subjects, which are compared, or brought into a relationship of similarity (or contiguity). In *The Philosophy of Rhetoric*, I. A. Richards calls the two terms "vehicle" and "tenor."[3] The tenor in a figure of speech is its underlying subject; the vehicle is the mode in which the tenor is expressed. In the familiar metaphor from Psalm 23, "The LORD is my shepherd," the tenor is "the Lord," and the vehicle is "my shepherd." The primary subject of the metaphor is in fact "the

---

1. E. W. Bullinger, *Figures of Speech Used in the Bible: Explained and Illustrated* (London: Eyre & Spottiswoode, 1898; repr. Grand Rapids: Baker, 1968), xix–xlvi and vi.

2. Ian Paul, "Metaphor," in *Dictionary for Theological Interpretation of the Bible*, ed. Kevin J. Vanhoozer, Craig G. Bartholomew, Daniel J. Treier, and N. T. Wright (Grand Rapids: Baker, 2005), 507.

3. I. A. Richards, *The Philosophy of Rhetoric* (New York: Oxford University Press, 1936), 96–97.

Lord," not "my shepherd"; the way (mode) in which the Lord is spoken of in the metaphor is as the psalmist's shepherd.

Put another way, we see the subject ("the Lord," in this instance) in the vocabulary of the mode ("my shepherd"). The remainder of the twenty-third Psalm fills in the details of what it means that the Lord relates to his people as a shepherd does to his sheep. A figure of speech, then, is a new way of seeing, or understanding, that applies the ideas and associations of one term (the vehicle) to the other (the tenor). The new understanding comes from the "complete unit of tenor and vehicle";[4] that is, it takes the combination, or interpenetration, of the two terms of the figure of speech to make sense.[5]

Figures of speech may be subdivided into figures of similarity and figures of contiguity.[6] *Figures of similarity* are those in which there is no logical connection between the two terms of the comparison (vehicle and tenor). To return to the phrase, "The LORD is my shepherd," there is no logical connection inherent in the comparison between the Lord and a shepherd, though our familiarity with the metaphor may desensitize us to this fact. At first glance, then, it may appear that figures of similarity defy logical thinking. What is important for us to understand here is that figures of speech do indeed express a cognitive idea, even when there is no internal logic to the comparison of the terms (more on this later). Figures of similarity include simile, metaphor, image, and symbol.

Figures of contiguity, on the other hand, are based on some kind of logical association. The psalmists' frequent uses of "throne," for instance, to represent God's authority and majesty are figures of contiguity. There is a logical link between a throne on the one hand and authority and majesty on the other. In the psalmists' use of the throne of God to represent his authority, there is a substitution of one word ("throne") for another

---

4. Janet Martin Soskice, *Metaphor and Religious Language* (Oxford: Clarendon, 1987), 48.
5. Another example of a biblical figure of speech is the image of the New Testament church as the "body" of Christ. In this comparison, Christ is the tenor, and the body is the vehicle. In this image, we understand at the least that the church is (a) under the "headship" or authority of Christ; (b) dependent on Christ for its life; and (c) composed of many and different parts that function together for the good of the whole. Figures of speech communicate a great deal of theology in a short expression.
6. Rene Wellek and Austin Warren, *Theory of Literature*, 3d ed. (New York: Harcourt, Brace & World, 1956), 194.

("authority"). Specifically, the substitution of one word for another with which it is logically connected is called *metonymy*—one of the figures of contiguity. The other common figure of contiguity is *synecdoche*, the substitution of a part for the whole. An example of a synecdoche is the representation of sinners' ways as "their feet rush into sin" (Prov. 1:16). It is obvious that the whole person has chosen evil, not just his feet. The comparisons in figures of contiguity, then, turn on a logical connection that exists between vehicle and tenor of the figure of speech, while figures of similarity have no such logical connection between the two terms. Whether they are figures of similarity or contiguity, however, these figures of speech ultimately associate two objects or ideas in ways they could not otherwise have been found to have anything in common.

Figures of Speech and Meaning

Do figures of speech in the Bible articulate theology—or even propositional ideas, for that matter? Or did they merely assist illiterate pre-Enlightenment people who could not understand propositional ideas and who did not have a written text in any event? How can we know that figures of speech are not merely language decorations in the text or rhetorical flourishes to effect the reader's emotions? In his classic textbook, *Basic Bible Interpretation*, Roy Zuck states, "Figurative language . . . is not antithetical to literal interpretation; it is a part of it."[7] That is, figurative language does not conflict with propositional language in the sense that it is false and propositional language true. Rather, figurative language conveys "literal truth" in the sense that the ideas in a biblical figure of speech are literally true. The idea here is that figures of speech refer in some way to cognitive thought. Zuck calls such a figurative use of language "figurative-literal" as opposed to propositional language, which he calls "ordinary literal" language.[8] For Zuck, there is no inherent antithesis between figures of speech and truth, and it would be naïve for us to say that they do not convey truth in some way. But this claim does not take us very far in understanding meaning in figures of speech.

To appreciate how figures of speech create meaning, we have to consider how we actually think. Specifically, we need to take into account the

---

7. Roy B. Zuck, *Basic Bible Interpretation* (Colorado Springs: Chariot Victor, 1991), 147.
8. Ibid.

way analogies work in our thinking. If it is true that no learning occurs unless a new idea to be grasped is related significantly to something we already know, then all learning is in some sense a process of analogy. We understand a new idea when we see that it is (1) connected to an idea we already know; and (2) different from the old idea. Thinking is essentially analogical. The process of analogy is basically the way metaphor works. In metaphors—and by extension all figures of speech—two ideas are related in such a way that a new thought emerges. E. D. Hirsch is helpful here: "No one would ever invent or understand a new type of meaning unless he were capable of perceiving analogies." All thinking is, "in other words, the process of metaphor."[9] If Hirsch is correct, the principle of metaphor is at the heart of cognition. This view is a long way from the purely rhetorical and affective views of metaphor in previous centuries. Far from dismissing figures of speech as mere language decorations or emotional stimuli, we must understand that figures of speech do indeed express cognitive content. Other writers put it differently, but they all agree that metaphor and thought are closely connected. In *Words of Delight: A Literary Introduction to the Bible*, Leland Ryken remarks, "Metaphor and simile are not 'poetic devices'; they are a new way of thinking and formulating reality."[10] Literary critic Northrop Frye states flatly, "We clearly have to consider the possibility that metaphor is, not an incidental ornament of Biblical language, but one of its controlling modes of thought."[11] In all these cases, the common ground is that figures of speech can indeed communicate thought and often do so in the Bible.

To understand that figures of speech in the Bible can convey cognitive concepts or theology alleviates the question of their function. They are not to be understood as imaginative pictures; rather, they are to be conceived as part of the theology of a given pericope. That figures of speech communicate meaning, however, does not answer the question of how they do so. In beginning to formulate an answer, we turn to the role of context in helping the exegete interpret figures of speech. How, for example, is the reader to interpret the thunder, lightning, thick cloud, and loud rumbling

---

9. Hirsch, *Validity in Interpretation*, 105.
10. Leland Ryken, *Words of Delight: A Literary Introduction to the Bible*, 2d ed. (Grand Rapids: Baker, 1992), 169.
11. Northrop Frye, *The Great Code: The Bible and Literature* (San Diego: Harcourt, Brace & Co., 1982), 54.

at Mount Sinai when God called Moses up the mountain to receive the Decalogue? To be sure, these phenomena occurred historically. But is there anything figurative about the description? In the scene at Mount Sinai, the Lord expresses his holiness and commands that the people not come near or touch the mountain. God is entirely holy and "other," and the events surrounding the mountain underscore his holiness. The connection of God with "clouds" and "thick darkness," however, does not end at Mount Sinai. The psalmists speak of God in the same way (e.g., Ps. 97:2). In this psalm, the Holy Spirit takes historical events and in later writings molds them into images. While context certainly involves the immediate discourse, it also often relates to a larger context, even the whole canon of Scripture. For this reason, interpreters must be circumspect in the way in which they understand figures of speech in their respective contexts.

Figures of Speech and Contexts

One reason why it is impossible to escape the shaping role of context in interpreting figures of speech is that there are two terms in every figure of speech. Because there is more than one term, there is of necessity a context in which the terms are related (though the actual nature of such relationships is debated). In his comments on metaphor, Aristotle does not appeal explicitly to context, in large measure because there is no need for him to do so. By its nature, metaphor is constituted by a relationship of two nouns (albeit "deviant" from normal meaning, in Aristotle's view).[12] Still, when he goes on to elaborate the types of analogous relationships between nouns that metaphors establish, he tacitly acknowledges the significance of context in appreciating the metaphor and its effects.

Grant Osborne seems to agree that figures of speech work at the level of sentence structure, for he places his discussion of figures of speech in *The Hermeneutical Spiral* in the chapter on syntax.[13] To be sure, Osborne makes it clear that "grammatical and semantic analysis [and] syntactical research will occur at several levels."[14] Osborne understands there to be a "continuous spiral upward" in hermeneutics that includes figures of speech. According to Osborne, the spiral of contexts includes "semotaxis,

---

12. Aristotle, *Poetics*, 2332.
13. Osborne, *Hermeneutical Spiral*, 121–30.
14. Ibid., 139.

the influence of the surrounding ideas,"[15] and may allow for the interpretation of figures of speech in a context larger than syntax.

Writing earlier in the twentieth century in the area of literary theory, I. A. Richards understands the context of figures of speech in a larger sense than either Aristotle or Osborne. In *The Philosophy of Rhetoric*, Richards states that "the rest of the discourse" around the metaphor will provide "hints" as to which interpretation, of many, is appropriate for a given metaphor.[16] By "discourse," Richards means context in a larger sense than the syntax of the sentence in which the metaphor is found. That is, for Richards, the context of a metaphor limits the interpretation and provides a means of interpreting the meaning of the metaphor correctly. In Richards' view, metaphor is an interaction of meanings that produces its own meaning—a meaning governed by context.

Janet Martin Soskice clarifies the nature of context for how we understand figures of speech further when she states that meaning in figures of speech occurs at "the level of complete utterance, taking context into consideration."[17] This is to say that it is the author's intention that regulates the meaning of the figures of speech he uses. To assert that a statement such as "I am the bread of life" is false because there is no logical connection between the speaker and bread is to miss the point of the metaphor. Taken in its context of Jesus' claims regarding himself—that is, in the context of the "complete utterance"—it makes perfect sense. It is context that provides the clues as to what a given figure of speech means, and this is so because it is the context that illuminates the author's intention in using the figure of speech.

Figures of Speech and the Inexpressible

Nowhere is the significance of figures of speech greater than in the Bible's language about God. If God had not chosen to reveal himself to human beings, we would know very little about him. True, we can ascertain something of his divinity and power from nature, as Paul asserts in Romans 1:19–20. What is more, we know something about our moral bankruptcy from our conscience (Rom. 2:15). Beyond these "general"

---

15. Ibid.
16. Richards, *Philosophy of Rhetoric*, 126.
17. Soskice, *Metaphor and Religious Language*, 86.

revelations of God, however, we must rely on his self-revelation for what we know about him. Psalm 19 makes the point beautifully and unequivocally: the creation reveals something about God, but it takes the "law" of God—or, more broadly, the Word of God enscripturated—to reveal God's character. In the descriptions of God as Creator in the psalm, David employs figures of speech quite readily. When he turns to the "law of God" section in the psalm, however, he uses fewer figures and more propositional language. We need both propositional statements and figures of speech if we are to understand God as he reveals himself in Scripture. At least this is what the writers of the books of the Bible and the Holy Spirit who inspired them thought.

One purpose of this chapter has been to demonstrate how significant figures of speech are in biblical meaning. Ian Paul says it well:

> How do we describe an encounter with the Transcendent that has only been made possible by the Transcendent's own self-revelation? The answer, at the level of language, is by metaphorical extension.[18]

The Bible frequently uses figures of speech in its language—its words—about the person and work of God. If we do not give these figures their due attention, we attenuate our understanding and grasp of the attributes and actions of God.

How can finite man refer to a transcendent and infinite God? Biblical figures of speech are one way the Holy Spirit mediates spiritual things to us. Think of the many images for deity in the Old and New Testaments. In the Old Testament, God is presented as a warrior, a shepherd, a king, as thunder and lightning, and as a husband. Other spiritual matters in the Old Testament are mediated through figures of speech, as for instance in Ezekiel's vision of the living creatures that portray something of the glory of the Lord. In the New Testament, Jesus is presented, among other figures, as the good shepherd, the living water, the bread of life, and the lamb of God. The book of Revelation mediates spiritual things in vision after vision, in many instances using figurative language.

In fact, if there were no figures of speech in the Bible to represent God (Father, Son, and Holy Spirit—all three persons of the Trinity), our

---

18. Paul, "Metaphor," 508.

understanding of him would be narrowed and incomplete. To think of these many figures of speech about God as inaccurate or untrue because they are not direct propositional statements would be to reduce God to the level of a human syllogism. God accommodates himself to us in all of the words in the Bible, and he presents himself to us often in figures of speech. Tremper Longman asks why there are so many images of God in the Psalms and answers his own question as follows:

> Briefly, the answer is this: images, particularly metaphors, help to communicate the fact that God is so great and powerful and mighty that he can't be exhaustively described. Metaphor . . . may be accurate, but is less precise than literal language. Metaphor preserves the mystery of God's nature and being, while communicating to us about him and his love for us.[19]

Rather than seeing through the figures of speech about God in the Bible as if they were transparent and insignificant, we would be wise to understand the theology they contain.

One final question about the nature of figures of speech remains before we turn to a hermeneutic of figures of speech, and that is the limits of their expression. Figures of speech teach us hermeneutical humility, because it is often difficult to determine the precise ideas they communicate. In the above quotation, Longman states that metaphors are less precise than literal language. Longman touches on an important point here, for propositional prose is linear and univocal—at least, that is the ideal. The purpose of propositional prose is to minimize ambiguity and maximize clarity; it does so by allowing for only one interpretation. The statement "Salvation is by grace alone through faith alone in Christ alone" leaves little room for misunderstanding, even while not everyone accepts it as true.

Figures of speech, on the other hand, open up the range of meanings, requiring the reader to use context precisely to determine the appropriate meanings of the utterance. It would be inappropriate, for example, for a reader to elaborate on details of "scorpions" and other figures in the book of Revelation when the emphasis is clearly on the person and work of Jesus Christ, not on the mode or means by which the end of the age will be

---

19. Tremper Longman III, *How to Read the Psalms* (Downers Grove: InterVarsity, 1988), 121.

ushered in. Janet Martin Soskice says that figures of speech allow us to "depict" reality, but not to "describe" it precisely.[20] That is, we may not be able to understand a comprehensive description of God from the Bible; he would not be God if we could. Rather, we can express something about his reality in words, and very often we are forced to use figures of speech to say what little we can say. There are limits, then, to determining meaning in figures of speech, limits set by the comparison itself and by the contexts in which it is used. When it comes to figures of speech, readers cannot remain passive; they must engage the figure and be actively engaged by it.

ISSUES IN INTERPRETING FIGURES OF SPEECH IN THE BIBLE

The above discussion makes clear that interpreters of Scripture should not ignore figures of speech on the assumption that figurative language, other than propositional language, lacks theological content. To the contrary, figures of speech are often found in reference to God in the biblical material, because figurative language, as mentioned, lends itself particularly well to discourse dealing with God. Ian Paul outlines the stakes involved in interpreting figures of speech, which, like Longman, he represents by the one archetypal figure, metaphor:

> The interpretation of metaphor is often overlooked. Nevertheless, it is one of the most crucial areas in the whole of hermeneutics since so much biblical theology hangs on metaphors, and metaphor is at the heart of philosophical problems with religious language.[21]

This section presents some principles that will help us read figures of speech appropriately in order to determine how they express the theology of a given writer.

Figures of Speech and Literal Meaning

Simply because a word has figurative meanings in *one* context does not mean that it is figurative in *all* contexts. The same word can be literal in one context and figurative in another. One simple example is the word "day."

---

20. Soskice, *Metaphor and Religious Language*, 141.
21. Paul, "Metaphor," 507.

"Day" has multiple meanings in Scripture, some of them figurative in the sense that they reference long periods of time. In Daniel, the days represent years, as they do in Revelation. Again, in one of the psalms, one day is like a thousand years. But when we are told that on the next day Jesus and his disciples went to such-and-such a place and did such-and-such, we are to interpret "day" literally as a 24-hour period. Context demands it.

A more difficult example is the bread and wine in the Last Supper. The question of whether or not these words are figurative, as mentioned, has separated entire denominations. The context requires us to read these words figuratively, for Jesus uses a metaphor when he speaks. He tells the disciples that the bread *is* his body and the cup *is* his blood in the new covenant (Matt. 26:26–28; Mark 14:22–24; Luke 22:19–20). It is clear that he cannot be speaking literally here, or there would have had to have been a miraculous transformation in front of the disciples' eyes—and nothing of the sort happened. It is evident, then, that these words are meant figuratively—just as much so as Jesus' earlier claims to be the "bread of life" and "living water."

Vehicle and Tenor in Meaning

As we established above, figures of speech contain two terms, or subjects—the "vehicle" and the "tenor." It is important for the interpreter to understand each of the terms in itself before he or she attempts to understand how their interaction produces a meaning. In this regard, it will be important for you to do your linguistic and historical homework well. Understanding the meanings and associations of important words in their historical contexts—in short, the diachronic dimension to semantics—will spare you error in interpretation.[22] The famous camel and the "eye of the needle" (Matt. 19:24 and parallels) is a case in point; knowing something of what the latter phrase meant in its historical milieu will save fanciful interpretation when we are so far removed from the cultural context which produced the expression.

Connotations and Denotations

One reason why figures of speech can be difficult to interpret is that they often express a range of connotations as well as a denotation.[23] *De-*

---

22. See the discussion elsewhere in the present work.
23. Ryken, *Words of Delight*, 161.

notation refers to the simple definition of the word in the dictionary, *connotation* to the associations made with a word. "Shepherd," for instance, denotes a caretaker of sheep; it connotes loving care, sacrifice, provision, and constant attention. The difficulty of connotation in biblical figures of speech is made more acute for modern readers because some connotations are cultural, and we have lost the cultural contexts of ancient Near Eastern life. This is the reason it takes a thorough knowledge of Old Testament sacrifices, for instance, to appreciate the New Testament statements about Jesus as the "Lamb of God, who takes away the sin of the world" (John 1:29) and the image of the Lamb sitting on the throne in the book of Revelation (Rev. 5:6–14). The book of Hebrews, to cite another example, would not carry its full meaning to a reader who is ignorant of the figurative import of Jesus as a high priest after the order of Melchizedek. It is not simply emotional and decorative enrichment that knowing the Old Testament sacrificial system brings to the reading of the New Testament; it is rather a whole context and range of meanings—in short, theology—that it brings with it.

Active Participation by the Reader

Figures of speech demand active reading on the interpreter's part. Such reading is no spectator sport for the hermeneutically lazy or indifferent exegete. Leland Ryken states that figures of speech "require far more activity than a direct, propositional statement does."[24] One reason why figures of speech demand active reading relates to the question of which meanings are appropriate in any given figure. For instance, the writer of Hebrews plays on multiple meanings of the word "rest" in chapters three and four. Quoting Psalm 95:7–11, he refers to God's warning to the Israelites that, because of their unbelief, they would not enter the Promised Land, meaning the literal land of Canaan (Heb. 3:7–11). The writer of Hebrews, however, uses the term "rest" to signify spiritual peace with God through salvation in Jesus Christ (Heb. 4:1–3, 10). He even goes on to emphasize the certainty of spiritual rest in Christ by making reference to the divine rest subsequent to creation (Heb. 4:3–10). Here, in a few short verses, the writer's shifting contexts and allusions require careful attention if the reader is to interpret the theology of the passage correctly.

---

24. Ibid., 168.

Context

We have already alluded to the importance of context in interpreting figures of speech and only reiterate the matter here to underscore its significance.[25] In fact, of all the hermeneutical principles outlined in this chapter, context is the determinative factor in meaning. An interesting example comes from the Gospel of Matthew where Jesus tells the parable of the tenants who kill the servants and then the son of the master (Matt. 21:33–45). Using two important Old Testament images—the vineyard and the cornerstone—Jesus condemns the chief priests and Pharisees of his day. How did the religious leaders understand that he was speaking against them (Matt. 21:45)? It was because they understood the figurative meanings of the vineyard (God's people) and the stone (taken from Ps. 118:19–23) related to a righteousness to which they could not attain without Messiah.

In this example, it is clear that context in its near and far dimensions is necessary for proper interpretation. Context provides the limits of valid interpretation and helps the interpreter select the appropriate meanings from within those limits. Grant Osborne rightly notes, "Theology rarely stems from the metaphor itself but rather from the whole context of which it is a part."[26] Context involves the immediate linguistic setting, the historical setting (and meanings of those words in that historical setting), and the canonical context of such important images as lamb, shepherd, groom, and king. It is for these reasons that contextual clues in interpreting figures of speech are theological as well as semantic, syntactic, and canonical. All three dimensions of context are important in interpreting figures of speech.

Figures of Speech and Propositional Explanations

When a figure of speech is explained in its own context, there is no excuse for misconstruing its meaning.[27] Using the image of leaven, for instance, Jesus condemns the Pharisees for their unholy pollution of God's people. In Matthew's account, the incident ends with the statement, "Then they understood that he was not telling them to guard against the yeast

---

25. Paul, "Metaphor," 507–8.
26. Osborne, *Hermeneutical Spiral*, 239.
27. Zuck, *Basic Bible Interpretation*, 146.

used in bread, but against the teaching of the Pharisees and Sadducees" (Matt. 16:12). The point is driven home. Jesus explains some of his parables, such as the parable of the soils, in order to make his teaching plain for his disciples (Matt. 13:18–23). When the writer provides an interpretation of a figure of speech, it is normative.

TYPES OF FIGURES OF SPEECH IN THE BIBLE

Anthropomorphism

Anthropomorphism is the ascription of human characteristics to God. For instance:

> The eyes of the LORD are on the righteous
> and his ears are attentive to their cry;
> the face of the LORD is against those who do evil,
> to cut off the memory of them from the earth. (Ps. 34:15–16)

In this reference, the writer indicates God's regard for his people and rejection of the unrighteous. In verse 15, "the eyes" indicate God's active protection of his people, and "the ears" represent his responsiveness to their cries. In verse 16, "the face" signifies God's whole person in opposition to the unrighteous people who do evil. In all three anthropomorphisms, God is given human characteristics, with the result that his different attitudes toward the righteous and the unrighteous are made personal—and pointed.

Euphemism

Euphemism is the substitution of a less offensive term for an offensive one. The classic example of euphemism is Elijah's taunt of the prophets of Baal at Mount Carmel. When Baal does not answer his prophets' petitions, Elijah mocks, "At noon Elijah began to taunt them. 'Shout louder!' he said. 'Surely he is a god! Perhaps he is deep in thought, or busy, or traveling. Maybe he is sleeping and must be awakened'" (1 Kgs. 18:27). Here, the reference to Baal's being "busy" is a polite way of saying that he is "relieving himself" (compare ESV, where the euphemism is even more evident).

Hypocatastasis

Hypocatastasis is a device in which the comparison is implied by direct naming. In the prophet's taunt song against Nineveh in the book of Nahum, the vulnerability of the soon-to-be-defeated Ninevites is expressed in the hypocatastasis of the lions' den (Nahum 2). The lion was Nineveh's symbol. In saying that the lions' den is ravaged, the prophet mocks the Ninevites at their proudest point.

Image

Image is a word picture that makes an abstract idea concrete and reified. The imagery in the first chapter of the book of Revelation is a prime New Testament example. Here the golden lampstands and the Son of Man among them represent the glory and truth of the glorified churches in the presence of Christ. The effect of the imagery is to create awe. An Old Testament image is that of the four living creatures in the opening chapter of Ezekiel. The four faces, each one in itself symbolic, represent the omniscience of God, the wings and feet their ability to carry out God's commands, and the "appearance ... like burning coals of fire or like torches" (Ezek. 1:13) the holiness and glory of God. It is appropriate that the writings of the prophets contain so many images, for imagery makes the abstract concrete and brings the eternal into the temporal. The prophecies in the Old Testament and in the New Testament Apocalypse would not be nearly as accessible to us, were it not for the figures of speech they employ.

Metaphor

Metaphor is the imaginative identification of two distinct objects or ideas. The psalmist's declaration, "For the LORD God is a sun and shield" (Ps. 84:11), is an example of a double metaphor. The Lord is compared to the sun which provides life, and the psalmist takes the same idea explicitly in the same verse in that God "bestows favor and honor" and withholds "no good thing" from his people. As for the shield, no explanation is necessary; not only does God provide, he protects.

Metonymy

Metonymy is the substitution of one word for another. The great wedding song in Psalm 45 contains a vivid metonymy:

Your throne, O God, will last for ever and ever;
    A scepter of justice will be the scepter of your kingdom. (Ps. 45:6)

There are actually two metonymies in this verse. The first is "the throne of God," for "throne" represents the rule of a king. Thus this metonymy reminds us of God's eternal reign or authority over all things. "The scepter" is the second metonymy, referring to the power of the king. In ancient cultures, the scepter represented authority—as, for instance, in Esther's case (Est. 5:1–3). Here, the scepter of God's authority is his righteousness, or holiness—his essential attribute. In two brief metonymies, the psalmist expresses something of the majesty and dominion of God.

SAMPLE EXEGESIS: PSALM 18

History

Psalm 18 is replete with figures of speech and will therefore serve as a fitting illustration of how figures of speech work in context. According to the superscription, David wrote the psalm as a thanksgiving after the Lord had rescued him from Saul and his other enemies. The comments on the psalm that follow here do not represent a full exegesis of the passage at hand; they relate only to the figures of speech in the first part of the psalm. Also, we will address only the immediate context of the figures of speech but not their larger canonical context.

Language

In the first 19 verses, David comments on two primary subjects: his hopeless condition in the face of Saul's attacks and the Lord's rescue of him from certain death. The structure of these verses presents itself as follows:

14.1. STRUCTURE OF PSALM 18	
Verses 1–3	The Reason for the Psalmist's Thankfulness Announced
Verses 4–5	The Psalmist's Problem
Verses 6–15	The Lord's Response to the Psalmist's Cry for Help
Verses 16–19	The Results of the Lord's Response

Understanding the structure of these verses in this way draws attention to at least two of the overall effects of the verses. First, the psalmist uses a number of figures of speech regarding himself and his condition (vv. 4, 5, 16). Second, the psalmist presents the Lord essentially through a series of consecutive figures of speech (vv. 6–15).

As the structure of the psalm suggests, the figures of speech related to the psalmist himself are clustered primarily in the second section of the psalm (vv. 4–5). In an *image*, the psalmist speaks of himself as being "entangled" in "the cords of death" and "overwhelmed" by the "torrents of destruction" (v. 4). The vehicle in these images is "the cords," presumably a sort of rope, and the tenor is "death." The effect of the image is to suggest that possible imminent death has paralyzed the psalmist—itself an example of *litotes*, for if he were to be killed, he certainly could do nothing more to defend himself. The same effect is achieved in the subsequent images of the "cords of the grave" which are "coiling" around the speaker, and the "snares of death" which "confront" him (v. 5).

The accumulation of these images of restraint and despair conveys the fact that the speaker feels entirely beleaguered by the enemies he faces. As far as he can see, he is trapped, restrained, and consigned to an imminent demise. Add to these the image in verse 16, following the long section about Yahweh (vv. 6–15), and the reader has a clear understanding of how hopeless the psalmist felt. In verse 16, the Lord rescues the speaker from "deep waters," echoing the "torrents of destruction" (v. 4), providing something of a book-ending as a frame, and underscoring the speaker's complete inability to support and rescue himself. The overall effect of the images related to the psalmist in the early part of Psalm 18, then, is his complete hopelessness; he has nothing to defend and rescue himself from his enemy's attack.

In sharp contrast to the figures of speech that communicate the psalmist's utter hopelessness are the figures about the Lord—Yahweh. Whereas the images relating to the psalmist are clustered primarily in the second section of the psalm, the figures relating to the Lord are found throughout the entire passage. In verses 1–3 and 6–16, the psalmist accumulates figures of speech about the Lord and then states the thesis of the passage in verses 17–18. Coming after the many figures of speech about God, the propositional statement in verses 17–18 that God rescues him from his enemies is almost anticlimactic. It is as if the reader has to say, "Of course he rescued the speaker from his enemies; how could he not, given all that we have just read about him?"

The psalmist begins the figurative language about God immediately after the opening pronouncement of his love for God. Early in the psalm, God is described as a "rock," a "fortress," a "shield," "the horn of [the psalmist's] salvation," and a "stronghold" (v. 2). The fact that all of these figures are presented in rapid fire in one verse asserts unequivocally that God is able to protect the speaker who cannot protect himself.

The figures in this verse are all metaphors, for they are framed in the "(a) is (b)" pattern characteristic of metaphors. Where the copula verb "is" is missing, it is assumed (*ellipsis*). What is more, the writer patterns these metaphors carefully: God is (1) a rock; (2) a fortress; (3) a rock again; (4) a shield; (5) a horn of salvation; and finally (6) a stronghold. Even a superficial reading of this pattern suggests that the speaker sees God as his support and defense—support in the metaphors of "rock" and "stronghold," defense in the metaphors of "fortress" and "shield."

It is significant that these declarations of God's support and defense precede the psalmist's lament in verses 4–5 regarding his own utter helplessness. This structure places the fears of verses 4–5 within a framework of God's omnipotence toward the psalmist. Overwhelming though his fears may be, when he remembers the Lord, the psalmist is assured of comfort. In fact, one reason the psalm was written was to express this confidence in Yahweh and to praise him accordingly.

The metaphors about the Lord in the early part of the psalm all reflect stability and protection; they are *static*. In these metaphors, God is the same as he always has been, and the speaker's approaching enemy does not change his attributes or love. A number of other figures of speech in the passage, however, are *dynamic*. Specifically, the Lord is "a warrior." Based on the *metonymy* of the temple (v. 6), which portrays the Lord's majesty and power, the figures of speech that depict God as a warrior indicate that he comes to the speaker's rescue (vv. 7–15).

The predominant impression in these verses is of God's great power harnessed in the cause of the psalmist. He portrays the awesome power of God in the *hyperboles* of the earth "trembling" and "quaking" and the "foundations of the mountain" shaking (v. 7). It is true that God's power could do all of this and more to the mountains and the earth, such as are mentioned in the reflections on the exodus in Psalm 77 where the waters "writhed" and "were convulsed" (Ps. 77:16) and "the earth trembled and quaked" (v. 18).

In Psalm 18, however, these cataclysms are hyperboles because no such upheavals occurred in the psalmist's life. In an *anthropopathism*, the mountains "tremble" because of God's "anger" (v. 7). Verse 7 depicts a God who rouses himself actively in defense of his anointed one. The psalmist continues, presenting the Lord in the *imagery* of a warrior coming in the clouds of the sky, awesome to behold and terrible in his aspect (vv. 9–14). All of God's omnipotence is marshaled in the psalmist's defense, for he "parts" the heavens and descends with "dark clouds under his feet" (v. 9).

The image of this verse is of a powerful warrior rushing to battle, and contained within the image is the *anthropomorphism* of God's "feet" subduing even the clouds of the sky. The writer underscores the power and majesty of this warrior-God, for he rides the cherubim, and then expresses God's great speed as he "soars" on the "wings of the wind" (v. 10).

Next, the psalmist turns to the visual imagery of light and dark (vv. 11–12) and the auditory imagery of thunder (v. 13) to underscore the invincible power and strength of God. The Lord "thunders from heaven" and his "voice" resounds throughout the earth. While it is true that God can create thunder and lightning to announce his presence, as he did at Mount Sinai with Moses, here these are images. Because of the historical record in the Pentateuch of the Sinai event, however, these images are all the more powerful. The reference to the "voice" of God is an *anthropomorphism* announcing God's presence and judgment.

Last in these verses, which depict God as a descending and advancing warrior, is the metaphor of his "arrows" that "scatter the enemies" (v. 14). Note the statement that follows, identifying the arrows as lightning. Here is a warrior with an arsenal of all creation at his disposal and directed against the psalmist's enemies. The overall effect of these figures of speech about the Lord is kinesthetic in the extreme. He is "on the move," and his advance is inevitable and terrible.

The figures of speech in the first 19 verses of Psalm 18 strike a sharp contrast between the helpless and hopeless psalmist who sees himself at the mercy of a merciless enemy and the omnipotence of Yahweh the warrior rushing to his rescue. We know these are figures of speech—images, metaphors, anthropomorphisms, anthropopathism, metonymy and hyperbole—if for no other reason than that there exists no record of such meteorological events surrounding the conflict of David and Saul or any other similar conflict in the Old Testament apart from the exodus.

Theology

What theology do the figures of speech in this passage teach? They instruct us that when we are without hope in this world, Yahweh defends his chosen ones and nothing can resist his power. More than that, we learn that the proper response to the God who delights in us and redeems us is one of love and praise, for the psalmist begins with a declaration of his love for the Lord, praises him throughout the entire passage, and concludes with a declaration of God's love for him—"because he delighted in me"—forming an *inclusio* of love.

GUIDELINES FOR INTERPRETING FIGURES OF SPEECH IN THE BIBLE

1. Take the literal meaning of statements of comparison unless there are compelling reasons to interpret them figuratively.

2. Interpret each of the terms of the figure of speech (vehicle and tenor) before attempting to interpret what is intended by their figurative association.

3. Pay due attention to connotations, as well as denotations, of the terms involved in the figure of speech.

4. Read the figure of speech carefully for all of its import; do not "skim read" figures of speech in the Bible.

5. In cases where an explanatory propositional statement follows a figure of speech, interpret it in the light of the propositional statement.

6. Pay careful attention to contexts—immediate and far, linguistic and historical—in the interpretation of figures of speech.

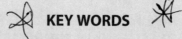

KEY WORDS

Anthropomorphism: the ascription of human characteristics to God

Anthropopathism: the ascription of human emotions to God

Antithesis: direct contrast, terms set in opposition to each other

Apostrophe: direct address to imaginary object or person, or to an object or person not present

Contiguity: figure of speech based on association, not similarity; in figures of contiguity, there is a logical comparison between the terms of the figure; metonymy and synecdoche are figures of contiguity

Epizeuxis or Epanadiplosis: repetition of a significant word for emphasis

Euphemism: substitution of a less offensive or explicit term for a stronger term

Figure of Speech: any use of language in which two terms are compared or brought into some relationship other than, or in addition to, a literal or logical connection; any use of language in which one term is spoken of in language suggestive of the other term

Hypocatastasis: figure of speech in which the comparison is implied by direct naming

Image: word picture in which the reader can, as it were, see, taste, touch, smell or hear what is being described

Irony: device in which the writer states the opposite of what is intended

Litotes: deliberate understatement for effect

Merism: type of synecdoche in which the whole is suggested by contrasting parts

Metaphor: figure of speech in which one term is imaginatively identified with another, or in which one object represents another object or idea

Metonymy: substitution of one word for another

Paronomasia: similar-sounding words placed side by side for emphasis

Personification (also Prosopopoeia): type of metaphor in which human characteristics are ascribed to inanimate objects, animals, or other non-human beings

Similarity: figure of speech based on comparison apart from any logical connection between the terms; figures of similarity include simile, metaphor, image and symbol

Simile: simple comparison, usually linked by "like" or "as"

Symbol: type of metaphor in which the vehicle, as well as the tenor, is broadly suggestive in itself

Synecdoche: figure of speech in which a part represents the whole

Tenor: underlying subject in a figure of speech

Term: subject of a figure of speech; there are two terms in a figure of speech, the "vehicle" and "tenor"

Vehicle: mode in which the tenor is experienced

STUDY QUESTIONS

1. How do you define the various figures of speech in Scripture? Read the list of definitions and be familiar with terms that are new to you. Understand these terms in reference to the interpretation of the Bible discussed in the present chapter.

2. What are some examples of figurative speech given in this chapter? Summarize new insights you have gained from these.

3. Explain why it is important to follow the guidelines for interpreting figurative speech. What interpretive danger is there if one is ill-equipped in reading figurative language in the Bible?

ASSIGNMENTS

1. Explain briefly important distinctive elements in dealing with figurative language such as: (1) basic types of figure of speech; (2) vehicle and tenor; and (3) denotation and connotation, and give examples of each.

2. Discuss the role of context in determining whether a given word or phrase is to be understood as literal or figurative. Granting that meaning is involved in whether what is under consideration is to be understood literally or as figurative speech, what additional information vital to the interpreter is conveyed by the author's use of figurative language?

3. Identify and explain the type of figures of speech being used in the following passages and explain their meanings.
    a. Hosea 7:6–12
    b. Hosea 14:5
    c. John 10:1–18

CHAPTER BIBLIOGRAPHY

Aristotle. "Poetics." In *The Complete Works of Aristotle*, vol. 2. Edited by Jonathan Barnes. Princeton: Princeton University Press, 1984.
_____. "Rhetoric." In *The Complete Works of Aristotle*, vol. 2. Edited by Jonathan Barnes. Princeton: Princeton University Press, 1984.

Black, Max. "More about Metaphor." In *Metaphor and Thought*. Ed. Andrew Ortony. Cambridge: Cambridge University Press, 1979.

Bullinger, E. W. *Figures of Speech Used in the Bible: Explained and Illustrated*. London: Eyre & Spottiswoode, 1898; repr. Grand Rapids: Baker, 1968.

Frye, Northrop. *The Great Code: The Bible and Literature*. San Diego: Harcourt, Brace & Co., 1982.

Hirsch, E. D. *Validity in Interpretation*. New Haven: Yale University Press, 1979.

Longman, Tremper III. *How to Read the Psalms*. Downers Grove: InterVarsity, 1988.

Paul, Ian. "Metaphor." Pp. 507–10 in *Dictionary for Theological Interpretation of the Bible*. Edited by Kevin J. Vanhoozer, Craig G. Bartholomew, Daniel J. Treier, and N. T. Wright. Grand Rapids: Baker, 2005.

Richards, I. A. *The Philosophy of Rhetoric*. New York: Oxford University Press, 1936.

Ryken, Leland. *Words of Delight: A Literary Introduction to the Bible*. Grand Rapids: Baker, 1992.

Soskice, Janet Martin. *Metaphor and Religious Language*. Oxford: Clarendon, 1987.

Stanford, William B. *Greek Metaphor*. Oxford: Basil Blackwell, 1936, 1972.

Wellek, Rene and Austin Warren. *Theory of Literature*. 3d ed. New York: Harcourt, Brace & World, 1956.

Zuck, Roy B. *Basic Bible Interpretation*. Colorado Springs: Chariot Victor, 1991.

PART 3

THE GOAL:
THEOLOGY

CHAPTER 15 OBJECTIVES

1. To acquaint the student with the nature of biblical theology.

2. To acquaint the student with some of the major issues in biblical theology.

3. To introduce the student to important questions related to the method of biblical theology.

4. To survey the history and approach taken to the study of biblical theology.

5. To familiarize the student with important issues related to the use of the Old Testament in the New.

CHAPTER 15 OUTLINE

A. Nature of Biblical Theology

B. Issues in Biblical Theology

C. Method of Biblical Theology

D. History of Biblical Theology

E. Approaches to Biblical Theology

F. Use of the Old Testament in the New

G. Sample Exegesis: John 12:37–41

H. Guidelines for the Study of Biblical Theology

I. Guidelines for Studying the Use of the Old Testament in the New

J. Key Words

K. Study Questions

L. Assignments

M. Chapter Bibliography

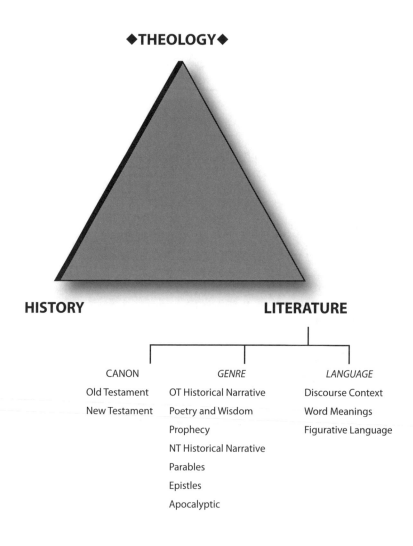

◆THEOLOGY◆

HISTORY

LITERATURE

CANON

Old Testament

New Testament

GENRE

OT Historical Narrative

Poetry and Wisdom

Prophecy

NT Historical Narrative

Parables

Epistles

Apocalyptic

LANGUAGE

Discourse Context

Word Meanings

Figurative Language

CHAPTER 15

MAKING THE CONNECTION: GETTING

OUR THEOLOGY FROM THE BIBLE

NATURE OF BIBLICAL THEOLOGY

AT LONG LAST, WE HAVE arrived at the mountain top in our interpretive journey and reached the goal of our quest to interpret Scripture accurately. Having grounded our interpretation of Scripture in the first dimension of the hermeneutical triad, history, and having focused on interpreting the various literary facets of Scripture in descending order from the macro- to the micro-level—(from canon to genre to language), we have come to our final destination: the third and crowning aspect of the hermeneutical triad, theology. If we are not only grounded in the historical setting and well versed in the various literary dimensions of Scripture but develop a firm grasp of its theological message, we will indeed be workers who need not be ashamed but who correctly handle God's Word.

In our day, theology, or doctrine, is often given a negative connotation, as people look for an authentic expression of biblical Christianity.[1]

---

1. In his November 2009 Page lectures at Southeastern Baptist Theological Seminary, Kevin Vanhoozer lamented the disappearance of doctrine in the church. He asked, "Is doctrine really irrelevant, divisive, unspiritual, and boring?" His answer: "No—doctrine is inevitable." What is more, doctrine, rightly understood, is anything but boring and irrelevant. Vanhoozer develops this thesis in his seminal work *The*

Doctrine is often viewed as a lifeless listing of a creed or confessional statement and contrasted with a vital spiritual first-hand experience of God. "Just give me Jesus," some say, but spare me doctrine and theology. Rather than viewing theology as nurturing and stabilizing elements in their journey of faith, many today view it as the enemy, or are skeptical at best if not indifferent or outright antagonistic. For reasons such as these, it is vital that we make sure that we derive our theology from the Bible rather than imposing our own preferred viewpoints onto Scripture. The quest for a sound, *biblical*, theology has in recent years come to be dealt with under the rubric "biblical theology."

What is "biblical theology"? The shortest possible answer is this: "Biblical theology is the theology of the Bible."[2] That is, biblical theology is theology that is biblical, or, in other words, theology that is derived from the Bible rather than imposed onto the Bible by a given interpreter of Scripture. If so, then it follows that Old Testament theology is the theology of the Old Testament, and New Testament the theology of the New Testament.

The theologian Adolf Schlatter put the issue well almost a century ago when he wrote: "In speaking of 'New Testament' theology, we are saying that it is not the interpreter's own theology or that of his church and times that is examined but rather the theology expressed by the New Testament itself."[3] In light of this definition, how are we to go about discerning the theology of the Bible?

Again, Schlatter's words are apropos: "We turn away decisively from ourselves and our time to what was found in the men through whom the church came into being. Our main interest should be the thought as it was conceived *by them* and the truth that was valid *for them*. We want to see and obtain a thorough grasp of what happened historically and existed in

---

Drama of Doctrine: A Canonical-Linguistic Approach to Christian Theology (Louisville: Westminster John Knox, 2005). See also his work *Remythologizing Theology: Divine Action, Passion, and Authorship* (Cambridge: Cambridge University Press, 2010).

2. Charles H. H. Scobie, *The Ways of Our God: An Approach to Biblical Theology* (Grand Rapids: Eerdmans, 2003), 3, citing Ebeling and noting that this is the definition preferred by most scholars.

3. Adolf Schlatter, *The History of the Christ*, trans. Andreas J. Köstenberger (Grand Rapids: Baker, 1997), 18.

another time."[4] This, Schlatter calls "the historical task," which is subsequently complemented by the "doctrinal task" of systematizing the Bible's teachings on a given subject.

As Schlatter reminds us, it is important not to blur the line unduly between these two tasks, lest our perception be muddied and our application rendered imprecise or even invalid: "The distinction between these two activities thus turns out to be beneficial for both. Distortions in the perception of the subject also harm its appropriation, just as conversely improper procedures in the appropriation of the subject muddy its perception."[5] In other words, we must put first things first. Before we can apply Scripture, we must first interpret it correctly, and this involves what Schlatter calls "the historical task."

ISSUES IN BIBLICAL THEOLOGY

Defining biblical theology as the theology of the Bible, and our task as discerning that theology from the point of view of the biblical writers themselves, may seem clear enough. However, in practice there are several potential problems in this regard. First, it is commonly acknowledged today that no interpreter approaches Scripture without *presuppositions*. How, then, is it possible to "turn away decisively from ourselves and our time," as Schlatter suggests?

In response, we may note that not all presuppositions are necessarily problematic. For example, the presupposition that Scripture is trustworthy is in keeping with its own self-attestation and with its nature as the inspired Word of God (e.g., Psalms 19; 119; 2 Tim. 3:16–17; 2 Pet. 1:21–22). Likewise, Scripture itself assumes the existence of God when it says in its opening words that, "In the beginning, God created the heavens and the earth" (Gen. 1:1). The existence of angels (including Satan) is assumed as well; the Bible does not narrate the creation of angels.

Other presuppositions, however, may derive from tradition, personal experience, or prejudice, or other possibly questionable sources that must be checked so that they do not become hindrances to a proper apprehension of the biblical message. For example, I have often found that my

---

4. Ibid.
5. Ibid.

students tend to assume that the interpretation of a given passage of Scripture by their favorite preacher (John Piper, Chuck Swindoll, John MacArthur, and so on) is correct. This may well be, but it is still important to be open to all the evidence relevant for biblical interpretation, whether or not this supports the interpretation of our favorite Bible expositor.

In today's postmodern environment, the impression is often given that our subjectivity is so inescapable that the apprehension of absolute truth and interpretive objectivity are complete impossibilities—except, of course, in apprehending the postmodern contention that objectivity is impossible, which is held as absolutely true![6] In this regard, it will be helpful for us to distinguish between the intended meaning of a passage itself and the degree of confidence to which we can reasonably expect to attain in having arrived at this meaning.

In other words, the meaning itself may be clear; the problem is our lack of equipment in ascertaining it. If so, however, repeated reading, diligent study, and biblical education can be expected to close the gap. What is more, while 100-percent confidence will often be elusive, this does not mean that we cannot be reasonably confident that a given interpretation accurately approximates the originally intended meaning. To use an analogy from life in general, we are regularly called to make decisions on less than 100-percent certainty or complete information. But this does not mean that we cannot make good decisions, such as buying a reliable vehicle or entering responsibly into marriage.

Second, how does one determine the theology of the Bible? This raises the issue of *hermeneutical method* and procedure. As a survey of the history of doctrine and of biblical theology reveals, different interpreters have interpreted Scripture differently with regard to its major or central themes, resulting in at times conflicting theological systems. Issues such as the relationship between Israel and the church, the fulfillment of Old Testament prophecy, and the end times have been adjudicated differently.[7]

---

6. For a helpful critique of postmodernism see D. A. Carson, *The Gagging of God* (Grand Rapids: Zondervan, 1996). See also Vanhoozer, *Drama of Doctrine.*

7. See esp. David L. Baker, *Two Testaments, One Bible: A Study of Some Modern Solutions to the Theological Problem of the Relationship between the Old and the New Testaments*, rev. ed. (Downers Grove: InterVarsity, 1991). See also Craig A. Blaising and Darrell L. Bock, eds., *Dispensationalism, Israel and the Church: The Search for Definition* (Grand Rapids: Zondervan, 1991).

This is not the place to deal with any of these issues in detail. In essence, this entire book is designed to set forth a responsible hermeneutical method that will enable the interpreter to derive the Bible's own theology through patient, repeated study. As we explore the three major aspects of the hermeneutical triad, history, literature, and theology; as we interpret a given passage in its larger canonical context; and as we familiarize ourselves with the characteristics of the various biblical genres, we will be equipped not merely to analyze individual biblical passages but also to develop a synthesis of the biblical teaching on the major topics it addresses.

Third, our apprehension of the theology of the Bible hinges on various other important foundations, such as the extent and composition of the biblical canon; the way in which the New Testament writers use the Old Testament; the relationship of the Testaments more broadly conceived; the issue of the unity and diversity of Scripture; and the question of whether or not the Old Testament, the New Testament (and certain New Testament writers such as Paul), and the Bible have a center and, if so, what it is. All of these are important issues which are dealt with in the relevant literature.[8]

METHOD OF BIBLICAL THEOLOGY

How should we go about doing biblical theology? While we may be agreed in principle as to the purpose and goals of the discipline, the question remains as to the means and method of arriving at an accurate representation of the theology of the Bible on its own terms. As we seek to

---

8. On the canon, see Lee Martin McDonald, *The Biblical Canon: Its Origin, Transmission, and Authority* (Peabody, MA: Hendrickson, 2007). On the use of the Old Testament in the New, see esp. D. A. Carson and H. G. M. Williamson, eds., *It Is Written: Scripture Citing Scripture* (Cambridge: Cambridge University Press, 1988); and G. K. Beale and D. A. Carson, eds., *Commentary on the New Testament Use of the Old Testament* (Grand Rapids: Baker, 2007). On the relationship between the Testaments, see esp. Baker, *Two Testaments, One Bible*. On the major issues in biblical theology see Gerhard F. Hasel, *Old Testament Theology: Basic Issues in the Current Debate* (Grand Rapids: Eerdmans, 1972); idem, *New Testament Theology: Basic Issues in the Current Debate* (Grand Rapids: Eerdmans, 1978). On the unity and diversity of Scripture see David Wenham, "Appendix: Unity and Diversity in the New Testament," in George Eldon Ladd, *A Theology of the New Testament*, 2d ed. (Grand Rapids: Eerdmans, 1993), 684–719; and Andreas J. Köstenberger, "Diversity and Unity in the New Testament," in *Biblical Theology: Retrospect and Prospect*, ed. Scott J. Hafemann (Downers Grove: InterVarsity, 2002), 200–23.

determine the best way to move forward methodologically, two important considerations must be stated at the very outset.

First, the method of biblical theology must be *historical*. That is, unlike systematic theology, which tends to be abstract and topical in nature, biblical theology aims to understand a given passage of Scripture in its original historical setting.[9] For example, when interpreting the well-known passage, "'For I know the plans I have for you,' declares the LORD, 'plans to prosper you and not to harm you, plans to give you hope and a future'" (Jer. 29:11), we must ask who were the original recipients of this promise, and at what stage of Israel's history was this prophecy uttered.

Or consider another familiar passage on the issue of tithing: "Will a man rob God? Yet you rob me. But you ask, 'How do we rob you?' In tithes and offerings. You are under a curse—the whole nation of you—because you are robbing me. Bring the whole tithe into the storehouse, that there may be food in my house. Test me in this,' says the LORD Almighty, 'and see if I will not throw open the floodgates of heaven and pour out so much blessing that you will not have room enough for it" (Mal. 3:8–10). Biblical theology will seek to understand this passage in its original historical context before asking questions regarding its applicability for today.[10]

Second, biblical theology will seek to study Scripture *on its own terms*, that is, pay special attention, not merely to the concepts addressed in Scripture, but to the very words, vocabulary, and terminology used by the biblical writers themselves. Rather than investigating "sanctification" as a broader topic, the biblical theologian will study the individual words that are used in the Bible to express what may be called the subject of Christian growth, words such as "set apart" (*hagiazō*) or "grow" (*auxanō*). This is

---

9. We hasten to add that once exegesis and biblical theology have done their work, systematic theology certainly has a place. See esp. the very helpful essay by D. A. Carson, "The Role of Exegesis in Systematic Theology," in John D. Woodbridge and Thomas Edward McComiskey, eds., *Doing Theology in Today's World: Essays in Honor of Kenneth S. Kantzer* (Grand Rapids: Zondervan, 1991), 39–76. I have previously spoken of a "systematized biblical theology," that is, systematic theology proceeding on the basis of a theologian having done his or her biblical-theological work. See Andreas J. Köstenberger, "The Challenge of a Systematized Biblical Theology: Missiological Insights from the Gospel of John," *Missiology* 23 (1995): 445–64.

10. See on this the two-part series by Andreas J. Köstenberger and David A. Croteau, "'Will a Man Rob God?' (Malachi 3:8): A Study of Tithing in the Old and New Testaments," *Bulletin of Biblical Research* 16 (2006): 53–77; and "Reconstructing a Biblical Model for Giving: A Discussion of Relevant Systematic Issues and New Testament Principles," *BBR* 16 (2006): 237–60.

part of the express purpose of biblical theology: to initially seek to understand the theology of the Bible before systematizing its teaching on certain
subjects and making application.

In light of these general observations, it will be helpful for us to survey
the various ways in which people in the past and the present have gone
about the task of practicing biblical theology. As we will see, biblical theology is a relative new theological discipline that has been defined variously by interpreters in the past. A concise survey of this past history of
biblical theology will help crystallize the issues and aid us in our quest to
arrive at a proper understanding of the most suitable method for biblical
theology. After this I will provide a brief survey of major approaches taken
to biblical theology.[11]

HISTORY OF BIBLICAL THEOLOGY

The recent history of biblical theology as an academic discipline is
commonly traced to J. P. Gabler's inaugural address at the University of
Altdorf, Germany, in 1787 entitled "An Oration on the Proper Distinction
between Biblical and Dogmatic Theology and the Specific Objectives of
Each." In this seminal address, Gabler distinguished between biblical and
what he called "dogmatic theology" (i.e., systematic theology) and called
upon scholars to observe this distinction in their work. While Gabler himself did not contribute significantly to the actual implementation of this
program, his foundational contribution was the postulation of the above-
mentioned distinction between biblical and dogmatic theology as such.[12]

The decades and centuries that followed saw the emergence and full-
blown development of the historical-critical method in biblical studies
under F. C. Baur and the Tübingen School.[13] Increasingly, the study of
Scripture was conceived not in theological but in historical terms. The

---

11. For a thorough survey of the history of New Testament theology see D. A. Carson,
"NT Theology," in *Dictionary of the Later New Testament & Its Developments*, ed.
Ralph P. Martin and Peter H. Davids (Downers Grove: InterVarsity, 1997), 796–814;
see also Ladd, *Theology of New Testament*, 1–28; Hasel, *New Testament Theology*,
9–139; and Scobie, *Ways of Our God*, 9–28.
12. On J. P. Gabler see William Baird, *History of New Testament Research*, Vol. 1: *From
Deism to Tübingen* (Minneapolis: Fortress, 1992), 184–87.
13. See ibid. See also Robert W. Yarbrough, *The Salvation-Historical Fallacy? Reassessing
the History of New Testament Theology* (Leiden: Deo, 2004).

study of the Old Testament often became a study in comparative religions where Israel's cult was compared to that of its neighbors and the New Testament church was discussed in relation to the mystery religions in the Hellenistic world and its practices of sacred meals and initiation and other rites (the history-of-religions school). In the end, in the hands of some of its practitioners such as William Wrede (*Concerning the Task and Method of "So-Called NT Theology,"* 1897), New Testament theology had become a completely historical enterprise almost entirely devoid of the category of divine revelation or theology.[14]

In due course, this one-sided preoccupation with history led to widespread disillusionment with the historical-critical method. Some, such as Oscar Cullmann, sought to salvage theology by proposing a salvation-historical (*heilsgeschichtliche*) method; others, such as Ernest Wright, pointed to God's mighty acts as the locus of revelation (*The God who Acts*).[15] One writer, Gerhard Maier, even wrote a book called *The End of the Historical-Critical Method* in which he declared the entire approach bankrupt.[16] Eta Linnemann, likewise, wrote off the method as hopelessly ideological and tainted with the anti-supernatural bias of many of its practitioners in the past and present.[17]

A crisis was reached in 1970 when Brevard Childs, in *Biblical Theology in Crisis*, declared that biblical theology was itself in crisis.[18] Childs himself, as well as Hans Frei (in his *Eclipse of Biblical Narrative*), sought refuge in the text or canon of Scripture, calling for a study of the Bible's literary feature while holding historical issues in abeyance.[19] Others pursued a study of the theologies of the various biblical writers, accentuating the New Testament's diversity. Recent years have shown signs of a revival

---

14. See Robert Morgan, *The Nature of New Testament Theology: The Contribution of William Wrede and Adolf Schlatter* (London: SCM, 1973).

15. G. Ernest Wright, *God Who Acts: Biblical Theology as Recital*, SBT 8 (London: SCM, 1952).

16. Gerhard Maier, *The End of the Historical-Critical Method* (St. Louis: Concordia, 1977; orig. German ed. 1974); but see more recently Gerhard Maier, *Biblical Hermeneutics*, trans. Robert W. Yarbrough (Wheaton: Crossway, 1994), in which Maier argues for a judicious approach he calls "historical-biblical."

17. Eta Linnemann, *Historical Criticism of the Bible: Methodology or Ideology?*, trans. Robert W. Yarbrough (Grand Rapids: Baker, 1990).

18. Brevard S. Childs, *Biblical Theology in Crisis* (Philadelphia: Westminster, 1970).

19. Ibid. and Hans Frei, *The Eclipse of Biblical Narrative: A Study of Eighteenth and Nineteenth-Century Hermeneutics* (New Haven: Yale University Press, 1980), Frei's work being part of the postliberal "Yale school."

of the discipline through the work of James Dunn, N. T. Wright, and D. A. Carson, among others.[20]

We conclude this brief survey of the history of biblical theology with the observation that the historical dimension of the biblical text can never be relegated to the sidelines since Christianity is by its very nature a historical religion whose truthfulness depends on the historical nature of events such as the incarnation or Jesus' bodily resurrection from the dead (see esp. 1 Corinthians 15).[21] For this reason, the literary study of Scripture, while a legitimate part of biblical interpretation, must be grounded in historical study and Scripture be seen not merely as a human witness or as an autonomous entity but as inspired, historically-grounded divine revelation. Thus we have argued that history, language, and theology form a hermeneutical triad with theology at the apex.

APPROACHES TO NEW TESTAMENT THEOLOGY

Practically, then, what are some possible approaches to discerning and presenting biblical theology? First, there is what may be called the "Systematic/Biblical" approach. This approach can be seen in the work of scholars such as Donald Guthrie. In his *New Testament Theology*, Guthrie discusses the contribution of the various biblical writings under broad topical headings such as "The Christian Life," "The Future," or "Ethics."[22] Thus the reader is introduced to the unfolding biblical teaching on several major topics of Scripture.

Second is what may be called "Biblical, One Author at a Time." Practitioners of this approach include George Eldon Ladd and Leon Morris.[23] In essence, these writers provide separate biblical-theological treatments of each New Testament writer, such as each of the four evangelists or Paul. It should be noted, however, that Ladd in addition also discusses Jesus'

---

20. James D. G. Dunn, *The Theology of Paul the Apostle* (Grand Rapids: Eerdmans, 1997); N. T. Wright, *The New Testament and the People of God* (Minneapolis: Augsburg Fortress, 1992); D. A. Carson, ed., New Studies in Biblical Theology series. See also the Biblical Theology of the New Testament series edited by Andreas J. Köstenberger.

21. See, e.g., Carson, "New Testament Theology," 807, who contends that "a proper emphasis on history is essential to NT theology."

22. Donald Guthrie, *New Testament Theology* (Downers Grove: InterVarsity, 1981).

23. Ladd, *Theology of the New Testament*; Leon Morris, *New Testament Theology* (Grand Rapids: Baker, 1990).

teaching directly, such as in the case of Jesus' teaching on the kingdom. Also, he often conflates the teaching of Matthew, Mark, and Luke, dealing more broadly with the Synoptic Gospels.[24]

Third, we find the approach that may properly be labeled "Biblical, One Theme at a Time." An outstanding example of this procedure is Charles Scobie's massive New Testament theology, *The Ways of Our God*.[25] The various contributions to the NSBT (New Studies in Biblical Theology) series edited by D. A. Carson also fit in this category as they typically take up a given theme and explore its development throughout Scripture in chronological order and on its own terms. Outstanding examples include Craig Blomberg's *Neither Poverty nor Riches* (on the biblical teaching regarding wealth and poverty) or David Peterson's *Possessed by God* (on sanctification).[26]

Yet another, fourth, approach may be called "Integrative: The Symphonic Approach." This includes the creative model employed by G. B. Caird, in which he "moderates" a roundtable discussion between the various writers of the New Testament on particular topics such as sin, Christ, or the end times.[27] Everyone has a voice at the table (including James or Jude), though some voices (Paul, John) may be weightier than others. The diversity and unity of perspectives represented in the New Testament is revealed as these voices interact and engage each other in this creative format.

Other approaches may be labeled "Historical-Theological" (Rudolf Bultmann) or "Biblical-Historical" (I. Howard Marshall).[28] In the former case, a history-of-religions model is blended with an existentialist approach to theology and a program of "demythologization." In the latter instance, an author is seeking to explore the biblical teaching in its original historical setting book by book or corpus by corpus. While it is not possible here to provide a thorough critique of each of these approaches,

---

24. This has been remedied, and separate treatments of the theology of Matthew, Mark, and Luke been provided, in the 1993 second edition of Ladd's work under the editorship of Donald A. Hagner.
25. Scobie, *Ways of Our God*.
26. Craig L. Blomberg, *Neither Poverty nor Riches: A Biblical Theology of Possessions*, NSBT (Downers Grove: InterVarsity, 2001); and David W. Peterson, *Possessed by God: A New Testament Theology of Sanctification and Holiness*, NSBT 1 (Leicester: InterVarsity, 2001).
27. G. B. Caird, *New Testament Theology* (Oxford: Oxford University Press, 1995).
28. Rudolf Bultmann, *A Theology of the New Testament*, 2 vols. (New York: Charles Scribner's Sons, 1951, 1955); I. Howard Marshall, *New Testament Theology: Many Witnesses, One Gospel* (Downers Grove: InterVarsity, 2004).

the above listing illustrates the variety of models used and underscores that these are not necessarily mutually contradictory or exclusive.

USE OF THE OLD TESTAMENT IN THE NEW

One important question in interpreting a given New Testament passage is, "Does the New Testament writer quote or allude to an Old Testament text?" In fact, the Old Testament is the major source of theology for the New Testament. Jesus frequently quoted the Old Testament, as did Paul, Peter, the author of Hebrews, and others. As a result, it is hard (if not impossible) to understand the New Testament apart from the Old. In what follows, we provide some important observations for interpreting passages involving the use of the Old Testament in the New.

(1) There are times when the New Testament's use of the Old is *structurally, thematically, and theologically significant*. In these cases, the New Testament writer establishes important structural connections between a given Old Testament theme and its New Testament counterpart or fulfillment. An example of this is Matthew 1–4, where the evangelist uses several "fulfillment quotations" to show that Jesus in the early stages of his ministry acted as the paradigmatic new Israel. In the temptation narrative, for example, Jesus repeats yet supersedes Israel's wilderness experience (Matt. 4:4, 6, 7, 10 citing Deut. 8:3; Ps. 91:11–12; and Deut. 6:16; 6:13, respectively). In these cases, we must not miss the Old Testament connection lest we miss the entire message of the New Testament passage in question. In other cases, a New Testament writer may use the Old Testament merely to establish a more limited exegetical point.

(2) While references to the Old Testament in the New are *frequent*, they are *not evenly spread.* For example, half of Paul's Old Testament citations are found in the book of Romans, and of these, half are found in chapters 9–11.[29] This means that a given New Testament writer, such as Paul, did not quote the Old Testament in every case but only when he believed this was warranted in the context of his theological argument and his original readership. For example, in Galatians Paul dealt with Judaizers who claimed that Gentile converts to Christianity must be cir-

---

29. For a helpful resource in this area see Richard N. Longenecker, *Biblical Exegesis in the Apostolic Period*, 2d ed. (Grand Rapids: Eerdmans, 1999).

cumcised. Since his opponents were Jews, Paul used the Old Testament
to show on scriptural grounds that the Judaizers' theology was mistaken,
even on the basis of the Scriptures they cited in support of their view (see
esp. Gal. 3:6–16 citing Gen. 15:6; Hab. 2:4; Deut. 21:23; etc.). In other cases,
especially when dealing with a Gentile audience, Paul referred to the Old
Testament less frequently, if at all (e.g., Colossians, Philippians).

(3) An important question to ask in the case of the New Testament's
use of the Old is that of *warrant*: Why does a given New Testament writer
use the Old Testament at all rather than making a certain pronouncement
on his own (apostolic) authority or stating a rationale that does not involve
using Old Testament Scripture? In many cases, the reason is that his audience already accepted the authority of the Hebrew Scriptures. If he could
show that his teaching was in accord with Old Testament teaching, his
audience would be convinced and satisfied (cf., e.g., Paul's repeated references to Gen. 15:6 in support of his gospel of salvation by faith apart from
works; see, e.g., Gal. 3:6; Rom. 4:3).

(4) Beginning students of Scripture sometimes assume that there is only
one way in which the New Testament writers use the Old Testament. (Most
commonly, the assumption is that this one way is prediction-fulfillment,
that is, a New Testament writer citing an Old Testament passage to show
that a given passage has been fulfilled in Christ.) Nothing could be further
from the truth. While it is true that the *prediction-fulfillment* pattern accounts for a significant number of New Testament references to the Old
(such as Matt. 2:6 citing Mic. 5:2), it is by no means the only type of usage.

Another important use involves *typology*, that is, the argument that an
original pattern in Scripture—a "type," be it an historical person, event, or institution—has found a corresponding "anti-type" in the messianic or church
age.[30] An example of this is Jesus' reference to the serpent lifted up in the wilderness in John 3:14. Just as Moses lifted up the serpent in the wilderness and
those survived who looked at the raised-up serpent in faith, so Jesus would be
lifted up on the cross and everyone who looked at him in faith would live.[31]

---

30. On typology, see the classic work by Leonhard Goppelt, *Typos* (Grand Rapids: Ee-
    rdmans, 1982; orig. German ed. 1939). See also Richard M. Davidson, *Typology in
    Scripture: A Study of Hermeneutical Typos of Structures* (Berrien Springs, MI: An-
    drews University Press, 1981).
31. For an analysis see Andreas J. Köstenberger, "John," in *Commentary on the Use of the
    Old Testament in the New*, 434–37.

The discerning reader will detect in this pattern an analogy (Moses-Jesus; looking/believing/life-looking-believing-eternal life). Indeed, analogy is present, but in the case of typology there is also the additional historical grounding which relates an earlier incident in the history of God's dealings with his people to an end-time corresponding event which is likewise historical. This typological usage proved exceedingly convincing in a Jewish context where people believed that God acted consistently throughout the course of history. If it could therefore be shown that God had acted in a certain way in ages past, there was a high likelihood that he had acted similarly in more recent history or would act again in a similar way in the future.

An example of the latter case is for the book of Jude, where the author shows that God consistently punished rebellion and immorality in Old Testament times and that it was therefore certain that he would similarly punish the false teachers in his day, even though he had not yet done so, on the basis of typological correspondence (a Jewish technique called "midrash," or commentary).

Yet other ways in which New Testament writers use the Old include those of *allegory* (e.g., Gal. 4:21–31), *analogy*, or *illustration* (Eph. 5:32). What all these uses of the Old Testament in the New have in common is that they add persuasiveness to the argument of a given New Testament author by seeking to demonstrate on the basis of the commonly accepted authority of the Hebrew Scriptures the truthfulness of their teaching regarding Christ or the church.

(5) *Direct citations* of the Old Testament in the New are only one form of the New Testament's use of the Old. Other forms of usage involve the employment use of *allusions or echoes*.[32] In the case of allusions, the question of criteria arises. In the absence of an extended literal quote, how can we be sure that a given New Testament writer intended to cite an Old Testament text? In response, the following constraints should be noted.

(a) *Authorial intent.* In order for a given use to qualify as an allusion, it must be authorially intended. Otherwise, we are no longer operating on the basis of an authorial intent hermeneutic but are moving into the realm

---

32. See esp. the seminal work by Richard B. Hays, *Echoes of Scripture in the Letters of Paul* (New Haven: Yale University Press, 1989); and the treatment of allusions and echoes in chapter 13 above.

of reader response. A New Testament passage may evoke the reminiscence of a certain Old Testament passage in the mind of the contemporary reader, but if it cannot be plausibly demonstrated that the New Testament writer intended to evoke this association, we should refrain from speaking of an "Old Testament allusion" in the particular New Testament passage in question.

(b) *Verbal similarity.* In order for a passage to qualify as allusion, there must be sufficient verbal similarity between the New Testament passage and the possible Old Testament source reference. In some cases, this may be only one or two words, perhaps even in different grammatical forms, possibly even involving the use of synonyms. But nevertheless, unless specific New Testament words can be matched with particular Old Testament words, any alleged allusions must normally remain in the realm of speculation, and caution should be exercised in those cases. Depending on the strength of these verbal similarities, it may be appropriate to distinguish in this category between *allusions* on the one hand (stronger similarity) and *echoes* (weaker, fainter similarity).

(6) A helpful indicator signaling the presence of an Old Testament quotation is the use of one of several *introductory formulas.* Examples of this are the following: "it is written"; "this took place in order that the words spoken by Isaiah the prophet might be fulfilled"; or a variety of other formulas. If such an introductory formula can be identified, the presence of an Old Testament citation is virtually certain, though in a few isolated cases it may be difficult to pinpoint the exact Old Testament passage quoted.

(7) In some cases, the study of the use of the Old Testament in the New involves *more technical biblical studies skills* where a particular question hinges on which version of the Old Testament a given New Testament writer used, the Greek Septuagint (LXX) or the Hebrew Masoretic text (MT), and in some cases which particular textual variant or even an unattested text form. In these cases, it is best to consult more technical commentaries or reference works in order to make sure one adequately understands the issues involved. An example of this is the use of Habakkuk 2:4 in Romans 1:17 where the Septuagint and the Masoretic text differ in their rendering and this is of some possible importance for the way in which Paul quotes this passage in Romans.[33]

---

33. See, e.g., James D. G. Dunn, *Romans 1–8*, WBC 38A (Dallas: Word, 1988), 40–46.

(8) In other cases, the difficulty may not be so much on the level of source text and biblical languages but on the level of *theology*. It may be unclear how a given New Testament writer derives a particular point from the Old Testament passage he cites. How does Matthew find support for Jesus' parent's flight to Egypt in the statement in Hosea 11 that God would call his son out of Egypt? (The answer probably involves the use of typology; see above.) Or how can James at the Jerusalem Council in Acts 15:16–18 cite Amos 9:11–12 in support of the conversion of the *Gentiles* when the original text speaks of restoring the house of *David*? (Part of the answer is the reference to "all the nations" in Amos 9:12.) And who among us would have detected a possible reference to God giving gifts to the church in Psalm 68:18 as Paul argues in Ephesians 4:9? We could multiply examples. In those cases posing an exegetical difficulty, it will be wise not to jump to conclusions or to give up but to educate yourself by consulting a technical commentary or good reference work and to weigh the different options before coming to a more settled conclusion.

(9) A helpful distinction in the study of the use of the Old Testament in the New is that between a *hermeneutical axiom* and an *appropriation technique*.[34] The former constitutes an underlying assumption which leads a given New Testament writer to use a particular Old Testament passage in a certain way. Most notably, such an axiom may be the conviction that Jesus is the Messiah predicted in the Old Testament. Paul, for example, became convinced of this when he met the risen Christ on the road to Damascus (Acts 9) and as a result reread the Old Testament in light of this newly-found hermeneutical axiom.

This made all the difference in the way Paul read the Hebrew Scriptures. Rather than believe that Jesus was crucified because he was cursed—in keeping with the statement in Deuteronomy 21:23 that "cursed is everyone who hangs on a tree"—Paul concluded that, on the premise that Jesus was the Messiah, Jesus' death was not for himself but for others—sinners in need of redemption—so that Jesus was not cursed but rather became a "curse *for us*"—for our salvation (Gal. 3:13). What a difference a new hermeneutical axiom makes!

---

34. To my knowledge this distinction was first proposed by Douglas J. Moo, *The Old Testament in the Gospel Passion Narratives* (Sheffield: Almond, 1983).

Appropriation techniques, on the other hand, are specific ways in which the Old Testament is appropriated by a New Testament writer as part of his theological argument: prediction-fulfillment, typology, analogy, illustration, and so on. We have already discussed this matter under point (4) above.

(10) One final question relates to whether or not we should expect to be able to duplicate the use of the Old Testament by the New Testament writers.[35] This is a difficult question to answer. On the one hand, we would expect the New Testament use of the Old to conform to historical-grammatical principles of exegesis that are reproducible by contemporary interpreters. At the same time, the New Testament writers operated under divine inspiration. Not that this inspiration necessarily overrode normal human thought processes, but it provides the New Testament interpretation of specific Old Testament passages with a type of authority that cannot legitimately be claimed by anyone today. For this reason, we will do well to exercise caution and to claim authority only for interpretations of the Old Testament that are made explicit in the New Testament.

SAMPLE EXEGESIS: JOHN 12:37–41

An example of an instance where the New Testament use of the Old Testament is both structurally and theologically significant is the use of Isaiah in John 12:37–41. This unit forms part of John's conclusion to the "Book of Signs," where the evangelist presents seven selected signs of Jesus in order to convince his readers that Jesus was the promised Messiah.[36] The first three signs are found in the opening "Cana Cycle" (chaps. 2–4): (1) the turning of water into wine (2:1–11); (2) the temple clearing (2:13–22);[37] and (3) the healing of the royal official's son (4:46–54). The next three signs are narrated as part of the "Festival Cycle" (chaps. 5–10): (4) the healing of the lame man (5:1–15); (5) the feeding of the multitude (6:1–15); and (6) the

---

35. On opposite sides of the question are Richard Longenecker, (*Biblical Exegesis in the Apostolic Period*; no) and Richard Hays (*Echoes of Scripture in the Letters of Paul*; yes); see the introduction to the second edition of *Biblical Exegesis in the Apostolic Period*.

36. For a detailed analysis, see Andreas J. Köstenberger, "John," in *Commentary on the New Testament Use of the Old Testament*, 477–83.

37. This is disputed; others identify the walking on the water (6:16–21) or some other event as a Johannine "sign." For a thorough discussion, see Andreas J. Köstenberger, *A Theology of John's Gospel and Letters*, BTNT (Grand Rapids: Zondervan, 2009), 323–35.

healing of the man born blind (chap. 9). The climactic seventh sign, the raising of Lazarus, takes up most of chapters 11–12.

At the culmination point of these messianic signs, John the evangelist draws the following conclusion: "Even after Jesus had done all these signs in their presence, they still would not believe in him" (12:37). He continues,

> This was to fulfill the word of Isaiah the prophet:
>   "Lord, who has believed our message
> and to whom has the arm of the Lord been revealed?"
>   For this reason they could not believe,
> because, as Isaiah says elsewhere:
>   "He has blinded their eyes
> and deadened their hearts,
>   so they can neither see with their eyes,
> nor understand with their hearts,
>   nor turn—and I would heal them."
> Isaiah said this because he saw Jesus' glory and spoke about him.
> (12:38–41)

In the overall scheme of John's Gospel, his use of not one, but two passages from Isaiah—Isaiah 53:1 in John 12:38 and Isaiah 6:10 in John 12:40, plus his global reference to Isaiah in verse 41—has a vital purpose: to show that Israel's rejection of her Messiah, far from proving Jesus to be an impostor, in fact took place in fulfillment of Old Testament prophecy.

In the first of these two quotes, Jesus' messianic ministry is aligned with the message Isaiah proclaimed to Israel regarding the Lord, who was high and exalted (Isa. 6:1). Did the Jews listen to the prophet? They did not, and the Babylonian exile ensued. Similarly, John argues, centuries later the Jews did not listen to Jesus' message but rejected it just like they did that of Isaiah. This reveals a pattern of obduracy on the part of Israel that had remained constant throughout history. When the Jews failed to recognize Jesus as Messiah, therefore, this should not have come as a surprise. Rather, the Jewish rejection of Jesus should have been expected and in no way constitutes proof that Jesus' messianic claim was false. Instead, it confirmed Jesus' true identity.[38]

---

38. See Jesus' teaching in the Parable of the Wicked Tenants (Matt. 21:33–46 and parallels).

The second quote, strung together with the first one in keeping with a Jewish device called *gezera shavah* ("equivalence of expression"), further intensifies John's point. The Jews *could not* believe, because, in keeping with Isaiah's prophecy, God had blinded their eyes (12:40; cf. 9:39–41). This, of course, raises an important theological point, because if it was *God* who hardened the heart of the Jewish authorities, then how can he still justly hold them accountable for their sin? For our present purposes, however, we cannot be detained by this discussion; fortunately, Paul takes up this point in Romans 9.[39] Suffice it to say that, according to John, the Jewish rejection of Jesus and his messianic signs was brought about ultimately by the providential will and purposes of God.

The second half of John's Gospel, then, tells the rest of the story: the Jews, with Pilate's help, had Jesus crucified, but God raised him from the dead, and he appeared repeatedly to his followers and commissioned them to spread the good news of salvation and eternal life for those who put their trust in him (John 13–21). Especially for John's Jewish readers, John's use of Scripture is absolutely critical, because they must be convinced that John's message was in keeping with the Hebrew Scriptures—the Old Testament—which they considered authoritative. If John could show that the Jewish authorities had rejected Jesus in keeping with the Old Testament prophetic message, and that Jesus really was the Messiah foretold in Scripture, he had fulfilled his purpose (see 20:30–31). Thus a judicious study of John's use of the Old Testament is absolutely essential for a proper understanding of John's message regarding Jesus.

On a note of personal application, I might add that this passage is deeply reassuring and comforting for believers who are faced with various kinds of adversity. It may appear that God's good purposes are thwarted in a given situation, but Jesus' examples inspires faith that, contrary to what it may appear, to quote Paul, "in all things God works for the good of those who love him, who have been called according to his purpose" (Rom. 8:28). Equipped with this kind of faith perspective, we will be able to recognize more readily that even adversity and rejection are ultimately ordained by God for his sovereign purposes.

---

39. See also D. A. Carson, *Divine Sovereignty and Human Responsibility: Biblical Perspectives in Tension* (Atlanta: John Knox, 1981).

GUIDELINES FOR THE STUDY OF BIBLICAL THEOLOGY

1. Determine the focus of your study: Is it the study of a particular theme in one or several biblical books? The study of a theme in one Testament or the entire Bible? Is it a study of two or several related themes?

2. Determine the relevant passages that need to be studied by means of lexical study, concordance work, study Bibles, and other reference works.

3. Engage in careful contextual study of each of the relevant passages in light of their historical context and the salvation-historical stage in the life of God's people Israel or the church.

4. Determine the original message to the intended recipients at the respective stage of salvation history.

5. Trace the Bible's teaching on your chosen theme throughout the respective books of the Bible or Testament or Scripture as a whole, carefully observing the terminology used by the respective biblical authors.

6. If desired, systematize the biblical teaching in the form of a systematized biblical theology and make proper application.

GUIDELINES FOR STUDYING THE USE OF THE OLD TESTAMENT IN THE NEW

1. Discern the hermeneutical axiom underlying a given use of the Old Testament in the New.

2. Determine the appropriation technique, whether prediction-fulfillment, typology, allegory, analogy, illustration, or other.

3. Ask the question of warrant: Why did the New Testament writer use the Old Testament in his argument?

4. Seek to determine the place the Old Testament quote or allusion has in the argument of the New Testament writer in the New Testament context.

5. Study the Old Testament context of the source quote and determine what role (if any) the original context has in its New Testament appropriation.

6. Engage in comparative study of the Hebrew text, the Septuagint version, and the New Testament citation. Note any important differences and attempt to explain their significance, in consultation with relevant commentaries and reference works.

7. Try to resolve any theological difficulties posed by a given New Testament use of the Old, in consultation with relevant commentaries and reference works.

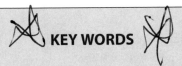

KEY WORDS

Allusion: an authorially intended reference to a preceding text of Scripture involving verbal or, at a minimum, conceptual similarity

Anti-type: a later pattern of God's dealings with his people that corresponds to an earlier instance (see Type below)

Appropriation technique: specific ways in which the Old Testament is appropriated by a New Testament writer as part of his theological argument

Biblical theology: a discipline of biblical study which seeks to investigate Scripture as originally given in its historical context and on in its own terms (in distinction from Systematic theology; see below)

Direct quotation: an explicit, verbatim citation of an Old Testament passage, usually fronted by an introductory formula (in distinction to Allusions or Echoes; see definition of these)

Dogmatic theology: older (German) term for "Systematic theology"

Echo: an authorially intended reference to a preceding text of Scripture which exhibits a proportionately lesser degree of verbal similarity than an allusion (see definition above)

Hermeneutical axiom: an underlying assumption which leads a New Testament writer to use an Old Testament passage in a certain way (e.g., Jesus is the Messiah)

Introductory formula: a phrase preceding a direct Old Testament quotation in the New Testament, such as "It is written"

Midrash: Jewish commentary

Prediction-fulfillment: a phenomenon by which an Old Testament prediction is fulfilled in the New Testament

Systematic theology: a form of presentation of biblical teaching which is essentially topical in nature (in distinction from biblical theology; see above)

Type: an instance of a historical person, event, or institution that exhibits a pattern of God's dealings with his people in salvation history

Typology: an escalating pattern in salvation history in which a later antitype is found to correspond to one or several original types

STUDY QUESTIONS

1. What is biblical theology?

2. What are the major issues involved in biblical theology?

3. What are some key ingredients in a proper method for biblical theology?

4. What are several milestones in the history of biblical theology?

5. What are some of the major approaches to biblical theology?

6. What are some important questions to ask when studying the use of the Old Testament in the New?

7. What are some proper guidelines for studying the New Testament use of the Old Testament?

ASSIGNMENTS

1. Study the theme of stewardship in Scripture. Decide on key terms to study, locate major passages, and sketch a biblical theology of stewardship. As you present your findings, explain and defend the method you used in arriving at your conclusions.

2. Imagine that you were asked to write a biblical theology by a major evangelical publisher. Weighing the different possibilities for presenting such a biblical theology, provide an annotated table of contents in order to sketch the flow of your presentation. Make sure to learn from the history of biblical interpretation and place yourself in the context of previous attempts at writing an account of biblical theology.

CHAPTER BIBLIOGRAPHY

Alexander, T. Desmond and Brian S. Rosner, eds. *New Dictionary of Biblical Theology*. Downers Grove: InterVarsity, 2000.

Balla, Peter. *Challenges to New Testament Theology*. Peabody, MA: Hendrickson, 1998.

Barr, James. *The Concept of Biblical Theology: An Old Testament Perspective*. Minneapolis: Fortress, 1999.

Baker, David L. *Two Testaments, One Bible: A Study of Some Modern Solutions to the Theological Problem of the Relationship between the Old and the New Testaments*. Rev. ed. Downers Grove: InterVarsity, 1991.

Barr, James. *Old and New in Interpretation. : A Study of the Two Testaments*. New York: Harper & Row, 1966.

Beale, G. K. and D. A. Carson, eds. *Commentary on the New Testament Use of the Old Testament*. Grand Rapids: Baker, 2007.

Blaising, Craig A. and Darrell L. Bock, eds. *Dispensationalism, Israel and the Church. : The Search for Definition*. Grand Rapids: Zondervan, 1991.

Bockmuehl, Markus N. A. *Revelation and Mystery*. Wissenschaftliche Untersuchungen zum Neuen Testament 2/36. Tübingen: Mohr-Siebeck, 1990.

Bruce, F. F. *The New Testament Development of Old Testament Themes*. Grand Rapids: Eerdmans, 1968.

Bultmann, Rudolf. *Theology of the New Testament*. New York: Scribner, 1955.

Caird, G. B. *New Testament Theology*. Oxford: Oxford University Press, 1995.

Carson, D. A. "New Testament Theology." Pp. 796–814 in *Dictionary of the Later New Testament and Its Developments*. Edited by Ralph P. Martin and Peter H. Davids. Downers Grove: InterVarsity, 1997.

_____. "Current Issues in Biblical Theology: A New Testament Perspective." *Bulletin of Biblical Research* 5 (1995): 17–41.

Carson, D. A. and H. G. M. Williamson, eds. *It Is Written: Scripture Citing Scripture. Essays in Honour of Barnabas Lindars, SSF.* Cambridge: Cambridge University Press, 1988.

Carson, D. A., ed. *From Sabbath to Lord's Day. A Biblical, Historical and Theological Investigation.* Grand Rapids: Zondervan, 12.

Croteau, David A. *You Mean I Don't Have To Tithe? A Deconstruction of Tithing and a Reconstruction of Post-Tithe Giving.* Eugene, OR: Pickwick, 2010.

Daube, David. *The New Testament and Rabbinic Judaism.* London: Athlone, 1956.

Davidson, Richard M. *Typology in Scripture: A Study of Hermeneutical Typos of Structures.* Berrien Springs, MI: Andrews University Press, 1981.

Davies, W. D. *Paul and Rabbinic Judaism. Some Rabbinic Elements in Pauline Theology.* London: SPCK, 1962.

Dodd, C. H. *According to the Scriptures: The Sub-Structure of New Testament Theology.* London: SCM, 1952.

_____. *The Apostolic Preaching and Its Developments.* New York: Harper, 1935.

Dyrness, William. *Themes in Old Testament Theology.* Downers Grove: InterVarsity, 1979.

Efird, James M., ed. *The Use of the Old Testament in the New and Other Essays. Studies in Honor of William Franklin Stinespring.* Durham, NC: Duke University Press, 1972.

Evans, Craig A. and William F. Stinespring, eds. *Early Jewish and Christian Exegesis. Studies in Memory of William Hugh Brownlee.* Atlanta: Scholars Press, 1987.

Feinberg, John S., ed. *Continuity and Discontinuity: Perspectives on the Relationship between the Old and New Testaments. Essays in Honor of S. Lewis Johnson, Jr.* Westchester, IL: Crossway, 1988.

Fitzmyer, Joseph A. *Essays on the Semitic Background of the New Testament.* Chico, CA: Scholars Press, 1974.

France, R. T. *Jesus and the Old Testament: His Application of Old Testament Passages to Himself and His Mission.* London: Tyndale, 1971.

Goldsworthy, Graeme. *According to Plan: The Unfolding Revelation of God in the Bible*. Leicester: InterVarsity, 1991.

Goppelt, Leonhard. *Typos: The Typological Interpretation of the Old Testament in the New*. Grand Rapids: Eerdmans, 1982 (orig. German ed. 1939).

Guthrie, Donald. *New Testament Theology*. Downers Grove: InterVarsity, 1981.

Hafemann, Scott J., ed. *Biblical Theogy: Retrospect & Prospect*. Downers Grove: InterVarsity, 2002.

Hasel, Gerhard. *Old Testament Theology: Basic Issues in the Current Debate*. Rev. ed. Grand Rapids: Eerdmans, 1975.

_____. *New Testament Theology: Basic Issues in the Crent Debate*. Grand Rapids: Eerdmans, 1978.

Hays, Richard B. *Echoes of Scripture in the Letters of Paul*. New Haven: Yale University Press, 1989.

Horbury, William. *Jewish Messianism and the Cult of Christ*. London: SCM, 1998.

Juel, Donald. *Messianic Exegesis. Christological Interpretation of the Old Testament in Early Christiani*. Philadelphia: Fortress, 1988.

Kaiser, Walter C. Jr. *The Uses of the Old Testament in the New*. Chicago: Moody, 1985.

Köstenberger, Andreas J. and Peter T. O'Brien. *Salvation to the Ends of the Earth: A Biblical Theology of Mission*. New Studies in Biblical Theology 11. Downers Grove: InterVarsity Press, 2001.

Ladd, George Eldon. *A Theology of the New Testament*. Revised edition. Grand Rapids: Eerdmans, 1993.

Lindars, Barnabas. *New Testament Apologetic. The Doctrinal Significance of the Old Testament Quotations*. London: SCM, 1961.

Longenecker, Richard N. *Biblical Exegesis in the Apostolic Period*. 2d ed. Grand Rapids: Eerdmans, 1999.

McComiskey, Thomas Edward. *The Covenants of Promise. A Theology of the Old Testament Covenants*. Grand Rapids: Baker, 1985.

Moo, Douglas J. *The Old Testament in the Gospel Passion Narratives*. Sheffield: Almond, 1983.

Morgan, Robert, ed. *The Nature of New Testament Theology*. Studies
     in Biblical Theology 25. London: SCM, 1973.

Pryor, John W. *John: Evangelist of the Covenant People. The Narrative
     and Themes of the Fourth Gospel*. Downers Grove: InterVarsity,
     1992.

Schlatter, Adolf. *The History of the Christ* and *The Theology of the
     Apostles*. Translated by Andreas J. Köstenberger. Grand Rapids:
     Baker, 1997, 1999.

Vanhoozer, Kevin J. *The Drama of Doctrine: A Canonical-Linguistic
     Approach to Christian Theology*. Louisville: Westminster John
     Knox, 2005.

Wilcox, Max. "On Investigating the Use of the Old Testament in the
     New Testament." Pp. 231–43 in *Text and Interpretation: Studies in
     the New Testament presented to Matthew Black*. Edited by Ernest
     Best and Robert McLachlan Wilson. Cambridge: Cambridge
     University Press, 1979.

Wright, G. E. *God Who Acts: Biblical Theology as Recital*. Studies in
     Biblical Theology 8. London: SCM, 1952.

Wright, N. T. *The New Testament and the People of God*. Minneapolis:
     Fortress, 1992.

APPLICATION
AND PROCLAMATION:
God's Word Coming to Life

CHAPTER 16 OBJECTIVES

1. To impress on the student the need to set aside sufficient time for study.

2. To equip students with the most helpful resources for serious Bible study and sermon/lesson preparation.

3. To show a clear path from text to sermon.

4. To build on the interpretive principles discussed for the different genres in the previous chapters and to set forth a sound methodology for preaching or teaching from the various biblical genres.

5. To discuss ways in which biblical interpreters can apply Scripture to their own lives and help others to do the same.

CHAPTER 16 OUTLINE

A. Introduction
B. Preparing for Study
   1. Time Management
   2. Resources
      a. English Bibles
      b. Language Tools
         i. Hebrew and Greek Grammars
         ii. Lexicons
         iii. Language-Specific Concordances
         iv. Theological/Exegetical Dictionaries
         v. Bible Encyclopedias/Dictionaries
         vi. Bible Atlases
         vii. Old and New Testament Introductions
         viii. Charts
         ix. Commentaries
         x. Systematic and Biblical Theologies
         xi. Communicator's Tools
      c. Electronic Resources
C. From Study to Sermon
   1. Old Testament Narratives
      a. Major Mistakes
      b. Preaching Old Testament Narrative
      c. Lesson/Sermon on 1 Kings 17–19
   2. New Testament Narratives (Gospels and Acts)
      a. Major Mistakes
      b. Preaching New Testament Narratives
      c. Lesson/Sermon on Luke 8:22–25
   3. Special Genres in Narratives
      a. Speeches/Exchanges
      b. Lesson/Sermon on John 2:23–3:21
      c. Parables

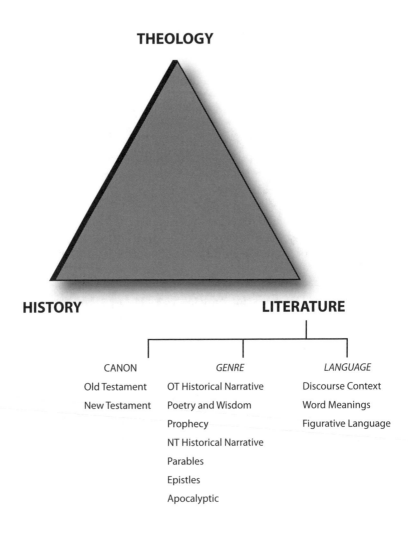

THEOLOGY

HISTORY

LITERATURE

CANON

Old Testament

New Testament

GENRE

OT Historical Narrative

Poetry and Wisdom

Prophecy

NT Historical Narrative

Parables

Epistles

Apocalyptic

LANGUAGE

Discourse Context

Word Meanings

Figurative Language

Chapter 16

GETTING DOWN TO EARTH: USING THE TOOLS, PREACHING AND APPLYING THE WORD

INTRODUCTION

A**T THE END OF A** semester's journey, which is any course in college or seminary, I often wonder what my students will take with them. I wonder this particularly in the case of classes in hermeneutics and Greek. What will the students do with the information they have learned? Will they methodically use it in their ministry, or will they check the class off the list of degree requirements and return to whichever method they were using for interpreting the Bible before they took the class? The latter is really a tragedy (not to mention the waste of time and money), but I fear it happens all too often. At times, the fault lies with us who teach. In the classroom, we didn't really connect the study of Scripture to the real life of personal application and proclamation.

This final chapter is designed to be a practical application of the paradigm presented in this book in order to facilitate and encourage its future use. It will not be the final word on the subject but rather may serve as the point of departure for a lifetime of studying and preaching or teaching the Bible. It is our hope that, as you begin preaching and teaching God's Word, you will start with the suggestions given below, adapt them, expand them, improve them, and if needed abandon them for something that better embodies the principles of exegesis in this book and better communicates the Word of God.

PREPARING FOR STUDY

Time Management

I once had a conversation with an unsatisfied church member regarding their pastor. One of the complaints was that he planned his sermons too far in advance. Upon further inquiry, I found that the parishioner thought it would be much more spiritual for this pastor to "pray a sermon down" on Saturday night rather than engaging in methodical study. Nothing could be further from the truth. By his grace, God can use "Saturday night specials," but a steady diet of these "microwave dinners" will be sure to starve a congregation spiritually. If you are a pastor, you should set aside regular time each week to study God's Word seriously, to contemplate its message prayerfully, and to make detailed preparations to deliver it. Whichever method you use, you must set aside *time* for study. In the long run, it is impossible to be effective in proclaiming God's Word without spending quality time in serious study and preparation.

This is no small task. Time management in day-to-day living is difficult enough; managing time for your study of Scripture requires you to jump over a series of even more difficult hurdles (not the least being spiritual warfare, since Satan has no interest in you studying God's Word and teaching it to others!). Those who engage in a regular preaching ministry in addition to holding down a regular job must juggle the demands of work, family, and the need for regular time to study the Bible. This calls for a considerable measure of commitment and self-discipline.

Pastors, for their part, have to balance the duties of a shepherd and those of a prophet. All the while, Sunday is always coming. People have crises, babies, deaths in the family, and other unscheduled needs. Count on these unexpected demands to occur at the worst possible moments. For this reason, planning a schedule that includes time for study requires flexibility. Occasionally, the schedule will need to be adjusted. You'll just have to squeeze the balloon to find the time, and occasionally you won't get to spend the time you wanted or even needed. However, this will be the exception rather than the rule if you have a general schedule that you set, guard, and keep.

Resources

Delving into your study assumes that there are good materials once you get there. Gathering good resources is half the battle. Every Christian ought to have a few reference works to help them understand the Bible. To be sure, those who work in God's vineyard need to fear him, love his Word, and be faithful in character—but what would a worker be without his or her tools? We will list eleven essential types of reference works and suggest a couple of standards in the field.[1]

English Bibles

At last count, there were ninety English Bibles produced in the twentieth century and nine produced in the twenty-first century. What is more, with many translations available on the internet, you have a wide variety at our fingertips. All you need is an internet connection.[2]

Regarding English translations, there are a wide variety of approaches. Suffice it to say here that the spectrum has "easy to read" at one end and "accurate" at the other. Translations at each end of the spectrum can be of value. With regard to interpretation, accurate is preferred. The freer translations often help you see the big picture better and help in applying the message. A good interpreter of Scripture will have several English translations on hand. You may want to use a translation using a formal equivalence approach ("word for word") such as the NASB alongside one employing using a dynamic equivalence approach ("phrase by phrase"; e.g., the NIV).[3]

---

1. This list is adapted from Paul D. Wegner, *Using Old Testament Hebrew in Preaching: A Guide for Students and Pastors* (Grand Rapids: Kregel, 2009), 29-65.
2. See, e.g., www.bible.logos.com; www.biblegateway.com; or http://unbound.biola.edu/. These have multiple English Bibles available to the student.
3. For a concise survey, see Andreas J. Köstenberger, L. Scott Kellum, and Charles L. Quarles, *The Cradle, the Cross, and the Crown: An Introduction to the New Testament* (Nashville: B&H, 2009), 35–38 (with further references).

Language Tools

Hebrew and Greek Grammars

Pay close attention to the section on Old Testament Hebrew and New Testament Greek in chapter 12. Most of us will have a beginning grammar as required in our basic Greek course. In addition, the student should have one or several more advanced grammars. Dan Wallace's *Greek Grammar Beyond the Basics* (also available in an abridged version) and Blass and Debrunner are two standards in the field.[4]

Lexicons

It pays to have a good lexicon for both Greek and Hebrew. Many Greek lexicons are available to the student of Scripture. The general rule of thumb is that you get what you pay for. The standard in the field for Greek is affectionately known as BDAG, that is, the Bauer, Danker, Arndt, and Gingrich lexicon.[5] In Hebrew, there is the two-volume work known as *HALOT* and the Brown-Driver-Briggs lexicon (a.k.a. BDB).[6] Another valuable resource is Louw and Nida's Greek-English lexicon based on semantic domains (i.e., it groups related words together); it is supremely useful when performing a semantic field study.[7]

Language-Specific Concordances

A concordance is invaluable in determining where a Greek or Hebrew word is used in the respective Testament because few English translations

---

4. Daniel B. Wallace, *Greek Grammar beyond the Basics* (Grand Rapids: Zondervan, 1996); and F. Blass and A. Debrunner, *A Greek Grammar of the New Testament and Other Early Christian Literature*, trans. and ed. Robert W. Funk (Chicago: University of Chicago Press, 1961).
5. Frederick W. Danker, Walter Bauer, and William Arndt, *A Greek-English Lexicon of the New Testament and Other Early Christian Literature*, 3d ed. (Chicago: University of Chicago Press, 2000).
6. Ludwig Köhler, Walter Baumgartner, M. E. J. Richardson, and Johann Jakob Stamm, *The Hebrew and Aramaic Lexicon of the Old Testament* (Leiden: E.J. Brill, 1994); Francis Brown, Edward Robinson, S. R. Driver, Charles A. Briggs, and Francis Brown, *The New Brown, Driver, Briggs, Gesenius Hebrew and English Lexicon: With an Appendix Containing the Biblical Aramaic* (Peabody, MA: Hendrickson, 1979); and Andreas J. Köstenberger, and Raymond Bouchoc, *The Book Study Concordance of the Greek New Testament* (Nashville: B&H, 2003).
7. J. P. Louw and Eugene Nida, *Greek-English Lexicon of the New Testament Based on Semantic Domains*, 2 vols. (New York: United Bible Societies, 1988, 1999).

will be consistent in translating a given word (nor should they always be!). The standard Greek concordance is Moulton and Geden's 6th edition.[8] Another valuable resource is Köstenberger and Bouchoc's *Book Study Concordance*, which collects the lexical stock of each New Testament book. For Hebrew, you may want to purchase the *Concordance to the Hebrew Old Testament* by Lisowski, Roost, and Rüger, or the less expensive work by Kohlenberger and Swanson, *The Hebrew-English Concordance to the Old Testament*.[9]

Theological/Exegetical Dictionaries

A theological dictionary is a collection of in-depth word studies that are designed to show the theological content of a given concept. Although such a compilation can be quite valuable, each entry should be critically evaluated. Regarding the New Testament, the standard in the field is the *Theological Dictionary of the New Testament*, known as *TDNT*, and Colin Brown's *New International Dictionary of New Testament Theology* (*NIDNTT*) is also well respected.[10] Regarding the Old Testament, there is a companion volume to the *TDNT* referred to as *TDOT*. The work by Harris, Archer, and Waltke, *Theological Wordbook of the Old Testament*, is also highly regarded.[11] The new standard is the five-volume *Dictionary of Old Testament Theology and Exegesis* edited by Willem VanGemeren.[12]

---

8.   W. F. Moulton, A. S. Geden, and I. Howard Marshall, *Concordance to the Greek New Testament*, 6th ed. (London: T&T Clark, 2002).

9.   Gerhard Lisowksy, Leonhard Rost, Hans Peter Rüger, *Concordance to the Hebrew Old Testament: Konkordanz zum Hebräischen Alten Testament* (Peabody, MA: Hendrickson, 2010); John R. Kohlenberger and James A. Swanson, *The Hebrew-English Concordance to the Old Testament: With the New International Version* (Grand Rapids: Zondervan, 1998).

10. Gerhard Kittel, Geoffrey Bromiley, and Gerhard Friedrich, eds., *Theological Dictionary of the New Testament*, 10 vols. (Grand Rapids: Eerdmans, 1964); and Colin Brown, ed., *The New International Dictionary of New Testament Theology*, 3 vols. (Grand Rapids: Zondervan, 1975).

11. G. Johannes Botterweck and Helmer Ringgren, eds., *Theological Dictionary of the Old Testament*, 10 vols. (Grand Rapids: Eerdmans, 1977); and R. Laird Harris, Gleason L. Archer, and Bruce K. Waltke, *Theological Wordbook of the Old Testament* (Chicago: Moody, 1980).

12. Willem A. VanGemeren, gen. ed., *New International Dictionary of Old Testament Theology & Exegesis*, 5 vols. (Grand Rapids: Zondervan, 1996); see esp. the index of semantic fields at the beginning of volume 5.

Bible Encyclopedias/Dictionaries

A solid essay-length treatment of various matters pertaining to the Old and New Testaments is very helpful. The standard in the field is the *Anchor Bible Dictionary*. We would also recommend the new *Zondervan Encyclopedia of the Bible*.[13]

Other helpful resources are *The Holman Illustrated Bible Dictionary* and *The New Bible Dictionary*.[14]

Bible Atlases

Knowing biblical geography is often quite helpful in exegesis. For example, knowing geography really helps one to gauge the impact of Samson's act in Judges 16:3. The text assumes that we know that the mount opposite Hebron is a whopping 38 miles from Gaza! The juggernaut of Bible atlases is the *Tübingen Bibelatlas* (not to worry, it has English subtitles!).[15] Other well-respected atlases are the *Holman Bible Atlas* and the *Kregel Bible Atlas*.[16]

The most recent atlases are the massive *ESV Bible Atlas*, which is exceptionally well produced and comes highly recommended, and the revised *Zondervan Atlas of the Bible*.[17]

Old and New Testament Introductions

A solid, conservative introduction to the Testaments is invaluable tools to the exegete. With regard to the New Testament, we are partial to *The Cradle, the Cross, and the Crown* by Köstenberger, Kellum, and Quarles. In the Old Testament, Longman and Dillard's *Introduction to the Old Testament* is a standard.[18]

---

13. David Noel Freedman, ed., *The Anchor Bible Dictionary*, 6 vols. (New York: Doubleday, 1992); and Merrill C. Tenney and Moisés Silva, eds., *Zondervan Encyclopedia of the Bible*, 5 vols. (Grand Rapids: Zondervan, 2009).

14. *The Holman Illustrated Bible Dictionary* (ed. Charles W. Draper et al.; Nashville: B&H, 2003); *The New Bible Dictionary* (ed. I. Howard Marshall; Downers Grove: intervarsity, 1996)

15. Siegfried Mittmann and Götz Schmitt, eds., *Tübinger Bibelatlas* (Stuttgart: Deutsche Bibelgesellschaft, 2001).

16. Thomas V. Brisco, *Holman Bible Atlas*, Holman Reference (Nashville: B&H, 1998); and Tim Dowley, *The Kregel Bible Atlas* (Grand Rapids: Kregel, 2003).

17. John D. Currid and David P. Barrett, *ESV Bible Atlas* (Wheaton: Crossway, 2010); Carl G. Rasmussen, *Zondervan Atlas of the Bible* (rev. ed.; Grand Rapids: Zondervan, 2010).

18. Köstenberger, Kellum, and Quarles, *Cradle, the Cross, and the Crown*; Tremper Longman III and Raymond B. Dillard, *An Introduction to the Old Testament*, 2d ed.

Charts

Both Kregel and Zondervan have a series of books of charts that summarize chronological, archaeological, thematic, and other very good information in an easy-to-access format. Often these are both thought-provoking and informative.[19]

Commentaries

To paraphrase the ancient teacher, "Of the making of commentaries, there is no end." Today, we have both academic and lay commentaries, preaching commentaries, application commentaries, background commentaries, and ever further subsets. With regard to buying commentaries, we suggest caution. First, avoid devotional commentaries in preparing an exegetically-based message (their place is in application—not interpretation). Academic exegetical commentaries (i.e., commentaries that deal with the original languages verse by verse) are the best for exegesis. They will cover the issues and debates that impact exegesis.

However, here the buyer must beware. The value of a commentary is often in the eye of the beholder. Few are written from a solidly evangelical perspective, and some series are mixed in this regard (e.g., the Word Biblical Commentary). What is more, a commentary series will also inevitably be uneven with regard to how well the individual volumes handle the text. It will benefit you to do some research on these matters before buying a commentary.[20] Overall, the rule is: don't buy an entire series, but

---

(Grand Rapids: Zondervan, 2006). See also D. A. Carson and Douglas J. Moo, *An Introduction to the New Testament*, 2d ed. (Grand Rapids: Zondervan, 2005); and Andrew E. Hill and John H. Walton, *An Introduction to the New Testament to the Old Testament?*, 3d ed. (Grand Rapids: Zondervan, 2009).

19. One of the more recent examples is Mark Wilson, *Charts on the Book of Revelation: Literary, Historical, and Theological Perspectives* (Grand Rapids: Kregel, 2007).

20. I often recommend that people just starting to build their academic libraries peruse D. A. Carson's *New Testament Commentary Survey*. It is now in its 6th edition from Baker at a very reasonable price. There is also an Old Testament version by Tremper Longman III. John Glynn's *Commentary and Reference Survey: A Comprehensive Guide to Biblical and Theological Resources* is also a good reference tool, as is as is Daniel L. Akin's *Building a Theological Library* (available online at http://apps.sebts.edu/president/wp-content/uploads/2008/08/building-a-theological-library-revised-81208.pdf). When using these resources, keep in mind that not all will agree with the opinion of a given writer, but these will give you a representative evangelical perspective. You can also often see previews of books at google books or read reader reviews on www.amazon.com, so you can see for yourself before you buy.

pick the best commentaries on any given book of the Bible based on the credentials of the author of the commentary and on the available reviews of a particular volume.

Systematic and Biblical Theologies

A Systematic Theology book with a Scripture index is often a very helpful resource to discern what matters of theology are germane to your text. This is not a fool-proof method, but one that will get you thinking about the theological implications of your passage. Sometimes you will discover aspects of your passage that you would not have considered otherwise. A standard in the field is Wayne Grudem's *Systematic Theology* that comes in both an unabridged and abridged versions. Also highly competent is Millard Erickson's *Christian Theology*.[21]

Communicator's Tools

The ultimate job of the exegete is to communicate what he or she has learned to his or her hearers. To do this, there are a few items that ought to be in your library. The first group is a series of works on English grammar. You should have a good English dictionary to help you use words correctly. You should also have a good thesaurus to choose the correct word. Finally, since bad grammar is a hindrance to good communication, you should have an English grammar to articulate your message using proper English grammar.[22]

Beyond these basic grammar tools, the good wordsmith will also have a series of books, databases, or services that will prove helpful in finding quotes and illustrations.[23] Sadly, your hearers will remember your illustra-

---

21. Wayne Grudem, *Systematic Theology: An Introduction to Biblical Doctrine* (Grand Rapids: Zondervan, 1994); idem and Jeff Purswell, *Bible Doctrine: Essential Teachings of the Christian Faith* (Grand Rapids: Zondervan, 1999); Millard J. Erickson, *Christian Theology*, 2d ed. (Grand Rapids: Baker, 1998).

22. We recommend the following: *Merriam-Webster Collegiate Dictionary* and *Merriam-Webster Collegiate Thesaurus* (in print, on CD-ROM, or via online subscription); Diana Hacker, *A Writer's Reference*, 6th ed. (Boston: Bedford/St. Martin's, 2009), idem, *Rules for Writers*, 6th ed. (Boston: Bedford/St. Martin's, 2009); idem, *The Bedford Handbook*, 8th ed. (Boston: Bedford/St. Martin's, 2009); see also this author's website, http://www.dianahacker.com.

23. Our recommendation is *Nelson's Complete Book of Stories, Illustrations & Quotes*; *1001 Quotes, Illustrations, and Humorous Stories for Preachers, Teachers, and Writers* (Nashville: Thomas Nelson, 2000); see also http://www.autoillustrator.com. Thanks

tions longer than your sermon content, so make every effort to illustrate the text well. Do not subscribe to the urban preaching legend method of getting sermon illustrations. That is, do not simply repeat the things you've heard other preachers say or your have read in anthologies of their sermons. Verify the content of a given illustration as best you can.

Electronic Resources

There are a great many electronic resources available to you either on the internet (in both free and for-pay varieties) or through applications for your computer. Let's talk about the internet first. There are quite a few sites that will help you with Hebrew and Greek (frankly, more with Greek than with Hebrew). One of the most helpful sites on the web regarding the Greek New Testament is the laparola site. (http://www.laparola.net/greco/index.php; yes, it's an Italian website in English about the Greek New Testament). On the Greek New Testament page, you have access to and can compare several editions of the Greek New Testament, including the UBS4 text, Westcott and Hort, and the Byzantine text type. Other options include searching for individual Greek and English words and even by Louw and Nida's semantic domains. You also have access to the textual variants and a description of the age and text type of each witness through a tool tip that appears when pulling the cursor over the witness. Though put together by one individual, it is an amazingly sophisticated site.[24]

By way of brief assessment, one should consider laparola like other open-source platforms in other fields—it is constantly being updated and corrected. What we are able to access that is otherwise unavailable in electronic format is amazing (e.g., the Münster textual variants). However, a great number of language works cannot be linked to the website because of copyright restrictions. Thus, for example, the lexicons hyperlinked to the individual words are Thayer's and Strong's rather than the more detailed, technical works.

Other internet sites could easily take up the rest of our space. Although information from the internet can be obtained quickly, be careful about internet sources. First, avoid blogs. To paraphrase Dale Carnegie, "Any

---

are due John Burkett, director of the writing center at Southeastern Seminary, for the recommendations in this and the previous footnote.
24. Richard Wilson, according to the website.

fool can blog, and most fools do."[25] Only a blog from a recognized scholar or a person whose materials have been proven valuable over time should be seriously considered—and then verified. In other words, a non-refereed post can only alert you to potentially valuable information; you still have to check out whether or not it is accurate.

Second, avoid websites by individuals who do not provide detailed documentation for their information. Johndoeonline.com may have some good information, but unless it is independently verified, you have no choice but to consider it useless.

Third, sites such as Wikipedia (www.wikipedia.com), that is, user-generated information, are a good place to begin searching for information but insufficient to use by itself. In other words, the lack of refereeing leaves such sites open to various sorts of problems, if not malicious manipulation and egregious error. You must verify every piece of information found on these sites by other reliable means.

Sites from trusted sources are the most valuable information. Some are trusted because of their institutional connection (e.g., www.bible.org/ Dallas Seminary). Others are relied upon for having been useful over a long period of time (e.g., www.laparola.net/greco) or come from a trusted scholar (e.g., www.reasonablefaith.org/William Lane Craig). The good news is that there are more valuable sites than we could reasonably list here. But for every good site, there are many others that should be held at arm's length or be ignored altogether.

Another exceedingly valuable source of information is google books.[26] At this website, you may search the contents of some seven million books (and growing). The books in public domain are available to download for free. Many standard works in the field of biblical studies (such as the ICC commentary series) are available in this manner. Truly, you could fill your hard drive with the works available to you. But the problem with works in public domain is that they are rather old (by law). Not only do older works run the danger of being outdated, they will not reference the latest linguistic and archaeological discoveries, deal with current debates, or always have updated paradigms. The reader must be discerning about what he or she finds there.

---

25. The actual quote is "Any fool can criticize, condemn, and complain—and most fools do."
26. http://books.google.com.

Newer books are often accessible as a "limited preview." Here a large portion of the book is available to view online. Regarding commentaries, the passage you are exegeting may very well be in an accessible portion of the text. Many are given in a "snippet view," which is virtually useless for research. Great is the rejoicing of the pastor who finds his passage in a limited preview!

In the near future, due to a lawsuit settlement, this is going to change.[27] The public domain books will still be available as a full review and be downloadable. The current books that are out of print but still under copyright will eventually be available for purchase online, as well as books currently in print. In short, the future looks bright for electronic publishing. Largely gone are the days of having to travel to the bookstore to get your hands on a book, or wait feverishly for the mail to deliver it to you (though there will always be exceptions).

Amazon.com has pioneered the downloading of books through their Kindle platform. Currently, some 360,000 volumes are available to download at a reduced price.[28] In addition to the Kindle, e-readers are available from Sony and Barnes and Noble, which has a version called "Nook." Eventually, there will be more and more e-readers that enter the market. Like the Kindle and the Nook, one expects these e-readers will feel and look increasingly like the pages of a book. Though pricey at present, it is likely that the price will drop as production mounts. In the meantime, amazon.com has released a free reader application for the PC and the iPhone, with no expensive e-reader necessary (mac and blackberry due out shortly). When we need a book, we now have the option of purchasing it at a discount price and for immediate use.

While you are spending money for your library, do include a Bible software program. While the investment seems high, you may replace several resources such as concordances, atlases, Gospel synopses/harmonies, lexicons, and other reference works by using software. Generally, for the professional exegete, low-end, low-cost software you see in many general

---

27. For the full description of the settlement and how things will change, see http://books.google.com/googlebooks/agreement.

28. For example, at the time of writing, our New Testament Introduction *The Cradle, the Cross, and the Crown* is available through amazon.com for $59.99 plus shipping and handling. The Kindle edition is available immediately for $39.41. No waiting, no shipping costs, less money.

outlets and bookstores is insufficient. These products simply will not include the resources that will make them very useful to you. Although free resources such as Olivetree and E-sword have a place (especially in the smart-phone market), they will, for the most part, prove insufficient for serious exegetes who engage the original languages. The general rule should be, pay as much as you can afford on your choice of Bible software. If what you can afford are the free and lower-priced versions, they will still be helpful.[29]

The GRAMCORD Institute's GRAMCORD for Windows was the first major player in Bible software tools. It is still available in a Windows and a Mac version but has been integrated into the Accordance software that many find quite satisfying. The GRAMCORD Lite, however, may be the best app for a smart phone. Accordance is the premier Bible software for the Mac environment, although PC programs can be run in a Mac through certain programs such as Microsoft Virtual PC, Boot Camp, or a simple Mac emulator.

Logos and BibleWorks are the major players right now in the premier Bible software category.[30] Both BibleWorks and Logos can do all the grammatical and lexical searches that the serious exegete will ever need. Each has a concordance function that goes beyond anything a printed concordance can do. For example, searches involving grammatical constructions, paired words, or semantic domains are difficult, if not impossible, in a printed concordance. These typically take less than a second electronically.[31]

You can also diagram sentences; compare text types, versions, and translations; reference paradigms quickly; hear both modern and Erasmian pronunciations of Greek; parse words immediately; use lexicons at the click of the mouse; quickly look up a grammatical issue in a Hebrew or Greek grammar; use and/or create cross references and notes; connect to external links (like laparola); do textual criticism; examine major biblical manuscripts (visually and lexically); and browse exegetical resources.

---

29. For an example of a free but very useful website, see www.NLTinterlinear.com, which features the complete NLT text with Hebrew and Greek word studies and many, many other useful features.
30. At the time of writing, the versions are Logos 4 and BibleWorks 9. New upgrades appear at the approximate rate of one every two years (as is the nature of technology today). See also www.mystudybible.com.
31. This depends on the speed of your computer, of course.

I could continue, but suffice it to say that research, lexicography, and personal Bible study are both quick and affordable through a premier Bible software program such as Accordance, Logos, or BibleWorks.[32]

The major difference, to the non-technical pastor or seminary professor, is the philosophy behind each program. Logos is part of the Libronix library system. That is, it is a library program with a very good Bible module. It is a massive database. At the time of writing, the platinum version of Logos offers 1,150 e-books with 1,000s more available to purchase. It comes in a variety of forms with matching prices (from $150.00 for a bare-bones home version to nearly $1,700.00 for the platinum version). It can be a virtual pastor's study. Through the i-Phone version, this library can go on the move with you even more easily.

BibleWorks, on the other hand, uses a different philosophy. It is all about exegesis and has little interest in being a virtual library. You will find digitized books, but these are usually confined to exegetical works (such as Metzger's 2d edition of his textual commentary, or Archer and Chirichigno's *Old Testament Quotations in the New Testament*). BibleWorks is blazing fast compared to Logos because it is searching a database and not a digitized manuscript. BibleWorks also has some built-in flexibility with external programs. That is, it does not have an up-to-date list of New Testament textual variants available in the analysis window but can be linked to the laparola website, so that by right-clicking on a Greek verse you get all the text-critical information at laparola. Its price (less than $400), speed, and focus make BibleWorks a very attractive choice.

The competition between software companies spells good news for the consumer. If one comes up with an innovation, another will not be far behind. So which software should you choose? My recommendation usually hinges on the needs and desires of the consumer. You should make your choice based on what you can afford and how the philosophy of the program fits your needs.

If you want a digital library, Logos is for you. I often recommend it to students who are preparing to go to the mission field. Shipping hundreds of books is expensive, bulky, and time-consuming. Through a digital

---

32. Personally, I find my sermon preparation time has been cut by half to a quarter by using Bible software.

library, you can take your library on your laptop or smart phone. Others, though not going to the mission field, simply love the ease and speed of a digital library. More than one pastor has begun selling his print books to buy the less expensive digital versions. If you want it all in one program, Logos is for you. Just make sure you have a backup! The computer crash is fast becoming the equivalent of the house burning down.

If all you want is exegesis, BibleWorks is your choice.[33] The focus, speed, and powerful tools in BibleWorks make it the ideal version in this regard. You also might want to diversify the programs you use. An e-reader (perhaps employing google books), in combination with Bible-Works (or another language program) and the Theological Journal library could be a powerful combination for the serious student of the Bible.

Whatever version you choose (and each will have its vigorous proponents), there are several mistakes you should avoid. First, avoid thinking that the programs are perfect. All are dependent on human data entry at some point. Thus there can and will be errors in them. A computer program that parses verbs and nouns for you is only as good as the person tagging them. Second, the language tools are useless to you unless you know at least the basics of grammar (or know how to look up its significance). The program may facilitate your reading of Hebrew and Greek, but it will not replace it. Third, you must be familiar with the terminology employed by the program. For example, some will describe deponents as "middles" without really denying the existence of deponents. Being unfamiliar with the program's terminology might stimulate some bizarre heresies! Fourth, never be satisfied with one search. The search is only as good as the parameters you set. Think about other options that you might have left out. For example, when searching through a semantic domain, do not neglect to look for negated antonyms. The concept expressed by "not condemned" and "forgiven" is essentially the same. Fifth, remember the distinction between formal grammatical constructions and their actual usage. For example, the Greek word *oida* is perfect in form but used as a present. Most software will tag it as a perfect by virtue of its form. Always think critically when using such tools!

---

33. Logos does offer an original languages module, but in my opinion BibleWorks is better for pure exegesis.

FROM STUDY TO SERMON

Once you have done your exegesis, you are ready to begin preparing your sermon or Bible study. While a study or sermon may take many forms—topical, textual, or expository—our primary concern is to prepare an expository message. It is our conviction that the majority of preaching should be expository, that is, explaining a biblical text. A steady diet of topical messages or unconnected texts is hazardous for the health of your audience. We must hear the Word of God in context. What follows is a suggestion for generating a study or sermon outline from your exegetical study.[34]

We often wrestle with the outline of our sermon study, but this is really unnecessary. The task is to *discover* our outline (again, remember Schlatter's hermeneutic of perception), not to *come up with one*. That is, if we have done our job in exegesis, we have our outline: it is the literary shape of the text. Since the literary shape is determined by the genre, we will examine the process genre by genre. We will begin with narratives.

Both Old Testament and New Testament narratives have similar structures and interpretative procedures. However, each brings its own distinctive issues that must be carefully navigated in order to faithfully proclaim the message of Scripture. Therefore, we will begin with Old Testament narratives and then build off its foundation to discuss their New Testament equivalent.

Old Testament Narratives

The issues pertaining to interpreting Old Testament narratives are covered in chapter 5. What follows is a suggestion building off the discussion in that chapter. Old Testament narratives are told to make a theological point of one kind or another. They are often longer than their New Testament counterpart and more subtle. For this reason, paying attention to the details is important. It should be the aim of the communicator of God's Word to

---

34. For an excellent treatment of preaching consistent with the hermeneutic triad proposed in the present volume, see Sidney Greidanus, *The Modern Preacher and the Ancient Text: Interpreting and Preaching Biblical Literature* (Grand Rapids: Eerdmans, 1988). Chapters 3–5 in Greidanus's work are devoted to literary, historical, and theological interpretation, respectively. Another helpful volume containing chapters on preaching from the different genres of Scripture is Graeme Goldsworthy, *Preaching the Whole Bible as Christian Scripture: The Application of Biblical Theology to Expository Preaching* (Grand Rapids: Eerdmans, 2000).

teach the story without losing the effect or the point of the narrative. Your privilege is to tell the same story as that told by the biblical author.

Major Mistakes

There are at least five major land mines to avoid when teaching or preaching an Old Testament narrative.

1. Be careful not to preach or teach a text while being ignorant of its literary context (e.g., how do the accounts of Noah and the flood or of David slaying Goliath fit into the bigger picture?). A joke is no good without the punch-line, and a story is incomplete without its component parts. There is no portion of a story that is not important to the story (or else it wouldn't be there!).

2. Be careful not to impose alien structural divisions on the text. This is the problem with most macro-chiastic structures applied to Old Testament narratives. Chiasm is more likely to be found in poetic literature than in narrative genres. But this is not the only potential stumbling block. The redaction-critical studies popular in the last century often dismembered the story for what ultimately seemed to be arbitrary reasons while violating the actual biblical narrative.

3. Be careful not to allegorize Old Testament narratives. Picking out elements to impose a "deeper" level of meaning is not particularly helpful, not to mention unfaithful to the text. Excluded here is the issue of typology (on which see the previous chapter).

4. Be careful not to impose unstated elements onto the narrative. Unless the text actually states these, we cannot know the feelings, thoughts, motives, and other sentiments of any given character. Be careful not to project onto the characters and events things that you are not specifically told. This does not mean that it is always improper to read empathetically between the lines. It is important, however, to be keenly aware of

what the text explicitly says and what we supply by our own imagination. Only what is in keeping with the authorial intention expressed in the text carries with it biblical authority.

5. Be ready to address familiar characters from a fresh perspective. Gideon is not a positive role model throughout his life. Samson was not a negative example *all* his life. All human beings are fallen and complex creatures. True stories will depict them in this way, warts and all. Do not let popular opinions sway you in this matter one way or another. Read the story with fresh eyes.

Preaching Old Testament Narratives

The controlling philosophy for all that follows is this: *the rhetorical structure of your lesson or sermon should be based on the literary structure of your text*.[35] Thus, building an expository study or sermon from a narrative begins by identifying each individual scene of a narrative cycle (sometimes called an "episode"). The scenes cluster together to form the cycle. In doing so, the biblical author (under the guidance of the Holy Spirit) is making a theological point. Thus, we should ask: what is the main idea of each scene, and what point is made when these scenes are stitched together to form a cycle?

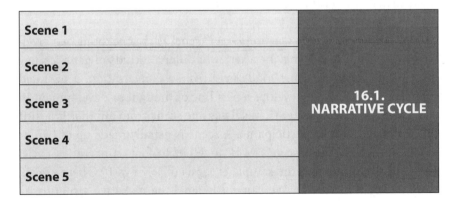

Step 1: Identify and interpret the scenes of the narrative cycle. Step 1 is applying what you have learned in this book. (Specifically, consult the

---

35. For an excellent discussion of preaching Hebrew narratives, see Greidanus, *Modern Preacher*, chapter 9.

Guidelines for Interpreting Old Testament Historical Narrative.) To tell the same story, your sermon or lesson structure should match the structure of the text. As to the structure of a narrative, most are built on what we will call "cycles" that consist of scenes related by character, place, setting, or incidents. Mildred Larson and Richard Young are particularly helpful in this regard.[36] There are two basic plot structures: problem-resolution plots and occasion-outcome plots. The major difference is whether or not there is a problem.

If the text does not describe a problem but a simple event, the structure is essentially quite simple: setting, occasion, and outcome; there may or may not be a sequel. The basic structure is that of a series of actions performed. There are a number of stimulus-response events that occur. These may or may not have a variety of different genres and imbedded genres such as dialogue. They are generally the "reporting of events" type described in the chapter on Old Testament historical narrative.

Most plot structures in biblical narrative take the problem-resolution form. Larson lists setting, problem, resolving incident, complication, and resolution as the backbone of a problem-resolution plot structure (there may or may not be a complicating factor, and if there is, it may be placed before or after the resolution). Note that both scenes and cycles employ these structures to varying levels of complexity.

a. Identify the component scenes. A "scene" is the backbone of a given narrative. These scenes may be a series of different kinds of genres. They may not all have the same mode (a speech, a conversation, a narrated event, etc.). Each scene develops a new line of thought or development in the story. The main marker that isolates one scene from another is a shift in time, place, and/or participants. A scene is usually made up of two or more characters. These scenes work together to form a narrative cycle. For example, remember the sample exegesis of 1 Kings 19. There are six basic scenes to the cycle. We can easily label the narrative structure as follows:

---

36. The following is adapted from Mildred L. Larson, *Meaning-Based Translation: A Guide to Cross-Language Equivalence*, 2d ed. (Lanham, MD: University Press of America, 1998), 401–4. See also Richard A. Young, *Intermediate New Testament Greek: A Linguistic and Exegetical Approach* (Nashville: B&H, 1994), 249–50.

Scene 1 *Prologue (Setting):* Elijah's call (17:1–6)	
Scene 2 *Development (Preliminary incident):* Elijah at Zarephath (17:7–24)	
Scene 3 *Crisis (Problem):* Elijah's message to King Ahab (18:1–19)	**16.2.** **NARRATIVE CYCLE**
Scene 4 *Climax (Resolving incident):* Elijah vs. the prophets of Baal and Asherah (18:20–46)	
Scene 5 *Denouement (Complication):* Elijah's flight to Horeb (19:1–18)	
Scene 6 *Epilogue (Sequel):* Elijah and the call of Elisha (19:19–21)	

But notice that each scene also has a narrative structure. We could outline it as follows:

I.   *Prologue (Setting):* Elijah's call (17:1–6)

    Setting and preliminary incident (17:1): God declares a drought through Elijah

    Problem (17:2–4): Elijah must hide and the ravens will feed him

    Resolution (17:5–7): God uses the ravens to feed Elijah but the brook dries up

II.   *Development (Preliminary incident):* Elijah at Zarephath (17:7–24)

    Setting (17:7–9): God instructs: "Go to the widow of Zarephath"

    Preliminary incident (17:10–11): Elijah asks for provisions

Problem (17:12): The widow and her son have only enough for a last little meal

Resolving incident (17:13–16): The Lord caused a miraculous provision

Complication (17:17–21): The Widow's son dies

Resolution (17:22–24): The Lord raises the boy—the widow's statement that Elijah is truly a man of God hammers home the point of the scene[37]

III. *Crisis (Problem):* Elijah's message to King Ahab (18:1–19)

Setting (18:1): After three years, God instructs Elijah to announce rain to Ahab.

Preliminary incident (18:2–8): Elijah meets and tells Obadiah to report to Ahab that he is coming to meet him

Problem (18:9–15): Obadiah is hesitant

Resolution (18:16–19): Elijah meets Ahab[38]

IV. *Climax (Resolving incident):* Elijah vs. the prophets of Baal and Asherah (18:20–46)[39]

Setting (18:20): They meet at Mount Carmel

Preliminary incident (18:21–24): Elijah challenges God's people

---

37. Note the progression in the miraculous. Droughts often happen, and being fed by ravens is unusual, but not overtly miraculous. The unending oil and flour and raising the boy from the dead is clearly God's approval on the man of God.
38. This scene lets us know the difficulty the people of God experience from Ahab, Ahab's evil heart, and sets the stage for the next scene.
39. This section is clearly the peak of the narrative. Note especially the length of the scene.

Problem (18:25–29): The Contest: the God that answers by
fire is the true God

Complication (18:30–37): Elijah makes the offering of God
difficult[40]

Resolution (18:38–40): God consumed the sacrifice, the
altar, and the water

Sequel (18:41–46): God sends the rain

V.   *Denouement (Complication):* Elijah's flight to Horeb (19:1–18)

Setting (19:1–3): Jezebel seeks the life of Elijah

Problem (19:4): Elijah is fearful and discouraged

Complication (19:11–14): God speaks to Elijah

Resolution (19:15–18): Elijah is rebuked

VI. *Epilogue (Sequel):* Elijah and the call of Elisha (19:19–21)

Setting (19:19a): Elijah departs

Occasion (19:19b–20): Elijah calls Elisha to be his servant

Outcome (19:21) Elisha follows Elijah

As you identify the scenes and observe how they build the cycle, remember that there may be varying levels of complexity. For example, a
narrative cycle may employ a series of complicating factors before the

---

40. Here we note that Elijah does just the opposite of the prophets of Baal. There is no
mention of them having to build an altar like Elijah had to build his. Their offering
was dry and on dry surroundings. Elijah's was soaking wet. They prayed for hours,
Elijah only uttered a few words. Their "god" had it easy; Yahweh showed that things
that are difficult for human beings are no trouble for him.

problem is resolved. Once you are comfortable with the structure of the cycle, examine the text for the main message. Ask yourself the question: What is it communicating beyond the brute facts of history?

b. Discover the main message (or point) of the narrative cycle. Each narrative cycle has an intended point and purpose. The scenes will build to develop the intended point and purpose of the cycle. Follow the Guidelines for Interpreting Old Testament Historical Narrative to guide your investigation. Explore the history, literature, and theology presented. The bulk of your work will be here!

Now we telescope out to look at the point of the whole cycle. The book of Kings is ordered around the ascension and fall of Solomon (1 Kings 1–11); the account of the two kingdoms (1 Kings 12–2 Kings 17); and the fall of Judah (2 Kings 18–25).[41] The "Elijah cycle" takes place in the large center section and brings a ray of hope to the people of God in the midst of an apostate culture.

Specifically, after the death of Omri, Ahab takes the throne and goes beyond Omri's abominations so that "Ahab . . . did more to provoke the LORD, the God of Israel, to anger than did all the kings of Israel before him" (1 Kgs. 16:33). The very next verse sets the stage for the "Elijah cycle": "In Ahab's time, Hiel of Bethel rebuilt Jericho. He laid its foundations at the cost of his firstborn son Abiram, and he set up its gates at the cost of his youngest son Segub, in accordance with the word of the LORD spoken by Joshua son of Nun" (1 Kgs. 16:34). Regardless of how Hiel lost his children, whether by sacrifice or tragedy, this took place in fulfillment of the prophecy in Joshua 6:26. The point was that God was still in charge; his word was still valid. This theme will be dramatically underlined through the "Elijah cycle" by highlighting the certainty of God's Word.

Elijah declares that there will be no rain except by his word (1 Kgs. 17:1), and the word of the Lord sends Elijah to Cherith (17:2) and then to Zarephath (17:8). There, the word of the Lord announces the miraculous provision of oil and flour (17:14) and makes clear that the word of the Lord was efficacious (17:16). At the raising of her son, the widow exclaims what

---

41. J. G. McConville, "Books of Kings," in *Dictionary of the Old Testament: Historical Books* (Grand Rapids: InterVarsity, 2005), 626–27.

the reader should know about Elijah: "Now I know that you are a man of God and that the word of the LORD from your mouth is the truth" (17:24). After this, God's Word tells Elijah to confront Ahab and his prophets (18:1). Two perspectives are contrasted in the interchange between Elijah and Ahab: Elijah is not the "troubler of Israel"—it is Ahab, on account of his apostasy (18:18).

The contest in the next scene is to show who the true God is: the one who sends fire to consume the offering. Particularly prominent is the statement at the end of the characterization of the efforts of the prophets of Baal: "Midday passed, and they continued their frantic prophesying until the time for the evening sacrifice. But there was no response, no one answered, no one paid attention" (18:29). In stark contrast, Elijah's simple request for the Lord to answer him is powerfully followed by a flash of fire (18:37–38). The scene powerfully shows that "The LORD— he is God! The LORD—he is God!" (18:39). Then, the Lord sends the rain.

One would expect a more confident Elijah upon such a victory, but Jezebel's threat sends him into the wilderness, where he ultimately (through angelic intervention) arrives at Horeb, the mountain of God at Sinai. There the word of the Lord comes to Elijah and asks him, "What are you doing here?" (19:9). God passes by him, but he is not in the wind, the earthquake, or the fire (reminiscent of the signs at the giving of the law at Mount Sinai). At the sound of a small whisper, Elijah recognizes the voice of God. God asks him again, "What are you doing here?" (19:13). When Elijah complains of being persecuted and alone, God gives him three pieces of instruction. The point here seems clear: although Elijah is at Sinai, and although supernatural signs are manifested, God's voice is even more powerful. God may not repeat Sinai, but he still speaks, and his word is true.

Although these events are often portrayed as Elijah's last actions, the prophet is active throughout the rest of 1 Kings and until 2 Kings 2:12 when Elisha succeeds him. God does not let Elijah get his wish to die. To the contrary, he rebukes him and encourages him. The command "Go back the way you came" provides more than a travel itinerary; it urges an attitude adjustment. The command to anoint Hazael and Jehu shows God's sovereignty over the kings of this earth. Elijah's complaint of being alone is answered with the summons of Elisha. At last, Elijah is corrected and comforted: there are 7,000 who have not bent the knee to the baalim (1 Kgs. 19:15–18).

The power of the Lord and his word is highlighted throughout these scenes. The point of the narrative seems to be an encouragement to the people of God that God is still on his throne in spite of their gloomy present circumstances. The writer seems intent on encouraging faithfulness in the midst of people's desire to retreat. God's Word is true and powerful. Thus, the main idea of the cycle is this: *God's Word is sure even in uncertain times.*

Scene 1 Drought by the word of God	
Scene 2 "...the word of the LORD from your mouth is the truth" (1 Kgs. 17:24)	
Scene 3 Elijah confronts Ahab	**16.3.** **NARRATIVE CYCLE**
Scene 4 Contest at Carmel—God answers "The LORD—he is God! The LORD—he is God!" (18:39)	
Scene 5 Elijah's flight to Horeb: God is in the still small voice	
Scene 6 Elisha's commitment to follow Elijah	

Step one is now complete. We are ready to prepare the outline of our message or series of messages.

Step 2: Analyze the scenes to determine the span of text for the sermon. The communicator must first decide the scope of the message. Your first decision will be to what extent you will delimit the text you will cover. Your text will need to be a self-contained unit, true to the divisions you discovered in following step 1. As much as possible, I prefer to preach the whole cycle in one setting. Because some cycles are so large, in some cases preaching the whole cycle and doing justice to the text is virtually impossible.

If you are led to preach a smaller section, it is best to limit your-self to the individual scene as the smallest textual unit of the sermon. This is more palatable if you are preaching a series of sermons. As you can see, you are building on the foundation you laid at the point of interpretation.

Step 3: Determine the structure of the textual unit. This step is only nec-essary if you have decided to preach an individual scene rather than the whole cycle. Here we return to our examination of the structure of the text and pore over the textual unit. Look for major shifts and movements. Look for the peak or climax of the scene. Look for threads that will illuminate the point of the scene. If you have done good work in step 1, most of this step has already been completed, but often closer inspection brings deeper insight.

Step 4: Design the sermon around the structure of the textual unit. It remains a marvel to me that an exegete will do all the work of exegesis to get to the point of the outline of his sermon, then abandon the structure of the text for something else. It is not the preacher's job to come up with a memorable, creative outline of his own making, but to discover the out-line in the text.

Going back to your exegesis of the passage, find the main point of the textual unit. If you are preaching or teaching on the whole cycle, the scenes will build to the point. If you are presenting an individual scene, it will have a point that fits organically within the cycle as a whole. Your message should build to the same point.

The suggestions below are mainly concerned with the overall structure of the sermon. Development within the individual points can be accomplished in a variety of ways and still be faithful to the text. My favorite way of devel-oping a sermon is to explain the text, then apply it within the same point.

Regarding the cycle we have been examining, the six scenes cluster by twos. The first two scenes set the stage for God's revelation of himself. God sends the drought and proves his word is true through his miraculous provision. The next two scenes set up and explicate the resolving incident. Yahweh is the true God; Ahab is the troubler of Israel. The last two scenes, finally, resolve the point of the cycle by highlighting Elijah's poor response to Jezebel's threat (flight), God's response to Elijah, and Elisha's commit-ment to follow Elijah. This suggests a three-point outline for preaching the cycle.[42] We will therefore develop such an outline, keeping in mind the structure of the text and the purpose of each section.

Our preference is to frame the study's structure around the response of the hearer to the ultimate point of the passage. So we begin with the main idea of the passage. We state it as succinctly as possible. Regarding the "Elijah cycle," it is as follows: "the Word of God is sure in uncertain times." But this doesn't entirely capture the purpose of the cycle, which seems to be an encouragement to the people of God not to turn back. Note especially at the end of the cycle that Elijah is reprimanded for desiring to give up and Elisha abandons his past life in order to follow Elijah. The thesis or purpose of the lesson or sermon is therefore as follows: *People should trust in the sure word of God even in uncertain times.* Finally, we pose a question to the audience that helps accomplish the purpose of the text in their lives. Thus, we plot out the study as follows:

Lesson/Sermon on 1 Kings 17–19

Main Idea: The Word of God is sure in uncertain times.

Thesis/Purpose: People should trust in the sure Word of God even in uncertain times.

Outline:
Introductory Question: How do you respond in a crisis?

I.   Expect God to Provide in the Crisis (17:1–24)
     Prologue (Setting): Elijah's call
     Development (Preliminary incident): Elijah at Zarephath

II. Expect God to Reveal Himself in the Crisis (18:1–46)
     Crisis (Problem): Elijah's message to King Ahab (18:1–19)
     Climax (Resolving incident): Elijah vs. the prophets of Baal/
     Asherah (18:20–46)

---

42. Three is not the mandatory number of points to a study. The text should design the overall structure of the text, but since it is difficult for hearers to follow a large number of sub-points, it seems reasonable to limit oneself to just a few.

III. Don't Abandon Ship (19:1–21)
   Denouement (Complication): Elijah's flight to Horeb
   Epilogue (Sequel): Elijah and the call of Elisha

Conclusion: Next time you face a crisis, don't expect God necessarily to deliver you *out of the crisis* immediately. Expect him to provide and to reveal himself *in the crisis.* Don't quit: Winston Churchill illustration.

New Testament Narratives (Gospels and Acts)

Old Testament narratives are usually longer and more subtle that their New Testament counterparts, but all the same major issues are involved in interpreting the text and presenting it in a lesson or sermon.[43] New Testament narratives, too, will be built in scenes and cycles to make a theological point.

Major Mistakes

Similar to when preaching Old Testament narratives, we must pay close attention to literary context; we must not impose alien structural divisions on the text; and we must not impose unstated elements onto the narrative. There are a few land mines that are more common to New Testament narratives. We must resist preaching a harmony instead of the text. Redaction criticism can be a very useful tool in exegesis, but sometimes, instead of illuminating a text, we import items from another Gospel's telling of the story. At that point, we are preaching reconstructed history and not the text. In essence, then, we are doing something we have not been given the privilege to do: create our own Gospel account. The final land mine we will mention here pertains especially to the book of Acts. We often mistake a description of an event for a command to the church. For example, Acts 1:26 describes the casting of lots to make a decision; it does not prescribe it as a way to know the will of God.

Preaching New Testament Narratives

As with Old Testament narratives, the controlling principle, the highest commitment of the exegete, is to preach and teach the Gospels and Acts with the same theological points and purposes as the text. We are to *preach the Word*, not *use the Word* in our preaching.

---

43. On preaching the Gospels, see especially Greidanus, *Modern Preacher*, Chapter 11.

Like Old Testament narratives, New Testament narratives are built on the scene→cycle structure. Scenes build to cycles, each theological point building to an overarching theological point. So, then, we will follow similar steps in the preparation of our lesson or sermon. For common, straightforward narrative genres, we can follow similar procedure used for Old Testament narratives. For example, let's say we are led to preach Luke 8:22–25, the pericope of Jesus stilling the storm. We will quickly apply the four steps to the outline of the lesson or sermon.

Step 1: Identify and interpret the scenes and the narrative cycle.

a. Identify the component scenes. Similar to Old Testament narratives, each scene has an intended point and purpose. These work into the intended point and purpose of the cycle. Technically, "scenes" are usually called "pericopes" in the Gospels (but not in Acts). In the Gospels, we are used to looking only at the individual pericopes, but we must train ourselves to look at the whole cycle. In the main, we have no problem identifying Gospel pericopes. In fact, we have names for most of them (especially the parables). There is the Temple Clearing, the Man with the Withered Hand, the Man Born Blind, the Parable of the Wheat and the Tares, and so on. (It is a little more difficult to do this in the book of Acts, since we are not as familiar with it as we are with the Gospels.)

Our example, as mentioned, will be the pericope of Jesus stilling the storm in Luke 8:22–25. Our first step is to look at the whole cycle. The scenes are easily identified, and each displays a component domain of the authority of Jesus.

Luke 8:22–25: Jesus has authority over nature	
Luke 8:26–39: Jesus has authority over the demons	**16.4. NARRATIVE CYCLE**
Luke 8:40–48: Jesus has authority over sickness and death	
Luke 9:1–6: Jesus gives authority to his disciples to proclaim the kingdom of God	

Once we have identified the scenes, the next step can take place.

b. Discover the main message (or point) of the narrative cycle. Here, the main point of the cycle has been linking the cycle together. Not overly subtle, Luke weaves these stories together not only to show Jesus' authority, but the extension of his authority to his disciples to proclaim the kingdom of God.

Step 2: Analyze the scenes to determine the span of text for the sermon. We have already decided to preach the first pericope, the stilling of the storm. Of course, we should keep the point of the whole cycle in mind as we preach it.

Step 3: Determine the structure of the textual unit. It is a simple problem-resolution narrative scene. We plot the structure as follows:

Setting
22 One day Jesus said to his disciples, "Let's go over to the other side of the lake." So they got into a boat and set out.

Problem
23 As they sailed, he fell asleep. A squall came down on the lake, so that the boat was being swamped, and they were in great danger.

Resolution
24 The disciples went and woke him, saying, "Master, Master, we're going to drown!" He got up and rebuked the wind and the raging waters; the storm subsided, and all was calm.

Sequel
25 "Where is your faith?" he asked his disciples. In fear and amazement they asked one another, "Who is this? He commands even the winds and the water, and they obey him."

This pericope is not about Jesus calming the storms of your life. The punchline is found at verse 25, where Jesus rebukes his followers' lack of faith and the disciples ask, "Who is this . . .?" So, then, the main idea is that Jesus is the one with all authority. Consequently, the purpose of the pericope is to engender faith in Jesus, the all-powerful one.

Lesson/Sermon on Luke 8:22–25

Main Idea: Jesus is the one who has the authority over nature.

Thesis: Because Jesus is the one who has authority, we should always have faith in him.

Outline:
Introduction: Fighting the elements—in your own strength or God's?

1. Man vs. Wild (vv. 22–23)
    Point: The best people can do is survive the elements. The disciples feared they wouldn't survive.

2. The Son of Man vs. Wild (v. 24)
    Point: The Son of Man has authority over nature.

3. The Proper Perspective (v. 25)
    Point: Jesus is more than a human being; he is God. Therefore, we should trust in him.

Conclusion: Nature will ultimately win, unless you have faith in the one who has authority over nature.

Special Genres in Narratives

Narratives will also have portions that are not necessarily narrated events. These "imbedded genres" include parables and speeches (discourses), including speech exchanges (dialogues). Parables are a special form, which requires us to approach them a little bit differently than other narrative forms. We will examine parables below.

Speeches/Exchanges

First, we will deal with speeches/exchanges. For these, it is best to follow a course similar to the Epistles (see below), tracing the flow of thought. Our four steps are different only in how we perceive the structure of the pericopes. We will examine the familiar scene in John 3, where Nicodemus comes to Jesus by night. Before looking at this scene, we should place it within its narrative cycle.

Step 1: Identify and interpret the scenes of the narrative cycle.

a. Identify the component scenes. Due to our familiarity with the individual scenes, we often miss the narrative cycle. For example, most Christians are very familiar with the pericope of Nicodemus at John 3 but are completely unaware that it is part of a longer cycle. Because of this, we often miss the point of Nicodemus' interchange with Jesus.[44] Earlier on, we identified the section the Nicodemus exchange occupies in the first trio of signs in John's Gospel, "The Forerunner, Jesus' Inaugural Signs, and Representative Conversations" (1:19–4:54).[45] Let's take a look at the whole cycle.

The first and second signs ostensibly show who Jesus is, and each sign concludes with a statement of belief. In 2:11, we read, "and his disciples put their faith in him." In 2:23–25, after the second sign, the evangelist writes, "Now while he was in Jerusalem at the Passover Feast, many people saw the signs he was doing and believed in his name. But Jesus would not entrust himself to them, for he knew all men." So, then, there are some who "believe" but do not have saving faith. In 3:2, Nicodemus is featured as an example of these individuals. (We'll return to Nicodemus in a moment.)

The chapter concludes with the final testimony of John the Baptist: "Whoever believes in the Son has eternal life, but whoever rejects the Son will not see life, for God's wrath remains on him" (3:36). An example of one who truly believes is found in the startling account of the woman at the well in John 4. She and her whole village receive Christ: "They said to the woman, 'We no longer believe just because of what you said; now we have heard for ourselves, and we know that this man really is the Savior of

---

44. For a thorough analysis of this pericope, see Andreas J. Köstenberger, *John*, BECNT (Grand Rapids: Baker, 2004), 113–32.

45. We could easily identify the "Book of Signs" as a problem-resolution narrative structure: Setting and Preliminary incident(s) (Section A); Problem (Section B: Rising Opposition); "Solution" (Section C: The Climactic Sign); Sequel (chapter 12) that leads to the Book of Exaltation.

the world'" (4:42). The next sign shows a royal official (a Gentile?) putting his faith in Jesus.

b. Discover the main message (or point) of the narrative cycle. Again, the main idea of the cycle emerges as we examine the scenes. In this case, we can identify the main message of the narrative cycle (the first trio of signs a.k.a. the "Cana cycle") is about who Jesus is and the proper (believing) response to him.

Step 2: Analyze the scenes to determine the textual unit for the sermon. Preaching the whole cycle is more difficult because of the theological density of the Gospel stories. I prefer preaching the individual scenes in many of these instances. However, preaching individual pericopes must be done with the whole cycle in view. It is here that we suggest preaching through the whole cycle one pericope at a time.

Step 3: Determine the structure of the textual unit. Structure and genre are closely related. In the case of the "Elijah cycle," we have already seen an example of common (or straightforward) narrative (i.e., the narrator tells a story). But that is not the only type of genre found in narrative. In the Nicodemus pericope, we see an example of a reported conversation. The conversation is driven by three questions: an implied question, "What must I do to be saved?" (3:1), followed by two stated questions by Nicodemus: "What is the new birth?" (3:4) and "How does it take place?" (3:9).[46]

Step 4: Design the sermon around the structure of the text. Using the questions by Nicodemus as the backbone of the lesson or sermon and remembering that Nicodemus is an example of one who believed but didn't really have saving faith, we propose to structure the outline as follows.

Lesson/Sermon on John 2:23–3:21

Main Idea: Saving faith is entrusting yourself to Jesus, the Son of God.

---

46. Whether we translate Nicodemus' use of *ginomai* "How can these things be?" or "How can these things happen?" (our preference), Jesus' answer describes saving faith as entrusting oneself to Jesus.

Thesis: To have saving faith, we must entrust ourselves to Jesus, the Son of God.

Outline:

Introduction: "What went wrong?" Apollo 13 illustration: we spent millions to find out what went wrong. The greatest tragedy would be to claim to have faith, but not really have it. Nicodemus is an example of "believing" but not really believing. We must clearly understand what saving faith really is.

Setting: Not All Faith Is Saving Faith (2:23–25)
I.   What Everybody Needs: The New Birth (3:1–3)
      A. Nicodemus' Question
      B. Jesus' Answer
      C. Application

II.   What is the New Birth? (3:4–8)
      A. Nicodemus' Question
      B. Jesus' Answer
      C. Application

III. How Can These Things Happen? (3:9–21)
      A. Nicodemus' Question
      B. Jesus' Answer
      C. Application

Conclusion: The trouble with Apollo 13 was caused by a defect in a little rubber o-ring. It's time to examine ourselves to see if something is wrong with our faith.[47]

Parables

Another genre found in narratives is the parable. We discussed the interpretation of parables in chapter 9 of this book. This is not the place

---

47. It is worth noting that many believe that 3:16–21 represents the evangelist's commentary on Jesus' interchange with Nicodemus (see Köstenberger, *John*, 113–14). If so, this section can provide us with the framework for our suggested application.

to repeat our discussion there. We will simply add a few preliminary considerations that the communicator of the truths of Scripture should consider.

Major Mistakes

The cardinal mistake I have often encountered in sermon on the parables is that preachers treated them as historical narratives. That is, they made no difference whatsoever between the "story element" in parables and the type of "reporting" that goes on in historical narratives. In preaching the Parable of the Good Samaritan, for example, such a preacher would tell the story as if the events and characters of the parable were actually real. In fact, as mentioned in chapter 9, parables are typically made-up, albeit realistic, stories invented by Jesus to teach a certain lesson. In this case, parables are closer to fables than to historical reporting.

Also, we must not domesticate the stories when preaching the parables. They are not just quaint agrarian illustrations of heavenly truths. They are often shocking and greatly offend those to whom they are directed. Most often, they involve some kind of reversal of expectation where the expected hero of a story turns out to be the villain and vice versa. The Parable of the Good Samaritan is an excellent example of this, because Samaritans were looked down upon by Jews. While people may not immediately recognize this today—hence the role of the preacher—this all-important detail would not have been missed by Jesus' first-century audience. The communicator of the parable should keep this in mind when crafting the Bible lesson or sermon.

Preaching the Parables

First, we should note the function of the parables in the structure of the whole book. There are no formal parables in John's Gospel. Luke features numerous parables throughout his Gospel. Matthew and Mark cluster most of their parables in single chapters, which necessitates a study of their sequence of parables.

Second, the parable often has embedded allegorical principles. These are usually built around the central character(s) of the parables. These then can become the organizing principles for our sermons.

Structurally, most parables are either problem-resolution or occasion-outcome narratives. However, the interpreter has the added task of keeping the deeper level of meaning in mind. We will use the Parable of the Prodigal Son in Luke 15:11–32 as our example.

Following our steps to the outline, we first of all locate the parable in its narrative cycle. The parable is the last of three parables introduced by the Pharisees' criticism that Jesus eats with sinners. The first two parables (The Lost Sheep and The Lost Coin) each repeat the significant idea of joy in heaven over sinners who repent.

The parable presents three characters: the father, the prodigal son, and the older brother. The narrative parable follows the occasion-outcome pattern in two cycles, the younger brother and then the older brother. Ultimately, the parable is not about the prodigal and/or elder son, but about the loving father. The point here is that both sons were wrong in their actions, but the father loves them both. Thus, our proposed outline for this lesson or sermon has two main points.

Lesson/Sermon on Luke 15

Main Idea: The father longs for the repentant sinner.

Thesis: Expect the Father to lovingly receive the repentant sinner.

Outline:
Introduction: Recount personal experience of rejection by earthly father. Contrast God as our heavenly Father who will never reject us.

I.   The Father Amazingly Loves the Lost Son in the World (15:11–23)
II.   The Father Lovingly Reproves the Self-Righteous Son in the House (15:24–32)

Conclusion: Parting challenge: Are you and I complacent? Are we so used to enjoying all the comforts of being in the Father's house that we fail to rejoice when sinners repent?

Non-narrative Literature
Poetic Literature

Most poetic literature occurs in the Psalter, but a great deal of poetic literature is found throughout the Old Testament and especially in the

Prophets. The variety of the manner of expression in poetic literature is expansive, and there is no single way to preach the form.

Major Mistakes

Regarding the Psalter, there are quite a few mistakes made on the way to the pulpit. We often mishandle the frequent figurative language found in poetry. We often impose historical situations as the context of the Psalm. We often preach the Psalms coldly, antiseptically, mining it for theological gems when the emotive content is often at the foreground. Sometimes we domesticate the intent of the Psalm because it is insensitive to modern ears or we have forgotten that they were written under another covenant.

Preaching the Psalms

Pay attention to the type of psalm you are communicating. Grant Osborne locates eight different types of Hebrew poetry,[48] but in broad practical terms, the Psalms can be classified into three broad categories: (1) praise; (2) thanksgiving; and (3) lament.[49] Walter Kaiser treats the Psalter in two categories: praise and lament.[50] Since thanksgiving and praise are similar in content and form, we will follow Kaiser here.[51]

When considering the scope of your textual unit, the Psalms are self-contained units and one should strongly consider preaching an entire Psalm. This, of course, is virtually unworkable in the case of the 176 verses of Psalm 119. We suggest a series of messages or lessons on this and other longer Psalms.[52] Another consideration is that scholars are paying close attention to the shape of the Psalter as well, that is, how the individual psalms are

---

48. Grant Osborne, *The Hermeneutical Spiral: A Comprehensive Guide to Biblical Interpretation*, 2d ed. (Grand Rapids: Zondervan), 231–36.

49. Terry G. Carter, J. Scott Duvall, and Daniel Hays, *Preaching God's Word: A Hands-On Approach to Preparing, Developing, and Delivering the Sermon* (Grand Rapids: Zondervan, 2005), 278.

50. Walter C. Kaiser, *Preaching and Teaching from the Old Testament: A Guide for the Church* (Grand Rapids: Baker, 2003).

51. Kaiser divides praise into "descriptive praise" (our praise) that extols God's person and "declarative praise" (our "thanksgiving") that declares what God does. "Thus, whether the psalmist praised God for who he is (descriptive) or for what he does (declarative), he was praising God" (*Preaching and Teaching from the Old Testament*, 153).

52. As do Carter, Duvall, and Hays, *Preaching God's Word*, 280.

arranged.[53] Carter, Duvall, and Hays note that Psalm 1 and 2 serve together to introduce the whole Psalter collection. More germane to the preaching task, certain Psalms cluster together (e.g., Psalm 22 and 23; Psalms 103 and 104). There is also a progression from lament to praise in the Psalter (lament dominates Psalms 3–41, while the latter Psalms focus on praise).[54]

Step 1: Identify the classification of the Psalm. Is the Psalm praise or lament? This is easily discernible; there is little joy and excitement in the laments of Israel. But more than the emotional content, the classification of the Psalm will usually have a distinctive structure as well. A word of caution, however, is necessary: not every Psalm neatly fits into these cat-egories. Be prepared for some to be far less streamlined.

Step 2: Identify the structure of the Psalm. The Praise Psalms gener-ally have a three-part schema (slightly different in praise and thanks-giving psalms). They typically feature (1) a call to praise; (2) the cause for praise; and (3) a conclusion or recapitulation of praise.[55] The Thanksgiving Psalms have a similar threefold structure but are more focused on the psalmist's praise for God's deliverance. They feature (1) a specific call to praise; (2) a specific cause for praise (the psalmist's dis-tress); and (3) a testimony to God's help and prayer for the future (or thanksgiving).[56]

Look for the structural items mentioned in chapter 6 on poetry and wisdom literature either making these divisions or within these divisions. Pay close attention within the divisions for complexity and subtlety. Not every psalm classified as praise will fit neatly into this schema. Be ready to see more complicated schemes such as acrostics or chiasms marking the whole Psalm or its component parts (e.g., Psalm 119 is a massive acrostic psalm).

If the Psalm is a lament, the speaker is suffering and expresses his sen-timents to God regarding his situation (whether personal or corporate).

---

53. See the fine essay by Georg P. Braulik, "Psalter and Messia :Towards a Christolog-ical Understanding of the Psalms in the Old Testament and the Church Fathers," in _Psalms and Liturgy_, ed. by Dirk J. Human and Casparus J. A. Vos (London: T&T Clark, 2004), 17.

54. Carter, Duvall, and Hays, _Preaching God's Word_, 273.

55. Kaiser, _Preaching and Teaching the Old Testament_, 154.

56. Adapted from ibid., 155.

These are brutally honest expressions of faith that have resonated in the hearts of believers going through trials in every century. Kaiser locates seven common elements of lament: (1) an invocation; (2) a plea to God for help; (3) one or more complaints; (4) confession of sin or an assertion of one's innocence; (5) an imprecation on one's enemies; (6) confidence that God will respond; and (7) a hymn or blessing. Do not expect every element to appear in every occurrence of a lament; the form is flexible. (See figure entitled Is the Psalm Praise or Lament?)

Step 3: Design the sermon around the structure of the Psalm. The Psalms are some of the easiest texts in the Old Testament to connect to modern hearers, for they deal with the things that are part of everyday human experience. They deal with the issues common to all humanity, such as joy, sadness, redemption, grief, sin, righteousness, guilt, forgiveness, etc.

Once you have done your exegesis of the Psalm and have discovered its classification and content, use its structure to design your sermon. Below is an example based on Psalm 66, a Praise Psalm. We can identify its structure as follows: (1) A Call to Praise (vv. 1–4); (2) The Cause for Praise (vv. 5–12); (3) Conclusion or Recapitulation of Praise (vv. 13–20).

We observe that the assertion at the beginning of the Psalm that God's enemies will feign praise and the reference at the end that if we regard wickedness God will not hear us (v. 18) form a literary *inclusio*. Thus, while the psalmist affirms with great skill the call to praise and its reasons, there is a not-so-subtle warning that we will not get the intimacy that normally comes from praising God if we harbor a wicked heart.

The sermon preliminaries and outline present themselves as follows.

Lesson/Sermon on Psalm 66
Main Idea: God is deserving of our praise but will only hear it from the righteous

Thesis: People need to praise God from a pure heart

Outline:

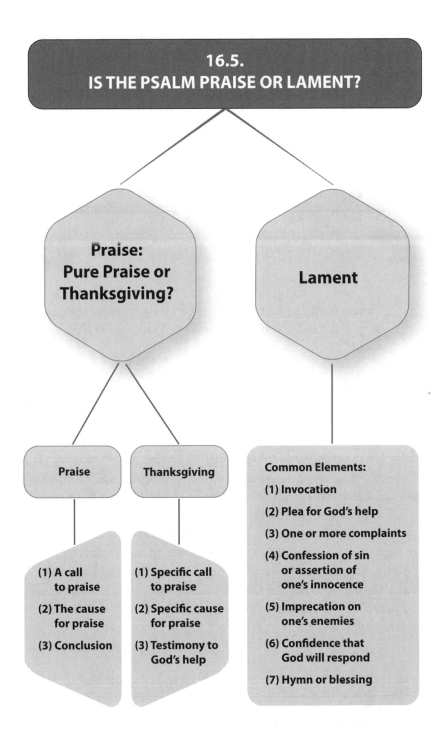

**16.5.
IS THE PSALM PRAISE OR LAMENT?**

**Praise:
Pure Praise or
Thanksgiving?**

Lament

Praise

Thanksgiving

Common Elements:

(1) A call
  to praise

(2) The cause
  for praise

(3) Conclusion

(1) Specific call
  to praise

(2) Specific cause
  for praise

(3) Testimony to
  God's help

(1) Invocation

(2) Plea for God's help

(3) One or more complaints

(4) Confession of sin
  or assertion of
  one's innocence

(5) Imprecation on
  one's enemies

(6) Confidence that
  God will respond

(7) Hymn or blessing

Introduction: Jesus regularly told demons to be quiet about his true identity. He didn't need fallen angels to sing his praises.

I.   Lift Your Voice to Praise God (vv. 1–4)
     God is so awesome, even his enemies pretend to praise him

II. Understand the Awesome Works and Person of God (vv. 5–12)
     A. His Redemption from Slavery (v. 5)
     B. His Rules over the Nations (v. 6)
     C. His Providence is Constant (vv. 7–12)

III. Understand that Only the Righteous Have Intimacy with God (vv. 13–20)

Conclusion: The Christian life is an intimate personal relationship with God. We have an awesome God: are you praising him today?

Wisdom Literature

Job, Ecclesiastes, Song of Songs, and Proverbs are usually the main books of the Old Testament that are classified as wisdom literature.[57] Ecclesiastes and Job are book-length treatment of a sustained topic and should be treated similarly to other expository literature (such as epistles and speeches), keeping in mind the poetic substructure. With this in mind, we will deal mainly with what is perhaps the most difficult portion of wisdom literature to preach: the book of Proverbs. The fact they these proverbs, on the whole, seem to be isolated chunks of wisdom layered one after the other runs counter to the systematic mind-set of the preacher. As Walter Kaiser notes, "How is one to give even the semblance of an expository sermon . . . when the material seems to resist such an approach at every point?"[58] The truth is, as we will see, this degree of despair need not be warranted.

---

57. Although note well that we have pointed out that wisdom as a genre occurs outside of these books and even the New Testament.
58. Kaiser, *Preaching the Old Testament*, 85.

Major Mistakes

First, don't preach a proverb as if it had no time or covenantal constraints. Second, preaching a single proverb and paying no attention to its context is unwise. This disregards the fact that at least two sections of Proverbs manifestly have a literary structure (chaps 1–9 and 31). Similarly, preaching groups of similar proverbs apart from their canonical setting creates a new anthology of wisdom. This may be permissible if the preacher is careful to look at the context of each individual proverb, but preachers rarely do.[59] Be careful here. Third, importing foreign historical or background information is a mistake (especially when good, simple exegesis will solve most "problems"). For example, parents of wayward children have often (falsely) been comforted by 22:6, "Train up a child in the way he should go, and when he is old he will not turn from it," as if it meant that the prodigal will always come home. But this is simply not the case in life or Scripture. To import late Arabic cognates or, even worse, popular preaching to explain the difficulty is an act of desperation that helps nobody, especially the grieving parent. We will instead offer a better look at the proverb and its context below.

Preaching from Proverbs

Step 1: Note where your passage is found within the overall structure of the book. The overall structure of the book of Proverbs can easily be arranged by noting the superscription attached to each section. This leads to the following divisions: chapters 1–9; 10:1–22:16; 22:17–24:22; 24:23–34; 25–29; 30:1–9; and 31:10–31. Duane Garrett divides these into fewer larger units based on other ancient Near Eastern wisdom texts, featuring the wisdom of Solomon (chaps. 1–24), Hezekiah (chaps. 25–29), Agur (chap. 30), and Lemuel (chap. 31).[60]

---

59. See, e.g., the treatment of the sluggard in Proverbs in H. Wayne House and Daniel Garland, *God's Message, Your Sermon: Discover, Develop, and Deliver What God Meant by What He Said* (Nashville: Thomas Nelson, 2007), 188.

60. Duane Garrett, *Proverbs, Ecclesiastes, Song of Songs*, NAC 14 (Nashville: B&H, 1993), 39–43, bases his observations on K. A. Kitchen, "Proverbs and Wisdom Books of the Ancient Near East," *TB* 28 (1977): 69–114; and idem, "The Basic Literary Forms and Formulations of Ancient Instructional Writings in Egypt and Western Asia," in *Studien zu altägyptischen Lebenslehren*, ed. E. Hornung and O. Keel, OBO 28 (Göttingen: Vandenhoeck & Ruprecht, 1979), 278–80. He locates the entirety of Proverbs 1–24 in what Kitchen calls "Type B" patterns or features: titles, prologues, subtitles, and titular interjections (such as an author addressing his audience; e.g.,

Proverbs 1–9 is a carefully constructed expository discourse that should be approached with the hermeneutical tools discussed in chapter 6 on Poetry and Wisdom. With regard to expository discourses, you should also employ the tools of discourse analysis to understand the major divisions and flow of thought within these sections (see the relevant portions on discourse analysis in chapter 12). Proverbs 31:10–31 should be treated as poetry (actually, an acrostic based on the Hebrew alphabet). If this is your text, you may skip to step 3 below.

If your text is found in chapters 10–30, the game changes somewhat, for the genre switches to the more typical proverb form.[61] These individual proverbs make sense by themselves, but also function in small sets of collections.[62] If preaching from this section of proverbs, go to step 2.

Step 2: Identify the type of collection. Instead of preaching on one or two proverbs, we suggest you take a hard look at the surrounding context of these proverbs and consider preaching the whole collection. So what are we looking for in these collections? Garrett lists five types of collections that occur in Proverbs:

1. *Parallel collection:* proverbs grouped in an A-B-A-B pattern. The elements of the pattern may be individual cola (two-proverb collection; 11:16–17) or whole proverbs (four-proverb collection; 10:27–30).

2. *Chiastic collection:* proverbs grouped in an A-B-B-A pattern. Again, the elements of the pattern may be individual cola (two-proverb collection; 18:6–7) or whole proverbs (four-proverb collection; 12:19–22).

3. *Catchword collection:* A group of proverbs that contain a common catchword (15:15–17).

4. *Thematic collection:* A group of proverbs that maintain a common theme (10:31–32). These are proverbs dealing with a similar subject matter.

"Solomon" in 22:17 and 24:23). Hezekiah, Agur, and Lemuel follow a simpler "Type A" pattern.

61. Note that chapters 10–30 do not constitute a literary section but a notation of what kind of proverbial material is found there.

62. Garrett, *Proverbs,* 46.

5. Inclusio collection: This is a group of proverbs bracketed by an inclusion, in which the first and last proverbs are similar or contain common catchwords. For example, 11:23–27 is set off by the catch-word "good" as an *inclusio* in verses 23 and 27, with verses 24–26 within that *inclusio* dealing with the theme of generosity and its rewards. A variation on the *inclusio* is the A-B envelope series, which consists of two juxtaposed collections with similar proverbs at the beginning and the end (as in 15:1–16:8).[63]

At times, we also find clusters of proverb collections working together. For example, 25:16–27 hold together by the *inclusio* of eating honey in excess (25:16, 27), but is made up of individual small collections of different types. Altogether, this collection deals with "exercising caution with people." The individual proverbs deal with overstaying your welcome (vv. 16–17); warnings about the perjurer, the liar, and the tactless (vv. 18–20); being kind to your enemies (vv. 21–22); warning about sly looks (v. 23); warning about a quarrelsome wife (v. 24); and the effect of the righteous man who falls into sin (vv. 25–26).[64]

Step 3: Design your sermon or study around the structure of the text. The basic structure of 22:6–16 is that of an *inclusio* between verses 6 and 7 (training and wealth) and verses 15 and 16 (training and wealth). What is more, if we understand that verse 6 states a negative pattern (i.e., train a child as he wants to be trained), continuity can be seen throughout the section. The individual proverbs between the two literary brackets seem to center around cause and effect—stereotypically stated at verse 8 as sowing and reaping. The collection features two contrasting self-imposed cause-and-effect relationships. Beginning at verse 11, the collection features three very negative examples, the treacherous man, the sluggard, and the cursed man—who are revealed by their outcomes—that is, what they managed to produce.

Here, we advise great caution. These proverbs are collected works placed in this context. We are assuming the editors had a reason for the arrangement. However, we run the risk of imposing a meaning on the text that does not exist if we interpret the individual proverbs haphazardly.

---

63. Ibid., 47–48.
64. Ibid., 207–10. Immediately following this collection are portraits of the fool (25:28–26:12); the sluggard (26:13–16); the busybody (26:17–22); and the liar (26:23–28; ibid., 211–15).

The caution we advise is that how we understand the overall collection must be built on the authentic exegesis of the individual proverbs. In other words, the component of proverbs must make the same sense standing alone and in the collection. But viewed in the collection, the proverb takes on a meaning in context that is not contrary to the individual proverb but transcends the constraints the individual proverb brings to its literary environment.[65]

Our proposed sermon outline here is as follows:

Lesson/Sermon on Proverbs 22:6–16
Main Idea: You reap what you sow.

Thesis: Sow righteousness in your children early to head off a crop of incredible misery.

Outline:
Introduction: Everybody looks forward to payday, but for those who have foolish and self-centered lives, payday brings a rude awakening.

I.   Principle Stated (vv. 6–7)
     6   *Train a child in the way he should go, and when he is old he will not turn from it.*
     7   *The rich rule over the poor, and the borrower is servant to the lender.*

II. Principle Revealed: A Contrast of Ways (vv. 8–11)
     A. Sowing and Reaping
          8 *He who sows wickedness reaps trouble, and the rod of his fury will be destroyed.*

---

65. Tremper Longman makes a good point for us to consider reserve in the matter. Referencing K.M. Heim's understanding of structure within the proverbs, Longman states, "Once he delineates the units, he then interprets individual proverbs within the cluster. This last point is the interpretive payoff of his ideas, and unfortunately, if he is wrong, it means that he is imposing meaning on these texts." Tremper Longman, III, "Proverbs 1: Book of," in *Dictionary of the Old Testament Wisdom, Poetry & Writings: A Compendium of Contemporary Biblical Scholarship* (Grand Rapids: InterVarsity, 2008), 548.

>   9 *A generous man will himself be blessed, for he shares his*
>   *food with the poor.*

>   B. Cause and Effect

>   10 *Drive out the mocker, and out goes strife; quarrels and*
>   *insults are ended.*

>   11 *He who loves a pure heart and whose speech is gracious*
>   *will have the king for his friend.*

> III. Principle Illustrated (vv. 12–14)

>   12 *The eyes of the LORD keep watch over knowledge, but he frus-*
>   *trates the words of the unfaithful.*

>   13 *The sluggard says, "There is a lion outside!" or, "I will be mur-*
>   *dered in the streets!"*

>   14 *The mouth of an adulteress is a deep pit; he who is under the*
>   *LORD's wrath will fall into it.*

> IV. Principle Restated (vv. 15–16)

>   15 *Folly is bound up in the heart of a child, but the rod of disci-*
>   *pline will drive it far from him.*

>   16 *He who oppresses the poor to increase his wealth and he who*
>   *gives gifts to the rich—both come to poverty.*

Conclusion: Reinforce main idea· what you recap is what you sow. You'll either pay attention to your family life and other responsibilities now, or you will regret it later.

Prophecy

Major Mistakes

Generally, the modern preaching from the Old Testament prophetic material suffers from two major problems. First, we are often completely ignorant of the different elements and/or forms of the prophetic genre. As a result, we mishandle a lawsuit complaint or a satire, because we approach the prophets as a flat rather than a multi-faceted genre. Second, we suffer from certain popular misconceptions about the very nature of the prophet and prophecy. More than once, we have seen preachers waxing eloquent about a modern event having been fulfilled in the Old

Testament prophets when the oracle itself has, at best, only limited affinities with the event.[66] Closely related to this error is the fallacy of understanding the prophet more like a fortune-teller than a biblical prophet.[67]

Another common mistake is to assume a chronological arrangement of the individual oracles. Ezekiel, Haggai, and Zechariah are chronological and supply such indicators through the text. But the latter prophets, especially, are not concerned so much with chronology but display a topical arrangement.[68] Another, more subtle mistake is to fail to recognize that a given oracle is employing poetry. Thus, the rules for interpreting poetry are ignored (including the use of parallelism, figurative language, etc.). Finally, a common mistake is to misconstrue the actual limits of the oracle (i.e., finding the beginning or end of the passage).

Preaching Old Testament Prophecy

The preacher of prophetic literature should pay careful attention to the historical dimension of the hermeneutical triad.[69] As the prophet enforces the covenant with Israel, it is very helpful to know where in the process the nation is found. The text itself will often set the prophet within his milieu; the careful preacher investigates this aspect thoroughly.

When preaching the prophets, we are faced with a variety of forms, genres, and sub-genres. Narratives in prophetic books should be interpreted and preached as narratives (see above). For example, the book of Jonah is a narrative about a (wayward) prophet. Keeping in mind the nature and purpose of prophecy and the office of prophet, the interpreter should handle the book as a narrative. The preacher or teacher should follow the guidelines for preaching narratives, keeping these factors in mind.

---

66. One of my "favorites" is the rant against the Christmas tree using Jeremiah 10:2–4. I, more than anyone, would love to strip Christmas of its pagan trappings, but this is a misuse of Scripture. The Jeremiah text knows nothing of a Christmas tree, but does roundly condemn idolatry (chopping, carving, decorating, and worshiping a piece of wood.

67. Note the main message of the prophets as discussed in chapter 7 on prophecy. It is also important to remember that prophets were more than mere "seers"; their primary role was that of "covenant enforcers," that is, calling the people of Israel to obey their covenant obligations toward Yahweh.

68. Marvin A. Sweeney, *Isaiah 1–39: with an Introduction to Prophetic Literature*, Vol. XVI: *The Forms of the Old Testament Literature* (Grand Rapids: Eerdmans, 1996), 17.

69. On preaching prophetic literature, see especially Greidanus, *Modern Preacher*, Chapter 10.

Other narrative accounts are even more adapted to the prophetic office and message. As a result, the reader will find divine pronouncements ("Thus says the LORD"), symbolic actions, vision reports, and both autobiographical and third-person accounts.[70] These will often overpower the normal structure of problem-resolution, etc.[71] The interpreter must keep these dimensions in mind as he or she approaches a prophetic narrative.

Apart from narratives portions in prophetic literature, the basic interpretive unit is the oracle, the divine speech presented through the prophet.[72]

Step 1: Determine the limits of the individual oracles and it place in the larger structure. Most prophetic books are collections of oracles. Delimiting the oracle is at times a subtle enterprise. Follow the Guidelines for Interpreting Prophetic Literature in chapter 7 in recognizing the divisions of the prophetic oracle.

These oracles are also arranged in a purposeful sequence. For example, Isaiah 1–12 is built in a triad of oracle collections.[73] Chapters 1–5 describe the failure of Judah and God's judgment with oracles, describing Judah as foolish children, a rebellious city, and an unproductive vineyard. Chapter 6 places Isaiah's own call as the demonstration of the awesome holiness of God. Finally, chapters 7–12 use the historical crisis embodied by Assyria's threat to announce Yahweh's rejection of the house of Ahaz for a later son of David, the Messiah. The collection ends with a song of the redeemed in chapter 12.[74]

The threefold purpose of this section clearly is (1) to show a round denunciation of Ahaz and his godless political machinations and those who follow suit; (2) to declare Yahweh as the Holy One of Israel; and (3) to give hope for Israel's preservation and future restoration. Yet the book does so with a stunning variety of genres including parables, woes, lawsuits, vision reports, and hymns. The preacher of prophetic literature must be able to place the oracle in its broader literary context. Ideally, one should preach or teach the whole collection, but similar to New Testament narratives, the

---

70. Ibid., 18–22.
71. David L. Petersen, *The Prophetic Literature: An Introduction* (Louisville: Westminster John Knox, 2002), 19.
72. Sweeney, *Isaiah 1–39*, 22.
73. Willem A. VanGemeren, *Interpreting the Prophetic Word: An Introduction to the Prophetic Literature of the Old Testament* (Grand Rapids: Zondervan, 1990), 254. VanGemeren calls it a "triptych."
74. Ibid., 254–63.

prophetic books are so theologically rich that this is often very difficult. We will assume that we are communicating the individual oracle.

Step 2: Determine the genre and/or subgenre of the oracle and its structure. In chapter 7, the genre or subgenres of prophetic literature were presented as follows: announcements of judgment (woe oracle, lament, covenant, lawsuit); salvation oracles (promise of deliverance, kingdom oracles, apocalyptic); instructional accounts (disputation, exhortation speeches, satire, wisdom sayings, prophetic narratives); and miscellaneous subgenres (vision/dream reports, prophetic hymns/songs, prophetic prayers, prophetic letters). Carefully identify your text's genre or subgenre. Do not be influenced by previous or following oracles; the prophets loved variety.

Once you have identified what kind of oracle your passage represents, search it carefully for the component parts of the genre (listed in chapter 7). For example, we identified Micah 6:1–16 as a covenant lawsuit and outlined it as follows: (1) Summoning of Witnesses (6:1–2); (2) List of the Charges against the Accused (6:3–12); (3) Final Divine Sentence of Judgment (6:13–15); and (4) Concluding Summation (6:16). Once you are comfortable with this, move on to step 3.

Step 3: Design the sermon around the structure of the text. The commitment, as usual, is to make the shape of your text the shape of your sermon. The content of the complaint illuminates the purpose of the text: to highlight the sin of God's people with an urge to repent. Using the structure already proposed for Micah 6:1–16, we discover the following outline for our sermon.

Lesson/Sermon on Micah 6:1–13
Main Idea: God's requirements are not burdensome and the only path of security.

Thesis: God requires us to act justly, to love mercy, and to walk humbly with him.

Outline:
Introduction: Followers of Ignatius bishop of Smyrna wanted to rescue

him when he was on his way to being martyred. Ignatius refused because he wanted to die a martyr's death. What is your motivation for living the Christian life?

I.   The Announcement of God's Displeasure (6:1–2)
      Summoning of witnesses: God calls the mountains and the foundations of the earth as witnesses, showing the solemnity of the charge and the smallness of the indicted.

II.   The Indictment (6:3–8)
      A. Has God Burdened His People? (6:3–5)
         Point: The people of God charge God with being too burdensome for them. You demand too much! Instead, Judah's history with God is one of amazing generosity.
      B. The Nation's Question (6:6–7)
         Point: The nation is seemingly willing to sacrifice things to the point of abomination, but this is not what pleases God.
      C. God's Answer (6:8)
         Point: What God truly requires of his people is acting justly, loving mercy, and walking humbly with their God; this is not burdensome.

III. The Sentence (6:9–13)
      Point: Because Judah has grown wealthy through corruption, violence, and dishonesty, what they get will not satisfy; what they store will be taken from them. Their idolatry will lead to ruin.

Conclusion: Recognize that God has been very generous to you. Have you been generous to God? Do you act justly, love mercy, and walk humbly with your God? Illustration of life of quiet, daily faithfulness.

Apocalyptic Literature

As mentioned in chapters 7 and 11, apocalyptic literature arose out of the prophetic genre. As noted as well, apocalyptic passages occur in both the Old Testament prophets and in the New Testament apocalypse. It seems appropriate, then, to deal with preaching and teaching the genre at this point.

Major Mistakes

When preaching the book of Revelation, communicators often make the mistake of approaching the text with one—and only one—interpretive grid. While I definitely approach the apocalypse with a futurist bent, for example, there are clearly places where the past is in view (chaps. 2–3). As always, we should take the passage at face value and not impose an interpretive grid on it. Related to this is the common practice of preaching Revelation strictly from the preacher's own theological framework without acknowledgment that there are other legitimate viewpoints held by respectable scholars and biblical communicators. This kind of indoctrination may work well when the doctrine at stake is clearly taught in Scripture—such as the way of salvation or the deity of Christ. In cases where matters are less clear—such as in the case of the end times, including the timing of the rapture—the preacher or teacher should be more tentative and willing to concede the possibility that others with whom he disagrees may have a point.

Second, we spend far too much time trying to figure out when the rapture will occur in the book. The cold, hard fact is that the rapture is not mentioned in Revelation. So why do we try our hardest to find it in the book? Maybe Revelation is not about the church's escape, but about the triumph of the Lamb? Another major mistake that happens when preaching the apocalypse is that we do not make sufficient connections to the Old Testament through the literary visions. This interpretive failure seriously undermines preaching and teaching on the apocalypse. A third mistake frequently made in preaching the Revelation is that we only preach up to chapter 3, for obvious reasons. The final mistake we often make is hubris. As mentioned, we could use more humility in our preaching and teaching of apocalyptic literature. Make a clear delineation between what is definitely true and what is only possibly true. There are enough definitive truths to feed and encourage your hearers. Clearly understanding what is probably or possibly true helps us all reassess the times as we get nearer to that day!

Preaching the Apocalypse

Steps 1–4 are congruent with the Guidelines for Interpreting Apocalyptic Literature. The following are highlighted not only for the need in interpretation, but they often form or inform the rhetorical structure of your lesson or sermon.

Step 1: Carefully identify the boundaries of your passage. Pay careful attention to both the macro-and micro-structure of your passage. Apply the Guidelines for Interpreting Apocalyptic Literature carefully. One cannot simply preach the four visions of the apocalypse. After the first vision, they are simply too large and complicated. Because of the narrative structure, your textual unit will be based more on the intermediate literary structures (i.e., episodes and paragraph clusters but not whole lengthy visions or merely a single paragraph).

Step 2: Carefully identify and interpret the Old Testament allusions in your passage. Remember, there are no formal Old Testament citations in the apocalypse. However, there are many Old Testament allusions. Once you have identified an allusion, determine the level of its impact on the text by identifying whether it is an embedded, implied, or an incidental allusion. Remember: the more probable an allusion, the more weight it has.

Step 3: Cautiously identify and interpret the symbols in your passage. Symbolism abounds. Some symbols are Old Testament allusions or themes. Other symbols are cultural or political. Others simply add color. Identifying and sorting through these symbols requires checking and double checking through quality resources. Where there is strong doubt, be less insistent on your conclusions.

Step 4: Fit your passage into the overall structure of its context (and book) and identify the passage's structure. Here is where you will be discovering the purpose of your passage. What is the author trying to accomplish with it? Does it wrap up a vision? Does it introduce a vision? Does it comfort the persecuted? For example, take the sample exegesis of the vision of Christ among the churches in Revelation 1:12–16. It is introduced by verse 11, when the voice John hears says, "Write on a scroll what you see and send it to the seven churches: to Ephesus, Smyrna, Pergamum, Thyatira, Sardis, Philadelphia and Laodicea." This vision is immediately followed by the letters to the seven churches, connected to the vision by the Lord giving the command to write at 2:1. So, then, this vision of Christ is intimately associated with the churches. By extension, we can understand that this is important to every church not just the seven.[75]

The vision itself is a narrative of what John saw. As such, it follows the structure of an occasion-outcome narrative. I plot it as follows: The Setting (1:9–11); the Occasion (1:12–16); the Outcome (1:17–18); Sequel (1:19–20). The sequel identifies the lamps and the stars and serves as a transition to the letters beginning in chapter 2. Greg Beale correctly identifies the purpose of this passage ". . . the initial vision he receives demonstrates that the saints' confidence is grounded in Christ's installation as cosmic judge, priest and ruler of the church as a result of his victory over death."[76]

Step 5: Design your message around the structure of your passage. By this time, you knew this would be the final step! At the end of your exegesis, you can now take your discovery and form your message. My sermon outline and preliminaries are as follows:

Lesson/Sermon on Revelation 1:9–20

Main Idea: Christ is our divine high priest and eternal judge.

Thesis: Christians should confidently submit to Christ.

Outline:
Introduction: Use the setting to introduce the lesson or sermon (1:9–11)

I.   He is the Divine Judge and High Priest in Their Midst (1:12–16)

    A. Intimately Connected with the Churches
       Image: The Son of Man among the seven lampstands (intimate connection with the churches: not a line of churches with one nearer to Jesus than the others, but a circle; cf. Zechariah 4; Dan. 7:9)

---

75. Just as the whole book of Revelation is written to the seven churches, but ultimately addressed to all the churches.
76. G. K. Beale, *Revelation*, NIGTC (Grand Rapids: Eerdmans, 2005).

B. The Great High Priest
   Image: Robe and golden sash (cf. Exod. 25:7; 28:4–43, 31; 29:5; Zech. 3:4)

C. The Ancient of Days
   Image: Head and hair: Son of Man identified as Ancient of Days (cf. Dan. 7:9)

D. Penetrating Vision
   Image: Eyes like blazing fire (cf. Dan. 10:6)

E. Fierce in judgment
   Image: Feet like bronze (cf. Dan. 10:6; Ezek. 1:27)

F. Speaks with Absolute Authority
   Image: Voice like the sound of rushing waters (cf. Ezek. 1:24; 43:2)

G. Cosmic Sovereign over the Churches
   Image: Angels in the place of power, privilege, and protection (cf. Gen. 37:6?)

H. Speaks the Devastating Word of God
   Image: Sharp two-edged sword coming out of his mouth (cf. Isa. 11:4; 49:2)

I. Displays the Glory of God
   Image: Face shining like the sun (cf. Dan. 10:6; Exod. 34:29–35)

II. He is the Sovereign God over All Forces, the Trailblazer through Death, and the Master of Eternity (1:17–18)
     A. The Divine Sovereign
        Point: He is the first and the last

     B. The Trailblazer through Death
        Point: He is the ever-living one

C. Master of Eternity
   Point: He holds the keys of death and Hades

D. Conclusion: Only proper response is confident submission

III.   Sequel (1:19–20): John uses the sequel to identify the mystery of the lampstands and the stars, but also transitions to the Letters to the Seven Churches, where one or more of the individual elements of the vision are applied to the church. Let's apply these to our life as individuals and to our lives as the family of faith.

Hortatory and Expository Literature (Epistles and Speeches)

Prose often takes the form of a more intentional literature. When dealing with these kinds of non-narrative literature, this will take the form of one of three subgenres. *Hortatory literature* exists when the speaker/writer is suggesting or commanding an action the reader should take. *Expository literature* explicates a thesis; it defends an argument. Finally, there is *procedural literature* where the writer or speaker gives step-by-step directions. This is extremely rare in the Bible but does occur in some Old Testament texts (e.g., Exodus 25). For these types of literature, it is most important to track the flow of thought and then to use that structure to build your message.

Major Mistakes

Several mistakes often show up when preaching expository and hortatory literature. First, a communicator will often ignore the historical context. Because epistles are occasional documents, one of the main questions one should ask regarding an epistle is: What's the problem here?[77] Not ascertaining the historical grounds that spawned the letter can create a "system failure" with our interpretation. The second major mistake is that we often ignore the literary context. The paragraphs and sentences in a letter or speech have a higher level function within the letter. Knowing these functions illuminates the meaning of the text. A third mistake is a related phenomenon, ignoring the thought flow of the text. Picking out a few key words

---

77.   Sometimes this is a multi-faceted issue that is difficult to express simply. Take 1 Corinthians, for example. A simply stated historical context is difficult to express. "Hey, I've got some problems with you" doesn't seem to work very well.

or subthemes and making your points from them is a common approach from pulpits. The truth is that you wouldn't handle any other literature that way; so why would we do so with Scripture? Another common error is that, especially in epistles arguing a thesis, we are tempted to preach a theological grid rather than the text. The text mentions our chosen status before God, and the preacher waxes eloquent for or against the five points of Reformed doctrine. There are more, but one more mistake in preaching expository or hortatory literature will have to suffice: the preacher or teacher will often make his or her study a series of word studies. The tragedy here is that the words in context are lost in favor of free-floating "theological concepts."

Preaching Hortatory and Expository Literature

When preaching or teaching this literature, be sure to recreate the historical situation for your hearers.[78] If we all know what spawned the letter or speech, then we can grasp meaning more easily. Another necessity is to know how your passage works in its section and to know how your section works in the whole letter. This, more than anything, will help you keep from importing foreign ideas into the text and will identify the function and purpose of the text. Above all, know the flow of thought in your passage. A clause-by-clause analysis of a narrative is not all that helpful; the story is told in larger sections. When crafting an argument or encouraging an action, however, a given writer or speaker will build a case line by line. As detailed in chapter 12, discourse analysis on the clausal level is extremely helpful here.

Step 1: Identify the structure of the whole letter. Read the whole letter through several times. As you are doing so, develop a basic outline for the whole letter. Most ancient occasional letters follow the basic three-part outline discussed in chapter 10. The greatest variation comes in the body of the letter. Play close attention to how the writer structures his arguments. It is helpful to consult good evangelical commentaries to see what the scholars are saying about the outline (beware of artificial arrangements, however).

Step 2: Analyze the structure to determine the textual unit for the lesson or sermon. Choose a passage of appropriate length for the treatment you

---

78. For an excellent discussion of preaching from the epistles using the hermeneutic triad, see Greidanus, *Modern Preacher*, Chapter 12.

wish to give and the time you have to give it. In this type of literature, it is best to think in paragraphs and paragraph clusters. Use the details of finding boundary features in chapter 12 to isolate self-contained units of thought. It is possible to preach the larger sections, but much of the detail is lost when we do so. However, many times the needs of the congregation call for broader brush strokes.

Step 3: Examine the text clause by clause. Once you have isolated your textual unit, apply a clause-by-clause analysis of the text. There are a variety of ways to examine a paragraph's clause structure. For the sake of space, I have chosen to simplify the semantic structure analysis model presented most recently in Larsen.[79] I have chosen 1 John 1:5–10 for analysis below.[80] Although this is from an epistle, the same procedures are suggested for a long speech in a narrative (e.g., John 13:31–16:33).

John's paragraph is in a simple principle-implication structure. The principle is that God is light, followed by two implications of that principle. In this case, the principal truth that God is light leads to implications of a person's relationship to God, indicated by the conduct of his or her life. Our main idea of the text, then, is this: "Since God is light; how a person lives indicates their relationship with God."

Step 4: Design a lesson or sermon outline from the structure of the text. The general principle here is to make the highest level structures in your paragraph the points of the lesson or sermon. In our case, the structures farthest to the left are the main points. Keeping this rule also helps keep the structure simple when you come to more complicated texts. When expressing the points, always ask: What is the essence of the relationships? The essence here is that the implications answer the question about the personal ramifications of the nature of God on his followers. So I turn it into a question: God is light—so what?

---

79. Larson, *Meaning-Based Translation*, 205–477.
80. The larger unit descends to 1 John 2:2, but I am simply treating this paragraph and not the whole paragraph cluster. For a defense of the section ending at 2:2, see J. Callow, "Where Does 1 John1 End?" in *Discourse Analysis and the New Testament*, 392–406. For a thorough analysis of the structure of 1 John, see L. Scott Kellum, "The Semantic Structure of 1 John: a Modest Proposal," *Faith and Mission* 23 (2008):34–82.

16.6. DISCOURSE ANALYSIS OF 1 JOHN 1:5–10

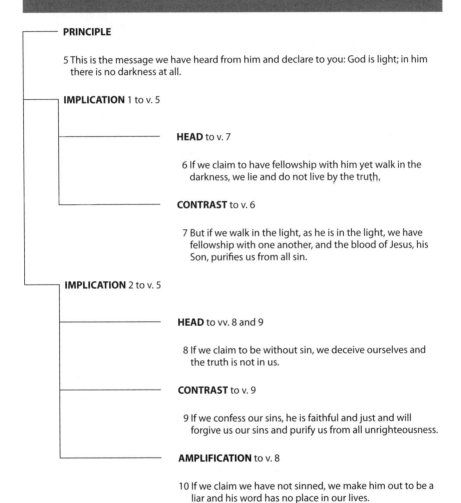

PRINCIPLE

5 This is the message we have heard from him and declare to you: God is light; in him there is no darkness at all.

IMPLICATION 1 to v. 5

HEAD to v. 7

6 If we claim to have fellowship with him yet walk in the darkness, we lie and do not live by the truth,

CONTRAST to v. 6

7 But if we walk in the light, as he is in the light, we have fellowship with one another, and the blood of Jesus, his Son, purifies us from all sin.

IMPLICATION 2 to v. 5

HEAD to vv. 8 and 9

8 If we claim to be without sin, we deceive ourselves and the truth is not in us.

CONTRAST to v. 9

9 If we confess our sins, he is faithful and just and will forgive us our sins and purify us from all unrighteousness.

AMPLIFICATION to v. 8

10 If we claim we have not sinned, we make him out to be a liar and his word has no place in our lives.

Lesson/Sermon on 1 John 1:5–9

Main Idea: Since God is light, how a person lives indicates his or her relationship with God.

Thesis: Real Christians have a changed walk and a changed assessment of their lives.

Outline:

Introduction: Tell own testimony of radical conversion from worldly pursuits to Christ. Talk about moral transformation that ensued, including breaking up ungodly relationships.

I.   Understand the Nature of God (1:5)
     Point: He is light (understood in an Old Testament context)
II. The Nature of the Believer's Walk (1:6–7)
     Point: The believer's life is conducted in the light—that is, in a righteous (although not sinless) manner
III. The Nature of the Believer's Confession (1:8–9)
     Point: Because believers walk in the light, they recognize their sin

Conclusion: Martin Luther's quote that Christians are beggars who know where to find bread. Christians are not better persons; they are forgiven sinners who are saved by grace.

APPLICATION

This textbook has been occupied with the (often nuanced) task of interpreting the Scripture. Yet, if we become experts at interpreting Scripture *only*, we lose the battle of glorifying Christ with our lives. We glorify Christ when we live out what we know. What is more, if we interpret 100 percent accurately and even stun our audience with our eloquence and skill in preaching or teaching the text but do not tell our people how to apply the truths we have taught, we have failed. To paraphrase our Lord, "Half done, you poor and unfaithful servant."

The prince of preachers, Charles Spurgeon, made the following statement in his *Lectures to my Students*: "We have all heard the story of the man who preached so well and lived so badly, that when he was in the pulpit everybody said he ought never to come out again, and when he was out of it they all declared he never ought to enter it again. From the imitation of such a Janus may the Lord deliver us."[81] Fundamentally, this is not

---

81. Charles Spurgeon, *Lectures to my Students: A Selection from Addresses Delivered to the Students of the Pastor's College, Metropolitan Tabernacle*, first series (New York: Sheldon & Company, 1875), 27–28.

necessarily a failure of good hermeneutics, but a failure to apply the truths we proclaim to our lives.

Application, then, is the believer's obedience to the correct interpretation of God's Word. The two together enable the believer to glorify Christ. Knowledge apart from application leads to hubris. But overt obedience is impossible without knowledge. In the preceding pages, we have repeatedly addressed the question of how to apply various portions of Scripture, such as the Law or the Epistles, in light of the complex hermeneutical issues involved.[82] As we conclude, it seems appropriate to give some general instruction regarding the application of the Bible to our lives.

Foundation

The foundation for mature obedience to Scripture begins with the conviction that it is the word of God. For most of us, this conviction is one of the reasons why we are reading this book. That Scripture is the word of God strongly implies that we should obey it. Notice that Paul connects inspiration and obedience in 2 Timothy 3:16–17: "*All Scripture is given by inspiration of God, and is profitable for doctrine, for reproof, for correction, for instruction in righteousness, that the man of God may be complete, thoroughly equipped for every good work.*"

The second motivation is that Scripture presents propositional truths to be obeyed by those who desire to follow God. Jesus summed up his teaching in Matthew 7:24: "Therefore everyone who hears these words of mine and puts them into practice is like a wise man who built his house on the rock." He habitually closed his parables with the words, "He who has ears to hear, let him hear" (e.g., Mark 4:9). Similarly, James wrote, "Do not merely listen to the word, and so deceive yourselves. Do what it says" (Jas. 1:22).

The third conviction is that Scripture is as relevant to us as it was to its first readers. The Bible everywhere assumes this. In fact, the very existence and preservation of the Bible attest to the conviction that people of all times and places need the word of God. Paul made this point repeatedly with regard to the OT. In Romans 15:4, he wrote, "For everything that was written in the past was written to teach us, so that through endurance and the encouragement of the Scriptures we might have hope." In 1

---

82. See chapters 3 and 11, respectively.

Chapter 16

Corinthians 10:6, he maintained, "Now these things occurred as examples to keep us from setting our hearts on evil things as they did."

We might say more, but we will close our foundational discussion with one last principle: obedience is the way to please God and glorify him in this life. The last book of the Bible twice makes this point: "Blessed is the one who reads the words of this prophecy, and blessed are those who hear it and take to heart what is written in it, because the time is near" (Rev. 1:3); "Behold, I am coming soon! Blessed is he who keeps the words of the prophecy in this book" (Rev 22:7).

Complications

That said, there are some complicating factors when it comes to applying the Scriptures. First, not every direct command found in the Bible is directly relevant for us today. Some might object to our above-stated conviction that Scripture is applicable for us by pointing out that believers under the new covenant are no longer under the Law, so certain laws no longer apply to us today. For example, the dietary laws are directly abrogated by Jesus in Mark 7:19: "in saying this, Jesus declared all foods clean." Are not the dietary laws, then, irrelevant for Gentile Christians? Or, for that matter, consider the matter of eating meat that had previously been sacrificed to idols. To be sure, this was a pressing issue for first-century Christians living in a pagan environment. But how is this matter still relevant for believers in the Western world at the beginning of the twenty-first century?

To complicate matters yet further, the Bible does not directly address many of the ethical issues facing modern civilization. Euthanasia, genetic manipulation, and cloning are just a few of the issues we face that the ancients did not. How are we to address these issues? Is it pointless to look to the Bible when grappling with these questions?

Human beings have lived and continue to live is a variety of circumstances and cultures. Even in our lifetime, we have experienced varying levels of technological sophistication. My parents (Andreas Köstenberger) did not own a car until I was eight, and I did not see a movie until I was 13. In fact, due to technological advances, in 20 years we may be facing ethical dilemmas that, at present, we could have never predicted. Because life is not stagnant, no book could give a single command for every possible situation. Not only would such a work be highly unwieldy, it would also be incredibly boring, resembling an auto-parts catalogue rather than our Bibles (e.g., Cloning sheep: Book 3, section A, part 1, law 3,034,578: You shall not monkey with the genomes of animals). Thankfully, God had another plan.

The book God delivered to us embodies, in a variety of genres, the story of creation, fall, and redemption. Along the way, numerous principles applying the word of God to our place within this story line are clearly delineated. God is our Creator; we fell in disobedience; Christ paid the price for our sins; repentance and faith in him secure our position in him. In cases where the situation described in Scripture matches our own, the biblical instructions are directly applicable to us. In cases where a given scenario in Scripture differs from the one we might be facing today, we should look for the underlying *principle* beneath a given command. That said, many (if not most) of the situations and commands contained in Scripture are very germane by virtue of our common humanity (and sinfulness!).

For example, Jesus issued the following invitation to his hearers in John 7:37–38, "If anyone is thirsty, let him come to me and drink. Whoever believes in me, as the Scripture has said, streams of living water will flow from within him." Jesus' offer is addressed to anyone who is thirsty for salvation, which is directly applicable to every human being who is aware of his or her sin and desires redemption. While the metaphor of "thirst" is involved, the application is nonetheless both direct and intuitively transparent: Come to Jesus and drink. Likewise, when Jesus told his disciples, "Whoever wants to be first must be slave of all" (Mark 10:44), the application for us is direct: go serve everyone you meet (that is, consider everyone else to be more important than you!).[83] If you do that, you'll be great in the kingdom. Or take the repeated biblical injunctions to forgive as another example. Because we are still sinners, we still sin, and still need to extend, and ask for, forgiveness. Many, many commands in Scripture operate in this way.

Nevertheless, it is true there are some passages in Scripture that are less directly applicable to us. A little while ago, we mentioned the food laws in Deuteronomy 14 and observed that in Mark 7:19, Jesus declared

---

83. The application is direct, notwithstanding the fact that Jesus' statement involves a reference to slavery, which is culturally constrained.

all foods clean. Should we, then, ignore these kinds of Old Testament passages because the teachings they contain have been superseded? Or do we find some health value in the dietary restrictions and strive to abide by these? Neither option seems entirely satisfying. A solution emerges once we consider the purpose of the dietary laws. Upon closer scrutiny, we discover the principle that is given as the grounds for these commands: "But you are a people holy to the LORD your God" (Deut. 14:21). This mirrors the statement made at the beginning of the same chapter: "You are the children of the LORD your God. Do not cut yourselves or shave the front of your heads for the dead, for you are a people holy to the LORD your God. Out of all the peoples on the face of the earth, the LORD has chosen you to be his treasured possession" (Deut. 14:1–2). Thus, the food laws were a sign of Israel's separation from the pagan world around them and her consecration for God. The Jewish people were not to be like the other surrounding nations. With the arrival of the new covenant, the inclusion of the Gentiles renders this particular badge of separation outmoded. God makes both Jew and Gentile one new entity in Christ. But *the principle* is not abrogated. The people of God are *not* to be like everyone else, but are to remain separate from the world and holy for God. Like Israel of old, they are to be his treasured possession.[84] The obvious application, then, is that it is not the surrounding culture that should dictate our behavior; it is to be the will of God.

At times, the procedure we have suggested here is called "principlization." Not everyone, however, agrees with this methodology. Jeannine Brown prefers what she calls "contextualization" (which likewise involves understanding and applying underlying principles). The main complaint again principlization, woodenly conceived, is that we should not elevate any principle or methodology, no matter how well-intentioned, over the word of God. This concern is well taken. Brown poses four questions to the proponents of principlization: (1) If something is *enculturated* truth, is it not still truth? (2) Does principlization not run the danger of elevating timeless abstracted truths over the canonical text? (3) Does not the transcultural principle in fact reflect the culture of the interpreter? and (4) Is

---

84. See Christopher J. Wright, *Deuteronomy*, NIBC 4 (Grand Rapids: Zondervan, 1996), 181–84.

such a methodology not at odds with entering the world of the text (reflecting an incarnational understanding of Scripture)?[85]

Brown's warrants are well taken and should help us put some controls on what we do in pursuing appropriate biblical application. The first question reminds us not to devalue the milieu of the text. Agreed; but we must still contextualize the meaning of the text in our lives and culture. Question #2 is also well taken, but our proposal here is not for us to look for *timeless abstracted* truth but for *concrete universal* principles that are expressed in the text in such a way that they are valid for the people of God in all cultures. Question #3 is a valid reminder to make sure that our principles are truly universal. Regarding the fourth question, we certainly would not advocate that at all. The principle we are after will emerge *after* we have entered the world of the text (as best as we can) and have exegeted the text to the best of our ability.[86]

Brown correctly cautions us as we move forward in our quest to apply biblical truth because the effort to make the connection between injunction and principle is fraught with danger. One can easily misread the correspondence between the original scenario addressed in Scripture and our situation. For instance, just because something is *in the Old Testament* does not automatically mean we must dispense with the direct injunction and look for a general principle. Surely no one would advocate a departure from the command "you shall not murder" (Deut. 5:17) in favor of some other universal truth. In this case, at least, the application today is just as direct as it was in Moses' day. At the same time, we do see this kind of application made frequently with texts in whose case direct application is not as readily apparent. I suggest we use the following steps to guard us from drawing questionable applications from the text.

---

85. Jeannine K. Brown, *Scripture as Communication: Introducing Biblical Hermeneutics* (Grand Rapids: Baker, 2007), 261–64.
86. And in keeping with sound hermeneutical method, such as the one presented in the present volume!

GUIDELINES FOR APPLICATION[87]

Steps of Application

Step 1: Apply the correct historical-grammatical exegesis of the text to find the intended purpose of the author. Application is always built on interpretation. If the interpretation is wrong, the application will be wrong as well. Use the tools you have learned in this book to determine the original meaning of the text. Enter its world, drink deeply from the well of Scripture. What is the main idea of the text? How does the author communicate it to us? What was his purpose and intent? It is imperative that you understand your passage for its own sake before you move on to formal application. I say "formal application," because it is impossible for anyone to read God's Word dispassionately at any level wondering how it is to be lived out in our individual and corporate lives. We read, posit tentative applications, read again, adjust what the Holy Spirit is saying to us through the word, and so on. This is a healthy and proper process. But formal finalized application comes at the end of this process.

Step 2: Evaluate the level of specificity of the original application(s). The major question here is whether the passage is dealing with an issue that is so conditioned by cultural or covenantal issues that it is impossible to apply the text directly. Generally, it is not terribly difficult to discern these culture-bound matters. But be careful. Make sure that you do not make culture something that rules over us and not God over culture. Mark Strauss, like Brown preferring the term "contextualization," posits five criteria to help us to determine whether or not a command in Scripture is specific to one particular culture.[88]

---

87. The following is adapted from William W. Klein, Craig L. Blomberg, and Robert L. Hubbard Jr., *Introduction to Biblical Interpretation*, 2d ed. (Nashville: Thomas Nelson, 2003), 482–503.

88. The following is adapted from Mark L. Strauss, "A Reflection," in Gary T. Meadors, ed., *Four Views on Moving Beyond the Bible to Theology*, Counterpoints (Grand Rapids: Zondervan, 2009), 294–97.

a. Criterion of purpose. The issue here is that the purpose of the rule generates the rule. So, then, it supersedes the rule itself. The good news is that the biblical authors (including the Holy Spirit) had a purpose in mind when they wrote the text. Discover that purpose. It will guide you to the application for today's hearers. So, for example, Peter's injunction to "Greet one another with a kiss of love" (1 Pet. 5:14) is generated by the desire for people in the body of Christ to show warm affection for one another, not just press lips.

b. *Criterion of cultural correspondence.* In determining whether or not a given biblical injunction is culturally conditioned (most are to one degree or another), we must ask, what is the correspondence to our culture? Are these cultural practices present in our culture? If the answer is yes, then we can apply the principle more directly. If no, then we look to the underlying principle to apply it to our situation. For example, meat sacrificed to idols (1 Corinthians 8) is not a direct problem in Western culture (though it is in some non-Western contexts), but having a government over us certainly is (1 Pet. 2:13–14). Thus we can directly apply Peter's command, "Submit yourselves for the Lord's sake to every authority instituted among men" (whether or not it is literally "kings" or "governors" who rule over us as it says in the passage), for the abiding reason he cites: these authorities "are sent by him [i.e., God] to punish those who do wrong and to commend those who do right." In the case of the injunction not to eat meat previously sacrificed to idols, on the other hand, a more indirect application will be called for (at least in the Western world), along the lines of not violating the conscience of other, less spiritually mature believers, who may be offended (rightly or wrongly so) by what they see us do (such as drink a glass of wine for dinner).

c. *Criterion of countercultural witness.* If a command runs counter to Jesus' own culture, then it runs counter to ours as well. For example, Jesus' command to love your enemies and Paul's command for husbands to love their wives so runs counter to their culture that they are clearly transcendent principles for us today as well. If you have an enemy or a wife, love them![89]

d. *Criterion of canonical consistency.* Is the ethical imperative consistent throughout the whole Bible? Then it applies today as well. For example, homosexuality is condemned throughout Scripture; thus it is still a sin today.[90]

e. *Criterion of creation principle.* An injunction is considered to be transcultural if it is defended by the author on the grounds of the original creation. See, e.g., 1 Timothy 2:12–14 "I do not permit a woman to teach or to have authority over a man; she must be silent. For Adam was formed first, then Eve. And Adam was not the one deceived; it was the woman who was deceived and became a sinner." The appeal to Adam and Eve regarding a woman teaching or having an ongoing authoritative or teaching ministry over men in a church, would strongly imply that the prohibition is not limited to the situation in Ephesus. The basis is universal, so too, then the command.

Step 3. Identify cross-cultural principles. This step is unnecessary if our passage treats a situation that is part of our experience. Prohibitions against sin, invitations to enjoy the salvation afforded in Christ, treatments of loneliness, betrayal, fortitude in the face of

---

89. Strauss lists the criterion of cultural limitations as his fifth criterion. In it he suggests "that caution must be exercised when an author is operating within strong cultural or societal constraints." He lists the example of slavery, contending that Paul fails to call for the dissolution of the institution because of societal constraints. He concludes "Just as countercultural statements in Scripture are likely to transcend specific situations, so imperatives that appear to be concessions to culture are less likely to have universal application" ("Reflection," 297). My problem here is that Paul never advocates slavery. In fact, nowhere in the New Testament is the institution itself explicitly addressed, and the only time Paul mentions an individual instance he all but demands the slave's manumission.

90. See on this Andreas J. Köstenberger, *God, Marriage & Family: Rebuilding the Biblical Foundation,* 2d ed. (Wheaton: Crossway, 2010), chapter 10.

trials, suffering for the cause of Christ, are all universally possible experiences for the believer. The main idea of the text applies directly in such situations.

However, if a particular command, example, promise, or waning cannot be applied universally without alteration, as identified in step 2 above, what do we do? First, we identify the principle underlying the command, example, promise, or warning. Here, we must be careful. One can easily identify a principle that is too broad or only part of the main idea of the text. Scott Duvall and Danny Hays give sound advice when identifying such a principle:[91]

a. *The principle should be reflected in the text.* That is, the text is pointing to this principle. It is often stated in the text itself. See, for example, the grounds given for the dietary laws in Deuteronomy 14 mentioned above. The principle underlies the text; it is not just tangential to the passage.

b. *The principle should be timeless and not tied to a specific situation.* This is moving into the area of application before you are ready. Avoid being specific regarding the distinction between modern and ancient. It should apply readily to both.

c. *The principle should not be culturally bound.* It is extremely easy to remove an item from a foreign culture. It is far more difficult to remove ourselves from ours. We believe the key here is to work at envisioning the principle from the ancient context.

d. *The principle should correspond to the teaching of the rest of Scripture.* Use the whole canon to test your principle. If your principle is in violation of clear teaching elsewhere, your principle is flawed.

---

91. The following points are taken from J. Scott Duvall and J. Daniel Hays, *Grasping God's Word*, 2d ed. (Grand Rapids: Zondervan, 2005), 24.

e. *The principle should be relevant to both the biblical and the contemporary audience.* If an ancient reader were to be able to read your principle, it should make absolute sense to him or her just as it does to you.

Discerning principles in culturally loaded contexts is not something to take lightly, nor do we elevate them above the text itself. If we have exegeted well, having accurately determined the meaning of the text, then the underlying principle should be easy to recognize.

Step 4: Find appropriate applications that embody broader principles. The communicator has clearly explained the meaning and purpose of the biblical text and now has discerned the underlying principle (often given directly in the text). It is time to suggest applications first for ourselves and then for our hearers. It is not as if there are generally two applications but the first one to apply the application and to respond to the invitation is the preacher or teacher.

Now a caveat: we do not discern principles, cut them free from their text, and arbitrarily apply them to all kinds of situations. We apply them to legitimately similar situations today. The principle that generated the command or action in the text should be applied appropriately in similar situations today. As Klein, Hubbard, and Blomberg observe, "[T]hus, we may give a hearty handshake instead of a holy kiss; we may set up inexpensive food banks instead of leaving our fields to be gleaned; and we should be concerned about the effect of consuming alcohol in the presence of a recovering alcoholic, even if we are never faced with the dilemma of whether or not to eat meat sacrificed to idols."[92]

In application, we no longer deal in theory, but with practice. We no longer describe the abstract, but the concrete. You should give practical suggestions of how the text applies to your audience today and suggest specific points of application. You should be persuading

---

92. Klein, Blomberg, and Hubbard, *Introduction to Biblical Interpretation*, 501.

your listeners to conform their lives to the truths of the passage of Scripture you have just presented.

Here is where you let the imagination run free. Imagine how your text impacts all of your hearers: children and adults; married, single, and single again; those caught in sin and those caught in self-righteousness; the employed, underemployed, unemployed, and the overemployed. You must investigate your culture (within the bounds of propriety). Know what's going on in the high school and in the nursing home. Read, study, and reflect on the collision of world views between your culture and the biblical world view.[93]

As a final example, consider the following portion of a lesson/sermon from Philippians 1:12–21:

Lesson/Sermon on Philippians 1:12–18

Main Idea: Paul expressed his confidence in the gospel in the midst of difficult circumstances.

Thesis: Believers should look at their circumstances from the perspective of a Christ-centered, gospel-focused life.

Outline:

Introduction: If you live long enough, bad circumstances are going to come your way. What should you do?

I.   Principle Stated: Paul's Circumstances Were Being Used by God (1:12–14)

Main Point: "Now I want you to know, brothers, that what has happened to me has really served to advance the gospel" (v. 12)

Although Paul's circumstances were bad for him, they were good for the progress of the gospel.

II.   Three Outcomes of Paul's Circumstances (1:15–17)

---

93. A classic work here is John R. W. Stott, *Between Two Worlds: The Challenge of Preaching Today* (Grand Rapids: Eerdmans, 1994).

A. The cause of Christ became known throughout the
Praetorian Guard 1:13)
B. Most of the brothers were preaching Christ more
boldly 1:14)
C. Some of the brothers were proclaiming Christ more
coldly (1:15–17)

III. Paul's Response to Adversity: Joy in the Gospel (1:18)
Conclusion: Paul's circumstances were bad, but they
turned out to the furtherance of the gospel. He saw
beyond his problems to God's purposes—and so should
we.

General Application: From this passage, the following points of
general application emerge.

1. God works not *in spite* of adverse circumstances but *through*
them.
General principle: All of our circumstances are a platform for
the glory of Christ and for the gospel of Christ.

2. We can trust that this is true without knowing all the reasons.
Because of the sovereignty of God
Because of goodness of God

3. We should not ask, "Why me, Lord?" but "What now, Lord?"
The first prayer we should utter is, "Lord, use this situation to
make yourself known and to bring glory to yourself."

Specific Points of Application:

• When someone hurts you

• When you can't pay the bills through no fault of your
own

- When loved ones are hurting

- When you get cancer

- When a child dies

- When you get a bad haircut, when you fail a test, when you don't get a promotion . . .

- Could God be using that to glorify himself? yes, Yes, YES!

Conclusion: When God uses your troubles, then they are not pointless. Joy comes when we understand that our afflictions are a platform for the redemption of others and we respond in submission to him. Yes, it is an act of faith, but one well grounded in the God's Word and borne out by our experience. He is faithful, and he will do it.

CONCLUSION

Having applied the truth of God's Word to our lives and communicated it to others, our interpretive journey has come to an end, at least as far as this book is concerned. The challenge of interpreting and applying Scripture, of course, is the task of a lifetime. In the preceding pages, we have sought to lay the foundation for the interpretation of Scripture within a proper biblical framework. On the basis of the recognition that the Bible was given to us by revelation from God under the inspiration of the Holy Spirit, we have used the hermeneutical triad of history, literature, and theology as the basic grid for biblical interpretation. We noted that before we turn to the task of interpretation, it is vital that we engage in proper preparation, which includes an awareness of our presuppositions and personal background, a prayerful disposition and a high view of Scripture, and a suitable method.

In Part I, we focused on the first dimension of the hermeneutical triad: (1) history. Chapter 2 explored the study of the historical setting and cultural background of a given passage of Scripture. Part II took up the bulk of our canonical journey, dealing with the second dimension of the hermeneutical triad, literature. We began this section with a canonical survey of both Testaments (chapters 3–4). After this, we focused on the study of the different genres of Scripture: in the Old Testament, narrative, poetry and wisdom, and prophecy (chapters 5–7); in the New Testament, narrative (Gospels/Acts), parables, epistles, and apocalyptic (chapters 8–11). The final portion of our discussion of literature was concerned with various entailments of the language of Scripture, whether discourse context (chapter 12), word meanings (chapter 13), or figurative language (chapter 14). In chapter 15, we reached the goal of our interpretive journey: theology, the third dimension of the hermeneutical triad. With this, we were ready to "get down to earth" (chapter 16): using the tools, moving from text to sermon, and applying God's Word to our lives.

Our prayers are with you as you hone your interpretive competencies for the glory of God, seeking to grow in (1) historical-cultural awareness; (2) canonical consciousness; (3) sensitivity to genre; (4) literary and linguistic competence; (5) a firm and growing grasp of biblical theology; and (6) an ability to apply and proclaim passages from every biblical genre to your own life and to the life of your congregation. In the spirit of 2 Peter 1:3–11, we would also encourage you to cultivate the following interpretive virtues:[94]

- Be submissive: Take on a submissive stance toward Scripture. Do not domesticate Scripture, or use biblical interpretation to serve your own ends. Approach Scripture with reverence as the Word of God.

---

94. If you are interested in pursuing this subject further, you should also read Andreas J. Köstenberger, *Excellence: The Character of God and the Pursuit of Scholarly Virtue* (Wheaton, IL: Crossway, 2011), which discusses a dozen or so scholarly and personal virtues (for additional helpful resources, see also the selected annotated bibliography at the end of that volume). An excellent, albeit more advanced, treatment of virtue is N. T. Wright, *After You Believe: Why Christian Character Matters* (New York: HarperOne, 2010).

- Be humble: Don't be dogmatic or arrogant. Focus on issues, not people.

- Be spiritual: Read 1 Cor 2:10b–16. Ask God to illumine your study of Scripture.

- Be sensible: Be mindful of the importance of balance. In your interpretation of Scripture, do not go out on a limb. Distinguish between possible, plausible, and probable interpretations. Beware of exegetical fallacies.

- Be seasoned. Be knowledgeable, develop experience. Be aware of the relevant issues and any potential pitfalls.

- Be committed to proper interpretive procedure: Make the hermeneutical triad your own and use it regularly. Look at every passage you study from the vantage point of history, literature, and theology.

- Be intentional and deliberate. Don't be haphazard in your interpretation of Scripture. Good hermeneutics does not happen by chance. It takes careful thought, planning, and effort, and requires the use of a sound interpretive method.

- Be consistent: Make sure your interpretive outcome and application are coordinated, not arbitrary. If 1 Timothy 3 applies to today, so does 1 Timothy 2. If certain patterns in the book of Acts apply (or don't apply), so do others (or they don't).

- Be perceptive: Remember Schlatter's hermeneutic of perception. Be quick to listen and slow to speak (Jas. 1:19; Eccl 5:1–2). Listen to God's Word carefully and aim to perceive what is there. Cultivate the ability of seeing and perceiving.

- Be conservative: Exercise interpretive restraint. Do not unduly exaggerate, illegitimately extrapolate, or otherwise exceed the evidence.

- Be courageous: If necessary, be prepared to swim against the stream of tradition. Scripture must have priority and be in a place of ultimate authority.

- Be exegetical: Don't cover up bad exegesis by generalizations, grand theories, or other improper interpretive moves.

We close this volume the way we started—with a call to all of us to heed Paul's exhortation to Timothy: "Do your best to present yourself to God as one approved, a workman who does not need to be ashamed and who correctly handles the word of truth" (2 Tim. 2:15). In a day when man-made solutions to the world's problems abound, those who are called by God to shepherd his flock must be faithful to his charge: "Preach the Word; be prepared in season and out of season; correct, rebuke and encourage—with great patience and careful instruction. For the time will come when men will not put up with sound doctrine" (2 Tim. 4:2–3).

These are indeed times when the truth of God's Word is regularly rejected, ridiculed, and set aside as irrelevant. But God's Word is not bound—it is "living and active," and "sharper than any double-edged sword, it . . . judges the thoughts and attitudes of the heart. Nothing in God's creation is hidden from his sight. Everything is uncovered and laid bare before the eyes of him to whom we must give account" (Heb. 4:12). God's Word has real authority and power, but only to the extent that it is faithfully and properly interpreted and proclaimed. To this end, may this book make a small contribution, for the good of God's people and for God's greater glory.

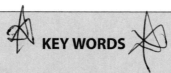

KEY WORDS

Catchword collection: group of proverbs that contain a common catchword

Chiastic collection: proverbs grouped in an A-B-B-A pattern

Expository literature: type of writing that explicates a thesis or defends an argument

Hortatory literature: type of writing in which the writer is suggesting or commanding an action the reader should take

Inclusio collection: group of proverbs bracketed by an inclusion, in which the first and last proverbs are similar or contain common catchwords

Parallel collection: proverbs grouped in an A-B-A-B pattern

Principlization: method of application that seeks to understand the principle underlying the biblical text in order to apply it properly to the reader's present context

Procedural literature: type of writing in which the writer provides step-by-step directions

Thematic collection: group of proverbs that maintain a common theme, dealing with the same subject matter

STUDY QUESTIONS

1. Which are some of the tools every interpreter should have?

2. What is the key principle for moving from text to sermon?

3. What are some of the mistakes to avoid in preaching Old and New Testament narratives, poetic and wisdom literature, prophecy and apocalyptic, and hortatory and expository literature?

4. What are the major steps in preaching Old and New Testament narratives, poetic and wisdom literature, prophecy and apocalyptic, and hortatory and expository literature?

5. What are some of the major challenges in applying the biblical text to life, and what are the basic steps in application?

ASSIGNMENTS

1. Write out your schedule for this coming week. Make sure you plan for sufficient time to study God's Word. Then, check to see if you were able to stick to your plan and continue setting realistic goals.

2. Look up Romans 1:16–17 in five different Bible translations, including the NIV, the NASB, and the CEV. Note any significant differences and then consult at least two of the Romans commentaries recommended in the appendix of this textbook to see what accounts for the differences. Then, indicate your preference for a given rendering and explain why you prefer it over the alternative renderings.

3. Repeat the process outlined in the previous assignment for John 1:16–18. Make sure to look up the passage in the NIV, the NASB, and the ESV. Again, compare translations and then consult at least two commentaries on John's Gospel to account for the differences. After this, identify which translation is preferable in this instance.

4. Use all the resources at your disposal to study John 2:23–3:21. Use background reference works to research any historical-cultural elements; prepare an outline of the passage; use a concordance and other lexical tools to study any relevant words; and then prepare a lesson or message on this passage. Conclude with a list of points of practical application.

5. Plan a series of lessons or messages on the book of Esther. Read through the entire book at least twice. Then, follow the steps outlined for teaching or preaching from Old Testament narratives in preparing your series of messages. Make sure to break down the book into an appropriate number of individual lessons or messages and to include a series of points of contemporary application, following the steps of application outlined in the course text.

6. Develop a message or series of messages on Colossians 1:9–23. Conduct a discourse analysis of this passage and then develop a lesson or sermon outline from your discourse analysis of this text. Make sure your lesson or sermon retains the shape of the epistolary text. Again, include a list of contemporary applications, following the guidelines in the course text.

CHAPTER BIBLIOGRAPHY

Adam, Peter. *Speaking God's Words*. Leicester: InterVarsity, 1996.

Akin, Daniel, David L. Allen, and Ned Mathews, eds. *Text-Driven Preaching*. Nashville: B&H, 2010.

Akin, Daniel, Bill Curtis, and Stephen Rummage. *Engaging Exposition*. Nashville: B&H, 2011.

Bauer, David R. *An Annotated Guide to Biblical Resources for Ministry*. Peabody, MA: Hendrickson, 2003.

Brown, Jeannine K. *Scripture as Communication: Introducing Biblical Hermeneutics*. Grand Rapids: Baker, 2007.

Carson, D. A. *New Testament Commentary Survey*. 6th ed. Grand Rapids: Baker, 2007.

Carter, Terry G., J. Scott Duvall, and Daniel Hays. *Preaching God's Word: A Hands-On Approach to Preparing, Developing, and Delivering the Sermon*. Grand Rapids: Zondervan, 2005.

Chapell, Bryan. *Christ-Centered Preaching: Redeeming the Expository Sermon*. 2d ed. Grand Rapids: Baker, 2005.

Clowney, Edmund P. *Preaching and Biblical Theology*. Grand Rapids: Eerdmans, 1961.

Doriani, Daniel M. *Getting the Message: A Plan for Interpreting and Applying the Bible*. Phillipsburg, NJ: Presbyterian & Reformed, 1996.

Duduit, Michael, ed. *Handbook of Contemporary Preaching*. Nashville: Broadman, 1992.

Duvall, J. Scott and J. Daniel Hays. Chapter 13. "Application" in *Grasping God's Word: A Hands-On Approach to Reading, Interpreting, and Applying the Bible*. 2d ed. Grand Rapids: Zondervan, 2005.

Goldsworthy, Graeme. *Preaching the Whole Bible as Christian Scripture: The Application of Biblical Theology to Expository Preaching*. Grand Rapids: Eerdmans, 2000.

Greidanus, Sidney. *The Modern Preacher and the Ancient Text: Interpreting and Preaching Biblical Literature*. Grand Rapids: Eerdmans, 1988.

_____. *Preaching Christ from the Old Testament: A Contemporary Hermeneutical Method.* Grand Rapids: Eerdmans, 1999.

Heisler, Greg. *Spirit-Led Preaching: The Holy Spirit's Role in Sermon Preparation and Delivery.* Nashville: B&H, 2007.

House, H. Wayne and Daniel Garland. *God's Message, Your Sermon: Discover, Develop, and Deliver What God Meant by What He Said.* Nashville: Thomas Nelson, 2007.

Johnson, Darrell W. *The Glory of Preaching: Participating in God's Transformation of the World.* Downers Grove: InterVarsity, 2009.

Kaiser, Walter C. Jr. *Toward an Exegetical Theology: Biblical Exegesis for Preaching and Teaching.* Grand Rapids: Baker, 1981.

_____. *Preaching and Teaching from the Old Testament: A Guide for the Church.* Grand Rapids: Baker, 2003.

Klein, William W., Craig L. Blomberg, and Robert L. Hubbard Jr. Chapters 11 and 12 in *Introduction to Biblical Interpretation.* 2d ed. Nashville: Thomas Nelson, 2003.

Longman, Tremper. *Old Testament Commentary Survey.* 4th ed. Grand Rapids: Baker, 2007.

Meadors, Gary T., gen. ed. *Four Views on Moving Beyond the Bible to Theology.* Counterpoints. Grand Rapids: Zondervan, 2009.

Merida, Tony. *Faithful Preaching.* Nashville: B&H, 2009.

Osborne, Grant R. Chapters 17 and 18 in *The Hermeneutical Spiral: A Comprehensive Introduction to Biblical Interpretation.* 2d ed. Downers Grove: InterVarsity, 2006.

Packer, James I. "The Preacher as Theologian." Pp. 79–95 in *When God's Voice Is Heard: Essays on preaching Presented to Dick Lucas.* Edited by C. Green and D. Jackman. Leicester: InterVarsity, 1995.

Robinson, Haddon R. *Biblical Preaching: The Development and Delivery of Expository Messages.* 2d ed. (Grand Rapids: Baker, 2001).

Stott, John R. W. *Between Two Worlds: The Challenge of Preaching Today.* Grand Rapids: Eerdmans, 1994.

Sunukjian, Donald R. *Invitation to Biblical Preaching: Proclaiming Truth with Clarity and Relevance.* Grand Rapids: Kregel, 2007.

Wegner, Paul D. *Using Old Testament Hebrew in Preaching: A Guide for Students and Pastors.* Grand Rapids: Kregel, 2009.

APPENDIX: BUILDING A BIBLICAL
STUDIES LIBRARY

GENERAL RESOURCES

Bibliographic Aids
General
Akin, Daniel L. *Building a Theological Library*. Wake Forest, NC: SEBTS, n. d.

Bauer, David R. *An Annotated Guide to Biblical Resources for Ministry*. Peabody, MA: Hendrickson, 2003.

Glynn, John. *Commentary & Reference Survey*. 10th ed. Grand Rapids: Kregel, 2007.

Old Testament
Longman, Tremper. *Old Testament Commentary Survey*. 4th ed. Grand Rapids: Baker, 2007.

New Testament
Carson, D. A. *New Testament Commentary Survey*. 6th ed. Grand Rapids: Baker, 2007.

Jewish Second Temple Literature
Köstenberger, Andreas J. and David W. Chapman, "Jewish Intertestamental and Early Rabbinic Literature: An Annotated Bibliographic Resource," *JETS* 43 (2000): 577–618. An update will appear in 2012.

Software
Accordance

BibleWorks

Bibloi

Logos

SESB (Stuttgart Electronic Study Bible)

Thesaurus Linguae Graecae (TLG Workplace)

Study Bibles

The ESV Study Bible.

The HCSB Study Bible.

The NET Bible.

The NIV Study Bible.

The NLT Study Bible.

REFERENCE WORKS

Introductions and Surveys
Old Testament

Arnold, Bill and Bryan Beyer. *Encountering the Old Testament.* Grand Rapids: Baker, 1999.

Hill, Andrew E. and John H. Walton. *A Survey of the Old Testament.* 3d ed. Grand Rapids: Zondervan, 2009.

LaSor, William, David A. Hubbard, and Frederick W. Bush. *Old Testament Survey: The Message, Form and Background of the Old Testament.* 2d ed. Grand Rapids: Eerdmans, 1996.

Longman, Tremper and Raymond B. Dillard. *An Introduction to the Old Testament.* 2d ed. Grand Rapids: Zondervan, 2007.

New Testament

Carson, D. A. and Douglas J. Moo. *An Introduction to the New Testament.* 2d ed. Grand Rapids: Zondervan, 2005.

Elwell, Walter A. and Robert W. Yarbrough. *Encountering the New Testament: A Historical and Theological Survey.* 2d ed. Grand Rapids: Baker, 2005.

Gundry, Robert H. *A Survey of the New Testament.* 4th ed. Grand Rapids: Zondervan, 2003.

Guthrie, Donald. *New Testament Introduction.* 4th ed. Downers Grove: InterVarsity, 1990.

Köstenberger, Andreas J., L. Scott Kellum, and Charles L. Quarles. *The Cradle, the Cross, and the Crown: An Introduction to the New Testament.* Nashville: B&H, 2009.

Specialized Commentaries

Arnold, Clinton E., ed. *Zondervan Illustrated Bible Backgrounds Commentary: New Testament.* 4 vols. Grand Rapids: Zondervan, 2002.

Beale, G. K. and D. A. Carson, eds. *Commentary on the New Testament Use of the Old Testament.* Grand Rapids: Baker, 2007.

Walton, John H., ed. *Zondervan Illustrated Bible Backgrounds Commentary: Old Testament.* 5 vols. Grand Rapids: Zondervan, 2009.

Background

Both Testaments

Drane, John, ed. *Illustrated Encyclopedia of the Bible.* Nashville: Thomas Nelson, 1998.

Metzger, Bruce M. and Michael D. Coogan, eds. *The Oxford Guide to People & Places of the Bible.* Oxford: Oxford University Press, 2001.

Packer, J. I., Merrill C. Tenney, and William White, Jr. *The Bible Almanac.* Nashville: Thomas Nelson, 1980.

Porter, J. R. *The Illustrated Guide to the Bible.* London: Barnes & Noble, 2000.

Old Testament

Arnold, Bill T. and Bryan E. Beyer, eds. *Readings from the Ancient Near East: Primary Sources for Old Testament Study.* Encountering Biblical Studies. Grand Rapids: Baker, 2002.

Hoerth, Alfred J., Gerald L. Mattingly, and Edwin M. Yamauchi. *Peoples of the Old Testament World.* Grand Rapids: Baker, 1994.

Kaiser, Walter. *A History of Israel: From the Bronze Age through the Jewish Wars.* Nashville: Broadman & Holman, 1998.

Long, V. Philips, David Baker, and Gordon Wenham, eds. *Windows into Old Testament History.* Grand Rapids: Eerdmans, 2002.

Long, V. Philips, Tremper Longman III, and Iain W. Provan. *A Biblical History of Israel.* Louisville: Westminster John Knox, 2003.

Merrill, Eugene H. *Kingdom of Priests: A History of Old Testament Israel.* Grand Rapids: Baker, 1996.

Millard, Alan. *Discoveries from Bible Times.* Oxford: Lion, 1990.

Sparks, Kenton L. *Ancient Texts for the Study of the Hebrew Bible: A Guide to the Background Literature.* Peabody, MA: Hendrickson, 2005.

New Testament

Barnett, Paul. *Jesus and the Rise of Early Christianity: A History of New Testament Times.* Downers Grove: InterVarsity, 1999.

Barrett, C. K. *New Testament Background: Selected Documents.* 2d ed. San Francisco: HarperCollins, 1989.

Burge, Gary M., Lynn H. Cohick, and Gene L. Green. *The New Testament in Antiquity: A Survey of the New Testament within Its Cultural Contexts.* Grand Rapids: Zondervan, 2009.

Elwell, Walter A. and Robert W. Yarbrough, eds. *Readings from the First-Century World: Primary Sources for New Testament Study.* Encountering Biblical Studies. Grand Rapids: Baker, 1998.

Evans, Craig A. and Stanley E. Porter, eds. *Dictionary of New Testament Background.* Downers Grove: InterVarsity, 2000.

Evans, Craig A. *Ancient Texts for New Testament Studies: A Guide to the Background Literature.* Peabody, MA: Hendrickson, 2005.

Ferguson, Everett. *Backgrounds of Early Christianity.* 2d ed. Grand Rapids: Eerdmans, 1993.

Porter, Stanley E., ed. *Dictionary of New Testament Background.* Downers Grove: InterVarsity, 2000.

BIBLICAL LANGUAGES

Texts
Both Testaments

Biblia Sacra: Utriusque Testamenti Editio Hebraica Et Graeca. Peabody, MA: Hendrickson, 2006.

Old Testament

Biblia Hebraica Stuttgartensia. K Elliger and W. Rudolph, eds. Stuttgart: Deutsche Bibelstiftung, 1967–1977.

Septuaginta. 2 vols. A. Rahlfs, ed. Stuttgart: Württemburgische Bibelanstalt, 1935/1971.

New Testament

Aland, Barbara and Kurt, et al., eds. *The Greek New Testament.* 4th ed. New York: United Bible Societies, 1993.

Introductory Grammars
Hebrew

Fuller, Russell T. and Kyoungwon Choi. *Invitation to Biblical Hebrew: A Beginning Grammar*. Invitation to Theological Studies Series. Grammar and Workbook. Grand Rapids: Kregel, 2006.

Pratico, Gary D. and Miles V. Van Pelt. *Basics of Biblical Hebrew*. Grammar, Workbook, and Study Aids. Grand Rapids: Zondervan, 2001.

Ross, A. P. *Introducing Biblical Hebrew*. Grand Rapids: Baker, 2001.

Seow, C. L. A. *Grammar for Biblical Hebrew*. Nashville: Abingdon, 1995.

Greek

Baugh, Steven M. *A New Testament Greek Primer*. 2d ed. Phillipsburg, NJ: Presbyterian & Reformed, 2009.

Black, David Alan. *Learn to Read New Testament Greek*. 3d ed. Nashville: Broadman & Holman, 2009.

Mounce, William D. *Basics of Biblical Greek*. Grand Rapids: Zondervan, 1993.

Intermediate/Advanced Grammars
Hebrew

Joüon, Paul and T. Muraoka. *A Grammar of Biblical Hebrew*. 2 vols. Rome: Pontifical Biblical Institute, 1993.

Kautzsch, E., ed. *Gesenius' Hebrew Grammar*. Translated by A. E. Cowley. 2d ed. Oxford: Clarendon, 1910.

Waltke, Bruce K. and M. O'Connor. *An Introduction to Biblical Hebrew Syntax*. Winona Lake, IN: Eisenbrauns, 1990.

Greek

Baugh, Steven M. *A First John Reader: Intermediate Greek Reading Notes and Grammar*. Phillipsburg, NJ: Presbyterian & Reformed, 1999.

Mounce, William D. *A Graded Reader of Biblical Greek*. Grand Rapids: Zondervan, 1996.

_____. *The Morphology of Biblical Greek*. Grand Rapids: Zondervan, 1994.

Wallace, Daniel B. *Greek Grammar Beyond the Basics: An Exegetical Syntax of the New Testament*. Grand Rapids: Zondervan, 1996. Abridgement: *The Basics of New Testament Syntax*. Grand Rapids: Zondervan, 2000.

Textual Criticism
Both Testaments
Wegner, Paul D. *A Student's Guide to Textual Criticism of the Bible: Its History, Methods and Results.* Downers Grove: InterVarsity, 2006.

Old Testament
Scott, William R. *A Simplified Guide to the BHS.* 3d ed. N. Richland Hills, TX: Bibal, 1987.

Würthwein, Ernst. *The Text of the Old Testament: An Introduction to the Biblia Hebraica.* 2d ed. Grand Rapids: Eerdmans, 1995.

New Testament
Aland, Kurt and Barbara. *The Text of the New Testament.* 2d ed. Grand Rapids: Eerdmans, 1989.

Metzger, Bruce M. *A Textual Commentary on the Greek New Testament.* 2d ed. New York: United Bible Society, 1994.

Metzger, Bruce M. and Bart Ehrman. *The Text of the New Testament: Its Transmission, Corruption, and Restoration.* 4th ed. Oxford/New York: Oxford University Press, 2005.

Lexical and Syntactical Study
See also Bible Software above and Dictionaries below.
General
Carson, D. A. *Exegetical Fallacies.* 2d ed. Grand Rapids: Baker, 1996.

Cotterell, Peter and Max Turner. *Linguistics and Biblical Interpretation.* Downers Grove: InterVarsity, 1989.

Silva, Moisés. *Biblical Words and Their Meaning: An Introduction to Lexical Semantics.* Rev. ed. Grand Rapids: Zondervan, 1994.

Both Testaments
Green, Jay P., gen. ed. *The Interlinear Bible.* 2d ed. Peabody, MA: Hendrickson, 1986.

Hebrew
Brown, Francis, S. R. Driver, and Charles A. Briggs. *The New Brown-Driver-Briggs-Gesenius Hebrew-English Lexicon.* Peabody, MA: Hendrickson, 1979.

Harris, R. Laird, Gleason L. Archer, and Bruce Waltke. *Theological Wordbook of the Old Testament.* 2 vols. Chicago: Moody, 1980.

Kohlenberger, John R. and James A. Swanson. *Hebrew-English Concordance to the Old Testament.* Zondervan. Grand Rapids: Zondervan, 1998.

Rudolph, W. and H. P. Rüger, eds. *Biblia Hebraica Stuttgartensia.* 2d ed. Stuttgart: Deutsche Bibelgesellschaft, 1983.

Wigram, George V. *The New Englishman's Hebrew Concordance.* Peabody, MA: Hendrickson, 1986.

Greek

Bauer, Walter, Frederick W. Danker, William F. Arndt, and F. Wilbur Gingrich. *A Greek-English Lexicon of the New Testament and Other Early Christian Literature.* 3d ed. Chicago: University of Chicago Press, 2000. (BDAG)

Goodrick, Edward W., John R. Kohlenberger, and James A. Swanson. *Exhaustive Concordance to the Greek New Testament.* Grand Rapids: Zondervan, 1995.

Köstenberger, Andreas J. and Raymond P. Bouchoc, *The Book Study Concordance.* Nashville: Broadman & Holman, 2003.

Louw, Johannes P. and Eugene A. Nida. *A Greek-English Lexicon of the New Testament.* 2 vols. New York: United Bible Society, 1988, 1989.

Wigram, George V. and Ralph D. Winter. *Word Study New Testament and Concordance.* 2 vols. Wheaton: Tyndale House, 1978.

DICTIONARIES

Both Testaments

Alexander, T. Desmond, Brian S. Rosner, D. A. Carson, and Graeme Goldsworthy, eds. *New Dictionary of Biblical Theology.* Downers Grove: InterVarsity, 2000.

Freedman, David Noel, ed. *The Anchor Bible Dictionary.* 6 vols. Garden City: Doubleday, 1992.

Marshall, I. Howard, Alan R. Millard, J. I. Packer, and Donald J. Wiseman, eds. *New Bible Dictionary.* 3d ed. Downers Grove: InterVarsity, 1996.

Ryken, Leland, James C. Wilhoit, and Tremper Longman III, eds. *Dictionary of Biblical Imagery.* Downers Grove: InterVarsity, 1998.

Vanhoozer, Kevin J., ed. *Dictionary for Theological Interpretation of the Bible.* Grand Rapids: Baker, 2005.

Old Testament

VanGemeren, Willem A., gen. ed. *New International Dictionary of Old Testament Theology and Exegesis.* 5 vols. Grand Rapids: Zondervan, 1997.

New Testament

Balz, Horst and Gerhard Schneider, eds. *Exegetical Dictionary of the New Testament.* 3 vols. Grand Rapids: Eerdmans, 1990–93.

Brown, Colin, ed. *New International Dictionary of New Testament Theology.* 4 vols. Grand Rapids: Zondervan, 1986.

Green, Joel B., Scot McKnight, and I. Howard Marshall, eds. *Dictionary of Jesus and the Gospels.* Downers Grove: InterVarsity, 1992. 2d ed. forthcoming.

Hawthorne, Gerald F., Ralph P. Martin, and Daniel G. Reid, eds. *Dictionary of Paul and His Letters.* Downers Grove: InterVarsity, 1993.

THEOLOGIES

Biblical Theology

Alexander, T. Desmond. *From Eden to the New Jerusalem: An Introduction to Biblical Theology.* Grand Rapids: Kregel, 2009.

Goldsworthy, Graeme. *According to Plan.* Downers Grove: InterVarsity, 2002.

Hafemann, Scott J., ed. *Biblical Theology: Retrospect and Prospect.* Downers Grove: InterVarsity, 2002.

Scobie, Charles H. H. *The Ways of Our God: An Approach to Biblical Theology.* Grand Rapids: Eerdmans, 2003.

Old Testament

Dempster, Stephen. *Dominion and Dynasty: A Biblical Theology of the Hebrew Bible.* NSBT. Downers Grove: InterVarsity, 2003.

Dumbrell, William J. *The Faith of Israel: A Theological Survey of the Old Testament.* Grand Rapids: Baker, 2001.

House, Paul R. *Old Testament Theology.* Downers Grove: InterVarsity, 1998.

Kaiser, Walter. *Toward an Old Testament Theology.* Grand Rapids: Zondervan, 1978.

Martens, Elmer A. *God's Design: A Focus on Old Testament Theology.* 2d ed. Grand Rapids: Baker, 1994.

Merrill, Eugene H. *Everlasting Dominion: A Theology of the Old Testament* (Nashville, Broadman & Holman, 2006.

Waltke, Bruce K. *An Old Testament Theology: An Exegetical, Canonical, and Thematic Approach.* Grand Rapids: Zondervan, 2006.

New Testament

Caird, George B. *New Testament Theology.* Completed and edited by L. D. Hurst. Oxford: Clarendon, 1994.

Guthrie, Donald. *New Testament Theology.* Downers Grove: InterVarsity, 1981.

Ladd, George Eldon. *A Theology of the New Testament.* Rev. ed. Grand Rapids: Eerdmans, 1993.

Marshall, I. Howard. *New Testament Theology: Many Witnesses, One Gospel.* Downers Grove: InterVarsity, 2004.

Schreiner, Thomas R. *New Testament Theology: Magnifying God in Christ.* Grand Rapids: Baker, 2008.

Thielman, Frank. *Theology of the New Testament: A Canonical and Synthetic Approach.* Grand Rapids: Zondervan, 2005.

Wright, N. T. Vol. 1: *The New Testament and the People of God.* Vol. 2. *Jesus and the Victory of God.* Vol. 3: *The Resurrection and the Son of God.* Christian Origins and the Question of God. 5 vols. (in progress). Minneapolis: Fortress,1992, 1996, 2003.

Systematic Theology

Akin, Daniel, ed. *A Theology for the Church.* Nashville: B & H, 2007.

Erickson, Millard J. *Christian Theology.* 2d ed. Grand Rapids: Baker, 1998

Grudem, Wayne A. *Systematic Theology.* Grand Rapids: Zondervan, 1994.

HERMENEUTICS

Duvall, J. Scott and J. Daniel Hays. *Grasping God's Word: A Hands-On Approach to Reading, Interpreting, and Applying the Bible.* 2d ed. Grand Rapids: Zondervan, 2005.

Goldsworthy, Graeme. *Gospel-Centered Hermeneutics: Foundations and Principles of Evangelical Biblical Interpretation*. Downers Grove: InterVarsity, 2006.

Klein, William W., Craig L. Blomberg, and Robert L. Hubbard. *Introduction to Biblical Interpretation*. 2d ed. Dallas: Word, 2004.

Osborne, Grant R. *The Hermeneutical Spiral: A Comprehensive Introduction to Biblical Interpretation*. 2d ed. Downers Grove: InterVarsity, 2006.

Thiselton, Anthony. *Hermeneutics: An Introduction*. Grand Rapids: Eerdmans, 2009.

Vanhoozer, Kevin J. *Is There a Meaning in This Text?* Grand Rapids: Zondervan, 1998.

_____. *The Drama of Doctrine: A Canonical-Linguistic Approach to Christian Theology*. Louisville: Westminster John Knox, 2005.

COMMENTARIES

Commentary Series

Anchor Bible (AB)

Baker Exegetical Commentary on the New Testament (BECNT)

Eerdmans Critical Commentary (ECC)

Expositor's Bible Commentary, revised edition (EBC)

Hermeneia

Historical Commentary on the Old Testament (HCOT)

International Critical Commentary (ICC)

Interpretation

IVP New Testament Commentary (IVPNTC)

New American Commentary (NAC)

New Century Bible Commentary (NCBC)

New International Biblical Commentary (NIBC)

New International Commentary on the New Testament (NICNT)

New International Commentary on the Old Testament (NICOT)

New International Greek Testament Commentary (NIGTC)

NIV Application Commentary (NIVAC)

Pillar New Testament Commentaries (PNTC)

Tyndale New Testament Commentaries (TNTC)

Tyndale Old Testament Commentaries (TOTC)

Word Biblical Commentary (WBC)

One-Volume Commentaries

Elwell, Walter A., ed. *Evangelical Commentary on the Bible*. Grand Rapids: Baker, 1989.

Wenham, Gordon J., J. A. Motyer, D. A. Carson, and R. T. France, eds. *New Bible Commentary*. Downers Grove: InterVarsity, 1994.

Individual Commentaries

Old Testament

Genesis

Arnold, William T. *Encountering the Book of Genesis*. Grand Rapids: Baker, 1998.

Hamilton, Victor P. *The Book of Genesis*. NICOT. 2 vols. Grand Rapids: Eerdmans, 1990, 1995.

Mathews, Kenneth A. *Genesis*. NAC. 2 vols. Nashville: Broadman & Holman, 2005.

Wenham, Gordon J. *Genesis*. WBC. 2 vols. Nashville: Thomas Nelson/Word, 1987, 1994.

Exodus

Kaiser, Walter C. Jr. "Exodus." EBC 2. Grand Rapids: Zondervan, 1990, 285–497.

Stuart, Douglas K. *Exodus*. NAC. Nashville: Broadman & Holman, 2006.

Leviticus

Harrison, R. K. *Leviticus*. TOTC. Downers Grove: InterVarsity, 1980.

Rooker, Mark F. *Leviticus*. NAC. Nashville: Broadman & Holman, 2000.

Wenham, Gordon J. *The Book of Leviticus*. NICOT. Grand Rapids: Eerdmans, 1979.

Numbers

Ashley, Timothy R. *Numbers*. NICOT. Grand Rapids, Eerdmans, 1993.

Cole, R. Dennis. *Numbers*. NAC. Nashville: Broadman & Holman, 2000.

Wenham, Gordon J. *Numbers*. TOTC. Downers Grove: InterVarsity, 1981.

Deuteronomy

Craigie, Peter C. *Deuteronomy*. NICOT. Grand Rapids, Eerdmans, 1976.

Merrill, Eugene. *Deuteronomy*. NAC. Nashville: Broadman & Holman, 1994.

Wright, Christopher J. H. *Deuteronomy*. NIBC. Peabody, MA: Hendrickson, 1996.

Joshua

Hess, Richard S. *Joshua*. TOTC. Downers Grove: InterVarsity, 1996.
Howard, David, Jr. *Joshua*. NAC. Nashville: Broadman & Holman, 1998.
Woudstra, M. H. *The Book of Joshua*. NICOT. Grand Rapids: Eerdmans, 1981.

Judges/Ruth

Block, Daniel. *Judges, Ruth*. NAC. Nashville: Broadman & Holman, 1999.
Boling, R. G. *Judges: A New Translation with Introduction and Commentary*. AB. Garden City: Doubleday, 1975.
Younger, K. Lawson. *Judges/Ruth*. NIVAC. Grand Rapids: Zonde
Block, Daniel I. *Judges, Ruth*. NAC. Nashville: Broadman & Holman, 1999.
Bush, Frederic W. *Ruth, Esther*. WBC. Dallas: Word, 1996.
Hubbard, Robert L Jr. *Ruth*. NICOT. Grand Rapids: Eerdmans, 1988.

1–2 Samuel

Arnold, William T. *1 and 2 Samuel*. NIVAC. Grand Rapids: Zondervan, 2003.
Baldwin, Joyce G. *1 & 2 Samuel*. TOTC. Downers Grove: InterVarsity, 1988.
Youngblood, Ronald F. "1, 2 Samuel." EBC 3. Grand Rapids: Zondervan, 1992.

1–2 Kings

House, Paul R. *1, 2 Kings*. NAC. Nashville: Broadman & Holman, 1995.
Patterson, Richard D. and Hermann J. Austel. "1 and 2 Kings." EBC 4. Grand Rapids: Zondervan, 1988. 2d ed. forthcoming.
Provan, Iain W. *1 and 2 Kings*. NIBC. Peabody, MA: Hendrickson, 1995.
Walsh, Jerome T. *1 Kings*. Berit Olam. Collegeville, MN: Liturgical Press, 1996.
Wiseman, Donald J. *1 & 2 Kings*. TOTC. Downers Grove: InterVarsity, 1993.

1–2 Chronicles

Dillard, Raymond B. *2 Chronicles*. Waco, TX: Word, 1987.
Hill, Andrew E. *1 Chronicles/2 Chronicles*. NIVAC. Grand Rapids: Zondervan, 2003.

Payne, J. Barton. "1 and 2 Chronicles." EBC 4. Grand Rapids: Zondervan, 1988.

Williamson, H. G. M. *1 and 2 Chronicles*. NCBC. Grand Rapids: Eerdmans, 1982.

Ezra/Nehemiah

Fensham, F. C. *The Books of Ezra and Nehemiah*. NICOT. Grand Rapids: Eerdmans, 1982.

Williamson, H. G. M. *Ezra, Nehemiah*. WBC. Waco, TX: Word, 1985.

Yamauchi, Edwin. "Ezra, Nehemiah." EBC 4. Grand Rapids: Zondervan, 1988.

Esther

Baldwin, Joyce G. *Esther*. TOTC. Downers Grove: InterVarsity, 1984.

Bush, Frederic W. *Ruth, Esther*. WBC. Dallas: Word, 1997.

Jobes, Karen. *Esther*. NIVAC. Grand Rapids: Zondervan, 1999.

Job

Anderson, Francis I. *Job: An Introduction and Commentary*. TOTC. Downers Grove: InterVarsity, 1976.

Clines, David J. *Job 1–20* and *Job 21–37*. WBC. Dallas: Word, 1989 and Nashville: Thomas Nelson, 2006.

Hartley, John F. *The Book of Job*. NICOT. Grand Rapids, Eerdmans, 1988.

Smick, Elmer B. "Job." EBC 4. Grand Rapids: Zondervan, 1988.

Psalms

Craigie, Peter C. *Psalms 1–50*. WBC. Waco, TX: Word, 1983.

Kidner, Derek. *Psalms 1–72*. TOTC. 2 vols. Downers Grove: InterVarsity, 1973, 1975.

VanGemeren, Willem A. "Psalms." EBC 5. Grand Rapids: Zondervan, 1991.

Proverbs

Fox, Michael V. *Proverbs: A New Translation with Introduction and Commentary*. AB. 2 vols. New York: Doubleday, 2000, 2003.

Kidner, Derek. *Proverbs*. TOTC. Downers Grove: InterVarsity, 1964.

Waltke, Bruce K. *The Book of Proverbs*. NICOT. 2 vols. Grand Rapids: Eerdmans, 2004, 2005.

Ecclesiastes

Eaton, Michael A. *Ecclesiastes: An Introduction and Commentary.* TOTC. Downers Grove: InterVarsity, 1983.

Longman, Tremper III. *Ecclesiastes.* NICOT. Grand Rapids, Eerdmans, 1998.

Provan, Iain. *Ecclesiastes and Song of Songs.* NIVAC. Grand Rapids: Zondervan, 2001.

Seow, Choon-Leon. *Ecclesiastes: A New Translation with Introduction and Commentary.* AB. New York: Doubleday, 1997.

Song of Songs

Carr, G. Lloyd. *The Song of Solomon.* TOTC. Downers Grove: InterVarsity, 1984.

Longman, Tremper III. *Song of Songs.* NICOT. Grand Rapids, Eerdmans, 2001.

Provan, Iain. *Ecclesiasts and Song of Songs.* NIVAC. Grand Rapids: Zondervan, 2001.

Isaiah

Oswalt, John N. *The Book of Isaiah.* NICOT. 2 vols. Grand Rapids: Eerdmans, 1986, 1997.

Motyer, J. A. *The Prophecy of Isaiah: An Introduction and Commentary.* Downers Grove: InterVarsity, 1993.

Watts, John D. W. *Isaiah.* WBC. 2 vols. Waco: Word, 1985, 1987.

Jeremiah/Lamentations

Craigie, Peter C., Page H. Kelley, and Joel F. Drinkard Jr. *Jeremiah 1–25.* WBC. Dallas: Word, 1991.

Harrison, R. K. *Jeremiah and Lamentations: An Introduction and Commentary.* TOTC. Downers Grove: InterVarsity, 1981.

Hillers, Delbert. *Lamentations: A New Translation with Introduction and Commentary.* AB. Rev. ed. Garden City: Doubleday, 1992.

Keown, Gerald L., Pamela J. Scalise, and Thomas G. Smothers. *Jeremiah 26–52.* WBC. Dallas: Word, 1995.

Provan, Iain. *Lamentations.* NCBC. Grand Rapids: Eerdmans, 1991.

Thompson, John A. *The Book of Jeremiah.* NICOT. Grand Rapids: Eerdmans, 1980.

Ezekiel

Alexander, Ralph H. "Ezekiel." EBC 6. Grand Rapids: Zondervan, 1986.

Allen, Leslie C. *Ezekiel 1–19* and *Ezekiel 20–48*. WBC 28 and 29. Nashville: Nelson, 1990, 1994.

Block, Daniel I. *The Book of Ezekiel*. NICOT. 2 vols. Grand Rapids, Eerdmans, 1997, 1998.

Duguid, Iain M. *Ezekiel*. NIVAC. Grand Rapids: Zondervan, 1999.

Greenberg, Moshe. *Ezekiel: A New Translation with Introduction and Commentary*. AB. 2 vols. Garden City: Doubleday, 1983, 1997.

Daniel

Baldwin, Joyce G. *Daniel: An Introduction and Commentary*. TOTC. Downers Grove: InterVarsity, 1978.

Goldingay, John. *Daniel*. WBC. Dallas: Word, 1989.

Longman, Tremper III. *Daniel*. NIVAC. Grand Rapids: Zondervan, 1999.

Miller, Stephen R. *Daniel*. NAC. Nashville: Broadman & Holman, 1994.

Minor Prophets

General

Achtemeier, Elizabeth. *Minor Prophets*. NIBC. 2 vols. Peabody, MA: Hendrickson, 1996.

Craigie, Peter C. *Twelve Prophets*. DSB. 2 vols. Philadelphia: Westminster, 1984.

Hill, Andrew E. and Richard D. Patterson. *Minor Prophets*. Carol Stream, IL: Tyndale, 2007.

McComiskey, Thomas E. *The Minor Prophets*. 3 vols. Grand Rapids: Baker, 1998.

Sweeney, Marvin A. *The Twelve Prophets*. Berit Olam. 2 vols. Collegeville, MN: Liturgical Press, 2000.

Hosea

Anderson, Francis I. and David N. Freedman. *Hosea: A New Translation and Commentary with Introduction and Commentary*. AB. Garden City: Doubleday, 1980.

Garrett, Duane A. *Hosea, Joel*. NAC. Nashville: B & H, 1997.

Hubbard, David Allan. *Hosea*. TOTC. Downers Grove: InterVarsity, 1989.

Stuart, Douglas K. *Hosea–Jonah*. WBC. Waco, TX: Word, 1987.

Joel

Garrett, Duane A. *Hosea, Joel.* NAC. Nashville: B & H, 1997.

Hubbard, David Allan. *Joel and Amos.* TOTC. Downers Grove: InterVarsity, 1989.

Patterson, Richard D. "Joel." EBC 7. Grand Rapids: Zondervan, 1985.

Stuart, Douglas. *Hosea–Johah.* WBC. Dallas: Word, 1987.

Amos

Andersen, Francis I. and David N. Freedman. *Amos: A New Translation with Introduction and Commentary.* AB. Garden City: Doubleday, 1980.

Hubbard, David Allan. *Joel and Amos.* TOTC. Downers Grove: InterVarsity, 1989.

Obadiah

Alexander, Desmond, David W. Baker, and Bruce K. Waltke. *Obadiah, Jonah, Micah.* TOTC. Downers Grove: InterVarsity, 1988.

Stuart, Douglas. *Hosea–Jonah.* WBC. Dallas: Word, 1987.

Jonah

Alexander, Desmond, David W. Baker, and Bruce K. Waltke. *Obadiah, Jonah, Micah.* TOTC. Downers Grove: InterVarsity, 1988.

Baker, David W., T. Desmond Alexander, and Bruce K. Waltke. *Obadiah, Jonah, Micah: An Introduction and Commentary.* TOTC. Downers Grove: InterVarsity, 1988.

Stuart, Douglas K. *Hosea–Jonah.* WBC. Waco, TX: Word, 1987.

Micah

Andersen, Francis I. and David Noel Freedman. *Micah: A New Translation with Introduction and Commentary.* AB. New York: Doubleday, 2000.

Baker, David W., T. Desmond Alexander, and Bruce K. Waltke. *Obadiah, Jonah, Micah: An Introduction and Commentary.* TOTC. Downers Grove: InterVarsity, 1988.

Barker, Kenneth L. "Micah." NAC 20. Nashville: Broadman & Holman, 1999.

Waltke, Bruce K. "Micah: An Introduction and Commentary." In D. W. Baker, D. Alexander, and B. Waltke, *Obadiah, Jonah, and Micah.* TOTC. Downers Grove: InterVarsity, 1998.

Nahum

Meier, Walther A. *The Book of Nahum: A Commentary*. Reprint. Grand Rapids:
  Baker, 1980.
Patterson, Richard D. *Nahum, Habakkuk, Zephaniah*. Dallas: Biblical Studies
  Press, 2003.
Roberts, J. J. M. *Nahum, Habakkuk, and Zephaniah*. OTL. Louisville:
  Westminster/John Knox, 1991.
Robertson, O. Palmer. *The Books of Nahum, Habakkuk, and Zephaniah*.
  NICOT. Grand Rapids: Eerdmans, 1990.

Habakkuk

Baker, David W. *Nahum, Habakkuk and Zephaniah: An Introduction and
  Commentary*. TOTC. Downers Grove, InterVarsity, 1988.
Patterson, Richard D. *Nahum, Habakkuk, Zephaniah*. Dallas: Biblical Studies
  Press, 2003.
Roberts, J. J. M. *Nahum, Habakkuk, and Zephaniah*. OTL. Louisville:
  Westminster/John Knox, 1991.
Robertson, O. Palmer. *The Books of Nahum, Habakkuk, and Zephaniah*.
  NICOT. Grand Rapids: Eerdmans, 1990.
Smith, Ralph L. *Micah–Malachi*. WBC. Dallas: Word, 1984.

Zephaniah

Baker, David W. *Nahum, Habakkuk and Zephaniah: An Introduction and
  Commentary*. TOTC. Downers Grove, InterVarsity, 1988.
Berlin, Adele. *Zephaniah: A New Translation with Introduction and
  Commentary*. AB. Garden City: Doubleday, 1994.
Patterson, Richard D. *Nahum, Habakkuk, Zephaniah*. Dallas: Biblical Studies
  Press, 2003.
Roberts, J. J. M. *Nahum, Habakkuk, and Zephaniah*. OTL. Louisville:
  Westminster/John Knox, 1991.
Robertson, O. Palmer. *The Books of Nahum, Habakkuk, and Zephaniah*.
  NICOT. Grand Rapids: Eerdmans, 1990.

Haggai

Baldwin, Joyce G. *Haggai, Zechariah, Malachi*. TOTC. Downers Grove:
  InterVarsity, 1972.
Meyers, Carol L. and Eric M. Meyers. *Haggai and Zechariah 1–8: A New Translation
  with Introduction and Commentary*. AB. Garden City: Doubleday, 1987.

Petersen, David L. *Haggai and Zechariah 1–8: A Commentary*. Old Testament Library. Louisville, KY: Westminster John Knox, 1984.

Verhoef, Pieter A. *The Books of Haggai and Malachi*. NICOT. Grand Rapids: Eerdmans, 1987.

Zechariah

Baldwin, Joyce G. *Haggai, Zechariah, Malachi*. TOTC. Downers Grove: InterVarsity, 1972.

Merrill, Eugene G. *Haggai, Zechariah, Malachi*. NAC. Nashville: Broadman & Holman, 1994.

Meyers, Carol L. and Eric M. Meyers. *Haggai and Zechariah: A New Translation with Introduction and Commentary*. AB. 2 vols. Garden City: Doubleday, 1987, 1993.

Malachi

Baldwin, Joyce G. *Haggai, Zechariah, Malachi*. TOTC. Downers Grove: InterVarsity, 1972.

Clendenen, E. Ray. "Malachi." NAC 21a. Nashville: Broadman & Holman, 2004.

Hill, Andrew E. *Malachi*. AB. New York: Doubleday, 1998.

Kaiser, Walter C., Jr. *Malachi*. Grand Rapids: Baker, 1984.

Merrill, Eugene G. *Haggai, Zechariah, Malachi*. NAC. Nashville: Broadman & Holman, 1994.

Verhoef, Pieter A. *The Books of Haggai and Malachi*. NICOT. Grand Rapids: Eerdmans, 1987.

New Testament
Matthew

Blomberg, Craig L. *Matthew*. NAC. Nashville: Broadman, 1992.

Carson, D. A. "Matthew." EBC 8. Grand Rapids: Zondervan, 1984, 3–599.

Davies, W. D. and Dale C. Allison. *A Critical and Exegetical Commentary on the Gospel according to Saint Matthew*. ICC. 3 vols. Edinburgh: T. & T. Clark, 1989, 1991, 1997.

France, R. T. *The Gospel of Matthew*. NICNT. Grand Rapids: Eerdmans, 2007.

Hagner, Donald A. *Matthew*. 2 vols. WBC. Dallas: Word, 1993, 1995.

Keener, Craig S. *A Commentary on the Gospel of Matthew*. Grand Rapids: Eerdmans, 1999.

Turner, David. *Matthew*. BECNT. Grand Rapids: Baker, 2008.

Wilkins, Michael. *Matthew*. NIVAC. Grand Rapids: Zondervan, 2004.

Mark

Evans, Craig A. *Mark 8:27–16:20*. WBC. Nashville: Thomas Nelson, 2001.

France, R. T. *The Gospel of Mark: A Commentary on the Greek Text*. NIGTC. Grand Rapids: Eerdmans, 2002.

Garland, David E. *Mark*. NIVAC. Grand Rapids: Zondervan, 1996.

Guelich, Robert A. *Mark 1–8:26*. WBC. Dallas: Word, 1989.

Gundry, Robert H. *Mark: A Commentary on His Apology for the Cross*. Grand Rapids: Eerdmans, 1993.

Lane, William L. *Commentary on the Gospel of Mark*. NICNT. Grand Rapids: Eerdmans, 1974.

Stein, Robert H. *Mark*. BECNT. Grand Rapids: Baker, 2008.

Luke

Bock, Darrell L. *Luke*. 2 vols. BECNT. Grand Rapids: Baker, 1994, 1996.

Fitzmyer, Joseph A. *The Gospel According to Luke*. AB. 2 vols. New York: Doubleday, 1981–85.

Green, Joel B. *The Gospel of Luke*. Rev. ed. NICNT. Grand Rapids: Eerdmans, 1997.

Marshall, I. Howard. *Commentary on Luke*. NIGTC. Grand Rapids: Eerdmans, 1978

Nolland, John. *Luke*. WBC. 3 vols. Dallas: Word, 1990–93.

John

Carson, D. A. *The Gospel According to John*. PNTC. Grand Rapids: Eerdmans, 1991.

Keener, Craig S. *The Gospel of John: A Commentary*. Peabody, MA: Hendrickson, 2003.

Köstenberger, Andreas J. *John*. BECNT. Grand Rapids: Baker, 2004.

_____. *A Theology of John's Gospel and Letters: The Word, the Christ, the Son of God*. BTNT. Grand Rapids: Zondervan, 2009.

Morris, Leon. *Commentary on the Gospel of John*. Rev. ed. NICNT. Grand Rapids: Eerdmans, 1995.

Ridderbos, Herman N. *The Gospel of John: A Theological Commentary*. Grand Rapids: Eerdmans, 1997.

Acts

Barrett, C. K. *A Critical and Exegetical Commentary on the Acts of the Apostles.* ICC. 2 vols. Edinburgh: T. & T. Clark, 1994–98.

Bock, Darrell L. *Acts.* BECNT. Grand Rapids: Baker, 2007.

Bruce, F. F. *Commentary on the Book of Acts.* Rev. ed. NICNT. Grand Rapids: Eerdmans, 1988.

Fitzmyer, Joseph A. *The Acts of the Apostles.* AB New York: Doubleday, 1999.

Longenecker, Richard N. "Acts." EBC 9. Grand Rapids: Zondervan, 1981, 207–753.

Peterson, David G. *The Acts of the Apostles.* PNTC. Grand Rapids: Eerdmans, 2009.

Romans

Cranfield, C. E. B. *A Critical and Exegetical Commentary on the Epistle to the Romans.* ICC. 2 vols. Edinburgh: T. & T. Clark, 1975–79.

Dunn, James D. G. *Romans.* WBC. 2 vols. Dallas: Word, 1988.

Moo, Douglas J. *The Epistle to the Romans.* NICNT. Grand Rapids: Eerdmans, 1996.

Schreiner, Thomas R. *Romans.* BECNT. Grand Rapids: Baker, 1998.

Wright, N. T. "The Letter to the Romans." *New Interpreter's Bible.* Nashville: Abingdon, 2002, Vol. 10, 393–770.

1 Corinthians

Barrett, C. K. *A Commentary on the First Epistle to the Corinthians.* Harper's New Testament Commentary. New York: Harper, 1968.

Blomberg, Craig L. *1 Corinthians.* NIVAC. Grand Rapids: Zondervan, 1994.

Fee, Gordon D. *The First Epistle to the Corinthians.* NICNT. Grand Rapids: Eerdmans, 1987.

Garland, David E. *1 Corinthians.* BECNT. Grand Rapids: Baker, 2003.

Hays, Richard B. *1 Corinthians.* Interpretation. Louisville: Westminster/John Knox, 1997.

Thiselton, Anthony C. *The First Epistle to the Corinthians: A Commentary on the Greek Text.* NIGTC. Grand Rapids: Eerdmans, 2000.

2 Corinthians

Barnett, Paul. *The Second Epistle to the Corinthians.* NICNT. Grand Rapids: Eerdmans, 1997.

Furnish, Victor. *II Corinthians*. AB. New York: Doubleday, 1984.

Garland, David E. *2 Corinthians*. NAC. Nashville: Broadman & Holman, 1999.

Hafemann, Scott J. *2 Corinthians*. NIVAC. Grand Rapids: Zondervan, 2000.

Harris, Murray J. *The Second Epistle to the Corinthians*. NIGTC. Grand Rapids: Eerdmans, 2005.

Martin, Ralph P. *2 Corinthians*. WBC. Waco: Word, 1986.

Galatians

Bruce, F. F. *Galatians*. NIGTC. Grand Rapids: Eerdmans, 1982.

Dunn, James D. G. *The Epistle to the Galatians*. HNTC. Peabody, MA: Hendrickson, 1993.

Fung, R. Y. K. *The Epistle to the Galatians*. NICNT. Grand Rapids: Eerdmans, 1988.

George, Timothy. *Galatians*. NAC. Nashville: Broadman & Holman, 1994.

Hays, Richard B. "The Letter to the Galatians." *New Interpreter's Bible*. Nashville: Abingdon, 2000, Vol. IX, 181–348.

Longenecker, Richard N. *Galatians*. WBC. Dallas: Word, 1990.

Martyn, J. Louis. *Galatians*. AB. New York: Doubleday, 1997.

Ephesians

Best, Ernest. *A Critical and Exegetical Commentary on Ephesians*. ICC. Edinburgh: T. & T. Clark, 1998.

Bruce, F. F. *The Epistles to the Colossians, to Philemon, and to the Ephesians*. NICNT. Grand Rapids: Eerdmans, 1984.

Hoehner, Harold W. *Ephesians: An Exegetical Commentary*. Grand Rapids: Baker, 2002.

Lincoln, Andrew T. *Ephesians*. WBC. Dallas: Word, 1990.

O'Brien, Peter T. *The Letter to the Ephesians*. PNTC. Grand Rapids: Eerdmans, 1999.

Philippians

Bockmuehl, Markus. *The Epistle to the Philippians*. Black's NT Commentaries. Peabody, MA: Hendrickson, 1998. Paperback edition New York: Continuum, 2006.

Fee, Gordon D. *Philippians*. NICNT. Grand Rapids: Eerdmans, 1995.

Hansen, G. Walter. *The Letter to the Philippians*. PNTC. Grand Rapids: Eerdmans, 2009.

Hawthorne, Gerald. *Philippians*. WBC. Rev. and exp. by Ralph P. Martin. Nashville: Nelson, 2004.

O'Brien, Peter T. *The Epistle to the Philippians*. NIGTC. Grand Rapids: Eerdmans, 1991.

Silva, Moisés. *Philippians*. BECNT. Grand Rapids: Baker, 2005.

Thielman, Frank. *Philippians*. NIVAC. Grand Rapids: Zondervan, 1995.

Colossians and Philemon

Bruce, F. F. *The Epistles to the Colossians, to Philemon, and to the Ephesians*. NICNT. Grand Rapids: Eerdmans, 1984.

Dunn, James D. G. *Epistles to the Colossians and to Philemon: A Commentary*. Grand Rapids: Zondervan, 1998.

Garland, David E. *Colossians and Philemon*. NIVAC. Grand Rapids: Zondervan, 1998.

Martin, Ralph P. *Colossians and Philemon*. New Century Bible. Grand Rapids: Eerdmans, 1973.

O'Brien, Peter T. *Colossians, Philemon*. WBC. Waco, TX: Word, 1982.

Wright, N. T. *The Epistles of Paul to the Colossians and to Philemon*. TNTC. Grand Rapids: Eerdmans, 1986.

1–2 Thessalonians

Bruce, F. F. *I and II Thessalonians*. WBC. Waco, TX: Word, 1982.

Fee, Gordon D. *The First and Second Letters to the Thessalonians*. NICNT. Grand Rapids: Eerdmans, 2009.

Green, Gene L. *The Letters to the Thessalonians*. PNTC. Grand Rapids: Eerdmans, 2002.

Marshall, I. Howard. *I and II Thessalonians*. New Century Bible. Grand Rapids: Eerdmans, 1983.

Morris, Leon. *The First and Second Epistles to the Thessalonians*. Rev. ed. NICNT. Grand Rapids: Eerdmans, 1991.

Wanamaker, Charles A. *The Epistles to the Thessalonians*. NIGTC. Grand Rapids: Eerdmans, 1990.

1–2 Timothy, Titus

Johnson, Luke Timothy. *Letters to Paul's Delegates: 1 Timothy, 2 Timothy, Titus*. New Testament in Context. Valley Forge, PA: Trinity Press International, 1996.

Knight, George W. III. *The Pastoral Epistles*. NIGTC. Grand Rapids: Eerdmans, 1992.

Köstenberger, Andreas J. "1 and 2 Timothy, Titus." EBC 12. Rev. ed. Grand Rapids: Zondervan, 2006, 487–625.

Marshall, I. Howard. *The Pastoral Epistles*. ICC. Edinburgh: T. & T. Clark, 1999.

Mounce, William D. *Pastoral Epistles*. WBC. Nashville: Thomas Nelson, 2000.

Quinn, Jerome D. and William C. Wacker. *The First and Second Letters to Timothy*. ECC. Grand Rapids: Eerdmans, 2000.

Towner, Philip H. *The Letters to Timothy and Titus*. NICNT. Grand Rapids: Eerdmans, 2006.

Hebrews

Attridge, Harold. *The Epistle to the Hebrews*. Hermeneia. Philadelphia: Fortress, 1989.

Bruce, F. F. *The Epistle to the Hebrews*. NICNT. Grand Rapids: Eerdmans, 1990.

Ellingworth, Paul. *The Epistle to the Hebrews*. NIGTC. Grand Rapids: Eerdmans, 1993.

Hagner, Donald A. *Hebrews*. NIBC. Peabody, MA: Hendrickson, 1990.

Lane, William L. *Hebrews*. WBC. 2 vols. Dallas: Word, 1991.

O'Brien, Peter T. *The Letter to the Hebrews*. PNTC. Grand Rapids: Eerdmans, 2010.

James

Davids, Peter H. *Commentary on James*. NIGTC. Grand Rapids: Eerdmans, 1982.

Johnson, Luke Timothy. *The Letter of James*. AB. New York: Doubleday, 1995.

Martin, Ralph P. *James*. WBC. Waco, TX: Word, 1988.

McCartney, Dan G. *James*. BECNT. Grand Rapids: Baker, 2009.

Moo, Douglas J. *The Letter of James*. PNTC. Grand Rapids: Eerdmans, 2000.

Richardson, Kurt. *James*. NAC. Nashville: Broadman & Holman, 1997.

1–2 Peter, Jude

Bauckham, Richard J. *Jude, 2 Peter*. WBC. Waco, TX: Word, 1983.

Davids, Peter H. *The First Epistle of Peter*. NICNT. Grand Rapids: Eerdmans, 1990.

Green, Gene L. *Jude & 2 Peter*. BECNT. Grand Rapids: Baker, 2008.

Grudem, Wayne A. *The First Epistle of Peter*. TNTC. Grand Rapids: Eerdmans, 1988.

Jobes, Karen H. *1 Peter*. BECNT. Grand Rapids: Baker, 2005.

Michaels, J. Ramsey. *1 Peter*. WBC. Waco, TX: Word, 1988.

Moo, Douglas J. *2 Peter and Jude*. NIVAC. Grand Rapids: Zondervan, 1996.

Schreiner, Thomas R. *1, 2 Peter and Jude*. NAC. Nashville: Broadman & Holman, 2003.

1–3 John

Akin, Daniel L. *1, 2, 3 John*. NAC. Nashville: Broadman & Holman, 2001.

Bruce, F. F. *The Epistles of John*. Grand Rapids: Eerdmans, 1979.

Kruse, Colin G. *The Letters of John*. PNTC. Grand Rapids: Eerdmans, 2000.

Marshall, I. Howard. *The Epistles of John*. NICNT. Grand Rapids: Eerdmans, 1978.

Smalley, Stephen S. *1, 2, 3 John*. WBC. Waco, TX: Word, 1984.

Stott, John R. W. *The Epistles of St. John*. Rev. ed. TNTC. Grand Rapids: Eerdmans, 1988.

Thompson, Marianne Meye. *1–3 John*. IVPNTC. Downers Grove: InterVarsity, 1992.

Yarbrough, Robert W. *1–3 John*. BECNT. Grand Rapids: Baker, 2008.

Revelation

Aune, David E. *Revelation*. WBC. 3 vols. Dallas: Word, 1997; Nashville: Thomas Nelson, 1998.

Beale, G. K. *The Book of Revelation*. NIGTC. Grand Rapids: Eerdmans, 1999.

Ladd, George Eldon. *A Commentary on the Revelation of John*. Grand Rapids: Eerdmans, 1972.

Mounce, Robert H. *The Book of Revelation*. Rev. ed. NICNT. Grand Rapids: Eerdmans, 1997.

Osborne, Grant R. *Revelation*. BECNT. Grand Rapids: Baker, 2001.

GLOSSARY

*A **fortiori** argument*: argument from the lesser to the greater

Account: presentation of history that includes theological interpretation

Aktionsart: German for "kind of action"

Allegory: series of related metaphors

Alliteration: subsequent words starting with the same letter

Allonymity or allepigraphy: the theory that a later author edited what the original author wrote while attributing the writing to the original author or writing in another person's name without intent to deceive

Allusion: an authorially intended reference to a preceding text of Scripture involving verbal or, at a minimum, conceptual similarity

Amanuensis: scribe or secretary who wrote down the message of the author of an epistle, whether by way of word-by-word dictation or by filling out the sense of a missive

Anaphora: pronouns and other terms referring back to a previous clause or textual unit

Announcement of judgment: a prophetic oracle involving the stating of an accusation and the pronouncement of the ensuing judgment

Antagonist: the person opposing the protagonist

Anthropomorphism: ascription of human characteristics or qualities to God

Anthropopathism: the ascription of human emotions to God

Antithesis: direct contrast, terms set in opposition to each other

Antithetic parallelism: two poetic lines expressing sharp contrast

Antitype: a later pattern of God's dealings with his people that corresponds to an earlier instance (see Type below)

Apocalypse: a genre of literature with a narrative framework in which a revelation is mediated by an otherworldly being to a human recipient, disclosing a transcendent reality that is both temporal and spatial

Apocalyptic: a world view anticipating God's climactic and cataclysmic intervention in human history at the end of time

Apocalypticism: denotes a worldview, ideology, or theology merging the eschatological aims of particular groups into a cosmic and political arena

Apophthegm: short, witty, and instructive saying

Aposiopesis: the breaking off of a speech or statement owing to strong emotion, modesty, or other reasons

Apostrophe: direct address to imaginary object or person, or to an object or person not present

Appropriation technique: specific ways in which the Old Testament is appropriated by a New Testament writer as part of his theological argument

Aretalogy: string of "I am" statements

Aspect: a writer's choice to present a given action from a particular vantage point

Assonance: see Alliteration

Asyndeton: lack of a conjunction at the beginning of a sentence

Augustinian proposal: theory that Matthew wrote first, then Mark using Matthew, then Luke using both Matthew and Mark

Biblical theology: a discipline of biblical study that seeks to investigate Scripture as originally given in its historical context and on its own terms (in distinction from Systematic theology; see below)

Bicolon: parallel thought over two successive lines of poetry

Bifid structure: the poet's structuring of his material in two parts, each answering to the other in similar or corresponding fashion and in the same basic order (e.g. Psalm 135; Nahum; Zephaniah)

Bookending: the technique of returning at the end of a unit to a theme, subject, or word(s) mentioned at the beginning of that section

Brachylogy: the omission, for the sake of brevity, of an element that is not necessary for the grammatical structure but for the thought

Bultmannian: in conformity with the teachings of Rudolf Bultmann, a noted twentieth-century German theologian

Canonical Edition of the New Testament: the notion that the individual(s) responsible for the compilation of the books of the New Testament in a particular order shaped this document in a particular way

Characterization: the depiction of major and minor figures in the narrative

Chiasm: a literary device in which the second half of a composition takes up the same words, themes, or motifs as in the first half, but in reverse order (A B B′ A′ pattern)

Chreia: pronouncement story

Clause: any meaningful cluster of words that includes a verb

Closure: the concluding statement in a given discourse unit

Cohesion: the glue that holds a discourse together

Concreteness: a feature of Hebrew poetry that involves a graphic description appealing to the reader's senses

Connotation: the meaning added to the lexical meaning or denotation by the context

Contiguity: figure of speech based on association, not similarity; in figures of contiguity, there is a logical comparison between the terms of the figure; metonymy and synecdoche are figures of contiguity

Covenant lawsuit: a type of prophetic judgment speech in which God summons his people to appear before him for covenant violations

Crux interpretum: a passage that is difficult to interpret

Deliberative speech: exhorts or dissuades the audience regarding future actions by seeking to show the expediency or lack thereof of one's future actions

Denotation: the "dictionary" definition of a word apart from a particular context

Denouement: the final clarification or resolution of a narrative or dramatic plot

Diachronic: the study of language "over time"

Diatessaron: Grk. "through four"; first parallel presentation ("harmony") of the four canonical Gospels Matthew, Mark, Luke, and John by the second-century church father Tatian

Diatribe: a technique for anticipating objections to an argument, raising them in the form of questions and then answering them (e.g., Romans 6–7)

Direct quotation: an explicit, verbatim citation of an Old Testament passage, usually fronted by an introductory formula (in distinction to Allusions or Echoes; see definition of these)

Disclosure formula: indication that author wants to inform his readers about a given subject (e.g., "I do not want you to be ignorant")

Discourse: any coherent sequence of phrases or sentences, whether a narrative, logical argument, or poetic portion of text

Discourse analysis: a study of a textual unit for the purpose of discerning various features of the text such as boundary markers, cohesion, prominence, relations, and situatedness

Discourse boundary: the opening and closing phrases or devices marking the beginning and end of a given discourse unit

Disputation: a literary device that deals with a given topic by way of presenting different sides of an argument, often involving declaration, discussion, and refutation

Dogmatic theology: older (German) term for systematic theology

Echo: an authorially intended reference to a preceding text of Scripture that exhibits a proportionately lesser degree of verbal similarity from the preterist, historicist, idealist, and futurist approaches

Ellipsis: a feature by which an incomplete idea requires the reader to supply a missing element that is self-evident

Emblematic parallelism: two poetic lines showing progression of thought involving simile

Emperor cult: the mandated, enforced worship of the Roman emperor as deity

Epideictic discourse: affirms communal values by praise or blame in order to affect a present evaluation

Epizeuxis or Epanadiplosis: repetition of a significant word for emphasis

Eschatological: end-time

Eternal State: heaven

Etymology: the root (i.e. original) meaning of a word

Euphemism: substitution of a less offensive or explicit term for a stronger term

Exhortatio: refutation of the opponents' arguments

Exhortation speech: an instructional message in which the recipients are urged to follow the Lord and his standards

Exodus event: historical details concerning God's deliverance of the Hebrews out of Egypt, his guidance of them through the wilderness, and eventual bringing them into the Promised Land

Exordium: introduction defining the character of the speaker and the central issue(s) addressed

External elements of narratives: features outside the narrative, such as author, narrator, and reader

Farewell Discourse: final period of Jesus' instruction to his followers per John 13–17 or, more narrowly conceived, John 13:31–16:33

Figure of speech: any use of language in which two terms are compared or brought into some relationship other than, or in addition to, a literal or logical connection; any use of language in which one term is spoken of in language suggestive of the other term

Forensic or judicial speech: defends or accuses someone regarding past actions by seeking to prove that one's actions were just or unjust

Form criticism: study of the Gospels that focuses on the period of oral transmission

Four Source hypothesis. modification of the Two-Source hypothesis by B. H. Streeter, which adds "M" and "L" for material unique to Matthew and Luke as sources

Futurist approach: interpretation of Revelation as primarily depicting future events

Gallio inscription: ancient artifact mentioning the name of the governor of Achaia by that name

Gezera shawah: rule of equivalence, that is, the principle of Scripture interpreting Scripture

Graffiti: informal sketch or scribbling

Grammar: specific features of syntax, such as a certain kind of genitive or participle (form)

Griesbach hypothesis: theory popularized by J. J. Griesbach that Matthew wrote first, then Luke using Matthew, then Mark using both Matthew and Luke

Hapax legomenon (pl. *hapax legomena*): a word occurring only once in the Old or New Testament

Haustafel: household code delineating the responsibilities of the various members of the ancient household such as wives, parents, slaves, and masters

Hendiadys: an arrangement of two or more expressions that essentially convey the same idea

Hermeneutical axiom: an underlying assumption that leads a New Testament writer to use an Old Testament passage in a certain way (e.g., Jesus is the Messiah)

Highlighting: the literary technique of drawing attention to a particular detail in the story

Historicist approach: interpretation of Revelation as forecasting the course of history in Western Europe

Horizontal reading: comparison of the presentations of a given event by the different Gospels

Hyperbole: a form of overstatement in which literal fulfillment or portrayal is impossible

Hypocatastasis: figure of speech in which the comparison is implied by direct naming

Idealist approach: interpretation of Revelation focusing on the symbolic portrayal of spiritual and timeless truths regarding the end times

Illegitimate totality transfer: the improper assumption that a word in a given context means everything the word can mean in a variety of different contexts

Image: word picture in which the reader can, as it were, see, taste, touch, smell, or hear what is being described

Implicature: implicit yet necessary information for understanding a given discourse

Implied author: persona created in text by real author

Inaugurated eschatology: aspects of the end times that have already begun to be a present reality in the lives of believers

Inclusio: the occurrence of a given word or phrase at the beginning and at the end of a discourse unit for the purpose of marking this portion of material as a textual unit

Instructional account: various forms of prophetic material, including disputation and exhortation speeches, satire, or wisdom sayings

Interlude: a literary feature interspersing additional material into a given unit

Internal elements of narrative: features of the narrative itself, including setting, plot, and characterization

Intertextuality: relationship between texts

Introductory formula: a phrase preceding a direct Old Testament quotation in the New Testament, such as "it is written"

Irony: device in which the writer states the opposite of what is intended

Ladder parallelism: two or more poetic lines displaying progression in form of numerical sequence

Lament: a special type of a prophetic announcement of judgment similar to the woe oracle in which the prophet deplores the state of affairs among God's people

Law: in the Bible an expression of God's will and moral standards for human conduct delivered as instructional material

Lexis or lexical meaning: a word's meaning as listed in a dictionary

Linguistics: the study of the nature of language

Litotes: deliberate understatement for effect

Markan priority: theory that Mark was the first to write his Gospel

Matthean priority: theory that Matthew was the first to write his Gospel

Maximalist-minimalist debate: controversy as to whether the Bible is an accurate source of historical-cultural background information

Merism: type of synecdoche in which the whole is suggested by contrasting parts

Messiah: God's promised, anointed, and divine representative who would deliver his people and rule as king in earth's final state

Metaphor: figure of speech in which one term is imaginatively identified with another, or in which one object represents another object or idea

Metonymy: substitution of one word for another

Midrash: Jewish commentary-style interpretation or exposition of a religious text

Millennium: the one-thousand-year reign of Christ at the end of time depicted in Revelation 20

Mirror-reading: the (often doubtful) interpretive practice of inferring the circumstances surrounding the writing of a given text from explicit statements made in the text

Monocolon: an individual poetic line that does not combine closely with another line

Narratio: unit presenting the events related to the central issue

Narrative: a literary genre that builds its sentences and paragraphs around discourses, episodes, or scenes

Narrator: person telling the story

Nero *redivivus* myth: the belief that the Roman emperor Nero (A.D. 54–68) did not truly die but was still alive and would return

New covenant: in Old Testament prophesies, God's future bestowal of blessings upon his redeemed people in the Promised Land

***nomina sacra*:** contracted words for deity in early Greek New Testament manuscripts

Old Testament Canon: that body of writings accepted as reflecting divine inspiration and authority

Orienter: an initial marker indicating a boundary feature in a given discourse

Ossuary: ancient bone box containing the remains of a deceased

***par excellence*:** the most perfect example

Parable: true-to-life or realistic story told in form of an extended simile, short story, or allegory to teach a spiritual lesson

Paradox: a statement that appears to be contradictory

***Paraenesis*:** exhortation

Parallelism: the practice of using similar language to express corresponding thoughts in succeeding lines of poetry

Parallelomania: the adducing of parallels of questionable value

Parataxis: unconnected juxtaposition of sentence units or clauses

Paronomasia: similar-sounding words placed side by side for emphasis

***parousia*:** second coming of the Lord Jesus Christ

Peaking: the height of action reached in a particular discourse unit

Pericope: narrative unit

Peroratio: recapitulation of the basic points aimed at evoking a sympathetic response

Personification (also Prosopopoeia): type of metaphor in which human characteristics are ascribed to inanimate objects, animals, or other non-human beings

Pesher: Jewish verse-by-verse commentary

Phrase: any meaningful word cluster that lacks a verb form

Pleonasm: a form of redundancy by which a previously expressed idea is repeated as a way of speaking

Plot: the arrangement of events in the story

Prediction-fulfillment: a phenomenon by which an Old Testament prediction is fulfilled in the New Testament

Preterist approach: interpretation of Revelation that focuses on the book's message to its contemporary, first-century readers

Probatio: confirmation setting forth logical arguments

Progressive dispensationalism: belief that the various eras of salvation history (dispensations) progressively overlap in keeping with the "already/not yet" tension of inaugurated eschatology

Progressive parallelism: a succeeding line (or lines) supplements and/or completes the first line

Prominence: elements in a discourse that stand out, be it by way of natural or marked prominence

Prophetic narrative: an account of the prophet's calling, life, and work

Prophetic-apocalyptic: the likely genre of the book of Revelation, combining prophetic and apocalyptic features

Propositio: a summary of the central thesis or theses to be proved

Protagonist: the main character of a story

Proverb: short memorable statement of the true state of things as perceived and learned by human observation over extended periods of experience

Pseudonymity: a writing in which a later follower attributes his own work to his revered teacher in order to perpetuate that person's teachings and influence

Pun: a play on words in which one word may have more than one meaning or two similar-sounding words intentionally used to suggest two or more different meanings

Q: hypothetical document containing material common to Matthew and Luke (from the German *Quelle,* meaning "document")

Qal wahomer: argument from the lesser to the greater (lit. "light and heavy")

Quod erat demonstrandum: Latin for "that which needed to be demonstrated"

Rapture: meeting between believers alive at the time of Christ's return and their risen Lord per 1 Thessalonians 4:13–18

Real author: actual writer of a given document

Reference: the linguistic procedure by which a word points to an extra-textual object

Referent: the object to which a word points

regula fidei: Latin, "rule of faith," i.e. the apostles' teaching as a standard for orthodox doctrine

Relations: various ways in which statements or propositions are conjoined in a given text

Report: a narrative providing historical information

Riddle: a simple statement with a hidden meaning that the hearer must uncover

Royal grant treaty: privileges or benefits granted by a king to a vassal or servant for faithful and loyal service

Salvation oracle: prophecy that deals with God's saving work, such as a promise of deliverance, a kingdom oracle, or apocalyptic

Satire: an attempt to demonstrate through ridicule or rebuke the vice or folly of that which appears to be improper or ill-conceived

Second Temple period: time between the rebuilding of the temple subsequent to the return from the exile and the destruction of the temple in A.D. 70

Semantic anachronism: the imposition of the later meaning of a word onto earlier uses

Semantic field: a group of words that are related in meaning

Semantic field study: the study of the meaning of a word and related words

Semantic obsolescence: rendering a word with a meaning it once possessed but that has since fallen into disuse

Semantic range: the variety of meanings of which a word is capable in different contexts

Semantics: concerned with the meaning of individual words based on the recognition that word meaning is to be discerned in context

Sense: the meaning of a word in context including the word's connotation

Sentence: any complete thought expressed in form of one or several independent clauses

Setting: information as to the place, time, and circumstances of a given event

Similar parallelism: two poetic lines conveying closeness of thought and expression

Similarity: figure of speech based on comparison apart from any logical connection between the terms; figures of similarity include simile, metaphor, image, and symbol

Simile: simple comparison, usually linked by "like" or "as"

Similitude: extended simile

Sitz im Leben: the life-setting of a given literary unit in history (e.g. of a parable)

Sitz im Leben der Kirche: the life setting of the church at the time of composition

Sitz im Leben Jesu: the life setting of a story or parable in Jesus' day

Staging: the presentation of setting of a given action or event

Staircase parallelism: a thought stated in the first line is completed by a succeeding line beginning with similar phraseology

Stitching: an author's practice of linking successive units or subunits of a poem by means of repeating a word, phrase, or idea

Suzerainty treaty: an agreement whereby the enacting party imposes covenant stipulations upon a vassal

Symbol: type of metaphor in which the vehicle, as well as the tenor, is broadly suggestive in itself

Synchronic: the study of language "together with" (i.e. at the same) time

Synecdoche: figure of speech in which a part represents the whole

Synoptic Gospels: Grk. "seeing together"; common designation for Matthew, Mark, and Luke owing to the similarities between these Gospels

Syntax: refers more broadly to relationships between words in the larger scheme of discourses and sentence structures

Systematic theology: a form of presentation of biblical teaching which is essentially topical in nature (in distinction from Biblical theology; see above)

Tail-head link: mention of a topic at the end of a section to be developed in the following unit

Targum: the Aramaic paraphrase of the Hebrew Bible used in the synagogue liturgy

Tenor: underlying subject in a figure of speech

Term: subject of a figure of speech; there are two terms in a figure of speech, the "vehicle" and "tenor"

terminus ad quem: latest possible date

Terrace pattern parallelism: type of staircase parallelism in which the beginning of the second line repeats the end of the first line

Terseness: feature of Hebrew poetry that involves succinctness of stating a point

Theodicy: vindicating the righteousness of God and his ways when called into question

Thought flow: discourse structure as conveyed by various discourse features per discourse analysis

Transitivity: the ability of the audience to grasp and comprehend an allusion and its source text

Tricolon: three lines of poetry forming a distinct unit

Two-Document hypothesis: theory that Mark (written first) and "Q" served as the 2 sources for Matthew and Luke

Type: an instance of a historical person, event, or institution that exhibits a pattern of God's dealings with his people in salvation history

Typology: an escalating pattern in salvation history in which a later antitype is found to correspond to one or several original types

Vehicle: mode in which the tenor is experienced

Vertical reading: initial study of a given incident in the Gospel in which it is narrated

Vision or dream report: instance in which a prophet receives God's message in a vision, which he in turn is to proclaim to his people

Woe oracle: a special type of a prophetic announcement of judgment that involves (1) invective (the pronouncement of woe); (2) threat (the details of coming judgment); and (3) criticism (the reason for the coming judgment)

Zeugma: a special type of ellipsis in which a different verb is to be supplied

Zoomorphism: ascription of animal qualities to God

SCRIPTURE INDEX

SUBJECT INDEX

PERSON INDEX